UNIVERSITY CASEBOOK SERIES®

U.S. INTERNATIONAL TAXATION

CASES AND MATERIALS

FOURTH EDITION

REUVEN S. AVI-YONAH
Irwin I. Cohn Professor of Law
The University of Michigan

DIANE M. RING
Professor of Law and Dr. Thomas F. Carney Distinguished Scholar
Boston College

YARIV BRAUNER
Hugh Culverhouse Eminent Scholar Chair and Professor of Law
The University of Florida

FOUNDATION
PRESS

University Casebook Series is a trademark registered in the U.S. Patent and Trademark Office.

© 2002, 2005 FOUNDATION PRESS
© 2011 By THOMSON REUTERS/FOUNDATION PRESS
© 2019 LEG, Inc. d/b/a West Academic
    444 Cedar Street, Suite 700
    St. Paul, MN 55101
    1-877-888-1330

Printed in the United States of America

ISBN: 978-1-68328-650-9

For Orli, Michael and Shera (R.A.Y.)

For Liam, Caroline and Anna (D.M.R.)

For Ruthie and Noga, Leehee and Omri (Y.B.)

PREFACE

International taxation is an area of increasing importance in a world in which cross-border capital flows exceed $1 trillion per day. Twenty years ago, international tax was the specialty of a small number of attorneys, most of whom practiced in the large financial centers like New York, Washington or Los Angeles. Today, almost any transaction over a certain dollar amount will involve an international component, and focusing solely on the U.S. domestic aspects is a luxury few tax lawyers can afford. In addition, the international tax rules are constantly changing as new areas of business develop (such as electronic commerce and derivatives) and an attempt is made to fit them into a framework that in its basic contours is now almost 100 years old.

This book is an effort to provide law teachers with a relatively simple, easy to use casebook to teach U.S. international taxation. The field is notoriously complex—more so, perhaps, than any other area of Federal tax law. Thus, we have made a conscious effort to try to stick to the essentials: How does the U.S. tax law treat foreign investors deriving income from sources within the U.S. (inbound transactions), and how it treats U.S. taxpayers deriving foreign source income (outbound transactions). Throughout, the focus is on how the details of the tax law fit into a broader structure, which is described in the introduction. Thus, the book will hopefully enable students to fit the particular issues they are working on into a larger context, so as to develop an intuition for where the problem areas may lie. The rest they can learn (much faster) in practice.

The book is divided into an introduction and five parts. The introduction summarizes the entire course; it can be read profitably both before and after learning the details. Part A addresses general problems such as jurisdiction to tax and the source rules for income and deductions. Part B deals with inbound tax issues (which come first primarily because they are simpler). Part C is concerned with transfer pricing, which is common to inbound and outbound transactions and lies at the heart of the essential international tax problem of how to divide the revenue pie among competing jurisdictions. Part D is the hardest one since it involves deferral and the foreign tax credit, which are the most complicated topics in international taxation. Part E concludes by examining special topics like section 367 and the foreign exchange rules, and then discussing the relationship between the U.S. rules and the international tax regime, as embodied in the over 3,000 bilateral tax treaties. Part E also addresses some policy issues as to where international taxation may be headed in the 21st century, such as tax competition and tax arbitrage. For the fourth edition, we have up-dated the entire text with recent cases and administrative rulings, as well as reflecting the significant changes enacted in the Tax Cuts and Jobs Act of 2017.

This first edition of this book had its origins in a joint project with Charlie Kingson and Phil West, and even though we ultimately decided to separate, it still benefits from their wisdom and advice, for which the first author is grateful. We would also like to thank Michael Graetz and Dan Shaviro for helpful comments on a draft of the book. We have benefited tremendously from the input of our students who wrestled with earlier drafts at Arizona State, Boston College, Florida, Harvard, Penn, Michigan, Northwestern, and NYU. We would particularly like to acknowledge the work of Shay Moyal in summarizing the TCJA changes. Finally, we would like to thank our editors at Foundation Press for their outstanding work in bringing this fourth edition to print.

SUMMARY OF CONTENTS

TABLE OF CONTENTS

TABLE OF CASES

The principal cases are in bold type.

UNIVERSITY CASEBOOK SERIES®

U.S. INTERNATIONAL TAXATION

CASES AND MATERIALS

FOURTH EDITION

INTRODUCTION: THE INTERNATIONAL TAX REGIME

When one of the authors was a second year student in law school, he enrolled in a course that was known as "international taxation." Being young and naive, he assumed (without thinking too much about it) that there was such a thing as international tax rules. Only when he was actually in the course did he discover that its real title was "International Aspects of U.S. Income Taxation," and that this, and not some "international tax regime," was the topic.

It is a commonplace to assert that there is no such thing as international tax rules; only nations have the power to prescribe tax laws, and some of these laws have international aspects—that is, they relate to the taxation of income earned by foreigners or of foreign income earned by residents. And on some basic level, this assertion is of course true, which is why this book is called "U.S. International Taxation" and not simply "International Taxation".

Nevertheless, it is our belief (now that we're older and hopefully wiser) that our colleague's initial intuition as a second year student was actually correct. That is, we believe there is an international tax regime that is a coherent set of principles that in many ways constrain the ability of countries to adopt any international tax laws that they please. This regime is embodied principally in the more than 3,000 existing bilateral tax treaties, but it is also incorporated in the domestic international tax laws of most countries, including the United States.

The purpose of this book is to enable students to learn the principal contours of the international tax regime, and how the U.S. Internal Revenue Code fits with that regime as it relates to non-residents earning U.S. source income ("inbound" transactions) and U.S. residents earning foreign source income ("outbound" transactions).

The following text describes the main features of the international tax regime, and how U.S. tax law fits in with that regime.

Avi-Yonah, The Structure of International Taxation: A Proposal for Simplification
74 Texas L. Rev. 1301 (1996).

The current international tax regime is a flawed miracle. It is a miracle, because taxes are the last topic on which one would expect sovereign nations to reach a consensus, since to some extent international taxation is a zero-sum game and one country's gain in revenue is another's loss. When income is derived by a resident of one country from sources in another, and both countries have a legitimate claim to tax that income and the ability to enforce that claim, either country will lose revenue by granting the other the primary right to tax that income.

Nevertheless, and contrary to *a priori* expectations, a coherent international tax regime exists, which enjoys near universal support, and which underlies the complexities of the international aspects of individual countries' tax systems. This regime was developed since the 1920s, when the League of Nations first undertook to study ways to avoid international double taxation, and has been embodied in the model tax treaties developed by the OECD and the UN and in the multitude of bilateral treaties that are based on those models. The existence of this regime shows that despite each country's claim to sovereignty in tax matters, it is possible to reach an internationally acceptable consensus that will be followed by the majority of the world's taxing jurisdictions. This international tax regime, based on voluntary consensus, can be regarded as one of the major achievements of twentieth-century international law.

Yet the miracle is flawed. The current regime suffers from significant weaknesses, especially in two areas in which the development of the world economy has made the principles that were agreed upon in the 1920s and 1930s obsolete: The growth of internationally mobile capital markets for portfolio investment, and the rise of integrated multinational enterprises (MNEs).[1] Thus, as this century nears its end, it is time to re-examine the prevailing international tax regime and to ask whether a new consensus can be reached to remedy its major weaknesses, and to ensure its continued viability in the next century.

I.   The Structure of International Taxation.

a.   The Active/Passive Distinction in International Taxation.

In 1923, a committee of four economists submitted to the League of Nations a report that for the first time set out the basic principles underlying international tax jurisdiction. The report pointed out that an income tax based on ability to pay does not answer the question of whose ability to pay is to be considered in each taxing jurisdiction. To answer this question, the report developed the "doctrine of economic allegiance," which underlies modern discussions of jurisdiction to tax. Fundamentally, the report endorsed two bases for economic allegiance which justify a country's imposition of tax: Where income is produced, or the source jurisdiction, and where it is consumed or saved, or the residence jurisdiction.

The 1923 report also addressed the issue of double taxation: As between the source and residence jurisdictions, which should have the primary claim to tax income produced in the other, and which should have the obligation to prevent double taxation by giving up its claim? On

---

[1] We currently believe there are additional challenges facing the regime, such as international tax competition and tax arbitrage. These topics are explored in Ch. 12.

practical grounds, the source jurisdiction has the primary right because it can generally impose its taxes on income deriving from within it first. However, the 1923 report recommended that in future negotiations between tax jurisdictions, income items should be classified according to whether the primary economic activity giving rise to the income takes place in the source or in the residence country, and the prior right to tax the income be divided accordingly between them.

These principles underlay the development of the current consensus regarding the proper allocation of taxable income among taxing jurisdictions. While the source country is granted the prior right to tax all income and the residence country has the primary obligation to prevent double taxation, this is a concession to the source country's ability to impose taxes first, and does not reflect the optimal allocation. Instead, the ultimate goal underlying the international tax regime is that *active* business income should be taxed in the country in which it originates (the source country), while *passive* income should be taxed in the country in which the recipient of the income resides (the residence country). The rationale for this division is discussed below.

This consensus can best be seen in operation by examining the extensive tax treaty network. Tax treaties reflect the active/passive distinction in two ways. First, they define what constitutes an active business operation in a given country (a "permanent establishment") and give the source country the primary right to tax the profits from that operation. The residence country is required to exempt those profits from tax, at least to the extent they were taxed by the source country, either by exempting foreign source business income or by granting a foreign tax credit. Second, the tax treaties seek to reduce as much as possible the taxes levied by the source country on passive income (such as dividends, interest, and royalties) derived from within it, leaving the right to tax that income to the residence country.

The tax treaties do not completely achieve their goal of dividing the worldwide taxing jurisdiction between source and residence countries along active/passive lines. First, the "permanent establishment" concept reflects a compromise: not all active business income is taxable primarily in the source country, but only income that is attributable to a permanent establishment, because otherwise international business would be subject to burdensome administrative requirements of filing returns and paying tax in every country in which it has a minimal presence. However, the threshold of what constitutes a permanent establishment is quite low: A single office, or even a single agent with authority to conclude sales, is generally sufficient. Second, the taxation of passive income at source is not completely abolished, but is reduced in most treaties to the lowest possible levels. For example, the 1992 OECD Model Income Tax Treaty recommends tax rates of 5% to 15% on dividends, 10% on interest, and 0% on royalties; the 1996 U.S. Model Income Tax Treaty recommends tax rates of 5–15% on dividends, and 0% on interest and royalties. These low withholding tax rates represent a compromise between the desire of source countries to levy some tax on income derived by foreigners from within the country, and the international consensus that such income should be primarily taxed in the residence country. In the absence of a treaty, much higher withholding tax rates may apply; but these rates reflect the fact that in the absence of a treaty the source country has no assurance that the income will in fact be taxed by the residence country, and therefore arrogates to itself the taxes that should be paid to the residence country.

The distinction between active and passive income is thus a fundamental element of the current regime. Is this a distinction that reflects a real difference? There are three arguments that it does. First, from an economic perspective, one may conceive of the pool of worldwide income as produced by value-adding firms. A firm is a joint venture of persons who invest in it, seeking returns. The value added by each firm is the sum of its undistributed profits, plus the dividends, interest, royalties and rents which it pays, and which represent different ways of distributing the firm's income among the persons who invest in it. The investment may be in the form of equity capital, debt capital, or tangible and intangible assets, depending on the level and type of risk that the investor is willing to undertake.

From this perspective, the taxation of active business income represents the taxation of the profits of the firm, while the taxation of passive income represents the taxation of the division of those profits among investors in the firm. The active/passive distinction in international taxation reflects this economic analysis.

Second, the active/passive distinction reflects to some extent the degree of control exercised over the activity. Active business income is generally derived from economic activities under the taxpayer's direct control. In the international sphere, it is usually linked with foreign direct investment. Passive income, on the other hand, is frequently derived from activities in which the taxpayer has only a very small degree of voting control. Examples would be a small shareholder in a corporation, or a third-party lender whose relationship contains no elements of control. However, passive income (in the sense of distributions of a firm's earnings) may also be earned by persons who control the underlying operations, such as when a controlling shareholder derives dividends or interest from her corporation. This type of passive income (associated with direct investment) is frequently treated differently from passive portfolio income, but under the current consensus it is still taxed primarily in the country of residence of the controlling shareholder, and not in the country where the corporation engages in business. In the following discussion, the term "portfolio income" will be reserved for passive income that is not linked with control.

Third, the active/passive distinction is significant because to a substantial extent it overlaps with the distinction between publicly traded corporations on the one hand, and individuals, close corporations, and other legal entities on the other hand. Much of the world's active income is earned by large, publicly traded corporations, and in the international context, by MNEs; much of the world's passive income is earned directly by individuals or through close corporations or pass-through entities. We shall discuss the importance of this empirical distinction below.

b. Is the Consensus Justified?

If the active/passive distinction reflects some economic reality, why should active income be taxed on a source basis, while passive income is taxed on a residence basis? The 1923 League of Nations report attempted to justify this distinction by means of an analysis of which types of income derive more from activities performed in each jurisdiction, but this type of analysis has been rejected by modern economists, who cast doubt on whether income can meaningfully be said to derive from one source rather than another. Instead, a better understanding of the logic behind the active/passive distinction can be reached if one examines the two extreme alternatives: Taxing all income in the country of residence, and taxing all income in the country of source.

Robert Green has argued for the abolition of source based taxation on the ground that it is incompatible with the modern notion of ability to pay. Indeed, since ability to pay is not adequately measured by income from one source, but rather by "all income from whatever source derived," it seems difficult to reconcile source jurisdiction with an income tax based on ability to pay. However, this argument by itself does not explain why the residence jurisdiction should have the sole claim to tax global income. In terms of the taxpayer's economic allegiance, she owes taxes to both residence and source countries. Each contributes to her ability to earn, and therefore each has the right to tax her entire income, which reflects her global ability to pay. However, since this result is impracticable and would result in complete multiple taxation, one sensible route would be to permit each jurisdiction to tax the income derived from within it (that is, on a source basis), resulting in the taxpayer being taxed on her global income according to her ability to pay. Of course, each of the source jurisdictions may have a different tax rate (including a zero rate), but the fact that a taxpayer may not be taxed or may be taxed at a lower rate in one jurisdiction does not automatically give the residence jurisdiction the residual right to tax that income.

There appear, however, to be several solid grounds for preferring residence over source taxation *for individuals*. The first is a pragmatic ground: Individuals can only be in one place at any given time. Thus, residence for individuals is a relatively easy concept to establish, and in fact it is possible to set down bright line rules (based, as is the case in the United States, on counting days) for determining fiscal residence of individuals. On the other hand, the establishment of the source of income is a highly problematic endeavor, and in most cases income will have more than one source. Thus, if one jurisdiction is to be given the primary right to tax individuals, or at least the residual right to tax income that is untaxed at source, the residence jurisdiction is an obvious candidate.

Second, because most individuals have only one residence jurisdiction, and are part of one society, distributional concerns can be effectively addressed only in the country of residence. If the personal income tax is to have a significant redistributive function through progressive rates, it is necessary to include all income (including foreign source income) in the measurement of ability to pay. There may be no horizontal equity problem in taxing differently two equivalently situated taxpayers, only one of whom invests abroad and earns low-taxed income there, as long as the other has the same choice of investments open to her. There is, however, a significant vertical equity problem in taxing an investor with low domestic and high foreign earnings which are not taxed abroad the same as a person with only low domestic earnings. This problem can be resolved if the residence jurisdiction is allowed to tax on a residual basis only foreign source income that is not taxed abroad (or is taxed at lower effective rates), and allow a credit for foreign taxes, but it is much simpler to address the issue if the residence jurisdiction is given the primary right to tax all income of its residents.

Third, the residence of individuals to some extent overlaps with their political allegiance. In democratic countries, it is considered important for individuals to have a right to participate through their representatives in deciding how much tax they have to pay. The converse is even more significant: Democratic legislatures have a preference for raising taxes on foreigners precisely because they cannot vote. Thus, taxation based on residence is a useful, though far from perfect, proxy for taxation with representation.

Finally, economists have pointed out that residence based taxation is compatible with the goal of capital export neutrality (CEN). This goal requires that the decision to invest in a given location not be affected by tax rates; otherwise, investments that yield the highest returns on a pre-tax basis will not be made because the after-tax return will be lower, and global welfare (based on allocative efficiency) will be diminished. In a world with many taxing jurisdictions with varying rates, CEN is best achieved by taxing all investors at their residence country rate.

Why, then, not follow the path of pure residence based taxation, as suggested by Professor Green? There are two major grounds for rejecting this position. The first is that to implement full residence based taxation, it is necessary either to artificially determine the residence of corporations, which cannot be determined the way the residence of individuals can be, or to impute the earnings of publicly traded MNEs to their shareholders (the alternative supported by Professor Green), which is a very complex task and may be administratively impossible.

The second objection to pure residence based taxation is that it results in too much revenue being collected by developed countries and too little by developing countries. To illustrate this, it is convenient to refer to a stylized model world made up of only three jurisdictions: a developed country (e.g., the U.S.), a developing country (e.g., India), and a tax haven (e.g., the Caymans). The residents of the U.S. earn active income from the U.S., earn passive income from investments in the U.S. and in the Caymans, and earn passive income from investments in X, a MNE headquartered in the U.S. The residents of India earn active income from India, earn passive income from working for X in India, and, in the case of the elite, earn investment income from the U.S. and the Caymans. X develops products in the U.S., manufactures them in India, and sells them in the U.S., but its profits are to a large extent channeled to investments in the Caymans.

In this stylized world, if all taxation were based on residence, the U.S. would receive the taxes from the income of its residents (active and passive), as well as the entire taxes from X, either because X is headquartered there (if corporations are to have a fiscal residence) or because all of X's shareholders are residents of the U.S. and none are residents of India. India, the developing country, would thus be left only with the taxation of the local income of its residents and with the taxes due on the income of its elite from the U.S. and the Caymans, which are very difficult for India to collect. This would likely be an insufficient amount of income for India, which would therefore refuse to cooperate in the residence based system.

The other extreme alternative, taxing all income on a source basis, appears more appealing in this regard. In the simplified world, it would result in the U.S. collecting taxes on active and passive income from the U.S., including X's income from the U.S., and India collecting taxes on active and passive income from India, including X's income from India (assuming that X can be effectively taxed on a source basis). In comparison with a regime under which each country has the right to tax passive income of its residents and active income earned within its borders, India would not lose from this arrangement, except for the taxes it forgoes on passive income from the U.S. and the Caymans, which are difficult for India to collect. Moreover, it would gain to the extent that there is some portfolio income derived by investors from India.

However, as was indicated earlier, pure source based taxation is also unattractive. It undermines the ability to use the income tax as a redistributive mechanism in the country of residence, unless a complicated residual residence based taxation with a foreign tax credit mechanism is implemented; it severs the connection between taxation and participation in the political process; and it is incompatible with CEN.

None of these reasons apply with the same forcefulness to active business income as they do to passive income, precisely because much of the active income in the world is earned by MNEs, which do not vote and which are not residents of a single society. Moreover, capital export neutrality does not apply with the same forcefulness to MNEs as it does to portfolio investments. Consider three reasons for this. First, most of the world's international investment is now portfolio investment, and the role of MNEs, while still growing in absolute terms, is diminishing relative to the growth of portfolio investment. For example, in 1970, foreign direct investment accounted for 75% of U.S. receipts of foreign income; in 1990 U.S. receipts from foreign portfolio investments exceeded receipts from direct investment, even though direct investment rose from 10.8% of corporate profits in 1970 to 17.9% in 1990. The same phenomenon is true for foreign portfolio investment into the U.S., which in 1990 was almost three times as high as foreign direct investment into the U.S.

Second, MNEs have the ability, through debt financing and transfer pricing manipulation, to achieve effective CEN by lowering the rate of tax they pay in high tax jurisdictions. It has been suggested that as long as MNEs can deduct interest expense, they will expand to the point where the return to capital in a given country equals the global rate of interest paid by the MNE (plus a risk premium specific to the particular country and project), and that the combined source and residence rates of tax are irrelevant to this decision.

Finally, the U.S. debate about CEN is misguided as applied to MNEs, because it applies CEN only to MNEs whose parent happens to be incorporated in the U.S., which is increasingly a purely formal distinction. As Joel Slemrod writes, it would be just as significant to tax corporations whose names begin with the letters A through K differently than corporations whose names begin with L through Z, and forbid name changes! For true CEN to apply to MNEs, either the U.S. would have to tax *all* MNEs on their worldwide income, or all MNEs would have to be subject to worldwide taxation by their country of residence (assuming that one country is determined uniformly to be the country of residence); neither of these conditions is likely to be fulfilled.

The taxation of active business income by the source jurisdiction and of passive portfolio income by the residence jurisdiction would appear to address most of the issues identified above. The taxation of passive income on a residence basis is congruent with the need to preserve redistribution and representation for individuals, who earn most of this income (especially if one ignores passive income earned by affiliated corporations), and with achieving CEN. It appears unlikely that source countries would be harmed significantly by giving up source based taxation of passive income earned by individuals and close corporations. The taxation of active income by the source country is congruent with the need to preserve some source of revenue for the source country, and if most such income is earned by MNEs, the arguments for taxing it on a residence basis do not apply. Thus, it appears that the current international consensus has significant advantages, which should be borne in mind when considering ways to simplify and modernize it.

II. The Active/Passive Distinction and U.S. International Taxation.

This part of the article describes how the structure of U.S. international taxation reflects the active/passive distinction outlined above. . . .

The fundamental distinction underlying the U.S. international tax regime is between domestic taxpayers (U.S. citizens, residents, domestic corporations, partnerships and trusts), who are taxed on their world-wide income, and foreign taxpayers (all others), who are only taxed on their U.S. source income. Domestic taxpayers are taxed by the U.S. because of their personal connection to the U.S., i.e., on a residence basis, although the U.S. includes in this category non-resident U.S. citizens. Foreign taxpayers are taxed by the U.S. on the basis of their territorial connection to the U.S., i.e., on a source basis. One problem that is raised by this distinction is that the choice between being taxed on a residence or source basis is initially left to the taxpayer, because corporations are classified as domestic or foreign based on their formal place of incorporation, and therefore it is possible for a domestic taxpayer to shift income from residence to source-based taxation by routing it to a corporation incorporated abroad; if the income is foreign-source, the result is the avoidance of current U.S. taxation (because it is foreign source income of a foreign corporation). Much of the complexity of the current U.S. international tax regime stems from attempts to address this problem.

a. Foreign Taxpayers.

The active/passive distinction is reflected in the two ways in which the U.S. taxes foreign taxpayers on income derived from sources within the U.S.: Income that is effectively connected with a U.S. trade or business, i.e., active income, is taxed on a net basis in the same way as it would have been taxed if earned by a domestic business. "Fixed or determinable, annual or periodic" (FDAP) income, i.e., passive income, is nominally taxed on a gross basis at a relatively high rate (30%). However, a combination of source rules, statutory exemptions, and tax treaties results in such income generally being taxed only when earned by foreign businesses as part of their active business operations. Portfolio investors who earn such income are generally not taxed.

The taxation of active business operations in the U.S. is relatively straightforward. Income that is "effectively connected" with a U.S. "trade or business" is taxed at the regular rates and on the same net base as income earned by domestic taxpayers. The crucial terms, "trade or business" and "effectively connected", are not defined in the Code, but a series of rulings and court cases have sought to distinguish active business operations subject to this regime from mere investment activity not subject to it. In particular, from 1966 onward the U.S. generally does not treat passive earnings of foreign businesses in the U.S. as subject to tax on a net basis unless the assets or operations of the business participated in generating the income. In addition, a specific Code provision excludes investments through a U.S. broker from being treated as a trade or business for this purpose.

In general, the definition of income subject to tax as effectively connected income corresponds to the economic definition of active business income. However, effectively connected income is in some respects broader and in others narrower than active business income from U.S. sources. First, the source rules operate to exclude from the U.S. taxing jurisdiction income that would not be subject to U.S. tax under the permanent establishment threshold of tax treaties. In particular, income from sales is generally sourced based on the residence of the seller, and income from sales of purchased inventory is sourced based on where title passes (a formal attribute totally within the taxpayer's control), *unless* such income is attributable to a U.S. office or other fixed place of business. Similarly, income from international communications and from activities in space (two of the newer additions to the source rules) is sourced by residence of the seller (and thus not subject to U.S. tax if the seller is foreign), unless attributable to a U.S. office or fixed place of business. These rules reflect the international consensus that source based taxation of active business income should be limited to business operations that exceed a certain minimal standard in the host country.

In certain cases the U.S. treats passive income (income that reflects the division of the profits of the business enterprise among investors) as effectively connected income. For example, capital gains from the sale of real property located in the U.S. is treated as effectively connected income even when the foreign investor plays an entirely passive role. In other cases, income that is not clearly active or passive is treated as active: This is the case of U.S. source income that is not effectively connected but is not FDAP or capital gain (e.g., inventory sales that are not effectively connected).

It is more difficult to see how the U.S. follows the international consensus regarding the taxation of passive income, since the statute provides for a heavy 30% withholding tax on gross passive income from U.S. sources. However, in this case it is necessary to look beyond the basic statutory rate and determine in how many cases the current regime actually imposes it. In effect, through a combination of source rules, treaties, and statutory exemptions, little foreign portfolio investment ends up being subject to the 30% tax, and little revenue is collected from this tax. In 1990, the U.S. collected only about $2 billion from all its withholding taxes together on a total of $16 billion in passive income earned by foreigners (i.e., an effective rate of only 12.5%), including passive income earned by controlling shareholders, while an additional $42 billion of passive income was exempt from tax under the provisions described below.

The most obvious exception to the nominal 30% withholding tax is interest, which under an exception enacted in 1984, is not subject to tax when earned by foreign portfolio investors. The exceptions to this exception are instructive: One concerns foreign banks making loans into the U.S. in the ordinary course of their business, when the interest represents active business income. Another exception concerns interest paid to foreign shareholders whose interests exceed 10%. This rule reflects the distinction outlined above between active and portfolio income on the basis of control, and it also provides some deterrent against the ability of those shareholders to disguise dividends as interest. Similarly, another rule restricts the application of the exception to contingent interest, which is too similar to dividends, and thus subject to abuse in the hands of controlling shareholders.

In addition, yet another rule restricts the deductibility of interest paid to foreign related parties (generally, under a 50% common ownership threshold) if the payor's ratio of debt to equity is too high. This "earnings stripping" rule is also designed to backstop the interest/dividends distinction and prevent too high a percentage of U.S. business profits to be paid out as deductible interest to controlling shareholders.[2] The combination of the 10% foreign shareholder limit and the limits on deductibility means that a foreign enterprise engaged in an active business operation in the U.S. through a subsidiary cannot escape U.S. tax by means of interest payments that reduce the profits of the subsidiary and are not subject to withholding, although that result can be achieved by financing the subsidiary from an unrelated foreign entity (as long as it is not a "bank"). The emphasis on relatedness in both the earnings stripping rule and the 10% exception to the portfolio interest exemption reflects the sense that a related foreign party is really engaged in active business in the U.S. through its control of its subsidiary, so that the interest income it receives represents more than purely passive income. Thus, these rules run contrary to the formal distinction between the foreign parent and the subsidiary, even though the internationally accepted definition of a permanent establishment excludes a parent from being treated as engaged in an active business in the U.S. merely because it controls the subsidiary, but they are congruent with a view that restricts passive income to portfolio income.

The situation in the case of dividends is more complicated. First, unlike interest, which is not subject to withholding under the U.S. model treaty, dividends are subject to taxation at source (at 5% or 15%, depending on whether they are paid to shareholders owning 10% of the payor or not) even when a treaty is in place.[3] Second, dividends are subject to potential triple taxation, because they are not deductible to the

---

[2] The December 2017 tax reform significantly revised this earnings stripping rule to expand its reach. For example, the post-2017 version applies to payments made to both related *and* unrelated parties.

[3] Some recent US treaties (e.g., with the UK) have a 0% rate for dividends paid within a corporate group.

payor, are subject to withholding, and are potentially subject to tax in the hands of the recipient (with no foreign tax credit or exemption if, for example, they are treated as domestic source dividends under a foreign country's source rules, which frequently are less formal than the residence of the payor rule followed by the U.S.). Thus, dividends are a very tax-inefficient way of repatriating the earnings of U.S. corporations.

Nevertheless, even in the case of dividends, certain rules operate to reduce the likelihood that portfolio dividends will be subject to effective source based taxation. The source rule for dividends, as for interest, is formal: Dividends are sourced based on the residence of the payor. This means that a foreign corporation whose entire income is effectively connected with its U.S. trade or business can pay dividends to foreign shareholders without withholding tax being imposed. In fact, the source rule has been modified to make such dividends U.S. source in certain cases; but in practice the U.S. Treasury has found it impossible to enforce withholding on dividends paid by a foreign corporation to foreign shareholders, and is forbidden from doing so by many U.S. treaties. To counteract this result, Congress in 1986 enacted a branch profits tax which seeks to impose an equivalent tax on the earnings of the foreign corporation that are withdrawn from its U.S. trade or business. While the branch profits tax operates as a replacement for withholding on dividends (and interest) paid by the foreign corporation from its U.S. business, it should be noted that (unlike a withholding tax on dividends) it is an additional tax on the corporation engaged in the active U.S. business, which may or may not be passed on to the passive investors in that corporation.

Finally, in many cases, dividends can be disguised as interest, which can benefit from the portfolio interest exemption in the hands of small investors. While the 1993 Tax Act reduced somewhat the size of this loophole, it still exists, for example, in the case of interest based on the value of publicly traded stock. The combination of these rules means that dividend withholding is infrequent in the case of portfolio investors.[4]

The withholding tax on royalties and rents is slightly harder to avoid than the tax on dividends or interest, because the source rule is less formal and more tied to economic reality: Royalties and rents are sourced based on the place of use of the asset that gives rise to them. However, it should first be noted that the U.S., like most industrialized countries, negotiates for a 0% withholding rate on rents and royalties in its tax treaties. Moreover, even in the absence of a treaty, royalties can frequently be recharacterized as sale proceeds or as income from services, and in both cases favorable source rules can then be used to avoid U.S. withholding taxes altogether.

---

[4] An additional technique to avoid dividend withholding is through the use of financial derivatives that mimic dividends, such as equity swaps. New legislation enacted in 2010 treats certain dividend equivalent payments as U.S. source and potentially subject to U.S. withholding tax. Section 871(*l*).

To sum up, the taxation of foreign taxpayers generally follows the active/passive distinction outlined above. Active income (income effectively connected with a U.S. trade or business) is subject to U.S. tax at source. Passive income (FDAP) is nominally subject to withholding taxes, but because of the operation of statutory rules (like the portfolio interest exemption), source rules (like the formal rules for sourcing dividends, interest, and wages), regulatory rules, and treaties (like the 0% rate on interest and royalties), such income is frequently not taxed by the U.S. in the hands of portfolio investors.

Commentators have suggested that the 30% U.S. withholding rate is too high, reflecting as it does an attempt to roughly equate net rates of 70% or 90%. In fact, the refusal to lower the rate when the net rates were lowered in 1986 may reflect Congress' recognition that in practice the withholding regime is filled with loopholes and that the 30% rate is rarely imposed in practice upon portfolio investors, but that it is a useful bargaining chip in treaty negotiations. However, if the proper U.S. policy is not to tax passive income at source, this can be achieved in simpler ways than the hodge-podge of rules and exceptions outlined above.

b. Domestic Taxpayers.

Domestic U.S. taxpayers are taxed on their world-wide income, but a foreign tax credit is given for foreign taxes on foreign source income up to the U.S. tax rate. This suggests that the U.S. policy is to give the source country primary tax jurisdiction over all types of income. While this is true to some extent, a combination of statutory rules results in passive foreign income being treated far less favorably than active foreign income, so that in practice the U.S. is more likely to respect the primary right of the foreign jurisdiction to tax the latter than the former.

The first distinction between active and passive income involves deferral. The possibility to defer current U.S. tax on foreign source income results from the basic distinction outlined above between foreign and domestic taxpayers (only domestic taxpayers are taxed on their worldwide income), and the ease by which taxpayers can choose between classification as foreign or domestic based on the formal jurisdiction of incorporation. Because of this rule, a taxpayer can defer current U.S. tax on foreign source income by the simple expedient of routing it to a subsidiary incorporated abroad. If the subsidiary is incorporated in a tax haven, the result is no current taxation of the foreign source income of the subsidiary, which is equivalent to a tax exemption for the interest on these earnings for the period of deferral, and to virtually complete exemption in present value terms if the deferral lasts long enough.

Such favorable treatment of foreign source income would encourage U.S. taxpayers to route their income to foreign "incorporated pocketbooks." To counter this tendency, the U.S. has a complex set of overlapping anti-deferral regimes, all of which result in either current taxation of the foreign source income to controlling U.S. shareholders, or in an interest charge on the income when it is repatriated to the U.S. The earliest of these regimes (dating from 1937) applied only to foreign corporations controlled by five or fewer U.S. individuals.[5] In 1962, the anti-deferral mechanism was applied to foreign corporations controlled by U.S. corporate as well as individual shareholders, and in 1986, it was extended to all U.S. shareholders of foreign corporations, even if they only hold a minuscule percentage of the shares.

It should be noted, however, that the common feature of all of these regimes, as well as a currently proposed, simplified regime uniting most of them, is that they only apply to passive foreign income. In 1962, the original Kennedy administration proposal for eliminating deferral on all the foreign earnings of controlled foreign corporations was defeated, as were similar proposals in the 1970s; most recently, in 1992, a similar proposal by former Chairman Rostenkowski also did not meet with any enthusiasm, and no movement in this direction seems to be likely. Instead, various recent enactments have expanded the scope of deferral, e.g., by treating interest income of banks and investment income of insurance companies as active.

The result of this regime is that active foreign income enjoys a privileged position over passive foreign income. While passive foreign income is taxed currently even to non-controlling U.S. shareholders, most active foreign income can avoid current U.S. tax, even if it is not currently taxed overseas. Thus, the U.S. unilaterally grants the source jurisdiction the primary right to tax active income, and does not assert residual jurisdiction even if the foreign country does not exercise that right, as long as the income stays abroad; but it asserts its jurisdiction to currently tax passive foreign income, albeit with a foreign tax credit (up to the U.S. tax rate) to avoid double taxation of that income.

A second significant distinction in favor of source based taxation of active foreign income involves the operation of the foreign tax credit. As revised in 1986, the limitation on the credit (by which the credit is limited to the U.S. tax rate on foreign source income) is further limited by applying it separately by categories of income ("baskets"). In particular, several categories of passive income are segregated from each other, so that high foreign taxes on one type of passive income cannot be averaged with low foreign taxes on another type of passive foreign income.[6] For example, if Germany imposes a high withholding tax on interest and India does not, these two categories of income are segregated into separate baskets and cannot be combined to bring the average foreign tax below the limitation. This rule means that if the high withholding tax on the gross interest from Germany translates into a rate on the net interest income that is higher than the U.S. rate, the excess foreign taxes cannot be credited, resulting in a permanent bias against such

---

[5]   This regime was finally abolished in 2004 because it was redundant with more modern ones.

[6]   Under the American Jobs Creation Act of 2004, those baskets are reduced to two (active and passive) from 2007.

investments. Similarly, dividends from each foreign corporation in which the taxpayer controls between 10% and 50% of the shares are segregated, so that high withholding taxes on such dividends from one country cannot be averaged by low withholding taxes on dividends from a different country (e.g., a treaty partner of the U.S.).

The exception to this "basket" system is active foreign source income, which is all lumped into one residual category. This means that high foreign taxes on active income can usually be credited in full if the U.S. corporation can find a low taxed source of active foreign income. For example, suppose that U.S. corporation X has 100 in U.S. source income and 100 in foreign source income from Germany, which bears a German tax rate of 50%. In that case, X's ability to credit the foreign tax will be limited by the formula to the U.S. tax rate times its foreign source income, or 35% × 100 = 35, and its overall tax liability will be 35% × 200 (worldwide income) = 70 (tentative U.S. tax), minus 35 (foreign tax credit allowed by the limitation), for a residual U.S. tax of 35 and total worldwide tax liability of 50 + 35 = 85, an effective tax rate of 42.5%, with 15 of excess foreign tax credits. If X can in this situation find a foreign country which does not tax active income (e.g., Malaysia, which grants tax holidays to foreign investors), and from which it can earn an additional 100 of foreign source income, its foreign tax credit limitation will be 35% × 200 = 70, its overall U.S. tax liability will be 35% × 300 = 105 (tentative U.S. tax) minus 50 (foreign tax credit allowed by the limitation) = 55, and its worldwide tax liability will be 55 + 50 = 105, or an effective worldwide tax rate of only 35% (or 7.5% less than in the previous case).

The ability to thus average active foreign income from several sources for foreign tax credit limitation purposes means than there is a significant incentive for U.S. taxpayers who operate abroad to invest in foreign jurisdictions that levy low effective tax rates on foreign investments, since this will enable them to credit the frequently higher foreign taxes imposed on other business operations.

To sum up: Active foreign business income of domestic taxpayers is not taxed by the U.S. currently if earned through a foreign subsidiary, even if there is no source based taxation, until it is distributed to the U.S. taxpayer (as a dividend, interest, or even as a loan).[7] Moreover, even when distributed, such active income retains its privileged positions because the averaging rules generally mean that all foreign taxes on such income can be credited, so that the U.S. will rarely get to levy even residual taxes on this income. Passive foreign income, on the other hand,

---

[7] As discussed further in note 4 below, the December 2017 tax reform ended deferral on a significant portion of foreign income earned through a controlled foreign corporation. Income not captured by this new anti-deferral regime can benefit from a 100% dividends received deduction (the participation exemption) when received by a 10% U.S. corporate shareholder as a dividend (section 245A)—and thus be exempt from any U.S. income tax. Dividends received by individual shareholders cannot benefit from the dividends received deduction and are taxed on receipt of a dividend from a foreign corporation.

is taxed currently (or with an interest charge), and taxpayers are discouraged from investing such income in countries imposing heavy taxation at source by effectively denying foreign tax credit for such taxes by segregating them in a separate basket. As a result, the U.S. most often will get to tax such passive income currently and fully. While the U.S. retains the residual right to tax active income as the residence country, and recognizes the primary right of other countries to tax passive income at source, the incentives provided by these rules tend toward source taxation of active income and residence taxation of passive income, as the international consensus would indicate, even in the absence of a tax treaty with the U.S.

. . .

NOTES AND QUESTIONS

1. The above is a highly summarized description of the international tax regime and of the U.S. international tax rules. Thus, you do not need to worry if you fail to understand some of it at present. We will come back to this description throughout the course.

2. The structure of international taxation, as described above, can be summarized in the following table, which you may want to refer back to as you study the materials to come.

3. The principles underlying the above scheme can be summarized as follows:

Reuven S. Avi-Yonah, Full Circle? The Single Tax Principle, BEPS, and the New US Model, 1 Global Taxation 12 (2016).

1.   Introduction: The Single Tax Principle

Since 1997, I have argued that a coherent international tax regime exists that is embodied in both tax treaties and the domestic laws of most countries, including the United States, and that limits the practical ability of countries to adopt any international tax rules they choose. I further argued that the core of the international tax regime is two principles, which I call the benefits principle (active income should be taxed primarily at source and passive income primarily at residence) and the single tax principle (all income should be subject to tax once at the rate derived from the benefits principle, i.e., active income at the consensus corporate rate and passive income at the residence rate for individuals).

This formulation has been highly controversial. While most commentators would agree that the benefits principle has been the core of the international tax regime since 1923, many deny the validity of the single tax principle and some doubt its coherence. In particular, the single tax principle suggests that whenever the country that has primary jurisdiction under the benefits principle refrains from taxing cross-border income, the other country (residence for active income, source for passive) should tax it instead. This seemed to fly in the face of observed reality because residence countries typically exempt or defer active income, and source countries refrain from taxing many forms of passive income unilaterally without regard to whether it is taxed at residence.

There are, however, elements of US international tax that seem consistent with the single tax principle. The decision in 1918 to prevent double taxation by granting a foreign tax credit rather than an exemption was justified by Thomas Adams in terms of the single tax principle. The adoption of the foreign passive holding company rule in 1935, followed by the PFIC rule in 1986, seems intended to ensure effective residence based taxation of passive income that is unlikely to be taxed at source. The adoption of Subpart F in 1962 was premised on the assumption that the type of income that can be deferred (active income) is likely to be taxed at source at rates comparable to the US rate, and that other types of income (passive and base company income) for which this assumption does not hold should be taxed on a residence basis regardless of the benefits principle (since some of them, especially base company income, are active income that should generally be taxed primarily at source). . .

4. The above text represents the US international tax regime before 2018. The Tax Cuts and Jobs Act (TCJA), as passed by Congress and signed into law on December 22, 2017, represents the most far reaching reform of the US international tax rules since Subpart F was enacted in 1962.[8] Most importantly, TCJA for the first time since the income tax was enacted in 1913 changes the rule that US resident taxpayers have to pay tax on all income "from whatever source derived" (US Constitution, Amendment XVI; IRC section 61). Under the TCJA, dividends paid to US corporate shareholders from non-Subpart F income of their foreign subsidiaries are exempt from US tax. That remains true even if the dividend was not subject to a withholding tax at source and was paid out of earnings that were not subject to foreign tax in the country where the subsidiary is incorporated.

This "participation exemption" is similar to the tax rules of our main trading partners in Europe and Asia. On the face of it, the participation exemption represents a glaring deviation from what the first author has called the "single tax principle". The single tax principle states that all income should be subject to tax once, at the residence country rate if it is passive income and at the average source country rate if it is active income. The participation exemption violates this principle because it exempts dividends from residence taxation even if they were not taxed at source.

But the violation is less blatant than it appears. First, the participation exemption only applies to 10% corporate shareholders. Portfolio US investors still are taxed on foreign source dividends. Moreover, when the US parent distributes a dividend to its taxable US shareholders or buys back their shares, the distribution is fully taxable at the dividend/capital gains rate (usually 23.8%, calculated as the statutory capital gains rate plus the "net investment income" tax of 3.8%).

Second, in conjunction with adopting the participation exemption, TCJA significantly expanded Subpart F. Specifically, IRC section 951A now

---

[8] The name of the act was stricken from the final version as enacted, but it is still commonly referred to as the TCJA.

currently taxes US parents of controlled foreign corporations (CFCs) on their "global intangible low-taxed income", or GILTI, at a 10.5% rate. GILTI is defined broadly as any income that exceeds a 10% return on the CFCs' basis in their tangible assets (the "hurdle rate"), with a credit for foreign taxes. Thus, the US parents of CFCs are effectively subject to a minimum tax of 10.5% on their offshore earnings that exceeds the hurdle rate. The tax on GILTI is consistent with the single tax principle because contrary to pre-TCJA law it ensures that offshore earnings that exceed the hurdle rate are taxed at 10.5%, and that a residence-based tax applies to those earnings to the extent they are not taxed at source.

Third, there is a new anti-base erosion anti-abuse tax (BEAT) imposed at 10% on deductible payments made by US corporations to their foreign affiliates (which can be foreign parents or CFCs). The BEAT upholds the single tax principle because it imposes tax at source under circumstances where they may not be a tax at residence.

Because of these and other provisions of the TCJA, it can actually be seen as more consistent with the single tax principle than previous law. On the outbound front, prior law permitted US-based multinationals to accumulate over $2.6 trillion in low tax jurisdictions offshore without current US or foreign tax, which was a blatant violation of the single tax principle. On the inbound front, prior law only had a weak limit of interest deductions to foreign related parties, so that massive earnings stripping out of the US could occur.

PART A

GENERAL

CHAPTER 1

JURISDICTION TO TAX AND DEFINITIONS

1.1 JURISDICTION TO TAX: IN GENERAL

Read IRC sections 61(a), 63(a), 1(a) and 11(a). Is there anything strange about the legislative language when considered from the perspective of a world having more than one taxing jurisdiction? (Hint: To whom do those sections apply?)

Now read sections 2(d) and 11(d). As you can see, the general scheme of the Code is to apply the U.S. taxing jurisdiction to everyone, but then limit it in the case of "nonresident alien individuals" and "foreign corporations." (We shall discuss the meaning of those terms later in this chapter). Why does the Code do this, instead of limiting the application of the U.S. income tax up front to residents and domestic corporations?

* * *

Bruins et al., *Report on Double Taxation, Submitted to the Financial Committee*, League of Nations Doc. E.F.S. 73 F. 19 (1923), reprinted in LEAGUE OF NATIONS PUBLICATIONS, II ECONOMIC AND FINANCIAL (No. 28), 22–23 (1923)

* * *

The taxes, though measured by things, eventually fall upon persons and ought to fall upon them in the aggregate according to the total resources of the individual. . . . When the money has left the pocket of the individual, its destination is not a single one but is due to all those governments to whom the individual owes economic allegiance. . . .

In the attempt to discover the true meaning of economic allegiance, it is clear that there are three fundamental considerations: that of (1) production of wealth; that of (2) possession of wealth; that of (3) disposition of wealth. We have to ask where wealth is really produced, i.e., where does it really come into existence; where is it owned; and, finally, where is it disposed of?

By production of wealth we mean all the stages which are involved up to the point of wealth coming to fruition, that is, all the stages up to the point when the physical production has reached a complete economic destination and can be acquired as wealth. The oranges upon the trees in California are not packed, and not even at that stage until they are transported to the place where demand exists and until they are put where the consumer can use them. These stages up to the point where wealth reaches fruition, may be shared in by different territorial authorities.

By disposition of wealth we mean the stage when the wealth has reached the owner, who is entitled to use it in whatever way he chooses. He can consume it or waste it, or re-invest it; but the exercise of his will to do any of these things resides with him and there his ability to pay taxes is apparent. By possession of wealth we refer to the fact that between the actual fruition of production into wealth and the disposing of it in consumption there is a whole range of functions relating to establishing the title to wealth and preserving it. These are largely related to the legal framework of society under which a man can reasonably expect to make his own what has been brought into existence. A country of stable government and laws which will render him those services without which he could not enter into the third stage of consumption with confidence is a country to which he owes some economic allegiance.

. . .

NOTES AND QUESTIONS

1. The three bases of economic allegiance identified by the League of Nations Committee eventually became two: (a) the acquisition of wealth from a <u>source</u> in a given country (the territorial connection) and (b) the location of wealth—the enforceability of the rights to it, and its consumption or accumulation by <u>residents</u> of a given country (the personal connection). Thus, U.S. taxing jurisdiction rests on two distinct bases. As to U.S. residents and domestic corporations, jurisdiction to tax is based on their *personal* connection with the United States (in personam jurisdiction), and is world-wide. As to non-residents and foreign corporations, jurisdiction to tax is based on the *territorial* connection of their income to the United States, and is limited to income from U.S. sources (in rem jurisdiction). These two bases of jurisdiction to tax are also called residence and source based taxation, respectively. (As explored in the next section, the U.S. expands the "personal" connection in tax jurisdiction to assert the right to tax U.S. citizens on a worldwide basis regardless of where they reside.)

Regarding nonresident aliens and foreign corporations, read sections 871(a)(1), 872(a) and 881(a).

2. The principal problem of international taxation, and the one the League of Nations Committee was set up to address, is the avoidance of double taxation when income is derived from one jurisdiction by a resident of another. For example, consider Taxpayer A who is a resident of Country A but visits Country B and earns $10,000 working there. To which country should Taxpayer A pay income tax on the $10,000? As between the two jurisdictions, source and residence, which has the better claim to tax the income? On practical grounds, which country is likely to get "the first bite"? We shall consider the ways in which international double taxation is mitigated in practice much more fully in chapters 8 and 11.

3. What is the relation between economic allegiance and ability to pay, which is usually considered the underlying rationale for the income tax? More specifically, how can source-based taxation, which only takes into account wealth produced in a given location, be reconciled with taxation based on taxpayer's overall ability to pay the tax? Consider the following:

> In most of the modern literature the "ability to pay" theory is preferred. In the international context, however, the "ability to pay" is meaningless until one has identified the persons or the enterprises whose wealth is to be taken into account. . . . As a generalizing principle to deal with the questions of selecting from among a world full of potential taxpayers those who will be taxed by a particular nation, the "cost-benefit" analysis remains valuable. When the focus turns to the question of how much tax should be imposed, the concepts of relevant wealth and ability to pay play their part.

> D. Tillinghast, *Tax Aspects of International Transactions,* 3 (1984).

Do you agree? How is taxation by source countries related to benefits provided? To the taxpayer's wealth? What about taxation by residence countries?

1.2   DEFINITIONS

a. NONRESIDENT ALIEN

Read section 7701(b)(1) and (3). As we have seen, the taxes imposed by section 1 do not apply to nonresident alien individuals (section 2(d)); instead, they are taxed under section 871. What is the principal distinction between the tax imposed on residents and on nonresidents? As a U.S. tax planning matter, would taxpayers prefer to be considered residents or nonresidents of the U.S.

The mechanical definition of section 7701(b) was added to the Code in 1984; previously, the distinction between a resident and nonresident alien was based on a facts and circumstances test, such as whether a person intends to remain permanently in the jurisdiction, which is similar to the tests still used by the various states in distinguishing between residents and non-residents (and in the treaty context to resolve dual residency issues). What are the advantages and disadvantages of the mechanical approach of section 7701(b)?

All individuals other than nonresident aliens are citizens or residents of the United States and subject to tax under section 1. See section 7701(a)(1) and 7701(a)(30).

Can a U.S. citizen who lives abroad ever be considered a nonresident alien?

* * *

Cook v. Tait

Supreme Court of the United States.
265 U.S. 47 (1924).

* * *

■ MR. JUSTICE MCKENNA delivered the opinion of the Court. . . .

The tax was imposed under [the equivalent of section 1 of the Code], which provide[d] . . .: "That . . . there shall be . . . paid for each taxable year upon the net income of every individual a . . . tax of 8 per centum of the . . . net income . . ."[1]

Plaintiff is a native citizen of the United States and was such when he took up his residence and became domiciled in the City of Mexico. . . . The question in the case . . . is . . . whether Congress has power to impose a tax upon income received by a native citizen of the United States who, at the time the income was received, was permanently resident and domiciled in the City of Mexico, the income being from real and personal property located in Mexico.

. . . [T]he foundation of [plaintiff's argument] is the fact that the citizen receiving the income, and the property of which it is the product, are outside of the territorial limits of the United States. These two facts, the contention is, exclude the existence of the power to tax. Or to put the contention another way, as to the existence of the power and its exercise, the person receiving the income, and the property from which he receives it, must both be within the territorial limits of the United States to be within the taxing power of the United States. The contention is not justified. . . . In United States v. Bennett, 232 U.S. 299, the power of the United States to tax a foreign built yacht owned and used during the taxing period outside of the United States by a citizen domiciled in the United States was sustained. . . . It was pointed out [in Bennett] that there were limitations upon [the power of a State] that were not on the national power. The taxing power of a State, it was decided, encountered at its borders the taxing power of other States and was limited by them. There was no such limitation, it was pointed out, upon the national power; and the limitation upon the States affords, it was said, no ground for constructing a barrier around the United States "shutting that government off from the exertion of powers which inherently belong to it by virtue of its sovereignty."

The contention was rejected that a citizen's property without the limits of the United States derives no benefit from the United States. . . .

Judgment affirmed.

---

[1] The following regulation . . . under the Revenue Act of 1921, provides . . .: "Citizens of the United States . . . wherever resident, are liable to the tax. It makes no difference that they may own no assets within the United States and may receive no income from sources within the United States. Every resident alien individual is liable to the tax, even though his income is wholly from sources outside the United States. . . ."

NOTES AND QUESTIONS

1. The Court held that Congress had the legal power to tax U.S. citizens residing abroad. But did Congress exercise its power? The only citation offered is to the Treasury regulation, and the Code is silent on this point, except by implication from the sweeping language of section 1. This situation is striking, given that almost no other country seeks to tax its citizens residing abroad on their worldwide income (the Philippines eliminated taxation on the basis of citizenship in the 1990s; Eritrea is sometimes mentioned as a jurisdiction that taxes on citizenship but it unclear whether tax on such grounds its actually imposed).

2. In essence, the taxpayer argued that for jurisdiction to tax to exist, there must be either residence or source jurisdiction. The Court, however, paraphrased this contention as follows: "or to put the contention another way, as to the existence of the power and its exercise, the person receiving the income and the property from which he receives it must both be within the territorial limits of the United States. (Emphasis added)" Is this the same argument? Which argument is best supported by *U.S. v. Bennett*, the case cited by the Court?

3. What do you think of the Court's contention that U.S. citizens residing abroad benefit from the U.S. government and therefore should pay taxes to support it?

4. The Court stated that the taxing power of U.S. states is limited by the power of other states and therefore cannot extend beyond their borders. How do you think Mexico felt about this decision?

5. What about U.S. citizens who relinquish their citizenship? See section 877A. Is this section an adequate solution? Note that section 877A, enacted in 2008, represents the latest effort to effectively tax expatriating citizens on economic value generated but not yet taxed while they were U.S. citizens (e.g., unrealized appreciation).

b. FOREIGN CORPORATIONS AND PARTNERSHIPS

(i) BEFORE "CHECK THE BOX"

Generally, why does it matter whether an entity is taxed as a corporation or as a partnership? How do we know whether an entity is a corporation? Read section 7701(a)(2), (3), (4), and (5). Many other jurisdictions (e.g., the U.K. and countries influenced by it) use a less formal definition of what is a domestic corporation, such as one based on its location of management and control. What are the advantages and disadvantages of each approach?

Domestic corporations are usually easy to identify because they are incorporated under the laws of one of the states, although the corporate income tax can apply to unincorporated domestic associations. What about foreign entities? Before the controversial check-the-box rules (discussed next) were enacted, the regulations relied on a multi-factor test to classify entities. As you read the following ruling under the pre check-the-box rules, consider the degree of flexibility the multi-factor test offered in tax planning.

Rev. Rul. 88–8

1988–1 C.B. 403.

* * *

ISSUE

Whether an entity organized under foreign law is classified for federal tax purposes on the basis of the characteristics set forth in section 301.7701–2 of the Procedure and Administration Regulations.

FACTS

In 1986, twenty-five United States citizens organized M in Great Britain as an unlimited company by registering M under the Companies Act 1985 (Act), Vol. 8, Halsbury's Statutes of England and Wales, (4th Ed., 1985). . . . Chapter I, Section 1(2) of the Act provides that a company may be:

(a) a company having the liability of its members limited by the [Memorandum of Association] to the amount, if any, unpaid on the shares respectively held by them ("a company limited by shares");

(b) a company having the liability of its members limited by the [Memorandum of Association] to such amount as the members may respectively thereby undertake to contribute to the assets of the company in the event of its being wound up ("a company limited by guarantee"); or

(c) a company not having any limit on the liability of its members ("an unlimited company").

A company is registered under the Act by delivering to the Registrar of Companies for England (Registrar) the company's Memorandum of Association (Memorandum) and Articles of Association (Articles). After registration, the Registrar provides a certificate which indicates that the company is incorporated. Thus, the Act represents Great Britain's "corporation" statute. The effect of registering a company is that, from the date of incorporation stated in the Certificate of Incorporation, the subscribers of the Memorandum, together with such other persons as may from time to time become members of the company, shall be a body corporate by the name contained in the Memorandum, capable of exercising all the functions of an incorporated company, but with such liability on the part of the members to contribute to the assets of the company in the event of its being wound up as provided by the Act.

The Memorandum sets forth the company's name, location, business objective, and share capital. The Memorandum also states the degree of liability assumed by the members of the company. The Memorandum of M provides that there will be no limit on the liability of its members.

The Articles contain regulations for the internal management of the company and for the conduct of its business. Under the Act, there are no restrictions on transfer except as imposed by the Articles of Association. The Articles provide that a member may not substitute a person who is not a member of M, unless the member obtains the consent of the other members.

LAW AND ANALYSIS

Section 7701(a)(3) of the Code provides that the term "corporation" includes associations, joint-stock companies, and insurance companies.

Section 301.7701–1(b) of the regulations states that the Code prescribes certain categories or classes into which various organizations fall for purposes of taxation. These categories or classes include associations (which are taxable as corporations), partnerships, and trusts. The tests or standards that are to be applied in determining the classification of an organization are set forth in sections 301.7701–2 through 301.7701–4.

Section 301.7701–2(a)(1) of the regulations sets forth the following basic characteristics of a corporation: (1) associates, (2) an objective to carry on business and divide the gains therefrom, (3) continuity of life, (4) centralization of management, (5) limited liability, and (6) free transferability of interests. Whether a particular organization is to be classified as an association must be determined by taking into account the presence or absence of each of these corporate characteristics.

Section 301.7701–2(a)(2) of the regulations further provides that characteristics common to partnerships and corporations are not material in attempting to distinguish between an association and a partnership. Since associates and an objective to carry on business and divide the gains therefrom are generally common to corporations and partnerships, the determination of whether an organization that has such characteristics is to be treated for tax purposes as a partnership or as an association depends on whether there exists centralization of management, continuity of life, free transferability of interests, and limited liability. Section 301.7701–2(a)(3) provides that an unincorporated organization shall not be classified as an association unless such organization has more corporate characteristics than noncorporate characteristics.

Rev. Rul. 73–254, 1973–1 C.B. 613, holds that the classification of a foreign unincorporated business organization for federal tax purposes will be determined under section 7701 of the Code and the regulations thereunder. However, it is the local law of the foreign jurisdiction that must be applied in determining the legal relationships of the members of the organization among themselves and with the public at large, as well as the interests of the members of the organization in its assets.

An entity organized under foreign law cannot be classified for federal tax purposes solely on the basis of the label attached to the entity by the statute under which it is established, without an inquiry into the legal relationships of the members of the entity as established under applicable local law. Accordingly, the applicable foreign statute and the entity's organization agreements must be examined to determined whether the entity is classified as a corporation for federal tax purposes. In order to ensure uniformity and certainty regarding the classification of an entity organized under foreign law for federal tax purposes, the standards set forth in section 301.7701–2 of the regulations must be applied. All foreign entities are considered to be "unincorporated organizations" for purposes of section 301.7701–2(a)(3) of the regulations. Consequently, no foreign organization or entity is classified as an association unless such organization or entity has more corporate than non-corporate characteristics.

In the present situation, M has associates and an objective to carry on business and divide the gains therefrom and, therefore, is properly classified as either an association or a partnership. M will be classified as a partnership for federal tax purposes unless the organization has a preponderance of the remaining corporate characteristics of continuity of life, centralization of management, limited liability, and free transferability of interests.

Section 301.7701–2(d)(1) of the regulations provides that an organization has the corporate characteristic of limited liability if under local law there is no member who is personally liable for the debts of or claims against the organization. Personal liability means that a creditor of an organization may seek personal satisfaction from a member of the organization to the extent that the assets of such organization are insufficient to satisfy the creditor's claim.

As permitted under the Act, the Memorandum provides that the members' liability to contribute to the payment of M's debts and liabilities is unlimited. Consequently, M lacks the corporate characteristic of limited liability.

Under section 301.7701–2(e)(1) of the regulations, an organization has the corporate characteristic of free transferability of interests if each of the members or those members owning substantially all of the interests in the organization have the power, without the consent of other members, to substitute for themselves in the same organization a person who is not a member of the organization. In order for this power of substitution to exist in the corporate sense, the member must be able, without the consent of the other members, to confer upon the substitute all the attributes of the member's interest in the organization. The characteristic of free transferability does not exist if each member can, without the consent of the other members, assign only the right to share in the profits but cannot assign the rights to participate in the management of the organization.

Under the Articles, no member may transfer any interest in M without the unanimous prior written consent of the other members.

Consequently, M lacks the corporate characteristic of free transferability of interests.

HOLDING

An entity organized under foreign law is classified for federal tax purposes on the basis of the characteristics set forth in section 301.7701–2 of the regulations.

M has associates and an objective to carry on business and divide the gains therefrom but lacks the corporate characteristics of limited liability and free transferability of interests. Therefore, M is classified as a partnership for federal tax purposes.

NOTES AND QUESTIONS

1.   In Rev. Rul. 93–4, 1993–1 C.B. 225 (under the pre check-the-box rules), the IRS held that a German GmbH which had both limited liability and centralized management, and which could opt for limited life, could qualify as a partnership for U.S. tax purposes if its charter provided that each member could ban the others from transferring their stock, even though the only two members were wholly owned subsidiaries of a U.S. parent company. The ruling reversed the IRS' previous position that restrictions on transferability were meaningless in this context. Do you agree? Why do you think the U.S. parent structured its holding of the GmbH in this way? What are the implications of the structure for limited life?

2.   The shareholders of the U.K. corporation planned to have the corporation be treated as a partnership for U.S. tax purposes. Can you envisage circumstances in which such treatment would be advantageous from a U.S. tax perspective? (Hint: What if the U.K. entity has losses?).

3.   More commonly, the U.S. shareholders would prefer a controlled foreign entity to be classified as a corporation for U.S. tax purposes. Why? What are the implications of the ease with which the choice can be made (as demonstrated by this ruling) for the reach of the taxing jurisdiction of the U.S.? Come back to this question after Chapter 7. Can you provide a more nuanced, and complicated, answer to this question now?

4.   How do you think the entity would be treated for U.K. tax purposes? Can you envisage circumstances in which inconsistent treatment may be advantageous for the taxpayer? (Hint: Consider the loss situation again, and see section 1503(d)). Generally, the U.K. follows a "substantive" (place of management and control) definition of corporate residency, while the U.S. follows a "formal" (place of incorporation) definition. What are the advantages and disadvantages of each approach?

(ii)   AFTER "CHECK THE BOX"

In 1996, the Treasury adopted a regulation (Treas. Reg. 301.7701–1, 2 and 3) that lets all shareholders choose whether entities they own (and which are not incorporated under the laws of one of the states) be treated as corporations or partnerships for U.S. tax purposes, unless the entities are incorporated under the laws of a state or appear on a list of foreign entities treated as corporations. Read the regulation. To what extent is this "check the box" approach only a recognition of reality under the ruling cited above? What are the implications for U.S. taxing jurisdiction? For the ability of shareholders to elect whether to take losses into account if the foreign entity has losses, but to defer paying tax on its foreign source income if it has profits?

We will return to consider the international implications of "check the box" as we proceed. In particular, you should keep it in mind when we discuss deferral (Ch. 7) and the foreign tax credit (Ch. 8).

c. FOREIGN TRUSTS AND ESTATES

Rev. Rul. 81–112
1981–1 C.B. 598.

* * *

ISSUE

Is the estate of the United States citizen who was a resident in a foreign country at the time of death a nonresident alien entity and, therefore, a foreign estate for purposes of section 7701(a)(31) of the Internal Revenue Code?

FACTS

A, a United States citizen by birth, was a resident of Country X for 20 years prior to dying in 1978. At the time of A's death A's spouse, who was the primary beneficiary of A's estate, was a citizen of Country X. A's children, who are equal residuary beneficiaries of A's estate, were citizens and residents of the United States. A's last will and testament was executed in Country X.

Upon A's death, A left an estate that consisted of several businesses incorporated and operated in Country X. The estate's assets also included certificates of deposit and accounts in foreign banks. A had no business interests or assets in the United States.

A company and a bank, both incorporated and operating under the laws of County X, were granted letters of administration and letters testamentary and hold legal title to all the assets of A's estate. The estate is not subject to ancillary administration in the United States or any other country. The administrator and executor are each represented by local counsel. All the income of the estate is from foreign sources.

LAW AND ANALYSIS

Section 7701(a)(31) of the Code provides that the terms foreign estate and foreign trust mean an estate or trust, as the case may be, the income of which, from sources without the United States that is not effectively connected with the conduct of a trade or business within the United States, is not includible in gross income under subtitle A. . . .

In determining whether an estate is a foreign estate under section 7701(a)(31) of the Code, the question is whether the estate is comparable to a nonresident alien individual. Thus, it must be decided whether the estate is alien and nonresident in the United States. Rev. Rul. 62–154, 1962–2 C.B. 148, concludes that the standards that have been developed for making these determinations in the case of trusts are equally applicable to estates. This ruling cites and relies on the case of B.W. Jones Trust v. Commissioner, 46 B.T.A. 531 (1942), aff'd, 132 F.2d 914 (4th Cir.1943), which sets forth standards for determining the alienage and residency of a trust.

B.W. Jones Trust concluded that the trust in question there was an alien entity. In reaching this conclusion, the Board of Tax Appeals considered 1) the country under whose law the trust was created, and 2) the alienages of the settlor, the trustees, and the beneficiaries.

Applying these standards in the instant case indicates that the estate is an alien entity. The assets of the estate are located in country X and are administered under the laws of that country. The company and the bank that hold legal title to the assets of the estate are both incorporated and operating under the laws of country X. Only the alienage of the decedent and the two residuary beneficiaries weigh against alien status for the estate. These factors by themselves, however, do not prevent the estate from being considered an alien entity.

With respect to the residency question, B. W. Jones Trust concluded that the trust in question there was a United States resident. In reaching this conclusion the United States Court of Appeals relied upon the following facts: 1) 90% of the trust property was securities of United States corporations, 2) these securities were held in the United States by a trustee who was a United States citizen, 3) these securities were traded by that trustee on United States exchanges, and 4) these securities returned income collected by the trustee in the United States and handled from an office maintained in the United States for that purpose.

The estate in the instant case had none of the indicia of residency that were present in B. W. Jones Trust. The assets of the estate are held in country X and their management involves no contact with the United States.

HOLDING

A's estate is a nonresident alien entity and, therefore, is a foreign estate for purposes of section 7701(a)(31) of the Code. Thus, the estate is only subject to federal income tax on income that is derived from sources within the United States or income that is effectively connected with the conduct of a trade or business within the United States.

NOTES AND QUESTIONS

1.   As a planning matter, how would you ensure that an estate is treated as a foreign estate?

2.   Under the facts and circumstances test envisaged in the ruling, are some factors more important than others? Which?

3.   In 1997, Congress revised section 7701(a)(31) and added sections 7701(a)(31)(B) and 7701(a)(30)(E) for trusts. Is this approach better than the one reflected in the ruling (and which still applies to estates)? How can you ensure that a trust is treated as a foreign trust under current law?

4.   Note that in some circumstances U.S. residents could also be considered residents of other countries. Why is this problematic from a policy perspective? The effect of tax treaties is elaborated on later, in Chapter 11, but note, in the meanwhile, that such treaties rely significantly on domestic definitions of residency, but also attempt to solve situations of dual-residency and provide a clear (single) treaty residency. Read, for instance, article 4 of the U.S. model tax treaty (reproduced in Ch. 11). Note the very different method of breaking a tie in the case of individuals in comparison to corporations.

1.3   REVIEW PROBLEMS—CHAPTER 1

1.   A is a U.S. citizen, whose parents left the U.S. when she was 1-year old to move to Argentina. She has not been to the U.S. since. She is now 35 and a successful lawyer in Buenos Aires. She asks you whether she will be taxed as a U.S. resident on capital gains she expects to make on stock of a U.S. corporation that she wishes to purchase through an online broker. She has no other income with any connection to the U.S. or U.S. residents.

2.   B is an individual citizen and resident of Brazil. His start-up company negotiates cooperation with a U.S. corporation, which requires him to visit the U.S. Shall he become a U.S. resident in 2019 in the following cases?

    a.   He spent the first three full months of 2017–2019 in the U.S.

    b.   He spent 360 days in the U.S. in each of 2017 and 2019, and the whole month of June in 2019.

    c.   He spent 20 days in the U.S. in each of 2017 and 2018. What is the maximum number of days he can stay in the U.S. in 2019?

3.   What if A (in question 1) was not a U.S. citizen, but had spent the months January-June (exactly) of 2017–2019 in the U.S., enjoying the sun in Miami's south beach and doing nothing else. She continued to practice law in Argentina the rest of the year.

4.   What if A alternatively decided after spending the first week of January 2019 on the beach in Miami to move to Miami and work as a commentator for a local Spanish-speaking radio channel? She returned to Buenos Aires, sold her practice and belongings over the next six

months and returned to Miami on July 1, 2019 for her first day at work. She has not left the U.S. since. She was present in the U.S 180 days in 2017 and did not visit in 2018. Will she be taxed as a U.S. resident on a sale of stock executed on June 1, 2019? On July 1, 2019?

5.   A GmbH is a German entity with limited liability and centralized management under German law. A BV is a similar entity under Dutch law. Assume that both entities do not allow for free transferability of ownership of shares and cease to exist (liquidate) upon the withdrawal or sale of interest by any member of the entity. NV is a Netherlands Antilles corporation. Assume that it is similar to a U.S. corporation in all characteristics. Now, USCO, a Delaware corporation, wholly owns an NV that owns all of the shares of a BV that owns all of the shares of a GmbH, which shall be the only operative entity. This structure was put in place 30 days ago and now the corporate lawyers ask you to assist in accomplishing the following: 1. Free (of U.S. tax) deployment of cash between BV and GmbH (and vice versa). Assume that dividends are free of withholding tax if between resident entities within the E.U.; and 2. Allow for a future IPO of the European operations of the group. Is it possible?

CHAPTER 2

THE SOURCE OF INCOME

2.1 INTRODUCTION AND OVERVIEW

Why does source of income matter? In Chapter 1 above, we have seen the importance of determining the source of income for nonresident individuals and foreign corporations, because (under sections 872(a) and 882(b), respectively) they are generally taxed only on their income from sources within the United States. As we will examine in detail in Chapter 8 below, the source of income is also important for United States persons. Although U.S. persons are generally taxed by the United States on their worldwide income, they can receive a credit for foreign taxes paid on their foreign source income, and this credit reduces their U.S. income taxes.

Question: Given the different ways in which source matters to taxpayers under U.S. law, would taxpayers generally prefer that their income be sourced inside or outside the United States? What if the taxpayer is a nonresident? A U.S. person?

What are the source rules and why do we need them? The source rules are provisions of the Code (and tax treaties) that designate rules for assigning income to a particular jurisdiction. Source rules are a necessity in a world in which most taxing jurisdictions prefer to tax nonresidents, since as a jurisdictional and practical matter they can only tax them on domestic source income. In addition, as long as source-based taxation persists, and some jurisdictions impose taxes on their residents' worldwide income, the best way to prevent double taxation is the foreign tax credit (i.e. the residence country grants its taxpayers a credit for income taxes paid to a foreign country on foreign source income, see Chapter 8). Economists would generally prefer a tax system without source rules, because they contend that defining the economic source of most types of income is a hopelessly complex if not meaningless task. But as long as countries tax nonresidents (which seems likely to continue), source rules will be necessary both to set limits on the scope of that taxation (a source country use of the rule) and to provide foreign tax credits to prevent double taxation (a residence country use).

As we look at the source rules, three basic and interconnected questions arise: (1) What are the different source rules (and their exceptions)? (2) How do we decide in which category an item of income belongs (which matters to the extent the source rules differ for different types of income)? and (3) What if income is earned partly in and partly out of the United States?

The basic source rules for income are given in sections 861–865. In general, the source rules are different for various categories of income, but there is generally no distinction between the rules applicable to U.S.

and to foreign persons. Neither of these results is absolutely necessary: It is possible to imagine a single source rule that would apply to all types of income, and it is conceivable to have different source rules apply to foreign and domestic taxpayers. At the end of this chapter, we will return to the question whether the policy choices reflected in having different rules for categories of income, but the same rules for U.S. and foreign persons, make sense.

Question: Can you think of any disadvantages that result from having different source rules apply to each of an enumerated list of categories of income? (Hint: Compare the list in Table 2.1 below to the categories of income enumerated in section 61(a)).

2.2   SUBSTANTIVE V. FORMAL RULES

The source rules can generally be divided into "formal" and "substantive" ones. Formal rules are rules which leave control over the source of income to the taxpayer and do not attempt to track the economic source of the income. For example, the source rule for dividends is generally residence of the payor. Since dividends are paid by corporations and corporate residence is defined in a way that is controlled by the taxpayer, this is a formal rule in that it lets the taxpayer control the source of dividend income. In addition, it is a formal rule because dividends paid by a foreign corporation are generally considered foreign source even if the corporation derives 100% of its income from the U.S. (and therefore in an economic sense the dividend is U.S. source income).

On the other hand, the source rule for royalties is place of use of the intangible property giving rise to the royalty. This is a substantive rule that seeks to track the economic source of the income, although most economists would contend that the jurisdiction where the research that produced the intangible was performed is also a source of the royalty income.

The major source rules and their exceptions are briefly outlined below (and summarized in Table 2.1):

Dividends: As noted above, dividends are generally sourced to the residence of the payor. Thus, dividends paid by a U.S. corporation are U.S. source, and those paid by a foreign corporation are foreign source. However, dividends paid by a foreign corporation can be U.S. source, at least in part, if a certain portion of income is earned in the United States. Section 861(a)(2)(B). This special source rule can impact U.S. shareholders of a foreign corporation, but post 2004 has limited effect on foreign shareholders.[1]

---

[1]   Until 2004, foreign shareholders could face U.S. withholding tax on these "re-sourced" dividends. The 2004 tax act repealed the withholding tax on foreign corporation dividends treated as U.S. source. Sections 871(i)(2)(D), 881(d). (The importance of this repeal is muted by the fact that these foreign shareholders of foreign corporations were and continue to be subject to the U.S. branch profits tax regime, which had generally superceded the withholding tax on re-sourced dividends. See chapter 5). However, even after the 2004 tax changes, these dividends

Question: ABC Co., a U.S. corporation which earns all of its income in Singapore, pays a dividend to all of its shareholders including U.S. persons and foreign persons. What is the source of that dividend? Are the foreign shareholders subject to U.S. tax on this dividend? After 2010,[2] such dividends are U.S. source income subject to the U.S. income taxation when earned by both U.S. and foreign shareholders.

Interest: Interest is generally sourced to the residence of the payor. Section 861(a). What alternative rules are possible? If a U.S. corporation, XYZ Co., has a branch in Mexico, and that branch borrows money from a Mexican bank, what is the source of the interest paid on the loan? Under the basic rule, it is U.S. source. There are, however, three major exceptions. First, interest paid on deposits with foreign branches of a U.S. corporation or partnership is not U.S. source, if the branch is engaged in the commercial banking business. Section 861(a)(1)(A)(i). Second, in the context of the branch profits tax regime, certain interest paid by the U.S. branch of a foreign corporation may be treated as U.S. source. For example, consider a Swedish corporation with a U.S. branch that borrows from a U.S. bank. Under the general rule—what is the source of the interest paid by the branch on the debt? Now read section 884(f). How does that provision change the result? (The reason for this change in source rule will become clearer when you examine the branch profits tax regime in Chapter 5.).[3]

Question: In the above example, 90% of XYZ Co.'s gross income earned over the past three years was active foreign business income. Under the Code, what is the source of interest paid by XYZ Co.'s branch

---

are still U.S. source under section 861(a)(2)(B)—a relevant fact for the U.S. shareholders of these foreign corporations as they calculate their foreign tax credits (recall that getting credits depends on having foreign source income—which these dividends would not be).

[2] Until new legislation was enacted in August 2010, if a U.S. corporation satisfying the "80/20" test (i.e. 80% or more of the corporation's gross income was active, foreign business income—see sections 871(i)(2)(B) and 881(d)) paid a dividend to a foreign person, then the percentage of the dividend matching the percentage of foreign source income earned by the U.S. corporation was not subject to U.S. withholding tax even though it was U.S. source. For example, if ABC Co. had $85 of foreign active business income and $15 of passive foreign income, then ABC Co. met the 80/20 test because 80% or more of its income was foreign active business income. But when ABC Co. paid a dividend to its foreign shareholders the percentage of the dividend that was excluded from income was the ratio of ABC Co. foreign source income to total ABC Co. income which here is a ratio o $100/$100. Thus, none of the dividend paid to ABC Co.'s foreign shareholders was subject to U.S. withholding tax. This example highlights the important distinction between an item of income being U.S. source and being subject to U.S. income tax. Effective December 31, 2010, the 80/20 exception from withholding on U.S. source dividends is repealed (although certain qualifying corporations and their dividend payments will be grandfathered).

[3] Note also that interest paid by an "80/20" corporation (same definition as above note 2 with respect dividends) traditionally was classified as not U.S. source if during the testing period (i.e. the last three years), 80% or more of the debtor's gross income was active foreign business income. Section 861(c)(1)(A). Thus, in the Mexican branch example above, the interest paid by XYZ Co. would not be U.S. source if XYZ Co. was an 80/20 corporation. However, the legislation enacted in August 2010 repeals these provisions that treated all or some of the interest paid by a U.S. corporation as foreign source. Certain qualifying interest payments will continue to be exempt from withholding under a grandfathering rule. Sections 861(a)(1)(A), 871(i).

to the Mexican bank if the Mexican bank owns 15% of XYZ Co.? (See section 861(c)(2)(A)).

Caveat: Note that the 80/20 test was used differently in the case of dividends as compared to interest. In the dividend context, dividends paid by an 80/20 corporation were still U.S. source, it was just that they could avoid some U.S. withholding tax, depending on the percentage of foreign source income earned. In contrast, interest paid by an 80/20 corporation was not U.S. source, thus it became unnecessary to seek a special exception to the withholding tax generally imposed on foreign lenders receiving dividends or from U.S. debtors. See how the net tax effect for foreign persons receiving dividends or interest from an 80/20 corporation was typically the same (the approaches were different for reasons related to the subtleties of dividend taxation of U.S. persons that were not at issue here). Why did Congress effectively eliminate the 80/20 rule for interest and dividends? Could Congress have achieved its goals without so comprehensively eliminating the 80/20 rules?

Question: When the full extent of the source rules for interest and dividends are considered, are they really based on residence? If not, what factors seem to shape the rules?

Services: Income from services is sourced to where the services are performed. Section 861(a)(3). (Certain exceptions apply—look at section 861(a)(3). How valuable is this exception given the monetary limit? This limit has not been changed in decades.) What alternative rules could have been considered instead of the location of performance? What issues are likely to arise in the case of services? What kinds of payments constitute income from services? See the discussions in Chapters 2.3, 2.4, and 2.5 below. While it may once have been clear where services were performed, the changing nature of commercial activity has put that clarity to the test. Consider two cases: Case #1—Bus Co., a U.S. corporation with an office in Chicago, has a broken computer. Repair Co. sends an employee to Chicago to fix the computer. These repair services are performed in the United States and hence are U.S. source. Case #2— Bus Co. has the same computer problem, but this time it calls Offshore Repair Co, a foreign corporation, to fix the problem. Offshore Repair Co. directs its employee, located outside the United States, to fix Bus Co.'s computer by long distance without entering the United States. What is the source of the repair services income? Does it matter that the offshore transaction replaces what would otherwise be U.S. services? Are there other arguments that a different rule should apply in the second case?

Rents and Royalties: For tangible property, rents are sourced to where the property is located; for intangible property, it is where it is used. Sections 861(a)(4), 862(a)(4). What is the source of royalty income paid for the right to show a film in London?

Property: Gain on the sale of property is sourced according to different rules depending on the type of property (real, inventory, other):

Real property sales income is sourced where the property is located. Sections 861(a)(5), 862(a)(5). The definition of what constitutes a sale of U.S. real property has expanded in response to perceived abuses. See section 897, discussed in Ch. 4.7.

The source of inventory sales income turns on whether the inventory is purchased or manufactured by the taxpayer. For the sale of purchased inventory (i.e. the taxpayer buys and resells) gain is sourced to where the sale takes place under a "title passage" rule. (Title passage refers to conventional rules for commercial contract that identify at what point title on the underlying goods passes). Read sections 861(a)(6) and 862(a)(6). Do the provisions speak of "title passage"? How can it be inferred from the language? What if the taxpayer buys inventory in the United States and sells it in the United States for a gain of $100. What is the source of the $100? Cf. Carding Gill, 38 BTA 669 (1938) (acknowledging the absence of statutory guidance in the entirely domestic case but affirming the use of the place of sale rule).

The source of income from the sale of manufactured inventory was changed in the TCJA to depend entirely on location of production. Under IRC section 863(b) as amended by the TCJA, income from the sale or exchange of inventory property that is produced in whole or in part within the United States and sold outside the United States (or vice versa) is allocated and apportioned between domestic and foreign sources solely on the basis of production activities with respect to the property.

What about the sale of property that is not real property or inventory—for example the sale of a painting hanging in a corporate office or in a private home? Generally such income is sourced to the residence of the taxpayer. Section 865. Note that in section 865, the term resident does not have its usual meaning under section 7701. Instead, section 865(g)(1)(A)(i) defines a U.S. resident as an individual who "is a United States citizen or a resident alien and does not have a tax home (as defined in section 911(d)(3)) in a foreign country" or a nonresident alien who "has a tax home (as so defined) in the United States." Who would like this definition of resident? How would it affect taxation in the following case: Taxpayer A, a U.S. citizen, has been sent by her employer to work in the Paris office for a few years. While she is there, Taxpayer A sells her Monet painting for a gain of $200,000.

A number of important exceptions exist, however to the general rule in section 865 sourcing gain on the sale of property to the taxpayer's residence. Review section 865 and try to map out these exceptions. Do they have anything in common?

Losses on the sale of property are not actually "sourced," rather losses, like deductions, are allocated and apportioned to the different classes of taxpayer income. The treatment of losses on the sale of property is considered further in Ch. 3.

"Newer" Types of Income: In 1986, Congress enacted several new source rules to codify the treatment of income derived from certain less traditional activities: (1) space, ocean, or Antarctica income, (2) transportation income, and (3) international communications income. Look at these rules in section 863(c), (d), and (e). What approach to sourcing do these rules employ? Why do you think Congress considered it necessary to add these specialized source rules to the Code? How would these items of income have been sourced under prior law?

These major source rules are summarized in the following table:

TABLE 2.1
SUMMARY OF SOURCE RULES

TYPE OF INCOME	RULE	EXCEPTIONS
Interest	Residence of payor	
861(a)(1)		
884(f)(1)(A)		
Dividends	Residence of payor	75% domestic business
861(a)(2)		
884(a)		
Services	Place of performance	$3000/90 day rule
861(a)(3)		
Rents/Royalties	Place of use of property	
861(a)(4)		
Sales (General)	Residence of seller	Real estate/Inventory depreciable prop.
865(a)		
865(c)		
Sales (R.E.)	Location of real estate	
861(a)(5)		
Sales (Inventory)	Purchased: Passage of title	
861(a)(6)		
863(b)	Produced: Formula (place of production)	
865(b)	(property/sales)	

These rules can be further divided into formal and substantive, as follows:

Formal Rules	Substantive Rules
Dividends—residence of the payor	Royalties—Place of use
Interest—residence of the payor	Rents—Place of use

Capital gains—residence of the seller	Services—Place of provision
Purchased inventory—title passage	Manufactured inventory—Place of production
	Real estate—location

Note that there is a tendency for the rules for active income (services, royalties, and inventory sales) to be substantive, while the rules for passive income (dividends, interest, capital gains) are formal. The exception is the formal rule for purchased inventory, which depends on where title passes—a purely formal event with no economic significance under the UCC. But when the rule was adopted in the 1920s, title passage had economic significance and therefore the rule was substantive rather than formal.

Does this distinction make sense? (Hint: think about which jurisdiction has the primary right to tax active and passive income under the consensus described in the introduction).

Note also that the source rules for dividends and interest are the same, thus eliminating the need for distinguishing debt from equity for this purpose (unfortunately they are treated differently for other purposes, thus creating both the need and the incentive to distinguish debt and equity). Observe, however, the different tax treatment of dividends and capital gains, although both represent the same economic income: a capital gain on stock represents either current earnings or the present value of future earnings available for distribution as dividends.

Clearly taxpayers have some control over the source of income governed by the formal rules. What about transactions governed by the substantive rules? Can they be avoided? Read the revenue ruling below and then see how the courts treat the same issue in the notes that follow. Which is the better approach?

Rev. Rul. 80–362

1980–2 C.B. 208.

* * *

ISSUE

Are royalties paid for the use of a patent in the United States, under the circumstances described below, subject to United States tax?

FACTS

A, a citizen and resident of a country other than the United States or the Netherlands, licenses the United States rights on a patent to X, a Netherlands corporation. X is a bona fide corporation unrelated to A. X agrees to pay A a fixed royalty each year in return for the patent license. X re-leases [sic] the patent to Y, a United States corporation, for use in the United States. Y agrees to pay X royalties based on the number of units produced by Y each year under the patent. X's fixed royalty to A is not contingent upon the receipt of royalties from Y. A's royalty income is not effectively connected with the conduct of a trade or business within the United States within the meaning of section 871(b) of the Internal Revenue Code.

Article IX(1) of the United States-Netherlands Income Tax Convention, . . . provides that royalties paid to a resident or corporation of the Netherlands shall be exempt from tax by the United States. There is no income tax convention between A's country of residence and the United States.

LAW AND ANALYSIS

Section 861(a)(4) of the Code provides that royalties for the privilege of using a patent in the United States are treated as income from sources within the United States.

Section 871(a)(1)(A) of the Code imposes a tax of 30 percent of the amount received from sources within the United States by a nonresident alien individual as interest, dividends, rents, salaries, wages, premiums, annuities, compensations, remunerations, emoluments, and other fixed or determinable annual or periodical gains, profits, and income.

Section 1.871–7(b) of the Income Tax Regulations provides that royalties, including royalties for the use of a patent, constitute fixed or determinable annual or periodical income to which the 30-percent tax rate imposed by section 871(a)(1)(A) applies.

Section 1441(a) of the Code provides that all persons, in whatever capacity acting, having the control, receipt, custody, disposal or payment of any of the items of income specified in section 1441(b) (to the extent that any of such items constitute gross income from sources within the United States), of any nonresident individual shall deduct and withhold from such items a tax equal to 30 percent thereof.

Section 1.1441–2(a) of the regulations provides that royalties are included in the items of income enumerated under section 1441(b) of the Code.

In the present factual situations, the royalties from Y to X are exempt from United States tax under Article IX(1) of the Convention. However, the royalties from X to A are not exempt from taxation by the United States because there is no income tax convention between A's country of residence and the United States providing for such an exemption. Since the royalties from X to A are paid in consideration for the privilege of using a patent in the United States, they are treated as income from sources within the United States under section 861(a)(4) of the Code and are subject to United States income taxation under section 871(a)(1)(A).

HOLDING

Royalties paid by X to A are subject to United States tax at the 30-percent rate pursuant to section 871(a)(1)(A) of the Code. X, under section 1441(a), is required to withhold from the royalties paid to A a tax equal to 30 percent of such royalties.

NOTES AND QUESTIONS

1. This revenue ruling is based on the U.S.-Netherlands income tax treaty. We will discuss treaties in Chapter 11, but you can already see that the treaty reverses the Code result to give the residence rather than the source country exclusive taxing jurisdiction. Why?

2. Assume that F, a foreign person generally taxable on United States source royalties, licenses a United States patent to X (a U.K. Corporation) for $100. X, in turn, re-licenses the patent for $110 to D, a United States corporation. X is exempt from U.S. tax on its royalty receipts because it is a U.K. corporation and the U.S.-U.K. treaty has a royalty provision similar in this regard to U.S.-Netherlands treaty). Royalties are paid as follows:

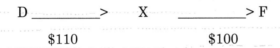

D _____ >   X _____ > F

$110 $100

What is the United States tax, and why?

3. In what way does the criterion of source for royalties differ from that for interest and dividends? That is, how would back to back loans, in contrast to the back to back licenses of Rev. Rul. 80–362, be treated for tax purposes? For example, consider the same transaction outlined above in question 2—but assume the transaction is a loan and not a licensing (with X exempt from any tax imposed by section 881 on United States source interest[4] receiving $110 of interest from D; and F—taxable on any United States source interest—receiving $100 of interest from X. If X were not considered a conduit (i.e. if X's role were respected), who would owe U.S. tax?

4. In SDI Netherlands v. Commissioner, 107 T.C. 161 (1996), the Tax Court held on facts similar to Rev. Rul. 80–362 (but with the royalties flowing among related parties) that the royalties paid by the Netherlands entity to Netherlands Antilles entity for the use of the license in the United States could not be treated as U.S. source because such a result could lead to the imposition of U.S. tax twice (first on the royalty payment from the U.S. entity using the license in the United States to the Netherlands entity, and second on the royalty payment from the Netherlands entity to the Netherlands Antilles entity). Of course this double tax would arise only if the U.S.-Netherlands royalties were not exempt under the treaty. What do you think of the court's argument? (Hint: If the U.S.-Netherlands royalties were not exempt from tax under the treaty, do you think the parties would have structured the transaction the way they did?)

---

[4] The interest exemption may be afforded either by the portfolio interest exemption of section 881(c) (discussed in Ch. 4), or by the U.S.-U.K. treaty.

5. Is the "source" of income always clear? In Arnett v. Commissioner, 473 F.3d 790 (7th Cir. 2007), the court held that income earned by a U.S. resident from employment in Antarctica was <u>not</u> foreign source income because Antarctica was not a foreign country for purposes of section 911. The taxpayer had sought to exclude the income earned in Antarctica under section 911, which grants a special, limited exclusion for labor income earned by a U.S. resident in a foreign country.

2.3   TO WHAT CATEGORY DOES INCOME BELONG?

Where source rules are relatively established but vary depending on income type, taxpayers will seek to characterize their payments as belonging to the category providing the best source result in their situation. The following cases illustrate the tension in classifying income for source purposes. As you read the cases, be sure to identify how the taxpayer and the Service each characterize the payment, and how that makes a difference in taxation.

a.   ROYALTIES V. SALES

The following case is a classic and one that outlines a number important points regarding the interpretation of FDAP. However, it is useful to bear in mind that certain aspects of related law were different, for example section 865 and its rules regarding certain contingent payments on the sale of property were not in the code. Additional differences are outlined in the notes that follow.

Commissioner v. Wodehouse
Supreme Court of the United States.
337 U.S. 369 (1949).

CERTIORARI TO THE UNITED STATES COURT OF APPEALS FOR THE FOURTH CIRCUIT.

* * *

■ MR. JUSTICE BURTON delivered the opinion of the Court.

The question before us is whether certain sums received in 1938 and 1941, by the respondent, as a nonresident alien author not engaged in trade or business within the United States and not having an office or place of business therein, were required by the Revenue Acts of the United States to be included in his gross income for federal tax purposes. Each of these sums had been paid to him in advance and respectively for an exclusive serial or book right throughout the United States in relation to a specified original story written by him and ready to be copyrighted. The answer turns upon the meaning of "gross income from sources within the United States" as that term was used, limited and defined in [sections 872(a), 871 and 861] . . . For the reasons hereinafter stated, we hold that these sums each came within those kinds of gross income from sources within the United States that were referred to in those Acts as "rentals or royalties for the use of or for the privilege of using in the United States . . . copyrights, . . . and other like property," and that, accordingly, each of these sums was taxable under one or the other of those Acts.

The respondent, Pelham G. Wodehouse, at the times material to this case, was a British subject residing in France. He was a nonresident alien of the United States not engaged in trade or business within the United States and not having an office or place of business therein during either the taxable year 1938 or 1941. He was a writer of serials, plays, short stories and other literary works published in the United States in the Saturday Evening Post, Cosmopolitan Magazine and other periodicals. . . .

Pursuant to . . . [an] agreement, the respondent received $40,000 from Curtis, December 13, 1938, for serial rights in and to his story "Uncle Fred in the Springtime." It was published serially in the Saturday Evening Post, April 22 to May 27, 1939. . . .

August 12, 1941, Curtis, through the same agent, paid the respondent $40,000 for the "North American (including Canadian) serial rights" to respondent's novel entitled "Money in the Bank." The agreement was in the form used by Curtis in 1938. . . .

For United States income tax purposes, the respondent's literary agent, or some other withholding agent, withheld from the respondent, or from his wife as his assignee, a part of each payment.

In 1944 the Commissioner of Internal Revenue, petitioner herein, gave the respondent notice of tax deficiencies assessed against him for the taxable years . . . 1938 . . . and 1941. . . . The respondent, . . . not only contested the additional taxes assessed against him, which were based upon the full amounts of those receipts, but he asked also for the refund to him of the amounts which had been withheld. . . .

The petitioner contends that receipts of the type before us long have been recognized as rentals or royalties paid for the use of or for the privilege of using in the United States, patents, copyrights and other like property. Keeping in mind that, before 1936, such receipts were expressly subject to withholding as part of the taxable income of nonresident alien individuals, he contends that those receipts remained taxable and subject to withholding in 1938 and 1941, after the standards for taxation of such aliens had been made expressly coterminous with the standards for subjecting this part of their income to withholding procedures.

In opposition, the respondent argues, first, that each sum he received was a payment made to him in return for his sale of a property interest in a copyright and not a payment to him of a royalty for rights granted by him under the protection of his copyright. Being the proceeds of a sale by him of such a property interest, he concludes that those proceeds were not required to be included in his taxable gross income because the controlling Revenue Acts did not attempt to tax nonresident alien individuals, like himself, upon income from sales of property. Secondly, the respondent argues that, even if his receipts were to be treated as royalties, yet each was received in a single lump sum and not "annually" or "periodically," and that, therefore, they did not come within his taxable gross income.

The petitioner replies that, in this case, we do not properly reach the fine questions of title, or of sales or copyright law, thus raised by the respondent as to the divisibility of a copyright or as to the sale of some interest in a copyright. . . . He claims [also] that the respondent cannot escape taxation of such receipts merely by showing that each payment was received by him in a lump sum in advance for certain uses of a copyright, instead of in several payments to be made at intermediate dates during the life of the copyright. . . .

A. These receipts unquestionably would have been taxed to a nonresident alien individual if received by him under the Revenue Act of 1934. . . .

[The predecessors of sections 871, 1441, and the regulations under section 1441] show that, under the Act of 1934, Congress sought to tax (and withhold all or part of the tax on) the income of a nonresident alien individual insofar as it was derived from payments for the use of or for the privilege of using copyrights in the United States. It also sought to tax (although it could not generally withhold the tax on) any gain which the taxpayer derived from the sale of personal property produced by him without the United States but sold within the United States. Accordingly, if the receipts now before us had been received by the respondent under the Act of 1934, they would have been taxable whether they were treated as payments in the nature of royalties for the use of the copyrights . . . or were treated as payments of a sale's price for certain interests in copyrights . . . The Regulations helpfully carried this analysis further. They showed that, while both forms of income were taxable, yet it was only the royalty payments (and not the sales' proceeds) that were subject to the withholding procedure. . . .

B. The Revenue Act of 1936 preserved the taxability of the several kinds of income of nonresident alien individuals which had been the subject of withholding at their respective sources, including receipts in the nature of royalties for the use of copyrights in the United States.

The Revenue Act of 1936 did not change materially the statutory definition of gross income from sources within the United States under [section 861]. It did, however, amend [section 871] materially in its description of the taxable income of nonresident alien individuals. . . . These amendments . . . limited the taxability of the income of each nonresident alien individual to those kinds of income to which the withholding provisions also applied. . . . By thus restricting the income tax to those specific types of income to which the withholding procedure had previously applied, Congress automatically relieved nonresident alien individuals from the taxation of their income from certain sales of real or personal property, previously taxed. . . . The practical situation was that it had been difficult for United States tax officials to ascertain the taxable income (in the nature of capital gains) which had been derived from sales of property at a profit by nonresident alien individuals, or by foreign corporations, when the respective taxpayers were not engaged in trade or business within the United States and did not have an office or place of business therein. This difficulty was in contrast to the ease of computing and collecting a tax from certain other kinds of income, including payments for the use of patents and copyrights, from which the United States income taxes were being, wholly or partially, withheld at the source. . . . There is no doubt that these steps sought to increase or at least to maintain the existing volume of revenue. No suggestion appears that Congress intended or wished to relieve from taxation the readily accessible and long-established source of revenue to be found in the payments made to nonresident aliens for the use of patents or copyrights in the United States. Much less was any suggestion made that lump sum advance payments of rentals or royalties should be exempted from taxation while at the same time smaller repeated payments of rentals or royalties would be taxed and collected at the source of the income. . . .

II. The receipt of the respective amounts by the respondent in single lump sums as payments in full, in advance, for certain rights under the respective copyrights did not exempt those receipts from taxation.

Once it has been determined that the receipts of the respondent would have been required to be included in his gross income for federal income tax purposes if they had been received in annual payments, or from time to time, during the life of the respective copyrights, it becomes equally clear that the receipt of those same sums by him in single lump sums as payments in full, in advance, for the same rights to be enjoyed throughout the entire life of the respective copyrights cannot, solely by reason of the consolidation of the payment into one sum, render it tax exempt. . . .

The argument for the exemption was suggested by the presence in [sections 871(a) and 1441(a)] of the words "annual" and "periodical." If read apart from their text and legislative history and supplemented by the gratuitous insertion after them of the word "payments," they might support the limiting effect here argued for them. However, when taken in their context . . . they have no such meaning. Those words are merely generally descriptive of the character of the gains, profits and income which arise out of such relationships as those which produce readily withholdable interest, rents, royalties and salaries, consisting wholly of income, especially in contrast to gains, profits and income in the nature of capital gains from profitable sales of real or personal property. . . .

For the foregoing reasons, we hold that the receipts in question were required to be included in the gross income of the respondent for federal income tax purposes. The judgment of the Court of Appeals accordingly is reversed and remanded for further proceedings consistent with this opinion.

Reversed and remanded. . . .

■ MR. JUSTICE FRANKFURTER, with whom MR. JUSTICE MURPHY and MR. JUSTICE JACKSON join, dissenting. . . .

By the Revenue Act of 1936, Congress changed the scheme of taxing nonresident aliens. . . . [A]s to those who are "not engaged in trade or business within the United States," the only type of proceeds to be taxed were those which were attributable to sources within the United States but only if there were "fixed or determinable annual or periodical gains, profits, and income." . . .

The specifically defined receipts—fixed or determinable annual or periodical gains, profits, or income—are not words giving rise to an exemption, and as such to be strictly construed. They are the controlling basis for taxation. To be taxable under [section 871(a)(1)(A)] the proceeds must be from sources within the United States, as set forth in [section 861(a)], but also of the nature defined in [section 871(a)(1)(A)]. . . . Since the reach of [section 871(a)(1)(A)] does not include the proceeds from a sale, receipts from a sale are not taxable even though such proceeds are from a source within the United States and, as such, are listed in [section 861(a)(5)–(6)]. . . .

The Regulations, to be sure, give "royalties" as an example of proceeds which are within the phrase "fixed or determinable annual or periodical gains, profits, and income." . . . But proceeds sought to be brought within the term "royalties" must be of a nature which justifies that classification. Royalties are within the section only because they meet the above description. It completely ignores the intrinsic character of "royalties," and therefore the basis of including them in the larger category of "fixed or determinable annual or periodical gains, profits, and income," to infer that proceeds which do not meet that description but result from the use of another method of realizing economic gain from a property right—that of sale rather than a license producing a recurring income—are also "royalties."

By such reasoning proceeds from the sale of a house would also be within [section 871(a)(1)(A)] because another way that the owner could have realized gain on the property would have been to have leased it over its lifetime. . . .

Therefore, the principle of tax evasion is irrelevant to the disposition of this case, except on the assumption that Congress itself evaded its own tax purposes and that the Court must close what Congress left open. It is taking too much liberty even with tax provisions to read out a defining clause that Congress has written in merely because Congress permitted desirable revenue to escape the tax collector's net. The only judicial problem is whether the proceeds constitute a type of income which Congress has designated as taxable. That type must have the characteristic of being "fixed or determinable annual or periodical gains, profits, and income." A lump-sum payment for an exclusive property right, transferable and transferred by the taxpayer, simply does not meet that qualification. Unless there is something inherent in the copyright law to prevent it, such a transaction is the familiar "sale of personal property." . . . Surely it is a sale of a capital asset. . . . As such it is not subject to the tax. . . .

Thus we are brought to the question which the Treasury, the courts and the parties here have regarded as determinative of this controversy: may serial rights under a copyright be sold in law as they constantly are sold in the literary market? Specifically, is there some inherent obstacle of law which precludes the sale of such serial rights from having the usual incidents of a commercial sale? If it were impossible to make a sale, then the proceeds arguably are "royalties" because in that event the transfer can have been only for the use. There would still remain the difficulty of getting the lump-sum payments within the reasonable meaning of [section 871](a)(1)(A). For, it is fair to recall, [861](a)(4) would only determine whether the payment is from a source within the United States, not whether it is taxable. There would be the further difficulty of calling a payment a "royalty" when its amount bears only that relation to the future proceeds obtained by the transferee in exploiting the literary product as would be reflected in the purchase price of any income-producing property. If, on the other hand, the valuable right that, commercially speaking, was in fact sold, may as a matter of law also be treated as a sale, the proceeds would not be included. . . . The "right to exclude others from interference with the more or less free doing with it as one wills" is precisely the right that Wodehouse transferred to Curtis. To the extent that the Copyright Law gave Wodehouse protection in the United States, he transferred all he had in property of considerable value—the serial rights in his novels—and Curtis acquired all of it. For the duration of the monopoly granted by the Copyright Law, Curtis could assert the monopoly against the whole world, including Wodehouse himself. . . .

To treat the transfer of any one of the various rights conferred by the Copyright Law as a sale would accord not only with analysis of their essential character and the scheme of the Copyright Law, but with the way these rights are treated by authors and purveyors of products of the mind for whose protection the Copyright Law was designed because of the belief that the interests of society would be furthered. The various exclusive rights have different attributes and therefore different significance. For that reason they may be sold separately and form the basis for a new copyright. The author "could sell separately the right to dramatize and the right to make a moving picture play." . . .

Thus it would seem as a matter of legal doctrine that where a person transfers absolutely to another, under terms of payment which do not depend on future use by the transferee, a distinct right conferred by the

Copyright Law granting the transferee a monopoly in all the territory to which the Copyright Law itself extends, legal doctrine should reflect business practice in recognizing that the proceeds are from "the sale of personal property," rather than amounts received as "fixed or determinable annual or periodical gains, profits, and income." . . .

Wodehouse made an absolute transfer of some of those rights. He did not receive royalties but instead gave up that chance in return for a lump sum, just as the seller of a house gives up the right to receive rent in return for the purchase price. That transaction can only be regarded as a sale. As the revenue laws now stand, it was nontaxable.

I would affirm the judgment below.

NOTES AND QUESTIONS

1. To put it mildly, the majority and the dissent framed the issues in the case somewhat differently. Articulate the differences.

2. Justice Frankfurter says that "surely" the transfer of Wodehouse's serial rights "is the sale of a capital asset." The definition of capital asset, then as now, excluded property described in section 1221(a)(1) (i.e., inventory). Some years later, General Dwight Eisenhower obtained capital gain treatment for his book *Crusade in Europe* under the so-called "gentleman author" doctrine—that is, a person not in the business of selling book rights. Congress then added section 1221(a)(3)(A) to the list of noncapital assets. What is there about an author's sale of book rights that might make you wary of capital gain treatment when the maximum tax on capital gains was 25% and that on compensation was 91%?

3. What does Frankfurter's concept of a sale require as to continuing control over economic participation in the transferred property? If those requirements are not met, what would he call the transfer and the consideration for the transfer?

4. Read section 871(a)(1)(D). To what extent does section 871(a)(1)(D) conflict with Frankfurter's concept of a sale? What section of the Code was *Wodehouse* interpreting? When section 871(a)(1)(D) was enacted in 1966, Congress did not amend that section. But did Congress assume that Frankfurter's dissent represented the law or that section 871(a)(1)(D) overruled the majority? Was *Wodehouse* overruled in 1966? How would *Wodehouse* come out today?

5. Was there any other possible characterization of the payment to Mr. Wodehouse, other than sale proceeds or royalties? What would be the result under that characterization?

b. SERVICES V. ROYALTIES

Karrer v. United States

United States Court of Claims.
152 F.Supp. 66 (1957).

* * *

■ LITTLETON, JUDGE, delivered the opinion of the court:

This is an action to recover $201,504.88 in Federal income taxes which plaintiff alleges were erroneously and illegally assessed and collected from him for the years 1941 to 1946, inclusive. The question presented is whether payments made by a domestic corporation to a nonresident alien under a contract between the nonresident alien and a nonresident foreign corporation constitute income to the individual from sources within the United States for the purposes of the income tax imposed by [section 871](a)(1)(A) of the Internal Revenue Code of 1939.

The plaintiff, Paul Karrer, is, and has been since 1918, a professor of chemistry at the University of Zurich, Zurich, Switzerland, where he is Director of the Chemical Institute. He won the Nobel Prize in 1937 for his work in the field of synthetic vitamin structure. Professor Karrer has not been in the United States since 1933, when he spent several weeks here delivering lectures, and does not maintain an office or carry on any business activities in this country.

Plaintiff's duties at the University of Zurich are to give lectures, direct and manage the Chemical Institute and to do scientific research work. Although the university requires him to devote full time to his work, he is free to do what he wishes in such spare time as he may have.

In the early 1930's, Professor Karrer became interested in the flavins, which are yellow dyestuffs that occur frequently in the plant and animal kingdom. Since some researchers had assumed that vitamin B-2 was identical with certain flavins, plaintiff undertook the investigation of the vitamin B group, especially vitamin B-2. Karrer's researches required the extraction of a flavin which could be most conveniently obtained from sweet whey, a by-product of the manufacture of cheese. This flavin substance extracted from whey was lactoflavin and is present in very small quantities only. It was therefore necessary for Karrer to make arrangements for the processing of large quantities of whey from which might be recovered the required amount of lactoflavin needed for his research in the vitamin B field.

On May 7, 1934, plaintiff approached the F. Hoffmann-LaRoche & Co. Ltd. of Basle, Switzerland, hereinafter referred to simply as Basle, and asked it to support his investigations in the vitamin B-2 field by processing a large quantity of whey in accordance with his instructions. At this time, the chemical structure of vitamin B-2 was not known and consequently no one knew whether a synthesis of vitamin B-2 could be made or if it would have any commercial value. On May 8, 1934, Basle wrote plaintiff that it would be glad to cooperate with him and, in July 1934, began processing whey in accordance with instructions received from the professor. Just before Basle began processing the whey, it wrote plaintiff that it was proceeding with the work on the assumption that he would grant Basle the sole right to exploit the manufacturing processes resulting from his investigations if his research proved to be of commercial value. Basle stated that if any process worked out by plaintiff as a secret process showed considerable improvement over existing knowledge, or if the process led to a patent, Basle would grant plaintiff a participation in the net proceeds of the sales of vitamin B-2 products manufactured and sold by it. Plaintiff accepted Basle's proposal by letter.

Under Swiss law the exchange of letters between plaintiff and Basle constituted a contract which may be designated as a special employment contract, under the terms of which all patents resulting from plaintiff's discoveries belonged to Basle, the employer. Both parties understood that plaintiff would be responsible for the scientific work, that Basle would develop the processes for commercial exploitation, that all commercial rights in secret processes or formulae discovered by plaintiff would belong to Basle, together with the right to patent and market products developed therefrom, and that Basle would pay plaintiff a percentage of the net proceeds of the sale of such products. The contract at that time stated the rights of the parties, including the compensation to be paid to plaintiff, in general terms only, because commercial prospects could not then be evaluated.

From the processed whey produced by Basle in accordance with its special employment contract with Karrer, the professor isolated natural vitamin B-2 and sent the prescription to Basle. In August 1934, plaintiff determined the chemical structure of natural vitamin B-2 and from this he proceeded to discover how vitamin B-2 could be produced synthetically in the laboratory. Plaintiff turned this discovery over to Basle, which proceeded to develop the manufacturing processes for the commercial exploitation of vitamin B-2. Basle did not begin marketing synthetic vitamin B-2 in quantity until 1940, because it was not clear until about that time that the vitamin had an important function in the human body or was of any real commercial value.

During the period in 1934, when plaintiff was doing research on synthetic vitamin B-2, Basle refused to allow plaintiff to work with others in vitamin B-2 experiments. From time to time plaintiff prepared scientific papers for publication in a Swiss chemical journal, but before he submitted such papers for publication he would send the paper to Basle for its approval. Basle would either approve the paper without change or suggest that certain statements be added or deleted.

During the period from 1934 to 1939, Basle filed applications in many countries for patenting the discoveries and syntheses of Karrer. The plaintiff actively assisted and materially aided Basle in preparing and filing the patent applications and also aided Basle during subsequent litigation involving the patents.

Early in 1939, plaintiff told Basle that he had heard that lactoflavin ampules were on the market and that he assumed Basle would give him a percentage of the sales. A representative of Basle stated that negotiations as to the extent of plaintiff's participation would be concluded as soon as certain patent questions were settled.

On December 9, 1940, after he heard that the sales of lactoflavin could be increased in the future, plaintiff wrote Basle to remind it of its agreement to grant him a participation in the net proceeds of vitamin B-2 sales. After some bargaining between the parties as to the extent of plaintiff's participation it was agreed that plaintiff was to participate in the sales for a period of twelve years. Basle gave the plaintiff the choice of starting participation either on January 1, 1940, or on January 1, 1941, and he selected the latter date. On January 15, 1941, the parties entered into a formal contract specifying the percentage of net proceeds to be paid by Basle to the plaintiff as 5 percent.   *amount of percent payment.*

In 1937, plaintiff began the study of vitamin E. He discovered that vitamin E substance occurs in the germ of wheat. Because his laboratory in Zurich did not have the equipment necessary to perform all of the experiments required in his research on vitamin E, the plaintiff asked Basle to perform certain experiments for him on extracts from the wheat germ. After isolating natural vitamin E, plaintiff determined the chemical structure of the vitamin and was thereafter able to establish the synthesis of vitamin E. Dr. Otto Isler, a Basle employee, performed extensive experiments in connection with the synthesis of vitamin E, and Basle kept plaintiff informed of Isler's work in that connection. Basle had the same relationship with plaintiff with respect to vitamin E as it had with respect to vitamin B-2. After Basle received the vitamin E synthesis from plaintiff, Basle proceeded to develop the manufacturing process that made it possible to exploit the synthesis commercially.

On August 11, 1938, plaintiff and Basle entered into a formal contract pertaining to the exploitation of the commercial possibilities of their work on vitamin E and fixing the percentage of the net proceeds of the sales which plaintiff was to receive. The contract provided that plaintiff and Basle would collaborate in the synthesis of vitamin E and referred to the parties as partners. Basle had the sole right to take out patents resulting from the collaboration either in its own name or that of Karrer. Patents that were taken in Karrer's name had to be transferred to Basle upon its request, irrespective of whether the patents were applied for before or during the collaboration. The collaboration was to extend for a period of three years and thereafter until one party gave six months' notice to end the agreement. Basle had the exclusive right to commercial utilization of the products of the collaboration and Karrer was to receive 3 percent of the net proceeds of synthetic vitamin E for a period of 12 years. In a supplement to the contract, plaintiff agreed to inform Basle before publishing any article with respect to vitamin E. Plaintiff received payments under the vitamin E contract from December 1, 1938 to November 30, 1950.

In all of his collaboration with Basle, plaintiff never was asked by Basle to participate in the manufacture or sale of the vitamins, nor did he direct or exercise any control over the marketing of the vitamin products.

Basle did not, at any time pertinent to this suit, have a place of business or a permanent establishment in the United States, nor did it engage in any trade or business in this country. On January 27, 1941, Basle and Hoffmann-LaRoche, Inc., of Nutley, New Jersey, hereinafter called Nutley, a New Jersey corporation doing business in the United States as a chemical manufacturing firm with emphasis in the fields of pharmaceutical specialties and vitamins, entered into a contract whereby Nutley was granted the exclusive enjoyment and use within the United States of all of Basle's secret processes and scientific developments pertaining to certain products, including the vitamins which had been synthesized by Karrer. In return, Nutley agreed to pay Basle 4 percent of the net proceeds of sales made by Nutley. This contract terminated a previous agreement between Basle and Nutley whereby for a stated consideration to be paid to Basle, Nutley was given the right to receive and commercially exploit in the United States the results of Basle's research activities. Plaintiff, who had no contractual relationship with Nutley, was not a party to the January 27, 1941, contract between Basle and Nutley.

In all countries other than the United States, Basle applied for patents covering plaintiff's discoveries in its corporate name. In the United States a patent application can be filed only by a natural person, the inventor, and Basle therefore required the plaintiff to file the applications on his vitamin B-2 and vitamin E discoveries. Plaintiff was reimbursed by Basle for all expenses that he incurred with respect to filing the patent applications. Also at Basle's request, plaintiff assigned the vitamin B-2 and vitamin E United States patent applications to Nutley before the patents were granted. The patent assignments to Nutley were thereupon recorded in the United States Patent Office, and the patents themselves were issued to Nutley as owner and assignee of plaintiff, and, in a few instances in the case of vitamin E, as assignee of Dr. Isler, who had worked with plaintiff in vitamin E research. The procurement of the United States patents was paid for by Nutley or Basle.

The termination dates of the participation contracts entered into between plaintiff and Basle with respect to vitamin B-2 and vitamin E precede the expiration dates of all the United States patents on the two vitamins.

Nutley, the American corporation, produced and marketed vitamin B-2 and vitamin E products and, although Nutley had no contract of any kind with plaintiff, it paid to plaintiff a percentage of all its sales of products containing vitamin B-2 and vitamin E. The percentage paid depended upon the type of preparation involved and was in the amounts specified in the contracts entered into between plaintiff and Basle. Nutley was aware at the time it entered into its contract with Basle that plaintiff was entitled to a percentage of the net proceeds of vitamin B-2 and vitamin E sales made by Basle. In fact Nutley had copies of the contracts entered into between Basle and Karrer, but no mention was made anywhere or at any time in writing of a liability on the part of Nutley to make payments to Karrer. These payments to plaintiff were made by Nutley pursuant to instructions by the president of Nutley. He thought that, although Nutley had no contract with Karrer, since it manufactured synthetic vitamin B-2 and vitamin E products under the Karrer inventions, Nutley should make the payments to Karrer called for by the inventor's contracts with Basle. These payments made to plaintiff by Nutley were characterized on the books of Nutley as royalties.

Nutley withheld and paid United States income taxes on behalf of plaintiff in the sum of $92,978.22 for the years 1941 through 1945. Plaintiff timely filed United States income tax returns for the years 1941 through 1946 and paid a balance shown to be due thereon of $108,526.66. Plaintiff has timely filed claims for refund amounting to $201,504.88, representing the total amount of United States taxes paid and withheld from plaintiff on account of the payments made by Nutley to plaintiff with respect to the sale in the United States of vitamin B-2 and vitamin E products. It is with respect to the payment of these taxes that plaintiff filed its claims for refund and now brings suit before this court. Switzerland accords to citizens of the United States the right to prosecute claims against the Government of Switzerland in its courts and therefore plaintiff has standing to sue in the United States in this court.

The defendant says that the payments from Nutley to Karrer were subject to Federal income tax because they were fixed, periodical income to plaintiff from sources within the United States falling within the provisions of section [871](a)(1)(A) of the Internal Revenue Code of 1939. . . .

It is plaintiff's position that the payments made to him by Nutley were for services performed outside of the United States and are therefore not from sources within the United States so as to provide a basis for the imposition of a United States income tax.

In order to determine this question we must define "gross income from sources within the United States" as that term is used in the context of the statutes imposing, limiting and defining the taxes on nonresident aliens.

Section [871](a)(1)(A), above quoted, prescribes a tax upon income from sources within the United States which consists of fixed or determinable, annual or periodical, income. There seems little question from the facts in this case that Karrer received fixed, periodical income as those terms are used in the Code. We must determine, therefore, whether or not as a matter of contract or law the income was from sources within the United States, since section [872](a) of the Code specifically includes gross income of a nonresident alien only income which is derived from sources within the United States. A definition of what is "gross income from sources within the United States" is contained in section [861] of the Code . . .

It is clear from the foregoing excerpt that if the payments to plaintiff by Nutley were for the use of plaintiff's property located in the United States, then those payments are properly characterized as income from sources within the United States and subject to the tax imposed by section [871]. On the other hand, should we determine, as plaintiff would have us do, that the payments were compensation for labor or services performed by plaintiff without the United States, we must necessarily hold that the income tax thereon was illegally assessed and collected on income exempted from taxation by section [872](a), supra. The issue is, therefore, directed to the precise nature of these payments.

The fact that the payments here in question were made by a United States corporation is not determinative of the right to tax the nonresident alien who is the recipient of such payments. The only criterion for imposing the tax is that the "source" of the income to be taxed must be within the United States. The "source" of income in this connection is not necessarily the payor, but may be the property or the services from which the particular income is derived as indicated in section [861] of the Internal Revenue Code. In the instant case the vitamin B-2 and vitamin E patents, together with the right to use and sell their commercial values, were income producing property and thus a "source" of income. Furthermore, the United States patents and Nutley's right to use and exploit their commercial value were property located within the United States so that payments made by Nutley for such use or for the privilege of such use, would be clearly taxable to the recipient of such payments under section [871]. However, we are of the opinion that the payment made by Nutley to Karrer were not payments for the right of Nutley to use any income producing property or interest therein belonging to Karrer.

The right to use and exploit in the United States the patents granted on the discoveries of Karrer was granted to Nutley by Basle pursuant to the terms of the contract of January 27, 1941, and not by Karrer. Basle was the owner of the commercial rights in Karrer's discoveries and it alone could convey this right to another. Plaintiff's only interest in the sales of the vitamins produced and sold arose out of his contractual relationship with Basle. Defendant urges that the payments made to Karrer were in the nature of royalty payments, but that argument is premised upon the assumption that Karrer's contracts with Basle were royalty contracts. The contracts between Karrer and Basle under which the payments in question were made were entered into in Switzerland between Swiss nationals, and their character and interpretation must be governed by Swiss law. The only evidence as to the nature of the contractual relationship between plaintiff and Basle under Swiss law was offered by plaintiff and was to the effect that the relationship was one of special employment. As such, all payments under the Swiss participation contracts to Karrer were payments of compensation for services rendered in Switzerland. Inasmuch as defendant has not refuted this testimony, we must accept it as a correct statement of Swiss law.

Under all the facts and circumstances, and regardless of the particular manner in which the parties to the two Swiss contracts may have referred to each other, it does not appear that there ever existed between Basle and Karrer any relationship other than that of special employment. The arrangement was analogous to the usual one of a person employed to make inventions for his employer, the employer thereby acquiring title to such inventions and to any patents secured thereon. Payments made to such an employee, even though based on a percentage of the proceeds of the sales of the invented process or object, would be compensation for the employee's services rather than royalties, because the employee's right to such payments derives from his services to his employer and not from any rights in inventions owned by the employee. If the services just described were rendered in a foreign country by a nonresident alien they would not be taxable under the clear wording of section [861(a)](3) and section [872](a) of the Internal Revenue Code.

It is true that Karrer received the payments in suit from Nutley, an American corporation, rather than from the Swiss corporation for which he had performed the services and which Swiss corporation was under contractual obligation to compensate him therefor. This circumstance, however, in no way alters the character of the obligation or of the payments made pursuant thereto. Since Nutley paid the plaintiff amounts due on an obligation owing to plaintiff by Basle for services performed for Basle by plaintiff in Switzerland, they do not represent payments for plaintiff's rights or interest in property located in the United States, but rather payments for services performed outside the United States, and are therefore exempt from taxation. Nutley's denomination of the payments as royalties on its books cannot change the true character of these payments.

Defendant cites several cases and urges that Commissioner v. Wodehouse, 337 U.S. 369 . . . [is] applicable to this case. In the Wodehouse case, P. G. Wodehouse, a nonresident alien, sold to a United States publishing house the rights to publish and sell certain stories written by him. The consideration paid for such rights were lump sum payments which the taxpayer contended were the proceeds of the sale of personal property not taxable to a nonresident alien under section [871] of the Code, and, in the alternative, that if the court should find that these payments were in fact royalties, they were not "annual" or "periodical" payments and should therefore be excluded from taxation. The Supreme Court reversed the lower court decision favorable to the plaintiff and held that the lump sum payments were in the nature of advances of royalty payments which were intended to be taxed under section [871]. The Court in the Wodehouse case necessarily found that the payments were from sources within the United States, and this finding would seem to follow readily from the fact that Wodehouse himself or his agent had sold the rights directly to a United States publishing house.

The situation presented in the case now before the court is clearly distinguishable on its facts since Karrer sold nothing to Nutley, the American corporation, nor did Basle sell anything to Nutley as the agent for Karrer. As we pointed out earlier herein, Karrer had nothing to sell to Nutley since all rights in his inventions and any patents thereon had vested in Basle. . . .

It is the opinion of the court that the payments received by Karrer from Nutley were income from sources without the United States and were not taxable under the internal revenue laws in effect during the period in suit.

Plaintiff is entitled to judgment in the amount of $201,504.88, together with interest provided by law. Judgment will be entered to that effect.

It is so ordered.

■ LARAMORE, JUDGE; MADDEN, JUDGE; WHITAKER, JUDGE; and JONES, CHIEF JUDGE, concur.

NOTES AND QUESTIONS

1. Why did Nutley pay Karrer directly, characterizing the payments as "royalties"? (Hint: What would have been the tax result if Nutley had paid Basle?)

2. Are you persuaded by the court's reliance on Swiss law? What was the evidence for Swiss law? Why was the "particular manner in which the parties to the two Swiss contracts may have referred to each other" irrelevant? Note that in general, U.S. courts follow U.S., and not foreign law, principles in determining the U.S. tax liability of foreign parties (see the *Biddle* and *Goodyear* cases in Ch. 8 below).

3. Could the transaction between Karrer and Basle been characterized in any way other than services or royalties? (Hint: Think of *Wodehouse*). What would have been the tax result under this characterization?

4. If one person thinks up cookie recipes, another bakes and sells the cookies, and they share the net proceeds, what sort of an arrangement is that? What would have been the result in *Karrer* of that characterization?

* * *

Boulez v. Commissioner

United States Tax Court.
83 T.C. 584 (1984).

. . .

■ KORNER, J.: Respondent determined a deficiency in petitioner's individual income tax for the calendar year 1975 in the amount of $20,685.61. After concessions, the sole issue which we are called upon to decide is whether certain payments received by petitioner in the year 1975 constitute "royalties," within the meaning of the applicable income tax treaty between the Federal Republic of Germany and the United States, and are therefore exempt from tax by the United States, or whether said payments constitute compensation for personal services within the meaning of that treaty, and are therefore taxable by the United States. . . .

OPINION

Petitioner contends that the payments to him in 1975 by CBS, Inc., were not taxable by the United States, because they were "royalties" within the meaning of the applicable treaty between the United States and the FRG. Respondent, as noted above, contends that the payments in question were taxable to petitioner by the United States because they represented compensation for personal services performed in the United States by petitioner. The parties are in agreement that the outcome of this dispute is governed by the effective income tax treaty between the United States and the FRG.

Under date of July 22, 1954, there was executed a "Convention Between the United States of America and the Federal Republic of Germany for the Avoidance of Double Taxation with Respect to Taxes on Income," 5 U.S.T. (part 3) 2768, T.I.A.S. No. 3133. As amended by a Protocol, dated September 17, 1965, 16 U.S.T. (part 2) 1875, T.I.A.S. No. 5920, this convention (hereinafter the treaty) was in effect during the year 1975, and undertook to govern, in stated respects, the income taxation of natural and juridical persons resident in either of the two nations, whose affairs might bring into play the taxing laws of both nations. Petitioner, a resident of the FRG, was a person within the coverage of the treaty. The relevant portions of the treaty provide, in part:

Article II

(2)   In the application of the provisions of this Convention by one of the contracting States any term not otherwise defined shall, unless the context otherwise requires, have the meaning which the term has under its own applicable laws

* * *

Article VIII

(1) Royalties derived by a natural person resident in the Federal Republic or by a German company shall be exempt from tax by the United States.

* * *

(3) The term "royalties", as used in this Article,

(a) means any royalties, rentals or other amounts paid as consideration for the use of, or the right to use, copyrights, artistic or scientific works (including motion picture films, or films or tapes for radio or television broadcasting), patents, designs, plans, secret processes or formulae, trademarks, or other like property or rights, or for industrial, commercial or scientific equipment, or for knowledge, experience or skill (know-how) and (b) shall include gains derived from the alienation of any right or property giving rise to such royalties.

* * *

Article X

* * *

(2) Compensation for labor or personal services (including compensation derived from the practice of a liberal profession and the rendition of services as a director) performed in the United States by a natural person resident in the Federal Republic shall be exempt from tax by the United States if[3]—

Acknowledging that the provisions of the treaty take precedence over any conflicting provisions of the Internal Revenue Code of 1954 (sec. 7852(d); see also sec. 894), we must decide whether the payments received by petitioner in 1975 from CBS, Inc., constituted royalties or income from personal services within the meaning of that treaty. This issue, in turn, involves two facets:

(1) Did petitioner intend and purport to license or convey to CBS Records, and did the latter agree to pay for, a property interest in the recordings he was engaged to make, which would give rise to royalties?

(2) If so, did petitioner have a property interest in the recordings which he was capable of licensing or selling?

The first of the above questions is purely factual, depends upon the intention of the parties, and is to be determined by an examination of the record as a whole, including the terms of the contract entered into between petitioner and CBS Records, together with any other relevant and material evidence. . . .

---

[3] The treaty then enumerates several conditions which must be fulfilled before the exemption from tax by the United States is effective. The parties are in agreement that the exceptions do not apply in the present case, so that the payments in question, if held to be income from personal services, are taxable by the United States to petitioner.

The second question—whether petitioner had a property interest which he could license or sell—is a question of law. The treaty is not explicit, and we have found no cases or other authorities which would give us an interpretation of the treaty on this point. We are therefore remitted to U.S. law for the purpose of determining this question. Treaty, supra at art. II (2).

We will examine each of these questions in turn.

1.   The Factual Question

By the contract entered into between petitioner and CBS Records in 1969, as amended, did the parties agree that petitioner was licensing or conveying to CBS Records a property interest in the recordings which he was retained to make, and in return for which he was to receive "royalties?" Petitioner claims that this is the case, and he bears the burden of proof to establish it. Welch v. Helvering, 290 U.S. 111 (1933); Rule 142(a).

The contract between the parties is by no means clear. On the one hand, the contract consistently refers to the compensation which petitioner is to be entitled to receive as "royalties," and such payments are tied directly to the proceeds which CBS Records was to receive from sales of recordings which petitioner was to make. Both these factors suggest that the parties had a royalty arrangement, rather than a compensation arrangement, in mind in entering into the contract. We bear in mind, however, that the labels which the parties affix to a transaction are not necessarily determinative of their true nature (Kimble Glass Co. v. Commissioner, 9 T.C. 183, 189 (1947)), and the fact that a party's remuneration under the contract is based on a percentage of future sales of the product created does not prove that a licensing or sale of property was intended, rather than compensation for services. Karrer v. United States, 138 Ct. Cl. 385, 152 F. Supp. 66 (1957).

On the other hand, the contract between petitioner and CBS Records is replete with language indicating that what was intended here was a contract for personal services. Thus, paragraph 1 (quoted in our findings of fact) clearly states that CBS Records was engaging petitioner "to render your services exclusively for us as a producer and/or performer *** It is understood and agreed that such engagement by us shall include your services as a producer and/or performer." Paragraph 3 of the contract then requires petitioner to "perform" in the making of a certain number of recordings in each year. Most importantly, in the context of the present question, paragraph 4 of the contract (quoted in our findings) makes it clear that CBS considered petitioner's services to be the essence of the contract: petitioner agreed not to perform for others with respect to similar recordings during the term of the contract, and for a period of 5 years thereafter, and he was required to "acknowledge that your services are unique and extraordinary and that we shall be entitled to equitable relief to enforce the provision of this paragraph 4."

Under paragraph 5 of the contract (quoted supra), it was agreed that the recordings, once made, should be entirely the property of CBS Records, "free from any claims whatsoever by you or any person deriving any rights or interests from you." Significantly, nowhere in the contract is there any language of conveyance of any alleged property right in the recordings by petitioner to CBS Records, nor any language indicating a licensing of any such purported right, other than the designation of petitioner's remuneration as being "royalties." The word "copyright" itself is never mentioned. Finally, under paragraph 13 of the contract, CBS Records was entitled to suspend or terminate its payments to petitioner "if, by reason of illness, injury, accident or refusal to work, you fail to perform for us in accordance with the provisions of this agreement."

Considered as a whole, therefore, and acknowledging that the contract is not perfectly clear on this point, we conclude that the weight of the evidence is that the parties intended a contract for personal services, rather than one involving the sale or licensing of any property rights which petitioner might have in the recordings which were to be made in the future.

2. The Legal Question

Before a person can derive income from royalties, it is fundamental that he must have an ownership interest in the property whose licensing or sale gives rise to the income. Thus, in Patterson v. Texas Co., 131 F.2d 998, 1001 (5th Cir.1942), the Court of Appeals adopted the definition of a "royalty" as "a share of the product or profit reserved by the owner for permitting another to use the property." Likewise, in Hopag S.A. Holding De Participation, etc. v. Commissioner, 14 T.C. 38 (1950), this Court held that in order for a payment to constitute a "royalty," the payee must have an ownership interest in the property whose use generates the payment, citing the definition of royalties in section 119(a)(4) of the Internal Revenue Code of 1939 (section 861(a)(4) in the 1954 Code is the same), which states:

> Rentals or royalties from property located in the United States or from any interest in such property, including rentals or royalties for the use of or for the privilege of using in the United States patents, copyrights, secret processes and formulas, good will, trademarks, trade brands, franchises, and other like property,

* * *

See also Downs v. Commissioner, supra; Moore v. Commissioner, T.C. Memo. 1968–110.

In its definition of royalties, the treaty embodies the same fundamental concept of ownership. Thus, in article VIII(3)(a), "royalties" are defined to mean "amounts paid as consideration for the use of, or the right to use, copyrights, artistic or scientific works * * * or other like *property* or rights," and article VIII(3)(b) also states that the term "royalties" "shall include gains derived from the alienation of any right or *property* giving rise to such royalties." (Emphasis supplied.)

It is clear, then, that the existence of a property right in the payee is fundamental for the purpose of determining whether royalty income exists, and this is equally true under our domestic law as well as under the treaty.

Did the petitioner have any property rights in the recordings which he made for CBS Records, which he could either license or sell and which would give rise to royalty income here? We think not. . . .

Holding and Rule for royalties.

NOTES AND QUESTIONS

1.   An authoritative treatise states that under present law Boulez might have a copyrightable interest. Kuntz & Peroni, *U.S. International Taxation,* A2.03[6][e][i], n.254 (2010).

2.   What did Boulez receive?

3.   What was the legal issue?

4.   Why did it matter?

5.   Which country had the better right to tax? Does this depend on how the transaction is characterized?

6.   What would have happened if CBS had given a copyright interest to Boulez at the time he conducted? (Hint: Look at section 83(a)). A 2006 protocol to the 1989 U.S.-Germany tax treaty states that "[w]here an artiste resident in one Contracting State records a performance in the other Contracting State, has a copyrightable interest in the recording, and receives consideration for the right to use such recording based on the sale or public playing of such recording, then such consideration shall be governed by [the royalties article, providing for exemption from source country tax]."

7.   In the absence of the above treaty provision, how would a taxpayer in the same position as Boulez improve the likelihood that the payment would be characterized as royalty? (Note that taxpayers would not universally prefer a royalties label over a services label. Compare *Boulez* with *Karrer*.)

8.   In *Tobey v. Commissioner*, 60 T.C. 227 (1973), the Tax Court held that a painter who sold his own paintings through galleries had "earned income" for purpose of section 911(b). Section 911 grants a qualified U.S. citizen or resident an exclusion from gross income for a limited amount of foreign source "earned income" (i.e. income due to the performance of services). The taxpayer had both risk (his paintings were not commissioned) and control (his paintings were not commissioned, so he painted what he chose).

In *Boulez*, risk and control were split as outlined below. How should these factors impact the characterization of income? Even if these factors are relevant in cases like *Boulez* (which assess the characterization of a payment as dividend or sales income to determine withholding under the Code or a treaty), are these factors likely to be as relevant when characterizing a payment for purposes of other provisions, such as section 911? Why might it be different?

CONTROL		RISK	
CBS	BOULEZ	CBS	BOULEZ
The recording session, including choice of musicians	How to perform	Studio cost	Payment contingent
Manufacturing and distribution	What to perform	Manufacture & distribution costs	Effort, inability to compete

c. SERVICES V. INTEREST (THE TRANSFER OF MONEY)

The provision of money or credit has sometimes been considered a service. When you use a credit card, are you borrowing money, paying for a service, or both?

PRIVATE RULING 7808038

* * *

DATE: November 25, 1977.

. . .

Gentlemen:

This is in response to your letter, dated March 17, 1977, in which rulings are requested that the commitment fees paid by the United States branch of Corp. A to Corp. B constitute income from sources without the United States under section 862(a)(3) of the Internal Revenue Code of 1954, income not effectively connected with a United States trade or business under section 864(c)(4) of the Code, income not taxable under either section 881(a) or 882(a), and income not subject to withholding under section 1442.

The following facts were submitted for consideration. Corp. A is a corporation organized under the laws of country X and has its general offices there. Corp. A is engaged principally in the banking business in country X and throughout the world through branches and subsidiary companies. Corp. A has a branch in the United States and has been engaged in the banking business in the United States through its United States branch since date M.

Corp. B is a wholly-owned subsidiary of Corp. A organized under the laws of country Y. Its general offices are located in country Y and it has been represented that Corp. B has no permanent establishment in the United States.

Corp. B proposes to place at the disposal of the United States branch of Corp. A a standby amount of $50,000,000. Under the terms of an agreement, the United States branch shall be able to borrow upon five days notice, any amount up to $50,000,000 at currently prevailing interest rates. The funds will be available initially for one year and such availability may be renewed annually.

A commitment fee of 1/4 of one percent on the overall amount of the commitment will be charged by Corp. B for the service of maintaining the funds on a standby basis. The commitment fee is not to be a charge for the use of funds and it will be charged whether or not the funds are used. The "draw down" of funds under the line of credit will be determined by the cash needs of the United States branch, and the commitment fee is to be earned by having the funds available when the branch requires them. The commitment fee is not refundable in any event and will not be applied in reduction of any other charges such as stated interest or other fees. The services related to the authorization of the funds and the raising of the funds will be performed by Corp. B at its offices outside of the United States. It has been represented that Corp. B has no offices and does not conduct any business in the United States through the United States branch of Corp. A or through any other office.

Section 862(a)(3) provides that compensation for labor or personal services performed without the United States shall be treated as income from sources without the United States.

Section 881(a) of the Code provides, in part, for a tax of 30 percent of the amount of the items of income enumerated therein received from sources within the United States which is not effectively connected with the conduct of a trade or business within the United States.

Section 882(a)(1) of the Code provides, in part, that a foreign corporation engaged in a trade or business within the United States during the taxable year shall be taxable on its taxable income which is effectively connected with the conduct of a trade or business within the United States. Section 882(a)(2) provides that in determining taxable income for purposes of section 882(a)(1), gross income includes only gross income which is effectively connected with the conduct of a trade or business within the United States.

Section 864(b) of the Code and section 1.864–2 of the Income Tax Regulations define the term "engaged in a trade or business within the United States" to include the performance of personal services within the United States at any time within the taxable year. In addition, other guidelines are set forth therein to determine whether foreign corporations or nonresident alien individuals are engaged in the conduct of a trade or business within the United States in given situations. If a foreign corporation or nonresident alien individual is considered to be engaged in a trade or business in the United States during the taxable year, sections 864(c) and 1.864–4 set forth guidelines to determine whether income earned by that foreign corporation or nonresident alien individual is effectively connected with the United States trade or business. Section 864(c)(4) provides that no income, gain, or loss from sources without the United States shall be treated as effectively connected with the conduct of a trade or business within the United

States unless the nonresident alien individual or foreign corporation has an office or other fixed place of business within the United States to which the income, gain, or loss is attributable and the income, gain, or loss is of certain specific enumerated types or the foreign corporation is a life insurance company taxable under part I of subchapter L.

Section 1442 of the Code provides, in pertinent part, that in the case of a foreign corporation, there shall be deducted and withheld at the source in the same manner and on the same items of income as provided in section 1441 a tax equal to 30 percent thereof. Section 1441(a) provides, in pertinent part, that except as provided in section 1441(c) all persons, in whatever capacity acting having the control, receipt, custody, disposal, or payment of any of the items of income specified in section 1441(b) (to the extent any such items constitutes gross income from sources within the United States), of any nonresident alien individual or of any foreign partnership shall deduct and withhold from such items a tax equal to 30 percent thereof. Specified items of income in section 1441(b) include interest, dividends, rent, salaries, wages, premiums, annuities, compensations, remunerations, emoluments, or other fixed or determinable annual or periodical gains, profits, and income.

Rev. Rul. 54–43, 1954–1 C.B. 119, characterizes "commitment fees" as current charges for making business funds available on a standby basis and not charges for the use of such funds. Rev. Rul. 54–43 further states that such fees do not represent interest incurred.

Rev. Rul. 56–136, 1956–1 C.B. 92, distinguishes commitment fees from interest on indebtedness which is defined as compensation for the use or forbearance of money. See Deputy v. du Pont, 308 U.S. 488 (1940), Ct. D.1435, 1940–1 C.B. 118.

 Rev. Rul. 70–540, 1970–2 C.B. 101, concludes that under the specified circumstances therein, a commitment fee is a charge for the agreement to make funds available rather than for the use or forbearance of money and, therefore, is not interest.

In accordance with Rev. Rul. 54–43, Rev. Rul. 56–136, and Rev. Rul. 70–540, the commitment fees to be paid by the United States branch of Corp. A to Corp. B are not payments of interest but instead are payments made in order to secure the availability of funds upon need. It has been represented that all relevant services with respect to the available funds are to be performed at Corp. B offices outside of the United States. The commitment fees constitute income received by Corp. B for the performance of services performed without the United States.

Accordingly, the commitment fees to be paid by the United States branch of Corp. A to Corp. B constitute income from sources without the United States pursuant to section 862(a)(3) of the Code.

It has been represented, in effect, that Corp. B is not engaged in trade or business in the United States. Because the commitment fees to be paid by the United States branch of Corp. A to Corp. B constitute income from sources without the United States, pursuant to section 864(c)(1)(B) of the Code, such income is not effectively connected with the conduct of a trade or business within the United States. Section 862(a) taxes only effectively connected income.

Accordingly, the commitment fees to be paid by the United States branch of Corp. A to Corp. B is income not effectively connected with the conduct of a trade or business within the United States pursuant to section 864(c)(1)(B) of the Code and is not taxable under section 882(a).

Section 881(a) of the Code taxes certain enumerated items of income provided such income is received from sources within the United States and is not effectively connected with the conduct of a trade or business within the United States. As discussed previously, the commitment fees to be paid by the United States branch of Corp. A to Corp. B is income received from sources without the United States pursuant to section 862(a)(3) and such income is not effectively connected with the conduct of a trade or business within the United States.

Accordingly, the commitment fees to be paid by the United States branch of Corp. A to Corp. B is income which is not subject to tax under section 881(a).

Section 1442 of the Code provides for the deduction and withholding of tax from the specified items of income only to the extent any of such items constitutes gross income from sources within the United States. The commitment fees to be paid by the United States branch of Corp. A to Corp. B have been held, pursuant to a ruling above, to constitute income from sources without the United States.

Accordingly, the commitment fees to be paid by the United States branch of Corp. A to Corp. B are not subject to withholding under section 1442 of the Code. . . .

Sincerely yours,

John L. Crawford

Chief, Corporation Tax Branch

NOTES AND QUESTIONS

1.   Having read this ruling, do you think that the extension of credit is a service or a borrowing or some combination of both? In *Deputy v. du Pont*, 308 U.S. 488, 498 (1940), the Supreme Court stated that "[i]n the business world 'interest on indebtedness' means compensation for the use or forbearance of money."[5] What, in the definition of interest as "compensation for the use or forbearance of money," is forbearance?

---

[5]   The case involved the deductibility (as trade or business expenses, or as interest) of expenses for borrowing stock to be used for executive compensation purposes. Frankfurter's concurrence would have excluded from the concept of "carrying on any trade or business" the incurring of expenses "in the active concern over one's own financial interest." Rather, he would

2. In Private Ruling 7808038, assume that A is a Dutch bank (Allegemeine) with a United States branch, and that B, the subsidiary of the Dutch bank, is incorporated in the Bahamas, a country that imposes no tax. Any commitment fees paid by the United States branch will reduce the branch's taxable income, saving the United States tax of 21 percent (in 2019) of the amount paid. The fee will not be taxed by the Bahamas.

3. For what is the commitment fee being paid? Why is this a service?

Bank of America v. United States

United States Court of Claims.
680 F.2d 142 (1982).

* * *

■ KASHIWA, J.: This case is before the court on the defendant's exceptions to the findings of fact and recommended opinion of Trial Judge John P. Wiese. We are faced with the question whether certain commissions received by the plaintiff, Bank of America, an Edge Act corporation, should be characterized as United States or foreign source income for purposes of the Internal Revenue Code. The trial judge held that all the commissions at issue should be classified as income from sources without the United States. We have given careful consideration to the trial judge's report, the parties' submissions, and oral argument. We find that although we agree with the result reached by the trial judge as to acceptance and confirmation commissions, our reasoning differs. With regard to negotiation commissions, we reverse the trial judge and hold such commissions are income from sources within the United States.

I.

Plaintiff is an Edge Act corporation organized and existing under the laws of the United States, 12 U.S.C. §§ 611–614 (1976). The Edge Act amended the Federal Reserve Act in 1919 to allow national banks to participate in international banking through qualified subsidiaries. These subsidiaries, such as plaintiff, are domestically organized corporations which are permitted to offer international banking services. As an Edge Act corporation, plaintiff is only permitted to transact international business and therefore is actively involved in financing of international trade. The financing of international trade often occurs through the issuance of short-term loans, confirmed letters of credit, and the issuance of banker's acceptances. We are concerned here with the commissions charged by the plaintiff for confirmed letters of credit, banker's acceptances, and negotiations in connection with export letters of credit. These commissions were paid to the plaintiff in the years 1958 through 1960 by foreign banks located in Germany, France, Guatemala, and Singapore.

---

have required a trade or business to involve "holding one's self out to others as engaged in the selling of goods or services."

The transactions at issue involve commercial letters of credit issued by a foreign bank on behalf of a foreign purchaser for the benefit of an American exporter. Such a transaction begins with an agreement by an American exporter to sell goods to a foreign purchaser. The foreign purchaser then requests a commercial letter of credit from a foreign bank. A commercial letter of credit is a mechanism whereby trade is facilitated; it is a document issued by a bank on behalf of its customer. This document commits the bank to pay the beneficiary of the letter when certain terms have been met. By issuing a letter of credit, a bank has substituted its credit for that of its customer. The bank issuing the letter of credit is commonly referred to as the opening bank. An opening bank will only issue a letter of credit when it has evaluated its customer's credit and found it satisfactory. Thus, the foreign bank issues the letter of credit for the benefit of the American seller if it finds the foreign purchaser creditworthy. The terms of such a letter typically include some of the terms of the sales agreement between the merchants. By issuing such a letter of credit, the foreign opening bank agrees to pay the American seller a specified amount when the American seller meets the terms of the letter of credit. The foreign opening bank, in turn, expects its customer, the foreign importer, to reimburse it.

The letter of credit the opening bank issues may be one of two different types known as sight and usance (or time) letters of credit. The beneficiary of a sight letter of credit is entitled to payment once it is determined he has met the terms of the letter. The beneficiary of a usance letter of credit, on the other hand, is not entitled to payment immediately upon the determination he has met the terms of the letter but, instead, will be entitled to payment at a specified time in the future. Plaintiff's transactions in the years in question involve both sight and usance letters of credit. A draft is the specific document that directs payment be made to the beneficiary. There are both sight and time drafts.

Any letter of credit a foreign bank issues on behalf of a foreign purchaser for the benefit of an American exporter can be advised by the plaintiff as a courtesy to the foreign bank. When a letter of credit is advised by the plaintiff, plaintiff simply informs the American beneficiary of the letter that a letter of credit has been issued in his favor and forwards the letter. The plaintiff does not undertake any credit commitment and so informs the letter's beneficiary. Uniform Customs & Practice for Commercial Documentary Credits Fixed by the Thirteenth Congress of the International Chamber of Commerce, Article 6 (effective January 1, 1952) (hereinafter UCP). See generally U.C.C. § 5–103. During the years 1958 through 1960, no fee was charged by the plaintiff for advisement.

Alternatively, a foreign bank can request that plaintiff confirm a sight letter of credit. If plaintiff agrees to confirm a sight letter of credit, it not only advises the letter but it irrevocably commits itself to pay the face amount of the letter. Payment is only made if the beneficiary has met the terms of the letter of credit. UCP, Article 5. Under ordinary circumstances, plaintiff is reimbursed by the foreign bank for paying the draft. Whether or not plaintiff agrees to confirm a letter of credit depends upon its evaluation and credit analysis of the opening bank. When plaintiff does agree to confirm, it notifies the beneficiary. At the time of notification, plaintiff becomes obligated to pay the beneficiary regardless of any changes that might take place affecting the ability of the opening bank to reimburse the plaintiff. Subsequent to notification, a beneficiary can present the letter of credit and supporting documents for payment at any time.

After plaintiff has paid the amount of the draft to the beneficiary, it will ordinarily debit the foreign bank's account. Occasionally, a foreign bank will prepay the amount of the draft. When prepayment occurs, plaintiff usually waives the confirmation commissions. During the years 1958 through 1960, plaintiff charged the opening foreign bank a commission for confirmation of 1/20 of 1 percent of the face amount of the draft for each calendar quarter or fraction thereof the draft was outstanding. If this amount was less than $2.50, a minimum commission of $2.50 was charged. Confirmation commissions are charged the opening bank upon confirmation.

A foreign bank can also request that plaintiff negotiate a letter of credit. This can be done with either advised or confirmed letters of credit. Negotiation is the process by which the beneficiary's papers are checked to see whether they meet the terms of the letter of credit. This process takes place at the offices of the plaintiff in the United States. The papers are then forwarded to the opening bank which independently checks the papers. Neither bank inspects the merchandise. In cases involving confirmed letters of credit, negotiation is always required. A separate commission was charged for negotiation of 1/10 of 1 percent of the face amount of the draft. If this amount was less than $5, a minimum of $5 was charged. With confirmed letters of credit, the negotiation commission is charged at the time the sight draft is honored.

The third type of commission we are concerned with is acceptance commissions. Acceptance financing can be used to obtain money directly, to finance the storage of goods, to refinance sight letters of credit, and to finance export/import trade. The acceptance commissions involved in this case were paid to plaintiff by foreign banks as a result of plaintiff's acceptance of time drafts drawn pursuant to usance letters of credit issued by those foreign banks or pursuant to lines of credit extended by plaintiff to the foreign banks. When a foreign bank requests plaintiff's involvement in acceptance, plaintiff first undertakes a credit analysis of the foreign bank. If plaintiff agrees, the following procedures take place.

In circumstances involving usance letters of credit, when the beneficiary presents the letter of credit and accompanying documents to the plaintiff, plaintiff examines the documents to see whether they conform to the terms of the letter of credit. If the documents conform, plaintiff places its acceptance stamp upon the draft. By placing its stamp upon the draft, plaintiff obligates itself to pay the face amount of the draft on the day the draft becomes due. Once the plaintiff's acceptance is stamped, the draft becomes a money market obligation and is freely tradeable. Plaintiff is obligated to pay any holder in due course on the date the draft becomes due.

Customarily, the foreign bank pays the plaintiff the face amount of the time draft on the day preceding the date of its maturity. This normally is done by debiting the account of the foreign bank. Whether or not the foreign bank makes the payment, plaintiff is obligated to pay the holder in due course of the draft. The acceptance commission charged by the plaintiff would vary from 1.5 percent to 2.5 percent per year of the face amount of the draft, depending upon the creditworthinesss of the foreign bank.

In circumstances involving lines of credit, these lines of credit are first established by plaintiff for its customer, the foreign bank, after a thorough credit evaluation is conducted by the plaintiff. Typically, such lines of credit provide a ceiling dollar amount for direct loans, letters of credit, and banker's acceptances. A foreign bank with such a line of credit can ask the plaintiff to refinance a letter of credit. In that situation, the foreign bank requests plaintiff provide financing in the form of a draft of a sufficient amount to reimburse the plaintiff for its payment of the original letter of credit. The present discounted value of this draft is equivalent to the face amount of the original draft. Plaintiff then accepts the newly issued draft. Upon its acceptance, the draft is immediately discounted and the proceeds used to reimburse the plaintiff for payment of the original draft. Under this type of financing, the foreign bank pays the plaintiff the same acceptance commissions it pays in acceptance transactions involving usance letters of credit. The foreign bank also pays the plaintiff the amount of the discount. The commission and the discount together approximate the interest charge the foreign bank would have paid if it had obtained a direct loan.

For the years 1958 through 1960, plaintiff paid income taxes on its international banking business to Germany, France, Guatemala, and Singapore. In its timely filed United States income tax return for the same years, plaintiff deducted foreign income taxes under 26 U.S.C. (Internal Revenue Code of 1954 as amended) § 164 (subsequent section references are to the Internal Revenue Code). In May 1963, plaintiff timely filed claims for refund for federal income taxes assertedly overpaid by it for its 1958 through 1960 taxable years. These claims were amended in June 1966. In its refund claims, plaintiff elected to take a foreign tax credit under section 901, rather than a deduction under section 164, for the foreign taxes it paid or accrued. In computing the per-country foreign tax credit limitation of section 904 for income taxes paid to Germany, France, Guatemala, and Singapore, plaintiff treated the confirmation, negotiation, and acceptance commissions it received from foreign banks in those countries as income from sources without the United States. The Internal Revenue Service partially disallowed plaintiff's refund claim. It determined the commissions in question were income from sources within the United States for purposes of computing the limitation under section 904. On May 11, 1971, plaintiff timely instituted this federal income tax refund suit. We must decide whether the confirmation, negotiation, and acceptance commissions at issue are United States or foreign source.

II.

Plaintiff as a domestic corporation is taxed on its worldwide income. Sections 11, 61; Great-West Life Assurance Co. v. United States, ante at 477. Under section 901, plaintiff receives a foreign tax credit for taxes it has paid on its income to foreign countries. The calculation of this credit is limited by section 904. . . . Thus before plaintiff's foreign tax credit can be calculated, it must be determined whether the commissions at issue are United States or foreign source income.

Sections 861, 862, and 863 provide rules for determining whether a particular class of income is United States or foreign source. Sections 861(a)(1) through (a)(7) provide rules as to when specific classes of income are sourced within the United States. Section 862(a) is a parallel section providing when those same classes of income are sourced without the United States. The classes of income specified in sections 861 and 862 include the following: interest, dividends, personal services, rentals and royalties, income derived from the disposition of real property, income from the sale or exchange of personal property, and underwriting income. Section 863 grants the Secretary authority to promulgate regulations allocating income not specified within sections 861(a) and 862(a) to sources within and without the United States. It is well settled that sections 861 through 863 and their predecessors were not intended to be all inclusive. . . . When an item of income is not classified within the confines of the statutory scheme nor by regulation, courts have sourced the item by comparison and analogy with classes of income specified within the statutes. . . .

The parties agree that to determine what class of income the commissions fall within or may be analogized to we must look to the substance of the transaction. Karrer v. United States, 138 Ct. Cl. 385, 152 F. Supp. 66 (1957). The Government takes the position that plaintiff is paid by the opening banks for services. If so, personal services are sourced under sections 861(a)(3) and 862(a)(3) where those services are performed. The Government contends the plaintiff performed the services relevant to the commissions at its offices in the United States. Thus, under the Government's theory the commissions are sourced as income from United States sources. The plaintiff, on the other hand, contends it is not being paid for personal services but instead for something similar to a loan (the use of its credit). Thus, plaintiff claims its income may be sourced by analogy to interest. Interest under sections

861(a)(1) and 862(a)(1) is in general sourced by the residence of the obligor. . . . Since the commissions in this case were paid by foreign banks, the plaintiff takes the position the income is foreign source. The trial judge found neither the plaintiff's nor the Government's analysis adequate. He found the substance of the transaction to be the plaintiff's promise to pay regardless of any change in circumstances, i.e., the assumption of risk of the foreign bank's default. Since the foreign bank and the risks associated with it are located abroad, the trial judge found the commissions to be foreign source. We do not fully agree with any single analysis proposed. Instead, to properly determine the source of the various commissions, we hold that each type of commission must be examined separately.

III.

We first consider acceptance commissions. As we have explained, the acceptance commissions at issue are paid by foreign banks to the plaintiff under two circumstances. The first is as a result of plaintiff's acceptance of time drafts drawn pursuant to usance letters of credit; the second is as a result of the acceptance of drafts drawn against a line of credit extended by plaintiff to the foreign bank. In either circumstance what occurs is similar to a loan transaction. In a direct loan a lender uses its credit resources to intermediate between investors who have money available and borrowers who need money. With direct loans a lender will assume the credit risk of the borrowers to its investors. Similarly, in the acceptance financing transactions at issue the plaintiff acts as an intermediate between the holder of the acceptance draft and the foreign bank. The plaintiff assumes the credit risk of the foreign bank and assures the draft's holder of its payment. The plaintiff on the day it accepts a time draft guarantees to the holder that it will pay the full amount of the draft at maturity at a specified date in the future. This promise is made regardless of any change in circumstances that may cause the foreign bank to default. The significance of the plaintiff's guarantee is evidenced by the fact the accepted draft is freely tradeable on the market. In Helvering v. Stein, 115 F. 2d 468 (4th Cir.1940), an income tax case that also involved a sourcing issue, the Fourth Circuit treated a transaction involving banker's acceptances as a loan transaction. The court said, "[we] do not think the use of drafts instead of promissory notes in these transactions goes beyond the form of the transaction." Id. at 472. Similarly, we find the use of banker's acceptances in the transactions at issue cannot mask their essence. The essence of the transactions, like that of a direct loan, is the use of plaintiff's credit.

The commissions charged the foreign banks by the plaintiff include elements covered by the interest charges made on direct loans. The evidence established that interest typically covers credit risk, credit administration, and cost of funds. See Noteman v. Welch, 108 F. 2d 206 (1st Cir.1939). If we examine an acceptance financing transaction, we find the commissions charged cover credit risk and credit administration. A holder of an accepted draft may present his draft for payment or trade it on the market at any time. If he does so prior to maturity, he will receive not the value of the draft at maturity but its discounted value. The discounted value is equivalent to the value at maturity less the time value of the money (cost of funds). Typically, the discount plus the acceptance commission will approximate interest charges made on direct loans. It is thus apparent that acceptance commissions cover the cost to the plaintiff of credit administration and credit risk. This notion is reinforced by the fact plaintiff varied its acceptance commissions from 1.5 percent to 2.5 percent dependant upon the creditworthiness of its customer. Cf. Sumitomo Bank, Ltd. v. Commissioner, 19 B.T.A. 480 (1930) (compensation received by a Japanese bank with a New York agency on transactions involving banker's acceptances was treated as interest).

We recognize the plaintiff performed services for the foreign banks as part of the acceptance transactions; e.g., advising the letter of credit and making the actual payment of money. We also realize foreign banks without United States branches cannot perform some of these services and require an agent in the United States to do that. We find, however, these functions are not the predominant feature of the transactions. Instead, the predominant feature of these transactions is the substitution of plaintiff's credit for that of the foreign banks. No one would question that lenders in making direct loans also perform personal services. Yet, Congress in section 861(a)(1) and 862(a)(1) has determined that all interest will be sourced under those sections and not as personal services under sections 861(a)(3) and 862(a)(3). We find acceptance commissions to be similar.

In Block v. Pennsylvania Exchange Bank, 253 N. Y. 227, 230–231, 170 N. E. 900, 901 (1930), then Chief Judge Cardozo said:

* * *

"The central function of a commercial bank is to substitute its own credit, which has general acceptance in the business community for the individual's credit, which has only limited acceptability."

* * *

A bank "manufactures credit by accepting the business paper of its customers as security in exchange for its own bank credit in the form of a deposit account."

* * *

"It stands ready to exchange its own credits for those of its customers."

* * *

Whatever is an appropriate and usual incident to this substitution or exchange of credits, instead of being foreign to the functions and activities of banking, is in truth of their very essence. It is the end for which a bank exists. [Citations omitted.]

We therefore hold that for the reasons discussed the acceptance commissions are sourced by analogy to interest under the provisions of sections 861(a)(1) and 862(a)(1). Interest should be used because it furnishes the closest analogy in the statutory sourcing provisions, although (as the trial judge held) the acceptance commissions here cannot be directly equated with interest. Since interest is sourced by the residence of the obligor and the obligors in all instances were foreign banks, we find the acceptance commissions are foreign source income.

IV.

We next consider confirmation commissions. In confirmation the plaintiff advises a sight letter of credit and adds to it its own obligation to pay the sight draft when the terms of the letter have been met. The plaintiff irrevocably commits itself to pay the draft at the time it notifies the beneficiary of the letter of credit that it has confirmed the letter. The beneficiary may present the letter and accompanying document to the plaintiff for payment at any time thereafter. The account of the foreign bank is ordinarily not debited until the sight draft is presented and paid. Thus, from the moment of confirmation the plaintiff has made an enforceable promise to pay regardless of any change in the foreign bank's financial condition. As in acceptance and loan transactions, the plaintiff here has acted as an intermediate, has assumed the risk of default of the foreign bank, and has assured the draft's holder of payment.

The services involved in confirmation are little different from those in advisement where no charge is made. The only service provided by plaintiff in confirmation that was not provided in advisement is the actual payment of dollars. It is important to note the plaintiff usually waived the confirmation commissions when a foreign bank prepaid the amount of the draft. Thus, it is apparent what plaintiff was really charging for was not the services performed but the substitution of its own credit for that of the foreign bank. The predominant feature of the confirmation transactions was the substitution of plaintiff's credit for that of the foreign banks. The services performed were subsidiary to this. Therefore due to the similarities between a confirmation and a loan transaction, we hold that the confirmation commissions should be sourced by analogy to interest. Again we point out that interest should be used because it furnishes the closest analogy in the statutory sourcing provisions, although confirmation commissions cannot be directly equated with interest. Since the obligors were all foreign banks, we hold the confirmation commissions are income from without the United States.

V.

Finally, we consider negotiation commissions. The analysis here is somewhat different. Negotiation is simply the process by which the plaintiff checks to see whether the documents the beneficiary presents conform to the terms of the letter of credit. A separate commission is charged for negotiation of advised letters of credit and confirmed letters of credit. Where negotiation commissions are charged for advised letters of credit, we find the commissions are charged for personal services. In those situations there is no assumption of any credit risk by the plaintiff. The plaintiff does not make any payments to the beneficiary of the letter of credit. The only risk present is that the plaintiff will improperly check the documents. No analogy can possibly be drawn to a loan situation. Since the negotiation commissions charged with advised letters of credit are clearly being charged for personal services, we hold they should be sourced as personal services.

Plaintiff contends, however, in instances where letters of credit are confirmed it must negotiate to protect itself from making payment to a party who has not met the terms of the letter of credit. Plaintiff therefore argues the risks of the confirmation process are dominant and should control the sourcing of the negotiation commissions. Although we agree plaintiff requires negotiation with confirmed letters of credit, we cannot agree the character of confirmation controls that of negotiation. Plaintiff's own method of structuring these transactions militates against its argument. Plaintiff does not charge just one fee for confirmation and negotiation but makes two separate charges at two separate points in time. It charges negotiation commissions when it completes the actual negotiation process. In addition, the negotiation commissions are twice that of confirmation commissions. We therefore cannot conclude the services of negotiation are so minor they are merely a part of the confirmation process. When a foreign bank pays the plaintiff a commission for negotiation, it is paying the plaintiff to perform the physical process of checking documents and nothing more.

We therefore hold negotiation is a personal service and negotiation commissions are therefore sourced under sections 861(a)(3) and 862(a)(3). Personal services are sourced where the services are performed. Plaintiff performed negotiation at its offices in the United States. Thus, negotiation commissions are income from sources within the United States.

VI.

In conclusion, we hold the acceptance and confirmation commissions at issue are income from sources without the United States and the negotiation commissions are income from sources within the United States. We remand the case to a trial judge under Rule 131(c) to determine in light of our holding the foreign tax credit and refund plaintiff shall receive for the taxable years 1958 through 1960.

NOTES AND QUESTIONS

1. What was the context in which the issue of source of income arose? Why does a U.S. resident taxpayer care about source? We will return to this question in Ch. 8.

2. What was the Service's position? Was it consistent with its position in PLR 7808038?

3. Whom was the accepting bank (Bank of America) benefiting? Just the opening bank? Did the opening bank bear the cost of the acceptance and confirmation commissions, or do you think it required its customer, the importer, to reimburse it for them? If so, is this decision based on the form of the transaction (that since the opening bank paid the commission, the guarantee must have been for the benefit of the payor)? If Bank of America had not in effect guaranteed the foreign bank's letter of credit, who would have been inconvenienced?

4. What asset of Bank of America was it bestowing on its recipients? Where is that asset located? Where was it being used?

5. If Bank of America is providing a service, should the income not be sourced under the services source rules?

6. What was the core of the Court's reasoning in *Bank of America*? Why did it reject the taxpayer's argument regarding the negotiation fees?

7. Assume that a United States bank with only domestic assets issues a credit card to a United States citizen and resident, who used it to charge a meal at a restaurant in Canada. In effect, the Canadian restaurant pays the United States bank a fee equal to two percent of the meal. The holder of the credit card may also pay a fee to the bank for the privilege of having such card. Now there are two payors. What is the source of the income?

8. The debates over characterizing payments extends beyond the cases examined above. For example, in Pinson v. Commissioner, T.C. Memo. 2000–208, the court held that payments from a foreign corporation to the taxpayer constituted compensation for services performed in the United States, not a foreign source dividend. More generally, having read the cases in this section, what do you think of the system in which each category of income has its own source rule? This system has its origin in the Seligman commission report (see introduction), dating from a time when economists believed they could define the economic source of each type of income. Economists no longer believe that, but the system is still with us, and it is embodied in the tax treaties (which have a separate article for each category) and thus very hard to change.

For a recent attempt to adapt this system to the realities of the modern world, look at Treas. Reg. Sec. 1.861–18 (dealing with the classification of income from transactions in software). In particular, look at the examples. What do you think about this regulation?

Container Corporation v. Commissioner

United States Tax Court.
134 T.C. 22 (2010).

■ HOLMES, JUDGE: The Code puts a 30-percent tax on "fixed or determinable annual or periodical" income received by foreign corporations from sources within the United States. Vitro, S.A. is a Mexican corporation that charged one of its U.S. subsidiaries a fee to guarantee the subsidiary's debt to U.S. lenders. The question presented in this case is whether that fee is from a source within the United States.

BACKGROUND

In 1901, Vitro, S.A. started making glass bottles for the local beer makers of Monterrey, Mexico. Over the next century, Vitro became one of Mexico's most successful businesses, eventually becoming a holding company and the corporate parent of a large number of consolidated and unconsolidated subsidiaries. . . . Vitro provides administrative and support services to its Mexican operating subsidiaries through a wholly owned management subsidiary, Vitro Corporativo, S.A. (Corporativo).

* * *

Vitro did not have glassmaking plants of its own in the United States, but had inched into the market by organizing marketing and distribution subsidiaries. In December 1988, Vitro reorganized these subsidiaries, and formed Vitro International Corp. as their U.S. holding company.

Then, in May 1989, Vitro organized C Holdings Corp. to be an acquisition company. Vitro merged C Holdings into Container Holdings Corp. in April 1990. (We refer to them collectively as Container.) Container's purpose was to help Vitro gain control of [two U.S. target corporations].

With the targets in sight and its squadron of acquisition vehicles ready to roll, Vitro next had to arm itself with financing. But here Vitro ran into a problem common to Mexican companies in the late '80s—an inability to rely on Mexican financing due to the peso devaluations of 1982 and 1987 which had left even the Mexican government unfinanceable. This made Vitro unfinanceable, because Standard & Poor or Moody's will not give a borrower a higher credit rating than that of its sovereign. Vitro needed to look elsewhere. It turned to two U.S. investment banks—Lazard, Freres & Co. and Donaldson, Lufkin & Jenrette (DLJ)—for help in negotiating the financing and strategy of what Vitro expected would be a hostile takeover.

Vitro wanted ultimately to finance the acquisition [of the U.S. targets] using a combination of bank debt, equity, and high-yield (or, as unwilling corporate targets usually called them, junk) bonds. But before Vitro could get permanent financing, it needed bridge financing for the tender offer. (Bridge financing is short-term financing that aims to provide money for a transaction. It is meant to be repaid after a borrower closes the transaction and can access the capital markets for a mix of short-and long-term debt and equity financing.) DLJ committed up to $295 million in bridge financing to Vitro. . . . Lazard and DLJ also lined up the components of what they expected would be the permanent financing for the acquisitions: hundreds of millions of dollars in bank loans and debt securities.

[The final steps of the acquisition of the U.S. targets were set to take place] on November 2, 1989, but on October 10, 1989 the junk-bond market collapsed when, in a completely unrelated development, the management of United Airlines found it could not finance its leveraged buyout. Without a market for junk bonds, Vitro's bridge financing looked like it might turn into bridge-to-nowhere financing. What followed was one temporary solution after another.

* * *

[Later, as Vitro's short term bridge financing came due, the group pursued a variety of other steps including ultimately moving some of the debt to a U.S. subsidiary ("International") outside of the Container group.] [Vitro] chose International because that company had enough cashflow from its operations to service at least part of the Note. DLJ requested that Vitro guarantee the debt as consideration for the restructuring. Vitro then restructured the Note through a series of transactions:

* * *

To make the first payment on the International 1990 Bridge note, International borrowed $31 million from Banca Serfin (Banca Serfin 1990 loan), a Mexican bank. Vitro guaranteed International's obligations under the Banca Serfin 1990 Loan. The Banca Serfin 1990 Loan matured in March 1991.

All this work on the financing side of the deal would have been fruitless without success on the operations side. And there the initial hopes that Vitro brought to the deal seemed to be justified. By 1991 the increased production capacity was having the desired effect, and Vitro's margins on glass containers were improving. With higher margins, the acquired U.S. target corporation increased its annual cashflow from $100 million to $200 million. But with the financial markets still depressed, Vitro and DLJ agreed that they needed to refinance one more time before they could finally move the debt to from International to [the acquired U.S. target corporation.]

To refinance the debt, International was to issue 21 senior notes (together, the International 1991 senior notes) worth a total of $155 million. The problem was that no one expected International to have sufficient cashflow to make the payments on the International 1991 senior notes unless [International's own related corporation made payments on its notes held by International.] DLJ advised that for International to take on that amount of debt it would need some credit support or the notes would not be marketable.

The needed credit support came from Vitro's guaranty of the International 1991 senior notes. The guaranty allowed the note purchasers to collect from Vitro if International defaulted. Vitro was chosen as guarantor over another U.S. subsidiary because it had a lower debt-to-equity ratio [and no restrictions on its ability to serve as a guarantor]. . . . On March 28, 1991, International issued the International 1991 senior notes to a group of U.S. insurance companies and Vitro guaranteed the notes pursuant to a guaranty agreement.

* * *

International used the proceeds to repay and cancel the International 1990 Bridge note and Banca Serfin 1990 Loan.

International made the following guaranty-fee payments to Vitro on the International 1991 senior notes:

Year	Amount
1992	$2,309,758
1993	1,912,867
1994	2,485,470

* * *

It is the tax treatment of these fees that is at issue in this case. The guaranty agreement set the fee at 1.5 percent of the outstanding principal balance of the notes per year. This 1.5-percent fee was standard—Vitro charged all of its subsidiaries the same fee no matter the subsidiary's capital structure or financial condition. And Vitro's willingness to guarantee its subsidiaries' debt was not limited to International: Vitro's policy was to give a guaranty to any subsidiary whenever it asked for one. The fees were not tied to the amount of work Vitro did to negotiate or monitor the guaranty. Vitro's estatutos (or bylaws) expressly provided that one of Vitro's business purposes was to guarantee the debts of its subsidiaries.

International did not withhold U.S. income taxes from the fees. And, as expected, it also did not have the cashflow to make the interest payments on the International 1991 senior notes. To make those payments, Vitro and Container contributed almost $80 million in capital to International from 1990 to 1994. But the money didn't help. At the end of 1993, soft-drink producers began switching to plastic containers, and in eighteen months the glass-container industry lost one-third of its demand. And then a merger of other glass-container producers knocked Vitro into third place in the U.S. market, a now-shrinking market where it turned out there was room for only two players. The acquired U.S. corporation's profits melted into losses. It filed for bankruptcy in 1997.

The Commissioner's response to this series of unfortunate events was to determine that International should have withheld 30 percent of the guaranty fees it paid to Vitro in 1992–94. . . .

DISCUSSION

Section 881(a) imposes a 30-percent tax on "fixed or determinable annual or periodical" (FDAP) income received from sources within the United States by a foreign corporation, "but only to the extent the amount so received is not effectively connected with the conduct of a trade or business within the United States." Taxes owed under section 881(a) are generally supposed to be withheld at the source. Sec. 1442(a). Thus, for Container to be liable under section 881(a) the guaranty fees must be: (1) FDAP income and (2) received from a U.S. source. See secs. 881(a), 1441(a) (b), 1442(a).

The parties agree that the guaranty fees, paid regularly in fixed amounts, are FDAP income . . . The key question in this case is whether the second requirement is met—was the source of the guaranty fees the United States or Mexico?

We determine FDAP income's source by using the rules in sections 861 to 863. Two rules are especially important here. The first is for interest— the rule is that the source of interest is the residence of the obligor. Secs. 861(a)(1), 862(a)(1); sec. 1.861–2, Income Tax Regs. The Commissioner would like the guaranty fees to be treated as interest, because International is a U.S. company.

Interest Rule

The second rule that's especially important here is the rule on services— that rule is that the source of services is where the services are performed. Sec. 861(a)(3), 862(a)(3); sec. 1.861–4, Income Tax Regs. Container would like the guaranty fees to be treated as payments by International for a service performed by Vitro in Mexico.

Services Rule

The sourcing rules are not comprehensive. If a category of FDAP is not listed, caselaw tells us to proceed by analogy. In other words, if the guaranty fees were neither interest nor payment for services rendered, we would still have to figure out whether they were more like interest or more like payment for services rendered (or, possibly, some other category of FDAP that has a specific sourcing rule). See Hunt v. Commissioner, 90 T.C. 1289, 1301 (1988); Howkins v. Commissioner, 49 T.C. 689, 693–95 (1968); Bank of Am. v. United States, 230 Ct. Cl. 679, 686, 680 F.2d 142, 147 (1982), affg. in part and revg. in part 47 AFTR 2d 81–652, 81–1 USTC par. 9161 (Ct. Cl. 1981).

A.   *Guaranty Fees as Interest*

Interest is "compensation for the use or forbearance of money." Deputy v. du Pont, 308 U.S. 488, 498, 60 S. Ct. 363, 84 L. Ed. 416, 1940–1 C.B. 118 (1940); Sharp v. Commissioner, 75 T.C. 21, 24 (1980), affd. 689 F.2d 87 (6th Cir. 1982). We agree with the parties that Vitro's guaranty was not a loan to International, so the guaranty fees are not interest.

B.   *Guaranty Fees as Payment for Services*

Sections 861(a)(3) and 862(a)(3) specifically source "labor or personal services," and Container argues that that is what Vitro performed for

International. Under the Guaranty agreement, Vitro was required to maintain records and supply information to the note purchasers. It performed these acts using Corporativo personnel, facilities, equipment, and capital—all located in Mexico. Container asks us to find that the guaranty fees were compensation for these services and are therefore Mexican source income. . . .

The Commissioner does not challenge Container's assertion that Corporativo performed services, but argues that services were not the predominant feature of the guaranty and should be ignored for sourcing purposes. See Bank of Am., 230 Ct. Cl. at 690, 680 F.2d at 149. Container responds by arguing that providing services is not a possible feature of a guaranty, but that a guaranty is itself a service; indeed, that the Code and regulations actually refer to guaranties as services.

We'll therefore analyze Container's arguments on this point at some length. They flow from four sections of the Code or regulations. The first is based on section 1.731–2(e)(3)(iii) of the Income Tax Regulations, which deals with partnership distributions. This section does include the words "services" and "guarantees of obligations," but it does not suggest that a guaranty is a service. And "guarantees of obligations" is actually tucked away in a parenthetical listing types of equity interests. Container's two other references are also of little help, but Container also asks us to look at transfer pricing of services under section 482.

This might be as a useful guide. Section 482's purpose "is to ensure that taxpayers clearly reflect income attributable to controlled transactions, and to prevent the avoidance of taxes with respect to such transactions." Sec. 1.482–1T(a)(1), Temporary Income Tax Regs., 58 Fed. Reg. 5272 (Jan. 21, 1993). For example, if a U.S. corporation guarantees a loan made to its foreign subsidiary by a third party without receiving compensation from the foreign sub, it could avoid the income it would have incurred had it charged a fee. But the guaranty adds some value, and the section 482 regulations tell taxpayers that the U.S. parent should recognize the amount it would have charged had the transaction been made at arm's length with an uncontrolled third party. See sec. 1.482–1T(b), Temporary Income Tax Regs., 58 Fed. Reg. 5272 (Jan. 21, 1993). But this is just a summary of a general rule. When it comes to deciding whether payments for a guaranty are services in particular transfer-pricing situations, the Commissioner has struggled.

In General Counsel Memorandum (GCM) 38499 (Sept. 19, 1980), the Commissioner agreed with a proposed revenue [but never published] ruling concluding that the "guarantee of the parent constitutes the performance of a service for the subsidiary." The Commissioner used section 1.482–2(b)(7)(v), Example (9), Income Tax Regs., to reach this result.

Example (9). X is a domestic manufacturing corporation. Y, a foreign subsidiary of X, has decided to construct a plant in Country A. In connection with the construction of Y's plant, X draws up the architectural plans for the plant, arranges the financing of the construction, negotiates with various Government authorities in Country A, invites bids from unrelated parties for several phases of construction, and negotiates, on Y's behalf, the contracts with unrelated parties who are retained to carry out certain phases of the construction. Although the unrelated parties retained by X for Y perform the physical construction, the aggregate services performed by X for Y are such that they, in themselves, constitute a construction activity. * * *

The proposed revenue ruling also concluded that guaranty fees should be sourced to the country where the financing is secured and where the subsidiary resides because that is the situs of the risk of default. In the General Counsel Memorandum, the Commissioner expressed reservations about that conclusion and suspended further consideration. GCM 38499 (Sept. 19, 1980).

We also have some caselaw. In Centel Commons. Co. v. Commissioner, 92 T.C. 612 (1989), affd. 920 F.2d 1335 (7th Cir. 1990), we decided that the guaranties were not a service, though in a very different context: A burgeoning telephone interconnect business got a loan to provide it with operating funds. Id. at 616. As a condition of the loan, the lender required guaranties from three of the company's shareholders. Id. The shareholders signed the agreements without compensation, but five years later they received stock warrants for their guaranties. Id. at 617–19. The issue we decided was whether the warrants were given for the performance of services under section 83(a). Id. at 626. We held that "within the meaning of section 83" the shareholder had not performed a service. Id. at 633.

"[W]ithin the meaning of section 83" is the key. We did characterize the guaranties as "shareholder/investor actions to protect their investment * * * [that] as such do not constitute the performance of services." Id. at 632–33. But we also stressed that our decision turned on a question of fact: whether the shareholders got the warrants in exchange for services rendered as employees or independent contractors. Id. at 629. The parties agreed the shareholders weren't employees, and we found that they were not independent contractors because they were not in the business of guaranteeing loans. Id. at 632. We did not hold that providing a guaranty is never a service, and noted that we were analyzing only the language of section 83. An analysis under that section is quite different from an analysis under the sourcing rules, but it nevertheless prompted the Commissioner to rethink his position when the problem came up in the transfer-pricing context again. This time he reasoned that

> The Centel decision increases the litigating hazards * * *. However, we do not read this case as contradicting the position of the Service as established in * * * G.C.M. 38499. Guarantees do not fit comfortably within normal tax law concepts in a number of areas and, consequently, there are substantial

arguments that can be made against any possible analysis of guarantees. * * *

1995 FSA LEXIS 135, 1995 WL 1918236 (IRS FSA May 1, 1995).

All we can conclude from this detour through transfer-pricing law is that it will not help us reach a reasonable conclusion on whether guaranties are services under section 861.

So we'll fall back on the dictionary. The common meaning of "labor or personal services" implies the continuous use of human capital, "as opposed to the salable product of the person's skill." Under this definition, we find that Container failed to prove that Corporativo performed sufficient "labor or personal services" to justify the $6 million International paid in guaranty fees over three years. Container presented very little evidence about the specific acts Corporativo performed and how much time it took to perform them. For example, Container's posttrial brief explains that the Guaranty agreement required Vitro to "take certain actions, confirm certain facts, provide certain information, and create and supply certain documents." The Guaranty agreement required only minimal accountings and reporting to the note purchasers. In any event, the fees were not tied to the amount of work that Vitro did, but to the amount of the outstanding principal that Vitro was standing behind. This leads us to hold that International did not pay the guaranty fees to Vitro as compensation for services. The value of Vitro's guaranty stems "from a promise made and not from an intellectual or manual skill applied." Bank of Am., 47 AFTR 2d at 81–657.

We therefore move on to reasoning by analogy, and ask whether guaranty payments are more like interest or more like services.

C.   *Guaranty Fees as Analogous to Interest or Payments for Services*

When we source FDAP income by analogy, our goal is to find the "source of income in terms of the business activities generating the income or * * * the place where the income was produced. Thus, the sourcing concept is concerned with the earning point of income or, more specifically, identifying when and where profits are earned." Hunt, 90 T.C. at 1301 (citation omitted).

There are only a few examples in the caselaw of sourcing by analogy. Alimony was the first. The question of its source arose when a U.S. resident paid alimony to his British ex from an English bank. We held that the alimony's source was the ex-husband's residence, and not where the funds were deposited or where the divorce decree was entered. See Manning v. Commissioner, 614 F.2d 815 (1st Cir. 1980), affg. T.C. Memo. 1979–146; Howkins, 49 T.C. at 694. Taking perhaps too modern a view of marriage, we reasoned that alimony, like interest, is not exchanged for property or services. And since interest is sourced to the residence of the obligor, so too would we source alimony. Howkins, 49 T.C. at 694.

Another example of sourcing by analogy came from the Court of Claims in Bank of America. In that case, the court sourced commissions received by Bank of America from foreign banks in connection with transactions involving commercial letters of credit. Bank of Am., 230 Ct. Cl. at 680–681, 680 F.2d at 143. The conflict in Bank of America, as in this case, was whether the commissions should be sourced by analogy to personal services or to interest. Id. at 686–687, 680 F.2d at 147.

To understand the holding in Bank of America requires some background in letters of credit. Such letters make trade easier by allowing a bank, rather than the seller, to examine a buyer's credit. For example, when a U.S. exporter wants to sell goods to a foreign buyer, assessing the creditworthiness of the foreign buyer can be a problem. So, instead of having the seller do it, the buyer requests a letter of credit from a foreign bank and the foreign bank does the job. If the buyer is creditworthy, the foreign bank (sometimes called the opening bank) substitutes its credit for the buyer's and commits to pay the seller when certain conditions are met, e.g., presentment of an inspection certificate and a bill of lading to the opening bank. After the opening bank pays the seller, the buyer reimburses it. There are two types of commercial letters of credit: sight and time. A sight letter of credit obligates the opening bank to pay as soon as the seller meets the conditions in the letter of credit. A time letter of credit obligates the opening bank to pay on a specific future date if the conditions were met. See id. at 681, 680 F.2d at 144.

BofA performed four kinds of transactions involving letters of credit, and charged the opening bank commissions for three of them. It's these three, and how the Court of Claims sourced each of them that are useful here. The first kind was an acceptance, and BofA received acceptance commissions in two situations—if BofA determined that the conditions of a time letter of credit had been met it would stamp the letter accepted, obligating itself to pay any holder in due course when the letter came due; or, if an opening bank with an established line of credit with BofA wanted to refinance a letter of credit, it would accept a time draft at a discount to the face amount of the letter of credit.

The Court of Claims began its analysis by noting that both these types of acceptance transactions are similar to a loan and that the commissions "include elements covered by the interest charges made on direct loans." Id. at 689, 680 F.2d at 148. The court also held that the predominant feature of an acceptance transaction was the substitution of BofA's credit for that of the opening bank and not the services BofA performed. Id. at 690, 680 F.2d at 149. These factors led the Court of Claims to source acceptance commissions by analogy to interest, with the obligor being the opening bank. Id. at 689, 680 F.2d at 148.

BofA also received confirmation commissions. It confirmed sight letters of credit by advising the letter and committing to pay the letter's face amount after the seller met its conditions. The opening bank reimbursed BofA by either prepaying it or by keeping an account that BofA could debit. When the opening bank prepaid, BofA didn't charge a commission. Otherwise it charged a commission that reflected its assumption of the risk that the foreign bank could default. The Court of Claims again found that the performance of services was a part of the deal but that its predominant feature was BofA's substituting its credit for the opening bank's. Id. at 691, 680 F.2d at 149–50. The court also thus sourced confirmation commissions, as it had acceptance commissions, by analogy to interest and with the obligor being the opening bank. Id. at 691–92, 680 F.2d at 150.

Finally, the Court of Claims examined negotiation commissions. Negotiations took place when BofA determined if the seller met the conditions for payment in the letter of credit. After BofA performed a negotiation, it would forward the papers to the opening bank, which would do an independent check. The Court of Claims found that negotiation commissions were paid for services performed in the United States and were distinguishable from the other two types of commission because the only risk that BofA assumed was that it might improperly determine that the seller met the conditions. Id. at 692, 680 F.2d at 150.

Commissioner

The Commissioner argues that Bank of America is controlling because acceptance and confirmation commissions, like guaranty fees, are uses of another's credit and are analogous to interest. But, as the Commissioner thoughtfully concedes, the "use" of credit is different in guaranties compared to acceptance and confirmation of letters of credit. When BofA confirmed or accepted a letter of credit, it assumed an unqualified primary legal obligation to pay the seller—it stepped into the shoes of the opening bank and substituted its own credit for the opening bank's. It was, in effect, making a short-term loan and the commissions approximated interest. Id. at 688–91, 680 F.2d at 148–50.

Vitro's case is different. It was augmenting International's credit, not substituting its own. But should this distinction matter? We conclude that it should, and begin our explanation by examining the effects of a default. When a debtor defaults on a loan, he is defaulting on an existing primary obligation. Default causes the creditor to lose the outstanding principal because he has already extended funds to the debtor. Interest is the creditor's compensation for putting his own money at risk. As in a loan, BofA put its money directly at risk when it paid the seller, and it charged for the risk-although it called that charge a "commission" rather then "interest". Vitro's obligation was, in contrast, entirely secondary. Unlike a lender, Vitro was not required to pay out any of its own money unless and until International defaulted. And Vitro's guaranty might not even put its money at risk after default, because if International defaulted and Vitro paid the 1991 International senior notes, it would step into the note purchasers' shoes and acquire any rights that they had against International. See Putnam v. Commissioner, 352 U.S. 82, 85, 77 S. Ct. 175, 1 L. Ed. 2d 144, 1957–1 C.B. 501 (1956). Vitro loses only if International defaults and Vitro repays the 1991 International senior notes (which transfers International's obligation from the note purchasers to Vitro) and then International defaults on the transferred debt.

Vitro's guaranty therefore lacks a principal characteristic of a loan because Vitro did not extend funds to International. To find otherwise would require us to assume that at the time of the guaranty, the 1991 International senior notes was somehow a loan to Vitro. Neither party makes this argument. http://www.lexis.com/research/retrieve? cc=&pushme=1&tmpFBSel=all&totaldocs=&taggedDocs=&toggleValue =&numDocsChked=0&prefFBSel=0&delformat=XCITE&fpDocs=&fpNo deId=&fpCiteReq=&fpSetup=0&brand=&_m=748a540e6863d7452dca17 3a7af556.&docnum=1&!1F_fmtstr=FULL&_startdoc=1&wchp=dGLzVz b-zSkAb&_md5=db78cd9218644c8fe46Fb4236fe=%22container+ corporation%22+and+bank+of+america&focBudSel=all-fnote18#fnote18 Vitro's later choice to subsidize International through capital contributions—instead of allowing International to default—does not affect our analysis. Capital contributions also lack a distinguishing characteristic of a loan—a promise to repay.

The Commissioner argues, however, that if guaranties are unlike loans because the guarantor does not have to hand over his money at the outset, guaranty fees may be like interest in some broader sense under Howkins. That case, the Commissioner argues, held that alimony is analogous to interest because it is not paid for property or services. Howkins, 49 T.C. at 694. Reading Howkins this way, however, is reading it less as a useful analogy than as creating a default rule. Property and services are listed in sections 861 and 862, so by definition, any unlisted type of income is not paid for property or services. And if we were to follow such reasoning without qualification, we would source all unlisted types of income by analogy to interest. But we read Howkins more narrowly; we reasoned there that alimony is analogous to interest because its source is the obligor. Howkins, 49 T.C. at 693. This logic also reminds us of the goal of sourcing by analogy: namely, find the location "of the business activities generating the income or * * * the place where the income was produced." Hunt, 90 T.C. at 1301. So we have to ask if there's a useful analogy to guaranty fees that would help us figure out, in some reasonable way, where they are produced.

International paid Vitro to guarantee the 1991 International senior notes. These fees compensated Vitro for incurring a contingent future obligation to either pay International's debt or make a capital contribution. Vitro was able to make this promise because it had sufficient Mexican assets—and its Mexican corporate management had a sufficient reputation for using those assets productively—to augment International's credit and enable the long and complex series of financings we charted at the beginning of this opinion to keep going as long as it did. So we conclude that it is Vitro's promise and its Mexican assets that produced the guaranty fees.

We do not choose International as the source of the income because the guaranty fees were not like alimony: Alimony is only an obligation to pay, because once a court orders one spouse to pay alimony, nothing more is required of the other spouse. Guaranty fees are different—they are payments for a possible future action.

We think that makes guaranties more analogous to services. Guaranties, like services, are produced by the obligee and so, like services, should be sourced to the location of the obligee. See secs. 861(a)(3), 862(a)(3); Hunt, 90 T.C. at 1301. We realize that we are deciding a close question, but an analogy to interest has too many shortcomings: Guaranty fees do not approximate the interest on a loan; Vitro, not International, produced the guaranty fees; and Vitro's guaranty was not an obligation to pay immediately, but a promise to possibly perform a future act.

CONCLUSION

We hold that International was not required to withhold taxes on the guaranty fees that it paid Vitro because those fees are Mexican source income. The parties settled various other issues, however, so

Decision will be entered under Rule 155.

[footnotes omitted].

NOTES AND QUESTIONS

1.   *Container Corp.* offers a window into the complex lending transactions that taxpayers pursue, and the circumstances driving these transactions. The Court's opinion also provides a rather frank examination of the task of sourcing a guaranty payment.

2.   Was the Court correct that the guaranty payment was not for services? Could it ever be? How much did it depend on the facts of this case? Should courts try to fit a payment into one of the existing source categories—or is resort to explicit analogizing appropriate? How should a court make its determination among competing analogies?

3.   In a footnote omitted from the above reprint of the Container Corp. case, the Court observed that although the parties did not address the following point—the guaranty fees "were somewhat analogous to rents or royalties for the use of Vitro's goodwill . . . which would also source them to Mexico rather than the United States." (footnote 19). What do you think of this argument? Is this analogy stronger than an analogy to interest? To services?

4.   The Court considers in detail the *Bank of America* case. Do you think the Court accurately characterizes that opinion? What do you think of the effort by the Court in *Container Corp.* to distinguish *Bank of America*?

5.   The decision in *Container Corp.*, which sources the guaranty fee to the foreign parent's jurisdiction, has been criticized as facilitating income stripping of U.S subsidiaries. [Income stripping essentially refers to the ability to withdraw money from one country through payments that are deductible in that jurisdiction but not taxable by it in the hands of the recipient. For example, if a U.S. subsidiary pays interest to its foreign parent,

that cash leaves the U.S. and reduces the U.S. tax base because the subsidiary is deducting the payment. There is no offsetting taxable income for the recipient of the interest (i.e. the foreign parent) in the U.S. to the extent that the foreign parent can rely on a U.S. treaty to reduce or eliminate taxation on its interest payment from its U.S. subsidiary.] The *Container Corp.* result arguably permits a foreign parent to avoid the anti-income stripping rules of section 163(j) by guaranteeing the subsidiary debt instead of loaning it money. From the subsidiary's perspective, how is paying a guaranty fee similar to paying interest? If they are similar, and if section 163(j) prevents abuse in the case of interest payments but not in the case of guaranty fees, then avoidance opportunity exists. We will revisit this issue in Ch.5.

6. Congress promptly legislated to reverse the result in *Container Corp.* See section 861(a)(9) as added by the Small Business Jobs and Credit Act of 2010.

2.4   WHAT ABOUT INCOME THAT DOES NOT BELONG TO ANY CATEGORY?

Korfund Co. v. Commissioner

United States Tax Court.
1 T.C. 1180 (1943).

* * *

■ DISNEY, J.: This proceeding involves the redetermination of a deficiency of $772.67 in income tax for 1938. The issue is whether petitioner is liable for withholding taxes on amounts paid to a nonresident alien and corporation.

Issue.

FINDINGS OF FACT

Petitioner is a New York corporation organized in 1924, with its principal place of business in New York City, for the purpose of manufacturing and selling foundation material, such as cork plates and vibration absorbers. Of the 1,000 shares of stock issued at that time, Hugo Stoessel, a nonresident alien and citizen of Germany, received 925 shares and Siegfried Rosenzweig the remaining shares. Petitioner filed its return for the taxable year on the accrual basis with the collector for the first district of New York.

The Emil Zorn Aktiengesellschaft, hereinafter referred to as Zorn, is a nonresident foreign corporation engaged in the same business as petitioner, with its principal office in Berlin, Germany. In 1928 its stock was held equally by Stoessel and Werner Genest, a nonresident alien and citizen of Germany. In 1932 or 1933 Stoessel became the sole owner of stock of Zorn.

On October 22, 1926, petitioner entered into a written contract in the United States with Zorn whereby Zorn agreed (a) not to compete with petitioner in this country and Canada or to form, or give any data for the purpose of forming, a competitive company in that territory until the end of 1945, and (b) to give technical and business advice to petitioner upon its request, and petitioner agreed (a) not to furnish material, for the isolation of noise and vibration, outside of the United States and Canada prior to December 31, 1945, except specified territory outside of European countries. Each party agreed to turn over inquiries received from territory of the other and to exchange without charge improvements, inventions, and patents involving isolation against noise and vibration. Zorn was to receive from petitioner quarterly "a royalty of 1 1/2% for the year 1926 and 2% thereafter of the sale of all cork plates with iron frames and of 4% of the sale of all vibration absorbers," computed in a specified manner, with a minimum payment of $400 for 1926, $1,000 for 1927, and $1,250 thereafter through 1940. Zorn did not own any patents at that time. One of the purposes of the contract was to eliminate competition. . . .

On September 21, 1928, petitioner entered into a written agreement with Stoessel in the United States whereby Stoessel undertook to act as consultant and adviser of petitioner in matters relating to the business of petitioner and to communicate to it information of value to petitioner's business until December 31, 1939, for 10 percent of the net earnings of petitioner payable at the end of each year. He also agreed not to act in a similar capacity for any other person, association, or corporation in the United States engaged in the same or a similar business. One of the purposes of the agreement was to eliminate competition. . . .

Zorn and Stoessel faithfully performed their agreements not to compete with petitioner and not to give advice to its competitors. On about January 1, 1933, petitioner canceled the contracts of September 21, 1928, and October 22, 1926, with Stoessel and Zorn, and refused to make further payments to them. The contract with Stoessel was canceled on account of his failure to communicate technical information relating to petitioner's business as required by the agreement. . . .

On July 30, 1934, Zorn assigned to Bernard Voges, New York City, all sums due it from petitioner under the agreement of October 22, 1926 . . . with power to recover the amounts for the account of the assignors. Voges instituted suit against petitioner in August 1934 under the assignments. An understanding was reached in 1934 to settle the claims by a payment of $2,750 to Stoessel and $3,250 to Zorn. . . . Final settlement was made in 1938 when $2,508 was paid to Stoessel and $2,964 to Zorn and $608 was withheld for payment of withholding taxes.

OPINION

In his determination of the deficiency the respondent held that the allowance of $2,786.67 to Stoessel and $3,293.33 to Zorn, . . . constituted income from sources within the United States on which petitioner, as withholding agent, should have paid a tax equal to 10 percent of the former amount and 15 percent of the latter amount in accordance with the provisions of sections 143 and 144 of the Revenue Act of 1938. . . .

Under their contracts Zorn and Stoessel agreed, in general, to act as consultants to petitioner. In addition Zorn agreed not to compete with petitioner or give any information for the formation of a competitive company and Stoessel agreed not to act as consultant to a competitor of petitioner. All of the amount paid to Zorn and the amount paid to Stoessel in excess of the surplus item were paid for these two general classifications of undertakings without any segregation of the amount paid for each. The respondent subjected the entire amounts to withholding tax, presumably in the absence of any basis of segregation, for he does not contend that the income from services performed as consultants is subject to the tax. Not only was no evidence offered on which to make an apportionment, but petitioner does not, upon brief, suggest or request an allocation. Under the circumstances, no apportionment is possible and we will regard all of the amounts in question under this point as having been earned by the nonresident aliens for obligations under the contracts other than service as consultants. See Estate of Alexander Marton, 47 B. T. A. 184.

The sole point of difference between the parties as to this income is whether it was earned from sources within the United States within the meaning of section [861] of the Revenue Act of 1938, and that, as already indicated, turns upon the source of the income derived from agreements not to compete with petitioner in the United States and Canada or give advice for the organization of, or to, a competitor.

The petitioner's contention is based upon the theory that the income was paid for agreements to refrain from doing specific things—negative acts. No defaults occurred and during the period of compliance the promisors were residents of Germany. Petitioner's contention is that negative performance is based upon a continuous exercise of will, which has its source at the place of location of the individual, and that, as the mental exertion involved herein occurred in Germany, the source of the income was in that country, not in the United States where the promise was given. The respondent's view of the question is, in short, that, as the place of performance would be in the United States if Zorn and Stoessel had violated their contractual obligations, abstinence of performance occurs in the same place. . . .

Zorn had a right to compete with petitioner in the United States and Canada and for that purpose to form a competitive company or to assist others in forming one. Likewise, Stoessel had a right to serve other corporations or individuals in the United States engaged in a business similar to petitioner's as a consultant and to furnish them information of value to their business. They were willing to and did give up these rights in this country for a limited time for a consideration payable in the United States . . . in our opinion, the rights of Stoessel and Zorn to do business in this country, in competition with the petitioner, were interests in property in this country. They might have received amounts here for services or information, but were willing to forego that right and possibility for a limited period for a consideration. What they received was in lieu of what they might have received. The situs of the right was in the United States, not elsewhere, and the income that flowed from the privileges was necessarily earned and produced here. Petitioner is merely using it, so to speak, for a specified time, subject to periodical payments to the owners of the rights. Upon the termination of the contracts the rights reverted to Zorn and Stoessel, and they were then free to exercise them independent of the agreements entered into with petitioner. These rights were property of value and the income in question was derived from the use thereof in the United States. . . .

We find and hold that the source of all of the income in question was in the United States and is subject to withholding tax in the taxable year.

Accordingly,

Decision will be entered for the respondent.

NOTES AND QUESTIONS

1. Why did Korfund cancel the contracts? (Hint: What happened in Germany on January 30, 1933?)

2. How does the Service characterize the payment in *Korfund*? How does the taxpayer? The taxpayer says the source is where he is physically located. Read section 865(a). Is the property at stake in *Korfund* independent property like goodwill, or property created for this time only? Is this the negative sending in of goods? Suppose it were the negative sending in of services?

3. If the taxpayer had competed by sending in goods, where would it have passed title? Would it have competed through a permanent establishment? Would it be relevant what the taxpayer had done historically?

4. When we examine the allocation of deductions in Chapter 3, we shall see that deductions are often allocated to domestic or foreign income based on the income that they were incurred to produce, even though that income never materializes. Is this analogous to the sourcing of income from a covenant not to compete?

5. What other categories of income are not enumerated in section 861? Compare the list to the categories enumerated in section 61. Any others? Consider Rev. Rul. 2004–75, 2004–31 I.R.B. 109 (concluding in the absence of statutory guidance that income paid by a U.S. life insurance company to a foreign person under a life insurance contract or annuity is U.S. source based on an analogy to interest, dividends and earnings on pension fund assets).

2.5   WHAT IF INCOME IS GENERATED BOTH INSIDE AND OUTSIDE THE UNITED STATES?

If income is sourced according to a formal rule such as residence of the taxpayer, then the location of any activities generating the income is irrelevant. However, for income sourced by a substantive rule such as performance of services, what is the result if those services are performed both inside and outside the United States?

Stemkowski v. Commissioner

Second Circuit Court of Appeals.
690 F.2d 40 (1982).

■ OAKES, J.:

This supposed test case involves the taxability of a Canadian citizen who formerly played professional hockey for the New York Rangers of the National Hockey League (NHL). As a nonresident alien, Stemkowski was subject to United States tax on that portion of his income connected with his performance of services in this country, and entitled to deduct expenditures relating to such United States income. The taxable year involved is 1971. After a trial in 1977, the Tax Court . . . filed an opinion . . . upholding the Commissioner on all major issues. . . . We affirm in part, and reverse and remand in part.

The five major issues on appeal are:

1. Whether the Tax Court correctly held that the stated salary in the NHL Standard Player's Contract covered only the services of taxpayer during the regular hockey season and not during the off-season, training camp, or the play-offs, so that only the time a player spent in Canada during the regular season could be used to calculate the portion of his salary excludable from his United States income. . . .

FACTS

Taxpayer was traded prior to the beginning of taxable year 1971 to the New York Rangers, who play their home games at Madison Square Garden in New York City. He had previously signed a two-year NHL Standard Player's Contract with the Detroit Red Wings, and this contract was assigned to and assumed by the Rangers. The contract provided for compensation of $31,500 in the 1970–71 season and $35,000 in the 1971–72 season plus various NHL bonuses, including a $1500 bonus for each round won in the play-offs. The player agreed to give his services in all "league championship" (i.e., regular season), exhibition, and play-off games, to report in good physical condition to the club training camp at the time and place fixed by the club, to keep himself in good physical condition at all times during the season, and to participate in any and all promotional activities of the club and the league that in the opinion of the club promoted the welfare of the club or professional hockey.

* * *

An NHL player's year is divided into four periods: (1) training camp, including exhibition games, beginning in September and lasting approximately thirty days; (2) the "league championship" or regular season of games beginning in October and lasting until April of the following year; (3) the play-off competition, which ends in May; and (4) the off-season, which runs from the end of the regular season for clubs that do not make the play-offs, or from a club's last play-off game, to the first day of training camp. Stemkowski lived in Canada during all of the off-season and most of the training camp period and played in Canada fifteen days out of 179 during the regular season and five out of twenty-eight days during the play-offs. When he was not living in Canada or travelling to games elsewhere, he lived in Long Beach, New York, near New York City, where he shared a rented house with other professional hockey players.

On his tax return, Stemkowski reported $44,271 in income, of which he initially excluded $10,625 as earned in Canada. . . . The Commissioner issued Stemkowski a notice of deficiency in February 1975, determining that Stemkowski had underestimated the proportion of his income derived from services in the United States. . . .

The less time Stemkowski was in the United States during the period covered by his contract, the less United States tax he owes. Thus, Stemkowski could reduce his tax liability either by showing that he was in Canada for a longer period during the time covered by the contract or, as is at issue here, that the contract covered a time during which he was in Canada. The Tax Court held that the total number of days for which Stemkowski was compensated under his contract was not 234 (all but the off-season) as he had claimed on his tax return, or 365 as he had claimed before the Tax Court, but only 179, the number of days in the regular season. The Tax Court held that Stemkowski could not use days spent in Canada during training camp, the play-offs, or the off-season in calculating his foreign-source exclusion from income. . . . Taxpayer has duly appealed. . . .

DISCUSSION

Allocation of Income

The first issue is the Tax Court's determination of the portion of Stemkowski's compensation under the NHL Standard Player's Contract that was drawn from United States sources. As a nonresident alien, Stemkowski was taxable on income connected with the conduct of a trade or business, including the performance of personal services, within the United States. I.R.C. Secs. 871(b), 864(b). Where services are performed partly within and partly outside the United States, but compensation is not separately allocated, Treas. Reg. Sec. 1.861–4(b) (1975) allocates income to United States sources on a "time basis":

> [T]he amount to be included in gross income will be that amount which bears the same relation to the total compensation as the number of days of performance of the labor or services within the United States bears to the total number of days of performance of labor or services for which the payment is made.

This regulation applies to Stemkowski because the NHL Standard Player's Contract does not distinguish between payments for services performed within and outside the United States.

The parties disagree on what components of a hockey player's year are covered by the basic compensation in the NHL Standard Player's Contract, and therefore on how to compute the time-basis ratio. The taxpayer contends here as he did before the Tax Court that the contract salary compensates him for training camp, play-off, and even off-season services. The Commissioner argues and the Tax Court held that the contract salary covers only the regular season, and therefore that contract salary should be allocated to United States income in the same proportion that the number of days played in the United States during the regular season (164) bears to the total number of days in the regular season (179).[4] We agree with the Commissioner and the Tax Court that the contract does not cover off-season services, but we hold that the Tax Court's finding that the contract does not compensate for training camp and the play-offs as well as the regular season is clearly erroneous. . . .

[handwritten margin note: Holding on time of contract.]

The Tax Court's holding was premised on provisions in the NHL contract and other players' agreements, and on the testimony of league and club officials. The first paragraph of the NHL Standard Player's Contract provides that if a player is "not in the employ of the Club for the whole period of the Club's games in the National Hockey League Championship Schedule," i.e., for the entire regular season, then he receives only part of his salary, in the same ratio to his total salary as the "ratio of the number of days of actual employment to the number of days of the League Championship Schedule of games." Paragraph 15 provides that if a player is suspended, he will not receive that portion of his salary equal to the ratio of "the number of days (of) suspension" to the "total number of days of the League Championship Schedule of games." The Tax Court concluded from these two paragraphs, and from the NHL's further agreements to pay players separate bonuses for participating in the play-offs and flat fees plus travel, room, and board for participating in training camp and pre-season exhibition games, that the basic contract salary did not cover play-off or training camp services.[5]

---

4   Although the Tax Court did not discuss separately the component of Stemkowski's total reported income representing play-off bonuses, the Commissioner concedes that Stemkowski's play-off compensation should be allocated separately from his contract salary, according to a ratio whose numerator contains the number of Ranger play-off days in the United States (23), and whose denominator contains the total number of Ranger play-off days in 1971 (28).

5   This interpretation was supported by the conflicting testimony of present or former league and club officials. The Commissioner's witnesses Clarence S. Campbell, a former NHL president, Vincent H.D. Abbey, a part owner and officer of the Seattle Totems of the Western Hockey League (WHL), and Emile Francis, former coach and general manager of the New York Rangers, all testified that the contract salary covered the regular season, not the off-season, training camp and exhibition games, or the play-offs. The Commissioner's witness George A. Leader, former president of the WHL, testified that the contract covered training camp as well as the regular season. The taxpayer's witness William H. McFarland, former player and coach and general manager of the Seattle Totems, testified that the contract salary covered all services named in the contract. . . .

We cannot uphold that finding, as we believe it clearly erroneous. The formulas for docking salary given in the contract's first and fifteenth paragraphs are not persuasive evidence that the salary compensates only for the regular season. These formulas may well use the number of days in the regular season in their denominators for administrative convenience (e.g., because the number of days to be spent in the play-offs cannot be known in advance) or to maximize the salary penalty per day lost. As to the testimony relied upon by the Tax Court, to a certain extent the owners and league officials have an interest in having the contract cover the shortest possible timespan so as to maximize loss to suspended or striking players. Furthermore, two of the league and club officials, Leader and McFarland, testified that at least training camp time was included in the contract. The contract's plain language, moreover, requires in Paragraph 2(a) that a player "report to the Club training camp . . . in good physical condition," and a player who fails to report to training camp and participate in exhibition games is subject under Paragraph 3 to a $500 fine, deductible from his basic salary. True, experienced players were paid $600 plus room and board for training camp under the Owner-Player Council minutes and Agreements, but we read those Agreements as providing that amount merely to cover the additional expenses of being away from home at training camp.

Paragraph 2 of the contract also plainly requires a player's participation in play-off games in exchange for basic contract salary. While it is true that bonuses are provided for play-off games won, these are simply added incentives, above and beyond salary, to get into and win the play-offs. In this respect, they are just like other incentive bonuses the contract provides to influence conduct during even the regular season, e.g., bonuses for the club's finishing in third place or better ($2500 in this case), or for the number of goals a player scores per season above certain minimums (at least $100 per goal over 20). Furthermore, players are required to participate in all play-off games for which they are eligible. Players may be terminated for failure to participate in the play-offs, but players receive nothing for the play-off games that they lose. Thus, we hold that the basic contract salary covered both play-off and training camp services.

 We agree, however, that the off-season is not covered by the contract. During the off-season, the contract imposes no specific obligations on a player. Stemkowski argues that the obligation to appear at training camp "in good condition" makes off-season conditioning a contractual obligation. Fitness is not a service performed in fulfillment of the contract but a condition of employment. There was no evidence that Stemkowski was required to follow any mandatory conditioning program or was under any club supervision during the off-season. He was required to observe, if anything, only general obligations, applicable as well throughout the year, to conduct himself with loyalty to the club and the league and to participate only in approved promotional activities.

* * *

Judgment affirmed in part; reversed and remanded in part.

NOTES AND QUESTIONS

1.   What is the core of the debate between the taxpayer and the Service in *Stemkowski*? Why does it matter?

2.   Apportionment between the U.S. and foreign sources is usually done on a time basis, unless that division does not reflect the underlying economic reality of the transactions. Section 863(b)(1).

3.   In Rev. Rul. 87–38, 1981–1 C.B. 176, the Service revoked Rev. Rul. 76–66 (maintaining that the contracts only covered the regular season) and adopted the position in *Stemkowski*.

2.6   HOW MUCH CONTROL DO TAXPAYERS HAVE OVER SOURCING INCOME?

Where income is sourced according to a formal rule, taxpayers have an incentive to structure the transaction to take advantage of the formal rule. The question is how much flexibility do taxpayers have in this regard?

United States v. Balanovski
United States Court of Appeals, Second Circuit.
236 F.2d 298 (1956).

* * *

■ CLARK, J.:

This is an appeal by defendants and a cross-appeal by the United States of America from a decision of Judge Palmieri, sitting without a jury, adjudging defendant-taxpayers liable for almost $1,000,000 in income taxes and interest for the year 1947, and directing two New York banks to pay over funds belonging to the defendant partnership in part payment of the judgment. D.C.S.D.N.Y., 131 F.Supp. 898. In our view the recovery granted was insufficient, and we are therefore reversing on the appeal of the United States only.

Defendants Balanovski and Horenstein were copartners in the Argentine partnership, Compania Argentina de Intercambio Comercial (CADIC), Balanovski having an 80 per cent interest and Horenstein, a 20 per cent interest. Balanovski, an Argentinian citizen, came to the United States on or about December 20, 1946, and remained in this country for approximately ten months, except for an absence of a few weeks in the spring of 1947 when he returned to Argentina. His purpose in coming here was the transaction of partnership business; and while here, he made extensive purchases and sales of trucks and other equipment resulting in a profit to the partnership of some $7,763,702.20.

His usual mode of operation in the United States was to contact American suppliers and obtain offers for the sale of equipment. He then communicated the offers to his father-in-law, Horenstein, in Argentina. Horenstein, in turn, submitted them at a markup to an agency of the Argentine Government, Instituto Argentino de Promocion del Intercambio (IAPI), which was interested in purchasing such equipment. If IAPI accepted an offer, Horenstein would notify Balanovski and the latter would accept the corresponding original offer of the American supplier. In the meantime IAPI would cause a letter of credit in favor of Balanovski to be opened with a New York bank. Acting under the terms of the letter of credit Balanovski would assign a portion of it, equal to CADIC's purchase price, to the United States supplier. The supplier could then draw on the New York bank against the letter of credit by sight draft for 100 per cent invoice value accompanied by (1) a commercial invoice billing Balanovski, (2) an inspection certificate, (3) a nonnegotiable warehouse or dock receipt issued in the name of the New York bank for the account of IAPI's Argentine agent, and (4) an insurance policy covering all risks to the merchandise up to delivery F.O.B. New York City. Then, if the purchase was one on which CADIC was to receive a so-called quantity discount or commission, the supplier would pay Balanovski the amount of the discount. These discounts, paid after delivery of the goods and full payment to the suppliers, amounted to $858,595.90, constituting funds which were delivered in the United States. After the supplier had received payment, Balanovski would draw on the New York bank for the unassigned portion of the letter of credit, less 1 per cent of the face amount, by submitting a sight draft accompanied by (1) a commercial invoice billing IAPI, (2) an undertaking to ship before a certain date, and (3) an insurance policy covering all risks to the merchandise up to delivery F.A.S. United States Sea Port. The bank would then deliver the nonnegotiable warehouse receipt that it had received from the supplier to Balanovski on trust receipt and his undertaking to deliver a full set of shipping documents, including a clean on board bill of lading issued to the order of IAPI's Argentine agent, with instructions to notify IAPI. It would also notify the warehouse that Balanovski was authorized to withdraw the merchandise. Upon delivery of these shipping documents to the New York bank Balanovski would receive the remaining 1 per cent due under the terms of the letter of credit. Although Balanovski arranged for shipping the goods to Argentina, IAPI paid shipping expenses and made its own arrangement there for marine insurance. The New York bank would forward the bill of lading, Balanovski's invoice billing IAPI, and the other documents required by the letter of credit (not including the supplier's invoice billing Balanovski) to IAPI's agent in Argentina.

Twenty-four transactions following substantially this pattern took place during 1947. Other transactions were also effected which conformed to a substantially similar pattern, except that CADIC engaged the services of others to facilitate the acquisition of goods and their shipment to Argentina. And other offers were sent to Argentina, for which no letters of credit were opened. Several letters of credit were opened which remained either in whole or in part unused. In every instance of a completed transaction Balanovski was paid American money in New York, and in every instance he deposited it in his own name with New York banks. Balanovski never ordered material from a supplier for which he did not have an order and letter of credit from IAPI.

Balanovski's activities on behalf of CADIC in the United States were numerous and varied and required the exercise of initiative, judgment, and executive responsibility. They far transcended the routine or merely clerical. Thus he conferred and bargained with American bankers. He inspected goods and made trips out of New York State in order to buy and inspect the equipment in which he was trading. He made sure the goods were placed in warehouses and aboard ship. He tried to insure that CADIC would not repeat the errors in supplying inferior equipment that had been made by some of its competitors. And while here he attempted "to develop" "other business" for CADIC.

Throughout his stay in the United States Balanovski employed a Miss Alice Devine as a secretary. She used, and he used, the Hotel New Weston in New York City as an office. His address on the documents involved in the transactions was given as the Hotel New Weston. His supplier contacted him there, and that was the place where his letters were typed and his business appointments arranged and kept. Later Miss Devine opened an office on Rector Street in New York City, which he also used. When he returned to Argentina for a brief time in 1947 he left a power of attorney with Miss Devine. This gave her wide latitude in arranging for shipment of goods and in signing his name to all sorts of documents, including checks. When he left for Argentina again at the end of his 10-month stay, he left with Miss Devine the same power of attorney, which she used throughout the balance of 1947 to arrange for and complete the shipment of goods and bank the profits.

When Balanovski left the United States in October 1947 he filed a departing alien income tax return, on which he reported no income. In March 1948 the Commissioner of Internal Revenue assessed $2,122,393.91 as taxes due on income for the period during which Balanovski was in the United States. In May 1953 the Commissioner made a jeopardy assessment against Balanovski in the amount of $3,954,422.41 and gave him notice of it. At the same time a similar jeopardy assessment, followed by a timely notice of deficiency, was made against Horenstein in the amount of $1,672,209.90, representing his alleged share of CADIC's profits on the above described sales of United States goods. The government brought the present action to foreclose a federal tax lien on $511,655.58 and $42,529.49—amounts of partnership funds held in two United States banks—and to obtain personal judgments against Balanovski and Horenstein in the sums of $6,722,625.54 (of which $5,050,415.64 is now sought on appeal) and

$1,672,209.90 respectively. Balanovski and Horenstein were served with process by mail in Argentina pursuant to 28 U.S.C. 1655; and Miss Devine, the purported agent of Balanovski, was personally served in New York. Defendants then appeared by their attorneys and proceeded to defend the action. . . .

The district court held that CADIC was not engaged in a trade or business within the United States within the meaning of [section 872] of the Internal Revenue Code of 1939, but that each of the partners was liable for certain taxes because Balanovski as an individual was so engaged in business and therefore taxable under [section 871(b)], while Horenstein received "fixed or determinable annual or periodical gains, profits, and income" within the meaning of [section 871(a)(1)(A)]. We, on the contrary, hold that the partnership CADIC was engaged in business in the United States and that hence the two copartners were taxable for their share of its profits from sources within the United States. . . .

CADIC was actively and extensively engaged in business in the United States in 1947. Its 80 per cent partner, Balanovski, under whose hat 80 per cent of the business may be thought to reside, was in this country soliciting orders, inspecting merchandise, making purchases, and (as will later appear) completing sales. While maintaining regular contact with his home office, he was obviously making important business decisions. He maintained a bank account here for partnership funds. He operated from a New York office through which a major portion of CADIC's business was transacted. . . .

We cannot accept the view of the trial judge that, since Balanovski was a mere purchasing agent, his presence in this country was insufficient to justify a finding that CADIC was doing business in the United States. We need not consider the question whether, if Balanovski (an 80 per cent partner) were merely engaged in purchasing goods here, the partnership could be deemed to be engaged in business, since he was doing more than purchasing. Acting for CADIC he engaged in numerous transactions wherein he both purchased and sold goods in this country, earned his profits here, and participated in other activities, pertaining to the transaction of business. Cases cited in support of the proposition that CADIC was not engaged in business here are quite distinguishable. . . .

As copartners of CADIC, Balanovski and Horenstein are taxable for the amount of partnership profits from sources within the United States under the statutory provisions cited above. The district court held them taxable only upon the "discounts" or "commissions" paid CADIC by the suppliers after completion of the sales transactions, not upon the total profits of the sales This solution of the problem is in seeming conflict with the usual rule that discounts received as inducements for quality purchasing are considered as reducing the purchasers' cost for tax purposes. . . . Further, isolation of the discount from the sales transaction is not in accord with preferred accounting technique. See, e.g., Paton, Essentials of Accounting 264–266 (Rev.Ed.1949). But see Finney,

General Accounting 247–250 (1946). Isolation of the discount for tax purposes would be more appropriate if the court considered the partnership as a broker receiving commissions, rather than as a vendor. Cf. Simon v. C.I.R., 2 Cir., 176 F.2d 230. See Note, 69 Harv. L. Rev. 567, 568–569. But we need not consider whether the circumstances here justified the segregation for tax purposes of the discounts from the remainder of the sales profits—see G. A. Stafford & Co. v. Pedrick, D.C.S.D.N.Y., 78 F.Supp. 89, affirmed 2 Cir., 171 F.2d 42—for we hold the total profits on these transactions, including the discounts, to be taxable in full.

Under [section 861(a)(6)] of the 1939 Code, a nonresident alien engaged in business here derives income from the sale of personal property in "the country in which (the goods are) sold." By the overwhelming weight of authority, goods are deemed "sold" within the statutory meaning when the seller performs the last act demanded of him to transfer ownership, and title passes to the buyer. . . .

Here, by deliberate act of the parties, title, or at least beneficial ownership, passed to IAPI in the United States. Under the letters of credit, Balanovski was paid in the United States and CADIC's last act to complete performance was done here. When Balanovski presented evidence of shipment—the clean ocean bill of lading made out to the account of an Argentine bank with the directive "Notify IAPI"—he had completed CADIC's work and he received the final 1 per cent of IAPI's contract price.

The time when title to goods passes depends, of course, upon the intention of the parties . . . When documents of title, such as a bill of lading, are given up, the presumption is that the seller has given up title, together with the documents. . . . In F.O.B. and F.A.S. contracts there is a presumption that title passes from the seller just as soon as the goods are delivered to the carrier "free on board" or "free alongside" the ship, as the case may be. . . . Both of these presumptions, which would tend to establish that title passed from CADIC to IAPI in the United States, are not altered by the use of a letter of credit. . . .

All the available evidence confirms, rather than rebuts, these presumptions of passage of title in the United States. All risk of loss passed before the ocean voyage. IAPI took out the marine insurance. CADIC performed all acts to complete the transaction, retained no control of the goods, and there was no possibility of withdrawal.

Judge Palmieri apparently did not contest that title to the goods passed in the United States. But he applied a test based upon the "substance of the transaction" to hold that Argentina was the place where the income-producing contracts were negotiated and concluded, the place of the buyer's business, and the destination of the goods. This led him to conclude that Argentina, rather than the United States, was the place of sale. The judge further buttressed this result by observing that IAPI, rather than CADIC, had insisted upon the passing of title in the United States.

Although the "passage of title" rule may be subject to criticism on the grounds that it may impose inequitable tax burdens upon taxpayers engaged in substantially similar transactions, such as upon exporters whose customers require that property in the goods pass in the United States—see Hearings before the House Committee on Ways and Means on Forty Topics Pertaining to the General Revision of the Internal Revenue Code, 83d Cong., 1st Sess., pt. 2, at 1458 (1953)—no suitable substitute test providing an adequate degree of certainty for taxpayers has been proposed. Vague "contacts" or "substance of the transaction" criteria would make it more difficult for corporations engaged in Western Hemisphere trade to plan their operations so as to receive the special deduction granted them if they derive at least 95 per cent of their income from sources outside the United States. Int.Rev.Code of 1954, §§ 921, 922; see also § 941. See Note, supra, 69 Harv.L.Rev. 567.

Careful study was given this problem by the experts working on the Income Tax Project of the American Law Institute. They did give consideration to an alternative test of "place of destination." But this was open to criticism on the ground that it unduly favored exporters. See Surrey & Warren, The Income Tax Project of the American Law Institute, 66 Harv.L.Rev. 1161, 1196–1198. After much deliberation the American Law Institute has retained the "title passage" rule in its 1954 draft of a model Internal Revenue Code. See American Law Institute, Federal Income Tax Statute, February 1954 Draft, vol. 2, § X906(c), and see comment at p. 483. Further, in substantially re-enacting [861(a)(6)] of the 1939 Code, Congress did not further define "the place of sale," thus apparently accepting the prevailing "passage of title" test. See Int.Rev.Code of 1954, §§ 861(a)(6), 862(a)(6).

Of course this test may present problems, as where passage of title is formally delayed to avoid taxes.[5] Hence it is not necessary, nor is it desirable, to require rigid adherence to this test under all circumstances. But the rule does provide for a certainty and ease of application desirable in international trade.[6] Where, as here, it appears to accord with the economic realities (since these profits flowed from transactions engineered in major part within the United States), we see no reason to depart from it. Hence we hold that the partners are liable for taxes on the entire profits of the partnership sales amounting to $7,763,702.20.

---

[5]   See Dean & Leake, How To Arrange Foreign Sales So Title Will Pass "Outside the U.S." for Tax Purposes, 94 J. Accountancy 457.

[6]   Treas.Reg. 111, §§ 29.119–8, promulgated under [section 861(a)(6)] of the Internal Revenue Code of 1939, provides that "the 'country in which sold' ordinarily means the place where the property is marketed."

The meaning of this definition is obscure, but surely we cannot construe it to mean the place of ultimate destination of the goods. Not only would such a construction be at variance with the decided cases, but it would make avoidance of American taxes not only simple but practically automatic.

NOTES AND QUESTIONS

1. Why did IAPI and Balanovski want title to pass to IAPI in the U.S.? (Hint: Who bore the risk of loss when the goods were on board in New York?) Note that under the UCC, risk of loss is independent of title passage.

2. Why did the ALI recommend against changing the passage of title rule? Why did Congress adopt this recommendation? (Hint: Western Hemisphere Trade Corporations, mentioned above, received a tax exemption for their income from exports designed for the western hemisphere. The same subsidy, in slightly different form, most recently existed in the qualifying foreign trade income provisions of sections 114, 941–943. However, this regime was repealed in 2004 and replaced with a more general incentive for U.S. production activities, section 199, that was itself repealed as part of the December 2017 tax reform) The Treasury has recently estimated that the passage of title rule costs the U.S. over $2 billion in tax revenues per year; other estimates put the correct amount as over $9 billion.

3. The court states (in a footnote) that a destination test "would make avoidance of American taxes not only simple but practically automatic". Do you agree? What about the passage of title test?

4. Do you think, in hindsight, the IRS should be pleased about appealing and winning *Balanovski*? The language at the end of *Balanovski* ("this test may present problems as where passage of title is formally delayed to avoid tax . . .") acknowledges the risk in this formal rule. The Service has not been successful in challenging transactions on these grounds, however. For example in Green Export Co. v. United States, 284 F.2d 383 (Ct. Cl. 1960), the sales contract specified that the title was to remain with the taxpayer until the goods reached their destination. The Service argued that the other terms of shipment evidenced an intent to pass title in the United States (contrary to the stated provisions on title). The court concluded that tax motivation alone would not bar the passage of title rule.

5. Can you envision a fact pattern in which the Service could successfully challenge the formal passage of title? Given the degree of taxpayer control for sourcing income subject to the title passage rule, why might Congress have retained this old rule for inventory?

2.7   CONCLUSION

Can the source rules be improved? The problems we have encountered stem for the most part from a scheme in which each category of income has its own source rules. As to foreign taxpayers, what would be your reaction to a rule that said that active income is U.S. source if attributable to an office or other fixed place or business in the U.S., while passive income is U.S. source if deductible by a U.S. taxpayer?

As to U.S. taxpayers, what would be your reaction to a rule that said that income is foreign source whenever a foreign country considers it domestic source for their tax purposes?

2.8   REVIEW PROBLEMS—CHAPTER 2

1.   A is a Brazilian lawyer (and citizen/resident), who visited the U.S. for the first time in 2019, staying 50 days, primarily for business reasons, in New York City. In 2019, A earned the following items of income:

   a. $100,000 salary paid (by his law firm) in Brazil to his Citibank account.

   b. $1,000 honorarium paid by a group of Latin American law students, for whom he was invited to lecture while in New York.

   c. $5,000 dividends paid on IBM stock he bought 5 years ago, through an online broker.

   d. $1,000 paid on a CD (certificate of deposit) paid by Citibank (a U.S. corporation) to his account in Brazil (in the Brazilian branch of Citibank).

   e. $1,000 gain on the sale of a zero-coupon bond of a U.S. corporation that he bought in 2009 and sold on Dec. 31, 2019, while in Brazil, to a Brazilian citizen and resident.

   f. $10,000 gain on a painting of the Grand Canyon that he found in the attic of his house, and sold to a U.S. business partner of his. He shipped the painting to the U.S. at his expense, including the insurance, by FedEx.

   g. $1,000,000 guaranteed payment on his money market account held in a Swiss bank and paid by the New York Branch of that bank while he was in New York.

   h.   B, his Brazilian friend, paid him (A) $20,000 with respect to a loan of $10,000 that A made to B last year and never thought about since.

   i. $10,000 profit on hand-made dolls that A produces at home and normally ships to the U.S. at the expense of his U.S. (one) customer, but this year brought into the U.S. by A in a suitcase and delivered by hand to the customer in New York. This is a hobby and A is under no obligation to produce these dolls—the customer will purchase whatever produced whenever produced at the agreed price and quality specifications. Alternatively, A purchases the dolls from a neighbor who regularly sells the dolls in his shop in Brazil.

   j. $1,000 for the exclusive worldwide distribution rights of a book he wrote in English for American lawyers with Brazilian customers.

How much U.S. source income does A have in 2019?

CHAPTER 3

THE ALLOCATION OF DEDUCTIONS

3.1 INTRODUCTION AND OVERVIEW

In Chapter 2 above, we saw that both foreign and domestic taxpayers would generally prefer to have their income sourced outside the United States. Where would they prefer to allocate their deductions?[1] Against U.S. or foreign source income?

The following table summarizes some of the major rules for allocating deductions, which are found in sections 861(b), 863(a), 864(e) and 864(g) and the regulations thereunder.

TABLE 3.1
SUMMARY OF ALLOCATION RULES FOR DEDUCTIONS

TYPE OF DEDUCTION	RULE
General 861(b), 863(a)	Allocate to class of income, then apportion on any reasonable basis
Interest 864(e)	Allocate based on assets, without regard to corporate entities
R & E 1.861–17	Allocate any government mandated research costs to that country; remaining expenses allocated either (1) 50% to research location, 50% based on sales, or (2) 25% to research location, 75% based on gross income

Unlike the rules for sources of income, which vary by category, the basic rule for sourcing deductions is the same: First, allocate the deduction to the class of income to which it relates (e.g., expenses incurred to earn sales income are allocated to that class); second, apportion the deduction between the two (or more) relevant groups (e.g., U.S. income and foreign source income) on the basis of some comparison between the two groups in that category. The apportionment methods permitted under the regulations use comparisons of amounts of gross income (the default category for deductions not related to a particular income class), of gross sales, or of expenses incurred. See Regs. sec. 1.861–8(b) and 1.861–8T(c)(1).

---

[1] The term "source" applies to income and the term "allocation" applies to deductions.

Example: Computer Co., a U.S. corporation, manufactures computers in the United States and sells them outside the United States, earning $90,000 of gross income. Computer Co. incurs $30,000 of manufacturing expenses and $10,000 of sales expenses. How are these expenses allocated and apportioned?

Analysis: As an initial matter, Computer Co. must source its income under the rules for manufactured inventory described in Chapter 2. Given the new 2018 source rule for produced inventory, Computer Co.'s $90,000 of gross income from produced inventory is sourced to the U.S., the place of production. Section 863(b) [step 1].

Because all of Computer Co.'s produced inventory income is sourced under one rule (place of production) and all production takes place in the U.S., there is no need for the second step of sourcing the different components of income: the production income is sourced in the United States. [step 2].

Step 1: Produced inventory gross income of $90,000 from the sale of manufactured goods sourced entirely to place of production (U.S.)

$90,000 $\longrightarrow$ Place of production

Step 2: Source each category
Production income   where production assets located, here all U.S.

Now the taxpayer is ready to allocate deductions against its income. Because the sale of produced inventory creates only one category of income (income at place of production) then all expenses are allocated against that $90,000. Thus, all $30,000 of manufacturing expenses and all $10,000 of sales expenses would be allocated to the $90,000 of gross income from sale of produced inventory [step 3].

Step 3: Allocate expenses

$30,000 Production expense

and

$10,000 Sales expenses allocated to $90,000 of gross income from sale of produced inventory

Next, the expenses allocated to each class of income (here, only one class—gross income from the sale of produced inventory) must be apportioned within that class as necessary to answer the relevant tax question. Typically, U.S. taxpayers need to determine what portion of their taxable income is U.S. source and what portion is foreign. However, in the original example above the facts are simplified; all production income is U.S. source so all expenses are apportioned to the United States. In more complicated fact patterns, portions of gross income may be earned both inside and outside the United States.

For example, if production in this hypothetical had occurred both inside and outside the United States then in step 2, gross income sourced on the basis of production (the $90,000) would not be all U.S. source. If 3/4 of the production assets were in the United States and 1/4 of the production assets were located abroad, then step 2 would be recalculated as follows:

Revised   *Step 2*: Source each category

           Production income $90,000—where production assets located so $67,500 would be U.S. source and $22,500 would be foreign source.

Step 3 would remain the same as before: the expenses would be allocated to the class to which they relate. There is only one class here, income from sale of produced inventory (in the amount of $90,000), so both the $30,000 of production expenses and the $10,000 of sales expenses would be allocated against the $90,000 of gross income. However, the taxpayer would next need to determine how the $40,000 of total expenses allocated to this class of income would be apportioned between the U.S. and foreign place of production [step 4]. Using a method based on gross income, the $40,000 of total expense would be apportioned against U.S. and foreign production income as follows:

Step 4:   Apportion the expenses between the U.S. and foreign source income in the category on the basis of gross income.

           Production income: 75% U.S. source, 25% foreign source, so the same ratio will be applied to the $40,000 of expenses— 75% or $30,000 will be apportioned to U.S. sources, and 25% or $10,000 will be apportioned to foreign sources.

Thus, for a taxpayer with $90,000 of gross income (in this revised version of the hypothetical where 75% of production takes place in the U.S.) the $50,000 of total taxable income ($90,000—$40,000 of expenses), is split such that $37,500[2] is U.S. source, and $12,500[3] is foreign source.

What if expenses relate to more than one category of income? How is the initial allocation step made? For example, in the above example, what if Computer Co. incurs $8,000 of general management expenses that relates to more than just the produced inventory income? The management expenses would be allocated to the class of income that includes all relevant income (including the produced inventory income and other income). Reg. sec. 1.861–8(d)(1). The $8,000 allocated to this

---

    [2]   The total U.S. source taxable income, calculated as $67,500–$30,000= $37,050.

    [3]   The total foreign source taxable income, calculated as [foreign source income of $22,500]—[foreign allocated expenses of $10,000]= $12,500.

class would then be apportioned within the class as necessary (e.g. to foreign and U.S source income).

What if an expense cannot be allocated to any class of gross income? Can you think of any example? How should such expenses be allocated and apportioned? See Reg. sec. 1.861–8(c)(3).

Question: Would taxpayers generally prefer the type of rule outlined above for allocating and apportioning deductions, or the set of specific rules for each category, exemplified by the sourcing of income?

There are two major statutory exceptions to the general rule, namely the rules for allocating and apportioning interest expense and those for research and experimental expense, which will be considered below in 3.3 and 3.4. The relevant sections provide for allocation generally based on a comparison of domestic to foreign assets (in the case of interest) or gross sales/gross income (in the case of R & E). Before turning to these exceptions, however, the following case demonstrates the application of the general rules for allocation of deductions.

3.2   ALLOCATION OF DEDUCTIONS

Black & Decker v. Commissioner

United States Tax Court.
T.C. Memo 1991–557 (1991).

* * *

■ COLVIN, JUDGE.

* * *

Petitioner, Black & Decker Corporation, sustained a $7,883,132 worthless stock loss for the taxable year ending September 27, 1981, when petitioner's stock in a wholly owned foreign subsidiary became worthless. The sole issue for decision is whether the loss is a deduction from United States or foreign source income in computing foreign source taxable income for purposes of the foreign tax credit limitation under section 904. We hold that the worthless stock loss is allocable against petitioner's foreign source income.

FINDINGS OF FACT

1.   Petitioner

Petitioner . . . is a United States corporation with principal offices in Towson, Maryland. . . . During the early 1970s, petitioner operated worldwide. . . . Petitioner operated through foreign subsidiaries or branches. Petitioner viewed itself as an effective competitor worldwide. Although petitioner's largest market share was in the United Kingdom, petitioner did substantially more business in the United States. During the early 1970s petitioner controlled a substantial portion of the United States market for professional and power tools.

2. Background . . .

During the early 1970s, two major Japanese tool manufacturers, Makita and Hitachi, competed with petitioner in several markets in which petitioner operated. During those years, Makita and Hitachi each possessed 40 percent of the Japanese power tool market. Makita and Hitachi began to expand their selling operations outside of Japan. Makita and Hitachi had sales activities worldwide, including Europe, the United States, Canada, Australia, and Southeast Asia.

In the early 1970s petitioner had significant concerns about Makita and Hitachi gaining United States market shares in the power tool industry, thereby posing a substantial threat to petitioner's business, not only in the United States but worldwide. Petitioner maintained a significant data bank on its Japanese competitors to closely monitor their activities.

3. Petitioner's Establishment of its Japanese Subsidiary (NBD) . . .

In 1972, petitioner formed [a] wholly owned foreign subsidiary, Nippon Black & Decker (NBD), in Japan to manufacture, purchase, sell, import, export, and provide repair service for power tools and accessories and related component parts. Petitioner acquired all of the shares of NBD for $249,838. NBD began operations in 1974.

NBD received approval from Japan's Ministry of International Trade and Industry (MITI) to build a manufacturing facility in Japan. The business plan presented to MITI anticipated that petitioner would obtain a 15 percent market share over the first 5 years. The approval granted by MITI was one of only a few approvals granted up to that time by MITI to a Japanese manufacturing corporation wholly owned by an American company. . . .

Because of NBD's continuing substantial losses in 1981 and petitioner's domestic financial reversals during the early 1980s, petitioner abandoned the NBD operations, liquidated the assets, and claimed a $7,883,137 worthless stock loss (the worthless stock loss), pursuant to section 165(g)(3) on its 1981 Federal income tax return. Respondent allowed petitioner's loss. The deficiency at issue is attributable to respondent's determination that the worthless stock loss was entirely allocable to sources outside the United States.

Petitioner's purpose in investing in NBD was to protect its market share in the United States and worldwide. Petitioner sought to achieve this purpose by competing aggressively with Makita and Hitachi in their home markets in Japan. Petitioner believed that competing with the Japanese companies in Japan would strengthen petitioner's ability to compete against their export activity to the United States and to other markets in which petitioner had sales operations.

Petitioner did not expect to receive dividends from NBD at the time of its investments in the stock of NBD (1972, 1974, and 1980) because of

NBD's losses. However, petitioner did intend to make a profit in Japan after establishing market share.

NBD operated at a loss for all but 2 years of its existence. NBD never declared or paid a dividend. NBD maintained a deficit in its retained earnings beginning with its taxable year ending September 30, 1975.

During the years in issue, all of NBD's business and assets were located in Japan. NBD operated solely in Japan and derived no United States source gross income on its sale of products or from any other activity during the years in issue. . . .

OPINION

The sole issue for decision is whether a loss from worthless stock in a wholly owned foreign subsidiary is deducted from U.S. source or foreign source income in computing the foreign tax credit limitation.

Petitioner contends that the worthless stock loss is entirely allocable to sources within the United States. Alternatively, petitioner contends that a portion of the worthless stock loss is allocable to sources within the United States.

Respondent agrees that petitioner is entitled to a worthless stock loss deduction under section 165(g)(3). However, respondent maintains that the deduction relates to petitioner's foreign source income and thus reduces taxable income from sources without the United States for purposes of the foreign tax credit limitation. . . .

Under sec. 1.861–8(a)(2), Income Tax Regs., a taxpayer is required to allocate deductions to a class of gross income, and then, if necessary, to apportion deductions within the class of gross income between the statutory grouping of gross income (foreign source income) and the residual grouping of gross income (U.S. source income). Allocations and apportionments are made on the basis of the factual relationship of deductions to gross income. Sec. 1.861–8(a)(2) and 1.861–8(a)(4), Income Tax Regs. If the deduction is allocable to a class of gross income which is contained in both the statutory and residual grouping, the deduction must be apportioned between the statutory and residual grouping of gross income within that class. Sec. 1.861–8(c)(1), Income Tax Regs.

In determining the class of gross income to which a deduction is allocated, section 1.861–8(b)(2), Income Tax Regs., provides:

(2) Relationship to activity or property. A deduction shall be considered definitely related to a class of gross income and therefore allocable to such class if it is incurred as a result of, or incident to, an activity or in connection with property from which such class of gross income is derived. Where a deduction is incurred as a result of, or incident to, an activity or in connection with property, which activity or property generates, has generated, or could reasonably have been expected to generate gross income, such deduction shall be considered definitely related to such gross income as a class whether or not there is

any item of gross income in such class which is received or accrued during the taxable year and whether or not the amount of deductions exceeds the amount of gross income in such class.

* * *

Section 1.861–8(e)(7)(i), Income Tax Regs., provides rules for allocation of losses on the sale, exchange, or other disposition of property. Such losses are considered definitely related and allocable to the class of gross income to which the property ordinarily gives rise. Section 1.861–8(e)(7)(i), Income Tax Regs., provides:

(7) Losses on the sale, exchange, or other disposition of property— (i) Allocation. The deduction allowed for loss recognized on the sale, exchange, or other disposition of a capital asset or property described in section 1231(b) shall be considered a deduction which is definitely related and allocable to the class of gross income to which such asset or property ordinarily gives rise in the hands of the taxpayer. Where the nature of gross income generated from the asset or property has varied significantly over several taxable years of the taxpayer, such class of gross income shall generally be determined by reference to gross income generated from the asset or property during the taxable year or years immediately preceding the sale, exchange, or other disposition of such asset or property.

* * *

3. Factual Relationship Approach v. Automatic Dividend Theory

Petitioner alleges that its purpose was not to generate dividend income but rather to protect and promote income from sales of its products in the United States, and that, accordingly, the stock loss is allocable to petitioner's U.S. source income from sales. However, we believe the record establishes that petitioner hoped to compete effectively against Japanese manufacturers in Japan and eventually to derive Japanese dividends.

In addition, petitioner asserts that since its investment in NBD did not give rise to any foreign source dividends, the loss is properly allocable to petitioner's U.S. source income.

Petitioner disagrees with respondent's argument that a loss on a stock investment is ordinarily allocable to the dividend class of income, noting that a stock investment also gives rise to capital gain income. Petitioner claims this approach is antithetical to the application of section 1.861–8(e)(7)(i), Income Tax Regs. Petitioner interprets the regulation as relating the loss to the income ordinarily produced in the hands of the taxpayer. Petitioner characterizes respondent's position as tantamount to an automatic dividend approach under which an investment in stock automatically gives rise to income (or loss) in the dividend category. If an automatic dividend approach were intended, petitioner contends, the phrase "in the hands of the taxpayer" would have been wholly unnecessary.

Respondent claims that petitioner misinterprets the regulations as providing a subjective test for allocating losses. Respondent maintains that the phrase "ordinarily gives rise" does not imply that the classification of income is determined by the intent of the taxpayer, and that the kind of income to which an asset ordinarily gives rise does not vary from taxpayer to taxpayer depending on their intent.

Respondent argues that although a stock investment can yield capital gain income, an investment in stock in a wholly owned subsidiary ordinarily gives rise to dividend income in the hands of the taxpayer. Respondent asserts that petitioner's investment in the NBD stock was an investment which would ordinarily have generated dividend income from sources without the United States, and that, under section 1.861–8(e)(7)(i), Income Tax Regs., the worthless stock loss is thus allocable to foreign source dividend income. Respondent also argues that the fact that petitioner's investment generated no dividend income does not preclude a finding that the class of gross income to which the loss should be allocated is dividend income from NBD. Sec. 1.861–8(b)(1)(2), 1.861–8(c)(1), and 1.861–8(d)(1), Income Tax Regs.

We believe the regulations require objective consideration of the facts and circumstances relating to the relationship of the worthless stock loss to the class of income to which the stock would ordinarily give rise in the hands of the taxpayer. Sec. 1.861–8(a)(2), Income Tax Regs.

Here, petitioner incurred a substantial worthless stock loss from its investment in NBD, its wholly owned foreign subsidiary. Although NBD did not pay or declare a dividend during the years of its existence, petitioner did contemplate taking profits from NBD once it established market share. For example, the business plan presented to MITI anticipated that petitioner would obtain a 15 percent market share over the first 5 years. On the basis of the facts, we conclude that petitioner's investment in the stock of NBD would ordinarily give rise to dividend income; accordingly, the worthless stock loss is allocable to dividend income. . . .

4.   Allocation Method

Petitioner argues in the alternative that, pursuant to the factual relationship test of the regulations, its worthless stock loss should be allocated against the classes of gross income received by petitioner directly from NBD, i.e., gross profit on sales, interest income, and royalty income. . . .

Having found that petitioner's worthless stock loss is allocable to foreign source income under section 1.861–8(a)(2), Income Tax Regs., we conclude that the loss is not allocable between U.S. source and foreign source income by reference to the classes of gross income received by petitioner directly from NBD.

5.   Apportionment of Worthless Stock Loss

Alternatively, petitioner asserts that since dividends from NBD were never received, the worthless stock loss is not definitely related to any class of gross income and the loss should be apportioned on the basis of the respective ratios of petitioner's U.S. source and foreign source income to its total gross income for the year of the loss.

Petitioner recognizes that section 1.861–8(b)(2), Income Tax Regs., states that a loss is allocated to a class of gross income even though the taxpayer realizes no gross income for that class during the year of the loss, but argues that it does not sanction the allocation of a loss to a class of gross income never realized or contemplated. . . .

We are not convinced that apportionment under this provision is justified in this case. We note that the regulations favor the identification of categories of gross income to which deductions are "definitely related," section 1.861–8(b)(2), Income Tax Regs., and do not favor the placement of deductions in the "not definitely related" category. Sec. 1.861–8(b)(5) and 1.861–8(e)(9), Income Tax Regs. We do not allocate the worthless stock loss to all of petitioner's gross income because the loss bears a definite relationship to petitioner's foreign source dividend income.

To reflect the foregoing,

Decision will be entered for the respondent.

NOTES AND QUESTIONS

1.   In *Commissioner v. Ferro-Enamel Corp.*, 134 F.2d 564 (6th Cir.1943), the taxpayer was an Ohio corporation that purchased stock in a Canadian corporation to obtain a constant source of raw materials for its domestic business. The stock later became worthless when the Canadian corporation ceased operations. The sole issue was whether the taxpayer's worthless stock loss arose from sources within or without the United States. The Board of Tax Appeals held that because the investment was not made to obtain dividends from a foreign corporation but was made to enable the taxpayer to carry on manufacturing in the United States, the loss was properly allocable to sources of income within the United States. The Sixth Circuit reversed, using a geographical situs test to determine the source of the loss. It stated:

> The statute in question undertakes to classify the sources of income within the United States and without the United States by the nature and location of the activities of the taxpayer or his property which produces the income. If the income be from service, the place where the service is performed is decisive. If the income is from capital, the place where the capital is employed is controlling. If the income arises from the sale of a capital asset or a loss from its disposition, the place where the sale occurs, or the loss happens, is decisive. [Commissioner v. Ferro-Enamel Corp., 134 F.2d at 566.]

The taxpayer in *Black & Decker* argued that the adoption of Reg. 1.861–8 in 1977 reversed this ruling by requiring that the relationship between the deduction and the income to which it gives rise, and not the geographical situs of the deduction, was decisive, and therefore it should prevail under the analysis used by the Board of Tax Appeals in *Ferro-Enamel*. Do you agree? What, if any, is the advantage of the factual relationship test over the geographic situs test used by the Sixth Circuit?

2.   In *Korfund* (Ch. 2 above), the court held that the location of the hypothetical income which was not earned as a result of the covenant not to compete was decisive, rather than the location of the mental activity needed in order to refrain from competition. How is this analysis similar to the court's holding in *Black & Decker*? Which opinion is more persuasive?

3.   What about the taxpayer's argument that the deduction should be allocated and apportioned based on the income actually earned from NBD, i.e., sales and royalty income, rather than based on the dividend income which was not earned? What distinction does the court draw between the two? Do you find it persuasive?

4.   What if the court had found that Black & Decker never expected to earn any income in Japan, and was only engaged in a preemptive maneuver to force Hitachi to mind its home turf?

5.   Could the taxpayer have argued that the stock was an active trade or business asset? The Supreme Court's decision in *Arkansas Best Corporation v. Commissioner*, 485 U.S. 212 (1988), which held that stock generally is a capital asset, suggests otherwise. *Arkansas Best* applied at the time of the *Black & Decker* decision; however, in 1999 Congress amended section 1221 and narrowed the definition of capital asset. Now, section 1221(a) excludes several additional categories from the definition of capital asset including: (1) a hedging transaction clearly identified on the day entered into, and (2) "supplies of a type regularly used or consumed by the taxpayer in the ordinary course of a trade or business of the taxpayer". Section 1221(1)(7), (8). Would either of these statutory changes have helped the taxpayer in *Black & Decker* claim the stock as an active trade or business asset?

6.   What about the argument that losses from stock should be allocated the same way as gains from the sale of the same stock? What would be the result under this analysis? See Reg. sec. 1.865–2 (adopted in 1999).

3.3   THE ALLOCATION AND APPORTIONMENT OF INTEREST EXPENSE (SECTION 864(e))

a.   WHY A SPECIAL INTEREST EXPENSE RULE?

Most expenses are allocated and apportioned as described in 3.1. But not interest. Why? Interest expense has always posed a special problem in the tax system because of its fungible nature. From an economic (as well as practical) perspective, borrowings relate to all of a business's income and are supported by all of its assets. Borrowing for one set of income generating activities frees up a business's cash and assets to fund other activities. Given the fungibility of money, the choice of where and when to borrow can be strategically manipulated for tax purposes. Thus, a rule for interest expense that linked debt and interest expense to the direct use of the funds (i.e. comparable to using the basic allocation and apportionment rule for deductions) would be an invitation to inappropriate tax manipulations. Recognizing this risk, the Code provides a special rule for interest: "[a]ll allocations and apportionments of interest expense shall be made on the basis of assets rather than gross income." Sec. 864(e)(2). For purposes of this calculation, the regulations provide for assets to be valued either at tax book value or fair market value. Reg. sec. 1.861–9T(g)(1)(i). However, the TCJA abolished the fair market value method, so that only tax book value can be used. Section 864(e)(2).

Example: Returning to the initial example in 3.1, assume that Computer Co. has U.S assets with adjusted basis of $50,000, and foreign assets with adjusted basis of $10,000 . If Computer Co. incurs $60,000 of current interest expense, how is that expense allocated and apportioned?

Analysis: Consideration of Computer Co.'s gross income is not relevant, only assets matter. Computer Co. must allocate according to its adjusted basis of its assets. Section 864(e)(2).[4] Using adjusted basis values, $1,000 of the total of $6,000 of interest expense is allocated to foreign source income:

$$\$6,000 \text{ interest expense x } \frac{\$10,000 \text{ foreign asset adjusted basis}}{\$60,000 \text{ total asset adjusted basis}} = \$1,000$$

Exceptions to the interest expense rules: A few exceptions exist to this special interest expense allocation rule. Temp. Reg. Sec. 1.861–10T(b), (c), (e). For example, in some cases, interest expense on nonrecourse debt incurred on a specific property will be allocated exclusively to the income generated by the property (e.g., rental income). Temp. Reg. Sec. 1.861–10T(b)(1). What rationale likely justifies this exception? Separate rules also govern the calculation of interest expense allocation for U.S. branches of a foreign corporation (such taxpayers, which are taxed by the United States on a net basis, must determine their net U.S. source income). Reg. Sec. 1.882–5.

b. INTEREST EXPENSE OF U.S. AFFILIATED GROUPS—THE LOOK THROUGH RULE

A major area of controversy for interest expense allocation has been the treatment of U.S. consolidated groups, which have been viewed as a single entity for some purposes, but not for others. To understand how consolidated groups can be difficult, consider this hypothetical: P and D are domestic corporations filing a consolidated tax return. P owns D, which has $1,000 in U.S. assets and $1,000 in foreign assets.

---

    4   The TCJA revised the rules for the deduction of interest expense. Prior to the 2017 tax reform, interest allocations could be made based on either the fair market value of assets or the adjusted basis of assets. Tax reform eliminated the fair market value option. Section 864(e)(2).

Prior to 1986, the allocation of interest expense depended on whether P or D was the borrower. If P borrowed and had $100 of interest expense, it was allocated based on P's assets. Here, P's only asset (stock in D) generated U.S. source income (dividends from a U.S. corporation, see Ch. 2), thus the $100 interest expense was allocated to U.S. source income (a desirable result from the perspective of the taxpayer—why?).

If D borrowed and had $100 of interest expense, the allocation based on D's assets ($1,000 U.S. assets and $1,000 foreign assets) would result in an allocation of half the expense ($50) to U.S. source income and half ($50) to foreign source income. This inconsistent result derived from the D stock being respected as a separate asset in the interest allocation step when P borrows, although P and D are treated as a single entity in the final consolidation step.

If P and D are deemed a single entity, then arguably it should not matter whether P or D incurred the debt and the $100 interest expense. Look at section 864(e)(1) enacted in 1986 to provide consistency. Now, D stock is disregarded in asset based allocations when P borrows, and a "look-through" rule applies (treating P as owning the assets ($1,000 U.S. and $1,000 foreign) held by its consolidated subsidiary D. Thus, a borrowing by P would now generate interest expense allocated half to U.S income, and half to foreign source income.

c.   THE UNFAIRNESS OF NOT LOOKING—THROUGH FOREIGN AFFILIATES?

The look-through rule used to relieve the inconsistency in interest expense allocation in the domestic affiliated group context failed to resolve all allocation problems of U.S. multinationals. Consider the next scenario: D, a U.S. corporation, has $1,000 in U.S. assets' adjusted basis generating $100 in U.S. income and has $500 in debt. D also has a wholly owned foreign subsidiary, F (with $1,000 in foreign assets adjusted basis generating $100 in income and with $500 of debt).

If D has $50 of interest expense on its $500 deposit, how is that expense allocated? Historically, foreign affiliates have never been treated as members of the U.S. affiliated group. Section 1504. Therefore, D's expense of $50 would be allocated based on its assets ($1,000 U.S. and $500 foreign[5]). Of D's total interest expense of $50, 1/3 would be allocated to foreign income and 2/3 would be allocated to U.S. income. The final net taxable income picture would look as follows:

---

[5]   D's foreign asset is its stock in F with a value of $500, reflecting F's underlying foreign assets of $1,000 and the debt of $500.

TABLE 3.2

F			D		
	Foreign			U.S.	Foreign
Income	$100	Income		$100	$50[6]
Interest exp.	$50[7]	Interest Exp.		$33	$17
Net income	$50[8]	Net Income		$67	$33

This outcome raises two questions. First, why does this allocation matter? Recall that for U.S. taxpayers, the sourcing of income and the allocation of deductions directly impacts their ability to get a full credit for foreign income taxes paid (see Ch. 8). The more of a taxpayer's net taxable income that is considered foreign source, the more likely the taxpayer is to obtain full foreign tax credits. Taxpayers achieve this by maximizing the portion of income treated as foreign and minimizing the portion of their deductions allocated against foreign income. Thus, any deduction rule that results in more expense allocated against foreign source income can significantly reduce available foreign tax credits.

The second question emerging from this scenario is why is the result incorrect (D has $67 net U.S. source income and $33 net foreign source income)? The answer lies in the theory of fungibility. If money is fungible and the group's assets—including assets of the foreign affiliate—support all of the group's debt then we should not treat the foreign assets as supporting all foreign debt *plus* some U.S. affiliate debt.[9] If D and F were seen as a single entity (which is how domestic affiliates are viewed for these purposes) then that entity would have $1,000 of U.S. assets (adjusted basis), $1,000 of foreign assets (adjusted basis), $100 of U.S. source income and $100 of foreign source income. Under the view that all assets support all debt, the total interest expense for the year, $100[10], would be allocated and apportioned half to foreign source income and half to U.S. source income using asset based allocations. Taxable income for the "single entity" would be net $50 U.S. source income and $50 foreign source income. In contrast, Table 3.2 produces $67 of U.S. source income and $33 of foreign source income—overstating U.S. source and understating foreign source income, and reducing available foreign tax credits.[11]

---

[6]   Dividend from F.

[7]   Because there was no look-through to the foreign affiliates, F's interest expense is allowed to fully reduce its gross income before distribution of that income to D.

[8]   Generally speaking D will get a credit for the taxes paid on this income by F (see Ch. 8).

[9]   See how Table 3.2 treats foreign assets as bearing all foreign, plus some U.S., debt. The $50 of F interest expense is completely deducted against the $100 of foreign source income. Then, when the net $50 reaches D as a dividend, it is further reduced by $17 of U.S. interest expense. Thus, a total of $67 of the full $100 of group interest expense is allocated to foreign source income even through foreign assets are only 50% of the total group assets.

[10] $50 technically incurred by D and $50 technically incurred by F.

[11]   Table 3.1 seems to indicate a total of $150 of income for the group. However, the $50 of F income is the same $50 of D income from foreign sources. In most cases the $50 reported by F

In 2004, Congress finally responded to this overallocation of interest expense to foreign income, motivated by the observation that:

> Present-law interest expense allocation rules result in U.S. companies allocating a portion of their U.S. interest expense against foreign source income, even when the foreign operation has its own debt. The tax effect of this rule is that the U.S. companies end up paying double tax [and are less competitive]. H.R. Rep. No. 108–548 (Act. Sec. 401).

Under this new provision, section 864(f)(1), domestic affiliates would be able to make a one-time election to calculate their interest expense allocations by treating all the members (foreign and domestic) of the worldwide affiliated group as if they were a single entity (with some adjustments). However, the effective date of section 864(f)(1) has been postponed several times—most recently by tax legislation in 2010 which sets the effective to begin for taxable years after December 31, 2020. The new rule is expected to be a revenue loser and its delay in implementation reflects recent budgetary pressures. The new section 864(f)(1) comprises a two-step process that better accounts for the role of foreign debt.

In step 1, the taxpayer determines the worldwide group's 3rd party interest expense[12] and then multiples it by the ratio of worldwide group foreign assets/worldwide group total assets. This calculation determines what fraction of the group's total interest expense is supported by foreign assets—"the worldwide group foreign interest expense". In step 2, the taxpayer subtracts from this foreign interest expense total, the amount of interest expense incurred by the foreign affiliates that would be allocated to foreign sources if in fact the foreign affiliates were the only entities (i.e. if the foreign affiliates have only foreign assets, then all of their interest expense under this inquiry would be allocated to foreign source income). The resulting number is the amount of the U.S. group's interest expense that will be allocated against foreign source income.

---

ultimately does not bear its own additional tax burden because income tax paid by F to its home jurisdiction will be credited by the United States against the U.S income tax owed by D. Thus, the group effectively pays tax on $100 of income. The problem with Table 3.1 is **how** that net taxable income of $100 is divided between foreign and U.S sources for the calculation of the foreign tax credit.

12 The rule is not available for related party debt.

Applying the new rule to the facts in Table 3.1:

Step 1:

$$\text{worldwide group interest expense (\$100)} \quad \times \quad \frac{\text{worldwide group foreign assets} \quad (\$1{,}000)}{\text{adjusted basis}} {\Large/} \frac{\text{worldwide group total assets} \quad (\$2{,}000)}{\text{adjusted basis}}$$

=$50 total group interest expense allocated to foreign source income

Step 2: the taxpayer subtracts from this group total of $50, the interest expense of the foreign members (here, F) that would be allocated to foreign source income if F were the only entity and the allocation rules applied to it. Because F has only foreign assets, all of its interest expense ($50) would be allocated to foreign sources. Thus,

$50	(total group interest expense allocated to foreign sources)
–$50	(foreign member interest expense otherwise allocable to foreign sources)
$0	(total of U.S. affiliate (D) interest expense allocated to foreign sources)

Returning to Table 3.2, if D has $100 of U.S. source income and $50 of foreign source income, but D's interest expense of $50 is now allocated all to U.S. sources, then D has $50 of U.S. source taxable income and $50 of foreign source taxable income—a result that matches a full look-through approach for the affiliated group and does not overstate the allocation of interest expense to foreign source income.

3.4   THE SOURCING OF R & E EXPENSE

The other major category of expenditures with special rules is R & E (research and experimental—sometimes referred to as research and development) expense. To see why these costs can be difficult to allocate and apportion, consider the following scenario. In 2010 a taxpayer incurs $100 in R & E expense in the United States to develop a patented product. This research will generate both foreign and U.S. source income in the future. However, in 2010 it is unknown how much of the future income will be foreign or domestic. Taxpayers have strongly urged a rule that allocates as much R & E expense to U.S. source income as possible. Obviously, such a result increases U.S. taxpayers' ability to maximize their available foreign tax credit (see Ch. 8). To justify this treatment, taxpayers have argued that their research was primarily directed at the U.S. market, with foreign market sales being only marginal. In fact, however, some corporations took resulting patents and dumped them into a U.S. subsidiary, which because it manufactured the product in Puerto Rico, was exempt from tax. See section 936 of the Code. Before Congress cut back this benefit, some pharmaceutical companies—by transferring valuable drug patents—paid $100,000 less in tax for every person they hired in Puerto Rico. 1982 Senate Report on TEFRA. When you get to Chapter 6 and transfer pricing, consider how strategies under section 482 have effectively replaced the tax planning that U.S. pharmaceutical corporations used to pursue under section 936.

In addition, taxpayers argued that if R & E were not favorably allocated to U.S. source income, they would move their research abroad, to foreign companies, where they could get the benefit of the deduction. But, as discussed later in connection with section 367, they could not transfer their valuable staffs to a foreign subsidiary without U.S. tax; and besides, the staffs might not want to go.

Reflecting the political struggle on this issue, the formulation of allocation and apportionment rules for R & E has changed a number of times over the past 20 years. The current approach is contained in Reg. Sec. 1.861–17 (note section 864(g) is no longer controlling). The basic premise of the regulations is that R & E expenses are related to gross income "from product categories and are to be allocated between product categories." The result is a two-step process. First, if any research is conducted pursuant to a government mandate, and is not expected to generate foreign income, then the costs of that research may be allocated exclusively to that country. Second, all remaining R & E costs are allocated and apportioned according to either the "sales method" or the "gross income method". Under the sales method, half of the R & E expense is allocated to the place in which the research is conducted (assuming that more than 50% of the research takes place in one country). The remaining half is allocated and apportioned ratably based on current sales of the taxpayer (using broad product categories). Under the gross income method, 25% of the expense is allocated to the place in which the research is conducted (assuming more than 50% of the research takes place there) and the remaining 75% is allocated and apportioned based on gross income (but the amount allocated to the United States must be at least 50% of what would be allocated under the sales method). What do you think of these rules? What kinds of incentives do they create?

3.5   REVIEW PROBLEMS—CHAPTER 3

1.   Z is a publicly traded Delaware corporation headquartered in New Jersey City. It produces shrink wrapped software in New Jersey and sells it in the U.S. and France. F, its wholly-owned French subsidiary, produces and packages the software in France for the French market. A, Z's CEO, who has been trying unsuccessfully to convince the board to expand operations, took a loan (on behalf of Z) that he found extremely attractive (very low interest rate) in 2018, on which Z paid $100,000 of interest in 2019. The loan proceeds have not been put to use in 2019. Z traded at $4M, $1M of which is attributed to F—its sole non-U.S. asset. The value of its factory (building and equipment), assuming it is its only Section 168 property is estimated at $2M. The adjusted tax basis of such property, correctly computed according to the requirements of Treas. Reg. Sec. 1.861–9(i), is $500,000. Allocate and apportion Z's interest expense.

2.   X is a Delaware corporation in the business of developing and producing certain systems for cell phones. The inventor of X's proprietary system is its founder, A, a U.S. citizen, who has never left the state of Texas. All R&E and related engineering activity takes place in X's headquarters in Dallas. X wholly owns a Singapore subsidiary, Y, that manufactures and sells the systems throughout Asia. X manufactures and sells them in the U.S. There are no other markets for the product. In 2019, X had $1M in sales and $350,000 of gross income, $50,000 of which was a (arm's length) royalty from Y for the right to manufacture and sell the product in Asia, and $50,000 interest on governments bonds its holds. It incurred $100,000 R&E expenses in 2019. Y had $1M in sales as well. Allocate and apportion X's R&E expense.

PART B

U.S. INCOME OF FOREIGN TAXPAYERS

CHAPTER 4

THE TAXATION OF NON-BUSINESS INCOME

4.1 INTRODUCTION

This chapter and the next (Ch. 5) explore how the United States taxes nonresidents. As a preliminary matter, consider whether you think the United States should impose income tax in the following three scenarios:

(1) A French corporation owns and operates a furniture factory in the United States.

(2) An Argentinian corporation licenses its patented technology (for producing synthetic rubber) to a U.S. tire manufacturer.

royalty — Yes tax

(3) A Singapore corporation engaged in the manufacture of X-ray equipment sells one machine to a dental office in the United States.

Inventory — where title passes.

To the extent you reached different conclusions in these scenarios, what was your reasoning?

4.2 OVERVIEW

As stated in *Wodehouse* (Ch. 2, above), the U.S. originally applied its income tax to non-residents on the same basis (graduated tax rates on net income) as it applied to residents, except that non-residents were subject to tax only on their U.S.-source income. As stated by Justice Burton, this situation changed in 1936:

> The Revenue Act of 1936 . . . limited the taxability of the income of each nonresident alien individual to those kinds of income to which the withholding provisions also applied. . . . The practical situation was that it had been difficult for United States tax officials to ascertain the taxable income (in the nature of capital gains) which had been derived from sales of property at a profit by nonresident alien individuals, or by foreign corporations, *when the respective taxpayers were not engaged in trade or business within the United States and did not have an office or place of business therein.* This difficulty was in contrast to the ease of computing and collecting a tax from certain other kinds of income, including payments for the use of patents and copyrights, from which the United States income taxes were being, wholly or partially, withheld at the source. . . .

Wodehouse, supra (emphasis added).

The Revenue Act of 1936 thus created the very important dichotomy found in current sections 871(a) and (b) (for non-resident individuals), 881 and 882 (for foreign corporations). Non-resident individuals and foreign corporations not engaged in a trade or business in the United States are taxed by withholding a tax on their *gross* "fixed or determinable, annual or periodic" income ("non-business income") from U.S. sources. Non-residents engaged in a trade or business are taxed by applying the rates found in sections 1 and 11 to their *net* earnings from their U.S. trade or business. In this chapter, we shall focus on the former category (gross basis withholding), while the latter (net basis tax on business income) will be the focus of the next chapter.

Another significant change in the manner of taxing non-residents was enacted in 1966. Read sections 871 and 872, as enacted in 1954.[1] These sections embodied the so-called "force of attraction" principle, under which a non-resident engaged in a U.S. trade or business was taxed at the net rates of sections 1 and 11 on *all of his or her U.S. source income, whether or not derived from the trade or business*. That is, once a taxpayer was determined to have a trade or business, all U.S. source income was taxed as if it were part of the trade or business.

The force of attraction rule made crossing the threshold to having a U.S. trade or business change the entire method of taxing (and the resulting tax bill of) a non-resident. This should be borne in mind when reading the pre-1966 cases, included in Ch. 5, defining what constitutes a U.S. trade or business. In general, would a non-resident prefer to be taxed under section 871(a) or under section 871(b)? What would you need to know to make that determination? Assuming that the withholding tax rate is constant at 30 percent, how might you answer the question when the top net rate is (a) 70 percent (the rate until 1981), (b) 28 percent (the rate after 1986), or (c) 21 percent (the current rate)?

Assuming that Congress intended a 30 percent rate on gross income to be a rough equivalent to a 70 percent rate on net income, why do you think the section 871 rate was left unchanged when the section 1 rate was reduced to 28 percent in 1986?

---

[1]   1954 Code sec. 871(a):

(a) No United States Business—30 Percent Tax—

     (i)   Imposition of tax. Except as otherwise provided in subsection (b) there is hereby imposed for each taxable year, in lieu of the tax imposed by section 1, on the amount received, by every nonresident alien individual not engaged in trade or business within the United States, from sources within the United States, as interest . . . or other fixed or determinable annual or periodical gains, profits, and income . . . a tax of 30 percent of such amount.

1954 Code sec. 871(c):

(c) United States Business.—A nonresident alien individual engaged in trade or business within the United States shall be taxable without regard to subsection (a).

1954 Code sec. 872(a):

(a) General Rule—In the case of a nonresident alien individual gross income includes only the gross income from sources within the United States.

The effect of the old "force of attraction" regime, (former section 871(c)) was to make taxation depend on the status of the recipient (doing business) rather than looking to the nature of the specific transaction producing the income. In this respect, it resembled the section 861(a)(1) and (2) source rules for interest and dividends, which look to the status of the payor (domestic or foreign) rather than to where the loaned funds were used or distributed or profits earned.[2] Both the interest and dividend source rules and the old 871(c) treated all income in a category alike—regardless of where or how it was earned.

By contrast, *current* sections 871(a) and (b) generally determine tax treatment based on how the nonresident earned the item of income. Effectively, this approach traces the nonresident's income to the transaction, comparable to the approach taken with the source rules for royalties and services (sections 861(a)(3) and (4)). Those source rules make the payor's status irrelevant—they look to where the transaction occurred. Similarly, the current section 871 makes the recipient's status irrelevant—he or she is taxed on U.S. nonbusiness income under the nonbusiness section 871(a) gross income rates and on U.S. business income under the section 1 rates on taxable (that is, net) income.

The tax on net business income is computed with regard only to net income *effectively connected* with a U.S. trade or business. The rate does not take into account any U.S. nonbusiness income or any income that— because it is foreign income—section 872 excludes from gross income and therefore does not incur any United States tax at all. It is very important to observe that a nonresident could, in the same tax year, have some income subject to net basis taxation in the U.S. under section 872 (as attributable to a U.S. trade or business) and have some income subject to gross basis taxation under section 871 (because it is U.S. source, not effectively connected, and yet is picked up under the rules of section 871). Try to craft an example in which this would occur.

Although most of this chapter will focus on the two key issues in taxing nonresidents on their **nonbusiness** income,[3] the next two sections briefly walk through the complete statutory regimes for taxing nonresident individuals and corporations on both their nonbusiness and business income. Having this framework in mind will illuminate the important differences for nonresidents between the approaches for the two types of income. Chapter 5 will then examine in greater detail the taxation of nonresident **business** income.

---

[2] Either of these would present extremely complex questions with possibly unascertainable answers.

[3] These two major questions are: (1) what nonbusiness income is included, and (2) what problems arise in withholding to collect tax on that income?

4.3   TAXATION OF NONRESIDENT INDIVIDUALS

1.   *U.S. Nonbusiness Income.*

Section 871(a): "Income Not Connected With United States Business—30 Percent Tax."

A tax of *30 percent* is imposed on the "*amount received*" (no deductions allowed, i.e., a tax on gross income) "from sources within the United States" (i.e., an item of income must be characterized as U.S. source), "but only to the extent the amount received is not effectively connected with the conduct of a trade or business within the United States"—in other words, "*U.S. nonbusiness income*".

Why doesn't the United States tax nonresident alien individuals on a net basis with respect to their nonbusiness income? Do these types of income have associated deductions? Of what magnitude?

2.   *U.S. Business Income.*

Sections 1(a) and 1(c) impose a graduated rate of tax (up to 37 percent) on the *taxable* (i.e., net) income of every individual. Section 2(d) provides that in the case of non-resident aliens, the section 1 graduated tax applies only as provided in section 871. Regs. sec. 1.1–1(a)(1) spells out that the section 1 tax is imposed on all income of citizens and residents; section 1 tax is also imposed on nonresident aliens in respect of their section 871(b) income—i.e., taxable U.S. business income.

Section 871(b): "Income Connected With United States Business—Graduated Rate of Tax." Section 1 tax is imposed only on nonresident alien's *taxable* income that is "effectively connected with the conduct of a trade or business in the United States" ("U.S. business income"). In calculating taxable U.S. income, you begin only with gross income that is gross U.S. business income.

To arrive at *taxable* U.S. business income, you subtract from gross U.S. business income only those deductions that are connected with U.S. business income (section 873(a)). This means that you must first *characterize* items of gross income as U.S. business income, and then *allocate* items of deduction to U.S. business income or to other income.

Thus, as stated in section 872(a), for a non-resident alien gross income for United States tax purposes includes only U.S. Nonbusiness Income and U.S. Business Income. In fact, it is useful at this stage to classify income of a nonresident alien as falling into one of three mutually exclusive categories:

1.   U.S. source income not effectively connected with a U.S. trade or business;

2.   U.S. source income that *is* effectively connected with a U.S. trade or business; and

3. Foreign income—i.e., income that is not gross income under section 872 and that is therefore exempt from U.S. tax.[4]

Income of a nonresident alien therefore has to be characterized as U.S. nonbusiness income (on which there is a 30 percent flat tax on *gross income*); as U.S. business income (on which there is a tax graduated up to 37 percent on taxable, i.e., net income); or as other income—i.e., income which is not included in the U.S. gross income of a nonresident alien and therefore does not incur either gross or net U.S. income tax. This latter category can include U.S. source income that is not effectively connected to a U.S. trade or business (thus no net basis taxation) and is not subject to withholding under section 871 (because the income is either explicitly or implicitly excluded from taxation under section 871). Moreover, even if income would be subject to 30% withholding under section 871, that withholding rate might be reduced, in some cases to 0%, by an applicable treaty. (See Ch. 11).

Deductions have to be classified as allocable to U.S. business income or not so allocable. Deductions allocated to U.S. business income will reduce taxable (net) income, and therefore reduce U.S. tax. Deductions not allocable to U.S. business income will not reduce U.S. tax, for one of two reasons:

1. Deductions allocable to U.S. nonbusiness income generate no tax benefit because that nonbusiness income faces a *gross* income tax of 30 percent, which by definition means that any related deductions are ignored. (Recall that this treatment was originally justified by the lower rate of withholding tax (30% instead of a substantially higher rate on net income, e.g. 70%)). Section 871(a).

2. Deductions attributable to income which is neither U.S. source nonbusiness nor U.S. source business income do not reduce U.S. tax because there is no U.S. tax on such income to reduce. [Such income would not have been included in the U.S. gross income of a nonresident alien].

4.4   TAXATION OF FOREIGN CORPORATIONS

The U.S. approach to the taxation of foreign corporations is parallel to the steps outlined above for individuals.

1.   *U.S. Nonbusiness Income.*

Section 881(a): A tax of 30 percent of the amount received—i.e., gross income—which is U.S. nonbusiness income.

---

[4]   The original section 872, before amendment in 1966, included in a non-resident alien's gross income only income from sources within the United States. To prevent use of the United States as a tax haven—for example, because no country would tax loans by U.S. branches of foreign banks to Latin American countries—in certain limited circumstances the U.S. taxes foreign source income as effectively connected with a U.S. trade or business. That is why current section 872(a)(2) does not refer to *United States* income effectively connected with a U.S. trade or business. But this exception is quite limited.

2. *U.S. Business Income.*

Section 882(a): Section 11 tax imposed only on a foreign corporation's *taxable* income that is U.S. business income. In calculating taxable U.S. business income, you begin only with gross income that is gross U.S. business income.

Section 882(c): To arrive at *taxable* U.S. business income, you subtract from gross U.S. business income only those deductions that are connected with U.S. business income. Again, this means you must characterize gross income as U.S. business income or not, and then allocate items of deduction between gross U.S. business income and other income.

In the same way as with nonresident alien individuals, with respect to foreign corporations income must be characterized as U.S. nonbusiness income, U.S. business income, and other income; and deductions must be classified as allocable to U.S. business income or not so allocable.

4.5   THE HEART OF GROSS BASIS TAXATION OF NONRESIDENTS: "FIXED OR DETERMINABLE, ANNUAL OR PERIODICAL" INCOME

Up to this point, we have spoken in general terms about the scope of the "nonbusiness" income subject to the 30 percent withholding tax. However, a precise understanding of what is and is not covered by the term is central to the application of this tax rule. For individuals this income is defined in section 871(a); for corporations, 881(a). Although there are some differences in scope noted below, for both nonresident individuals and corporations the major component of nonbusiness income is "fixed or determinable annual or periodical gains, profits, and income," (FDAP) a phrase that has been in the statute since 1936. What precisely is FDAP—and how important are the words in specifying its scope? We have already seen in *Wodehouse* (Ch. 2 above), which considered whether lump sum payments received by a nonresident in exchange for rights to written material were FDAP, that income does *not* have to be **annual** or **periodical** in order to qualify as FDAP. What about "**fixed or determinable**"?

Fernando Barba v. United States
United States Claims Court.
2 Cl.Ct. 674 (1983).

* * *

■ MILLER, JUDGE:

Plaintiff claims a refund of federal income taxes withheld from his winnings at two Nevada gambling casinos, on the grounds that as a nonresident alien his winnings were not subject to such taxes, and if they were, they should be offset by his gambling losses during the same year. Both parties have moved for summary judgment.

I

Plaintiff is a citizen and resident of Mexico and has not been engaged in any trade or business in the United States. While vacationing in Nevada in 1980, he "hit" two keno tickets at the Las Vegas Hilton Hotel for a total of $59,480 in winnings, and one at Harrah's Inc. at Tahoe, for $2,100. Keno is a game of chance generally resembling bingo or lotto. As conducted at the Hilton Hotel casino (and presumably at Harrah's) for each game a player selects in sequence from one to 15 numbers out of a total of 80 on a printed card and places a bet on them. The management then randomly draws 20 numbers. If they coincide with those selected by the player, he wins. The amount he wins depends on the total numbers chosen per game, the total which coincide and the amount he bet. The casino provides a printed keno payment schedule which makes it possible for a bettor to determine precisely what he may win for any combination of 1 to 15 of his numbers drawn.

The casinos withheld and paid over to the Internal Revenue Service $18,474 of the total proceeds of $61,580 to which plaintiff was entitled.

On January 12, 1981, plaintiff reported his keno winnings from the three tickets on a Non—Resident Alien Income Tax Return form for 1980 and requested a refund of the withheld tax. Thereafter, on September 28, 1981, he filed a formal claim for refund, which the Internal Revenue Service disallowed on May 5, 1982.

Plaintiff also alleges that for the entire year 1980 he incurred in excess of $475,000 in gambling losses at the Hilton Hotel. Although this allegation is not supported by affidavit, for purposes of the decision herein it will be assumed to be true.

gambling losses.

II

The section of the Internal Revenue Code the application of which is at issue is [sec. 871] . . . The taxpayer's first contention in support of his claim for refund of the tax is that his gambling winnings do not come within the scope of sec. 871(a) because they are not "fixed or determinable annual or periodical gains, profits, and income." The words of this statute not having been changed substantially since their original enactment in § 211(a) of the Revenue Act of 1936 . . . to aid our understanding of its meaning we must go back to the purpose and circumstances of the earlier enactment.

π

Prior to 1936 the income of a nonresident alien was taxed in the same manner and at the same rates as was the income of a resident citizen, except that his gross income was limited to his "gross income from sources within the United States" and his deductions were likewise limited to those connected with the United States. . . . As a mechanism for collection of the tax, another section of the same 1934 Act provided for withholding of the entire normal tax (then 4 percent) at the source of payment of numerous classifications of income. . . .

Immediately prior to the enactment of the Revenue Act of 1936, there could have been no reasonable doubt as to the includability of gambling winnings in the gross income of nonresident aliens since the statutory definition of gross income for all taxpayers included "gains or profits and income derived from any source whatever." . . . Furthermore that was assumed in § 23(g) of the same Act, which allowed deductions from gross income for losses from wagering transactions only "to the extent of the gains from such transactions."

In the Revenue Act of 1936 Congress amended the method of taxation of nonresident alien individuals not engaged in trade or business within the United States and not having an office or place of business therein. The amendments (1) substituted a special flat tax rate of 10 percent on the amount received for the general normal tax and surtax rates on net income; (2) required this entire special tax, in the usual case, to be withheld at the source of the amount received; (3) enumerated the items to be taxed to the nonresident aliens in terms substantially identical to the items on which tax was to be withheld; and (4) except for the addition of dividends, required withholding of tax by the payers on the same items of income as were subject to tax withholding under the prior law. See Commissioner v. Wodehouse, 337 U.S. at 386–87.

The committee reports with respect to these 1936 changes reflect that the legislative purpose was not to decrease the tax on nonresident aliens' income from United States sources but to increase it while at the same time relieving the then Bureau of Internal Revenue of difficult or impossible administrative burdens of ascertaining the proper deductions from nonresident aliens' gross income necessary to arrive at their net income and for the basis of property sold in the United States necessary to arrive at capital gains. Accordingly, the tax was levied on amounts received other than as proceeds of sales of property, and without allowing the deductions from gross income generally allowed to citizens, resident aliens or those engaged in trade or business in the United States; but as a trade-off for the absence of such deductions the tax on such gross income was levied at a flat 10 percent rate, generally lower than the combined normal tax and surtax rates applicable to many taxpayers (those having more than $10,000 in surtax net income, see Revenue Act of 1936 §§ 11, 12). . . .

Thus, it may fairly be concluded that in enacting the language of sec. 871 of the Internal Revenue Code in the predecessor statute Congress had no intent to exclude from tax the gambling winnings of nonresident aliens from United States sources. Such would have been a gratuitous reduction in revenue inconsistent with the stated purpose of increasing it and not supported or explained by any statement in the legislative history.

Plaintiff argues that since gambling winnings are uncertain they are not within the scope of the statute's phrase "other fixed or determinable annual or periodical gains, profits and income." However, as Commissioner v. Wodehouse, supra, makes clear (337 U.S. at 393–94), the words "annual" and "periodical" do not mean actually recurring but are merely generally descriptive of the character of the gains, profits and income which arise out of such relationships as those which produce readily withholdable interest, rents, royalties and salaries, consisting wholly of income, especially in contrast to gains, profits and income in the nature of capital gains from profitable sales of real or personal property.

Further, there is no reason to construe "fixed or determinable" as meaning that the amount of income must be known before it is received. The legislative purpose is carried out if the income is sufficiently "determinable" to the payor so that he may readily compute at the flat rate the tax to be withheld before paying out the remainder. . . .

III

Plaintiff's second line of attack upon the tax is that he had no income subject to the sec. 871(a) tax because for the entire year 1980 he had net gambling losses of more than $400,000.

Plaintiff bases this argument initially upon the words of the statute: the tax is imposed on "the amount received," and plaintiff did not receive any net amount from gambling for the year. But the fact is that plaintiff did receive the $61,580 in keno winnings, and there is no allegation that the losses were from the same transaction nor that he was compelled as a condition of the receipt to put the money back or to gamble again.

. . .

Next plaintiff urges that I.R.C. sec. 861, 862 and 863 in combination require the deduction of gambling losses from gambling winnings before the winnings may be deemed United States source income. . . . The fallacy in plaintiff's argument is in his assumption that the flat tax in sec. 871 is on "taxable income." I.R.C. sec. 63 defines "taxable income" to mean adjusted gross income minus the deductions allowed by the chapter imposing income taxes, other than the standard deduction. However, as I have already noted in the previous portion of this opinion, sec. 871(a) imposes a flat tax (currently 30 percent) on "the amount received" by a nonresident alien which is not connected with his conduct of a domestic trade or business, and Congress intended this to mean "gross" not "taxable" income. Thus the portion of sec. 863 on which plaintiff relies is not pertinent to the issue herein.

Section 863 originated in substantially the same language in § 217(e) of the Revenue Act of 1921 . . . except that the term "net income" was used in lieu of "taxable income." As indicated in part II of this opinion, prior to 1936 nonresident aliens were taxed on their net income from U.S. sources in the same way as citizens were taxed. Thus, until

1936 the method of computing net income from U.S. sourced gross income set forth in the various predecessors of I.R.C. sec. 863, would have been applicable to the non-business income of nonresident aliens; but it is clearly not applicable now. . . .

NOTES AND QUESTIONS

1. If FDAP does not have to be (a) fixed, (b) determinable (in advance), (c) annual, or (d) periodical, what does it mean? Can you suggest any type of income that is not FDAP, other than sales or exchanges of property?

2. Read section 871(j). What are the implications of the last sentence for the meaning of FDAP?

3. How would *Barba* have come out if section 871(j) had been in the Code in 1981?

4. What about Mr. Barba's argument that he should be able to offset his losses against his gains? What result if Barba had been a U.S. resident? See section 165(d).

5. Could Barba have argued that he was in business in the United States? How could that claim have helped him? In *Commissioner v. Groetzinger*, 480 U.S. 23 (1987), the Supreme Court decided that a full time gambler was engaged in a trade or business for purposes of section 162 of the Code.

6. In 2004, Congress further specified the limits of U.S. taxation of nonresident gambling income. New subsection 872(b)(5) now provides that "gross income" from a nonresident individual's "legal wagering transaction initiated outside the United States in a parimutuel pool with respect to a live horse race or dog race in the United States" will **not** be included in the nonresident's gross income. Previously, wagers placed in parimutuel pools in foreign jurisdictions would not have been U.S. source because the payout would have come entirely from a foreign pool/source. But if foreign and U.S. pools were merged, the payout to a nonresident was U.S. source subject to withholding. The new law now eliminates any distinction between winnings from an exclusively foreign parimutuel pool and from a co-mingled U.S. and foreign pool. What justifications support the change? Who benefits from the new rule?

4.6   BEYOND FDAP

Although FDAP is the most significant type of income subject to withholding under sections 871(a) and 881(a), several other categories are also included. First look at section 871(a). For individuals, the major items also facing a 30% withholding tax are: (1) gains from the sale/exchange of patents, copyrights, formulas, goodwill, trademarks, and similar property "to the extent such gains are from payments which are contingent on the productivity, use or disposition of the property or interest sold;" (2) capital gains earned by nonresident alien individuals present in the United States for 183 days or more during the year; (3) certain social security income.

A number of caveats and observations apply. First, as to gains from patents and related property—why is this rule necessary? What tax avoidance behavior is the rule targeting? Consider the following scenario: a nonresident (with no activities in the United States) has a copyrighted book and seeks to license that copyright to a U.S. publisher (for distribution in the United States). The parties could enter into a direct licensing agreement—e.g. the nonresident grants the publisher a copyright license for 15 years in return for royalties equal to 10% of net sales. How would the nonresident's royalty income be treated for tax purposes? What if instead the nonresident sold the copyright in exchange for annual payments equal to 10% of sales? In the absence of section 871(a)'s special rule for sales of copyrights, how would the nonresident's income from this sale be treated for tax purposes? Does that result make sense? Are the nonresident's contingent payments based on sales more like a royalty or more like gain on a sale?

Second, in terms of the capital gains coverage, why is this rule unlikely to apply? [Hint: What typically happens to a nonresident individual who is present in the United States for 183 days?] Under what circumstances might capital gains bear the 30% withholding tax? Finally, although the Code provides for taxation of social security income received by nonresidents, in many cases a special treaty will apply that may modify this taxation.

Turning to nonresident corporations, review section 881(a). Like nonresident individuals, corporations may be subject to withholding on gains from certain patents and related property. And, not surprisingly, no mention is made of social security income, which is not received by corporations. However, a little more surprising is the absence of a subsection providing for the taxation of capital gains here. If a foreign corporation not otherwise engaged in business in the United States earns capital gains, how will it be taxed?

4.7   EXCEPTIONS

There are several important statutory exceptions to the application of the 30% withholding tax on nonbusiness income of nonresidents. The most significant are summarized in the following table:

TABLE 4.1

EXCEPTIONS TO TAXATION OF NON-BUSINESS INCOME

EXCEPTION[5]	LIMITATIONS ON EXCEPTION
1. Sale or Exchange of Property (865(a)(2))	Sale of inventory (865(b)) Sale through fixed office (865(e)) Sale of real property (897)

---

[5]   Until 2010, one additional pair of exceptions applied to interest and dividends paid by U.S. corporations that were 80/20 companies. Recall that prior to August 2010, if a U.S.

2. Portfolio interest (871(h), 881(c))	10 percent shareholders (871(h)(3), 881(c)(3)(B)) Contingent interest (871(h)(4)) Bank loans (881(c)(3)(A))
3. Interest on bank deposits (871(i)(2)(A),(3)(A), 881(d)) interest and certain short-term discount (871(g))	Effectively connected
4. Dividends from foreign corporations that were resourced under section 861(a)(2)(b) to be U.S. source,[6] no longer subject to withholding	
5. Payments on notional principal contracts Reg. 1–863–7(6)(1)	Securities lending Reg. 1.861–3(a)(6), 1.871–7(6)(2)

NOTES AND QUESTIONS

1.   Why do you think these exceptions exist? Try to formulate a rationale for each one.

2.   Why are some exceptions stated explicitly in the taxing sections (i.e. they are U.S. source income that would be FDAP but for the presence of a specific rule), while others are found only in the source rules (i.e. they avoid being subject to FDAP withholding by virtue of special sourcing rules which reclassify the income as foreign source, thus removing it from the reach of the 30% withholding tax)? (Hint: When would Congress prefer these exceptions to be visible?).

3.   Why do the limitations on the exceptions exist? Try to formulate a rationale for each one.

4.   Read section 897. This significant regime was enacted in 1980, amidst growing concern about foreign investment in U.S. real property. Should this be a source of concern? Recall that if a nonresident does not have business activities in the United States then any capital gain avoids U.S. tax. Section 897 overrides this result by identifying gains from the sale of U.S. real property (both direct and indirect) and then subjecting them to tax on a net

---

corporation earned at least 80% of its gross income from foreign sources over a 3 year period, then the **source** rules reclassified the interest paid by that corporation as foreign source (with some modifications depending on whether the gross income was 100% foreign source or less). See Chapter 2.2. Relatedly, until August 2010, where a U.S. corporation earned at least 80% of its gross income from foreign sources over a 3 year period, dividends paid by the corporation **were** U.S. source (unlike the interest it paid) but the dividends were excluded from the 30% withholding by the substantive taxing provisions (sections 871, 881). Thus, the substantive law achieved for nonresidents receiving dividends from 80/20 U.S. corporations what the source rules achieved for their receipt of interest.

[6]   If a foreign corporation has 25% or more gross income over a 3 year period from trade or business in the United States, then a portion of the dividend was resourced to the United States under section 861(a)(2)(B).

basis (as described in Ch. 5). In order to make the substantive rule of section 897 effective, a special withholding tax rule (**not related to the 30% gross withholding tax**) applies to ensure collection. Could this mechanism found in section 897 be extended to other types of capital gains of foreigners? (See section 1445 for the enforcement mechanism). Should it be so extended?

5.   Perhaps the most important of all of the exceptions to the withholding tax are the exceptions for portfolio interest and bank deposit interest. These exceptions were enacted in 1984, and resulted in a significant decrease in the revenues collected under the 30 percent withholding tax (ten years later in 1994, these amounted to under $2 billion). Are these exceptions justified? Who benefits from the existence of these provisions? Why are portfolio dividends not granted a similar exception? How might dividends (and their corresponding equity investment) be viewed differently from interest (and the corresponding debt investment)? Many other countries followed the United States in eliminating withholding tax on portfolio interest. Why do you think they did? What was the risk if they did not?

6.   If a nonresident alien owns stock in a U.S. corporation, dividends are generally subject to withholding tax. If she enters instead into a "notional principal contract" (a derivative, such as an equity swap) with a U.S. investment bank that entitles her to receive "dividend equivalent amounts" whenever the U.S. corporation pays a dividend, the payments were not U.S. source and hence not subject to withholding tax (**until** 2010, see below). Reg. 1.863–7(b)(1). However, if the nonresident lends its stock in a U.S. corporation to the U.S. investment bank, and receives dividend equivalents when the U.S. corporation pays a dividend, the dividend equivalent are U.S. source and subject to withholding. Regs. 1.861–3(a)(6), 1.871–7(b)(2). Does this make sense? Which approach is better? What about capital gains from selling stock in a U.S. corporation?

In response to the inconsistency in taxation here among actual dividend payments, equity swap payments replicating dividends, and substitute payments in a security lending that mimic underlying dividends, Congress amended section 871 in 2010. New section 871(*l*) provides that dividends equivalent payments (which include both substitute dividend payments in a securities lending and dividend equivalent payments in a notional principal contract where the payment is calculated by reference to a payment from sources within the U.S.) shall be treated as U.S. source for purposes of sections section 871(a) and section 881.

4.8   COLLECTIONS

It is one thing to impose a tax burden on a nonresident, especially one with no business activities in the United States. It is quite a different matter to ensure collection of that tax. Thus emerged the withholding tax regime for the taxation of nonresidents' nonbusiness income.

Read section 1441(a); the first sentence of 1441(b); 1441(c)(1); and the first sentence of 1442. What section does 1441(b) remind you of? Read section 1461. Notice the scope sections 1441 and 1442 in terms of who may be required to withhold the 30% gross tax owed by a nonresident.

Such persons, known as "withholding" agents, include any person (domestic or foreign) with "control, receipt, custody, disposal, or payment" of income subject to 30% withholding. More than one party could be deemed a withholding agent, although tax is not required to be withheld more than once.

The following case, reflecting the often complicated transactions of cross border business, considers the question of when a party may be a withholding agent, and thus liable for payment of the 30% gross tax.

* * *

Casa De La Jolla Park, Inc. v. Commissioner
United States Tax Court.
94 T.C. 384 (1990).

■ WRIGHT, JUDGE.

. . .

The issue[] for decision [is w]hether petitioner was responsible under section 1441(a) for withholding tax on interest income of its nonresident alien sole shareholder. . . .

FINDINGS OF FACT

. . .

In early 1981, Donald J. Blake Marshall (Marshall), a Canadian citizen and nonresident of the United States, was approached by the principals of Versatyme Controls Corp. (Versatyme), a California corporation, who were seeking "bridge financing" for a property Versatyme intended to acquire and market on a time-share plan. Marshall, an engineer by training, was the president of Blake Resources Ltd. (Blake Resources), a Canadian public company that was involved in oil and gas exploration. . . .

Versatyme was interested in acquiring a 16-unit motel located in La Jolla, California (the La Jolla property). Marshall negotiated with Versatyme until April 1981, when he agreed to participate in the project. . . . Rather than advancing Versatyme the funds, however, Marshall decided to purchase the property himself and give Versatyme the option to buy the property from him. . . .

On April 10, 1981, Marshall, in his individual capacity, borrowed $1 million from the Royal Bank of Canada (Royal Bank). The loan was to be repaid over a 5-year term. In a letter to Marshall dated April 10, 1981, the Royal Bank required . . . the hypothecation of 828,000 shares of Marshall's stock in Blake Resources. . . . The Royal Bank also required Marshall to assign . . . as security for the loan . . . all his rights and interests in all of the time-share promissory notes from third parties as such notes were executed.

Marshall acquired 100 shares of DJBM [a California corporation] on April 14, 1981, with the $1 million loan proceeds from the Royal Bank. Also on April 14, 1981, DJBM acquired the La Jolla property for $1 million. . . . Simultaneously with DJBM's April 14, 1981, acquisition of the La Jolla property, Marshall granted Versatyme an exclusive option to acquire all of his DJBM stock. Under the option agreement, Marshall granted Versatyme the right to acquire all the stock for $1,200,000 in notes secured by deeds of trust and one-third of the "net venture profits" as defined in the option agreement. Versatyme had until June 16, 1981, to exercise the option. Thereafter, Versatyme received an extension of time to exercise its option. . . .

On November 17, 1981, Versatyme exercised its option to purchase Marshall's DJBM stock and gave Marshall a promissory note for $1,200,000 payable in 60 monthly installments at an annual 15 percent interest rate, plus a percentage of profits upon the sale of the time-share units. . . . Versatyme also granted Marshall a deed of trust in the La Jolla property for the purpose of securing Versatyme's promissory note to Marshall.

The sale and purchase agreement covering Versatyme's exercise of its option detailed specific provisions relating to the collection and disbursement of all cash, time-share promissory notes, time-share promissory note proceeds, and time-share trust deeds relating to the La Jolla property. By an agreement dated November 23, 1981, amending the sale and purchase agreement, the Bank of California (BankCal) was named as the collection agent for the collection and disbursement of the proceeds from the time-share notes and trust deeds. The sales and purchase agreement called for BankCal to make the following distributions of its collected proceeds:

1. to Marshall for the principal and interest due on the $1,200,000.00 promissory note from Versatyme. . . .

In January 1982, Versatyme was unable to meet its obligation to Marshall on the promissory note. In anticipation of Versatyme's default, Marshall formed another California corporation, petitioner herein, to continue marketing the timeshare units. On January 14, 1982, Marshall purchased all of the issued stock of petitioner (100 shares) for $10,000. Marshall was petitioner's sole shareholder and director. Petitioner acquired all of Marshall's interests and rights to the La Jolla property in exchange for a promissory note (shareholder loan) from petitioner to Marshall in the amount of $1,627,335 with interest at 28 percent per annum. The amount of the shareholder loan was based upon Marshall's total expenditures for the La Jolla property as of that time—$1 million for the purchase of DJBM stock and his additional advances to DJBM. By a reconveyance agreement dated January 15, 1982, petitioner also acquired all of Versatyme's rights to the La Jolla property in return for a release of Versatyme's obligations to Marshall.

By letter dated January 21, 1982, Versatyme's attorney advised BankCal of the transfer of rights in the La Jolla property by Versatyme to petitioner. Petitioner requested BankCal to continue its collection functions relating to the La Jolla property. BankCal thereafter remitted to petitioner payments collected on the time-share notes until August 1982. Petitioner continued to market the remaining timeshare units until all the units were eventually sold.

In April 1982, Marshall, in his individual capacity, obtained an additional $500,000 line of credit from the Royal Bank to be used for the La Jolla property. As collateral for its outstanding loans to him, the Royal Bank required Marshall to give it a security interest in his property, including hypothecation of Marshall's 100 shares in petitioner.

In mid-1982, Blake Resources Ltd. went into the Canadian equivalent of a bankruptcy reorganization (Chapter 11) proceeding. Thereafter, the Royal Bank, which held 828,000 shares of Blake Resources Ltd. stock as collateral security on its $1 million loan to Marshall, sought further assurances of collection on Marshall's debts.

On July 15, 1982, petitioner, by Marshall as director, authorized BankCal to remit to the Royal Bank on a monthly basis the net proceeds of the timeshare notes, otherwise due and payable to petitioner. The authorization stated that BankCal might be directed by the Royal Bank, from time to time, to transfer funds to petitioner's operating account. Marshall, as sole shareholder and director of petitioner, also caused petitioner to assign to the Royal Bank all the timeshare unit promissory notes and/or mortgages relating to the La Jolla property. The Royal Bank further requested BankCal to hold the notes and/or mortgages in trust for the Royal Bank and to continue its monthly collection duties. The Royal Bank also advised BankCal that the monthly proceeds of the notes and/or mortgages could be accumulated in the account until the Royal Bank requested them.

. . .

Petitioner filed U.S. Annual Returns of Income to be Paid at Source (Forms 1042) for taxable years ended December 31, 1982, and December 31, 1983, on which it reported gross amounts paid of $326,538 and $528,242 for 1982 and 1983, respectively. The Forms 1042 also reflected that no tax had been withheld on the reported payments, nor were there any deposits of tax.

. . .

OPINION

Section 1441(a) generally places a duty on all persons having the control, receipt, custody, disposal, or payment of certain income items of nonresident aliens to withhold tax on such income items. The applicable income items, to the extent they constitute gross income from sources within the United States, include interest. Sec. 1441(a) and 1441(b). The required rate of withholding on interest is 30 percent, unless reduced by treaty. Sec. 1441(a); sec. 1.1441–1, Income Tax Regs. . . .

Section 1461 imposes liability on every person required to deduct and withhold the tax required under section 1441(a).

. . .

The rationale underlying the withholding provisions at issue is as follows:

In order to insure collection of tax, withholding is required by the person paying the income, rather than the one receiving it, in general and in the case of payments to nonresident aliens of fixed or determinable annual or periodical income from sources within the United States. . . .

Petitioner contends that it is not liable for withholding taxes because it is not a withholding agent under section 1441(a). . . .

Whether Petitioner had a Withholding Duty under Section 1441(a)

In contesting its liability as a withholding agent under sections 1441 and 1461, petitioner contends that it never possessed or controlled Marshall's interest income. Therefore it was impossible, petitioner argues, to withhold tax from something it did not possess or control. Moreover, petitioner asserts that withholding income at the source was impossible because Marshall never actually received any income from which petitioner could withhold.

Respondent, on the other hand, contends that Marshall constructively received the interest income because pursuant to petitioner's directions the monthly net proceeds otherwise payable to it were applied to Marshall's outstanding loans with the Royal Bank. In addition, respondent contends that petitioner did control the proceeds of the timeshare notes from which withholdings could have been made.

With respect to its first argument, petitioner contends that there never were payments from petitioner to Marshall from which withholdings could have been made. Petitioner reasons that it never actually "paid" Marshall the interest income. Rather, petitioner merely accrued in its records the interest owed Marshall in accordance with its accrual method of accounting. Furthermore, Marshall, a cash-basis taxpayer, never actually received any income. Therefore, argues petitioner, the transactions at issue are simply the result of accounting entries rather than any actual payment of interest.

We reject petitioner's assertion that withholding responsibility under section 1441(a) requires actual payment and receipt. Petitioner's contention contradicts the language of section 1441(a) which contemplates imposing responsibility on a broad spectrum of persons: "all persons, in whatever capacity acting * * * having the control, receipt, custody, disposal, or payment." Sec. 1441(a) (emphasis supplied). Moreover, even though Marshall did not actually receive the interest income, under the doctrine of constructive receipt, which we find is applicable here, he constructively received the income when the Royal Bank applied it to reduce his outstanding loan balances. . . . Therefore, for purposes of section 1441(a), Marshall did receive the interest income.

Petitioner next argues that it did not possess the required custody or control of Marshall's interest income because it was not the payor. Petitioner cites Tonopah & T. R. Co. v. Commissioner, 112 F.2d 970 (9th Cir.1940), revg. 39 B.T.A. 1043 (1939), in support of its position. In Tonopah, the taxpayer (Tonopah) was a New Jersey corporation that was owned by a British corporation (Borax). Tonopah issued bonds that were guaranteed by Borax. Some of the bondholders were nonresident aliens. Because of substantial losses it had suffered, Tonopah was unable to meet its interest obligations on the bonds and Borax paid the interest out of funds on deposit in England. In reversing the Board of Tax Appeals, the Court of Appeals for the Ninth Circuit held that Tonopah was not liable for withholding on the interest payments to nonresident aliens because Tonopah "never possessed the interest moneys from which [it] could withhold anything within the contemplation of the statute." 112 F.2d at 972.

Petitioner argues that it could no more control the Royal Bank than Tonopah could control Borax. Without the required control or custody, argues petitioner, it could not withhold the tax from the amounts paid.

We are not persuaded, however, that Tonopah & T. R. Co. v. Commissioner, supra, supports petitioner's position. In Tonopah Borax, a British corporation, as guarantor and using its own funds, paid the interest directly to the nonresident alien bondholders of Tonopah, a New Jersey corporation. Accordingly, the court held that Tonopah never possessed the interest moneys from which it could withhold anything. Of equal importance was the court's rejection of the Commissioner's claim that Borax first loaned the funds to Tonopah and then paid the funds to the bondholders, as Tonopah's agent. The Court of Appeals rejected this claim because it was first raised before them and was contrary to the ultimate facts contended by the Commissioner before the Board of Tax Appeals.

The instant case is distinguishable from Tonopah & T. R. Co. v. Commissioner, supra. The payments at issue were not made by a third party guarantor out of its own funds and after the default of the primary obligor. Rather, petitioner directed BankCal to remit the net proceeds of the timeshare notes, otherwise due and payable to petitioner, to the Royal Bank, which applied the remitted funds to Marshall's outstanding personal loans. In addition, the funds used were petitioner's. Indeed, the facts of the instant case are more like the claim rejected by the Court of Appeals in Tonopah. Therefore, the holding in Tonopah of a lack of control is not applicable in the instant case.

Moreover, we reject petitioner's contention that it lacked control over the funds at issue because Marshall, as petitioner's director, really had no choice in directing BankCal to remit the timeshare note proceeds to the Royal Bank. We first note that petitioner in this case is Marshall's corporation, an entity completely separate from him. Marshall's financial problems are not imputable to his corporation. Furthermore, the funds were petitioner's and its decision to remit them directly to the Royal Bank necessarily manifests that petitioner possessed the requisite control.

We also dismiss petitioner's argument that it did not possess the requisite control because it lacked access to the funds remitted from BankCal to the Royal Bank. The facts simply contradict petitioner's assertion. The July 15, 1982, authorization covering the remittances from BankCal to the Royal Bank expressly stated that BankCal might be instructed to transfer funds to petitioner's operating accounts. Indeed, the Royal Bank did, at petitioner's request, authorize BankCal to release the entire February and March 1983 note proceeds to petitioner for its operating expenses.

. . .

In light of the foregoing,

Decision will be entered for the respondent.

NOTES AND QUESTIONS

1. In view of the broad definition of "control" in section 1441, and in view of section 1461, what do you expect the attitude of U.S. payors to be upon remitting any funds to nonresident aliens? Assume, for example, that a corporation distributes funds which may be a taxable dividend or a tax-free return of capital (or capital gain), depending on a calculation of its earnings and profits, which cannot be determined as of the date of payment. What would be the typical course of action? What recourse does the nonresident have? Is this justified?

2. Could Marshall have made another argument? See section 1441(c)(1). In fact, this argument was made but dismissed on procedural grounds. Had these grounds been unavailable, should Marshall have prevailed?

3. Do you agree with the result in the *Tonopah* case? How is a payment by a guarantor to the lender distinguishable from a payment from the guarantor to the borrower, followed by a payment by the borrower to the lender? Should the two have different tax consequences?

4. What happens if the payment to the nonresident is in a form other than cash (e.g. stock dividend, or other noncash payment)? The withholding agent may not release the property to the nonresident until converted into funds sufficient to meet the withholding tax obligation through a cash payment. Treas. Reg. 1.1441–3(e).

Exceptions to Withholding

A number of exceptions to withholding are provided in the statute and regulations. In some cases a nonresident taxpayer must file a statement for the exception to apply, in others it is not required. The withholding tax exceptions include:

(1) complete exemption for income effectively connected to a U.S. trade or business of the nonresident (as described in Ch. 5)—other than compensation for an individual's services. Section 1441(c)(1). A statement must be filed. Treas. Reg. 1.1441–4(a)(2), 1.1441–1(b)(4)(viii).

(2) portfolio interest. Section 1441(c)(9).

(3) bank deposits and similar interest. Section 1441(c)(10); Treas. Reg. 1.1441–1(b)(4)(ii).

(4) gambling winnings exempt under section 871(j). Section 1441(c)(11); Treas. Reg. 1.1441–1(b)(4)(xx).

4.9   CONCLUSION

How would you respond to the following two similar, but diametrically opposed, proposals for revising the taxation of nonbusiness income earned by nonresidents?

A. "The taxation of FDAP is a mess. The United States has a right, under internationally accepted jurisdictional principles, to tax any income that economically derives from within its borders. Therefore, the source rules should be revised to tax dividends and interest based on where the payor earned the underlying profits which are being distributed, whether the payor is a U.S. or a foreign entity. Moreover, the various exceptions embodied in the source rules and in the statutory provisions, such as the portfolio interest exemption, should be abolished. Only in this way can some consistency be achieved in this area without turning the U.S. into a major tax haven."

B. "The taxation of FDAP is a mess. The enactment of the portfolio interest exemption, as well as the other exceptions in the source rules, show that the United States cannot effectively enforce source based taxation of nonbusiness income in a world characterized by immense flows of mobile capital. The only rational course is to abolish the withholding regime altogether, since it involves unnecessary complexity and raises a minuscule amount of revenue."

Which option would you favor?

4.10   REVIEW PROBLEMS—CHAPTER 4

1. A is a Peruvian citizen and resident who was present for 180 days in the U.S. in 2019. During his stay, he traded in foreign currencies using money deposited with his account in Citibank, Los Angeles. These trades resulted in $1,000 of capital gains in 2010. He also earned in 2019 $500 interest on his deposit with Citibank and $1,000 dividends from Coca Cola Co. shares that he owned throughout the year.

a. What are A's U.S. tax consequences of the above?

b.   How would your answer change if A was present in the U.S. 183 days in 2019?

2.   B is a Panamanian citizen and resident who was present for 30 days in the U.S. in 2019. She owns an apartment building on Venice Beach, California. The apartments were maintained and rented out by a management company that went out of business in 2018. Therefore, B needed to fly to L.A. and find a new management company. During her visit, she also took care of some minor issues related to the building and signed an extension of one rental agreement. All in all, she spent 15 hours on these activities and devoted the rest of her visit on vacation.

     a.   What are A's U.S. tax consequences of the above?

     b.   What if she spent $100,000 in building related expenses in 2019?

3.   C is a Nicaraguan citizen and resident who was present (for the first time in her life) for 30 days in the U.S. in 2019. She developed certain software that she licenses in 2019 exclusively to P, a Delaware corporation, in exchange for a payment of $1,000 paid to her Swiss bank account. P uses the software in its products that are sold in the U.S.

     a.   What are C's U.S. tax consequences of the above?

     b.   What if the license is for 10 years and $1,000 paid annually in these years?

     c.   What if in (b) the payment of $1,000 was due only if sales of the P product exceeded $100,000?

[handwritten annotations:] 871(a)(1)(D) Contingent amount so even if sold it's treated as royalty subject to w/holding under § 9.

CHAPTER 5

THE TAXATION OF BUSINESS INCOME

5.1 INTRODUCTION AND OVERVIEW

As explained in Ch. 4, non-resident individuals and foreign corporations not engaged in a trade or business in the United States are taxed by withholding a tax on their gross "fixed or determinable, annual or periodic" income ("non-business income") from U.S. sources. Non-residents engaged in a trade or business are taxed by applying the rates found in sections 1 and 11 to their net earnings from their U.S. trade or business. In this chapter, we shall focus on the latter category.

Before 1966 all the U.S. source income of nonresidents was taxed on a net basis if the nonresident had a U.S. trade or business; this "force of attraction" rule was repealed and replaced with the current "effectively connected" rule in 1966. Since 1966, the tax on net business income is computed with regard only to net income effectively connected with a U.S. trade or business. If a nonresident, otherwise engaged in a U.S. trade or business, earns U.S. source income that is not "connected" to its trade or business, that income will be assessed under the gross basis taxation rules of Ch. 4. Thus, there are two crucial questions that need to be answered to know the amount of U.S. source income on which a foreigner will face net basis taxation: First, does the foreigner have a U.S. trade or business? (If not, the foreigner will only be liable for gross basis taxation). Second, if the answer to the first question is yes, how much of the foreigner's U.S. source income is regarded as effectively connected with the U.S. trade or business? (The other U.S. source income will be analyzed under the gross basis tax rules). The first two sections of this chapter will address these questions. The remainder of the chapter addresses two regimes that were added to the Code since 1986 to address specific ways in which foreign taxpayers could minimize the tax on their U.S. trade or business: the branch profits tax and the BEAT (base erosion anti-abuse tax).

5.2 WHAT IS A U.S. TRADE OR BUSINESS?

The term "United States trade or business" is not defined in the Code, except for certain specific exclusions that are listed in section 864(b). Instead, the definition has evolved in a series of court opinions. In reading these opinions, pay attention to the relationship between the definition of a "U.S. trade or business" and a similar term, "permanent establishment", that is used in tax treaties to refer to the threshold of business activities that has to be exceeded before an enterprise can be taxed on a net basis on its business activity in a given source jurisdiction.[1] Also, remember that for the cases decided before 1966, a finding that the taxpayer had a U.S. trade or business meant that her entire U.S. source income would be subject to tax at the net rate (at that time, up to 90%) rather than the gross rate (30%). Moreover, because there are few deductions normally associated with the earning of non-business income, almost the entire gross amount of the nonbusiness income would bear the 90% rate.

a. INVESTMENT ACTIVITIES

An important area in which the trade or business issue arises is where nonresidents seek to invest in the U.S. securities and commodities markets. How much involvement can a nonresident have with our trading markets before triggering net basis taxation?

Chang Hsiao Liang v. Commissioner of Internal Revenue

Tax Court of the United States.
23 T.C. 1040 (1955).

Respondent determined a deficiency in petitioner's income taxes in the amount of $41,267.73 for the year 1946 . . . . The issue is whether petitioner, a nonresident alien, was engaged in a trade or business within the United States during the year in controversy as a result of his security transactions through a resident agent so as to permit taxation of his income therefrom under section 211(b) of the Internal Revenue Code of 1939. . . .

Petitioner is a nonresident alien individual. He was not present in the United States at any time during the year in controversy. . . . Sometime in 1928, petitioner became acquainted with Lamont M. Cochran, a United States citizen, who was manager of the Mukden, Manchuria, branch of the National City Bank of New York, hereinafter sometimes called National City. At that time, petitioner was military governor of the three eastern provinces of Manchuria. He devoted his full time to military activities and had no other occupation from 1928 through 1946. Cochran was trying to get new business for the bank in 1928 and he approached petitioner with a view to obtaining a securities account from him. As a result of Cochran's efforts petitioner opened a securities account with the main office of National City.

When the Japanese began their military action against the Chinese in Manchuria in 1931, Cochran believed that the Far East was no longer

---

[1]   The permanent establishment threshold is often considered to require more of a presence in the source country before net basis taxation is imposed (e.g., it is possible that a nonresident's activities in the United States could constitute a trade or business but not a permanent establishment). See Ch. 11 for discussion of the relationship between treaty and code provisions (such as permanent establishment and trade/or business).

a desirable place in which to live. He then tried to make an arrangement with petitioner whereby Cochran would return to the United States and supervise petitioner's securities.

On February 1, 1932, petitioner and Cochran entered into the following agreement as drafted by Cochran:

This agreement is made this first day of February 1932 between Chang Hsiao Liang of Peiping, China and L. M. Cochran of Moukden, Manchuria.

L. M. Cochran undertakes to supervise and care for the investments of Chang Hsiao Liang in the United States of America or elsewhere.

In consideration Chang Hsiao Liang binds himself to pay L. M. Cochran U. S. dollars fifteen hundred (say U. S. $1500.00) per month as salary and allowance for his services, together with a commission amounting to one percent of the profit, to be calculated at two year intervals.

This agreement to remain in force for a period of ten years after which it may be cancelled on six months notice from either party.

Cochran returned to the United States in April 1932 and commenced the task of managing petitioner's investments in this country. He continued to function in this capacity throughout the period 1932 to 1946, inclusive. Petitioner originally transmitted $3,000,000 in cash from Mukden to the National City main office to be invested in this country. Certain additional amounts were added between 1928 and 1932, but no additions were made thereafter.

Petitioner's investments were managed by Cochran in 1946 through a custodian account maintained at the Guaranty Trust Company of New York City, hereinafter sometimes called Guaranty Trust. . . . Guaranty Trust bought and sold securities upon directions from Cochran. He would usually send a telegram at night which would be received before the opening of the market in the morning and would be executed at the opening prices through brokers of the bank's own choosing. Cochran performed no similar services for any other person in 1946, and had no other occupation aside from supervising petitioner's account. He bought and sold securities through no agency other than the Guaranty Trust account in 1946.

Cochran exercised sole discretion as to the management of the account, including decisions as to the items and times of purchase and sale and the exercising of proxies. Securities owned by petitioner on which there was a liability on his part were registered in the name of Lamont M. Cochran, pursuant to the custody agreement. The custody agreement was signed on behalf of petitioner by Cochran as agent.

Petitioner had capital gain income in 1946, resulting from his security transactions and capital adjustments . . . Petitioner reported no capital gain income on his 1946 return.

Total sales in the amount of $442,886.63 were consummated by Cochran in 1946. The gross gain less gross losses from account activity in that year totaled $141,598.84. Of that amount, more than $132,000 was derived from the sale of securities held for more than 2 years; more than $93,000 from securities held for more than 3 years; and more than $60,000 from securities held for more than 5 years. During the years 1940 through 1945, the major portion of gains and losses were long-term in nature, and the dollar amount of sales and purchases in each year was small in relation to the market value of the portfolio. . . .

Petitioner reported gross income on his 1946 return in the total amount of $68,050.59, representing dividends and interest. . . .

OPINION

Petitioner, a nonresident alien, was not present in this country in 1946 nor, apparently, at any other time after he entered into the agency agreement in 1932. He left the management of his considerable account entirely to the discretion of his agent. The latter invested petitioner's funds in stocks and securities. He never acquired any hedges; never made short sales; and never purchased "puts" or "calls." His commission in excess of a fixed salary was based on total earnings of the account, regardless of source.

Purchase and sale activity in the account during 1946, the year in controversy, and during 1940, which far exceeded such activity in other years, is adequately explained by transitional changes in the industries represented by the securities immediately before and after American participation in World War II, when increased trading activity was not unusual in the routine conservation and management of investment portfolios. And, in spite of increased activity, even during the year in controversy the average holding period of the securities sold was 5.8 years. More than 90 per cent of the gross gain was derived from the sale of securities held for more than 2 years; and more than 40 per cent of the gross gain was realized from the sale of securities held for more than 5 years. The absence of frequent short-term turnover in petitioner's portfolio negatives the conclusion that these securities were sold as part of a trading operation rather than as investment activity.

Section [864(b)] of the Internal Revenue Code . . . was intended to exempt capital gains realized by nonresident aliens from transactions in commodities, stocks, or securities effected through a resident broker or commission agent, unless such transactions constitute the carrying on of a trade or business rather than mere incidents of a personal investment account.

Whether activities undertaken in connection with investments are sufficiently extensive to constitute a trade or business is a question to be decided on the particular facts. . . . In Fernand C. A. Adda, 10 T. C. 273 . . . extensive transactions in commodities which do not pay dividends and could have resulted in profit only by means of the gains on the purchases and sales were found to constitute a trade or business. For similar reasons Commissioner v. Nubar, (C.A.4) 185 F. 2d 584, reversing 13 T. C. 566, held that transactions in commodities and securities where the taxpayer was himself present in the United States throughout the period were sufficient to constitute the conduct of a trade or business.

The present situation is quite different. Petitioner never having been present in the United States, it is only through the activity of his agent that he could be held to have conducted a business. For the solution of this problem we look not solely to the year in controversy but to the entire agency and particularly to the 7 years shown by the record. These figures appearing in our findings satisfy us that the primary, if not the sole objective, was that of an investment account established to provide a reliable source of income. In fact in 4 of the 7 years the capital transactions resulted in losses rather than gains and only in the year for which respondent has determined the deficiency were the gains of any considerable consequence.

Granting that Congress "did not intend to permit a nonresident alien to establish an agent in the United States to effect transactions for his account and escape taxation of the profits" where such activity is in the nature of a trade or business, we are satisfied that here the agent did no more than was required to preserve an investment account for his principal. . . . We have found as a fact that petitioner was not engaged in a trade or business in this country during the year 1946. Consequently, respondent's determination was, in our view, erroneous.

. . .

Decision will be entered for the petitioner.

NOTES AND QUESTIONS

1. Mr. Chang is a famous figure in modern Chinese history—notorious primarily as the warlord who in 1936 kidnapped Chang Kai Shek to force him to fight against the Japanese (the so-called "Xian incident"). Chang Kai Shek later had him imprisoned for the duration of the war, which explains his absence from the United States. He ultimately retired to Hawaii and lived a long and peaceful life there (he died over 100 years old), presumably off his U.S. investments. What do you think was the likely source of Chang's funds?

2. Is the distinction between an "investor" and a "trader" a convincing one? In the domestic context, it is often better to be a trader than an investor; for example, a trader is not subject to the investment interest limitations of Section 163(d). Cf. Yaeger v. Commissioner, 889 F.2d 29 (2d Cir. 1989). How would you formulate the distinction? Remember that a capital gain is the present value of the future income stream expected to be derived from a security.

3. How would *Chang* come out under current section 864(b)(2)(A)(i)? (See the court's emphasis in this case on factors not relevant today).

4. Map out the full set of rules in section 864(b) governing when a nonresident will and will not be treated as engaged in a U.S. trade or business by virtue of securities and commodities trading. These rather precise formulations stand in sharp contrast to the otherwise vague guidance available (only in case law) for the trade or business concept generally. Why is such clarity extended just to this set of activities? Does it favor or disfavor such activities? Nonresident dealers cannot rely on the "trading for your own account" exception to trade or business status. Why?

Under section 864(b) what is the result if:

(a) a nonresident is trading in stocks on her own account while she is present in the United States, or

(b) same as above except the trading is handled by an employee of the nonresident located in the United States.

5. In addition to securities and commodities trading, the other major activity for which the code provides specific trade or business rules is the performance of personal services. What is the general rule of section 864(b)? What exception is provided? What do you think is the scope of its relevance today? Why? What about when the provision entered the Code in the 1950s?

b. REAL ESTATE

Taxpayers engaged in real estate activities have generated many cases asking whether such activities constitute a U.S. trade or business. Nonresidents contemplating real estate investments should review the case law in this area to assess the likely treatment of their own fact pattern.

Jan Casimir Lewenhaupt v. Commissioner of Internal Revenue

Tax Court of the United States.
20 T.C. 151 (1953).

. . .

The Commissioner has determined a deficiency in income tax for the year 1946 in the amount of $33,820.30. The petitioner contests the entire deficiency and claims overpayment of tax in the amount of $4,345.95. He was a citizen and resident of Sweden during and before the taxable year.

The deficiency results principally from the inclusion in the petitioner's gross income of a long-term capital gain in the amount of $152,555.87, realized upon the sale of real property located in the United States. Petitioner claims that the capital gain is not taxable. . . .

The issues presented for decision are:

. . . whether the petitioner, during the taxable year, was engaged in trade or business within the United States. If this question is decided affirmatively, it follows that the capital gain is taxable by reason of the provisions of section [871] (b) of the Internal Revenue Code.

Petitioner's full name is Jan Casimir Eric Emil Lewenhaupt. He is a Swedish Count. He was born on April 1, 1916. From the date of his birth to November 1948 he was a nonresident alien and a resident and citizen of the Kingdom of Sweden. Petitioner became a resident of the United States in November 1948. The petitioner was physically present in the United States during the calendar year 1946 only from November 20, 1946, to December 20, 1946. At no time prior to November 1948 did the petitioner perform any personal services within the United States. From 1941 through 1946, except for the periods during which he was in the Swedish Army, petitioner was engaged in the importing and exporting business in Sweden. During World War II, petitioner spent several periods in the Swedish Army, and for a portion of this time his regiment was located on the northern border of Sweden, an isolated location with which communication was difficult. From about 1939 through 1945, petitioner was unable to leave Sweden to come to the United States. . . .

In 1874, petitioner's great-grandfather, Serranus Clinton Hastings, the first Chief Justice of California, created an inter vivos trust for the benefit of himself, his wife, and their descendants. This trust, sometimes hereinafter referred to as the Hastings trust, terminated on June 2, 1942, when the last of the children of Judge Hastings died. At the time that this trust terminated, Clinton LaMontagne was the trustee. From June 2, 1942, to March 31, 1945, inclusive, LaMontagne acted as referee in the partition of the corpus of the trust. The corpus was liquidated and distributed to the remaindermen in cash. The last of the distributions of corpus was made on or before March 31, 1945.

Prior to the calendar year 1941, petitioner owned no real or personal property in the United States. He was, however, the beneficiary of a trust established under the will of his mother, Azelea Caroline Lewenhaupt, hereinafter sometimes referred to as the Lewenhaupt trust, the corpus of which comprised four parcels of real property and securities in the United States. . . .

On January 28, 1941, the petitioner appointed LaMontagne, who was a resident of California, as his agent for the purpose of managing the personal and real property petitioner was to receive upon distribution of the assets of the Hastings and of the Lewenhaupt trusts. LaMontagne was a second cousin of the petitioner and had been a trustee of the Hastings trust. The power of attorney dated January 28, 1941, executed by the petitioner in favor of LaMontagne conferred broad general powers on LaMontagne to manage petitioner's affairs and property in the United States, including the power to buy and sell real estate and securities, and "to do and transact all and every kind of business of what nature and kind so ever" for and in the name of the petitioner. On the same date, the petitioner executed a power of attorney with identical provisions in favor of his father, Count Eric Audley Hall Lewenhaupt, who at all times material hereto was a resident of Great Britain.

Petitioner gave LaMontagne a broad power of attorney so that he might be able to act for him in case both Sweden and the United Kingdom were cut off from the United States and so that he would have sufficient power to handle petitioner's funds should the funds of Swedish nationals be frozen in the United States. The funds of Norwegian and Danish nationals in the United States were frozen on April 10, 1940. The funds of Swedish nationals in the United States were frozen on June 14, 1941. Petitioner gave his father a power of attorney because it was feared that Sweden might be invaded or cut off from contact with the United States and England, so that he could no longer communicate with his father in England or with LaMontagne in the United States. . . .

It was understood among petitioner, his father, and LaMontagne that LaMontagne was to take no important action regarding petitioner's United States property, such as purchasing and selling real estate, without first consulting either petitioner or petitioner's father. Prior to taking any major action with respect to petitioner's property in the United States, LaMontagne would consult with petitioner's father and, where practicable, with petitioner. Prior to selling petitioner's Modesto real property, referred to hereinafter, LaMontagne sought and received Count Eric Lewenhaupt's approval of the proposed sale. LaMontagne corresponded frequently with Count Eric Lewenhaupt. They corresponded about once or twice a week during the period from April 1, 1941, to December 31, 1946, inclusive. LaMontagne furnished petitioner's father with monthly reports of petitioner's United States properties. Petitioner frequently corresponded with his father regarding his properties in the United States.

. . . LaMontagne, in the management of petitioner's properties, inter alia, executed leases, rented properties, collected the rents, kept books of account, paid taxes and mortgage interest, insured the properties, executed an option to purchase the El Camino Real property (referred to hereinafter), executed the sale of the Modesto property, and supervised repairs. . . .

All of the income from petitioner's United States real property and securities, after payment of the expenses thereof, was transmitted to petitioner and his father.

The petitioner at one time or another during the calendar year 1946 held legal title to and owned only the following real property situated in the United States:

a.   Lots 29, 30, 31 and 32 in Block 68, 10th and J Streets, Modesto, California, hereinafter referred to as "the Modesto property."

b.   1786B90 San Jose Avenue, San Francisco, California, hereinafter referred to as "the San Jose Ave. property."

c.   679B85 Sutter Street, San Francisco, California, hereinafter referred to as "the Sutter St. property."

    d. 114 West Poplar Avenue, San Mateo, California, hereinafter referred to as "the West Poplar property."

. . .

    The Modesto property consisted of a single structure containing several stores. This property was acquired by petitioner on April 1, 1941, upon termination of the Lewenhaupt trust created for his benefit under the will of his mother. The property was encumbered by a mortgage in the amount of $24,500. On January 12, 1938, while it comprised a part of the corpus of the Lewenhaupt trust, the Modesto property was leased to the Stelling Leasehold Corporation, a California corporation . . . for a 50-year term commencing January 1, 1938. On January 12, 1938, petitioner executed an agreement, in which, as beneficiary of the trust, he undertook to be bound by the lease. On December 20, 1945, petitioner through LaMontagne entered into an agreement with the Stelling Properties Corporation for the sale of the Modesto property to that corporation. LaMontagne communicated with petitioner's father before making the agreement and secured his approval thereof. Legal title to the Modesto property was transferred to the Stelling Properties Corporation on January 23, 1946. The long-term capital gain from the sale of the Modesto property was $152,555.87. . . .

    The lease on the Modesto property was a so-called "net lease" under which the lessee paid all property taxes, all charges for utilities, all insurance; made all repairs, and took care of maintenance. Also, the lessee had the right to make alterations, additions, and improvements, and he was permitted to sublease the property. Petitioner, accordingly, did not pay taxes, insurance, utilities charges, or expenses of maintenance, repairs, or janitor services.

    Petitioner through LaMontagne regularly made payments of interest upon the $24,500 mortgage on the Modesto property, but he made no payment of principal until the date of the sale of that property. Petitioner through LaMontagne paid the mortgage in full upon the date of the sale of the property.

OPINION

    . . . The remaining issue is whether the petitioner, during the taxable year, was engaged in trade or business in the United States within the meaning of section 211(b) of the Internal Revenue Code. If the petitioner was so engaged the capital gain in question is taxable under the provisions of section 871 of the Internal Revenue Code. Section 871(b) of the Code . . . provides that nonresident aliens who are engaged in a trade or business in the United States are taxable in the same manner as citizens of the United States with respect to income derived from sources within the United States.

    The issue here is whether the petitioner's activities with respect to certain parcels of improved real estate constituted engaging in a trade or business. The petitioner, during the taxable year, did not trade in, or realize gain from the sale or exchange of, securities or commodities. At the beginning of the taxable year, the petitioner owned United States securities of an approximate value of $100,000. His only security transactions during the taxable year were the purchase of additional securities with part of the proceeds from the sale of the Modesto real property, which gave rise to the capital gain in question. The respondent's argument on brief that petitioner failed to show that his security transactions did not constitute engaging in business is without merit. . . .

Whether the activities of a nonresident alien constitute engaging in a trade or business in the United States, is, in each instance, a question of fact. The evidence and record before us establish, and we have found as a fact, that the petitioner's activities during the taxable year connected with his ownership, and the management through a resident agent, of real property situated in the United States constituted engaging in a business. The petitioner, prior to and during the taxable year, employed LaMontagne as his resident agent who, under a broad power of attorney which included the power to buy, sell, lease, and mortgage real estate for and in the name of the petitioner, managed the petitioner's real properties and other financial affairs in this country. The petitioner, during all or a part of the taxable year, owned three parcels of improved, commercial real estate. The approximate aggregate fair market value of the three properties was $337,000. In addition, the petitioner purchased a residential property, and through his agent, LaMontagne, acquired an option to purchase a fourth parcel of commercial property, herein referred to as the El Camino Real property, at a cost of $67,500. The option was exercised and title to the property conveyed to the petitioner in January 1947.

LaMontagne's activities, during the taxable year, in the management and operation of petitioner's real properties included the following: executing leases and renting the properties, collecting the rents, keeping books of account, supervising any necessary repairs to the properties, paying taxes and mortgage interest, insuring the properties, executing an option to purchase the El Camino Real property, and executing the sale of the Modesto property. In addition, the agent conducted a regular correspondence with the petitioner's father in England who held a power of attorney from petitioner identical with that given to LaMontagne; he submitted monthly reports to the petitioner's father; and he advised him of prospective and advantageous sales or purchases of property.

The aforementioned activities, carried on in the petitioner's behalf by his agent, are beyond the scope of mere ownership of real property, or the receipt of income from real property. The activities were considerable, continuous, and regular and, in our opinion, constituted engaging in a business within the meaning of section 871(b) of the Code. . . .

We hold that the petitioner, during the taxable year, was engaged in a trade or business, and that his income from sources within the United States is taxable under section 871(b) of the Code.

NOTES AND QUESTIONS

1. How would you define the principal difference between Chang's and Lewenhaupt's activities in the United States?

2. In Evelyn M. L. Neill, 46 B.T.A. 197 (1942) the taxpayer inherited property which was leased for a long term to a tenant who was required to pay taxes and insurance and to maintain the property. No substantial activity on the part of the taxpayer or her agent was necessary. Under those circumstances it was held that the taxpayer was not engaged in business in the United States.

In Elizabeth Herbert, 30 T.C. 26 (1958), the Tax Court held that a nonresident alien was not engaged in trade or business in the United States through the ownership of real property in the United States in the circumstances there present:

In the instant case the real property consisted of one building rented in its entirety to one tenant who has occupied it since 1940, has complete charge of its operation, and is responsible for all repairs except as to outer walls and foundation. This property (the only real property owned by petitioner in the United States) was acquired by petitioner 50 years ago, not as the result of a business transaction entered into for profit . . . but by gift from petitioner's father when she was a very young girl . . . During the taxable years her only activities, in addition to the receipt of rentals, were the payment of taxes, mortgage principal and interest, and insurance premiums. The record also shows that petitioner executed a lease of the property in 1940 and a modified renewal thereof in 1946, and made minor repairs to the walls and roof in 1954 and 1955.

We are of the opinion that petitioner's activities with regard to the real property here involved, which might be considered as "beyond the scope of mere ownership of real property, or the receipt of income from real property," were sporadic rather than "continuous," were irregular rather than "regular," and were minimal rather than "considerable." We therefore conclude that petitioner was "not engaged in trade or business in the United States" during the taxable years. . . .

As a result of decisions like Neill, Herbert, and Lewenhaupt, conservative law firms frequently advise that ownership of more than one piece of real property in the United States, even on a net lease basis, may constitute engaging in a trade or business. Do you agree?

3. What would be the impact on Lewenhaupt of section 897 (enacted in 1980)?

c. ACTIVE BUSINESS

A taxpayer can be clearly engaged in a trade or business, but the activities in the United States might be too incidental or sporadic to constitute a U.S. trade or business, even though they contribute to the foreign business. The key is to evaluate the U.S. activities in isolation. Of course, that may not be so easy to do, as the following case demonstrates.

Spermacet Whaling & Shipping Co. S.A. v. Commissioner of Internal Revenue

Tax Court of the United States.
30 T.C. 618 (1958).

. . . Respondent determined a deficiency in income tax for the taxable year ended April 30, 1948, in the amount of $351,492.29, all of which is in controversy. The issues to be decided are:

(1) Was petitioner, during the taxable year, a "resident * * * foreign corporation engaged in trade or business within the United States" as that phrase is used in section 882, as amended? . . .

FINDINGS OF FACT

Some of the facts are stipulated. To the extent such stipulated facts are not set out herein, they are nevertheless found as facts and are incorporated herein by reference. Petitioner is a corporation organized and existing under the laws of the Republic of Panama. . . .

Archer-Daniels-Midland Company (hereinafter called A. D. M.) is a Delaware corporation with its principal office in Minneapolis, Minnesota. At all times pertinent hereto, it was engaged in the business of processing grains, seeds, and cereals, buying and selling various types of vegetable and other oils, and of conducting related manufacturing and processing operations. During the period from 1946 to 1948, inclusive, Werner G. Smith, a citizen of the United States and a resident of Cleveland, was a director and executive vice president of A. D. M . . . the Smith Division of A. D. M. had its headquarters in Cleveland and was engaged in the business of purchasing, processing, and selling certain special oils, including sperm oil.

Sperm oil is obtained from the sperm whale and is used for industrial purposes, primarily as an additive to lubricants. It is to be distinguished from the edible oils produced from baleen whales. In 1946, sperm oil was in short supply, primarily because the Norwegian whaling fleets had been depleted by enemy action during World War II, and because the whaling fleets then in operating condition were required to be used principally for the production of edible oils. At this time, as had been true for many years, Norway was the largest producer of whale oil in the world.

A typical whaling expedition to obtain crude sperm oil consists of a large mother or factory ship and a number of killer boats. These vessels customarily engage in pelagic whaling, which means deep-sea fishing in the open seas without operational contact with a base station located in coastal waters. The killer ships are used to catch the sperm whales and to tow them to the factory ship. After the whales have been hauled aboard the larger vessel, the sperm oil is extracted, partially from a cavity in the head of the sperm whale and partially by a cooking and refining process applied to the blubber and meat of the whale. Only the sperm liver (from which vital products are obtained) and the sperm oil, which is stored in large tanks on the mother ship, are preserved. Any sediment remaining after the cooking and refining process is discarded.

In the period from 1946 to 1948 A. D. M. was the largest refiner of sperm oil in the world. Neither it nor Smith, however, had any experience in whaling, nor had they ever participated in the operation of a sperm-whaling expedition. Instead, A. D. M.'s business consisted of buying crude sperm oil from the initial producer, refining it, and selling it to others for industrial use. The nature of its business was such that it was required to make long-term commitments to its customers and, as a consequence, it in turn sought to maintain large inventories of sperm oil and to establish assured sources of supply.

During this period from 1946 to 1948, there was a great demand for sperm oil. Of all the nations, Germany had the greatest demand and England likewise was a very large buyer. During this period nearly every country in Europe was interested in buying sperm oil.

Because of this great demand for sperm oil, coupled with the limited supply due to World War II, A. D. M. faced a critical business need. In an effort to meet this need, Smith contacted two Norwegian citizens by the names of Hans Bull Ovrevik and Magnus Konow. Hans Bull (as Ovrevik was known) was a broker in sperm oil, and Konow was a shipowner and a former manager of a large Norwegian whaling company. These individuals in turn approached Anders Jahre, one of Norway's leading whalers, and inquired whether he would be interested in organizing a new whaling company to engage in the production of sperm oil. They indicated that they would like to join Jahre in such a venture and that Smith, in the United States, would be interested if by that method he could secure sperm oil for A. D. M. Jahre was willing to organize such a company but suggested that it would be necessary first to secure a suitable factory ship.

Shortly thereafter Jahre caused the Falkland Shipowners Limited (hereinafter called Falkland), a British corporation which he indirectly controlled, to acquire from the British Government an old factory ship called the Anglo Norse. This ship had been converted to a tanker during World War II and required considerable work and capital to reconvert it into a factory ship. Jahre had at his disposal sufficient killer boats to outfit a whaling expedition.

On June 22, 1946, Jahre prepared a memorandum which he circulated among the parties interested in the proposed whaling expedition, including Smith, Bull, Konow, and one Anton Von der Lippe who was a citizen and resident of Norway and a close friend of Jahre's. As a result of this memorandum, Smith went to Europe and met with

Jahre, Bull, Konow, and Von der Lippe in Tonsberg, Norway, on July 4, 1946. At this conference the parties initialed a memorandum captioned "Proposed Agreement regarding Production of Sperm Oil and sale of Sperm Oil to the [Smith Division of A. D. M.]." Among other things, this proposed agreement provided that an operating company be formed; that the capital stock of the company ($200,000) be subscribed 40 per cent by Smith and 60 per cent divided between Jahre, Bull, Konow, and Von der Lippe; that the stockholders would also lend the company $200,000 in proportion to their stockholdings; that a syndicate be formed composed of the same stockholders; that the entire production of sperm oil by the operating company would first be sold to the syndicate and then resold by the syndicate to the Smith Division of A. D. M.; and that A. D. M. would lend the new company up to $500,000 for the purpose of enabling it to pay for provisions, fuel, wages, and similar items.

When Smith initialed the proposed agreement of July 4, 1946, he advised the other parties that he did so with reservations and would not consider himself bound until he had discussed it with his attorney Clayton A. Quintrell, of Cleveland, Ohio.

Upon Smith's return to the United States, he discussed the proposed agreement of July 4, 1946, with Quintrell. The latter objected to the syndicate arrangement, and these objections were later accepted by the parties interested in organizing the proposed operating company. . . .

Early in December 1946, Jahre, Bull, and Smith met in New York City and thereafter, on December 11 and 12, 1946, caused the petitioner to be incorporated under the laws of the Republic of Panama with the assistance of the law firm of Arias and Arias of Panama City, Panama. One of the reasons for causing petitioner to be incorporated in Panama was the hope of saving taxes.

Under petitioner's articles of incorporation, it was authorized to engage in the whaling and shipping industries with an authorized capital stock of 5,000 common shares without par value. Panama was fixed as the domicile of the corporation and the law firm of Arias and Arias of Panama City was named as its resident agent in Panama. The articles also provided that petitioner's initial board of directors would consist of Jahre, Bull, and Smith and, on the afternoon of December 12, 1946, they held their first board of directors' meeting in New York City.

Petitioner's capital stock was issued 40 per cent to Smith and 60 per cent to citizens and residents of Norway, and loans were made to petitioner in the same proportion. . . .

Smith made his investment in petitioner in order to obtain an adequate supply of sperm oil for A. D. M.

In accordance with authority vested in him at the first meeting of the board of directors, Jahre (acting in petitioner's behalf) signed on December 12, 1946, in New York City, a proposed sales contract between petitioner as seller and A.D. M. as buyer. Among other things, this contract provided that title to all sperm oil produced by the seller during the period of production "shall pass to and vest in the Buyer immediately upon the placing of such oil in the tanks of the said floating factory wherein it is produced by the Seller." For reasons hereinafter stated, this proposed sales contract was never signed by A. D. M. and never had any operative effect.

Shortly after the meeting of petitioner's board of directors in New York City on December 12, 1946, Jahre returned to Norway. Pursuant to the authority conferred upon him, he sought to formalize the prior arrangement existing with respect to the Anglo Norse by obtaining a charter for petitioner from Falkland. Since the latter was a British corporation, however, it could not execute such a charter to petitioner, a foreign corporation, without the approval of the British Government. When contacted, the British Government refused its consent on the ground that Panama (the country of petitioner's incorporation) had not subscribed to the International Whaling Agreement, a treaty to which both Great Britain and the United States were parties. The decision of the British Government jeopardized the entire sperm oil venture contemplated by petitioner's shareholders. Jahre first proposed that A. D. M. charter the Anglo Norse and then permit petitioner to manage the sperm oil expedition which had been planned, but A.D.M. refused to be a party to such an arrangement. After discussing the situation among themselves, petitioner's Norwegian shareholders proposed to Smith that Smidas Company, Inc.,(hereinafter called Smidas) charter the vessel and then work out some definitive relationship with petitioner for the conduct of the expedition. After some negotiation, Smidas accepted the proposal.[3]

On February 5, 1947, Smidas authorized Bull in Norway to charter the Anglo Norse in its behalf and to execute a supplemental charter contract in connection therewith. The authorization to Bull was signed "Smidas Inc by Werner G. Smith Secretary Treasurer." Pursuant to the authority thus conferred by Smidas, a "bare boat charter party" was negotiated in Europe on or about February 5, 1947, and was there signed by Falkland as the owner of the Anglo Norse, and by Bull, acting for Smidas, as charterers. On or about February 5, 1947, a supplemental contract was also entered into between Falkland and Smidas. This contract was also signed by Jahre and Bull, acting for petitioner. By these two instruments Smidas chartered the vessel for a period of 4 years, with options to renew for further periods totaling 6 years, for $50,000 per annum. Smidas assumed and agreed to pay all costs of the repairs and reconversion incurred since June 20, 1946, except for 25,000 British pounds sterling which Falkland agreed to pay.

. . .

---

[3] Smidas Company, Inc., was an Ohio corporation. The date of its incorporation was February 19, 1945. At the time of its incorporation, Smith acquired 54.5 per cent of its capital stock. The nature of its business was to promote export business of certain technical items. Its income is from commissions and fees.

On or about February 21, 1947, a new contract between petitioner as seller and A. D. M. as buyer was drafted and dated as of December 13, 1946. This proposed contract also provided that title to the sperm oil would pass to A. D. M. as the oil was produced by the Anglo Norse on the high seas and placed in the tanks of that vessel. This proposed contract was signed by both parties but due to circumstances hereinafter mentioned was mutually canceled and rescinded.

It still remained necessary for the parties to work out some definitive relationship between petitioner and Smidas (the charterer of the Anglo Norse) for the conduct of the contemplated sperm oil expedition. When the matter was discussed in Norway, Hans Bull proposed that petitioner enter into a management contract with Smidas, whereby petitioner would manage, finance, and operate the entire expedition without any interference from Smidas. In return, petitioner would be entitled to the entire proceeds from the sale of the oil to A. D. M., except for a certain amount which would be paid to Smidas for the part which it had played in making the venture possible. As a part of this proposal the Norwegian shareholders of petitioner contemplated that petitioner could, and would, itself sell the oil directly to A. D. M. When, however, the latter aspect of the proposal was called to the attention of Quintrell (who was in the United States), he took the position that if petitioner was merely to "manage" the sperm oil expedition, then Smidas (which was the charterer) necessarily was the producer and owner of the oil and had to be the one to enter into a contract with A. D. M. to sell the oil. Accordingly, the sales contract executed as of December 13, 1946, was canceled and rescinded, and two new contracts were executed. One contract, dated March 8, 1947, was between petitioner and Smidas, and the other contract, a sales contract dated May 26, 1947, was between Smidas and A. D. M.

The first contract, dated March 8, 1947, was in the form of a letter from Smidas to petitioner, wherein Smidas proposed and petitioner accepted. Under the terms of this arrangement, petitioner assumed all the obligations of Smidas under the charter party, agreed to furnish or procure for Smidas at least seven killer boats, completely outfit each vessel, hire all necessary personnel, procure adequate insurance, and pay all expenses necessary or incidental to the conduct of the contemplated expedition. Petitioner also agreed to comply in all respects with the International Whaling Agreement, to take such action as Smidas shall determine to be advisable for the delivery of the oil so produced at New York, and to keep Smidas advised of the actions taken by petitioner and the progress effected. The arrangement then recited that Smidas proposed to enter into a contract to sell to A. D. M. at $320 per long ton all sperm oil produced by the Anglo Norse to be delivered at New York on or before March 15, 1948, and that Smidas agreed to pay petitioner—for your services and for undertaking the burdens, expense and risks herein described the entire balance of the proceeds to be received by us from the sale of the oil produced under your management, which balance shall remain after deducting from such proceeds the sum of (a) $25,000 and (b) the amount of any expenses incurred directly by us in the sale and delivery of such oil. Petitioner agreed to exonerate Smidas from any liability for any obligation under any charter party relating to any of the vessels—and also from any liability or obligation for any tax upon the production, delivery and sale of such oil, including any income tax upon our alleged receipt of more than $25,000 of taxable net income from the sale of the oil produced hereunder. * * *

The second contract dated May 26, 1947, between Smidas and A. D. M. was drafted by Quintrell and sent to Jahre in Norway for approval. After the proposed instrument had been approved by Jahre, it was executed in the United States by Smidas and A. D. M. Quintrell signed the contract as vice president for Smidas, and the president of A. D. M., S. M. Archer, signed for A. D. M. The new sales contract, which was dated May 26, 1947, contained essentially the same provisions as the rescinded sales contract dated as of December 13, 1946, previously referred to, except that Smidas was the seller rather than petitioner and that the new contract provided that title to the sperm oil would pass to A.D. M., not as it was produced on the high seas aboard the Anglo Norse, but at the time that the sperm oil was delivered to A. D. M. in New York City. . . .

Pursuant to authority from Smidas, Bull negotiated and executed in Norway 7 separate charters for the 7 killer boats which were to accompany the Anglo Norse on the sperm oil expedition. Six of these charters were obtained from Norwegian corporations in the Jahre group and the seventh was obtained from Falkland. Neither Smith nor anyone else in the United States played any part in these transactions.

The Anglo Norse was reconverted to a factory ship and repaired and reconditioned entirely in Norwegian shipyards for the contemplated sperm oil expedition. All contracts for its reconversion, repairs, and equipment and for catch supplies, deck supplies, provisions, and engine room supplies to be used on the expedition, were negotiated, executed, and carried out in petitioner's behalf by Norwegians in Norway. Similarly, all officers and all members of the crews of the several vessels (aggregating about 300 men) were Norwegian and were employed pursuant to contracts negotiated in petitioner's behalf in Norway by Jahre or others under his supervision. Apart from the Guaranty Trust account matter hereinafter discussed, the only activity of any kind occurring in the United States with respect to the expenditures of this type made by petitioner related to certain fuel oil purchases. In those instances, Smith, at the direction of petitioner's Norwegian management, merely contacted certain brokers who, at prices acceptable to and confirmed by the Norwegians, secured fuel oil to be delivered to the Anglo Norse while it was on the sperm oil expedition off the western coast of South America. The Anglo Norse and the 7 killer boats left Norway on the sperm oil expedition in April 1947. The Anglo Norse and one of the killer boats (both of which were owned by Falkland) flew the British flag and were documented under the laws of Great Britain. The other 6 killer boats flew the Norwegian flag and were documented under the laws of Norway. The vessels proceeded directly to the fishing grounds off the western coast of South America and there on May 20, 1947, fishing for sperm whales and the producing of sperm oil was commenced. These operations continued until on or about January 4, 1948, at which time the killer boats returned to Norway. During this entire period the vessels were in constant contact with petitioner's management in Norway via shortwave radio and remained under Jahre's supervision.

As a result of the sperm oil expedition there was produced by the Anglo Norse 15,357.1508 long tons of sperm oil. A portion of this production was delivered to A. D. M. by the transport Peik in October 1947 and the balance by the Anglo Norse in January 1948. In this connection the transport Peik (which was owned by one of the Norwegian corporations controlled by Jahre) was a private carrier sent by petitioner in September 1947 to the Anglo Norse with a load of fuel oil for the expedition. After delivering the fuel oil to the Anglo Norse and its supporting vessels, the Peik received from the tanks of the floating factory 8,194.8245 long tons of sperm oil and in turn delivered that quantity to A. D. M. in New York on or about October 20, 1947. At such time A. D. M. was authorized by Smidas to pay petitioner the contract price for the sperm oil then delivered, that contract price being $2,622,343.84. Of this amount, A. D. M. paid $1,429,900 directly to Lazard to discharge that bank's lien on the sperm oil for funds advanced to petitioner and, after charging petitioner with one-half of the survey fee paid at the port of entry (or $480), paid the balance of $1,191,963.84 to petitioner which petitioner deposited in its account with the New York Guaranty Trust Company.

The Anglo Norse arrived at New York, New York, on or about January 27, 1948, and delivered to A. D. M. 7,162.3263 long tons of sperm oil. At such time A. D. M. was again authorized by Smidas to pay petitioner the contract price for the quantity then delivered, that contract price being $2,291,944.42. After offsetting against this amount one-half of the survey fee paid at the port of entry (or $487.50), A. D. M. paid petitioner $2,287,668.26, leaving a balance due of $3,788.66. Petitioner deposited the amount of $2,287,668.26 in its account with the Guaranty Trust Company of New York. After unloading her cargo of sperm oil the Anglo Norse returned to Norway. . . .

The bank account maintained by petitioner at the Guaranty Trust Company of New York was opened by it on or about February 8, 1947, with a deposit of $125,630.11 and was, at all times pertinent hereto, the only bank account maintained by petitioner in the United States. The deposits to that account consisted, generally speaking, of amounts paid in as Smith's participation in the capital stock and shareholder loans to petitioner, the individual loans to petitioner from Smith or A. D. M., [and] the money paid by A. D. M. for the sperm oil it purchased (except for the amount required to be paid to Lazard as previously stated). . . .

Petitioner did not at any time prior to April 30, 1948, have an office in the United States. During that same period it did, however, have an office in Norway in which and from which it directed and managed petitioner's operations. It did not at any time have any United States employees nor was it qualified to do business in any State in the United States. Smith, petitioner's sole officer in the United States, was paid a director's fee of $10,000 for the period prior to April 30, 1948. During this same period Quintrell was paid "the bulk" of $11,000 for his services as an officer and for legal fees. . . .

OPINION

Petitioner does not dispute the correctness of the amount of the net income of $924,979.72 determined by the respondent. It contends, however, that not any of such net income is taxable to it by the United States or, in the alternative, if any amount is taxable, the taxable portion did not exceed $65,804.14.

It is clear that before petitioner can be taxed by the United States upon any part of the net income in question two requirements must be met. First, it must appear that petitioner was a "resident" foreign corporation "engaged in trade or business within the United States" and, second, that it had "gross income from sources within the United States" under section [882], as amended. This presents a question of fact. . . .

The question we have will become clearer once we resolve the part played by Smidas in the transaction. As disclosed in our findings, it was Smidas who chartered the boats, contracted with petitioner to manage them, took title to the oil, and made delivery of it to A. D. M. pursuant to a written contract entered into between Smidas and A. D. M. If we read the contracts as they are written, Smidas engaged petitioner to perform services under which petitioner would be rewarded with "the entire balance of the proceeds to be received by us from the sale of the oil produced under your management" in excess of $25,000 and certain expenses to be incurred by Smidas in the sale and delivery of such oil.

Petitioner in its opening statement insisted on the genuineness of Smidas's part in the transaction and insists it (petitioner) was not to be held responsible for the acts of Smidas who, it was claimed, was guided in its action by its own board of directors. It is certainly difficult to accept respondent's argument that Smidas was no more than a strawman, and the part it played in the enterprise was a sham. It was not a corporation organized for tax purposes or, for that matter, for the particular part it played in this transaction. Smidas had been in existence for some time; it had ample assets and was at times engaged in various business activities. As far as we know, it is still in existence. It was reasonably compensated for its activities in this enterprise.

We think Smidas's part in the expedition was vital and cannot be disregarded in determining whether petitioner was engaged in business within the United States. It is true that until the time Jahre contacted the British Government with the view of chartering the Anglo Norse from Falkland for petitioner it was the intention of all concerned that petitioner would charter the vessels, proceed to the whaling area, catch the whales, produce the oil, and sell the oil to A. D. M., all on the high seas. But when the British Government refused to grant its consent to the chartering on the ground that Panama had not subscribed to the International Whaling Agreement, the entire sperm oil venture was jeopardized. New arrangements had to be made and were made and petitioner had to assume a different role. Smidas became the charterer of the vessels in its own behalf and entered into a contract, dated March 8, 1947, with petitioner under which petitioner was to manage the expedition for Smidas and assume the obligations mentioned in our findings for which Smidas agreed to pay petitioner for its services.

We think the chartering of the boats, the March 8, 1947, management contract between petitioner and Smidas, and the sales contract dated May 26, 1947, between Smidas and A. D. M. were all bona fide contracts serving a real business purpose, and were in fact what they appeared to be in form. We do not believe they can be disregarded and petitioner treated as if it were the owner and seller of the oil, notwithstanding a statement appearing in petitioner's initial brief that it had "refrained from making the contention that Smidas, Inc., rather than itself, was the owner and seller of the sperm oil" and, hence, is the one to be held taxable on any gain from the sale. . . .

We think the facts here clearly show that petitioner was not the owner and seller of the oil. It had no contract with A. D. M. for the sale of oil. The oil which petitioner produced was produced for Smidas, and it was Smidas that entered into the contract of sale with A. D. M. Smidas was a separate and independent entity and in no way could it be regarded as if it were petitioner's agent . . . Smidas, as charterer of the vessels, entered into a contract with petitioner to manage the expedition for Smidas, for which Smidas agreed to pay petitioner the income here in question. The business in which petitioner was engaged was that of managing the expedition for Smidas, and petitioner's activities which produced the income in question took place almost entirely on the high seas or in Norway.

The activities cited by the respondent as having taken place within the United States are, in our opinion, without substance. He says petitioner had an office in Cleveland, but this was the office of A. D. M. and Smidas and was not petitioner's office. Respondent refers to some services performed by Hans Bull, Quintrell, and Smith on petitioner's behalf within the United States. Hans Bull arranged for the discharge of the oil when it was delivered in New York City. He did this as a broker and was paid a broker's commission. Quintrell is a lawyer and performed some legal services for petitioner. His title as assistant secretary of petitioner was conferred upon him only as a matter of convenience and to enable him to perform certain ministerial acts which are related to the strict professional obligation he owes his client. The acts of Smith in receiving monthly statements or correspondence involving petitioner, or in paying a limited number of obligations requiring payment in American dollars out of a bank account with the Guaranty Trust Company maintained by petitioner, were ministerial and clerical in nature, involving very little exercise of discretion or business judgment necessary to the production of the income in question. The holding of the directors' meetings in New York City solely for the personal convenience of the directors was of no particular consequence. Nor do we think the fact that the whaling enterprise was under the management of petitioner at the time the Anglo Norse made a delivery of sperm oil in New York is enough to say petitioner was engaged in trade or business within the United States. As we have already pointed out, the Anglo Norse at the time was under charter to Smidas and the oil cargo belonged to Smidas.

We have consistently held that before a taxpayer can be found to be "engaged in trade or business within the United States" it must, during some substantial portion of the taxable year, have been regularly and continuously transacting a substantial portion of its ordinary business in this country. This it did not do.

Upon the entire record, we are convinced that petitioner was not engaged in any substantial, regular, or continuous ordinary business activity in the United States. We hold that petitioner is not a "resident * * * foreign corporation engaged in trade or business within the United States" and is, therefore, not taxable as provided in sections [882]. . . .

Decision will be entered for the petitioner.

■ ATKINS, J., dissenting: I find myself unable to agree with the majority in this case. The Supreme Court has repeatedly taken the position that the incidence of taxation depends upon the substance of a transaction. . . .

Upon the facts in this case it seems clear that in reality the petitioner conducted the whaling operations and the sale of the oil, and that Smidas was a mere agency or instrumentality used by the petitioner for chartering the Anglo Norse, which it could not charter directly. Petitioner assumed all the obligations of Smidas under the charter party, procured the killer boats, outfitted each vessel, hired all necessary personnel, procured the insurance, conducted all the whaling operations, paid all expenses, delivered at least a part of the oil, and directly received the proceeds from the sale of the oil. Whereas in form the contract provided that the petitioner would manage, finance, and operate the expedition for Smidas and receive payment of the entire proceeds from the sale of the oil, except for $25,000 which would be retained by Smidas, in reality it was the petitioner which received all the proceeds from the sale of oil and paid Smidas $25,000 for what appears to have been merely entering into the charter agreement.

All the oil was sold in the United States. Since the delivery and sale of products are among the most important functions of a business for profit, I think it is clear that the petitioner was engaged in trade or business within the United States within the meaning of section [882], and therefore taxable upon income from sources within the United States. . . .

NOTES AND QUESTIONS

1.   Why do you think Quintrell rejected the original arrangement, under which A.D.M. (through Smith) would have directly participated in the whaling venture?

2.   Try to make a list of all the activities a taxpayer is permitted under this case to engage in in the United States without being considered engaged in a U.S. trade or business. Does this make sense?

3.   Assuming the dissent's view is accepted, would the taxpayer have any U.S. source taxable income? Note the change in the location in which title to the oil passed, and cf. *Balanovski* (Ch. 2 above) and section 863(b)(2) (cf. section 864(a) for a definition of "produced"). Why was the title passage changed to New York?

4.   How do you think this case would have come out under section 865(e)(2)? Again note that this is similar (but not identical) to the permanent establishment provisions of a typical tax treaty restricting the ability of the U.S. to tax foreign corporations unless they (a) have a "permanent establishment" in the U.S. (generally, an office or fixed place of business), and (b) derive income attributable to the permanent establishment.

d.   OPERATION THROUGH AN AGENT

A critical question, both in the code's determination of trade or business under section 864 and the treaty level determination of permanent establishment, is how to assess activities undertaken by an agent of a nonresident, particularly where that agent is located in the United States.

Frank Handfield v. Commissioner of Internal Revenue

Tax Court of the United States.
23 T.C. 633 (1955).

. . . This proceeding involves a deficiency in petitioner's income tax for the fiscal year ended July 31, 1949, in the amount of $639.67. The 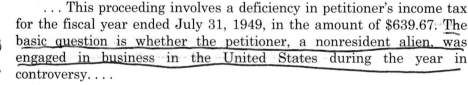basic question is whether the petitioner, a nonresident alien, was engaged in business in the United States during the year in controversy. . . .

FINDINGS OF FACT

The petitioner, Frank Handfield, is a nonresident alien individual residing in Montreal, Quebec, Canada. He was engaged in the manufacture of picture postal cards in Canada during the entire fiscal year ended July 31, 1949. The cards produced by the petitioner sold under the trade name "Folkards" and the business was operated under the style of Folkard Company of America. The business was organized and operated by petitioner as a sole proprietorship.

The petitioner managed the business and carried on his activities from his office in Montreal. He visited the United States for a total of 24 days in four trips in pursuit of his business activities during the fiscal year in issue. Petitioner also employed R. H. Hawken, now deceased, a resident of the United States, for the entire year involved. Hawken's duties were to check the vendors of the American News Company, under the contract below, to insure that the cards were being properly displayed.

Prints of Folkards were made in Canada from dies which, at all times material, were located in Canada. Sales of Folkards in the United States were effected under a contract between petitioner and the American News Company, Inc. The contract was embodied in a letter, dated November 18, 1940, from P. D. O'Connell, vice president of the News Company, to petitioner, the pertinent part of which follows:

This letter will confirm arrangements recently discussed for the exclusive distribution through our Company of Folkards, in any United States city in which it is mutually agreed to put these out. It is understood that each rack will contain 300 Folkards, and will be similar to those now being distributed in Canada. Folkards will be billed to The American News Company, Inc. at $2.40 per rack; trade price, $3.60 per rack; retail, $6.00 per rack or 2 cents per card; fully returnable. It is understood that transportation, both on shipments to branches and return shipments to you, is to be assumed by the manufacturer. It is also understood that you will accept for credit all unsold Folkards, regardless of condition. Payments will be made to you on the basis of actual check-ups of dealers' stock sixty days after distribution, and every thirty days thereafter. It is further understood as the distribution is extended, The American News Company will have exclusive rights to distribute Folkards in the United States. If, however, the sale in any city should be unsatisfactory, we will pick up stock from dealers and return it to you within sixty days after it is mutually agreed to discontinue the distribution. It is also understood that should Folkards be found to be an infringement of patent or copyright, or in any other way contrary to law, The American News Company reserves the right to withdraw them from sale without notice.

Under the above contract, all payments were sent to petitioner in Canada by check of the American News Company to the order of the petitioner. . . .

OPINION

The principal question in this proceeding is whether the petitioner, a nonresident Canadian, was engaged in business in the United States during the year in controversy. The determination of this question depends upon the nature of the arrangement which the petitioner had for selling in this country an item which he manufactured in Canada.

The petitioner manufactures a novelty item called Folkards which is a kind of postal card. He had a contract with the American News Company by which the latter distributed his cards to newsstands in the United States where they were sold to the public. The petitioner contends that the American News Company purchased the cards from him for resale. He further contends that the sale occurred in Canada when the cards were placed in transportation and at that time he surrendered all his right, title, and interest in the cards to the News Company.

The respondent contends that the arrangement between the petitioner and the News Company provided for an agency relationship, and that the News Company was petitioner's exclusive distributor in the United States.

The nature of the contract between petitioner and the News Company is to be determined from the intention of the parties. . . . It will be observed that the agreement between the petitioner and the News Company nowhere says that the News Company buys or will buy the petitioner's cards or that the company is or will be obligated for any definite number of cards or in any definite amount. The contract uses the word "sale" twice. In each instance it is clear that the word refers to transactions with the public, not between the petitioner and the News Company. . . . The contract speaks of its purpose as confirmation of "arrangements recently discussed for the exclusive distribution through our Company" in the United States where it is "mutually agreed to put these [cards] out." The contract specifies the rate at which the News Company will be billed for the cards, the rate at which the cards will be billed to the "trade," and the retail price at which the cards will be sold. But, payments were to be made "on the basis of actual check-ups of dealers' stocks sixty days after distribution, and every thirty days thereafter." The contract stated that all cards were "fully returnable" and that transportation on shipments to and from the United States was to be paid by the petitioner and that he would allow credit on all unsold cards, regardless of condition.

The contract gave exclusive rights to the News Company "to distribute Folkards in the United States" and, as noted above, the News Company could "pick up stock from dealers and return it" after it "mutually agreed to discontinue the distribution" in any city. . . .

From all the provisions of the contract and all the information on the operations of the petitioner in relation to it that are in this record, we think that the arrangement between the petitioner and the News

Company was one in which the News Company was his agent in the United States. We think that the cards were shipped on consignment to the News Company for sale to the public. All the aspects of the agreement point to this interpretation of the contract and none are inconsistent with this interpretation.

The features of the contract which are particularly persuasive in bringing us to the interpretation we have placed on it are: The News company does not obligate itself to buy any definite amount of merchandise from petitioner and it is obligated only to account for the merchandise which has been sold; all merchandise unsold may be returned; the petitioner will pay the transportation on the cards to and from Canada and give full credit for all cards unsold regardless of their condition; the agreement controls the retail price; and it gives the News Company the right to discontinue merchandising the cards when they move slowly or when they infringe copyright or patent provisions. All these, taken together, we think indicate that the arrangement was an agency relationship in the form of a contract of consignment. . . .

Decision will be entered under Rule 50.

NOTES AND QUESTIONS

1. What interpretations of the contract are possible?

2. How would you rewrite the agreement so as to achieve the underlying business aims of the parties, while preventing an agency relationship from arising?

3. As a policy matter, would it make sense to treat Handfield as engaged in a U.S. trade or business?

The following case considers the agency question from the treaty perspective—"Does the nonresident have a permanent establishment based on the activities of its agent?"

4. In 2009, the IRS issued a controversial General Legal Advice Memorandum 2009–010 which examined whether a foreign corporation was engaged in a U.S. trade or business where it relied on an agent in the U.S. to originate loans. In the memorandum, the taxpayer was a foreign corporation (in a non-treaty jurisdiction) which made loans to U.S. persons on the U.S. The foreign corporation did not have a U.S. office nor employees in the U.S. According to the memorandum:

To originate loans to the U.S. Borrowers, Foreign Corporation outsources the origination activities to a United States corporation (Origination Co."). Under a service agreement between Foreign Corporation and Origination Co., the activities performed by Origination Co. include the solicitation of U.S. Borrowers, the negotiation of the terms of the loans, the performance of the credit analyses with respect to U.S. Borrowers, and all other activities relating to loan origination other than the final approval and signing of the loan documents. Origination Co. conducts these activities on a considerable, continuous, and regular basis. Under the terms of the service agreement, Foreign Corporation pays Origination Co. an arm's length fee for its services. Origination Co. performs the origination activities through an office located in the United States, and Origination Co. is subject to U.S. federal income taxation. Although Origination Co. performs all of the origination activities on behalf of Foreign Corporation, Origination Co. is not authorized to conclude contracts on behalf of Foreign Corporation. Foreign Corporation's employees, who work in an office located outside of the United States, give final approval for the loans and physically sign the loan documents on behalf of Foreign Corporation.

The IRS concluded in this memorandum (which may not be used as legal precedent) that although Origination Co. does not have authority to conclude contracts for Foreign Corporation, it performed a significant number of functions related to Foreign Corporation's lending business, and that its activities can be attributed (by viewing Origination Co. as an agent) to the Foreign Corporation regardless of whether Origination Co. is nominally an independent contractor. In determining whether these activities, once attributed to Foreign Corporation were sufficient to rise to the level of trade or business in the U.S., the memorandum relied on several cases including *Lewenhaupt*, *Handfield*, and *Spermacet Whaling* to conclude that "[b]ecause the lending activities of Foreign Corporation, which were carried on by Origination Co., were considerable, continuous, and regular, Foreign Corporation is engaged in a U.S. trade or business."

Why do you think the safeharbors in section 864(b)(2) did not apply to help Foreign Corporation here?

The next question that the memorandum considered was whether the interest income received by Foreign Corporation was effectively connected to Foreign Corporation's trade or business. Remember these are two distinct questions—even if you have a U.S. trade or business, you are only taxed (with respect to that trade or business) on the income that is effectively connected under section 864. After you complete the reading below in Ch. 5.3 regarding effectively connected income, return this scenario and determine whether Foreign Corporation's income was in fact effectively connected (hint: look at Treas. Reg. sec. 1.864–4(c)(5)(ii)).

Tasei Fire and Marine Insurance Co., Ltd. v. Commissioner of Internal Revenue

United States Tax Court.
104 T.C. 535 (1995).

■ TANNENWALD, JUDGE: . . .

The principal issue in these consolidated cases is whether, during the years at issue, petitioners had a U.S. permanent establishment by virtue of the activities of a U.S. agent in accepting reinsurance on behalf of each petitioner. . . .

FINDINGS OF FACT

Some of the facts have been stipulated and are so found. . . .

Each petitioner is a Japanese property and casualty insurance company with its principal place of business in Japan. The stock of each petitioner is publicly traded on a Japanese exchange. There is no stock ownership relationship among petitioners.

The primary business of each petitioner is writing direct insurance in Japan. Each petitioner also assumes reinsurance ceded to it by insurers and reinsurers, including U.S. insurers and reinsurers, through a reinsurance department located in Tokyo. Each petitioner obtains foreign reinsurance through foreign brokers that bring reinsurance proposals to it, and from foreign insurers and reinsurers with which each petitioner has a direct relationship. . . .

Each petitioner has at least one representative office in the United States that provides information on the U.S. market to it and assists its clients in the United States, but which does not have authority to write any form of insurance. . . .

In addition, each petitioner grants authority to two or three different U.S. agents, including Fortress Re, Inc., to underwrite reinsurance on its behalf and to perform certain activities in connection therewith.

Fortress Re, Inc. (hereinafter referred to as new Fortress or Fortress) . . . acted as a reinsurance underwriting manager on behalf of various insurance companies with which it entered into management agreements. . . .

Fortress is a reinsurance underwriting manager, which involves acting as an agent for insurance companies in underwriting and managing reinsurance on behalf of such companies. Fortress is not licensed to conduct insurance or reinsurance business in any jurisdiction. Fortress underwrites reinsurance and places retrocessions only on behalf of the companies with which it enters into management agreements. Fortress enters into reinsurance and retrocession contracts on behalf of the companies it represents only through brokers; Fortress itself does not act as a broker.

Fortress enters into a separate management agreement with each insurance company it represents. The agreements with petitioners are identical except for the net acceptance limit. Since its inception, Fortress has been involved in as many as 10 management agreements in a management year. . . . Each agreement authorizes Fortress, among other things, to act as agent of each company to underwrite and retrocede reinsurance on behalf of each company. Under the agreement, the liability of the member with respect to each reinsurance contract, underwritten by Fortress on the member's behalf, is several and not joint with any other member.

Under the agreement, it is contemplated that Fortress may enter into similar, or substantially similar, management agreements with other insurance or reinsurance companies or other insurers. Fortress does not need permission of, or even to consult, the companies with which it has agreements, before entering into a new agreement. Although in practice, when a member terminated a management agreement, Fortress offered to increase the participation of the companies it already represented, it was not obligated to do so. . . .

Each reinsurance contract underwritten by Fortress, or old Fortress, on behalf of the companies it represented, is assigned to a management year. All premiums and losses, including claims settled in later years, associated with a particular reinsurance contract are allocated to the management year to which the reinsurance contract was assigned. Fortress is responsible for the handling and disposition of all claims against the companies it represents. In many cases, claims relating to the reinsurance underwritten by Fortress on behalf of companies it represents are not fully settled for many years. Fortress has total control over the handling and disposition of claims on behalf of petitioners.

Pursuant to each agreement, Fortress regularly exercises the authority to conclude original reinsurance contracts and to cede reinsurance on behalf of each petitioner. Each agreement provides Fortress with underwriting authority on a continuous basis until the agreement is terminated. The agreements can be terminated by either party, but only with 6 months' notice, although in practice the notice period has been waived. After termination of an agreement, Fortress continues to have obligations with respect to reinsurance previously underwritten. During the years in issue, Fortress had continuing duties to 13 insurance companies, excluding petitioners, for contracts underwritten in prior management years.

The only material limitation on Fortress' authority under the agreement is a "net acceptance limit," which is the maximum amount of net liability in respect of any one original reinsurance contract that Fortress can accept on behalf of a member. There is no gross acceptance limit in the agreements, so that Fortress can underwrite reinsurance contracts on behalf of a member that are greater than the net acceptance limit, provided that Fortress arranges for retrocessions of the excess over the net acceptance limit. In practice, Fortress sets its own gross acceptance limit, as to which it voluntarily advises petitioners. . . .

Mr. Kornfeld is the chief underwriter and, as such, decides what business Fortress will underwrite and retrocede on behalf of the members. The retrocession program for a management year was presented to each petitioner in advance, during an annual trip by Mr. Kornfeld to each petitioner's offices. However, Fortress does not need approval, and did not seek or receive input, from petitioners. . . .

Fortress was compensated for its services pursuant to compensation schedules set forth in each agreement. During 1986 to 1988, Fortress' income was derived from management fees, contingent commissions, and override commissions payable under management agreements entered into for management years I through XVI. Also, Fortress earned investment income on its own funds, which was not related to the management agreements. Fortress' compensation structure is the same as other reinsurance underwriting managers, although its management fees are slightly lower and its profit commissions slightly higher than the norm. . . .

OPINION

Under the Convention Between the United States of America and Japan for the Avoidance of Double Taxation and the Prevention of Fiscal Evasion with Respect to Taxes on Income, Mar. 8, 1971, 23 U.S.T. (Part 1) 969 (hereinafter referred to as the U.S.-Japan convention or convention), the commercial profits of a Japanese resident are exempt from U.S. Federal income tax, unless such profits are attributable to a U.S. permanent establishment. Convention, Art. 8(1). The relevant provisions of the convention whereby a Japanese resident will be deemed to have a U.S. permanent establishment due to the activities of an agent are as follows:

(4) A person acting in a Contracting State on behalf of a resident of the other Contracting State, other than an agent of an independent status to whom paragraph (5) of this article applies, shall be deemed to be a permanent establishment in the first-mentioned Contracting State if such person has, and habitually exercises in the first-mentioned Contracting State, an authority to conclude contracts in the name of that resident, unless the exercise of such authority is limited to the purchase of goods or merchandise for that resident.

(5) A resident of a Contracting State shall not be deemed to have a permanent establishment in the other Contracting State merely because such resident engages in industrial or commercial activity in that other Contracting State through a broker, general commission agent, or any other agent of an independent status, where such broker or agent is acting in the ordinary course of his business.

[Convention, Art. 9.]

Initially, it is undisputed that Fortress had the authority, which it exercised, to conclude contracts on behalf of petitioners, so that unless Fortress is "a broker, general commission agent, or any other agent of an independent status" within the meaning of Article 9(5), petitioners will be deemed to have U.S. permanent establishments. The parties are in agreement that Fortress was not a "broker" or "general commission agent", and respondent concedes that Fortress was acting in the ordinary course of its business when acting on behalf of petitioners. Thus, the issue before us is whether, during the years at issue, Fortress was an "agent of an independent status" in respect of each petitioner. In this connection, we note that neither petitioners nor respondent has argued that any petitioner should be treated differently from any other petitioner in resolving this issue.

Background

The U.S.-Japan convention itself does not define an "agent of an independent status". . . .

Our examination shows that the relevant provisions of the convention are not only based upon, but are duplicative of, Article 5, comments 4 and 5, of the 1963 O.E.C.D. Draft [model] Convention (hereinafter referred to as the 1963 model) . . . While the 1963 model itself provides no more definition than the convention, the model is explained in part by a commentary, which states in pertinent part:

15. Persons who may be deemed to be permanent establishments must be strictly limited to those who are dependent, both from the legal and economic points of view, upon the enterprise for which they carry on business dealings (Report of the Fiscal Committee of the League of Nations, 1928, page 12). Where an enterprise has business dealings with an independent agent, this cannot be held to mean that the enterprise itself carries on a business in the other State. In such a case, there are two separate enterprises.

19. Under paragraph 4 of the Article, only one category of dependent agents, who meet specific conditions, is deemed to be permanent establishments. All independent agents and the remaining dependent ones are not deemed to be permanent establishment. Mention should be made of the fact that the Mexico and London Drafts * * * and a number of Conventions, do not enumerate exhaustively such dependent agents as are deemed to be permanent establishments, but merely give examples. In the interest of preventing differences of interpretation and of furthering international economic relations, it appeared advisable to define, as exhaustively as possible, the cases where agents are deemed to be "permanent establishments."

* * *

20. * * * In the Mexico and London Drafts and in the Conventions, brokers and commission agents are stated to be agents of an independent status. Similarly, business dealings carried on with the co-operation of any other independent person carrying on a trade or business (e.g. a forwarding agent) do not constitute a permanent establishment. Such independent agents must, however, be acting in the ordinary course of their business. * * *

* * *

The special problems which can arise in the case of insurance companies dealing by means of intermediaries or variously qualified representatives shall be further studied.

[Commentary to Art. 5 of the 1963 model.] . . .

Based on the above, petitioners argue that the test of independent status is one of both legal and economic dependence and that, if we find that Fortress was either legally or economically independent of petitioners, it will necessarily follow that Fortress was not a permanent establishment . . . [T]he test for legal and economic independence [is] set forth in comment 37 to Article 5 of the 1977 model. That comment provides:

37. Whether a person is independent of the enterprise represented depends on the extent of the obligations which this person has vis-a-vis the enterprise. Where the person's commercial activities for the enterprise are subject to detailed instructions or to comprehensive control by it, such person cannot be regarded as independent of the enterprise. Another important criterion will be whether the entrepreneurial risk has to be borne by the person or by the enterprise the person represents. * * * [Comment 37 to Art. 5 of the 1977 model.]

It is obvious that the tests of "comprehensive control" and "entrepreneurial risk", as the determinants of legal and economic independence, involve an intensely factual inquiry, which does not lend itself to the articulation of a "definitive statement that would produce a talisman for the solution of concrete cases." . . .

Legal Independence

The relationship between Fortress and petitioners is defined by the management agreement that Fortress entered into separately with each petitioner. Petitioners have no interest in Fortress, and no representative of any of petitioners is a director, officer, or employee of Fortress. The agreements grant complete discretion to Fortress to conduct the reinsurance business on behalf of petitioners.

Respondent agrees that Fortress had independence with respect to day-to-day operations, but then argues that its actions were restricted by gross acceptance limits and limits on net premium income. However, even if there were such restrictions, they would not necessarily constitute control. The gross acceptance limit and net premium income both relate to the total exposure of petitioners, and even an independent agent only has authority to perform specific duties for the principal. It is freedom in the manner by which the agent performs such duties that distinguishes him as independent.

In any event, the record is clear that the gross acceptance limits were set by Fortress as part of its strategy to limit risk through diversification. Fortress advised petitioners of the gross acceptance limits for informational purposes and changed the limits without the advice or consent of petitioners. Fortress refused to put gross acceptance limits in the management agreements in order to retain flexibility. Respondent implies that the limit forced Fortress to enter into many small contracts instead of being able to enter into a few large contracts, but the pattern is consistent with Fortress' strategy of limiting risk through diversification, a strategy which Fortress was clearly in a position to implement through a plethora of available contracts. . . .

Respondent further argues there were restrictions on Fortress' corporate affairs not reflected in the agreements that gave petitioners comprehensive control of Fortress. As evidence, respondent relies on Fortress' consultations with petitioners in regard to the request of Dai Tokyo to become a client of Fortress, and to Fortress' intent to include Carolina Re in the reinsurance program. Respondent also points out that Fortress reported to petitioners more regularly than required by the agreements. However, these are actions of a company seeking to maintain good relations with longstanding clients, rather than one seeking approval. With respect to the Dai Tokyo and Carolina Re situations, Fortress had already made its decision before consulting with petitioners . . . Lewenhaupt v. Commissioner . . ., cited by respondent, not only involved a different test, i.e., whether the taxpayer was engaged in business in the United States through an agent, but involved continuous activity in managing U.S. real estate owned by the taxpayer which went beyond mere ownership or receipt of income. It is clearly distinguishable.

Respondent further argues that petitioners exercised "comprehensive control" over Fortress by acting as a "pool". However, there is no evidence that petitioners acted in concert to control Fortress. In only rare and isolated instances did petitioners communicate with one another regarding Fortress. Further, there are references to a "pool" throughout the history of Fortress, which period covers relationships with 17 separate U.S. and Japanese insurance companies. The inferences respondent would have us draw from the fact that petitioners are all from Japan and that petitioners are among the participants in regular industry conferences in Japan are simply insufficient to establish the existence of control by a "pool".

In a similar vein, we reject respondent's attempt to construct control from the fact that, during the years at issue, Fortress' activities were confined to the reinsurance it underwrote on behalf of petitioners. Pointing to Article 2(2) of the U.S.-Japan convention, respondent attempts to support her position by drawing upon the phrase "other agent of independent status" in section 864(c)(5)(A) and the regulation thereunder, section 1.864–7(d)(3) . . . Obviously, the statute simply repeats the phrase used in the convention. The regulations suggest two elements to be considered. The first is ownership or control, section 1.864–7(d)(3)(ii), Income Tax Regs., which the regulation specifically states is not determinative. The second, section 1.864–7(d)(3)(iii), Income Tax Regs., is whether the agent acts "exclusively, or almost exclusively, for one principal", in which event "the facts and circumstances of a particular case shall be taken into account in determining whether the agent, while acting in that capacity, may be classified as an independent agent." Assuming without deciding that these regulations, implementing a particular statute, should be accorded interpretative effect in respect of a treaty provision, it has no application herein where we have concluded that Fortress acted separately in respect of each of four petitioners and where respondent concedes that Fortress was acting in the ordinary course of its business, a position that seems inconsistent with both the "pool" and "exclusively" concepts. Moreover, we note that the number of principals for whom Fortress acted varied over the years and that, even during the years before us, Fortress carried on a substantial amount of activity in handling claims, etc., for several other insurance companies.

Finally, we note that all four petitioners, while not their primary business, did have reinsurance departments. Thus, petitioners had the ability to give detailed instructions to Fortress, yet they did not.

As an agent, Fortress had complete discretion over the details of its work. As an entity, Fortress was subject to no external control. In sum, Fortress was legally independent of petitioners.

Economic Independence

Fortress is owned solely by Mr. Sabbah and his family and Mr. Kornfeld. There was no guarantee of revenue to Fortress, nor was Fortress protected from loss in the event it had been unable to generate sufficient revenue. Fortress has management agreements with four separate clients, whereby any one of them can leave on 6 months' notice. If one of petitioners did end its relationship, Fortress would bear the burden of finding a replacement to subscribe to that client's share of reinsurance contracts.

Respondent argues that Fortress bore no entrepreneurial risk because its operating expenses were covered by a management fee, and because it was guaranteed business due to the creditworthiness of the reinsurers on whose behalf it acted, petitioners.

While the management agreements provided that Fortress earned a percentage of the gross premiums written which effectively covered Fortress' operating expenses, this did not mean that Fortress bore no risk. Fortress had to acquire sufficient business to produce the gross premiums. Further, it appears that this provision of the agreements is normal for an underwriting manager. That respondent's argument on this point misses the mark is illustrated, for example, by a large mutual fund that charges an annual management fee to cover operating expenses. Clearly, the mutual fund company would not be considered dependent on its thousands of investors. Under these circumstances, even with as few as four investors, Fortress cannot be considered dependent on petitioners to pay its operating expenses.

Nor do we agree with respondent's argument that Fortress is able to secure profitable reinsurance contracts only because its clients are petitioners. Although Fortress needs clients with a certain minimum capital to conduct its business, any of hundreds of other insurance companies worldwide would be adequate substitutes. Also, it cannot be denied that Fortress had access to the reinsurance contracts it considered good, in part because of Fortress' relationships and reputation in the industry. In fact, it appears that Fortress' access to profitable reinsurance contracts, as well as its experience and ability to choose profitable reinsurance contracts, attracted petitioners to Fortress, and would attract other insurance companies if Fortress needed another client to take a share of the contracts.

Finally, we think that the amount of Fortress' profits is significant . . . For the 3 years in issue, Fortress was paid over $27 million. This is not the kind of sum paid to a subservient company. In addition, petitioners were in effect forced to share reinsurance profits with Carolina Re, an entity owned by the same people who owned Fortress, by permitting Fortress to cede reinsurance to Carolina Re even though Carolina Re was not as well known or financially secure as other potential quota share reinsurers.

Conclusion

In sum, during the years at issue, Fortress was both legally and economically independent of petitioners, thus satisfying the definition of an agent of an independent status under Article 9 of the U.S.-Japan convention. . . .

We note that, in the commentary to the OECD's 1977 model, it is stated that an insurance company could do "large-scale business in a State without being taxed in that State on their profits arising from such business." Comment 38 to Art. 5 of 1977 model; see also comment 21 to Art. 5 of 1963 model. The commentary goes on to suggest that contracting states may want to contemplate that an insurance company will be "deemed to have a permanent establishment in the other State if they collect premiums in that other State through an agent established there", other than a dependent agent. Comment 38 to Art. 5 of 1977 model. However, the commentary notes that such a provision is not in the model and its inclusion should depend upon the factual and legal situation involved. Comment 38 to Art. 5 of 1977 model. . . .

The Convention between the United States of America and the Kingdom of Belgium . . . does include such an insurance provision. It provides that the independent agent provision "shall not apply with respect to a broker or agent acting on behalf of an insurance company if such broker or agent has, and habitually exercises, an authority to conclude contracts in the name of that company." U.S.-Belgium convention, Art. 5(6). Finally, we note that it was decided not to include reinsurance within the coverage of this provision . . . From the foregoing it appears that the resolution of the issue of the existence of an agent of independent status in the insurance arena turns, at least in part, upon the presence of a specific treaty provision. . . .

Given the absence of any provision dealing with insurance or reinsurance in the U.S.-Japan convention, our holding herein that Fortress is not a permanent establishment of petitioners is consistent with the approach suggested by the OECD model and the application thereof in the U.S.-Belgium convention.

NOTES AND QUESTIONS

1. Consider the relationship between the treaty standard for permanent establishment and the trade or business standard for non-treaty purposes. How would *Handfield* have been decided under the U.S.-Japan convention? See section 864(c)(5)(A).

2. Note that Fortress derived its entire income from the four petitioners. Given this fact, do you agree that the size of its income is relevant? How about the Court's mutual fund analogy?

3. Did Fortress bear any significant risk?

4. Given this decision, do insurance companies deriving income from insuring U.S. risks need to have any U.S. taxable income? Note that there is no discussion of where the insured property is located. In United States v. Northumberland Insurance Co., 521 F.Supp. 70 (D.N.J.1981), the court held that a foreign reinsurer was subject to an excise tax imposed on foreign insurance companies on premiums paid to another foreign insurance company that assumed certain casualty insurance written by the taxpayer, even though the taxpayer was not itself an "insured" under the statute (a term reserved to domestic entities), because the underlying risks were situated in the United States. How would *Taisei* come out under this type of analysis?

e. THE PHYSICAL PRESENCE REQUIREMENT

One possible hook upon which to place the trade or business definition is the presence of physical activity in the United States. However, as the following case suggests, such a bright line approach may provide an overly simplistic vision of how business may successfully be conducted in the United States. As you are reading *Piedras Negras* ask yourself about "modern" high tech businesses, including those conducted over the internet. How should the trade or business question be applied in those cases?

Commissioner v. Piedras Negras Broadcasting Co.

United States Court of Appeals, Fifth Circuit.
127 F.2d 260 (1942).

■ Opinion: Before HUTCHESON, HOLMES, and MCCORD, CIRCUIT JUDGES.

■ HOLMES, CIRCUIT JUDGE.

The respondent is a corporation organized under the laws of the State of Coahuila, Republic of Mexico, with its principal office and place of business at Piedras Negras, Mexico. Its business is the operation of a radio broadcasting station located at Piedras Negras, just across the Rio Grande from Eagle Pass, Texas. The decisive question presented by this

Issue?

petition for review is whether the respondent, from the operation of its business in 1936 and 1937, derived any income from sources within the United States subject to taxation by the United States.

The taxpayer conducted its affairs in the familiar manner. Its income was derived from the dissemination of advertising over the radio and from the rental of its facilities to customers, referred to as the sale of "radio time." All of its income-producing contracts were executed in Mexico, and all services required of the taxpayer under the contracts were rendered in Mexico. The company maintained a mailing address at Eagle Pass, Texas, and used a hotel room there in which it counted and allocated the funds received in the mails each day.

Contracts with advertisers in the United States were handled through an advertising agent, an independent contractor. The majority of the taxpayer's responses from listeners came from the United States, and ninety-five per cent of its income was from advertisers within the United States. Bank accounts were maintained in Texas and in Mexico. The books and records of the corporation were in Mexico, its only studio was there, and all of the broadcasts by the station originated in Piedras Negras. The broadcasts were equal in volume in all directions, and were heard by listeners in this country and elsewhere.

Holding

Section [882] . . . provides that the gross income of a foreign corporation includes only the gross income from sources within the United States. If this taxpayer, a foreign corporation, had no income from sources within the United States, no income tax was levied upon it. The Board of Tax Appeals concluded that none of the respondent's income was derived from sources within the United States, and we agree with that decision.

FDAP ?
B. Income

In Section [861] . . . Congress classified income, as to the source thereof, under six heads. Since the taxpayer's income was derived exclusively from the operation of its broadcasting facilities located in Mexico, or from the rental of those facilities in Mexico, its income therefrom was either compensation for personal labor or services, or rentals or royalties from property, or both, under the statutory classification. Section [861](a) (3) provides that compensation for personal services performed in the United States shall be treated as income from sources within the United States. By Section [861](c)(3), income from such services performed without the United States is not from sources within the United States. Likewise, rentals from property located without the United States, including rentals or royalties for the use of or for the privilege of using without the United States franchises and other like properties, are considered items of income from sources without the United States. Section [861](a)(4). . . .

We think the language of the statutes clearly demonstrates the intendment of Congress that the source of income is the situs of the income-producing service. The repeated use of the words within and without the United States denotes a concept of some physical presence, some tangible and visible activity. If income is produced by the transmission of electromagnetic waves that cover a radius of several thousand miles, free of control or regulation by the sender from the moment of generation, the source of that income is the act of transmission. All of respondent's broadcasting facilities were situated without the United States, and all of the services it rendered in connection with its business were performed in Mexico. None of its income was derived from sources within the United States.

The order of the Board of Tax Appeals is affirmed.

■ DISSENT: McCORD, CIRCUIT JUDGE, (dissenting).

I am unable to agree with the majority opinion.

Prior to March, 1935, many programs broadcast over the Mexican station originated in a remote control studio located in Eagle Pass, Texas. After the Communications Commission denied application for continuance of the studio, programs no longer originated in the United States, but the broadcasting company continued its business operations in much the same way that it always had. While the mere broadcasting of electromagnetic waves into this country may not constitute the doing of business which produces income derived from sources within the United States, I do not think the case is as simple as that. The actual broadcasting of message was not the only act, and the facts should be viewed as a whole, not singly, to see what was actually being done.

Various advertising contracts provided that the service to be rendered was to be from the station at Piedras Negras, but these contract provisions do not establish that the company was not taxable in this country. The programs of the Piedras Negras Broadcasting Company were primarily designed for listeners in the United States. Ninety per cent of its listener response came from this country, and ninety-five per cent of its income came from American advertisers. Through agents the broadcasting company solicited advertising contracts in this country, and it is shown that contracts were entered into by the company in the name of the Radio Service Co., an assumed name which for reasons beneficial to the company had been registered in Texas. The contracts also contained a provision that venue of any suit on such contracts would be Maverick County, Texas. Moreover, the company used Eagle Pass, Texas, as its mailing address, and its constant use of the United States mails was most beneficial to the company if not absolutely essential to the success of its operation. Money was deposited in American banks, obviously for convenience and to avoid payment of foreign exchange. Agents of the broadcasting company made daily trips to Eagle Pass where they met in hotel room with advertising representatives and opened the mail and divided the enclosed money according to their percentage contracts with advertisers, and it is shown that the company received much of its income in this manner. It was, therefore, receiving income by broadcasting operations coupled with personal contact in this country.

I am of opinion that all the facts taken together establish that Piedras Negras Broadcasting Company was doing business in the United States, was deriving income from sources within this country, and was taxable. I think the decision of the Board should be reversed. I respectfully dissent.

NOTES AND QUESTIONS

1. On what entity did the majority focus? Did it care whether the payments were for services or property?

2. On whom did the dissent focus? What jurisdiction to tax—source or doing business—primarily concerned the dissent?

3. Why did the majority state that "[t]he taxpayer conducted its affairs in the familiar manner"? What are the implications, if any?

4. Note that this is a source case, not a trade or business case. Nevertheless, the case is generally read to impose a physical presence requirement on the concept of U.S. trade or business. With respect to its role as a case on the question of source, how would *Piedras Negras* come out today? Consider section 863(e).

The physical presence question has emerged in another similar but entirely domestic context—the ability of one state to tax residents of another state. The Supreme Court's position on the issue, as revised in 2018, follows. Do you think the Court's reasoning should apply to cases like *Piedras Negras*?

South Dakota v. Wayfair, Inc., et al.

Certiorari to the Supreme Court of South Dakota.
___ U.S. ___, 138 S.Ct. 2080, 201 L.Ed.2d 40 (2018).

South Dakota, like many States, taxes the retail sales of goods and services in the State. Sellers are required to collect and remit the tax to the State, but if they do not then in-state consumers are responsible for paying a use tax at the same rate. Under National Bellas Hess, Inc. v. Department of Revenue of Ill., 386 U. S. 753, and Quill Corp. v. North Dakota, 504 U. S. 298, South Dakota may not require a business that has no physical presence in the State to collect its sales tax. Consumer compliance rates are notoriously low, however, and it is estimated that Bellas Hess and Quill cause South Dakota to lose between $48 and $58 million annually. Concerned about the erosion of its sales tax base and corresponding loss of critical funding for state and local services, the South Dakota Legislature enacted a law requiring out-of-state sellers to collect and remit sales tax "as if the seller had a physical presence in the State." The Act covers only sellers that, on an annual basis, deliver more than $100,000 of goods or services into the State or engage in 200 or more separate transactions for the delivery of goods or services into the State. Respondents, top online retailers with no employees or real estate in South Dakota, each meet the Act's minimum sales or transactions requirement, but do not collect the State's sales tax. South Dakota filed suit in state court, seeking a declaration that the Act's requirements are valid and applicable to respondents and an injunction requiring respondents to register for licenses to collect and remit the sales tax. Respondents sought summary judgment, arguing that the Act is unconstitutional. The trial court granted their motion. The State Supreme Court affirmed on the ground that Quill is controlling precedent.

Held: Because the physical presence rule of Quill is unsound and incorrect, Quill Corp. v. North Dakota, 504 U. S. 298, and National Bellas Hess, Inc. v. Department of Revenue of Ill., 386 U. S. 753, are overruled. *[handwritten: Holding]*

(a) An understanding of this Court's Commerce Clause principles and their application to state taxes is instructive here. (1) Two primary principles mark the boundaries of a State's authority to regulate interstate commerce: State regulations may no discriminate against interstate commerce; and States may not impose undue burdens on interstate commerce. These principles guide the courts in adjudicating challenges to state laws under the Commerce Clause. (2) They also animate Commerce Clause precedents addressing the validity of state taxes, which will be sustained so long as they (1) apply to an activity with a substantial nexus with the taxing State, (2) are fairly apportioned, (3) do not discriminate against interstate commerce, and (4) are fairly related to the services the State provides. See Complete Auto Transit, Inc. v. Brady, 430 U. S. 274, 279. Before Complete Auto, the Court held in Bellas Hess that a "seller whose only connection with customers in the State is by common carrier or . . . mail" lacked the requisite minimum contacts with the State required by the Due Process Clause and the Commerce Clause, and that unless the retailer maintained a physical presence in the State, the State lacked the power to require that retailer to collect a local tax. 386 U. S., at 758. In Quill, the Court overruled the due process holding, but not the Commerce Clause holding, grounding the physical presence rule in Complete Auto's requirement that a tax have a "substantial nexus" with the activity being taxed. *[handwritten: IC]*

(b) The physical presence rule has long been criticized as giving out-of-state sellers an advantage. Each year, it becomes further removed from economic reality and results in significant revenue losses to the States. These critiques underscore that the rule, both as first formulated and as applied today, is an incorrect interpretation of the Commerce Clause.

(1) Quill is flawed on its own terms. First, the physical presence rule is not a necessary interpretation of Complete Auto's nexus requirement. That requirement is "closely related," Bellas Hess, 386 U. S. at 756, to the due process requirement that there be "some definite link, some minimum connection, between a state and the person, property or transaction it seeks to tax." Miller Brothers Co. v. Maryland, 347 U. S. 340, 344–345. And, as Quill itself recognized, a business need

not have a physical presence in a State to satisfy the demands of due process. When considering whether a State may levy a tax, Due Process and Commerce Clause standards, though not identical or coterminous, have significant parallels. The reasons given in Quill for rejecting the physical presence rule for due process purposes apply as well to the question whether physical presence is a requisite for an out-of-state seller's liability to remit sales taxes. Other aspects of the Court's doctrine can better and more accurately address potential burdens on interstate commerce, whether or not Quill's physical presence rule is satisfied.

Second, Quill creates rather than resolves market distortions. In effect, it is a judicially created tax shelter for businesses that limit their physical presence in a State but sell their goods and services to the State's consumers, something that has become easier and more prevalent as technology has advanced. The rule also produces an incentive to avoid physical presence in multiple States, affecting development that might be efficient or desirable.

Third, Quill imposes the sort of arbitrary, formalistic distinction that the Court's modern Commerce Clause precedents disavow in favor of "a sensitive, case-by-case analysis of purposes and effects, West Lynn Creamery, Inc. v. Healy, 512 U. S. 186, 201. It treats economically identical actors differently for arbitrary reasons. For example, a business that maintains a few items of inventory in a small warehouse in a State is required to collect and remit a tax on all of its sales in the State, while a seller with a pervasive Internet presence cannot be subject to the same tax for the sales of the same items.

(2) When the day-to-day functions of marketing and distribution in the modern economy are considered, it becomes evident that Quill's physical presence rule is artificial, not just "at its edges," 504 U. S. at 315, but in its entirety. Modern e-commerce does not align analytically with a test that relies on the sort of physical presence defined in Quill. And the Court should not maintain a rule that ignores substantial virtual connections to the State.

(3) The physical presence rule of Bellas Hess and Quill is also an extraordinary imposition by the Judiciary on States' authority to collect taxes and perform critical public functions. Forty-one States, two Territories, and the District of Columbia have asked the Court to reject Quill's test. Helping respondents' customers evade a lawful tax unfairly shifts an increased share of the taxes to those consumers who buy from competitors with a physical presence in the State. It is essential to public confidence in the tax system that the Court avoid creating inequitable exceptions. And it is also essential to the confidence placed in the Court's Commerce Clause decisions. By giving some online retailers an arbitrary advantage over their competitors who collect state sales taxes, Quill's physical presence rule has limited States' ability to seek long-term prosperity and has prevented market participants from competing on an even playing field.

(c)   Stare decisis can no longer support the Court's prohibition of a valid exercise of the States' sovereign power. If it becomes apparent that the Court's Commerce Clause decisions prohibit the States from exercising their lawful sovereign powers, the Court should be vigilant in correcting the error. It is inconsistent with this Court's proper role to ask Congress to address a false constitutional premise of this Court's own creation. The Internet revolution has made Quill's original error all the more egregious and harmful. The Quill Court did not have before it the present realities of the interstate marketplace, where the Internet's prevalence and power have changed the dynamics of the national economy. The expansion of e-commerce has also increased the revenue shortfall faced by States seeking to collect their sales and use taxes, leading the South Dakota Legislature to declare an emergency. The argument, moreover, that the physical presence rule is clear and easy to apply is unsound, as attempts to apply the physical presence rule to online retail sales have proved unworkable.

Because the physical presence rule as defined by Quill is no longer a clear or easily applicable standard, arguments for reliance based on its clarity are misplaced. Stare decisis may accommodate "legitimate reliance interest[s]," United States v. Ross, 456 U. S. 798, 824, but a business "is in no position to found a constitutional right . . . on the practical opportunities for tax avoidance," Nelson v. Sears, Roebuck & Co., 312 U. S. 359, 366. Startups and small businesses may benefit from the physical presence rule, but here South Dakota affords small merchants a reasonable degree of protection. Finally, other aspects of the Court's Commerce Clause doctrine can protect against any undue burden on interstate commerce, taking into consideration the small businesses, startups, or others who engage in commerce across state lines. The potential for such issues to arise in some later case cannot justify retaining an artificial, anachronistic rule that deprives States of vast revenues from major businesses.

(d)   In the absence of Quill and Bellas Hess, the first prong of the Complete Auto test simply asks whether the tax applies to an activity with a substantial nexus with the taxing State. 430 U. S., at 279.

Here, the nexus is clearly sufficient. The Act applies only to sellers who engage in a significant quantity of business in the State, and respondents are large, national companies that undoubtedly maintain an extensive virtual presence. Any remaining claims regarding the Commerce Clause's application in the absence of Quill and Bellas Hess may be addressed in the first instance on remand.

5.3   WHAT IS EFFECTIVELY CONNECTED?

Having a U.S. trade or business is not sufficient to subject a nonresident to net basis taxation. Each item of income must meet the effectively connected income (ECI) test in order to be taxed on a net basis.

Read section 864(c). Note the two-part test used in section 864(c)(2): the asset test and the business activities test. These tests are further elaborated in Regs. sec. 1.864–4(c). Essentially, for "FDAP" type items (e.g., interest, dividends, rents, royalties, etc.) and capital gains, the income is ECI if it meets either the asset test or the activities test. Under the asset test, the income is ECI if "derived from assets used in or held for use in" the taxpayer's U.S. trade or business. Section 864(c)(2)(A). For example, a nonresident owns and operates a factory in the United States. As part of the U.S. trade or business, the nonresident has working capital deposited in a U.S. bank account generating interest income. This U.S. source interest income satisfies the asset test and would be ECI.

Under the activities test, income is ECI if the "activities of [the] U.S. business were a material factor" in producing the income. Section 864(c)(2)(B). For example, a nonresident develops and licenses software from its office in California. Royalties from these licensing activities are ECI under the activities test.

What about U.S. source income that is not "FDAP type" nor is capital gains? Such income is treated as ECI regardless of the reality of its connection to the U.S. trade or business. Section 864(c)(3). Known as the "residual force of attraction" rule, this is the only remnant of the old force of attraction regime. Since it excludes "fixed, determinable, annual or periodical" income and capital gains, can you envisage in what circumstances it would apply?

Can foreign source income be ECI? As a general matter, only U.S. source income can be ECI (see section 864(c)(4)(A)). However, in limited circumstances, foreign source income can be ECI, thus subject to U.S. net basis taxation. See section 864(c)(4)(B). As a preliminary matter, the nonresident must have a U.S. office and the foreign source income must be attributable to it. Section 864(c)(4)(B).

How would you structure the operations of a foreign entity that has a U.S. office to avoid having any effectively connected income under these tests?

Can a taxpayer have ECI for a year in which it is not engaged in a U.S. trade or business? Consider the following case:

Taxpayer, a nonresident corporation, is engaged in the business of manufacturing machine tools in Country X. Taxpayer established a branch office in the United States during 2010 which solicited orders from customers in the United States for tools manufactured by the taxpayer. Taxpayer sold tools on an installment basis in 2010, and in December 2010 closed the U.S. branch and ceased doing business in the United States. However, taxpayer continued to receive payments on the installment sales into 2011. How are these 2011 year payments received by the taxpayer treated for tax purposes?

First answer this question in the absence of any special rule. Then read section 864(c)(6) and answer the question.

5.4   REVIEW OF BASIC REGIME FOR NONRESIDENTS

The following flow chart maps the steps for determining how a nonresident will be taxed by the United States.

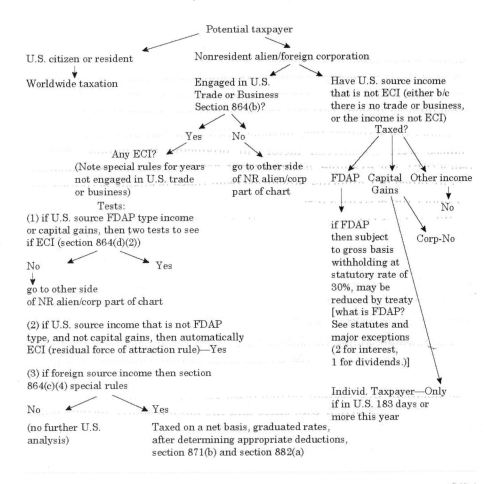

5.5   THE BRANCH PROFITS TAX

One way for a foreign taxpayer to avoid having a U.S. trade or business is to conduct its U.S. trade or business through a separately incorporated U.S. subsidiary. Under generally accepted principles (see, e.g., Reg. 1.864–7(f)) a trade or business carried on by one corporation is not attributed to another related corporation unless an agency relationship can be established under the principles set out in 5.3 above. However, before 1986 the establishment of such a subsidiary carried with it a definite tax disadvantage: While both a branch and a subsidiary were taxed on a net basis on their income from U.S. business activities, distributions from the subsidiary to its foreign parent were subject to a 30% withholding tax on dividends, while distributions from the branch to its head office were not taxable because they were made within the same legal entity. (As discussed in Ch. 2 above, the U.S. did attempt to impose tax on distributions from the foreign taxpayer with the U.S. branch to its foreign shareholders, but this "second-order dividend" tax proved impossible to collect in practice, since all the parties involved were foreign).

To remedy this situation, Congress in 1986 added section 884 to the Code. Read the section, paying particular attention to the following terms:

(a)   The "dividend equivalent amount";

(b)   "U.S. net equity";

(c)   "accumulated effectively connected earnings & profits".

Under the branch profits tax, the nonresident will be taxed currently on the "dividend equivalent amount" (DEA). The core idea behind the branch profits tax is that the United States is trying to determine what should be viewed as the branch's equivalent of the dividend paid by a U.S. subsidiary to its foreign parent and then taxing that amount like a dividend.

The challenge lies in determining what should constitute the "dividend" in the case of a branch. Why is it hard to decide what should be this equivalent? Why is it easier in the case of a subsidiary? The statute determines the branch's "dividend" by use of a formula that calculates the DEA. The starting point is the branch's U.S. earnings and profits (E & P). IF that entire amount is reinvested in the U.S. business, then no "dividend" is found (i.e. no funds are deemed repatriated to the home jurisdiction as a de facto dividend). If none of the branch's E & P is reinvested—then all of it is treated as a "dividend" repatriated home. (And to the extent a portion of the branch's E & P is reinvested, it reduces the amount treated as the branch's "dividend.")

formula

The branch profits tax can be expressed as follows:

Dividend Equivalent Amount = Effectively Connected E & P (Sec. 884(d))

PLUS: Any net decrease in investment in the United States (Sec. 884(b)(2))

OR, MINUS: Any net increase in investment in the United States (Sec. 884(b)(1))

Now solve the following problems:

1.   FC1, a foreign corporation using the calendar year, has $1000 U.S. net equity as of the close of year 1 and has $100 of effectively connected earnings & profits for year 2. During year 2, FC1 acquires $100 in additional U.S. assets. What is FC1's dividend equivalent amount?

2.   Assume the same facts as in question 1, except that FC1 only acquires $40 of U.S. assets by the end of year 2. What is FC1's dividend equivalent amount?

3.   Assume the same facts as in question 1 for year 2. In year 3, FC1 has no effectively connected earnings and profits, but its U.S. net equity decreases by $40. What is FC1's dividend equivalent amount for year 3?

4.   FC2 is a foreign corporation using the calendar year. As of the beginning of the current year, FC2 had aggregate effectively connected earnings and profits for years after 1986 of $100, and had prior dividend equivalent amounts of $60 for those years. As of the end of the prior year, FC2 had U.S. net equity of $1,040. In the current year, FC2 has $125 of effectively connected earnings and profits, and its U.S. net equity decreases by $50. What is FC2's dividend equivalent amount for the current year?

5.   The above examples refer to "U.S. assets"—but this is a precise term in the context of section 884. Look at question 1 again, and consider two different versions: in version (a) FC1 acquires $100 of U.S. bonds; in version (b) FCI acquires $100 of additional equipment used in the FC1's U.S. trade or business. In answering the question this time, look at section 884(c)(2) and Treas. Reg. sec. 1.884–1(d)(1)(i). Why do these provisions provide a narrower definition for U.S. asset under section 884 than the phrase might otherwise suggest?

In theory, under the branch profits tax, it should make no difference whether a foreign taxpayer operates its U.S. trade or business through a branch or through a subsidiary. Is that in fact true? Why might a U.S. subsidiary be preferable to a U.S. branch in terms of taxation of "dividends"?

The branch profits tax regime includes specific rules for "coordination with tax treaties." Section 884(e). We will discuss this section in the chapter devoted to treaties, but observe that this is a classic example of a "treaty override", i.e., a case in which Congress unilaterally changes the terms of treaties negotiated by the U.S. (through imposing a "qualified resident" requirement that is not found in the treaty itself). For qualified residents, the branch profits tax is preempted by treaties which forbid the imposition of a second order dividend tax, although post-1986 U.S. tax treaties generally permit the branch profits tax to be levied.

5.6   THE BEAT

The most important innovation in TCJA is the BEAT. Under new IRC section 59A, US corporate taxpayers have to pay a "base erosion anti-abuse tax" (BEAT), at 10% less any applicable credits (including the foreign tax credit, but the US taxpayer is unlikely to have them for the relevant income since any foreign tax is imposed on the foreign related party). The tax base is taxable income plus "base erosion payments", defined as any amount paid or accrued by a taxpayer to a foreign person that is a related party of the taxpayer and with respect to which a deduction is allowable, including interest (to the extent not otherwise disallowed) and, for inverted corporations, also cost of goods sold.

Withholding taxes (if any) are allowed as an offset. There is a safe harbor for smaller corporations with gross receipts below $500 million and another for base erosion ratio of less than 3%. The proposal applies to base erosion payments paid or accrued in taxable years beginning after December 31, 2017.

On its face, the BEAT does not violate tax treaties because the BEAT is applied only to the US party, so that the <u>savings clause applies</u> (US tax treaties Art 1(4): treaties cannot change US taxation of US residents). Still, it is likely that our trading partners will not view this provision favorably, since it appears substantively to be a violation of articles 11 (no withholding on interest),12 (no withholding on royalties), 9 (no denial of deduction for cost of goods sold if it is equivalent to the arm's length price), and 24 (no discrimination in denying deductions). If our trading parties respond by not allowing a tax credit for BEAT, double taxation could result.

Notes

BEAT is a new addition to the Code imposed primarily on large corporations ($500 million minimum in gross income). BEAT operates as alternative minimum tax that applies to domestic corporations and to foreign corporations with income effectively connected with a US trade or business. That means that BEAT applies to inbound transactions. It also applies on foreign corporations with U.S. branches. BEAT does not apply to individuals, S corporations, regulated investment companies or real estate investment trusts. BEAT is estimated to raise $149.6 billion over the 2018–2027 period, with nearly two-thirds of that amount collected in the last five years (because of an increasing BEAT rate).

Arguably, the BEAT implements the single tax principle, on the assumption that a taxpayer pays less in the foreign jurisdiction. It is an anti-abuse rule to ensure minimum payment and prevent U.S. tax base erosion with regards to inbound transactions. Arguably, it can make U.S. corporations more internationally competitive by eliminating the gap of U.S. domestic effective tax rate and those who operate internationally. It applies primarily to three types of tax base eroding payments: royalties, interest and depreciation.

The BEAT generally is calculated as 10 percent of modified taxable income less the regular tax liability (generally reduced by certain tax credits). The tax rate is 5 percent for 2018 as a sort of phase-in of the new regime, and eventually increases to 12.5 percent beginning in 2025 as one of several quantitative adjustments made by the legislation toward the end of the budget window in order to meet revenue targets. These rates are increased by one percent for certain banks and securities dealers. (They also don't have an exclusion for cost of goods sold, unlike other industries, and lower BE Percentage threshold). The BEAT calculations generally are made on a group basis (thus, for example, the related-party payments, deductions, and income of affiliated domestic corporations are aggregated for BEAT purposes).

The Base Erosion Minimum Tax Amount (BEMTA) is calculated as:

BEMTA = 10% * MTI – (RTL – BCREDs)

In the formula, MTI is the excess (if any) regular taxable income (before credits) less the sum of BETBs and the product of the base erosion percentage multiplied by NOL deductions. RTL is regular tax liability. BCREDs are credits that can increase BEMTA dollar-for-dollar. The amount ·in parentheses cannot fall below zero.

The BEAT applies to applicable taxpayers, which are corporations (other than a regulated investment company—RIC, such as ETF or REIT that are deemed to be pass through entities.) An applicable taxpayer has to have $500 million of gross receipts on average for the three prior taxable years. In addition, it has to have a Base Erosion Percentage of at least 3% of its total deductions. An aggregation Rule applies providing that certain related persons shall be treated as one person. Gross receipts of foreign persons only include effectively connected income. These rules (aggregation) appear to be intended to restrict the application of BEAT to large U.S. enterprises that have incurred substantial amounts of related party base eroding payments. (Because taking into consideration related parties transactions inflates gross receipts). Query: Would $499,999,999 gross receipt taxpayers be reluctant to sell an additional $1? The amount these taxpayers will sell is equal to the potential future BEAT liability.

Use of gross receipts rather than taxable income does not represent necessarily the wealth but the sales. It is similar to the test used to determine whether a corporation may use the cash receipts and disbursements method. Problems with gross receipts: a. Sales of products that are subject to return or allowance are generally netted against the original gross receipts. b. Highly leveraged institutions like Banks and Financial Intermediaries—gross receipts are not a true measure of the size a taxpayer's U.S. business. Possible way to overcome: Construct offsetting positions with unrelated persons to inflate the denominator of the Base Erosion Percentage. Or use sales conduits for both gross receipts and base erosion percentage.

Section 59A does not prescribe any rule for which entity might be required to pay the controlled group's BEAT. Per section 1504, only U.S. corporations of a 50% commonly owned controlled group that satisfy the 80% affiliation standard may join a consolidated return but not foreign corporate group member. In case of a controlled group commonly held 50% owned domestic and foreign corporations—the group may not have any mechanism under contract or law for collecting the liability from its co-owner since one will be calculated as the domestic is subject to controlled group rules and the other is not. The statute might literally be read as imposing a single tax on the entire controlled group. In that case, it should be apportioned among the group members for liability and E&P purposes. There are also considerations of tax credits and NOL's that are calculated on a single taxpayer basis.

The Base Erosion Percentage is calculated by comparing an Applicable Taxpayer's Base Erosion Tax Benefits to its total deductions. The same aggregation rules are used. The effectively connected income limitation is not specifically incorporated. Intra-group transactions should also be disregarded. However, there is a problem if we generally apply it to all payments of foreign affiliates, then all the payments to foreign affiliates would be excluded, causing the Base Erosion Percentage to be zero (if all the payments are to the same group. Solution to Base Erosion Percentage—apply ECI limitation—only ECI receipts of foreign corporations would be considered and only such ECI receipts and payments would be subject to intra-controlled group exclusion (means that only ECI receipts from intra-group transactions will be disregarded).

Base Erosion Payment-Aggregation rule and ECI limitation don't apply to Base Erosion Payment—its meaning stands alone. This inconsistency compounds when Base Erosion Payments are considered in the calculation of Modified Taxable Income. Base Erosion Percentage applicable to NOLs is calculated with the intra controlled group exclusion, but Base Erosion Payments are calculated without the exclusion. Reminder—Modified Taxable Income = Base Erosion Benefits + Base Erosion Percentage of NOLs + Taxpayer's taxable income. Example: A Base Erosion Payment of $100 would be calculated without the intra-controlled group exclusion to the extent utilized in Year 1, and then with the intra-controlled exclusion (on a consolidated level) when carried forward and utilized in Year 2. Solution: Apply the intra group exclusion if ECI to payments.

The BEAT and tax credits: Outside the BEAT context, credits reduce tax liability. For purposes of BEAT, reductions of regular tax liability through the utilization of Tax Credits increases the likelihood of there being a Base Erosion Minimum Tax Amount, effectively devaluating those credits for this purpose. Tax expenditure expenses for specific credits such as R&E, for tax years beginning on or before 2025 are not reduced, and BEMTA is not reduced by the full amount of certain other tax credits, thereby, preserving the value of those.

Modified Taxable Income: A corporation's modified taxable income is determined by adding back to taxable income current year deductions involving payments to related foreign persons. For this purpose, a foreign person is related if it is treated as owning at least 25 percent of the stock of the taxpayer (by vote or value) or satisfies various other relationship or control tests. Direct, indirect and constructive ownership is taken into account for purposes of the ownership tests (Changed section 318 and section 267). The BEAT's add-backs for deductible amounts paid or accrued to a related foreign person generally include payments for services, interest, rents and royalties. If a deduction for interest is limited by section 163(j), the reduction in the amount of deductible interest is allocated first entirely to interest on loans from unrelated persons. Depreciation and amortization from assets that were bought from related persons in 2018 onwards.

Modified Taxable Income is calculated without regard to any Base Erosion Tax Benefit or the Base Erosion Percentage of NOL's (This and the Base Erosion Benefits are "BEAT Deductions"). (Section 59(C)(1)). It is not clear how to calculate MTI. Two possibilities: (a) Top Up approach—merely adding back to taxable income the BEAT deductions. (less complexity and generally greater liability). (b) Recalculation approach—Recalculate taxable income as if BEAT deductions did not exist, resulting in lesser liability since certain deduction could be utilized. This arises because for purposes of determining taxable income, the deductibility of many items (including NOL's, interest expense under 163(j) and charitable donations) is limited to the percentage of the income. For example: disregarding BEAT deductions will result in greater income (in this stage top up and recalculation are the same) which in turn, will allow more interest for 163(j) purposes, that will reduce the modified taxable income. Section 163(j) was amended to apply on related and unrelated parties. Section 59A(c)(3) states that for purposes of calculating Modified Taxable Income, we should include first the deduction allocable to related parties (more related parties interest deductions allowed, and less unrelated interest deductions allowed). By that, it accelerates the application of the BEAT to such interest. That means that 163(j) carryforwards are treated for BEAT purposes will be first unrelated parties and then related parties. The issue is whether 163(j) carryforwards (not NOLs) should be treated as BE Tax Benefits in the year allowable (without regards to BE Percentage). Example: In Year 1 TP had 100 interest deductions, which consist of 35 related parties and 65 unrelated parties, and 100 ATI. In year 1 it utilized 30 interest deductions which were all considered tax benefit. It carried-forward 5 related parties and 65 unrelated parties interest). In Year 2 the TP had no interest deductions and 150 ATI. Result?

If the top-up approach is used and there is a loss (no taxable income) for the year, the issue is whether the taxable income—the starting point—can be below zero. If not—the add back of BE Benefits can give rise to BEAT liability, although the taxpayer would not have tax liability even without these benefits because of NOLs. Example: Gross income 300, and 600 NOL's which 80% can be offset (480). If taxable income is zero, then adding back 50 to the base will invoke BEAT although the taxpayer would not have tax liability even without these benefits.

IRC section 59A(c)(1)(B)—"means the taxable income of the taxpayer . . . for the taxable year, determined without regard to any base erosion tax benefit . . . or the base erosion percentage of any net operating loss deduction allowed under section 172 for the taxable year". The language of 59A(c)(1)(B) raises the question of whether the BE Percentage of any NOL is determined with respect to the year of its origination or the year of its utilization. It could have been also constructed as: "or without any net operating loss deduction allowed for the year to the extent of the BE Percentage for such year." Does taxable year modifies "deduction" (the nearest antecedent noun)? That will result in calculation without the relevant amount of NOL deduction allowed in a year. This is coherent with the wording of 59A(c)(4)(B) that explicitly excludes the NOL deduction in calculation of the BE Percentage, suggesting that NOL's imported into the year have a different Base Erosion Percentage than the BE Percentage for the year of the utilization. Example: Year 1—TP generates a loss entirely attributable to BE Payments. (Loss originated from BE Benefits). The loss exceeds taxable income and it is carried forward to Year 2. Year 2—TP has zero BE Percentage. The deduction of NOL's in Year 2 appears to be the utilization of the attribute that results in a BE Tax Benefit. If the BE Percentage were determined by reference to the year of utilization, the TP would add back none of such NOLs to Modified Taxable Income for purposes of calculating its Year 2 BEAT. (because of the zero BE Percentage). Using the alternative interpretation, will use NOL in Year 1, and it will carry-forward on Year 2. That is also the case with 50% or even less, since all of the NOLs were base eroding. On the other hand—the BE is limited to the tax benefit actually obtained and such benefit is determined in the year of utilization.

Base Erosion Payments are payments to related persons under Section 267(b) or Section 707(b). The statute includes entities that are treated as related under Section 482 standards. Section 482 might include two unrelated companies operating in concert or entities commonly owned by unrelated parties that operating in concert, or entities commonly owned by unrelated parties. Payments for this purpose do not include payments that reduce taxable income but are not treated as deductions—such as cost of goods, or certain service payments eligible for reimbursements at cost.

Once Base Erosion Payments have been identified—it is necessary to calculate Base Erosion Benefits. These are the deductions allowed by the code relating to those payments. (as oppose to the payments themselves). Example for a benefited payment: annual Base Erosion Tax Benefit is the depreciation (or amortization) deduction available with respect to that property for the taxable year in question. Interest expense limitation 163(j) or 267 deductions only to the extent allowable. Also include services expenses, and re-insurance premiums, which are not necessarily deductions but are reductions in gross income. Payments that are subject to withholding tax are excluded. (There are no benefits in them). Payments eligible for a reduced rate under an applicable treaty are treated as producing Base Erosion only to the extent no withholding tax is imposed (what about 0% rate w/t?) The withholding tax exception applies in computing Modified Taxable Income and Base Erosion Percentage, but not to gross receipts. Compare Section 245A.

Related Party: 25% related to the taxpayer by vote and value, and other persons related to the taxpayer or the 25% owner under Sections 267(b) or 707(b)(1), in addition to persons within the meaning of Section 482. This rule disregards different economic incentives of payments—reduction in US income taxed at the 21 payments does not economically make sense with a 75% unrelated person. Example: A TP paid 100 to a foreign 25% subsidiary. The U.S. tax benefit is 21 (generated by deducting the payment), and if the TP doesn't control the entity, it has lost 75 plus the tax in the foreign jurisdiction. Another problem is access to information when using Section 482 relationships for calculation of BEAT.

Cost of Goods Sold: The rule for Base Erosion Payment—"any amount paid or accrued by the taxpayer to a foreign person which is a related party of the taxpayer and with respect to which a deduction is allowable under this chapter". COGS payments for purposes of tax are not computed as a deduction but rather in a reduction to income. Therefore, it is not included in the definition. The joint committee and the legislative history recognized its exclusion. Other payments that reduce income and are not deductions are included, such as certain reinsurance payments. The exclusion of COGS is meant to provide relief for taxpayers who purchase raw materials, or partially manufactured components and assembly in the U.S. However—it applies to otherwise deductible royalties and other payments reflecting the value of intangibles that are capitalized under Section 263A. Or intangibles that are effectively embedded in the price of an imported tangible item, the value of which consists largely of IP (such as pharmaceutical products), and thus treated as COGS. That eliminates the BEAT effect to most payments related to IP to the extent the payments are connected to the production of goods. Consider the inequality in industries that generate revenue from licensing IP, advertising or services, and banks and financial services companies (where they pay more). The issue is whether or not to separate the embedded value of IP. One approach: If a full price to tangible and intangible product is consistent with Arm's length pricing, there is no reason for the U.S. to impose an additional tax cost—this views BEAT as aimed predominantly at financing arrangements. Second approach—BEAT targeted royalties, and the scope of it will be reduced if embedded royalties are not taxed. Also, there is no reason to prefer one industry over the other in this case.

Services Cost Method Payments: Section 59A(d)(5)—Service payments, which are permitted to be reimbursed at cost under Section 482 services cost method ("SCM") are excluded from Base Erosion Payments. Clause A— Services which meet the requirements for eligibility for use of the services cost method under Section 482 (determined without regard to the requirement that the services not contribute significantly to fundamental risks of business success or failure). SCM under Section 482—generic services not critical to the profit-making activity of an enterprise may be shared among members of a related party group and compensated at cost under the SCM, without profit element. Clause (B) states that "such amount constitutes the total services cost with no markup component". The issue is whether services can be differentiated from the markup component and be excluded, or an entire payment with profits is excluded. 2009—Issuance of regulations of AML—Service with no markup, but markup is available in some instances (4 prongs that make sure of no BE intent). Legislative history—discussion in the Senate between Sen. Orrin Hatch (Chair of the Finance Committee, R-Utah) and Sen. Chapman (R-Ohio) that emphasized that services can be separated from the markup component. The final statutory language in Section 14401 of the conference agreement adds one word (in italics below) to the relevant portion (of new section 59(d)(4)(B)) in the Senate amendment language: "such amount constitutes the total services cost with no *applicable* markup component." Not clear whether this addition change their intent. The joint explanatory statement released with the final statutory language: "A base erosion payment does not include any amount paid or accrued by a taxpayer for services if such services [meet certain requirements in the regulations] and only if the payments are made for services that have *no markup component*" (emphasis added). The draft added also this parenthetical in clause (A): "(Determined without regard to the requirement that the services not contribute significantly to fundamental risks of business success or failure)." Under Reg. 1.482–9(b)(5) significant services cannot qualify for the SCM and such services are required to have a profit component. The addition is a relaxation that permits the payor to exclude from BEAT any payments for services that normally would not qualify for the SCM because they are significant services for which service providers are required to charge a markup. Thus, if transactions that have profit will be excluded this addition doesn't make sense.

Exception for Derivative Payments: Qualified Derivative Payments (QDP) are exempted from both the Base Erosion Percentage and the Base Erosion Payments. Not stated in the legislative history, but the purpose of this requirement is to limit the QDP exemption to derivatives dealers, who generally mark their derivatives and treat them as OI under Section 475 (mark to market accounting method). That will potentially burden the financial industry. However, because it doesn't reference it applies to potential traders electing under Section 475(f) to mark to market. QDP has 4 prongs: 1. The payment made pursuant to a "derivative"; 2. the taxpayer must mark the derivative to market and recognize ordinary income, gain and loss with respect to it; 3. the payment must not be a Base Erosion Payment on a standalone basis or be allocable to a non-derivative component; and 4. certain reporting requirements must be met. What is a derivative for Section 59A purposes? (Read Section). Very broad because of (V). Section (V) makes (i)-(iv) redundant. Historically, it is similar to derivative definition such as in Camp's proposal (2014). The Mark-to-Market and Ordinary Requirement limits its scope. Two rules that are designed to prevent taxpayers from attempting to wrap a Base Erosion Payment into a derivative that raises uncertainty: ". . .Would be treated as a Base Erosion Payment if it were not made pursuant to a derivative, including any interest, royalty, or service payment. . ." However, if it would not be pursuant to a derivative, it doesn't qualify to the derivative exception. A rational interpretation is to aim at transactions or part of transactions that under general tax principles are treated as non-derivative transactions. That results in an overlap with the second requirement, that excludes a payment that is properly allocable to a non-derivative component, in the case of a contract that has both derivative and non-derivative components. (for example, if a taxpayer constructs a contract that functions as a total return swap, but built into the agreement a series of payments determined by reference to an unrelated aspect of the taxpayer's business).

Payments to a CFC: Payments between U.S. corporation and related CFCs within the same controlled group would be regarded as Base Erosion Payments, even if such amounts were immediately taxable to the U.S. SH. Example: A U.S. Corporation SH makes a payment to its 100% CFC. If such payment is not ECI might not be eliminated as a payment among members of the controlled group under the aggregation rule of Section 59A(e)(3). In this case—the payment would be treated as a Base Erosion Payment giving rise to Base Erosion Tax Benefits. (Layer of BEAT tax). This income to the CFC given certain conditions can be subpart F income or subject to GILTI (although relaxed a bit with FDII—provides 50% deduction) and be taxed immediately. (Another layer of tax). This GILTI income can be included in the modified taxable income of the U.S. SH for U.S. tax income purposes. (Another layer of tax?) This income is maybe taxed in the foreign jurisdiction, and BEAT disregard foreign tax credits. (Another layer of tax). NYSBA suggested to have an election to excludes these payments from BEAT. For example, if a U.S. SH holds 55% with a foreign 45%, it can elect to exclude 55% of the payments from the benefit.

Interest deductions of branches: U.S. branches of foreign corporations (with ECI) may be subject to the BEAT when they deduct payments made to related foreign persons. When U.S. branch of foreign corp. is entitled for deductions the BEAT can apply. Under Treas. Reg. 1.882–5 the Interest expense of a U.S. branch is calculated by: ECI US assets*actual world-wide debt-to-assets ration or the corporation or fixed ratio (95% for banks and 50% for other taxpayers) = U.S. liabilities. Then, under two different methods, an interest is allocated to the branch per the U.S. liabilities. Branch Interest allocated under both formulas is treated as it was paid by a domestic corporation, therefore, it will be subject to 59A.

Conduits: Fear of using unrelated intermediaries that will convert Base Erosion Payments by transferring payments to them, and in turn transferring it to the related parties. This leads to fear of reducing the $500m Threshold by assigning income, and to fear of inflating the amount of allowable non-base erosion deductions to reduce its Base Erosion Percentage. A solution might be to trace whether the unrelated party has a corresponding obligation to transfer the money to the taxpayer's related party. Problems to track these deductions—self reporting? What is the right standard to judge such transactions? But for (requiring the taxpayer to show that this payment would not be made "but for" the corresponding item of income)? Purpose of avoidance? Agent tests?

BEAT has a broad grant of regulatory authority: Prescribe such regulations as may be necessary and appropriate, in addition, to numerated issues. Because of a lot of inconsistencies, there is a chance for the Treasury to construe the provisions in ways that will fix logical inconsistencies.

BEAT and Treaties: Permanent Establishment—a foreign corporation protected by a treaty is taxed only on their income attributable to a U.S. PE. PE is not identical to Effectively Connected Standard, although they both have the same objective. We need more guidance to clarify that receipts attributable to U.S. PE should not be treated as a Base Erosion Payment. Those that are attributable to a US PE should have the benefit of the ECI limitation of Section 59A(e)(2).

5.7 HYBRID PAYMENTS

New Section 267A limits the deductibility of payments on hybrid instruments (treated as deductible in the US and exempt in the residence jurisdiction) or by hybrid entities (treated as corporations by the US and transparent in the residence jurisdiction, or vice versa). These provisions implement OECD BEPS Action 2 in accordance with the single tax principle.

NOTES

A new addition to the code: No deduction shall be allowed under this chapter for any disqualified related party amount paid or accrued pursuant to a hybrid transaction or by, or to, a hybrid entity. The Purpose: Avoid potential abuse of arbitrage between different jurisdictions, and by that create BE. Same as BEAT: Level the playing game for U.S. Domestic corporations in terms of effective tax rates (CIN). For BEAT—not a BE Benefit.

Section 267A applies only to interest and royalties (what about dividends to a person that is considered interest income in the foreign jurisdiction?) that was paid or accrued to a related party, and if one of the two prongs is satisfied: a. Such amount is not included in the income of such related party under the tax law of the country of which such related party is a resident for tax purposes or is subject to tax, or b. Such related party is allowed a deduction with respect to such amount under the tax law of such country. (Equivalent to not included in the tax).

First Prong Issues: Resident under which laws (U.S. or Foreign)? (e.g., incorporated in Ireland, but board meets in Bermuda). Subject to tax requirement—is it specifically on the income earned? If so, it contradicts the first words: "such amount is not included in the income of such related party". If not, then it is not clear since there many taxes that can be imposed.

What about CFC's? Importantly, any payment that is made to a CFC and included in the gross income of a 10% U.S. shareholder under Section 951(a) is not subject to Section 267A.

A related party means a related person as defined in Section 954(d)(3) (i.e., more than 50 percent vote or value standard). BEAT applies to payments to 25%–50%. Notice that there are different ways to calculate Related Parties for purposes of BEAT and Section 267A.

For purposes of this section, the term "hybrid transaction" means any transaction, series of transactions, agreement, or instrument one or more payments with respect to which are treated as interest or royalties for purposes of this chapter and which are not so treated for purposes the tax law of the foreign country of which the recipient of such payment is resident for tax purposes or is subject to tax. Use of conduits in foreign jurisdictions? (but for? Agent? Purpose of Avoidance? A corresponding obligation to transfer the royalty or interest?)

Hybrid entity: Any entity which is either—(1) treated as fiscally transparent for purposes of this chapter but not so treated for purposes of the tax law of the foreign country of which the entity is resident for tax purposes or is subject to tax, or (2) treated as fiscally transparent for purposes of such tax law but not so treated for purposes of this chapter. (reverse hybrid).

Fiscally transparent—checked the box, branches, partnerships—that's an assumption, but it is not defined. No cross reference and no definition. Currently, Regs. Sec. 1.894–1(d)(3)(ii) provides a definition of "fiscally transparent" for the purposes of claiming treaty benefits. Under this provision, an entity is fiscally transparent with respect to an item of income if, under the laws of its jurisdiction, its interest holder is required to separately take into account the item of income on a current basis with the same source and character as if the interest holder had realized the income directly from the originating source. In addition: Regs. Sec. 1.894–1(d)(3)(ii) further states that in determining whether an entity is fiscally transparent with respect to an item of income in the entity's jurisdiction, it is irrelevant that, under the laws of the entity's jurisdiction, the entity is permitted to exclude the item from gross income or that the entity is required to include the item in gross income but is entitled to a deduction for distributions to its interest holders (such as an exemption). Although rare, there are instances where for both U.S. and foreign purposes the payee and the payor are treated as the same type of entity. This transaction will result in deduction and non taxation—such as a European investments vehicles (special funds).

On the other hand, it can apply to certain transactions even if there aren't mismatch: Example: A U.S. corporation (USP) made a loan to a foreign disregarded entity (DRE) wholly owned by a U.S. subsidiary (USS) of USP. DRE is a hybrid entity (i.e., a corporation for non-U.S. tax purposes but fiscally transparent from a U.S. tax perspective). The interest expense generated by USS (via DRE) is offset by USP's interest income, resulting in a "wash" from a U.S. tax perspective, assuming no other limitations apply (e.g., dual-consolidated-loss limitations). Absent—the requirement that the recipient will be foreign under "disqualified related party-amount".

It could apply even to situations in which the amounts paid are subject to tax in the jurisdiction where the hybrid entity is resident. For example, assume FC is a U.K. limited liability partnership (LLP) that defaults into a corporation for U.S. federal income tax purposes under the check-the-box regulations. Further assume that all partners of the U.K. LLP are U.K. residents subject to tax on their share of the LLP's income. Section 267A would apply to any U.S.-source interest payments made to the U.K. LLP even though such amounts are fully taxable in the U.K. in the hands of the U.K. resident partners. While the statute indicates that Treasury may issue regulatory or other guidance dealing with exceptions to the anti-hybrid rules where the payment is taxed under the laws of another foreign country, the statute does not specifically direct Treasury to address situations involving taxation in the same country but as to a different taxpayer (such as the U.K. limited partners).

Hybrid entities and BEPS: Action 2 of the OECD's 2013 Action Plan on Base Erosion and Profit Shifting addresses hybrid mismatches that result in a deduction without inclusion. In such mismatches, the deduction should be denied in the member state that is the payer jurisdiction. Where the deduction is not denied in the payer jurisdiction, the amount of the payment that would otherwise give rise to a mismatch outcome is to be included in income in the member state that is the payee jurisdiction. How does this relate to Section 267A? To the single tax principle?

5.8   REVIEW PROBLEMS—CHAPTER 5

1. FC is a large multinational corporation organized under the laws of Argentina. It manufactures and sells various products related to the cellular telecommunication industry throughout the world. In 2018 and 2019 it had offices in New York City, Chicago and Atlanta, with 100 employees primarily engaged in (as yet unsuccessful in 2018) attempts to interest American carriers with its products. Also in 2018, A, the son of FC's founder, who just completed his MBA, traded in stock using FC's NYC office on behalf of FC and his own parents, using the family's private accounts and any free cash deposited with FC's banks in the U.S. He has been successful and generated $1m of gains for FC alone during 2018. He received $200,000 for this service to FC. He was not involved in FC's U.S. business otherwise. In 2019, A was asked by other friends and family to handle their stock portfolios in the U.S. He therefore rented a nicer loft in NYC, where he located his home office and handled the investments of these friends and family. He continued to invest for FC and generated another $1m of gains for FC during 2019. Again, he received $200,000 for this service to FC and was not involved in FC's U.S. business otherwise. Also in 2019, FC got its first contract in the U.S. when B, the CEO of D, a Delaware corporation met FC's CEO in Argentina and agreed on the supply of products that generated $10m to FC. The products were transferred (including title) to D's agent in Buenos Aires and were shipped on D's expense to the U.S. Neither B nor D were ever contacted or met any of FC's employees in the U.S. and none of these employees were involved in any way in the negotiation or conclusion of this contract. B did see their advertisement in the U.S. and D was helped by an Atlanta employee by phone in the process of delivery of the products from the ships to D's factory (this was technical assistance that took the employee approximately 2 hours and could be found on FC's website for free). What, if any, are FC's U.S. tax consequences of the above transactions?

    a. Assume, alternatively, that FC manufactures, in addition to the cellular equipment, large (and expensive) telecommunication equipment. It regularly sells between 500–1000 units of these products to the U.S each year, always to the same few clients and passing title in Argentina. FC's U.S. employees were never involved in this line of business, except that one of them sits on FC's board (she travels to Argentina for board meetings). FC's personnel visit their U.S. clients occasionally and sometimes pay visits to FC's offices to make unrelated phone calls, faxes and secure consultations with headquarters (in which the U.S. office's personnel never participate). Does FC have an office in the U.S. with respect to this line of business?

    b. Assume, alternatively that J, FC's President and controlling shareholder decided to purchase a NYC apartment in order to be closer to A, his son. He stays two months each year in that apartment and works in a home office established in that apartment. If an important meeting is required, he flies to Argentina for that purpose. He makes executive decisions, but does not participate in the daily management of FC, but he does insist on a having a final word (veto) regarding all large equipment sales contracts, which he views as sensitive and critical to the success of FC. Assume that he has the right to review each sale for 24 during which he can veto the sale. Does FC have an office in the U.S. with respect to its large equipment business because of J's actions above?

2.   Assume now, in addition to the facts of Q.1. that FC sold $1m of products to a Brazilian corporation, transferred by land (trucks) at the expense of FC. The Brazilian corporation was introduced to the product in one of the sales pitches conducted by FC's employees in NYC to a U.S. corporation in which the Brazilian corporation holds a stake. An FC U.S. employee convinced the Brazilians that FC's product fits their system and spent several hours to explain the pricing policy of FC. The Brazilian CFO then flew to Buenos Aires after the lawyers for both sides reviewed the standard sales agreement of FC, which was not extensively amended, and negotiated a discount during a two-hour meeting in the end of which the parties concluded and signed the agreement. Are there U.S. tax consequences to FC as a result of these new facts?

    a.   Assume, alternatively, that the role of FC's U.S. office was solely the display of the product in its Atlanta showroom, the provision of brochures and price lists, and direction of the Brazilians to the sales managers in Buenos Aires.

3.   N, a nonresident alien purchased a 10 floor fully-furnished NYC office-building from a domestic business that faced bankruptcy. She effectuated the purchase through her wholly owned U.S. corporation, which until that point of time had engaged in the sole activity of owning the rights to a patent that she intends to license in the future. She believes that the time has not yet come to exploit the patent despite her estimate of $10m value for that patent. She has never visited the U.S. and has performed all of the activities related to this business through unrelated persons that were paid in cash and at arms' length from her Swiss bank account. Her business model is to rent office space to anyone for whatever period required. She can divide the space almost at will with a set of moving walls already installed in the building when she bought it. In 2019, after 3 years of hefty profits from the building she found in one of her (building) clients a company that she believes would be a good match for the patent. Indeed, X, that (domestic) corporation immediately offers her $5m for the patent and an additional $5m for the whole office building that X expects to need upon the acquisition of the patent. She ends up selling the stock of her U.S. corporation to X realizing a $10m gain. Does she have any effectively connected income for the year of the stock sale?

PART C

THE TRANSFER PRICING PROBLEM

CHAPTER 6   The Transfer Pricing Problem

CHAPTER 6

THE TRANSFER PRICING PROBLEM

IRC section 482 encompasses the statutory transfer pricing rule. It reads:

"In any case of two or more organizations, trades, or businesses (whether or not incorporated, whether or not organized in the United States, and whether or not affiliated) owned or controlled directly or indirectly by the same interests, the Secretary may distribute, apportion, or allocate gross income, deductions, credits, or allowances between or among such organizations, trades, or businesses, if he determines that such distribution, apportionment, or allocation is necessary in order to prevent evasion of taxes or clearly to reflect the income of any of such organizations, trades, or businesses. In the case of any transfer (or license) of intangible property (within the meaning of section 936(h)(3)(B)), the income with respect to such transfer or license shall be commensurate with the income attributable to the intangible. For purposes of this section, the Secretary shall require the valuation of transfers of intangible property (including intangible property transferred with other property or services) on an aggregate basis or the valuation of such a transfer on the basis of the realistic alternatives to such a transfer, if the Secretary determines that such basis is the most reliable means of valuation of such transfers."[1]

This concise, and some may say, incomprehensible, short paragraph is supplemented by a long and elaborate body of treasury regulations which one cannot avoid in any attempt to deal with the transfer pricing problem. This problem is a product of the deviation of the law from the economic reality of multinational enterprises operating across-borders and through multiple entities as single economic units. The law, including the U.S. federal income tax law, "respects" the fiction that these multiple entities are separate. Therefore, transactions within the single economic enterprise are generally respected similarly to transactions between strangers. This creates an incentive for the MNEs to manipulate prices charged on such (enterprise) internal transactions—prices which are entirely in their discretion and not subject to market restrictions—to minimize the overall tax bill for the enterprise. They exploit, for instance, tax rate differences between countries, charging high prices to their entities in high tax countries, a strategy that results in profits being diverted to their entities subject to tax in relatively low tax jurisdictions. Concrete examples are explored throughout this chapter. No student of international tax can avoid this problem as it represents enormous risks

---

[1]   The last section of section 482 was added by the December 2018 tax reform.

and opportunities in the process of tax planning, and it is almost always intertwined with any tax planning technique employed. Keep that in mind while you read this and the following chapters.

6.1   THE ROOT OF THE PROBLEM

United States Gypsum Company and United States Gypsum Export Company v. United States of America

United States District Court for the Northern District of Illinois, Eastern Division.
304 F.Supp. 627 (1969).

■ CAMPBELL, DISTRICT JUDGE:

This is a consolidated action and involves three suits brought by the United States Gypsum Company ("USG") and its wholly owned subsidiary, the United States Gypsum Export Company ("Export") for refunds for federal income taxes paid by plaintiffs. The cases involve the tax liability of USG for the years 1954 and 1955 and again for 1957 and 1958, and the taxes of Export for the years 1957 and 1958. The defendant, ("government") not only denied all grounds for refund, but also claimed certain offsets as affirmative defenses. The basis for the alleged offsets is that USG paid one of its wholly owned subsidiaries excessive amounts for transporting its products and that it paid another subsidiary, Export, excessive amounts for crude gypsum rock, and undercharged it for finished products intended for resale by Export. . . .

The second issue involves the operations and earnings of United States Gypsum Export Co. Export purchased rock from Canadian Gypsum ("Canadian") another wholly owned subsidiary, organized under the laws of the Dominion of Canada, . . . which it in turn sold to USG. . . . This issue has generally been referred to as the "Export issue" and presents the questions: (a) Whether Export was a Western Hemisphere Trade Corporation under the Internal Revenue Code (26 U.S.C. §§ 921–922); and (b) Whether the income of Export earned from the sale of rock to USG . . . should properly be reallocated to USG again under section 482 (26 U.S.C. § 482) in order to clearly reflect the income of USG for federal income tax purposes. . . .

The Export Company Issues

These issues involve the operations of United States Gypsum Export Company, ("Export"), which, as previously stated, is a wholly owned subsidiary of USG. USG purchased gypsum rock from . . . its wholly owned Canadian subsidiary, Canadian Gypsum Company ("Canadian"), through its subsidiary Export. Specifically, the questions presented are: (1) Whether Export qualified as a Western Hemisphere Trade Corporation and was entitled to the special deduction accorded such corporations; and (2) Whether a portion of Export's income should be allocated to USG under section 482. . . .

The Operations of Export Company

Export was incorporated in 1954 as a result of a study USG conducted of its export-import operations. USG allegedly planned to explore and develop an export-import business through Export Company. Prior to that time USG had made substantial sales to Canadian, which operated a manufacturing plant and sales organization in Canada and also made some sales in Mexico, the Caribbean, South America and Europe. Sales were apparently also made to unrelated and independent purchasers when the purchasers initiated inquiry. USG in its evidence and in its briefs relates a number of business reasons for establishing the Export Company. It is quite clear, however, that a primary purpose was the tax advantage it could obtain as a Western Hemisphere Trade Corporation.

Through 1955 Export had only two employees, both "salesmen", in the Caribbean and Latin America. . . . USG personnel furnished accounting, billing and secretarial services for Export and also handled all of the details of credit, bills of lading, and made out customs papers and tax returns. All of these services were performed on "service contracts" entered into between USG and Export.

The purchase of crude gypsum rock by USG from its mining subsidiaries and through Export was facilitated by contracts entered into between USG and Export and between Export and the mining subsidiaries. Under the terms of the contract between Export and Canadian, Canadian agreed to produce, sell and deliver in Canada one million net tons of gypsum rock each year and whatever additional tonnage as Export might order. Export agreed to purchase the same amounts. Export agreed to pay Canadian its average costs per ton of producing the rock plus 25 cents per ton. This price incidentally was the same price which USG had been paying Canadian for crude gypsum. . . .

When Export entered into these purchase agreements with the mining subsidiaries it simultaneously entered into a sales agreement with the parent, USG. This contract in essence provided that Export would sell and USG would buy the same quantities (minimum and maximum) of gypsum rock as Export agreed to purchase from the mining subsidiaries.

Under the terms of the agreement with Canadian . . . Canadian was to deliver the rock to Export Company in Canada. Specifically, the contract provided that, "ownership, legal title to, risk of loss of, right to possession of, and all the property right in, the crude gypsum rock", was to pass from Canadian to Export when the crude rock passed across Canadian's dock in the course of delivery to the vessels. Under the terms of its agreement with USG, Export was to deliver the rock to USG in Canada. Title to the crude gypsum was to pass from Export to USG when it was loaded onto the vessel. Thus, Export held title and had possession of the crude gypsum only for the brief period from when the gypsum rock passed across the docks (when title passed to Export) until it was loaded onto the vessel (when title passed to USG). No one seems sure whether Export's ownership of the crude gypsum continued from the time it fell from the conveyor on the dock into the hold and until the vessel was fully loaded, or whether the ownership was only momentary, that is, that Export's ownership continued only from the time the gypsum rock fell from the conveyor until it landed in the hold, so that the ownership of Export was at the most a few hours, at the least a split second.

For accepting this momentary possession USG paid Export 50 cents per ton plus costs and administrative overhead. In other words Export was assured a profit of 50 cents per ton from USG. Export paid no Canadian tax because it did not take title on Canadian shore. As a United States corporation it claimed the benefits of a reduced tax as a Western Hemisphere Trade Corporation ... This deduction essentially reduces Export's tax rate from 52% to 38%. ...

The Western Hemisphere Trade Question. ...

The thrust of the government's argument, in contending that Export did not qualify for the deduction, is that Export's income from the sales of crude gypsum rock to USG was not "derived from the active conduct of a trade or business" as required. ...

Export owned the gypsum rock only for a brief moment while it fell from Canadian's dock into the hold of the waiting vessel—or possibly until the vessel was fully loaded. All of Export's dealings relating to the purchase and resale of crude gypsum rock were within the corporate family. The extent of its participation in the entire transaction is set forth in the post trial brief of the government:

"Export did not mine the gypsum (or own the mines), deliver the gypsum from the quarry to the dock, or load the gypsum from the dock into the vessel: CG (Canadian) did all of that. Export did not own or charter the vessels which carried the gypsum rock to the United States, order delivery, of the gypsum by CG (Canadian) at dockside in Canada, or notify CG (Canadian) of the vessel's arrival: Panama Gypsum Company and Gypsum Transportation Company did all of that. (TR. 199–200.) Export did not process the gypsum rock, manufacture it into finished products, or sell those finished products: USG did all of that.

(Stip. par. 11.) And Galileo taught us from his tower in Pisa that gravity—not Export—caused the gypsum rock to fall from the conveyor on CG's (Canadian's) dock to the stowage of the "Gypsum Prince." (Post-trial brief of gov't. p. 93).

My reading of the cases cited by the parties and my independent research on the subject lead me to conclude in agreement with the government's statement that the question, "whether Export's brief ownership of the gypsum rock and the subsequent resale could constitute the active conduct of a trade or business", is one of first impression. ...

In support of its position that it did conduct an "active trade or business", Export argues that the length of time it held title to the rock is irrelevant. Rather, it argues, that what is important is that Export did in fact purchase rock and resell the same and that these purchases and sales were made under long term contracts in which Export had no guarantee of resale to USG. In other words, Export took the risk of being able to resell the rock purchased from Canadian and the other mining subsidiaries. I agree that the purchase of goods with a concomitant risk of resale is the conduct of an active trade or business. I disagree with the statement of Export that there was in fact a risk of resale in this case. USG was obligated to purchase from Export the rock Export purchased from Canadian and the other mining subsidiaries. The only limit on this obligation was the most remote possibility that it would have no need at its many plants for this quantity of rock. Furthermore, considering the relationship of the companies, it would be naive to suggest that Export, a wholly owned subsidiary, was running any risk of resale in this operation.

On the ultimate issue, whether this was an active trade or business, on the basis of the evidence presented by Export itself, I am convinced that it was not an active trade or business and that, therefore, Export did not qualify as a Western Hemisphere Trade Corporation. . . .

Allocation of Export's Income to USG

Based on the same facts related in detail above, the government contends that the income or a portion thereof received by Export from the purchases of crude gypsum rock and the subsequent resales to USG should be allocated to USG under section 482 of the Internal Revenue Code. . . . The test [under section 482] is whether the price charged between the affiliated corporations basically reflects an arm's-length price, thus accomplishing the purposes of section 482 which is to place a controlled taxpayer on a tax parity with an uncontrolled taxpayer, by determining according to the standards of an uncontrolled taxpayer the true net income of the property and business of a controlled taxpayer. In short, the purpose of allocation is to charge income to the taxpayer who earned it.

As to the profits resulting from Export's purchases of crude gypsum from the mining subsidiaries and its resale to USG, the details of these operations have been adequately discussed. As I pointed out in my analysis of the Western Hemisphere Trade question, this scheme of "split second" ownership was devised solely to save USG 14% on its taxes. It had no other "substantial economic consequences and commercial significance." . . . Export assumed no liability for loss or damage in transit; it exercised no control over the goods; it ran no risks because it dealt only with controlled affiliates; and it performed no service. . . . As stated by our Seventh Circuit Court of Appeals in Local Finance Corp. v. Commissioner 407 F.2d 629, 632 (1969). The question is: "Whether * * * the companies would have entered into the same arrangements had they been uncontrolled corporations and bargained at arm's length". Certainly they would not.

On the basis of the facts fully presented and vividly illustrated, I can only conclude that the profits earned by Export as a result of its "split second" ownership of crude gypsum should be reallocated to USG to prevent tax avoidance and to clearly reflect its income. . . .

Holding ↑

* * *

NOTES AND QUESTIONS

1.   In broad terms, Canadian owned the gypsum until it was dropped from the dock to the ship, USG owned it from the moment it hit the ship, and Export, the Western Hemisphere Trade Corporation—think about it as a tax haven corporation for these purposes—owned the gypsum in between, as it falls (unassisted—by gravity) from the dock to the ship. Determine the contribution of each of these entities to the group's enterprise and compare it to the group's price allocation—the "transfer prices." Now try to define what is the root of the transfer pricing problem, as illustrated by this case.

    a.   How could USG set up a separate subsidiary purely in order to "own" the gypsum rock for a split second and argue that there was any substance to this ownership?

    b.   Should the tax law, in general, respect the separate identity of such a subsidiary, when it is by definition controlled by the parent? Is there a difference between accepting this legal fiction for tax purposes in general and accepting it in the specific context of transfer pricing?

2.   Assume a parent manufactures widgets at a cost of $20 each (manufacturing costs) and sells them to subsidiary, which is in another jurisdiction with a different tax rate. Subsidiary in turn sells the widgets to unrelated customers for $100 each, and incurs costs of $20 per widget in doing so (selling costs).

    a.   What is the net profit of the parent-subsidiary group? *60*

how to divide up profit?

    b.   Assuming each party seeks to recoup its costs (i.e., neither operates at a loss), what is the minimum price that parent would demand of subsidiary for each widget? What is the maximum price subsidiary would be willing to pay?

    c.   If you were the responsible officer at parent, how would you decide what price subsidiary should pay parent for each widget? What is your answer if the parent's tax rate is higher than the subsidiary's? What if the parent's tax rate is lower?

    d.   Assume now that both parent and subsidiary pay high rates of taxes. How much will you be willing to pay (bear costs) to effectively interpose another subsidiary that will not pay taxes at all? Recall Export in the above case, but remember that it is a relatively extreme case.

e.   If you were the IRS agent auditing the transaction, how would you go about deciding what the correct "transfer price" (as the price charged by the parent to the subsidiary is called) should be?

6.2   A CLASSIC EXAMPLE

E.I. Du Pont de Nemours and Company
v. United States

United States Court of Claims.
221 Ct.Cl. 333, 608 F.2d 445 (1979).

■ JUDGES: FRIEDMAN, CHIEF JUDGE, DAVIS, NICHOLS, KASHIWA, KUNZIG, BENNETT, and SMITH, JUDGES, en banc. DAVIS, JUDGE, delivered the opinion of the court.

Taxpayer Du Pont de Nemours, the American chemical concern, created early in 1959 a wholly-owned Swiss marketing and sales subsidiary for foreign sales—Du Pont International S.A. (known to the record and the parties as DISA). Most of the Du Pont chemical products marketed abroad were first sold by taxpayer to DISA, which then arranged for resale to the ultimate consumer through independent distributors. The profits on these Du Pont sales were divided for income tax purposes between plaintiff and DISA via the mechanism of the prices plaintiff charged DISA. For 1959 and 1960 the Commissioner of Internal Revenue, acting under section 482 of the Internal Revenue Code which gives him authority to reallocate profits among commonly controlled enterprises, found these divisions of profits economically unrealistic as giving DISA too great a share. Accordingly, he reallocated a substantial part of DISA's income to taxpayer, thus increasing the latter's taxes for 1959 and 1960 by considerable sums. The additional taxes were paid and this refund suit was brought in due course. Du Pont assails the Service's reallocation, urging that the prices plaintiff charged DISA were valid under the Treasury regulations implementing section 482. We hold that taxpayer has failed to demonstrate that, under the regulation it invokes and must invoke, it is entitled to any refund of taxes.

I.   Design, Objectives and Functioning of DISA

    A.   Du Pont first considered formation of an international sales subsidiary in 1957. A decreasing volume of domestic sales, increasing profits on exports, and the recent formation of the Common Market in Europe convinced taxpayer's president of the need for such a subsidiary. He envisioned an international sales branch capable of marketing Du Pont's most profitable type of products—Du Pont proprietary products, particularly textile fibers and elastomers specially designed for use as raw materials by other manufacturers. Du Pont had utilized two major marketing techniques to sell such customized products. One mechanism consisted of technical sales services: an elaborate set of laboratory services making technical improvements, developing new applications, and solving customer problems for Du Pont products. The other was "indirect selling," a method of promoting demand for Du Pont products at every point in the distribution chain. These two techniques were to be developed by DISA, Du Pont's international branch in Europe. DISA was not to displace plaintiff's set of independent European distributors, but rather to augment the distributors' efforts by the two marketing methods and to police the independents adequately.

B. Neither in the planning stage nor in actual operation was DISA a sham entity; nor can it be denied that it was intended to, and did, perform substantial commercial functions which taxpayer legitimately saw as needed in its foreign (primarily European) market. Nevertheless, we think it also undeniable that the tax advantages of such a foreign entity were also an important, though not the primary, consideration in DISA's creation and operation. During the planning stages, plaintiff's internal memoranda were replete with references to tax advantages, particularly in planning prices on Du Pont goods to be sold to the new entity. The tax strategy was simple. If Du Pont sold its goods to the new international subsidiary at prices below fair market value, that company, upon resale of the goods, would recognize the greater part of the total profit (i.e., manufacturing and selling profits). Since this foreign subsidiary could be located in a country where its profits would be taxed at a much lower level than the parent Du Pont would be taxed here, the enterprise as a whole would minimize its taxes. .... The new company's accumulated profits would be used to finance further foreign investments. The details of this planning are set forth in the findings, and they leave us without doubt that a significant objective of plaintiff was to create a foreign subsidiary which would be able to accumulate large profits with which to finance Du Pont capital improvements in Europe.[4]

---

[4] Du Pont is divided into a series of semi-autonomous departments which report to the Executive Committee. An early draft of a memorandum on this subject to the Executive Committee from the International Department (then known as the Foreign Relations Department) stated that the Treasury Department (responsible for Du Pont's tax planning) was considering the possibility of a "transfer of goods to a tax haven subsidiary at prices less than such transfers would be made to other subsidiaries or industrial Departments * * *" A memorandum from the Treasury Department reviewed the possibility of an IRS attack on such pricing and concluded:

"It would seem to be desirable to bill the tax haven subsidiary at less than an 'arm's length' price because: (1) the pricing might not be challenged by the revenue agent; (2) if the pricing is challenged, we might sustain such transfer prices; (3) if we cannot sustain the prices used, a transfer price will be negotiated which should not be more than an 'arm's length' price and might well be less; thus we would be no worse off than we would have been had we billed at the higher price."

A subsequent Treasury Department report on "Use of a Profit Sanctuary Company by the Du Pont Company" advised pricing goods to the "profit sanctuary" at considerably lower levels

C. Consistently with that aim, plaintiff's prices on its intercorporate sales to DISA were deliberately calculated to give the subsidiary the lion's share of the profits. Instead of allowing each individual producing department to value its goods economically and to set a realistic price,[5] Du Pont left pricing on the sales to DISA with the Treasury and Legal Departments. Neither department was competent to set an economic value on goods sold to DISA, and no economic correlation of costs to prices was attempted.[6] Rather, an official of the Treasury Department established a pricing system designed to leave DISA with 75 percent of the total profits. If the goods' cost was greater than DISA's selling price, the department would price the item at its cost less DISA's selling expense. This latter provision was designed to insulate DISA from any loss. On the whole, the pricing system was based solely on Treasury and Legal Department estimates of the greatest amount of profits that could be shifted to DISA without evoking IRS intervention.[7]

. . .

D. As it turned out, for the taxable years involved here, 1959 and 1960, the actual division of total profits between DuPont and DISA was closer to a 50:50 split. In 1959, DISA recognized 48.3% of the total profits, while in 1960, its share climbed to 57.1%. This departure from the original plan was the result of the omission of certain intercorporate transfers—a result not contemplated in the initial pricing scheme. In operation, DISA

than other intercorporate sales, suggesting that such prices could probably be sustained against an IRS challenge. In the spring of 1958, an International Department memorandum stated that the principal advantages of a "profit sanctuary trading company" (dubbed by its initials as a "PST company") depended "largely upon the amount of profits which might be shifted (through selling price) from Du Pont to the 'PST company.'" The report concluded that Du Pont could find "a selling price sufficiently low as to result in the transfer of a substantial part of the profits on export sales to the 'PST company.'" A corporate task force selected Switzerland as the best location for the foreign trading subsidiary, principally because of Swiss tax incentives.

The two industrial departments expected to provide the main source of DISA's sales were not overly enthusiastic about a new layer of company organization. However, both departments agreed to formation of DISA for tax reasons. The Elastomer Department concluded: "The decisive factor in our support of the organization is the potential tax saving." The Textile Fibers Department recognized that tax considerations "will command the establishment of lowest practical transfer prices from the manufacturing subsidiaries to Du Pont Swiss [DISA] * * * " A memorandum to the Executive Committee in late 1958 (shortly before the Committee approved DISA) spoke of the modest mark-up (emphasis in original) of goods sold to the foreign trading subsidiary. A prior draft of the memorandum used the phrase "the 'artificially' low price."

[5]   The individual industrial departments which manufactured goods sold to DISA had little reason to care about the pricing of such goods. Under a special accounting system DISA was ignored in computing departmental earnings, bonuses, etc. All profits from DISA were attributed to the department manufacturing the respective goods. This internal treatment of DISA's profits conflicted with Du Pont's standard practice of treating each subsidiary as a distinct profit center.

[6]   The responsible official did not solicit the views of the manufacturing departments as to an appropriate pricing system.

[7]   Finding 71 summarizes the testimony of the key Treasury Department official, who conceded he would have set prices so as to shift 99 percent of total profits to DISA if he had thought such an allocation would have survived IRS scrutiny.

enjoyed certain market advantages which helped it to accumulate large, tax-free profits. For its technical service function, the subsidiary did not develop its own extensive laboratories (with resulting costs and risks), but could rely on its parent's laboratory network in the United States and England. DISA was not required to hunt intensively (or pay as highly) for qualified personnel, since in both 1959 and 1960 it drew extensively on its parent's reservoir of talent. The international company's credit risks were very low, in part because of a favorable trade credit timetable by Du Pont. DISA also selected its customers to avoid credit losses, having a bad debt provision of less than one-tenth of one percent of sales. Unlike other distributor or advertising service agencies, DISA, because of its special relationship to the Du Pont manufacturing departments, had relatively little risk of termination.[8] And as explained supra, Du Pont's pricing formula was intended to insulate DISA from losses on sales.[9]

E. We have itemized the special status of DISA—as a subsidiary intended and operated to accumulate profits without much regard to the functions it performed or their real worth—not as direct proof, in itself, supporting the Commissioner's reallocation of profits under Section 482, but instead as suggesting the basic reason why plaintiff's sales to DISA were unique and without any direct comparable in the real world. As we shall see in Part II, infra, taxpayer has staked its entire case on proving that the profits made by DISA in 1959 and 1960 were comparable to those made on similar resales by uncontrolled merchandizing agencies. DISA's special status and mode of functioning help to explain why that effort has failed. It is not that there was anything "illegal" or immoral in Du Pont's plan; it is simply that that plan made it very difficult, perhaps impossible, to satisfy the controlling Treasury regulations under Section 482.[10]

---

[8] Du Pont's individual Industrial Departments could terminate sales with DISA, and two smaller departments did terminate. However, there is no evidence that Du Pont as an entity, particularly the important Elastomer and Textile Fiber Departments, would have seriously considered terminating DISA, a child of their own creation. Further, any such termination would have imposed less financial risk to DISA than for an independent distributor.

[9] In operating DISA, Du Pont also maximized its subsidiary's income by funneling a large volume of sales through DISA which did not call for large expenditures by the latter. Many of the products Du Pont sold through DISA required no special services, or already had ample technical services provided. Du Pont routed sales to Australia and South Africa through DISA although the latter provided no additional services to sales in these non-European countries. DISA made sales of commodity-type products and opportunistic spot sales to competitors temporarily short in a raw material, although neither type of sale required DISA's specialized marketing expertise. Du Pont also routed all European sales of elastomers through DISA, even though the parent had a well-established English subsidiary which had all the necessary technical services and marketing ability.

[10] The regulations make it clear (§ 1.482–1(c)) that they apply, not only to sham, fraudulent, or shady cases, but "to any case in which either by inadvertence or design the taxable

II. Section 482 and the "Resale Price Method" of Allocating Profits.

A. Section 482 gives the Secretary of the Treasury (or his delegate) discretion to allocate income between related corporations when necessary to "prevent evasion of taxes or clearly to reflect the income" of any of such corporations. The legislative history parallels the general purpose of the statutory text to prevent evasion by "improper manipulation of financial accounts", "arbitrary shifting of profits," and to accurately reflect "true tax liability." . . . The overall aim is to enable the IRS to treat controlled taxpayers as if they were uncontrolled. . . .

B. We do not, however, have the initial problem of considering this case on the words of Section 482 alone, or on comparable broad criteria. In 1968 the Secretary of the Treasury issued revised regulations governing action under the statute, and setting forth rules for certain specific situations. Treas. Reg. § 1.482–1, et seq. These regulations, which were issued before the trial here, were made retroactive to cover the taxable years before us (1959–1960), and both sides agree that the regulations must control. In some quarters these regulations have been faulted as not giving enough meaningful guidance in specific situations, or as being too narrow in the specific situations they do cover, but there is here no challenge to the validity of the regulations and we have to apply them as they are, with fidelity to both their words and their spirit.

For sales of tangible goods, the directive mandates determination of an arm's length price for the sale by one controlled entity to the other, and then sets out (in order of preference) four methods for calculating such an arm's length price: the comparable uncontrolled price method, the resale price method, the cost plus method, and any other appropriate method. The parties correctly agree upon the inapplicability of the comparable uncontrolled price method (which calls for comparison with an uncontrolled sale of an almost identical product). Plaintiff makes no argument as to the possible application of the cost plus method. Instead it posits its whole case on the resale price method (Treas. Reg. § 1.482–2(e)(3))— which we now consider.

C. Essentially, the resale price method reconstructs a fair arm's length market price by discounting the controlled reseller's selling price by the gross profit margin (or markup percentage) rates of comparable uncontrolled dealers. Thus, if DISA's gross profit margin for resale was 35% and the prevailing margin for comparable uncontrolled resellers was 25%, the Commissioner

---

income, in whole or in part, of a controlled taxpayer, is other than it would have been had the taxpayer in the conduct of his affairs been an uncontrolled taxpayer dealing at arm's length with another uncontrolled taxpayer."

could reallocate 10% of DISA's gross income. But the vital prerequisite for applying the resale price method is the existence of substantially comparable uncontrolled resellers. Subpart (vi) of Section 1.482–2(e)(3) requires determination of the "most similar" resale or resales, considering the type of property, reseller's functions, use of any intangibles, and similarity of geographic markets. Cases which have considered the regulation uniformly require substantial comparability. . . . Commentators agree on the need for close similarity of uncontrolled sales, and some criticize the regulation when no uncontrolled sales by the same party exist. . . . It is quite plain from the text of the regulation itself that the evident purpose for the use of the particular resale price method, as set forth in the regulation, is to proffer a relatively precise mechanism for determining a realistically comparable, uncontrolled, arm's-length resale price—not to leave the taxpayer, the Service, or the courts to grope at large for some figure drawn out of overly general indices or statistics.

The common starting point for our search in this case for a comparable meeting the requirements of the regulation is our finding 101 which states: "The parties agree, and their agreement is supported by the record, that there is not known to exist, presently or heretofore, an independent organization circumstanced as DISA was during the period in suit and performing the marketing functions that were assigned to it by plaintiff." That being so, the regulation requires us (§ 1.482–2(e)(3)(vi)(a), (b), and (d)) to look for the "most similar" resales and "in determining the similarity of resales" to consider as the "most important characteristics" the type of property sold, the functions performed by the seller with respect to the property, and the geographic market in which the functions are performed by the reseller. There is also special stress on the performance of "comparable functions" by the seller making the "most similar" resales. See Subpart (vii).

Taxpayer tells us that a group of 21 distributors, whose general functions were similar to DISA's, provides the proper base of comparison. Beyond the most general showing that this group, like DISA, distributed manufactured goods, there is nothing in the record showing the degree of similarity called for by the regulation. No data exist to establish similarity of products (with associated marketing costs), comparability of functions, or parallel geographic (and economic) market conditions. Rather, the record suggests significant differences. Defendant has introduced evidence that the six companies plaintiff identifies most closely with DISA all had average selling costs much higher than DISA. Because we agree with the trial judge and defendant's expert that, in general, what a business spends to provide services is a reasonable indication of the magnitude of those services, and because plaintiff has not rebutted that normal presumption in this case, we cannot view these six companies as having made resales similar to DISA's. They may have made gross profits comparable to DISA's but their selling costs, reflecting the greater scale of their services or efforts, were much higher in each instance. Moreover, the record shows that these companies dealt with quite different products (electronic and photographic equipment) and functioned in different markets (primarily the United States).

Other industrial group or individual resales relied on by taxpayer also fall short of comparability to DISA. We are cited to the gross profit margin of certain drug and chemical wholesalers contained in the Internal Revenue Service's Source Book of Statistics of Income for 1960. Because the gross profit for this group of undisclosed companies in 1960 averaged 21 percent, taxpayer infers that DISA's gross profit of 26 percent was reasonable. Again, the lack of any data establishing comparability between DISA and the category of Source Book companies precludes any such conclusion. The fact that, within the wholesaler category, gross profits varied from 9 to 33 percent indicates that to take a mere arithmetic average, without considering underlying factual details, would risk a total distortion. . . . Plaintiff tells us that the IRS itself used these Source Book figures for 1960 and later years (not now before us). But the Service utilized net profit figures, not those for gross profit or gross markup. Whether or not this use of net profit computations contravened the regulations (which call for comparisons of gross profits in using the resale price method) or means that the IRS was following the "fourth method" (see Part III infra), we cannot say, as plaintiff wants us to, that the Service must have considered these drug and chemical wholesalers as comparable companies making similar resales, but that the IRS simply made a mistake in using net profits. The little we have on the IRS practice does not permit us to conclude anything as to the Service's position on comparability of these companies for the purposes of the resale price method.

The lack of any significantly comparable resale (or group of resales) in this record is underscored by taxpayer's failure to suggest any means for adjusting for differences between DISA and the uncontrolled resellers. Subpart (ix) of section 1.482–2(e)(3) requires "appropriate adjustment" for "any material differences between the uncontrolled purchases and resales used as the basis for the calculation of the appropriate markup percentage and the resales of property involved in the controlled sale." Such material differences must be "differences in functions or circumstances" and must have a "definite and reasonably ascertainable effect on price." The trial judge premised his rejection of plaintiff's case on the failure to suggest appropriate adjustments under this subpart, particularly for DISA's lack of "entrepreneurial risk." Taxpayer mounts a vigorous assault on this position, arguing that DISA was exposed to all normal risks, including shipping and warehouse risks, sudden European market declines, or termination by manufacturing departments of Du Pont. Even if we assume arguendo that DISA did assume full market risks,[21] we think taxpayer cannot escape the ultimate point of subpart (ix)— assuming a roughly comparable uncontrolled reseller (or resellers), taxpayer still bears the burden of showing adjustments to arrive at an arm's length price. However, plaintiff proposes no adjustments for differences in marketing locations, selling functions, or production differences between DISA and the "comparable" 21 distributors. Taxpayer's brief selects one of the distributors, Superscope, as the company "most similar in function" to DISA, but fails to suggest the appropriate adjustments for such aspects as Superscope's different product line (tape recorders), different geographic market (the United States), or contractual obligation to make minimum purchases from the manufacturer.

This failure to proffer adjustments reflects the stark fact that, on this record, there is no company or group of companies so near and so comparable to DISA that the few material differences can be properly adjusted for under the regulatory pattern. Subpart (ix) and the example given under it (the same reseller selling two very similar products with only a difference in warranty coverage between the controlled and uncontrolled transactions) reinforce the view that under the resale price method the resales of uncontrolled companies must be substantially similar to those of the controlled reseller before that method can be used. And even if there is greater initial latitude in finding a comparable reseller than seems to us appropriate, subpart (ix) demands "appropriate adjustment * * * to reflect any material differences" which "have a definite and reasonably ascertainable effect on price." Plaintiff, which urges that the resale price method be used, bears the burden of fulfilling all the requirements of the regulation, but has failed to do so.

---

[21] This is not an easy assumption to accept, since Du Pont's pricing system for DISA was designed to protect the latter from losses, and DISA's operations seemed geared to help it make profits with little risk. See Part I, supra. Furthermore, the risk of complete termination by the parent which established and operated DISA for a number of particular purposes (including profit accumulation), seems substantially less than that of a wholly independent distributor.

Plaintiff contends, finally, that requiring it to prove the proper amount of adjustment is an unfair burden. The suggestion is that once Du Pont shows that its prices were arm's length prices (by demonstrating that DISA's gross profit margin was equivalent to that of uncontrolled distributors) any further readjustment should be left to the courts (or perhaps defendant). Our first response is, as we have said above, that taxpayer has not shown that, even apart from subpart (ix), any of its alleged comparables can be accepted as such under the resale price method portion of the regulation. And if we surmount that hurdle, we see no good reason why a taxpayer should be free from suggesting the appropriate adjustments under subpart (ix). As the opening words of the paragraph show, the adjustments called for by the subpart are integral to the determination of an "arm's length price," and the determination of an "arm's length price" is the essence of the resale price method which plaintiff invokes.

D. The upshot is that plaintiff has failed to bring itself within the resale price method. The record before us does not support use of that formula for this case.[24] Indeed, it may very well be that, because of DISA's unique position, the showing required by the regulation could simply not be made. At any rate, we have to conclude that, on this record, it is not possible to apply the resale price method.

As we have intimated in Part I, D, supra, this total failure of proof is no surprise. Taxpayer's prices to DISA were set wholly without regard to the factors which normally enter into an arm's length price (see Part I, C, supra), and it would have been pure happenstance if those prices had turned out to be equivalent to arm's length prices. This is not a case in which a taxpayer does attempt, the best it can, to establish intercorporate prices on an arm's length basis, and then runs up against an IRS which disagrees with this or that detail in the calculation. Plaintiff never made that effort, and it would have been undiluted luck—which under the regulation it probably could enjoy—if it had managed to discover comparable resales falling within the resale price method as set forth in the regulation (including adjustments to be made under subpart (ix)).

---

[24] Defendant says, somewhat weakly, that, although plaintiff made insufficient proof, the Government itself presented adequate evidence to comply with the resale price method by using as comparables Du Pont's independent distributors in Europe (to whom DISA resold)—and whose markup margins were normally much less than DISA's. But these "comparables" were not shown to be similar to DISA, which performed many other functions, and no effort was made by defendant to adjust upward for the differences. Therefore, we do not believe that the evidence as to the margin of these independent resellers enables us to apply the resale price method here.

III. Validity of the Commissioner's Allocation under the Regulation

In reviewing the Commissioner's allocation of income under Section 482, we focus on the reasonableness of the result, not the details of the examining agent's methodology. . . . Plaintiff contends that the Commissioner's result does not conform to any of the specific methods under the regulations and is therefore unreasonable per se. But the regulations (§ 1.482–2(e)(1)(iii)) specifically allow for another appropriate method—"some appropriate method of pricing other than those described * * * or variations on such methods"—when, as here, none of the three specific methods can properly be used. That alternative "fourth method" now comes into play, and we consider the reasonableness of the Commissioner's result under its very broad delegation. This other "appropriate method of pricing" must, of course, be consistent: "to place a controlled taxpayer on a tax parity with an uncontrolled taxpayer" and "in every case" to apply the standard "of an uncontrolled taxpayer dealing at arm's length with another uncontrolled taxpayer." See § 1.482–1(b)(1) and (c).

That some reallocation was reasonable is demonstrated by recalling the facts of DISA's operation. See Part I, supra. . . .

The amount of reallocation would not be easy for us to calculate if we were called upon to do it ourselves, but Section 482 gives that power to the Commissioner and we are content that his amount (totaling some $18 million) was within the zone of reasonableness. The language of the statute and the holdings of the courts recognize that the Service has broad discretion in reallocating income. . . . See, e.g., Eli Lilly & Co. v. United States, 178 Ct. Cl. Once past the three specific methods for computing intercompany prices of tangible property, the determiner of realistic intercompany prices is hardly exercising an economic art susceptible of precision. A "broad brush" approach to this inexact field seems necessary and conforms with this court's experience up to now under the Renegotiation Act, requiring post hoc and de novo determination of excessive profits on war and defense Government business. . . . Du Pont has not convinced us, on this record, that the Commissioner abused the broad discretion he possessed (the specific methods being inapplicable), or that he acted unreasonably.

. . .

NOTES AND QUESTIONS

1.   *Du Pont* is a classic for several reasons. First, the case (which took the government twenty years to win!) was a substantial incentive for enacting Subpart F, which at the time was seen as a very sharp departure from traditional principles of tax jurisdiction. That is because, in effect, it taxed the foreign source income of foreign corporations solely because they were controlled from the United States. Under current law, DISA's income would have been "foreign base company sales income" and taxed to Du Pont under Subpart F. See Ch. 7 below. Therefore, simply interposing a tax-haven

subsidiary and playing the transfer pricing game with it is not presently possible.

2. Secondly, *Du Pont* represents a classical tax planning technique of "breaking" a transaction into more than one segment and "channeling" it through a potentially unnecessary related entity. This is the fundamental story of some transfer pricing planning, as well as Subpart F planning, which was recently invigorated by the "check-the-box" regime. The use of a foreign regional (European, for instance) headquarter through which all transactions are channeled became standard for MNEs after the enactment of the "check-the-box" regime. Remind yourself why is it so? Do transfer pricing and "check-the-box" planning complement or collide with each other?

3. Finally, and most importantly for our purposes, *Du Pont* is a classic because it is the last major case which was completely won by the IRS. Clearly, one reason for the government's victory was the various "smoking guns" it discovered, as cited in Footnote 4, which may be the key for the decision in this case. What do you think about the ethical implications of those memoranda? Does section 482 require evidence of intent to misprice? Why might such evidence still be helpful?

4. In subsequent cases under section 482, no "smoking guns" were found. Why? Note that all subsequent cases (and there are many) were either won by the taxpayer or split. Read also sections 6662(e) & (h) that were enacted after *Du Pont*. How do you think they contributed to this phenomenon?

5. Why was it not possible to find comparables? It has been argued that one reason multinationals exist is to save taxes (see note 7 below). How does this relate to the facts of *Du Pont*?

6. If it is hard to find comparables, what do you think about the section 482 Treasury Regulations (particularly review Treas. Reg. 1.482–1(b)(1), 1.482–1(c)(2)(i) & 1.482–1(d))? A GAO study from 1981 found that of 403 transfer pricing cases it studied, direct comparables were found in only 3%. A Treasury study from 1988 reported that in 91% of the cases, the taxpayers did not use comparables in establishing transfer prices. The IRS used "fourth methods" (any "other" appropriate method . . .) in almost half the cases it audited.

Given the difficulty in determining arm's length pricing in many cases, the IRS instituted a program in 1991, the Advance Pricing Program, in which taxpayers could voluntarily approach the IRS to discuss the pricing of their related party transactions prior to executing those transactions. Under the program if the IRS and taxpayer reach agreement on the appropriate approach and method for pricing the transactions (but not the specific price) then they enter into an agreement outlining that approach. Assuming the taxpayer complies with the terms of the agreement, the IRS agrees to respect the resulting prices on audit. An added advantage of the APA program is the opportunity to reach agreement with not only the U.S. but also one or more other countries involved in the transactions. Why would this be a valuable opportunity?

7. Note the process of choosing the "best method" (as required by the regulations—see Treas. Reg. 1.482–1(c) & 1.482–8) in this case and the (failed) application of the "Resale Price Method" (skim Treas. Reg. 1.482–3(c)).

8.   Other than saving taxes, there may be another reason why comparables do not exist. As noted by one of the authors:

> Moreover, the very existence of integrated multinationals is evidence that the [arm's length standard] does not reflect economic reality. The predominant explanation for the existence of multinationals is the internalization theory which posits that, like any organization, multinationals exist because of market and non-market advantages that are derived from their structure. The multinational's structure allows it to avoid (internalize) transaction costs, which increases efficiency in raising capital, advertising products, achieving economies of scale, and protecting valuable intangibles. Thus, if one applies a market rate of return separately to each of the components of the multinational, the result is less than the actual return of the organization as a whole. This residual, the result of the interaction among the constituent parts of the organization, cannot be assigned to any component. Any transfer pricing rule which arbitrarily assigns the residual to one part of the organization distorts economic reality. No single correct transfer price exists in this situation; instead, there is a continuum which depends on how the residual is split among the parties, and any price on this continuum is correct.

> The implications of this "continuum price problem," as it is called in the economic literature, are profound. If comparables can be found, that fact indicates the multinational does not derive a large residual return from its structure because otherwise it could have driven its competitors out of the market. Thus, in these cases it would be possible to use functional analysis without having a comparable. On the other hand, where comparables cannot be found, such as in the majority of complex transfer pricing cases, that fact indicates a large residual is likely, and this residual advantage of the multinational has driven competitors out of the market. Thus, precisely in those situations arising in the majority of transfer pricing cases, where there are no comparables and therefore functional analysis is required, it will be impossible to find the "right" transfer price. Even if one performs a functional analysis based on the market returns of all the components of the multinational, a large residual will remain to be split arbitrarily among the parties. The IRS will seek to allocate all the residual to one party, the taxpayer to another, and it is likely some of it will not be taxed by any jurisdiction.

Avi-Yonah, "The Rise and Fall of Arm's Length: A Study in the Evolution of U.S. International Taxation," 15 Va. Tax Rev. 89, 148–49 (1995).

What does this imply for the chances of correctly resolving transfer pricing disputes under section 482?

6.3   THE PROBLEM OF COMPARABLES

The next case follows on this last point. Think about it as you read how U.S. Steel succeeded in taking advantage of the distorted economics behind the comparables rules.

United States Steel Corporation v. Commissioner of Internal Revenue

United States Court of Appeals, Second Circuit.
617 F.2d 942 (1980).

. . .

■ JUDGES: Before LUMBARD, MESKILL and NEWMAN, CIRCUIT JUDGES.

This consolidated appeal from two decisions of the Tax Court, Quealy, J., arises out of the development by United States Steel Corporation ("Steel") of newly discovered Venezuelan iron mines in the 1950's, and the financial arrangements resulting from the creation of two Steel subsidiaries to mine and transport ore. Two distinct questions of tax law are presented: first, what kind of evidence is sufficient for a taxpayer to challenge successfully the Commissioner's determination that payments between a parent and a subsidiary are not "arm's length" and thus are subject to reallocation under § 482 of the Internal Revenue Code. . . .

We find that the Tax Court, in the first case, T.C. Memo. 1977–140, did not give sufficient weight to the taxpayer's evidence supporting its contention that charges between the taxpayer and its subsidiary were arm's length, and for that reason we reverse the judgment of the Tax Court sustaining, with modifications, the Commissioner's reallocation of income. . . .

I

The Reallocation Issue

Taxpayer, United States Steel Corporation, is a major vertically integrated producer of steel. In addition to steel-making plants, it owns iron ore mines in the United States and elsewhere. In 1947, Steel discovered a vast new source of iron ore in Cerro Bolivar, a remote part of northeastern Venezuela on the Orinoco River. The transport of Orinoco ore to the Atlantic required the dredging of an extensive channel. Steel proceeded to develop these mines at a cost of approximately two hundred million dollars. In 1949, Steel formed Orinoco Mining Company ("Orinoco"), a wholly-owned Delaware subsidiary, to own and exploit the Cerro Bolivar mines.

Orinoco began selling ore from its mines in 1953. Initially, the ore purchased by Steel from Orinoco was transported to the United States in chartered vessels owned by two independent companies, Universe Tankships, Inc., ("Universe") and Joshua Hendy Corp. ("Hendy"). But in December 1953, Steel incorporated another wholly-owned subsidiary, Navios, Inc., ("Navios") in Liberia. Navios, with its principal place of business in Nassau, in the Bahamas, was a carrier which did not own any vessels. From July 1954 on, Navios, instead of Steel, chartered vessels from Universe, Hendy, and other owners, and Steel paid Navios for the transport of ore from Venezuela to the United States. Navios was an active company, having in the period 1954–60 between 53 and 81 fulltime employees.

Although Steel was by far the largest customer of Navios, Navios sold its transport services to other domestic steel producers (collectively "the independents") and to foreign steel companies. The prices charged by Navios to other domestic ore importers during the relevant period were the same prices charged to Steel, though the rates charged to companies importing ore to countries other than the United States were different.

Like Navios, Orinoco did not sell exclusively to Steel, although its parent was by far its largest customer. Orinoco sold to the independents and to foreign steel companies at the same prices it charged Steel.

Orinoco sold ore bound for the United States FOB Puerto Ordaz, Venezuela in an attempt to arrive at a fair market price in order to minimize conflict with the Venezuelan taxing authorities, who had the power to revalue, for taxation purposes, the price at which Orinoco sold its ore if they considered that price too low. United States prices of iron ore were set, during the period in question, by an annual auction of ore from the Mesabi range of Minnesota, which established the so-called "Lower Lake Erie" price. Through its subsidiary Oliver Mining Co., Steel sold significant amounts of Mesabi ore.

Orinoco was subject to a Venezuelan tax of up to 50% on income, and to a United States tax of 48% on any residue not offset by foreign tax credits. Steel was subject to a United States tax of 48% of net income. Navios was subject to a 2.5% excise tax in Venezuela and no tax in the United States. Dividends paid by Navios to Steel, of course, would be taxed at a rate of 48%.

Navios was a highly successful venture: Steel found itself in 1960 with a wholly-owned subsidiary possessing nearly $80 million in cash and cash equivalents. Navios paid no dividends to Steel during the period involved in this case. In effect, then, Navios became an offshore tax shelter. But, as the Tax Court found, Steel's decision to create Navios is not in itself a justification for the Commissioner's reallocation of income, since Navios served a major business purpose unrelated to tax-shifting: allowing Steel to reap the cost savings of using a non-United States-flag fleet.

In the tax years 1957 through 1960, Navios earned approximately $391 million in gross revenues, all on the transport of iron ore from Venezuela to various points in the eastern continental United States and in Europe. Of this total, revenues from Steel amounted to $286 million, or 73% of the total; and from independent domestic steel purchasers $21 million, or 5% of the total. . . .

During 1957–60, there was no information publicly available from which a "market price" for the carriage of iron ore by sea could be determined. Unlike the practice in the oil tanker industry, for example, ship charter contract prices for ore carriage were not published.

The Commissioner determined that Navios had overcharged Steel by 25%. . . .

The Tax Court reviewed the history of Steel's relations with its subsidiaries Navios and Orinoco and concluded that a § 482 reallocation was justified because Steel had caused Navios to charge rates such that, at all times, the delivered price of Orinoco-origin ore in the United States was equivalent of the Lower Lake Erie price. In the Tax Court's view, this equivalence served several purposes. First, it protected Steel's interest in the revenues of its subsidiary, Oliver Mining Co., by insuring that the Lower Lake Erie price was not undercut by cheaper foreign ore. Second, because Steel could be sure of selling its Orinoco production so long as the delivered United States price did not exceed the Lower Lake Erie price, it enabled Steel to earn "extra" profits. Third, such extra profits, because they were earned through Navios, were not subject to Venezuelan tax and were sheltered from United States tax.

Judge Quealy then reviewed the figures used by the Commissioner in his reallocation. The Commissioner had used an approach that looked to profits and determined that a certain percentage of Navios' profits was in excess of what would fairly reflect income. Judge Quealy, by contrast, used two alternative means of arriving at what Navios' revenues would have been had it charged a "market" price for its services. First, he extrapolated hypothetical rates for 1957–60 from what Universe and Hendy charged in their 1954 contracts with Steel, adding adjustments to account for increased costs, risk and profits. As a check on the accuracy of this historical approach, Judge Quealy also constructed hypothetical rates based on estimates of what Navios' costs had been in the taxable years in question, adjusting these estimates to allow for risk and profit. He then chose the method which, for each taxable year, would result in the lowest reallocation in favor of the government.

We are constrained to reverse because, in our view, the Commissioner has failed to justify reallocation under the broad language of section 482 . . . The Treasury Regulations provide a guide for interpreting this section's broad delegation of power to the Secretary, and they are binding on the Commissioner. Treas. Reg. 1.482–1(b) states in part that "(t)he standard to be applied in every (§ 482) case is that of an uncontrolled taxpayer dealing at arm's length with another uncontrolled taxpayer." This "arm's length" standard is repeated in Treas. Reg. 1.482–1(c), and this subsection makes it clear that it is meant to be an objective standard that does not depend on the absence or presence of any intent on the part of the taxpayer to distort his income.

§ 482
standard.

Treasury Reg. 1.482–2(b) governs the situation presented by the case at bar, in which a controlled corporation performs a service for a controlling corporation allegedly "at a charge which is not equal to an arm's length charge as defined in subparagraph (3) of this paragraph."

Subparagraph (3) defines an arm's length charge for a service which is an integral part of the business of the corporation providing it as "the amount which was charged or would have been charged for the same or similar services in independent transactions with or between unrelated parties under similar circumstances considering all relevant facts."

We think it is clear that if a taxpayer can show that the price he paid or was charged for a service is "the amount which was charged or would have been charged for the same or similar services in independent transactions with or between unrelated parties" it has earned the right, under the Regulations, to be free from a § 482 reallocation despite other evidence tending to show that its activities have resulted in a shifting of tax liability among controlled corporations. Where, as in this case, the taxpayer offers evidence that the same amount was actually charged for the same service in transactions with independent buyers, the question resolves itself into an evaluation of whether or not the circumstances of the sales to independent buyers are "similar" enough to sales to the controlling corporation under the circumstances, "considering all relevant facts." In our view, "considering all the relevant facts," the evidence was sufficient to show similar enough transactions with independent buyers to establish that the price Steel paid Navios was an arm's length price.

The evidence referred to above consists of Steel's uncontested showing that the amounts Steel paid Navios for ore transport were the same rates paid by other independent purchasers of Orinoco ore. The Commissioner argues that the payment of the same rates by Steel and by independent buyers does not alone show, "considering all the relevant facts", that Steel paid an arm's length price.

Judge Quealy found that although purchasers of Orinoco ore were not required to use Navios' transport services, "most purchasers would not be in a position to contract independently for transportation of the ore to the site of their mills." (T.C. Memo. 1977–140 at 62). But, as we have stated above, two steel companies, Bethlehem Steel and Eastern Fuel and Gas, did make such independent arrangements. Bethlehem was a large corporation with financial resources comparable to those of Steel, but Eastern was a relatively small company whose ability to do without Navios is persuasive evidence that Judge Quealy's reliance on the notion that independent steel buyers were somehow forced to use Navios out of economic necessity was misplaced.

... These figures show that the shipments of Orinoco ore to independent American buyers represented a series of transactions substantial in both frequency and volume. Although Steel's shipments were larger, transactions on the order of the carriage of 100,000 tons of ore (for which Navios would have charged approximately $1 million) cannot be dismissed as an arrangement a company would make without some attention to the possibility of securing more favorable terms. Nor can purchasers like Pittsburgh Steel, Sharon Steel, Jones & Laughlin and Youngstown Sheet & Tube be considered commercially unsophisticated or incapable of bearing the costs of seeking lower rates. It is true, as the Commissioner points out, that none of the independent domestic purchasers bought enough in one year to fill one of the very largest ore carriers chartered by Navios, but Navios also chartered smaller vessels, down to 20,000 ton capacity, and thus any argument that the independents were forced, in effect, to pool their transport requirements is untenable.

In sum, the record shows that over four years' time half a dozen large corporations chose to use the services of Navios despite the fact that they were not compelled to do so. In such circumstances, we think the taxpayer has met its burden of showing that the fees it paid (which were identical to those paid by the independents) were arm's length prices. We do not say that, had different or additional facts been developed, the Commissioner could not have countered the taxpayer's showing and sustained the validity of his reallocation. Such a counter-showing would have required evidence that Navios' charges, although freely paid by other, independent buyers, deviated from a market price that the Commissioner could have proved existed for example, if worldwide ore-shipping contracts had been recorded and published during the period in question.

The Commissioner also argues that the fact that Steel paid the same rates as the independents is itself sufficient evidence that Steel was overcharged. The reasoning behind this counter-intuitive argument is that, in essence, Steel's relationship to Navios was that of a long-term charterer while the independents were short-term charterers; and that it is axiomatic that a long-term charterer pays a lower annual rate than a short-term charterer, because a shipowner prefers the freedom from market vicissitudes offered by a long-term charter. We are not persuaded by this line of argument. The shipowner who locks himself into a long-term charter bears the risk that charter rates will go up. Moreover, Steel's relationship to Navios was not that of charterer at all; Navios chartered ships from Universe and Hendy, and Steel purchased Navios's services as a carrier. Thus the Commissioner's analogy is not persuasive.

The Commissioner also points out that some of the Orinoco ore was shipped to Great Britain; but that although the distance from Venezuela to Great Britain is, on the average, 54% greater than the distance to the United States, the rates charged by Navios were not 54% higher than the Venezuela-to-United States rates. We do not view this as persuasive. First, there is nothing in the record to support the premise of the Commissioner's argument that charter rates are or should be an arithmetical multiple of distance traversed, nor is there any expert evidence as to the additional marginal cost of transport to Britain. The British rates are therefore of only speculative relevance to this case. Second, it may be, as the Commissioner suggests, that Navios was constrained to set lower rates for its European customers than for its

American customers because the effective ceiling on the price of delivered ore in Europe was set by the price of Swedish ore, while the effective American ceiling was set by the Lower Lake Erie price. If the former was lower than the latter, shipping rates to Europe might have to be reduced. But the fact that sellers of ore, providers of ore transport, and ore buyers were all influenced by the price of a competing product does not mean that a price is not an arm's length price.

There is, however, a more sophisticated version of this argument which is entitled to scrutiny. Assume that an unrelated carrier would charge, as its Venezuela-U.S. rate, an amount which, when added to the price of Orinoco ore sold FOB, equaled the Lower Lake Erie price. Assuming further common ownership of Navios and Steel, but not of Orinoco, no case could be made out that Navios' rates were not arm's length, because for economic reasons unrelated to common ownership the price the carrier charged was the price any carrier would have charged and thus the price that would have been arrived at in a transaction between unrelated buyers and sellers. But add to this the fact that Steel also controlled Orinoco and therefore could reduce the price of Orinoco ore in order to increase Navios' share. The resulting price for Navios' services Lower Lake Erie price minus Orinoco FOB price would not be an arm's length price because it would have been affected by Steel's ownership of Orinoco, though not by Steel's ownership of Navios.

Attractive as this argument is in the abstract, it is a distortion of the kind of inquiry the Regulations direct us to undertake. The Regulations make it clear that if the taxpayer can show that the amount it paid was equal to "the amount which was charged . . . for the same or similar services in independent transactions" he can defeat the Commissioner's effort to invoke § 482 against him. The amount paid for Navios' services by Sharon Steel, Youngstown Sheet & Tube and other corporations was the same price paid by Steel. The only question, then, is whether the transactions were "independent."

We think that "independent" in this context must be viewed in contrast to the concept of joint ownership or control that is at the core of § 482. The transactions between Navios and Jones & Laughlin, Sharon and Youngstown were "independent" in that Steel had no ownership or control interest in any of these firms and thus was not in a position to influence their decision to deal with Navios. To expand the test of "independence" to require more than this, to require that the transaction be one unaffected by the market power of the taxpayer, would be to inject antitrust concerns into a tax statute. But in § 482, a tax statute, it is appropriate to limit the concept of what is not "independent" to actions influenced by common ownership or control.

We do not think that in order so to hold it must be shown that Navios' prices were the result of a perfectly competitive market. Prices arrived at by independent buyers and sellers in arm's length transactions may vary from such a perfect market price depending on factors extraneous to § 482.

Of course, in some markets, all "arm's length" transactions would occur at truly competitive prices. But the more imperfect the market, the more likely it is that "arm's length" transactions will take place at prices which are not perfect market prices. To use § 482 to require a taxpayer to achieve greater fidelity to abstract notions of a perfect market than is possible for actual non-affiliated buyers and sellers to achieve would be unfair. Thus, for example, Judge Quealy's reliance on the fact that Bethlehem did not use Navios' services ("Presumably, Bethlehem found that it could do the job for less." T.C. Memo. 1977–140 at 68.) even if correct factually, is irrelevant. The fact that transactions take place in the market place at different price levels does not, by itself, prove that transactions between unrelated buyers and sellers, such as Navios and Jones & Laughlin are not at "arm's length." The Regulations say that "independent transactions with or between unrelated parties" are enough to insulate a taxpayer's price from § 482. We decline to use the "all relevant facts" clause to transform this limited approach into a requirement that the taxpayer's price be the result of a perfectly competitive market.

Nor does the statute require that all independent transactions be at the price taxpayer charged or paid; therefore, the fact that Orinoco ore bought by Bethlehem Steel was transported to the United States at rates different from what Navios charged Steel and other customers is irrelevant. Since there were independent transactions significant in number and dollar amount and occurring over a long period of time, we need not address the question of how many such "independent transactions" at the taxpayer's price would be needed to insulate taxpayer from § 482 in a situation where a preponderance of the "independent" transactions take place at a price far different from the price paid or charged by taxpayer.

In at least one portion of Judge Quealy's opinion, however, it appears that the reason he relied upon to hold Navios' charges too high is not at all a matter involving the comparison of rates Steel paid to those paid by other steel companies. He said that what the rates paid by Steel must be measured against in order to see if a § 482 reallocation is justified is "what might be a reasonable charge for a continuing relationship involving the transportation of more than 10 million tons of iron ore per year." Jt. App. at 69. If this is indeed the inquiry, then the fact that other steel companies paid Navios the same rates Steel did is irrelevant. Judge Quealy explicitly recognized this:

The comparability tests in the regulations cannot be relied on because the transportation of iron ore on the basis proposed by the petitioner and Navios had never been done previously. There could be no "independent transactions with unrelated parties under the same or similar circumstances" within the meaning of section 1.482–1(d)(3) of the regulations. Jt.App. at 69–70.

We are constrained to reject this argument. Although certain factors make the operations undertaken by Navios for Steel unique (at one point, for example, Navios' ore-carriers were the largest of their kind in the world) the approach taken by the Tax Court would lead to a highly undesirable uncertainty if accepted.[11] In very few industries are transactions truly comparable in the strict sense used by Judge Quealy. Every transaction in wheat, for example, is more or less the same, except for standard variations in amount, time of delivery and place of delivery. But few products or services are as fungible as wheat. To say that Pittsburgh Steel was buying a service from Navios with one set of expectations about duration and risk, and Steel another, may be to recognize economic reality; but it is also to engraft a crippling degree of economic sophistication onto a broadly drawn statute, which if "comparable" is taken to mean "identical", as Judge Quealy would read it would allow the taxpayer no safe harbor from the Commissioner's virtually unrestricted discretion to reallocate.

NOTES AND QUESTIONS

1. Why do you think Judge Quealy did not think the comparables were comparable? What is the relevance of differences in (a) volume, (b) risk, and (c) Steel's control of Orinoco? Think about the differences between the case of Navios and "Export" in the *U.S. Gypsum* case.

2. If you were a decision maker in *U.S. Steel*, would you be willing to discount the shipping rates charged by Navios to your competitors below an otherwise accepted "market rate"? Why, and what does this tell us about comparables?

3. If Steel had a de facto monopoly and the operations of Navios were "unique", was this "economic reality" irrelevant? Does comparable have to mean identical under Judge Quealy's approach?

4. Part of the dispute was over services—the shipping services provided by Navios. Think about the difficulty of determining transfer prices for services in comparison to sales of ore, for instance. Did this difficulty play a major role in this case? We will elaborate on the transfer pricing rules regarding services in section 6.4 below.

5. In Bausch & Lomb v. Commissioner, 92 T.C. 525 (1989), the taxpayer licensed its unique process for manufacturing soft contact lenses to an Irish tax haven manufacturer. The Irish subsidiary manufactured the lenses for $1.50 each and sold them to the taxpayer for $7.50 each—the same price

---

[11] In addition to the resultant uncertainty as to whether or not the Commissioner would be justified in making an allocation, there is the second level of uncertainty present in all § 482 cases governed by a standard as general as that of "arm's length" transactions of how much of a reallocation the Commissioner will be entitled to. We need not criticize or endorse the calculating methods employed by either the Commissioner or the Tax Court in order to make this point; it is sufficient to point out that the Commissioner arrived at a total reallocation of $52 million, while the Tax Court arrived at a total of $25 million.

charged by unrelated parties with much higher manufacturing costs for the same products. The IRS reallocated the income to give the subsidiary its costs plus a 20% profit. The Tax Court, in an 86 page long opinion, reversed, relying on *U.S. Steel* to find that—

To posit that B & L, the world's largest manufacturer of soft contact lenses, would be able to secure a more favorable price from an independent manufacturer who hoped to establish a long-term relationship with a high volume customer may be to recognize economic reality, but to do so would cripple a taxpayer's ability to rely on the comparable uncontrolled price method in establishing transfer pricing by introducing to it a degree of economic sophistication which appears reasonable in theory, but which defies quantification in practice. 92 T.C. at 589–91.

Think, how would a court go about determining the correct price if it rejects both the taxpayer's and the IRS' positions?

6. The Second Circuit affirmed Bausch & Lomb v. Commissioner, 933 F.2d 1084 (1991), stating that—

The position urged by the Commissioner would preclude comparability precisely because the relationship between B & L and B & L Ireland was different from that between independent buyers and sellers operating at arm's length. This, however, will always be the case when transactions between commonly controlled entities are compared to transactions between independent entities. 933 F.2d, at 1091.

What are the implications for the arm's length standard? What are the efficiency implications of this judiciary insistence—who are the "winners" and "losers" from this rule?

7. The 1994 regulations under Section 482 attempt to reverse the result in *U.S. Steel* and *Bausch & Lomb* by requiring a much higher standard of comparability for the application of the comparable uncontrolled price method. When, if ever, do you think this method will apply? (read Treas. Reg. 1.482–3(b) & 1.482–4(c) [the latter refers to the comparable uncontrolled transaction method, which is the intangibles equivalent of the tangible property transactions' comparable uncontrolled price method] and revisit Treas. Reg. 1.482–1(c) & (d)).

8. Read Treas. Reg. 1.482–3(d), which describes the cost plus method—the last method introduced here of the three original transfer pricing methods (resale price, comparable uncontrolled price, and cost plus) which, by now are universally accepted, but rarely used effectively. Revisit the facts of *Bausch & Lomb* in question 5 above. Why do you think the IRS preferred this method originally? Is it realistically possible that cost plus and the resale price methods be equivalently appropriate? What does this say about these methods?

6.4   MORE ON THE OPERATION OF THE TRANSFER PRICING RULES

As you must realize by now, it is not enough to employ just one of the permissible methods to determine a transfer price. The regulations require that "[T]he arm's length result of a controlled transaction [ ] be determined under the method that, under the facts and circumstances, provides the most reliable measure of an arm's length result." Treas. Reg. 1.482–1(c)(1). This is the best method requirement (replacing a mandatory method ordering rule under prior regulations). You must also realize by now that this facts and circumstances' determination is quite problematic. Some of the newer transfer pricing rules attempt to assist in this process by provision of guidance targeted at different types of transactions.

a. TANGIBLE PROPERTY

This is where it all started. *Du Pont* can serve as a typical case in this category. Review Treas. Reg. 1.482–3 which governs the choice of methods for transfers of tangible property. It allows the three above-mentioned traditional methods (resale price, comparable uncontrolled price, and cost plus) and two newer methods: The comparable profits method, described in Treas. Reg. 1.482–5 (note that this method does not rely on price, but rather on operating profits) and the profit split method, described in Treas. Reg. 1.482–6, which evolved, although not explicitly, as a residual, "rough justice" method. See also the examples in Treas. Reg. 1.482–8.

In the IRS Annual Report on the Advance Pricing Agreement Program published in March 2019, the IRS reported that: "Consistent with prior years, in 2018, the primary transfer pricing method (TPM) used for both the sale of tangible property and the use of intangible property was the comparable profits method/transactional net margin method (CPM/TNMM). The CPM/TNMM was used for 86 percent of transfers of tangible and intangible property while all other methods combined accounted for the other 14 percent of such transactions." Why might it not be surprising that direct comparables—i.e. CUP or CUT—played a smaller role?

b. TRANSACTIONS WITH INTANGIBLE PROPERTY

Transactions involving intangible property present probably the biggest challenge to the transfer pricing rules. The following case presents a basic case that demonstrates this claim. Keep in mind that the applicable regulations were replaced with new regulations, which will be explored below.

DHL Corporation and Subsidiaries v. Commissioner of Internal Revenue

United States Court of Appeals, Ninth Circuit.
285 F.3d 1210 (2002).

■ WILLIAM A. FLETCHER, CIRCUIT JUDGE:

Petitioner DHL Corporation ("DHL") appeals the tax court's affirmance, in part, of the Commissioner of Internal Revenue's assessment of income tax deficiencies and penalties against petitioner for the tax years 1990–1992, based on the Commissioner's power to reallocate income between controlled entities under 26 U.S.C. § 482. Petitioner specifically appeals (1) the § 482 allocation to DHL of additional income arising from DHL's sale to Document Handling Limited, International ("DHLI") of the "DHL" trademark, which the tax court valued at $100 million; (2) the allocation of income to DHL for uncharged royalties from DHLI's use of the "DHL" trademark prior to the sale; and (3) the imposition of penalties under 26 U.S.C. § 6662 triggered by these deficiencies.

. . . We reverse the tax court's § 482 allocations to DHL of the value of the foreign trademark rights and unpaid royalties, and reverse the assessment of penalties under § 6662. We otherwise affirm.

I

The tax court opinion provides a detailed account of the various companies' histories, structures, and dealings. DHL Corp. v. Comm'r, 76 T.C.M. (CCH) 1122 (1998). Here we provide a summary of the relevant facts.

A. The DHL Network

Adrian Dalsey, Larry Hillblom, and Robert Lynn formed DHL Corporation ("DHL"), a package delivery company, in California in 1969. Document Handling Limited, International ("DHLI"), was incorporated in Hong Kong in 1972. Generally, independent local agents conducted the international operations and paid a network fee to DHLI. Middleston, N.V. ("MNV"), incorporated in 1979, owned most of the overseas local operating companies. At trial before the tax court, DHL conceded that, because of overlapping stock ownership, common control existed among DHL, DHLI, and MNV for all relevant times up to December 7, 1990.

From 1972 to 1992, DHL and DHLI/MNV were part of a global network in which DHL handled United States operations exclusively and DHLI/MNV handled foreign operations. DHL delivered DHLI's America-bound shipments, and DHLI delivered DHL's foreign-bound shipments. Until 1987, each company kept for itself the full amount paid by the local customer, and the companies did not exchange fees. Each company also paid for its own advertising expenses in its respective markets. A network steering committee, a specially formed corporation, and other mechanisms coordinated the worldwide DHL network. In 1988, a

Worldwide Coordination Center was established in Belgium, with the world operations of the DHL network divided into three regions, each with its own CEO. DHL struggled in the competitive American market, sustaining losses during the 1980s, but DHLI/MNV expanded rapidly and profitably.

B. The "DHL" Trademark

In 1974, DHL and DHLI entered into a Memorandum of Oral Agreement ("MOA"), under which DHL licensed the name "DHL" to DHLI for five years, terminable by DHL on 90 days notice. Under the MOA, DHLI would be prohibited from using the "DHL" name for five years after termination. The MOA did not include any provision for the payment of royalties by DHLI to DHL for use of the "DHL" trademark. Through a series of amendments, the MOA was extended through 1990.

In 1977, DHL began the process of registering the "DHL" trademark in the United States. DHLI commissioned the first "DHL" logo, which was then used worldwide. Beginning in 1983, DHLI incurred the expenses of registering the "DHL" trademark under DHLI's name in various foreign countries.

On December 7, 1990, DHL and DHLI entered into a new agreement. Under its terms, DHL had the exclusive right to use and sublicense the "DHL" trademark in the United States, and DHLI had corresponding rights overseas. The agreement included reciprocal performance standards, and DHL and DHLI agreed to compensate each other, at cost plus 2%, for any shipment imbalances between the two entities. The agreement was terminable only for cause and had a 15-year term, with an automatic 10-year renewal if both parties were satisfied. If the agreement was terminated, DHLI would be prohibited from using the "DHL" trademark for 5 years. The agreement contained no provision for payment of royalties for DHLI's use of the trademark.

C. Sale of DHLI/MNV and the "DHL" Trademark

From late 1986 to early 1988, DHL and DHLI negotiated with United Parcel Service ("UPS") concerning merger possibilities, but these negotiations broke down over price. UPS expressed little or no interest in the "DHL" trademark during these negotiations.

On December 21, 1988, Japan Airlines Co., Ltd. ("JAL") and Nissho Iwai Corp. ("NI") made an offer to purchase up to 80% of the combined DHL network. This offer was not well received, in part because Hillblom, a leading shareholder of both DHL and DHLI, did not want to give up his entire interest in DHL. A second offer was made on June 14, 1989. JAL and NI offered to purchase 60% of DHLI/MNV based on a total value for those companies of $450 million, and to purchase the trademark for $50 million. DHL counter-offered with a $100 million price for the trademark and a $500 million price for DHLI/MNV. However, in December 1989, the parties reached a memorandum of understanding for the sale based on the $450 million value for DHLI/MNV and the $50 million price, "subject to confirmation of the tax effect," for the trademark.

During the course of the negotiations, different parties provided a number of valuations of the DHL network and the "DHL" trademark. In February 1989, Robert Fleming Co. valued DHLI/MNV in a range of $392.2 to $680.4 million, and found that the "DHL" name, while intangible, was of some value that should be reflected in the final price. Peers and Co. produced a report on June 8, 1989, valuing DHLI/MNV at $522 to $580.9 million. In a revised report of September 14, 1989, it placed the value at $625 to $700 million. In June 1989, Nicholas Miller of Coopers & Lybrand valued the "DHL" trademark, outside the United States, at $25 million. This valuation was based in part on the view that DHL's trademark rights were diluted by its agreements with DHLI. On February 23, 1990, First Boston, retained by Lufthansa (JAL and NI's new partner), valued DHLI/MNV at $400 to $600 million and the trademark at $100 to $200 million. The First Boston trademark valuation, however, appears to have been done without knowledge of any ownership problems in the trademark.

On May 31, 1989, a Coopers & Lybrand report, commissioned by the foreign investors, raised the following concerns relevant to a possible purchase of DHLI/MNV: (1) DHL should receive an injection of capital via sale of the trademark; (2) DHL might be charged with imputed income based on prior uncharged royalties; and (3) DHL, in a trademark sale, should not have to pay royalties given its difficult financial position. DHL representatives also began to express concern about the tax consequences of the sale of the trademark, and they therefore sought a lower value for the trademark. As a result of these concerns, in July 1990, DHL sought a comfort letter from Bain & Co. on a $20 million trademark valuation. Bain supported the $20 million valuation after taking into account DHLI's possible ownership of the trademark and encumbrances in the form of royalty-free licenses to both DHLI (for the non-U.S. trademark interest) and DHL (for the U.S. trademark interest). On July 9, 1990, DHL and DHLI executed an agreement granting DHLI an option to purchase the "DHL" trademark for $20 million.

In late 1989, Lufthansa joined JAL and NI (collectively, the "Consortium"). On December 7, 1990, the Consortium and DHL/DHLI reached a final agreement under which the Consortium acquired (1) a 12.5% stock interest in DHLI/MNV, with an option to purchase an additional 45% interest based on a $450 million valuation of DHLI/MNV; (2) a 2.5% interest in DHL; and (3) an option to purchase the "DHL" trademark for $20 million, conditional upon the Consortium having first exercised its option to purchase the additional 45% interest.

The trademark option provided that DHL could use the "DHL" trademark in the United States royalty-free for 15 years. After 15 years, DHL would have the exclusive U.S. rights to the trademark for 10 years, but would have to pay a royalty fee of 0.75%. The final trademark purchase and sale agreement allocated the $20 million for the trademark in the following way: $17 million for the transfer of U.S. trademark rights, and $3 million for a quitclaim in the non-U.S. trademark rights. These two interests were to be transferred to separate entities.

The two-step acquisition process was designed to give the Consortium an opportunity to learn more about the DHL network prior to making a control commitment. During the interim period, the Consortium had the power to appoint 7 of the 13 directors of DHLI/MNV. The Consortium exercised this power, but the employees at the management level of DHLI/MNV remained the same. The Consortium did not exercise control over day-to-day management.

On June 7, 1992, the Consortium exercised its stock option, purchasing a majority stake in DHLI/MNV. The Consortium subsequently reorganized the entity into DHL International Ltd., incorporated in Bermuda. On September 17, 1992, the Consortium caused this new entity to exercise its option to purchase the "DHL" trademark rights for $20 million.

D.   The Commissioner's Deficiency Notice

The Commissioner's deficiency notice, issued June 30, 1995, listed deficiencies and penalties for the tax years 1990–1992. The initial deficiencies were based on a trademark valuation of approximately $600 million. The economist performing the valuation for the IRS was doing his first examination for the IRS; it was also his first effort at valuing a trademark. The total deficiency alleged in the notice was $194,534,167; the penalties in the notice totaled $74,777,222.

E.   The Tax Court's Decision

After an extended trial, the tax court upheld deficiencies and penalties totaling $59,427,093. Although the amount of the deficiencies and penalties was much less than had been contained in the original notice of deficiency, the tax court held that the Commissioner had not abandoned his valuation. Accordingly, the tax court held that the burden of proof did not shift from the taxpayer.

The tax court accepted the Commissioner's contention that DHL and DHLI were commonly controlled until 1992. The tax court upheld an income allocation to DHL under 26 U.S.C. § 482 based on a $100 million valuation of the trademark. Of this $100 million figure, $50 million was for the domestic trademark rights and $50 million was for the overseas trademark rights.

In addition, the tax court upheld an allocation to DHL based on imputed income from uncharged royalties for DHLI's prior use of the "DHL" trademark. It also upheld an allocation based on imputed income from uncharged transfer fees between DHL and DHLI. The transfer fees represented amounts to compensate DHL for the excess of packages that it delivered on DHLI's behalf as against those that DHLI delivered on DHL's behalf.

. . .

II

. . . we review the tax court's conclusions of law de novo and its factual findings for clear error. . . . We review the tax court's affirmance of a penalty for clear error.

"[T]he Commissioner has broad discretion under section 482, and neither we nor the Tax Court will countermand his decision unless the taxpayer shows it to be unreasonable, arbitrary or capricious." Foster v. Comm'r, 756 F.2d 1430, 1432 (9th Cir.1985) (citation omitted). Determinations with respect to valuation and common control are primarily factual determinations reviewed under the clearly erroneous standard. . . .

However, interpretations of Treasury Regulations are reviewed de novo. Dykstra v. Comm'r, 260 F.3d 1181, 1182 (9th Cir.2001). Furthermore, de novo review applies where "the primary issue . . . is whether the facts fall within the relevant legal definition." Paccar, Inc. v. Comm'r, 849 F.2d 393, 396 (9th Cir.1988). Determining whether DHLI qualifies as a "developer" or "assister" under the § 482 regulations (see infra Part V) constitutes such an inquiry.

III

. . . We first decide whether the tax court erred in finding sufficient common control between DHL and DHLI to justify application of § 482 to the sale of the "DHL" trademark rights.

A.   Timing of the Analysis

We agree with the tax court that the relevant time period for determining whether common control existed for purposes of § 482, given the particular business context here, is the period of negotiation and completion of the trademark option agreement between DHL, DHLI, and the Consortium. That is, the endpoint for the period over which there needed to be common control within the meaning of § 482 was the completion of the binding option agreement. The economic reality of the transaction was that the price of the trademark was established at the time the Consortium obtained the option to buy it at the specified price. The ultimate purchase of the trademark at that price merely ratified the price that had been established at the earlier time. Because both parties concede there was common control between DHL and DHLI during all relevant times up to December 7, 1990, and because DHL and DHLI—largely without objection by the Consortium, see infra Part III.B—set the price term of the Consortium's option to purchase the "DHL" trademark in July 1990, we find that § 482 applies here. Thus, we need not determine whether there was sufficient common control for § 482 purposes at the time the trademark option was exercised.

This transactional approach for determining common control under § 482 comports with common sense, and the regulations . . . we conclude

[handwritten margin note: The period of control relevant to § 482.]

that the time when the taxpayers (DHL and DHLI) were dealing with each other was when they set the terms of the option agreement.

B.   The Presence of the Consortium in the Negotiations

Because the price of the trademark was set at the time the option agreement was signed, the next question is who, in reality, set that price. DHL challenges the Commissioner's allocation of income by arguing that the presence of the Consortium on the other side of the negotiating table precludes a finding that income was shifted between DHL and DHLI. Unlike the usual case of two controlled taxpayers making a deal with each other, the deal in this case was made between two controlled taxpayers and an entity not controlled by the taxpayers. Nonetheless, we do not find the Consortium's presence sufficient ground to preclude a § 482 allocation, in light of the tax court's factual findings as to the Consortium's indifference to the specific trademark price term.

DHL cites R.T. French Co. v. Comm'r, 60 T.C. 836, 1973 WL 2530 (1973), in support of its argument that a third party's presence at the table ensures that a transaction is conducted at arm's length. In that case, the critical transfer consisted of royalty payments from R.T. French, a company jointly owned by two companies, to another company in which the joint owners had only a 51% interest. The tax court found that it was unlikely that there was any improper income shifting from R.T. French to the other company. Such shifting would have reduced the income of the joint owners of R.T. French, and enriched the 49% owners of the other company to the degree of that reduction. Because such shifting would have disadvantaged R.T. French and correspondingly advantaged the third-party 49% owners, the presence of the third parties ensured that the transaction was at arm's length.

This case is different from R.T. French because there is no such comparable advantage and disadvantage. Where a third party is indifferent to the terms of the transaction affecting the allocated items, its involvement does not interfere with the application of § 482. See GAC Produce Co. v. Comm'r, 77 T.C.M. (CCH) 1890, 1904 (1999). The one outside party in this case, the Consortium, would be neither advantaged or disadvantaged by the income-shifting between DHL and DHLI, as long as the total price it paid for DHLI and the trademark rights remained the same. On this view of the facts, the presence of the Consortium would not perform the same checking role that the presence of the third parties performed in R.T. French.

There was substantial evidence before the tax court supporting its conclusion that in the sale of DHLI and the trademark, the common owners of DHL/DHLI had considerable flexibility in structuring how the trademark price would be reflected in the deal terms. Without objection from the Consortium, the trademark price was reduced from $50 million in the initial agreement to $20 million in the final agreement. This reduction appears to have been based on considerations of DHL's potential tax liability and post-takeover viability rather than on the trademark's actual value. The trademark was initially priced at $50 million payable to DHL, "subject to confirmation of the tax effect." The price was then reduced to $20 million payable to DHL, with an accompanying addition to the agreement that DHL would be able to use the trademark royalty-free for the fifteen years following the sale to the Consortium, and to use it for a small royalty for ten years after that. If the value of the royalty-free and reduced royalty periods approximated the $30 million reduction in the sale price of the trademark, this was essentially a wash from the standpoint of the Consortium.

Perhaps more important, the Consortium had an interest in ensuring that tax consequences of the sale did not reduce the economic viability of DHL. On this view of the facts, the Consortium was not indifferent to the tax consequences of the sale. Rather, the Consortium was advantaged by the income-shifting, and therefore had an interest in facilitating that shifting.

IV

Under Treasury Regulation § 1.482–2(d)(1)(i), where intangible property is transferred between commonly controlled entities, "the district director may make appropriate allocations to reflect arm's length consideration for such property or its use." The tax court found that $100 million ($50 million for the U.S. rights, $50 million for the foreign rights), rather than $20 million, was the arm's length value of the "DHL" trademark. We do not find the tax court's valuation, a factual determination, to be clearly erroneous; thus we uphold the $100 million value.

DHL argues that the tax court's valuation is arbitrary and unreasonable and that the tax court failed to articulate its reasoning. . . .

. . . The tax court has complied with this standard by giving a step-by-step account of its reasoning. First, following the Commissioner's approach, the tax court reached a $300 million value for all unbooked intangibles, measuring the equity value of DHL and DHLI's intangibles based on what the Consortium paid for the company in excess of its book value. Although not without problems, this is a systematic, defensible approach. Second, the tax court determined that one-half of the total intangibles, or $150 million, was attributable specifically to the "DHL" trademark. The tax court, at several points, explained its belief that the trademark was worth at least as much as the other intangibles. Third, the tax court determined that two-thirds of the value of the trademark, or $100 million, was attributable to the non-U.S. rights to the trademark. Fourth, the tax court discounted the non-U.S. rights by 50% to reflect a marketability discount, based on potential problems with DHL's ownership of the foreign trademarks. The tax court therefore concluded that the foreign and domestic trademarks were each worth $50 million, for a combined value of $100 million.

Although the tax court painted with a broad brush, that is to be expected given the imprecise art of valuing an intangible asset. DHL may dispute the exact figures used by the tax court in reaching its valuation, but DHL fails to demonstrate clear error, either in the tax court's methodology or in its final result. We therefore affirm the tax court's valuation of the trademark at $100 million, based on a $50 million figure for the domestic rights and a $50 million figure for the overseas rights.

V

Having affirmed the application of § 482 to the trademark sale and the $100 million valuation for the trademark, we must next ask whether the tax court properly allocated the full $100 million to DHL. DHL does not appeal the tax court's finding that it was the legal owner of both the domestic and foreign trademark rights. Rather, DHL asserts that the tax court erred in applying the § 482 developer-assister regulations, which preclude the allocation to DHL of the $50 million value of the foreign trademark rights. We agree and reverse the tax court accordingly.

The 1968 Treasury Regulations for § 482 state:

> [W]here one member of a group of related entities undertakes the development of intangible property as a developer . . . no allocation with respect to such development activity shall be made . . . until such time as any property developed . . . is sold, assigned, loaned or otherwise made available in any manner by the developer to a related entity in a transfer subject to the rules of this paragraph.

Treas. Reg. § 1.482–2(d)(1)(ii)(a). DHL contends that DHLI was the developer of the overseas trademarks. If this is true, DHL argues, the tax court's allocation for the foreign trademark value was erroneous under § 1.482–2(d)(1)(ii)(a) because the transfer in this case was not "by the developer to a related entity," but rather from a related entity (DHL) to the developer (DHLI).

Alternatively, should the court find DHL to be the developer, DHL argues that DHLI should be allowed a set-off under § 1.482–2(d)(1)(ii)(b) for the amount of assistance that it provided to DHL in developing the foreign trademarks:

> Where one member of a group renders assistance in the form of loans, services, or the use of tangible or intangible property to a developer in connection with an attempt to develop intangible property . . . the value of such assistance shall be allowed as a set-off against any allocation that the district director may make under this paragraph as a result of the transfer of the intangible property to the entity rendering the assistance. Id. § 1.482–2(d)(1)(ii)(b). DHLI would be entitled to the setoff because the transfer under this scenario was from DHL (developer) to DHLI (assister).

Under the 1968 regulations governing this case, the tax court's determination of whether an entity is a developer or an assister in the development of an intangible asset requires a case-by-case approach:

> The determination as to which member of a group of related entities is the developer and which members of the group are rendering assistance to the developer in connection with its development activities shall be based on all the facts and circumstances of the individual case. Of all the facts and circumstances to be taken into account in making this determination, the greatest weight shall be given to the relative amounts of all the direct and indirect costs of development and the corresponding risks of development borne by the various members of the group. . . . Other factors that may be relevant in determining which member of the group is the developer include the location of the development activity, the capabilities of the various members to carry on the project independently, and the degree of control over the project exercised by the various members. Id. § 1.482–2(d)(1)(ii)(c).

The tax court found that DHLI was neither a developer nor an assister. However, we hold that the tax court applied the wrong legal tests under the developer-assister regulations in reaching its conclusions.

A. Legal Ownership/Licensor-Licensee Standard

For the tax court, the fact that in its view DHL was the legal owner of the "worldwide" trademark rights was decisive, in spite of the unusual circumstances of the licensing arrangement. The tax court stated, "[t]he related parties' relationship regarding the use of the DHL trademark was not a textbook example of a licensing agreement, but it was sufficient to bind these related parties and to effectuate control over the use of the trademark." Based on its resolution of the ownership question, the court then required DHL to demonstrate that DHLI's expenditures as either a developer or assister were more than the promotional expenses that a similarly situated licensee would expend at arm's length.

There are two problems with the tax court's approach. First, the tax court's ownership analysis and licensee-expenditure tests are in conflict with the plain language of the governing 1968 regulation, which lists four factors that the tax court should consider: (1) the relative costs and risks borne by each controlled entity; (2) the location of the development activity; (3) the capabilities of members to conduct the activity independently; and (4) the degree of control exercised by each entity. Treas. Reg. § 1.482–2(d)(1)(ii)(c). On a plain reading of the regulation, the principal focus appears to be not on legal ownership, but on equitable ownership based on economic expenditure. Legal ownership is not even listed among the factors.

Additional evidence that legal ownership is not the proper test under the 1968 regulations comes from the process of drafting the superceding

1994 regulations. The 1994 regulations appear designed to correct for the fact that the old regulations ignored legal ownership in favor of an economic approach. The critical language from the preamble to the 1994 regulations is as follows:

> The 1993 regulations provided that . . . intangible property generally would be treated as owned by the controlled taxpayer that bore the greatest share of the costs of development. This rule was criticized by many commenters, principally because it disregarded legal ownership. . . . For instance, a controlled taxpayer that was treated as the owner of an intangible for section 482 purposes might not be the legal owner. At arm's length, the legal owner could transfer the rights to the intangible to another person irrespective of the developer's contribution to the development of the intangible.

Intercompany Transfer Pricing Regulations Under Section 482, 59 Fed.Reg. 34,971, 34,984 (July 8, 1994) (emphasis added).

Although the preamble refers to the 1993 temporary regulations rather than the 1968 regulations, the relevant provisions in the 1993 temporary regulations were the same as those in the 1968 regulations. The 1994 regulations are completely different from both the 1968 and 1993 proposed regulations, explicitly stating that legal ownership is the test for identifying the intangible. See Treas. Reg. § 1.482–4(f)(3)(ii)(A) (1994) ("The legal owner of a right to exploit an intangible ordinarily will be considered the owner for purposes of this section."). The 1994 revision of the 1968 regulations thus strongly reinforces a plain-meaning reading of the 1968 regulations, with the result that legal ownership is not the analytical touchstone for those regulations.

Second, the tax court erroneously required DHL to demonstrate that DHLI's expenditures as either a developer or assister were more than the promotional expenses that a similarly situated licensee would expend at arm's length. The tax court appears to have found this requirement in the 1994 regulations. See id. § 1.482–4(f)(3)(iii) ("Assistance does not, however, include expenditures of a routine nature that an unrelated party dealing at arm's length would be expected to incur under circumstances similar to those of the controlled taxpayer."). However, the applicable 1968 regulations impose no such burden and simply turn on the relative amounts spent and risks borne by the related entities in developing the intangible.

Even if "arm's length" licensee expenditures were the correct standard, it does not fit the facts of the present case. Such a standard may work where there is a clear line between development and exploitation. For example, the development of a drug (the basic fact-pattern employed in the examples for the 1968 regulations) can be distinguished from the marketing of that drug. Or, even in the trademark context, if a company with a product already recognized in the target market incorporated a local subsidiary, the subsidiary's expenditures might be presumed to be exploiting this trademark rather than developing its value.

The tax court treated this case as one in which a well-established product or service is licensed to a licensee. This is a mistake, however, because the value of the DHL trademark was created only by virtue of the sustained and combined efforts of both DHL and DHLI. Although DHL began with domestic delivery, the ultimate value of the DHL trademark was dependent on demonstrating the company's ability to deliver internationally. DHLI was formed shortly after DHL began operations. The only entity that moved packages out of the United States, and between all foreign points, was DHLI. DHLI therefore both developed the trademark in foreign countries and developed the service network that was the foundation for the trademark. Given the growth and profitability of DHL's international operations, the history looks much more like an equal partnership than a subsidiary incurring advertising expenses to exploit the trademark of a parent company.

B. Four Factors under the 1968 Regulation

The tax court failed to apply the relevant factors mandated by the 1968 regulation for determining who is a developer or assister. First and foremost, the regulation provided that "greatest weight shall be given to the relative amounts of all the direct and indirect costs of development and the corresponding risks of development borne by the various members of the group." . . . Here, the relevant intangible is the foreign trademark rights. Trademark rights are created by registration and/or use in a given country and have a separate legal existence under each country's laws. . . . Trademark rights are further developed and strengthened by advertising and promotional activities. . . .

DHLI undertook the registration of the "DHL" trademark in numerous foreign countries and bore essentially all related costs. Furthermore, DHLI paid for all of the overseas marketing campaigns with the "DHL" trademark, an expense that exceeded $340 million. Since developing a trademark includes advertising that mark, it does not make sense to distinguish between typical marketing activity and development. See Marc M. Levey, Tax Court Sends Messages to Taxpayers in DHL, 482 PLI/Tax 775, 786 (2000) ("For trademarks connoting brand image, which is highly company and market specific, this test may be an impossible benchmark to quantify."). In addition, DHLI bore the costs of protecting the foreign trademarks against infringement and handled all disputes relating to trademark usage abroad. Conversely, it was undisputed at trial that DHL bore none of the costs and risks in developing the foreign trademark rights. Thus, the first and most important factor clearly favors DHLI as the developer of the foreign trademark rights.

The other three factors, less important but nonetheless relevant, further support DHLI's status as the developer. The location of the development activity was in the foreign countries which DHLI, not DHL, served. DHLI was better suited to carry on the advertising and marketing independently given its connections to the foreign countries. Finally, DHLI exercised greater, if not exclusive, control over the advertising and development of the foreign trademarks.

Even if we accepted the tax court's conclusion that DHL was the developer, DHLI would at least qualify as an assister under the aforementioned regulations. The tax court therefore clearly erred in saying that the Commissioner may not be compelled to set off the value of the assistance against any allocation. The 1968 regulation provides that "the value of the assistance shall be allowed as a set-off against any allocation." Treas. Reg. § 1.482–2(d)(1)(ii)(b) (emphasis added). Thus, the set-off is mandatory. Moreover, the petitioner need not show the precise amount of its development expenditures here, since presumably at least $50 million (the amount the tax court allocated to DHL for the foreign trademark rights) of the $340 million spent by DHLI in overseas advertising constitute development expenditures for the "DHL" trademark.

In summary, we hold that DHLI was the developer of the international trademark, in which case no allocation to DHL for the value of the foreign trademark rights was appropriate, or, alternatively, that DHLI provided assistance to DHL's development, thereby entitling DHL to a complete setoff against the $50 million allocation.

VI

The tax court upheld deficiencies based on allocated imputed income for the tax years 1990–1992 from uncharged royalties. The royalties were those the tax court held that DHL should have charged to DHLI for use of the "DHL" trademark from 1982 through 1992. Applying the same developer-assister regulations as in Part V, supra, we reverse the allocation of unpaid royalties to DHL.

The concept of the developer-assister regulations is that the party that incurred the costs and risks of developing the intangible should not be required to pay a royalty to use that intangible. Levey, supra, at 786; James P. Fuller, Jim Fuller's U.S. Tax Review, 18 Tax Notes Int'l 391 (1999). As we held in Part V, DHLI was the developer of the overseas component of the "DHL" trademark, and thus no royalty income should be allocated to DHL for DHLI's use of those rights. Since the trademark license was from a related entity (DHL) to the developer (DHLI) rather than a transfer by the developer, no allocation is permitted under § 1.482–2(d)(1)(ii)(a).

VII

The tax court upheld two types of penalties under 26 U.S.C. § 6662 against petitioner: (1) a substantial understatement penalty for the unpaid royalties, and (2) a gross valuation misstatement penalty on the additional $80 million that the tax court allocated to DHL for the sale of the "DHL" trademark to DHLI. Because we reverse the allocation of imputed income from the unpaid royalties in Part VI, we reverse the first penalty in its entirety without further discussion.

As to the second penalty. . . . No valuation misstatement penalty is warranted . . . if "there was a reasonable cause" for the underpayment and "the taxpayer acted in good faith" with respect to the underpayment. Id. § 6664(c). The key issue before the tax court was whether DHL showed good faith by obtaining a comfort letter from Bain & Co. regarding the $20 million valuation for the "DHL" trademark, or whether the comfort letter was an instrument in DHL's allegedly evasive scheme. The tax court rejected Bain's appraisal as a basis for demonstrating good faith reliance on an expert. The tax court stated that it was not reasonable for DHL to have relied on the comfort letter because DHL sought the letter only after choosing an artificially depressed price, which it then communicated to Bain. The tax court observed that "parties can find experts who will advance and support values that favor the position of the person or entity that hired them."

We are less inclined than the tax court to condemn a taxpayer who seeks a comfort letter from a respected financial firm in order to ensure compliance with IRS standards. There is no evidence that DHL manipulated Bain's appraisal or that Bain blindly affirmed DHL's desired figure. Indeed, the $17 million valuation of the domestic trademark rights which Bain supported was much closer to the tax court's valuation of $50 million than the IRS's own original valuation of over $350 million for the domestic rights. Accordingly, the tax court clearly erred in rejecting DHL's reliance on the Bain comfort letter as an indication of DHL's good faith, and we reverse its penalty assessment under § 6662.

Conclusion

For the foregoing reasons, we AFFIRM in part and REVERSE in part, and REMAND for further proceedings consistent with this opinion.

* * *

NOTES AND QUESTIONS

1.   *DHL* represents a significant taxpayer victory. It also illuminates the significance of the monetary stakes of transfer pricing planning. Note that in any case involving intangibles, two questions will almost always be raised: ownership and valuation.

    a.   What does ownership mean in the case of intangibles? Think about a case where an owner of software leases it to another for a period of 5 years (more than the expected effective economic life of the software). What was the ownership dilemma in this case? How did it affect the result of the case?

    b.   Prior regulations allowed multiple and mixed ownership, as evidenced in the *DHL* case. The new regulations attempt to solve this problem by requiring single, "legal" ownership, following private law. Read Treas. Reg. 1.482–4(f)(3). Does this solve the problem? Is the result under the new regulations less exploitable? Is it fairer?

c.   What does ownership mean in the case of intangibles? What is the price paid when such legal all-or-nothing definitions are employed, ignoring economic arrangements? What role did the bifurcation of payments play in *DHL*? Did the court understand the fungibility of money concept in your opinion?

d.   Note the number of different valuations of the trademark mentioned or used in this case. How did it affect the determination of the transfer prices in this case?

2.   Review Treas. Reg. 1.482–4, which governs the choice of methods for transfers of intangible property. In this case, the three traditional methods are basically abandoned, leaving a modified comparable uncontrolled price method, now called the comparable uncontrolled transaction method. The other two newer methods: The comparable profits method, described in Treas. Reg. 1.482–5 and the profit split method, described in Treas. Reg. 1.482–6, are also permissible. Think why were the cost plus and resale price methods dropped in the case of intangibles? Aren't these weaknesses shared by the surviving methods?

3.   Note the second to last sentence of Section 482 added in 1986. The "commensurate with income" (CWI) notion has not yet been developed in case law or transfer pricing practice, but it is a potentially potent concept which the IRS may decide to better exploit in the future. Why is there a specific reference to intangibles in this second to last sentence? The definition of intangibles covered by the last sentence was broadened by the TCJA to include goodwill, going concern value, and workforce in place as well as any other item the value of which is not attributable to tangible property or the services of any individual.

4.   An enormously important concession in the transfer pricing methods is the special regime in the Cost Sharing regulations permitted for transfers of intangibles. Review the recently revised rules in Treas. Reg. 1.482–7T. What is cost sharing? In this context it refers to an agreement between two related parties to jointly share the costs of creating an intangible and then sharing the ownership of that intangible pursuant to terms of an agreed contract.

To understand the appeal of "cost sharing," consider the situation of a hypothetical U.S. corporation with valuable intellectual property in the U.S—perhaps some type of software. The income generated, e.g. royalties, from that valuable IP will be subject to U.S. tax, even if it is foreign source income. (Why?) The U.S. corporation would be interested in a plan that would enable that income to avoid U.S. taxation. The "obvious" solution would be to sell the IP to a foreign subsidiary in a low tax jurisdiction and have that subsidiary license the IP globally. Ideally the income earned by the foreign subsidiary would not be taxable in the U.S. until dividends were paid to the U.S. parent. However, the basic Section 482 rules governing the transfers of intangibles to related parties, *along with the commensurate with income rule* in the second to last sentence of Section 482, make this strategy unappealing. If the U.S corporation tries to sell the IP to the subsidiary at a low price—it will be challenged either immediately—or later when the foreign subsidiary begins generating significant income from the intangible.

Another possibility would be to avoid a taxable transfer by contributing the property as a tax free contribution to capital to the foreign subsidiary. However, Section 367(d), which will be discussed in Chapter 9 below, makes this a very (tax) costly transfer. At this point, the prospect of entering into a cost sharing agreement with your foreign subsidiary is an attractive option—at least for the next generation of your IP.

Thus, returning to the hypothetical, the U.S. corporation would enter into an agreement with its foreign subsidiary to jointly create and own the next generation of the existing software. The two parties would contribute to the costs of developing the new software (such as employees, testing, etc.) in proportion to their ultimate ownership rights. (Thus, if the U.S. corporation has the right to use the resulting IP in the U.S, and the foreign subsidiary has the right to use it in the rest of the world, and these rights are of equal value, then the two parties must contribute equally to the costs of developing the new IP). But there is one big issue: if, as in this hypothetical, the new IP is a second generation product, then the sharing of new development costs is not enough. Why? The U.S. corporation is "bringing" to the joint endeavor its pre-existing intangible (the first generation IP) and allowing this intangible to be used to create the second generation IP—i.e. its own replacement! The U.S. corporation must be compensated by its foreign subsidiary for effectively allowing its foreign subsidiary to use the first generation intangible to create a replacement which the foreign subsidiary will partially own. [This payment has been referred to as the "buy-in" payment.] To appreciate the reality of this, ask yourself the following question? Would the U.S. corporation enter into THIS cost sharing agreement with its biggest rival (under which the rival would have the worldwide rights to the new intangible that would be replacing the first generation IP owned exclusively by the U.S. corporation)? The answer is likely no—and if the U.S. corporation were to do so, it would require the other party to pay for the rights to use the first generation software in the new development process and this price would be significant.

The cost sharing regulations permit related parties to enter into these agreements and have their joint ownership respected. It requires some information from the taxpayers and requires them to follow certain formalities, but in exchange permits a "cheap" transfer of rights (and future income) in intangibles to a related person. This is permitted even if the intangible is already in development, if an appropriate "buy-in" payment for the already developed value is made. The problem with the cost sharing regulations as they have evolved over time, is whether they are effective in requiring the related party to pay an appropriate (i.e. arm's length) buy-in amount. In 2009 the IRS introduced new temporary regulations aimed at ensuring that the buy-in payment (now labeled the "platform contribution" payment) is arm's length.

The transfer of intangibles, particularly in the context of a cost sharing agreement remains a highly contested area of international tax in which large amounts of money are at stake. The following case represents one example of the latest round in this struggle between taxpayers and the government.

Veritas Software Corp. v. Commissioner

United States Tax Court.
133 T.C. No. 14 (2009).

OPINION

■ FOLEY, JUDGE: On November 3, 1999, VERITAS Software Corp. (VERITAS US) and VERITAS Ireland entered into a cost-sharing arrangement (CSA), which consisted of a research and development agreement and a technology license agreement. Also on November 3, 1999, VERITAS US, pursuant to the CSA, transferred preexisting intangible property to VERITAS Ireland and VERITAS Ireland made a buy-in payment to VERITAS US as consideration for the preexisting intangible property. After concessions, the issue for decision is whether, pursuant to section 482, the buy-in payment was arm's length.

BACKGROUND

* * *

VERITAS US is in the business of developing, manufacturing, marketing, and selling advanced storage management software products. VERITAS US' products protect against data loss and file corruption, provide rapid recovery after disk or system failure, process large files efficiently, manage and back up systems without user interruption, and provide performance improvement and reliability enhancement features that are critical for many commercial applications.

In the mid to late 1990s VERITAS US expanded its business through corporate acquisitions and the establishment of foreign subsidiaries. On April 25, 1997, VERITAS US acquired and merged with OpenVision Technologies, Inc. (OpenVision). With the acquisition of OpenVision, VERITAS US obtained NetBackup; offices in the United Kingdom, Germany, and France; an engineering team; and skilled sales and marketing executives. By the end of 1997 VERITAS US had sales subsidiaries in Canada, Japan, the United Kingdom, Germany, France, Sweden, and the Netherlands. VERITAS US, on May 28, 1999, acquired Seagate Software Network and Storage Management Group, Inc. (NSMG). . . . On July 2, 2005, VERITAS US was purchased by Symantec Corp. (Symantec) and became one of Symantec's wholly owned subsidiaries. References to petitioner are to VERITAS US, its subsidiaries, and Symantec (successor in interest to VERITAS US and subsidiaries).

I.   Storage Management Software Products

All computer operating systems have "backup" and "restore" capabilities. Storage management software replaces the portion of a computer's operating system that organizes files and manages data storage devices. Stored data is preserved and protected against loss or corruption by the use of backup applications that copy, on secondary storage, the data, its organizational structure, and its ownership information. Secondary storage devices may be attached directly to a computer or accessed through a network server.

Prior to 1999 only one application could access a data file at any given time. Thus, to back up data on secondary storage, it was first necessary to shut down all applications using the data. Most secondary storage was on magnetic tape and directly attached to a single server. After the CSA, there were important technological advances relating to the data storage software industry. In response to 24-hour Web sites, backup technology advanced significantly, enabling backups to run at any time. In addition, exponential increases in file size and data volume and the plummeting cost of disk storage spurred the use of disks as secondary storage. The switch to disks as the primary backup medium required the source code of backup products to be rewritten. The advent of storage area networks allowed storage to be shared by numerous computers, allowed more than one server to access a particular piece of data, and enabled applications to run continuously without interruption. Other technological advances dramatically increased storage capacity and also facilitated disaster recovery by allowing storage resources to be replicated several times in different data centers. These advances reduced the cost of physical storage and made it possible for many systems to share storage devices.

During the years in issue, VERITAS US had one primary commercial product (i.e., a product with a low price point and high-volume sales), Backup Exec, and five primary enterprise products (i.e., products with a high price point and low-volume sales): NetBackup, Volume Manager, File System, Cluster Server, and Foundation Suite.

Backup Exec, which was targeted to small businesses . . . NetBackup, Volume Manager, File System, Cluster Server, and Foundation Suite were purchased by businesses with large sophisticated information technology systems. . . .

Many of VERITAS US' products were deemed "sticky" because after employing them it was difficult, costly, and time consuming for the user to change to a competing product. These products communicated with and controlled parts of the computer and its attached devices without support from standard application program interfaces (API) or device drivers. Consequently, the software code in these products included code inextricably tied to the most basic part of an operating system. . . . After the CSA, VERITAS US released numerous versions of its aforementioned products. Each version contained new features. When new features were added to a product, the source code relating to these features was either added to existing files or placed in newly created files. . . .

II.   Product Distribution Channels

. . . In 1999 VERITAS US sold its products directly to customers and through original equipment manufacturers (OEMs), distributors, and resellers. From 1997 to 2006 VERITAS US entered into OEM agreements with several entities including Sun, HP, Dell Products, L.P. (Dell), Compaq Computer Corp. (Compaq), Ericsson Radio Systems AB (Ericsson), Hitachi, Ltd. (Hitachi), NEC Corp. (NEC), Microsoft, NCR Corp. (NCR), and Siemens Nixdorf Informationssysteme AG (Siemens). VERITAS US provided the OEMs with the product and the OEMs sold the products either bundled with their operating systems or unbundled as an option. Bundled products were installed with, and sold as a part of, the operating system, while unbundled products were sold as separate products for customers to install. During the term of the license, OEMs generally received the current version of the products plus updates, upgrades, and new versions. After selling VERITAS US' bundled products, the OEMs often provided technical, engineering, and maintenance support. The OEMs' willingness to sell and support the bundled products was a tacit affirmation of the products' reliability and quality. VERITAS US benefited from this arrangement because the OEMs had better name recognition and more customers.

From November 1999 to 2006 OEM licensees paid VERITAS US $1.327 billion in royalties. The calculation of royalties was based on list price, revenues, or profits and the products were often sold at a discount off list price. VERITAS US generally received a one-time license fee upon entering into the agreement and additional license fees each time the OEM sold VERITAS US products bundled with an operating system. The royalty rates relating to VERITAS US' OEM licenses ranged from 10 to 40 percent for bundled products and 5 to 48 percent for unbundled products. Profit potential and sales volume were important factors in determining royalty rates. VERITAS US could not accurately predict the amount of its license revenue receipts attributable to OEM agreements because VERITAS US had no control over delivery dates or the number of VERITAS US products sold with OEM operating systems. This uncertainty led VERITAS US to explore other paths to market (i.e., distributors, resellers, and direct sales) for its products.

VERITAS US sold Backup Exec through distributors and resellers. . . . VERITAS US sold NetBackup, Volume Manager, File System, Cluster Server, and Foundation Suite directly to customers and through resellers. Between 1997 and 2005 VERITAS US entered into reseller agreements with operating system, hardware, and database vendors including Compaq, Hitachi, Fujitsu, Ericsson, Dell, HP, NCR, Bull S.A., and EMC Corp. (EMC). The royalty rates relating to the reseller agreements ranged between 32.5 and 70 percent.

III. Intensely Competitive Market

Prior to the CSA, VERITAS US products competed intensely with products manufactured by numerous companies. . . .

VERITAS US products competed with both comparable and free alternatives. The free alternatives included storage management products readily accessible on the Internet and those bundled with operating systems. Vendors sometimes incorporated storage management capabilities into their operating systems. Some customers preferred operating systems with built-in storage management software (i.e., integrated stacks). . . . VERITAS US continuously sought to offer products that were faster and more efficient than comparable products or free alternatives . . .

Between 1996 and 2006 the primary competition for VERITAS US products was products sold by operating system, hardware, and database vendors such as Sun and Oracle. Sun and Oracle had a similar objective—remove VERITAS US from their respective stacks and provide their respective customers with viable alternatives to VERITAS US products. . . .

IV. Product Lifecycles and Useful Lives

In the rapidly changing storage software industry, products with state-of-the-art function lost value quickly as that functionality was duplicated by competitors or supplanted by new technology. Even with substantial ongoing research and development (R&D), VERITAS US products had finite lifecycles. Intense competition (i.e., from OEMs offering comparable products) and the rapid pace of technological advances forced VERITAS US to innovate constantly. By the time a new product model became available for purchase, the next generation was already in development.

At the time of the CSA, VERITAS US products, on average, had a useful life of 4 years. . . .

VERITAS US typically updated its products but, on occasion, an OEM would pay VERITAS US to build a custom item that would not be further developed. In these instances, the related OEM agreements contained a royalty degradation or technology aging discount provision to account for obsolescence and decay. Some agreements provided for the royalties to be decreased at a steady rate while others required royalty rate reductions that increased during the term of the agreement. Generally, the agreements did not provide a royalty rate reduction of more than 75 percent over a 4-year period.

V. Geographic Expansion

Prior to 2000 VERITAS US had limited presence in EMEA and Asia Pacific and Japan (APJ). While VERITAS US had sales and service offices and resellers in North America, Europe, Asia Pacific, South America, and the Middle East, it had no manufacturing operation in these countries and only small sales subsidiaries in the United Kingdom, France, Germany, Sweden, the Netherlands, Switzerland, Japan, and Australia. . . . VERITAS US' management recognized that geographic expansion in EMEA and APJ presented an opportunity to increase sales. After evaluating the cost of labor, employment laws, quality of workforce, and tax considerations, VERITAS US' management decided to headquarter its EMEA and APJ operations in Ireland.

VI. The Cost-Sharing Arrangement

In January 1999 VERITAS Software Holding, Ltd. (VSHL) was incorporated as an Irish corporation. VSHL was a resident of Bermuda and a wholly owned subsidiary of VERITAS US. In August 1999 VERITAS Software International, Ltd. (VSIL) was incorporated as a resident of Ireland and a wholly owned subsidiary of VSHL. VERITAS Software, Ltd. (VERITAS UK) and VERITAS Software Asia Pacific Trading PTE, Ltd. (VERITAS Singapore), disregarded entities for U.S. income tax purposes, were also wholly owned by VSHL. In 2000 and 2001 VSHL, VSIL, VERITAS UK, and VERITAS Singapore (collectively, VERITAS Ireland) were subsidiaries of VERITAS US.

Effective November 3, 1999, VERITAS US assigned to VERITAS Ireland all of VERITAS US' existing sales agreements with European-based sales subsidiaries (i.e., VERITAS UK, VERITAS Sweden, VERITAS Switzerland, VERITAS France, and VERITAS Germany). Also effective on that date, VERITAS US, VERITAS Operating Corp., NSMG, and VERITAS Ireland entered into the Agreement for Sharing Research and Development Costs (RDA), and VERITAS US and VERITAS Ireland entered into the Technology License Agreement (TLA).

Pursuant to the RDA, the signatories agreed to pool their respective resources and R&D efforts related to software products and software manufacturing processes. They also agreed to share the costs and risks of such R&D on a going-forward basis. The RDA provided VERITAS Ireland with:

> the exclusive and perpetual right to manufacture Products utilizing, embodying or incorporating the Covered Intangibles within VERITAS Ireland's Territory, and the nonexclusive and perpetual right to otherwise utilize the Covered Intangibles worldwide, including in the marketing, sale, and licensing of Products utilizing, embodying or incorporating the Covered Intangibles, and in further research into similar technology.

The RDA defined "Covered Intangibles" as:

> any and all inventions, patents, copyrights, computer programs (in source code and object code form), flow charts, formulae, enhancements, updates, translations, adaptations, information, specifications, designs, process technology, manufacturing requirements, quality control standards, and other intangible

property rights arising from or developed as a result of the Research Program.

Pursuant to the TLA, VERITAS US granted VERITAS Ireland the right to use certain "Covered Intangibles", as well as the right to use VERITAS US's trademarks, trade names, and service marks in EMEA and APJ. The TLA defined "Covered Intangibles" as:

> any and all inventions, patents, copyrights, computer programs (in source code and object code form), flow charts, formulae, enhancements, updates, translations, adaptations, information, specifications, designs, process technology, manufacturing requirements, quality control standards, and other intangible property rights arising in existence as of the Effective Date of this Agreement, relating to the design, development, manufacture, production, operation, maintenance and/or repair of any or all of the Products.

In exchange for the rights granted by the TLA, VERITAS Ireland agreed to pay VERITAS US royalties. The TLA, which was amended on three occasions, specified the initial royalty rates, as well as a prepayment amount (i.e., a lump-sum buy-in payment). (emphasis added) The TLA provided that the parties "shall adjust the royalty rate prospectively or retrospectively as necessary so that the rate will remain an arm's-length rate."

In 1999 VERITAS Ireland paid VERITAS US $6.3 million and agreed to prepay VERITAS US, in 2000, the remaining consideration relating to the preexisting intangibles. In 2000 VERITAS Ireland made a $166 million lump-sum buy-in payment to VERITAS US, and in 2002 VERITAS Ireland and VERITAS US adjusted the payment to $118 million.

VII. VERITAS Ireland's Operations

. . . . In 1999 VERITAS Ireland began codeveloping, manufacturing, and selling VERITAS US products in the EMEA and APJ markets. . . . With VERITAS Ireland in control of the manufacturing process and managing the Lisle contractor, the supply chain became much more efficient.

VERITAS Ireland developed the EMEA and APJ markets without significant input from VERITAS US. . . .

VERITAS Ireland's operations and its presence in the EMEA territory grew substantially from 2000 to 2006 [in terms of facilities square footage, employees, foreign subsidiaries, and amount of money spent on sales and marketing].

VIII. Procedural History

VERITAS US timely filed Federal income tax returns for 2000 and 2001. On its 2000 return VERITAS US reported a $166 million lump-sum buy-in payment from VERITAS Ireland. In response to VERITAS Ireland's updated sales figures and forecasts, VERITAS US, on December 17,

2002, amended the 2000 return reducing the lump-sum buy-in payment to $118 million.

Respondent examined VERITAS US' 2000 and 2001 returns and concluded that the cost-sharing allocations reported did not clearly reflect VERITAS US' income. On March 29, 2006, respondent issued petitioner a notice of deficiency based on a report prepared by Brian Becker (Becker). In the notice, respondent stated:

> In accordance with Section 482 of the Internal Revenue Code, to clearly reflect the income of the entities, we have allocated income and deductions as a result of the transfer and/or license of pre-existing intangible property in connection with the cost sharing arrangement and technology license agreement, both effective November 3, 1999.

Becker employed the forgone profits method, the market capitalization method, and an analysis of VERITAS US' arm's-length acquisitions to arrive at a series of values, ranging from $1.9 billion to $4 billion, for the lump-sum buy-in payment. He ultimately decided that a $2.5 billion buy-in payment was appropriate. In accordance with Becker's calculations, respondent, in the notice to petitioner, made a $2.5 billion allocation of income to VERITAS US and determined deficiencies of $704 million and $54 million, and section 6662 penalties of $281 million and $22 million, relating to 2000 and 2001, respectively.

On June 26, 2006, petitioner timely filed its petition with the Court seeking redetermination of the deficiencies and penalties set forth in the notice. . . . Respondent, in his statement of position filed September 6, 2007, stated: "In view of the fact that information is still being collected and analyzed, Respondent cannot state which transfer pricing method(s) he intends to utilize at trial." On October 11, 2007, respondent, in a supplement to his statement of position, notified the Court and petitioner that he was going to employ the forgone profits method, but was not going to rely on the market capitalization method or call Becker as a witness. Respondent, in the October 11, 2007, statement also stated:

> Respondent will use the actual income figures and projections extrapolated from those figures to determine the value of the intangibles and, consequently, the total compensation due Petitioner from VERITAS Ireland for the intangibles. Based on a preliminary analysis of Petitioner's actual income figures, which are less than Petitioner's projections relied upon by Dr. Becker, Respondent anticipates that the resulting value will be less than the amount used in the notice of deficiency. In that case, Respondent will not contend that the value is greater than the amount determined by his experts at trial.

* * *

On January 11, 2008, the Court filed petitioner's motion for partial summary judgment. In the motion, petitioner contended that respondent had abandoned the $2.5 billion allocation and the methodologies set forth in the notice; the notice was fundamentally defective; and respondent's determination was arbitrary, capricious, and unreasonable. Petitioner further contended that, pursuant to precedent governing the Court of Appeals for the Ninth Circuit (Ninth Circuit), the burden of proof shifts to respondent. The Court, on February 6, 2008, filed respondent's notice of objection to petitioner's motion for partial summary judgment.

On March 7, 2008, respondent submitted to the Court an expert report prepared by John Hatch (Hatch). Hatch, employing a discounted cashflow analysis, concluded that the requisite lump-sum buy-in payment was $1.675 billion, and calculated, as an alternative, a 22.2-percent perpetual annual royalty. In determining the best method to calculate the buy-in payment, Hatch rejected the comparable uncontrolled transaction method (CUT method) and the profit split method. He contended that prior to November 3, 1999, VERITAS US had made several acquisitions of software companies that offered complementary, and in some cases, competing products. Hatch opined that those acquisitions were comparable to the CSA because VERITAS US received rights pursuant to the acquisitions that were similar to those which VERITAS Ireland received pursuant to the CSA. On the basis of his findings, Hatch characterized the CSA as "akin" to a sale or geographic spinoff ("akin" to a sale theory) and employed the income method to determine the requisite buy-in payment.

Hatch defined the buy-in payment as "the present value of royalty obligations expected to be paid under arm's length royalty terms applicable to the rights conferred on a go-forward basis." He did not individually value any of the specific items that were allegedly transferred to VERITAS Ireland. Instead, he employed an "aggregate" valuation approach that was based on a three-step analysis. First, Hatch estimated the arm's-length royalty amounts that would be due in each period (i.e., each calendar year or portion thereof after November 3, 1999) of the CSA. Second, Hatch chose a discount rate to convert estimated future royalty payments into November 1999 dollars. Third, Hatch calculated the buy-in payment as equal to the present value of the royalty payments estimated in step 1, discounted at the rate determined in step 2. Hatch concluded that the requisite buy-in payment was $1.675 billion and that a 22.2-percent perpetual annual royalty was economically equivalent to the requisite $1.675 billion payment. In calculating the requisite buy-in payment, Hatch assumed that the preexisting intangibles have a perpetual useful life. In addition, he concluded that 13.7 percent was the appropriate discount rate and 17.91 percent was the appropriate compound annual growth rate.

On March 21, 2008, the Court filed respondent's motion for leave to file amendment to amended answer and lodged respondent's amendment to amended answer. In the proposed amendment, respondent alleged that the requisite buy-in payment was $1.675 billion, payable as either a lump-sum payment or a 22.2-percent perpetual royalty. In paragraph 9.f of the proposed amendment, respondent asserted an adjustment relating to a transfer of "certain other intangible rights." Respondent specifically alleged a transfer of access to VERITAS US' marketing team; access to VERITAS US' R&D team; and VERITAS US' trademarks, trade names, customer base, customer lists, distribution channels, and sales agreements (collectively, paragraph 9.f items). . . .

On July 1, 2008, the trial commenced.

DISCUSSION

We must determine whether VERITAS Ireland made an arm's-length buy-in payment to VERITAS US as consideration for intangible property transferred to VERITAS Ireland in connection with the CSA. In addition, we must determine whether respondent's allocation is arbitrary, capricious, or unreasonable.

In essence, respondent's determination began to unravel with the parties' pretrial stipulations of settled issues. After the parties' settlement relating to the arm's-length value of the RDA, as a practical and legal matter respondent was forced to justify the $1.675 billion allocation by reference only to the preexisting intangibles. As discussed herein, he simply could not. Respondent, in a futile attempt to escape this dilemma, ignored the parties' settlement relating to the RDA and disregarded section 1.482–7(g)(2), Income Tax Regs., which limits the buy-in payment to preexisting intangibles. In addition, respondent inflated the determination by valuing short-lived intangibles as if they have a perpetual useful life and taking into account income relating to future products created pursuant to the RDA.

After an extensive stipulation process, a lengthy trial, the receipt of more than 1,400 exhibits, and the testimony of a myriad of witnesses, our analysis of whether respondent's $1.675 billion allocation is arbitrary, capricious, or unreasonable hinges primarily on the testimony of Hatch. Put bluntly, his testimony was unsupported, unreliable, and thoroughly unconvincing. Indeed, the credible elements of his testimony were the numerous concessions and capitulations.

Respondent's predicament was primarily attributable to the implausibility of respondent's flimsy determination. In calculating the $1.675 billion allocation, Hatch used the wrong useful life for the products and the wrong discount rate and admittedly did not know precisely which items were valued. Furthermore, respondent's trial position reflected sections 1.482–1T through 1.482–9T, Temporary Income Tax Regs., 74 Fed. Reg. 349 (Jan. 5, 2009)—regulations that were promulgated 10 years after the transaction and 5 months after trial. These regulations include specific examples involving "assembled workforce" and prescribe the income method as a specified method. In fact, after amending his amended answer, respondent began referring to the intangibles subject to the buy-in payment as "platform contribution" intangibles (i.e., the term used in sections 1.482–1T through 1.482–9T, Temporary Income Tax Regs., supra) rather than "pre-existing intangibles" (i.e., the term used in the applicable regulations). We further note that the Administration, in 2009, proposed to change the law, expanding the section 482 definition of intangibles to include "workforce in place", goodwill, and going-concern value. See Department of the Treasury, General Explanations of the Administration's Fiscal Year 2010 Revenue Proposals 32 (May 2009). For the years in issue, however, there was no explicit authorization of respondent's "akin" to a sale theory or its inclusion of workforce in place, goodwill, or going-concern value. Taxpayers are merely required to be compliant, not prescient.

Pursuant to the law in effect at the time of the CSA, respondent's determination is arbitrary, capricious, and unreasonable, and VERITAS US' CUT method, with some adjustments, is the best method to determine the requisite buy-in payment.

I.   Applicable Statute and Regulations

Section 482 was enacted to prevent tax evasion and ensure that taxpayers clearly reflect income relating to transactions between controlled entities. . . . In determining the true taxable income, "the standard to be applied in every case is that of a taxpayer dealing at arm's length with an uncontrolled taxpayer." Sec. 1.482–1(b)(1), Income Tax Regs.

Section 482 provides that in the case of any transfer of intangible property the income with respect to the transfer shall be commensurate with the income attributable to the intangible. In a qualified cost-sharing arrangement, controlled participants share the cost of developing one or more items of intangible property. See sec. 1.482–7(a)(1), Income Tax Regs. When a controlled participant makes preexisting intangible property available to a qualified cost-sharing arrangement, that participant is deemed to have transferred interests in the property to the other participant and the other participant must make a buy-in payment as consideration for the transferred intangibles. Sec. 1.482–7(g)(1) and (2), Income Tax Regs. The buy-in payment, which can be made in the form of a lump-sum payment, installment payments, or royalties, is the arm's-length charge for the use of the transferred intangibles. Sec. 1.482–7(g)(2), (7), Income Tax Regs.

Section 1.482–7(g)(2), Income Tax Regs., requires buy-in payments to be determined in accordance with sections 1.482–1 and 1.482–4 through 1.482–6, Income Tax Regs. Section 1.482–4(a), Income Tax Regs., provides:

> (a) In general. The arm's length amount charged in a controlled transfer of intangible property must be determined under one of the four methods listed in this paragraph (a). Each of the methods must be applied in accordance with all of the provisions of § 1.482–1, including the best method rule of

§ 1.482–1(c), the comparability analysis of § 1.482–1(d), and the arm's length range of § 1.482–1(e). The arm's length consideration for the transfer of an intangible determined under this section must be commensurate with the income attributable to the intangible. See § 1.4824(f)(2) (Periodic adjustments). The available methods are—

(1) The comparable uncontrolled transaction method, described in paragraph (c) of this section;

(2) The comparable profits method, described in § 1.482–5;

(3) The profit split method, described in § 1.482–6; and

(4) Unspecified methods described in paragraph (d) of this section.

If the recipient of the intangibles fails to make an arm's-length buy-in payment, the Commissioner is authorized to make appropriate allocations to reflect an arm's-length payment for the transferred intangibles. Sec. 1.482–7(g)(1), Income Tax Regs. The Commissioner's authority to make section 482 allocations is limited to situations where it is necessary to make each participant's share of costs equal to its share of reasonably anticipated benefits or situations where it is necessary to ensure an arm's-length buy-in payment for transferred preexisting intangibles. Sec. 1.482–7(a)(2), Income Tax Regs.

II. Respondent's Buy-in Payment Allocation Is Arbitrary, Capricious, and Unreasonable

Respondent's section 482 allocation must be sustained absent a showing of abuse of discretion. . . . If petitioner proves that respondent's allocation is arbitrary, capricious, or unreasonable but fails to prove that the allocation it proposes meets the arm's-length standard, the Court must determine the proper allocation for the buy-in payment. . . .

Respondent's determination as set forth in the notice of deficiency is presumptively correct. . . . Respondent made two determinations with respect to the requisite buy-in payment, one set forth in the notice of deficiency and one set forth in the amendment to amended answer. . . . Thus, we look to both the notice determination and the revised determination in the amendment to amended answer to decide whether respondent's section 482 allocation is arbitrary, capricious, or unreasonable.

A. Respondent's Notice Determination Is Arbitrary, Capricious, and Unreasonable

In the notice, respondent determined, using Becker's valuation, that the requisite buy-in payment was $2.5 billion. During trial respondent did not call Becker as a witness, place Becker's report in evidence, or present any evidence to support Becker's findings. Respondent, relying solely on the report prepared by Hatch, did not address Becker's $2.5 billion buy-in valuation but instead asserted a $1.675 billion buy-in valuation. The $825 million decrease in value with little explanation is just one of the factors we consider in evaluating the reasonableness of respondent's determination. There are other factors that collectively and convincingly establish that the notice determination was not only unreasonable but was also arbitrary and capricious. Using an income method, Becker and Hatch, respectively, employed a 12.8- and a 13.7-percent discount rate to calculate the requisite buy-in payment. Beta, a key component in the formula used to calculate the discount rate, is a measure of the tendency of a security's price to respond to swings in the market. In calculating their discount rates, Becker and Hatch used essentially the same beta, 1.4 and 1.42, respectively. Petitioner's finance expert established that 1.935 was the correct beta. . . . Hatch ultimately conceded that a 1.42 beta "could not, to a reasonable degree of economic certainty, be the correct beta." . . . In essence, Hatch admitted that both he and Becker employed the wrong beta. Indeed, the beta Becker employed was even further removed from the correct beta.

In sum, respondent, without meaningful explanation, conceded $825 million of the buy-in amount set forth in the notice and at trial failed to offer even a token defense in response to petitioner's critique of Becker's conclusions. Moreover, respondent cannot convincingly contend that the notice allocations are reasonable while adopting the opinion of an expert who admits that a critical factor relating to the calculation of the allocation is incorrect. Accordingly, respondent's notice determination is arbitrary, capricious, and unreasonable.

B. Respondent's Determination in Amendment to Amended Answer Is Arbitrary, Capricious, and Unreasonable

Respondent's amendment to amended answer set forth a revised determination of the requisite buy-in payment. The revised determination, which is based on Hatch's report, takes into account certain items (i.e., the paragraph 9.f. items) that respondent alleges were intangibles transferred to VERITAS Ireland. Hatch's valuation was based on the theory that the collective effect of the RDA, TLA, and conduct of the parties was "akin" to a sale of VERITAS US' business. Respondent's determination is erroneous for several reasons.

1. Respondent's "Akin" to a Sale Theory Is Specious

Respondent contends that VERITAS US' transfer of preexisting intangibles was "akin" to a sale and should be evaluated as such. Respondent further contends that because "th[e] assets collectively possess synergies that imbue the whole with greater value than each asset standing alone", it is appropriate to apply the "akin" to a sale theory and aggregate the controlled transactions, rather than value each asset. Hatch was certainly in a position to know whether his valuation method took into account the collective assets' "synergies", yet his defense, of respondent's "akin" to a sale theory was akin to a surrender. On redirect examination, Hatch testified:

Q   [Counsel for respondent] Do you believe your valuation methodology captured synergistic value?

A   [Hatch] I really don't have an opinion. It may have. It may not have.

At trial the Court asked respondent's counsel: "if [we] reject Dr. Hatch's approach that [we] should look at this in the aggregate and he hasn't valued any of the intangibles separately, where does that leave the Court?" Respondent's counsel replied: "That leaves the Court absolutely nowhere", and that is precisely where respondent is with this theory—absolutely nowhere. Petitioner astutely suggests that "The reason that respondent is placing an all or nothing bet on his aggregation theory is simple: software does not last forever, but Respondent's valuation approach does." Indeed, respondent's assertion of the "akin" to a sale theory and its assumption that the preexisting intangibles have a perpetual life are an unsuccessful attempt to justify respondent's determination.

Respondent contends that pursuant to section 1.482–1(f)(2)(i)(A), Income Tax Regs., he was authorized to aggregate the transactions and treat them as a sale. Transactions may be aggregated if an aggregated approach produces the "<u>most reliable</u> means of determining the arm's length consideration for the controlled transactions". <u>Id.</u> (emphasis added). Respondent's "akin" to a sale theory (i.e., a theory which encompasses short-lived intangibles valued as if they have a perpetual life and takes into account intangibles that were subsequently developed rather than preexisting) certainly does not produce the most reliable result. Thus, pursuant to section 1.482–1(f)(2)(i)(A), Income Tax Regs., respondent was not authorized to aggregate the transactions and treat them as a sale.

2.   Respondent's Allocation Took Into Account Items Not Transferred or of Insignificant Value

The parties agree that, on November 3, 1999, certain product intangibles (i.e., NetBackup, Backup Exec, Volume Manager, File System, Cluster Server, and Foundation Suite) were transferred from VERITAS US to VERITAS Ireland but disagree about the transfer of the nonproduct items alleged by respondent. With the exception of the trademarks, trade names, brand names, and sales agreements, the nonproduct items either were not transferred or had insignificant value.

With respect to distribution channels, VERITAS US had relationships with distributors and resellers prior to the CSA, but those relationships were weak and had little value. In fact, it was not until VERITAS Ireland hired the channel manager from Computer Associates that the distribution channels were strengthened and maximized. . . . Thus, to the extent VERITAS US' customer lists and customer base were transferred to VERITAS Ireland, they had insignificant value. With respect to "access to research and development team", Hatch testified that his valuation of the buy-in payment did not include access to R&D team and that access to R&D team "just was not on [his] radar screen or anything that [he] thought of." In addition, Hatch conceded that if he assumed that the agreement relating to the share of R&D expenses was arm's length, a fact that the parties stipulated, then access to the R&D team would have zero value. With respect to "access to marketing team", Hatch testified that he did not value VERITAS US' marketing team, did not know whether marketing support was provided by VERITAS US, and had no idea whether the alleged marketing intangibles existed or had been transferred. Hatch further testified:

> if those marketing intangibles did exist—and sometimes they don't, and they just have clauses in there, I don't know. But if they did exist, they were conferred when these related party seller contracts were assigned. Now did they have any value? I don't have any opinion on that. I have no idea. [Emphasis added.]

In short, there is insufficient evidence that access to VERITAS US' R&D and marketing teams was transferred to VERITAS Ireland or had value.

3. Respondent's Allocation Took Into Account Subsequently Developed Intangibles

Hatch's calculations of the requisite buy-in payment took into account rights to future codeveloped intangibles transferred pursuant to the RDA. Petitioner contends that respondent's buy-in payment allocation relating to subsequently developed products violates section 1.482–7(g)(2), Income Tax Regs. We agree.

Section 1.482–7(g)(2), Income Tax Regs., the regulatory authority requiring a buy-in payment, states:

(2) Pre-existing intangibles. If a controlled participant makes pre-existing intangible property in which it owns an interest available to other controlled participants for purposes of research in the intangible development area under a qualified cost sharing arrangement, then each such other controlled participant must make a buy-in payment to the owner. * * * [Emphasis added.]

The regulation unequivocally requires a buy-in payment to be made with respect to transfers of "pre-existing intangible property". No buy-in payment is required for subsequently developed intangibles. Yet Hatch unabashedly took such items into account in calculating the requisite buy-in payment rather than limiting the valuation to preexisting intangibles as prescribed by section 1.482–7(g)(2), Income Tax Regs. In fact, respondent readily and repeatedly acknowledged that his valuation took into account income relating to items other than the preexisting intangibles. Accordingly, respondent's allocation violates section 1.482–7(g)(2), Income Tax Regs.

4.   Respondent Employed the Wrong Useful Life, Discount Rate, and Growth Rate

Respondent, relying on Hatch's report, employed the wrong useful life, the wrong discount rate, and an unrealistic growth rate to calculate the requisite buy-in payment.

In calculating his valuation of the buy-in payment, Hatch assumed a perpetual useful life for the transferred intangibles, yet acknowledged that "if you had 1999 products that you left untouched, that technology would age and eventually become obsolete" and that the preexisting product intangibles would "wither on the vine" within 2 to 4 years without ongoing R&D. . . .

. . . Petitioner contends that respondent employed the wrong beta, the wrong equity risk premium, and therefore the wrong discount rate. Hatch employed an industry beta to calculate the discount rate. He opined that using an industry, rather than a company specific, beta was preferred because, with respect to an individual company, a beta relating to an earlier period is a very poor predictor of the beta for subsequent periods. Hatch ultimately admitted, however, that "to a reasonable degree of economic certainty, the beta he used could not have been the correct beta for VERITAS US as of November 3, 1999."

Hatch's 5-percent equity risk premium was much lower than the 1926 through 1999 historic average of 8.1 percent which Hatch stated was reported by Ibbotson Associates (i.e., the recognized industry standard of historical capital markets data). . . . . In sum, Hatch employed the wrong beta, the wrong equity risk premium, and thus the wrong discount rate to calculate the requisite buy-in payment.

Hatch also employed large and unrealistic growth rates into perpetuity. . . . Moreover, he could not provide a plausible explanation for the growth rate he employed. Further, petitioner notes that a buy-in payment based on Hatch's growth rate would require VERITAS Ireland to allocate a buy-in payment equal to 100 percent of its actual and projected operating income to VERITAS US through 2009, resulting in $1.9 billion in losses over that period. Simply put, the growth rate Hatch employed was unreasonable.

In sum, VERITAS Ireland prospered, not because VERITAS US simply spun off a portion of an established business and transferred valuable intangibles, but because VERITAS Ireland employed aggressive salesmanship and savvy marketing, successfully developed the EMEA and APJ markets, and codeveloped new products that performed well in those markets. For the foregoing reasons, we conclude that respondent's allocations set forth in the amendment to amended answer and at trial are arbitrary, capricious, and unreasonable.

III. Petitioner's CUT Analysis, With Some Adjustments, Is the Best Method

Petitioner used the CUT method to calculate the buy-in payment. The best method rule seeks the most reliable measure of an arm's-length result. Sec. 1.482–1(c), Income Tax Regs. "[T]here is no strict priority of methods, and no method will invariably be considered to be more reliable than others." Id. Respondent's income method, riddled with legal and factual miscalculations, is certainly not the best or most reliable method. Therefore, we must determine the propriety of petitioner's CUT analysis. If petitioner's CUT analysis does not meet the arm's-length standard, we must determine the requisite buy-in payment. See Sundstrand Corp. & Subs. v. Commissioner, 96 T.C. at 354; see also Eli Lilly & Co. v. Commissioner, 856 F.2d at 860 (and cases cited thereat).

The CUT method evaluates whether the amount charged for a controlled transfer of intangible property is arm's length by referencing the amount charged in comparable uncontrolled transactions. If an uncontrolled transaction involves a transfer of the same intangible under the same, or substantially the same, circumstances as a controlled transaction, the results derived from applying the CUT method will generally be the most reliable measure of the arm's-length result. Sec. 1.482–4(c)(2)(ii), Income Tax Regs. If, however, uncontrolled transactions involving the same intangible under the same circumstances cannot be identified, uncontrolled transactions that involve the transfer of "comparable intangibles under comparable circumstances" may be used to apply the CUT method, but the reliability of the results is reduced. Id.

Respondent contends that the CUT method is not the best method and that petitioner has not presented comparable uncontrolled transactions to prove that its buy-in payment is arm's length. Specifically, respondent asserts that the rights licensed under agreements between VERITAS US and unrelated parties are not comparable because they involved either rights that are not comparable to those licensed under the CSA or licensees who are not comparable to VERITAS Ireland. Petitioner contends that the CUT method is appropriate and that the value determined by its expert, William Baumol (Baumol), was arm's length.

Baumol calculated, using the CUT method, a range of estimates for the value of the transferred intangibles and concluded that the lump-sum buy-in payment was within or exceeded the arm's-length range. Baumol used four parameters to estimate a value for the buy-in payment: The expected economic life of the intangibles, the annual rate at which the value of the intangibles declines as a function of time and new software replacements (i.e., the rate of obsolescence), the parameter value selected to determine the value of the licenses (e.g., royalty rates as a percent of revenues, list price, or profits), and the appropriate discount rate.

Baumol chose particular agreements (i.e., some involving bundled products and some involving unbundled products) between VERITAS US and seven OEMs (i.e., Sun, HP, Dell, Hitachi, NEC, Compaq, and

Ericsson) to determine the appropriate starting royalty rate for the buy-in payment. Most of the product licenses that Baumol selected provide royalties as a percentage of list price (e.g., global list price, international list price, or U.S. list price). Based on his findings, Baumol derived a range of starting royalty rates of 20 to 25 percent of list price and opined that the low end of the range, 20 percent, was the appropriate starting royalty rate for the buy-in payment.

Baumol determined that the preexisting product intangibles had a useful life ranging from 2 to 4 years. Having determined both the starting royalty rate and the useful life, Baumol adjusted the royalty rate by ramping down (i.e., incrementally reducing) the rate over the buy-in period. . . .

Using the aforementioned findings, Baumol calculated a valuation range of $94 million to $315 million for the buy-in payment and concluded that "the preponderance of the values" fell between $100 million and $200 million.

A.   Comparability of OEM Agreements

Use of the CUT method requires that the controlled and uncontrolled transactions involve the same or comparable intangible property. Sec. 1.482–4(c)(2)(iii)(A), Income Tax Regs. In order for intangibles involved in controlled and uncontrolled transactions to be comparable, "both intangibles must—(i) Be used in connection with similar products or processes within the same general industry or market; and (ii) Have similar profit potential." Sec. 1.482–4(c)(2)(iii)(B)(1), Income Tax Regs.

In his CUT valuation, Baumol referenced, as comparables, agreements between VERITAS US and certain OEMs (i.e., Sun, HP, Dell, Hitachi, NEC, Compaq, and Ericsson). Respondent contends that the CSA involves the transfer of "platform contribution" intangibles and broad "make-sell rights" with respect to VERITAS US' full range of products, while the OEM agreements did not. We note that the term "platform contribution intangibles" does not appear in the regulations applicable to the CSA but is set forth in section 1.482–7T, Temporary Income Tax Regs., 74 Fed. Reg. 352 (Jan. 5, 2009)—regulations effective for transactions entered into on or after January 5, 2009. Thus, respondent's litigating position appears to mirror transfer pricing regulations promulgated 10 years after VERITAS US and VERITAS Ireland signed the CSA. In essence, respondent contends that, pursuant to section 1.482–4(c)(2)(iii)(A), Income Tax Regs., the CUT method is not appropriate because the OEM agreements involve substantially different intangibles. We disagree.

VERITAS Ireland, pursuant to the TLA, received broad rights for the full range of VERITAS US products. The rights licensed under the OEM agreements referenced by Baumol involved Backup Exec, NetBackup, Volume Manager, File System, Cluster Sever, and Foundation Suite. While none of the individual OEM agreements evaluated by Baumol included a license for the full range of VERITAS US' product line, collectively the agreements did involve essentially the same intangibles that were transferred from VERITAS US to VERITAS Ireland. The OEM agreements Baumol selected do not, however, provide the most reliable measure for calculating the requisite buy-in payment.

B. Unbundled OEM Agreements Were Comparable to the Controlled Transaction

VERITAS US entered into numerous OEM agreements prior to and during the CSA. Baumol chose to use only a select few of those OEM agreements (i.e., some involving bundled products and some involving unbundled products) to calculate the requisite buy-in payment. His justification for rejecting particular agreements was simply: "I didn't find the numbers that I could use." Respondent contends that the OEM agreements Baumol selected are not comparable to the controlled transaction because the circumstances surrounding the selected OEM agreements and the circumstances surrounding the controlled transaction are different. We conclude that, collectively, the more than 90 unbundled OEM agreements the parties stipulated are sufficiently comparable to the controlled transaction.

When OEMs sold VERITAS US products bundled with the OEMs' operating systems, VERITAS US gained credibility and improved brand identity. The OEMs actively marketed the bundled products; listed the products on their Web sites; and provided equipment, technical support, and engineering assistance for those products. Because of these factors, OEMs paid a lower royalty rate with respect to bundled products. VERITAS Ireland, on the other hand, did not have a trade name as widely recognized as the trade names of the OEMs, guaranteed sales like the OEMs, or an operating system with which to bundle VERITAS US products. Therefore, VERITAS Ireland would not be entitled to similar royalty rates. In contrast to bundled products, unbundled products were not directly associated with the OEMs' products and the OEMs did not provide the same level of assistance (i.e., technical and engineering support). Thus, customers did not perceive unbundled products to be more reliable or of greater quality than other comparable products. The OEMs merely listed the unbundled products as an option (i.e., customers could purchase VERITAS US products or other products). Because such agreements are more comparable to the transaction between VERITAS US and VERITAS Ireland, use of the OEM agreements involving unbundled products provides a more reliable arm's-length result. Thus, we compare VERITAS US' unbundled OEM agreements with the controlled transaction.

The degree of comparability between controlled and uncontrolled transactions is determined by applying the comparability standards set forth in section 1.482–1(d), Income Tax Regs. Sec. 1.482–4(c)(2)(iii), Income Tax Regs. Section 1.482–1(d)(1), Income Tax Regs., provides that the following factors shall be considered in determining comparability between controlled and uncontrolled transactions: Functions, contractual terms, risks, economic conditions, and property or services. An analysis employing these factors confirms that VERITAS US' unbundled OEM agreements are sufficiently comparable to the controlled transaction.

The first factor, functional analysis, compares the economically significant activities undertaken, or to be undertaken, in the controlled transactions with the economically significant activities undertaken, or to be undertaken, in the uncontrolled transactions. Sec. 1.482–1(d)(3)(i), Income Tax Regs. VERITAS Ireland and the OEMs undertook similar activities (e.g., manufacturing and production, marketing and distribution, transportation and warehousing, etc.) and employed similar resources in conjunction with such activities. See section 1.482–1(d)(3)(i), Income Tax Regs., for a list of functional analysis comparability factors. Respondent contends, however, that the OEM agreements and the controlled transactions are not functionally comparable because R&D is a particularly significant function in the controlled transactions (i.e., VERITAS US and VERITAS Ireland agreed to share in ongoing R&D costs relating to the development of new software products), whereas the OEM agreements did not involve ongoing R&D activities. Respondent contends that the R&D function is important because VERITAS Ireland "received ownership interests in future generations of technology which germinated from the pre-existing technology." Respondent's functional analysis is misguided. Respondent is relying on rights involving subsequently developed intangibles to support his assertion that the OEM agreements are not comparable to the controlled transaction. As previously determined herein, VERITAS Ireland was required to make a buy-in payment with respect to the transfer of "pre-existing intangible property", not subsequently developed intangibles. See sec. 1.482–7(g)(2), Income Tax Regs. Thus, the focus of the buy-in payment analysis should be on transactions involving preexisting intangibles. For the products in existence on November 3, 1999, there are no significant differences in functionality.

The second factor is the comparability of contractual terms. Determining the degree of comparability between the controlled and uncontrolled transactions requires a comparison of the significant contractual terms that could affect the results of the transactions (e.g., the form of consideration; the sales volume; the scope and terms of warranties; the right to updates, revisions, or modifications; the duration of the agreement; etc.). Sec. 1.482–1(d)(3)(ii)(A), Income Tax Regs. Respondent contends that the contractual terms of the OEM agreements are not comparable to the controlled transaction for two reasons. First, respondent contends that the OEMs often provided VERITAS US with APIs, source code, or information about their hardware so VERITAS US could adapt VERITAS US products to the OEMs' hardware and operating systems, whereas VERITAS Ireland did not have an operating system,

APIs, or source code. . . . The APIs and source code information did not change the essential functions of VERITAS US products but rather enabled VERITAS US products to run on the OEM's operating system. Second, respondent contends that the OEMs provided engineering assistance to VERITAS US in connection with the development of VERITAS US bundled products, whereas there is no evidence that VERITAS Ireland was in a position to provide engineering assistance to VERITAS US. While it is true that some OEMs did provide engineering support with respect to bundled products, the provision of engineering support was not a standard contractual term in OEM agreements relating to unbundled products . . . Thus, there are no significant differences in contractual terms.

The third factor compares the significant risks borne by the parties that could affect the prices charged or the profit earned in the controlled and uncontrolled transactions. Sec. 1.482–1(d)(3)(iii), Income Tax Regs. The parties to the controlled and uncontrolled transactions bore similar market risks, similar risks associated with R&D activities, similar risks associated with fluctuations in foreign currency exchange rates and interest rates, similar credit and collection risks, and similar product liability risks. See section 1.482–1(d)(3)(iii)(A), Income Tax Regs., for a list of risk comparability factors . . .

The fourth factor compares the significant economic conditions that could affect prices or profit in the controlled transaction to the significant economic conditions that could affect prices or profit in the uncontrolled transactions. Sec. 1.482–1(d)(3)(iv), Income Tax Regs. Respondent contends that the economic and market conditions affecting the OEM agreements are not comparable to those affecting the transaction between VERITAS US and VERITAS Ireland because, unlike VERITAS Ireland, the OEMs occupied significant positions in the market. . . . We agree with respondent that the OEMs and VERITAS Ireland were at dramatically different stages of development and held different positions in the market. We note, however, that both the OEMs and VERITAS Ireland competed in similar geographic markets, incurred similar distribution costs, marketed products that faced similar competition, and were subject to similar economic conditions. . . . While certain economic conditions (e.g., interest rate fluctuations, general vicissitudes of the market, etc.) affect prices and profits for both startups and established businesses, the impact on a particular business may certainly depend on the business' economic stability and market position. Our analysis of this factor narrowly weighs against a finding of comparability.

The fifth factor compares the property or services provided in the controlled transaction to that provided in the uncontrolled transactions. Sec. 1.482–1(d)(3)(v), Income Tax Regs. Respondent contends that under the OEM agreements, VERITAS US generally contracted to provide only the development work necessary to ensure its products would work with the OEMs' products, whereas under the CSA, VERITAS US provided make-sell rights and preexisting intangibles for research to produce future generations of technology. Specifically, respondent contends that "VERITAS U.S. and VERITAS Ireland contracted to share all the costs of future R&D on future software generations and for each to hold separate exploitation rights. * * * Neither the property nor services were comparable." Once again, respondent's contention is misguided. Respondent is relying on rights involving subsequently developed intangibles to support his assertion that the OEM agreements are not comparable to the controlled transaction. As previously determined herein, pursuant to section 1.482–7(g)(2), Income Tax Regs., the requisite buy-in payment need not take into account subsequently developed intangibles. With respect to the controlled transaction involving the transfer of preexisting intangibles and the uncontrolled transactions involving VERITAS US' unbundled OEM agreements, there are no significant differences in property or services provided.

Although VERITAS US' unbundled OEM agreements are certainly not identical to the controlled transaction, an analysis of the comparability factors establishes that the unbundled OEM agreements are sufficiently comparable to the controlled transaction and that the CUT method is the best method to determine the requisite buy-in payment. There are, however, certain adjustments we must make to petitioner's CUT analysis to enhance its reliability.

IV. Requisite Adjustments to Petitioner's CUT Analysis

Imperfect comparables serve "as a base from which to determine the arm's length consideration for the intangible property involved in this case." <u>Sundstrand Corp. & Subs. v. Commissioner</u>, 96 T.C. at 383, 393. Section 1.482–1(e)(2)(ii), Income Tax Regs., provides that

Uncontrolled comparables must be selected based upon the comparability criteria relevant to the method applied and must be sufficiently similar to the controlled transaction that they provide a reliable measure of an arm's length result. If material differences exist between the controlled and uncontrolled transactions, adjustments must be made to the results of the uncontrolled transaction if the effect of such differences on price or profits can be ascertained with sufficient accuracy to improve the reliability of the results. * * *

A.   The Appropriate Starting Royalty Rate

Respondent contends that if the OEM agreements are comparable to the controlled transaction, petitioner's calculation of the starting royalty rate is nevertheless erroneous. In determining the requisite buy-in payment, Baumol used 20 percent as the starting royalty rate and acknowledged that he did not use any "sophisticated calculation" or "higher mathematics" to arrive at that rate. He based the 20-percent royalty rate on rates found in select OEM agreements involving bundled and unbundled products. As previously determined, OEM agreements involving unbundled products are the appropriate comparables. As petitioner did not use sufficiently comparable transactions in determining the starting royalty rate to calculate the requisite buy-in payment, and respondent has not provided a royalty rate other than one based on a perpetual royalty, the Court must determine the appropriate royalty rate.

The parties provided the Court with the royalty rates for more than 90 unbundled OEM agreements. Because each unbundled OEM agreement standing alone does not involve the full range of intangibles referenced in the TLA, the agreements must be looked at collectively. The royalty rates relating to VERITAS US unbundled products range between 25 and 40 percent. The mean (i.e., the average) royalty rate for VERITAS US' OEM agreements involving unbundled products is 32 percent of list price. Thus, we conclude that the starting royalty rate for the transferred product intangibles is 32 percent of list price.

B. The Appropriate Useful Life and Royalty Degradation Rate

The appropriate useful life of the preexisting product intangibles is 4 years. Indeed, as previously discussed, VERITAS US products, on average, had a useful life of that duration. . . .

C. Value of Trademark Intangibles and Sales Agreements

Petitioner contends that VERITAS US' trademarks, trade names, and brand names (trademark intangibles) lacked value because in 1999 "VERITAS" was registered in only a few foreign jurisdictions and was relatively unknown in the EMEA and APJ markets. Regardless of the number of foreign jurisdictions in which the "VERITAS" trademark was registered, the "VERITAS" trademark and the individual product names, especially "NetBackup" and "Backup Exec", were well known, respected, and valuable. Thus, pursuant to section 1.482–7(g), Income Tax Regs., VERITAS Ireland was required to pay VERITAS US a buy-in payment as consideration for those trademark intangibles.

Petitioner's trademark expert found that as of November 3, 1999, VERITAS US had trade names for Backup Exec, NetBackup, Volume Manager, File System, Cluster Server, and Foundation Suite, as well as certain other products. He believed that the value of the trademark intangibles was zero but nevertheless calculated another value for those intangibles. In calculating a value petitioner's trademark expert opined that the useful life of the trademark intangibles in VERITAS Ireland's territory should be no more than 7 years, selected a range of royalty rates from 0.5 to 1 percent of revenue, and concluded that before taxes the value for the trademark intangibles was between $1.7 and $3.4 million. He assumed that VERITAS Ireland was entitled to royalty-free use of the trademark intangibles for the duration of the TLA and concluded that the TLA, which did not have a termination date, had a term of November 1999 through October 2003. Thus, his initial valuation included a royalty for only 3 years (i.e., from November 2003 through the end of 2006). During trial, in response to Hatch's criticism of his findings petitioner's trademark expert revised his calculations to include a royalty that covered the entire 7-year useful life that he projected. He ultimately concluded that the revised upper-end value for the trademark intangibles was $9.6 million.

Petitioner's trademark expert was not convincing and when he was questioned regarding the calculation of his lower range of values, his response was incoherent. Respondent failed to estimate a value for these intangibles, and the paucity of credible evidence relating to this issue is disconcerting. Nevertheless, we conclude that petitioner's trademark expert's upper-end value of $9.6 million is the best available approximation of, and thus, the arm's-length value of the trademark intangibles.

The buy-in payment must also be adjusted to take into account the value of the sales agreements transferred from VERITAS US to VERITAS Ireland. We do not, however, have sufficient evidence to determine the value of those agreements. Thus, this matter must be addressed in the parties' Rule 155 computations.

D.   The Appropriate Discount Rate

Petitioner's financial markets expert Burton Malkiel (Malkiel) applied the CAPM and concluded that 20.47 percent was a reasonable estimate of VERITAS US' WACC. There are two differences between Hatch's and Malkiel's applications of CAPM: The estimate of the beta and the equity risk premium. Malkiel, unlike Hatch, used reliable data to calculate both variables. . . .

Accordingly, the appropriate discount rate is 20.47 percent.

V.   Conclusion

With the aforementioned adjustments, the CUT method is the best method for determining the requisite buy-in payment relating to VERITAS Ireland's transfer of intangibles to VERITAS US.

Contentions we have not addressed are irrelevant, moot, or meritless. To reflect the foregoing,

Decision will be entered under Rule 155.

NOTES AND QUESTIONS

1.   In reaching its final decision, how much was the court influenced by its view that the Government seemed to talk the language of the new regulations that did not govern the years in questions? Was it simply a matter of terminology? Significantly different methods?

2.   How did the pricing approach advanced by the Government's expert differ from what the court considered to be the set available of appropriate pricing methods? Did the court object to the method used by the government? How it was used? With respect to what assets it was used?

3. What facts in the *Veritas* case do you think were most significant or persuasive to the court in framing their understanding of the underlying commercial events?

4. What method did the taxpayer use? As discussed earlier, it is can be quite difficult to support a CUT as best method. How was the taxpayer able to rely on a CUT? Did the court fully accept the taxpayer's position?

5. Does the court's opinion in *Veritas* (which applied older regulations) undermine the new temporary cost sharing regulations? Take a look at the court's discussion of valuing assets in the aggregate, of the "akin to a sale theory," and of whether and how R&E and marketing teams should be included in the buy-in determination.

The same issues arose more recently in Amazon v. Commissioner, 148 TC No. 8 (2017), and again the IRS lost on the valuation of the buy-in payment. How may the last sentence added to section 482 change these results?

6. The highest profile recent tax cases, Xilinx v. Commissioner and Altera v. Commissioner, both involved a cost sharing agreement. In *Xilinx*, a U.S. corporation engaged in researching, developing and manufacturing, and selling integrated circuit devices and related software, entered into a cost sharing agreement (CSA) with its wholly owned subsidiary. The major issue, as the case wound its way through the courts, was whether the stock based compensation costs that the U.S. parent Xilinx incurred where costs required to be shared with the Irish subsidiary pursuant to the cost sharing agreement. [What position do you think that the taxpayer Xilinx took? Why?] The Tax Court, ruling against the IRS concluded that Xilinx did not need to share these costs because unrelated companies do not share stock-based compensation costs. On appeal, the 9th Circuit reversed the Tax Court holding that the employee stock option costs must be included in the shared costs under the CSA because the relevant Section 482 analysis asks what is an accurate reflection of income. These stock based compensation costs were costs related to the new technology created pursuant to the CSA—and the regulations detailing taxation under a CSA state that "all costs" must be shared. To the extent this outcome conflicts with the application of an arm's length rule, the more specific rules of the cost sharing regime apply. The 9th Circuit decision created tremendous controversy. Some viewed the court as rejecting the arm's length standard in violation of long standing U.S. practice and in violation of international and treaty standards. Others suggested the court's reasoning was not ideal but that the outcome was appropriate under the statute because section 482 explicitly contemplates a departure from a formalistic view of arm's length by allowing the commensurate with income rule. In January 2010, the 9th Circuit withdrew its decision in *Xilinx*. Finally, in March 2010, the 9th Circuit issued a new decision affirming the Tax Court's conclusion that the stock based compensation costs do not need to be shared. The 9th Circuit rejected its own prior analysis which relied on rules of statutory construction that resolved conflict in favor of the more specific rule. Instead the court now argued that the important question did not concern an individual rule of statutory construction but rather the dominant purpose of the regulations in conflict. The court concluded the purpose was parity for transactions involving related parties and those involving unrelated parties. Achieving parity here would dictate that the stock based compensation be treated as simply a cost of Xilinx, not a cost under the cost sharing agreement.

In *Altera*, the same issue arose again after the IRS amended the regulation to specifically require the inclusion of stock option costs, but without amending the ALS language. The Tax Court sitting en banc unanimously held that the regulation was inconsistent with the Administrative Procedure Act because Treasury and the IRS did not receive any comments that supported the regulatory approach. On appeal the Ninth Circuit initially reversed, holding that the commensurate with income language was sufficient to support the regulation, but this opinion was withdrawn (in August 2018) due to the death of one of the judges.

c.   SERVICES

Determination of transfer prices for services can be difficult, inter alia, because many services, especially those performed within a MNE, are embedded in other transactions, and because their variety complicates any attempt of valuation. New regulation Treas. Reg. 1.482–9 (finalized in 2009) governing the provision of related party services outlines a new system for pricing services transactions that incorporates versions of many of the same methods used for sales tangibles and transfers of intangibles. Take a look at the regulations—what portions seem familiar? Note the introduction of the SCM—the services cost method, which is meant to be a safe harbor for low value or non-vital services. The adoption of the new rules was driven in part by the recognition that in today's world services can be a very high value part of business and the economy—and thus careful (and perhaps more sophisticated) attention to related party pricing is essential. See also Notice 2007–5.

6.5   THE INTERACTION WITH FOREIGN LAW

Procter & Gamble Company v. Commissioner of Internal Revenue

United States Tax Court.
95 T.C. 323 (1990).

■ OPINION BY: HAMBLEN

OPINION: Respondent determined deficiencies in petitioner's Federal income tax in the amounts and for the years as follows:

TYE	Deficiency
June 30, 1978	$765,649.04
June 30, 1979	1,188,033.02

The issue for decision in this case is whether respondent's allocations of gross income from Procter & Gamble Espana, S.A., to Procter & Gamble A.G., pursuant to section 482, were arbitrary, capricious, or unreasonable.

FINDINGS OF FACT . . .

Procter & Gamble Company (petitioner or P & G) is an Ohio corporation whose principal place of business at the time of the filing of the petition herein was in Cincinnati, Ohio. . . . At all times relevant to the issues in this case, petitioner was principally engaged in the business of manufacturing and marketing consumer and industrial products. Petitioner operated its business both directly and indirectly through domestic and foreign subsidiaries and affiliates.

Procter & Gamble A.G. (AG) is a Swiss corporation and at all relevant times was a wholly owned subsidiary of petitioner. During each of the years in issue, AG was engaged in the marketing of petitioner's products, generally in those countries in which petitioner did not have a marketing subsidiary or affiliate.

During the years in issue, petitioner and AG were parties to a License and Services Agreement, known as a "package fee agreement," under which AG paid royalties to petitioner for the nonexclusive use by AG and its subsidiaries of petitioner's patents, trademarks, tradenames, knowledge, research, and assistance in the fields of manufacturing, general administration, finance, buying, marketing, and distribution. Petitioner executed similar agreements with its other directly owned foreign subsidiaries during the years in issue. The royalty amounts paid by AG to petitioner were based principally on net sales of petitioner's products by AG and its subsidiaries, and certain other companies in Greece, Spain, Austria, Saudi Arabia, Morocco, Iran, Libya, and Lebanon. During the years in issue, AG executed technical assistance and other service agreements, similar to package fee agreements, with its directly owned active subsidiaries.

In 1967, petitioner made preparations to organize a wholly owned subsidiary in Spain to manufacture and sell its consumer and industrial products in that country. At that time, many laws, decrees, and orders were in effect in Spain regulating foreign investment in Spanish companies and limiting the payment or assignment of credits in pesetas in favor of residents of foreign countries.

Article First, paragraphs 14 through 17, of the First Title of the Spanish Law of Monetary Crimes of November 24, 1938 (Law of Monetary Crimes), in effect through 1979, provided broad authority for the regulation of payments from Spanish entities to residents of foreign countries. These provisions required governmental authorization prior to the making of payments or assignment of credits in pesetas in favor of residents of foreign countries. The making of such payments without governmental authorization constituted a crime. . . .

Decree 16/1959 of July 27, 1959, contained specific regulations concerning investment of foreign capital in corporations organized in Spain. Article 4 of Decree 16 classified investment of foreign capital based on whether the particular business was of "preferential economical and social interest." Article 4 provided, inter alia, that a foreign investment could be deemed preferential if directed towards the modernization or enlargement of existing plants. If the foreign investment was found to be of preferential economic interest, Article 6 provided that the company would have the "right to transfer abroad in foreign currency and—without any quantitative limitation, the benefits actually obtained by the foreign capital." Article 5 required prior authorization from the Spanish Council of Ministers in order for foreign participation to exceed 50 percent ownership of the capital of a Spanish corporation.

On September 23, 1967, P & G, upon the advice of competent Spanish counsel, submitted an application letter addressed to the "Presidency of the Spanish Government" requesting authorization to organize a Spanish company, Espana. The application recited that P & G intended to own directly, or through a wholly owned subsidiary, 100 percent of the capital stock of Espana. The application stated that Espana would have as its purpose the manufacture and sale of high quality consumer and industrial products, including synthetic detergents, soaps and toiletries, and other cleaning and washing products.

In an index attached to the application letter, P & G stated that Espana would employ up to 250 persons for its manufacturing operations and that an additional 120 persons could be employed if P & G were to construct a new synthetic detergent factory. However, P & G indicated that it might purchase an existing plant if one could be found meeting its technical specifications.

Paragraph 8 of the index set forth estimated annual requirements for foreign currency for the first 5 years of Espana's existence. Among the items covered was an annual amount of 7,425,000 pesetas necessary for royalty and technical assistance payments.

The final portion of the index related to P & G's justification for its desire to hold over 50 percent of the capital of Espana. P & G stated that its 100 percent ownership of Espana would allow Espana immediate access to additional foreign investment. Further, P & G indicated that it was in the best position to shoulder the formidable risks associated with mass-produced consumer products, and that 100 percent ownership of Espana would allow P & G to preserve the confidentiality of its technology.

The Spanish Government approved P & G's application for a 100 percent interest in Espana by a letter dated January 27, 1968. However, the letter expressly provided that Espana could not pay any amounts for royalties or technical assistance. After receipt of the letter, P & G's Spanish counsel advised that the limitation on royalty payments was within the power of the Spanish Government and reflected normal practice. Counsel further advised that there was no realistic possibility of appealing or protesting the decision as long as P & G intended to retain 100 percent ownership of Espana. Consistent with advice of counsel, P & G did not formally appeal the prohibition on royalty payments. At the time of its organization, Espana had several competitors in Spain who likewise could not make royalty payments abroad.

For reasons not clear in the record, a determination was made that AG, rather than P & G, would hold the entire interest in Espana. Espana's Deed of Incorporation was registered in the Mercantile Registry of the Province of Madrid on May 29, 1968. . . .

Counsel for Espana and an official from the Spanish Ministry of Industry met on May 19, 1970, to discuss the possibility of Espana's making technical assistance payments to AG. However, the Spanish Government would not approve or grant permission for such payments. To the contrary, such applications or appeals were discouraged by the Spanish Government due to concerns that similarly situated companies would abuse technical assistance payments to remove profits from Spain untaxed. On the other hand, this policy was not imposed as to companies with a majority of foreign capital where a clear and obvious benefit to Spain was demonstrated in terms of substantial exports, use of Spanish raw materials, and enhancement of Spanish technology. . . .

Among other adjustments contained in the statutory notice of deficiency, respondent determined that income should be allocated in the amounts of $1,232,653 and $1,795,005 for the years 1978 and 1979 respectively, from Espana to AG, pursuant to section 482, in order to clearly reflect AG's income. These allocations in turn increased petitioner's Subpart F income under section 951(a)(1)(A).

Respondent's determination is based on a royalty of 2 percent of Espana's net sales of petitioner's products for the taxable years in question. For purposes of this litigation, petitioner does not contest the amount of the allocation made by respondent or the use of 2 percent in calculating that determination, but contends that no allocation from Espana is proper under section 482. Thus, after concessions, the sole issue for decision is whether respondent's allocations of gross income from Procter & Gamble Espana, S.A., to Procter & Gamble A.G., pursuant to section 482, were arbitrary, capricious, or unreasonable.

OPINION . . .

Section 482 authorizes respondent to allocate income between controlled enterprises if he determines that such an allocation is

Procedure of §482

necessary to prevent evasion of taxes. . . . It is sufficient for purposes of this opinion to emphasize that section 482 is designed to prevent the artificial shifting of the true net incomes of controlled taxpayers by placing controlled taxpayers on a parity with uncontrolled, unrelated taxpayers

It is well established that respondent's authority to make allocations under section 482 is broad and that respondent's section 482 determination must be sustained absent a showing that he has abused his discretion. Thus, in order for this Court to redetermine the deficiency, the taxpayer must meet a heavier than normal burden of proof and demonstrate that respondent's determinations are arbitrary, capricious, or unreasonable.

Petitioner asserts that because Spanish law prohibited or blocked royalty payments from Espana to AG, petitioner did not improperly utilize its control to shift income, and thus section 482 does not apply. In this regard, petitioner relies primarily on Commissioner v. First Security Bank of Utah, supra, a case in which the Supreme Court denied the Commissioner's section 482 allocation of insurance premium income to taxpayers who were otherwise prohibited from receiving income of that nature by Federal law. As petitioner sees it, AG's income should not be increased by amounts which it could not and did not receive by virtue of Spanish law.

Respondent's primary argument is that Spanish law did not prohibit the payment of royalties by Espana to AG during the years at issue, and accordingly First Security Bank does not impact his allocation. In respondent's view, the prohibition on the payment of royalties from Espana to AG was merely an administrative decision, arbitrarily determined and subject to appellate review which Espana voluntarily waived.

Assuming we find that Spanish law did prohibit Espana from paying royalties to AG, respondent insists that First Security Bank does not control this case because it is factually distinguishable. In particular, respondent finds it significant that in First Security Bank, Federal law served to prohibit absolutely the taxpayers from receiving the income in question under any circumstance. On the other hand, respondent asserts that in the case sub judice Spanish law only prohibited royalty payments from a Spanish company to its foreign parent. Respondent contends that because AG could have received royalty payments from an unrelated Spanish company, and would have demanded royalties if bargaining at arm's length, the transaction cannot withstand the analysis associated with the second prong of section 482. That is, the transaction, albeit a product of Spanish law, effects an artificial shifting of income and does not clearly reflect income. Petitioner concedes that the Supreme Court did not consider within the context of First Security Bank whether section 482 would apply in the face of a foreign law which proscribes payments between companies with common ownership.

As we understand the positions of the parties, we are confronted with an issue of first impression. Specifically, the issue is whether a section 482 allocation is appropriately applied under the circumstances to correct the "shifting" of income associated with Spain's policy of prohibiting or blocking royalty payments from a Spanish subsidiary to its foreign parent. A review of First Security Bank will aid in establishing the framework for analysis of this issue.

In First Security Bank, two national banks, First Security Bank of Utah and First Security Bank of Idaho (the banks), wholly owned subsidiaries of First Security Corporation, made a practice of offering to arrange credit life, health, and accident insurance for their borrowers. The lending officer would explain the function and availability of credit insurance, complete the necessary forms, deliver a certificate of insurance, and collect the premium or add it to the customer's loan. At that point, the banks would forward the forms and premiums to an independent insurer. The independent insurer would then reinsure the policies with Security Life, another wholly owned subsidiary of First Security Corporation. Under this arrangement, Security Life retained 85 percent of the premiums paid for the insurance, and the independent insurer, which furnished actuarial and accounting services, received the remainder.

Security Life reported the entire amount of insurance premiums in its income for the years in issue. By virtue of the lower effective tax rate applicable to life insurance companies, the total tax liability for First Security Corporation and its subsidiaries was less than it would have been had Security Life paid a part of the premiums to the banks as sales commissions. Pursuant to section 482, the Commissioner determined that in order to reflect actual income, 40 percent of Security Life's premium income was allocable to the banks as compensation for originating and processing the insurance.

The Supreme Court framed the issue to be decided as follows: whether there was a shifting or distorting of the banks' true net income resulting from the receipt and retention by Security Life of the premiums in question. At the outset, the Court noted that Federal banking laws had been interpreted to prohibit the banks from receiving a share of the insurance premiums. In addition, the Court referenced the finding of the courts below that the banks, upon advice of counsel, believed that they would violate Federal banking law by receiving income from their customers' purchases of insurance.

In concluding that the Commissioner's allocation was unwarranted, the Supreme Court emphasized that there was no shifting or distorting of income because the banks simply could not receive insurance premium income. The Court stated that section 1.482–1(b)(1), Income Tax Regs., as applied to the facts—contemplates that [First Security Corp.]—the controlling interest—must have "complete power" to shift income among its subsidiaries. It is only where this power exists, and has been exercised in such a way that the "true taxable income" of a subsidiary has been understated, that the Commissioner is authorized to reallocate under sec. 482. But [First Security Corp.] had no such power unless it acted in violation of federal banking laws. The "complete power" referred to in the regulations hardly includes the power to force a subsidiary to violate the law. [Commissioner v. First Security Bank of Utah, 405 U.S. at 404–405. n4] . . .

We find First Security Bank . . . compelling with respect to the issue before the Court. As we understand these cases, section 482 simply does not apply where restrictions imposed by law, and not the actions of the controlling interest, serve to distort income among the controlled group. Accordingly, in order to decide whether respondent's allocation is appropriate in the case sub judice, we must determine whether Spanish law prohibited or blocked Espana from making royalty payments to AG. . . .

We find that Spanish law prohibited Espana from making royalty payments to AG. . . .

On this record, as was the case in First Security Bank, there is no evidence whatsoever that petitioner utilized its control over its subsidiaries to manipulate or shift income amongst them. Petitioner sought to maintain 100-percent control of Espana in order to ensure that the company had direct and immediate access to additional capital and to protect its proprietary rights in a technologically competitive industry. Although petitioner possibly could have organized Espana so that royalties could be paid, n6 it was not obligated to do so. . . . Moreover, section 482 does not impel the violation of a legal prohibition solely for the sake of matching income and expense. Commissioner v. First Security Bank of Utah, 405 U.S. 394, 404–405 (1972). Because the deflection of income in this case arose as a direct consequence of petitioner's valid business purposes and good faith compliance with Spanish law, an allocation under section 482 is inappropriate. . . .

* * *

NOTES AND QUESTIONS

1.   Would a taxpayer bargaining at arm's length agree to provide the data provided by AG to Espana without a royalty?

2.   Do you agree that *First Security Bank* is indistinguishable? Is Federal law and foreign law the same for these purposes?

3.   Is a legal prohibition relevant to the purposes of Section 482? Was First Security Bank correct?

4.   In Exxon Corp. v. Commissioner, 66 T.C.M. 1707 (1993), the Tax Court refused to allow the IRS to allocate intercompany oil sales between Exxon subsidiaries based on Saudi Arabian price controls set below market rates, despite the fact that the controls were set out in a letter by the Saudi minister to Exxon, which had questionable legal effect, and the fact that

Exxon had flouted the restrictions. The case was part of the so-called "Aramco Advantage" set of cases, which together form the largest deficiency ever litigated in tax court. Thus, the issue in *P & G* could end up costing the government billions of dollars.

5. New regulations under Section 482 attempt to reverse the result in these cases. Treas. Reg. 1.482–1(h)(2) accepts certain foreign legal restrictions, but requires information (provided in a formal tax return) in exchange and payment with interest of the original tax when the restrictions are moved. It is still unclear what the effect of these regulations may be. The issue may have to reach the Supreme Court again.

6.6   CONCLUSION: IS THERE A FEASIBLE ALTERNATIVE?

The key to transfer pricing disputes is the fundamental assumption that each subsidiary in a commonly controlled group is a separate taxpayer and separate from the parent, so that the price of inter-group sales matters. There is an obvious alternative: To treat a commonly controlled group as a single, unitary entity and allocate the total profit from each transaction to its members based on some formula. That is the approach taken by the U.S.' states, which allocate the income of unitary businesses by ignoring the separate existence of the constituent corporations and using a formula (usually based on assets, payroll and sales).

Do you think this is a feasible alternative? The main objection to it is that a formula is too mechanistic if applied across the board. Recall the "profit split" method (Treas. Reg. 1.482–6) that focuses on the entire profit of related parties, but does not contain a formula to allocate any residual left over after the normal returns have been allocated to routine functions performed by each party. "Profit split" and, to a larger extent, CPM were criticized as incompatible with the arm's length standard. In particular the OECD transfer pricing guidelines use a similar, yet arguably less "formulaic" version of CPM, coined: Transactional Net Margin Method ("TNMM"). Note also that both in the United States and in the other OECD countries these two "criticized" methods are clearly the most widely used in the practice of transfer pricing support.

One possibility would be to try to negotiate a separate formula for each taxpayer under the so-called "advance pricing agreement" initiative, which is an attempt by the IRS to prevent transfer pricing litigation by agreeing with taxpayers (and sometimes other taxing authorities) what the proper profit allocation should be in advance.[11] What do you think?

Note that an advance pricing agreement with the IRS may not, as such, be agreeable with tax authorities in other countries involved. Some multilateral advance pricing agreements have concluded, yet they are

---

[11] Under the existing APA structure, the IRS and the taxpayer negotiate directly the transfer price rather than a formula.

still the exception rather than the rule. This is a significant and reasonable development for multinationals seeking certainty. Increased international cooperation with regard to advance pricing agreements is inevitable and expected in the coming years.

6.7   REVIEW PROBLEMS—CHAPTER 6

1.   P, a U.S. drug company, is selling its product in the U.S. and foreign countries F and G. It also secured a patent on this drug in these countries. P licenses the right to manufacture and sell the drug in F to a local company L for an annual (lump sum) payment of $X. In G, a country that is three times the size of F (and 5 times its GDP per capita), P owns a subsidiary, S, which manufactures and sells the drug locally and pays P $X each year as well for the right to do that. Do you expect transfer price adjustment?

2.   Would your answer change if the agreements included also the rental of certain laboratory equipment (the same equipment for both S and L and the same payments)?

3.   Now assume that P provides (monthly) equipment and material to both S & L. L, however, pays for the transportation of this supply, whereas S gets the supply for virtually free because P's trucks that regularly travel between P's headquarters and country G, can add the small size monthly supply to their load without any additional cost.

4.   FP is a tax haven company that wholly owns D, a domestic corporation. Now assume that FP established D with equity of $100 (cash), that D has $100 of accumulated and current E&P and it owes FP $1,000 lent in the beginning of the year 2019. FP sold 100 units of product X to D in 2019—each unit of the product costs $100 to manufacture and transport into the U.S., including taxes and customs, and sells for $10,000 in the U.S. In 2019 D transferred $1,000,000 to FP and labeled the transfer as payment for the product. It filed its tax return accordingly. What was behind this label and what are the adjustment risks that D faces?

5.   X is an individual microbiologist working for D, a U.S. corporation. In the ordinary course of his work, X discovered a new groundbreaking process that promised to be very profitable to D. After a series of extensive tests and consultation with top management, D organized a wholly owned tax haven subsidiary, S, to engage in the development of the new process. D contributes $1,000,000 to the capital of S, which later is spent primarily to finance the development of the process. D also spent about $1,000,000 in the development of the process—all according to a cost-sharing agreement that D and S entered into upon S's organization and expected earnings from the license of the product to be 50% from the U.S. and 50% from outside the U.S. D received under the agreement all the rights to exploit the process in the U.S. and S outside the U.S. Assume that the agreement is a qualified cost sharing agreement. What are the

tax consequences of the parties' realization that foreign royalties will exceed U.S. royalties by 50%—so in years 1–5 40% of earnings came from the U.S. and 60% from abroad?

How would the fact that D secured a patent on the process while X, its employee, worked on its final marketability evaluation, change your answer?

PART D

FOREIGN INCOME OF U.S. TAXPAYERS

CHAPTER 7

DEFERRAL AND ITS LIMITS

7.1 THE PROBLEM OF DEFERRAL

As stated in Ch. 1 above, U.S. international taxation applies differently for U.S. and non-U.S. persons. U.S. persons (primarily U.S. citizens, residents, and domestic corporations) are taxed on their worldwide income "from whatever source derived" (sections 1, 11, 61). Non-U.S. persons are taxable only on U.S. source income (sections 2(b), 11(d), 871, 881). As we have also seen, while the line between individual U.S. residents and non-residents is a relatively meaningful one, the distinction between domestic and foreign corporations depends entirely on corporate formalities that are within the taxpayer's control.

Tax law's respect of corporations as (separate) legal persons causes a major deviation from the general norm of taxing U.S. persons on their worldwide income. Take, for illustration purposes, A, an individual U.S. citizen residing in Florida. She is in business importing widgets from abroad and selling them to customers in the United States. Her net income from the sale of the widgets is subject to U.S. tax.

On the advice of her tax lawyer, A sets up a Cayman Islands corporation (an act that can be done by phone with a minimal fee, courtesy of one of the many Cayman Islands law offices). A owns 100% of the shares of the corporation ("CayCo"). Thereafter, the purchase and resale of the widgets are done through CayCo, with title passing outside the United States.

Does A have to pay U.S. tax on the profit from the resale of the widgets by CayCo? Does CayCo? When, if ever, will A have to pay tax on such profits (hint: remember section 1014)?

A's ability not to pay current tax on CayCo's profit is called deferral. The value of deferral to the taxpayer results from the delay in paying the tax. In present value terms, it reduces the burden of the tax on the taxpayer; if deferral lasts long enough, the present value of the tax can approach zero. It is not hard to imagine that deferral is very costly in terms of U.S. revenue and can produce a huge (tax) incentive for U.S. persons to invest abroad rather than domestically, and invest through foreign subsidiaries rather than directly. This problem triggered the enactment of certain limitations on deferral (still—the general rule), which are the primary focus of this chapter. A major feature of the December 2017 tax reform was the inclusion of a significant further limitation on the ability to defer current U.S. taxation through the use of foreign corporations.

Finally, revisit the "check-the-box" regime described in chapter 1. Note that deferral can now be achieved even when the traditional business form is direct—through a foreign branch of the U.S. person—by simply checking-the-box to have the branch taxed as corporation (and therefore deferral-eligible) for U.S. tax purposes.

7.2   LIMITATIONS PRIMARILY FOR INDIVIDUALS

a.   EARLY LIMITATIONS ON DEFERRAL

Until 1937, there were no limitations on deferral in the Code.[1] In 1937, Congressional hearings showed that many wealthy U.S. individuals (including, e.g., all the partners in the J.P. Morgan bank) did not pay U.S. income tax by shifting their investment income to controlled corporations in Caribbean tax havens. For example, Jacob Schick, the inventor of the Schick electric razor, transferred his royalty income from the patent on the razor to a Bahamas corporation controlled by him. This corporation was described as an "incorporated pocketbook." Congress responded by enacting the Foreign Personal Holding Corporations' ("FPHC") regime in sections 551–558. Other anti-deferral regimes followed, attempting to stop tax avoidance schemes identified by the government. This trend has reversed in the last decade, when Congress attempted to simplify these regimes and eliminate common overlaps among them. Finally, the AJCA repealed some remaining regimes, including FIC and FPHC,[2] reflecting a belief that the remaining Subpart F and Passive Foreign Investment Companies ("PFIC") rules (see sections 7.2.c and 7.3.b below) would suffice.[3]

The following table summarizes the former anti-deferral regimes and their relationships to each other.

Summary of Anti-Deferral Rules

Rule	Requirements	Result	Priority
FIC (1246–47) (1962)	1. Engaged primarily in investment business 2. 50% of vote by U.S. persons	OI on sale of stock unless distrib. 90% of income	Subpart F
Subpart F (951–960) (1962)	50% by vote or value owned by 10% (by vote) U.S. shareholders (CFC)	Current inclusion of Subpt F income by U.S. sh, OI on sale (1248)	FPHC PFIC

---

[1]   The only possible exception is the accumulated earnings tax (sections 531–537), which by its terms applies to foreign as well as domestic corporations. However, because the tax applies at the corporate level, it was not considered applicable to foreign corporations in 1937. In addition, the tax is widely considered a paper tiger because of the difficulty for the IRS to show that earnings and profits were accumulated beyond the reasonable needs of the business.

[2]   AJCA § 413, effective for tax years beginning after December 31, 2004.

[3]   AJCA § 413 did adjust the scope of PFIC to include personal service contract income, previously covered by the FPHC rules.

FPHC (551–558) (1937)	1. 60% of gross income is FPHC income, and	Current inclusion of FPHC income	PFIC PHC AET
	2. 50% by vote or value held by 5 or fewer U.S individuals		
PFIC (1291–97) (1986)	1. 75% of gross income is passive, or	Current inclusion or interest charge or mark to market (all income)	PHC AET
	2. 50% of assets are passive (by value or basis)		
PHC (541–547) (1937)	1. 60% of gross income is PHC income, and income	20% tax on PHC	AET
	2. 50% by value held by 5 or fewer indivs		
AET (531–537) (1921)	Formed or availed of to avoid tax on sh by permitting e & p to accum.	20% tax on accum. taxable income	

Do you think having so many rules made sense? If yes, in what circumstances?

b. REALIZATION V. RECEIPT

Any anti-deferral regime essentially taxes income earned outside the Jurisdiction (U.S.), and therefore requires an authority to extend the jurisdiction to tax to such profits. Another way to look at this problem is to assert that jurisdiction to tax residents includes taxation of their income realized through certain foreign entities owned by such residents. The following case clarifies that receipt of income in the U.S. is not a prerequisite for U.S. taxation of such income.

Eder et al. v. Commissioner of Internal Revenue

United States Court of Appeals for the Second Circuit.
138 F.2d 27 (1943).

. . .

■ Before L. HAND, AUGUSTUS N. HAND, and FRANK, CIRCUIT JUDGES.

. . .

We do not agree with taxpayers' argument that inability to expend income in the United States, or to use any portion of it in payment of income taxes, necessarily precludes taxability. In a variety of circumstances it has been held that the fact that the distribution of income is prevented by operation of law, or by agreement among private parties, is no bar to its taxability . . . That the result under the statute here before us may be harsh is no answer to the government's position; the purpose of Congress was to deal harshly with "incorporated pocketbooks", and the motive of a particular taxpayer who has such a "pocketbook" we have held to be irrelevant . . . In *Porto Rico Coal Co. v. Commissioner, 2 Cir., 126 F.2d 212, 213,* we said: "It is apparent that the decision of the Board has brought about a harsh result by imposing a surtax, to say nothing of the penalty for failure to file a return, upon a corporation which had no net income to distribute; but if it finds itself, because of the way it was organized and did its business, within the scope of a statute primarily designed to make the failure to distribute actual net income too expensive to be worthwhile and was, therefore, taxed when it did not in fact do what the statute was aimed to discourage, it must endure its misfortune as best it may."

Interpreting the statute to bring about such a consequence does not render the statute unconstitutional; the Congressional purpose was valid and the method of taxation was a reasonable means to achieve the desired ends.

NOTES AND QUESTIONS

1. Why do you think the taxpayer argued that the statute was unconstitutional? Is Judge Frank's reply and his analogy convincing?

2. Do you think it makes a difference that the tax was imposed on a deemed dividend from a foreign corporation? Are there any limits on Congress' ability to tax the foreign source income of foreign corporations?

c. PASSIVE FOREIGN INVESTMENT COMPANIES (PFIC, SECTIONS 1291–1298)

Read sections 1291–1298. This regime was enacted in 1986, and so it is much more modern than the recently repealed FPHC regime. What is the principal difference between the two regimes? (Hint: compare the definition of PFIC in sec. 1297(a) with the definition of FPHC in 552(a). What is missing in the PFIC definition?) This unique feature of PFIC makes it complementary to the Subpart F regime in the case of (especially portfolio) individual investors abroad. Because of its potentially broad application rather than a pinpointed "anti-abuse" or "loophole closing" approach, which is so typical of the code and the other anti-deferral regimes. In an innovative extension of this feature of PFIC, some commentators have suggested abolishing the corporate tax and replacing it with a PFIC-like regime for all U.S. shareholders in domestic as well as foreign corporations (with no limitation to passive income). Do you think this is a good idea?

Familiarity with the operative rules of PFIC are crucial for its understanding. Note the choice of tax regimes available to the taxpayer (think whether the word "choice" is appropriate here?):

1. An interest charge on the deferred amount upon the receipt of a dividend or disposition of the stock (sec. 1291),

2. Current inclusion of the income if the PFIC is willing to supply the taxpayer (and the IRS) with the necessary information (sec. 1293, 1295), or

3. "Mark to market" of the PFIC stock if it is publicly traded (sec. 1296).

Which regime do you think most taxpayers prefer (note the different information required to be furnished by taxpayers to the service under the different regimes)? Which do you think is the most commonly applicable? Why was it considered necessary to give the taxpayer such a range of choices? Are they equivalent in their effects? Note that this is the primary anti-deferral regime for non-controlled situations, and the taxpayer may not have the power to generate cash (in the form of dividends, for instance) out of the investment. In practice, these choices compel taxpayers to restructure their investment by abandoning deferral or entering into different transactions that avoid PFIC in most cases where it applies. This effect made PFIC a significant tax friction rather than the broadly applied regime, which it may seem to be at a first glance.

The regulations under these sections are quite complex. Note, in particular, the "once a PFIC, always a PFIC" rule (Reg. 1.1291–1(b)(1)(ii)), and the deemed disposition rule for non-residents (Reg. 1.1291–3(b)(2)). The latter is a "trap for the unwary" for foreigners who become residents temporarily and own PFIC shares (e.g., as beneficiaries of a trust). PFIC has been criticized also for its other unintended consequences. Take, for instance a U.S. individual portfolio investor in a foreign technology start up corporation owned 99% by foreign individuals. Naturally, the corporation builds up business losses in the first few years, but earns some interest income on bank deposits of the capital raised for R & E and operation. Is the corporation a PFIC? Does it matter how many years of losses it suffered? What do you think may be the effect of the PFIC rules on American portfolio investors interested in such corporations? Is this effect intentional or desirable in your opinion? Would you change your mind if you knew that the taxpayer was able to ensure annual dividend to (at least) cover the U.S. (PFIC related) tax?

7.3   LIMITATIONS PRIMARILY FOR CORPORATIONS

a.   FROM EQUITY TO NEUTRALITY

The principal rationale for the enactment of the FPHC rules in 1937 was equity: It was considered unfair to tax individual A on $100 in wages earned domestically but not individual B on $100 in interest earned through a foreign "incorporated pocketbook."

In 1961, President Kennedy proposed ending deferral for foreign subsidiaries of U.S. multinationals. This time, the rationale was not based on equity, but rather on efficiency considerations.

PRESIDENT'S TAX MESSAGE ALONG WITH PRINCIPAL STATEMENT, DETAILED EXPLANATION, AND SUPPORTING EXHIBITS AND DOCUMENTS

SUBMITTED BY SECRETARY OF THE TREASURY DOUGLAS DILLON in connection with THE PRESIDENT'S RECOMMENDATIONS CONTAINED IN HIS MESSAGE ON TAXATION

at Hearings conducted by COMMITTEE ON WAYS AND MEANS, HOUSE OF REPRESENTATIVES

May 3, 1961.

(U.S. Government Printing Office, Washington, D.C., 1961).

* * *

II. EQUAL TAXATION OF FOREIGN INVESTMENT INCOME

The President in his tax message has cited the strains in our balance-of-payments position as one of the factors which have led us to reexamine our tax treatment of foreign income. Earlier, in his balance-of-payments message, the President made it clear that our concern relates to the *preferential* treatment of foreign investment income, tax treatment that has favored U.S. private investment abroad compared with investment in our own country. There is no thought of penalizing private investment abroad which rests upon genuine production or market advantages.

ROLE OF TAX DEFERRAL

The most important feature of our tax system giving preferential treatment to U.S. investment abroad is the privilege of deferring U.S. income tax on the earnings derived through foreign subsidiaries until those earnings are distributed as dividends. The lower the rate of foreign income tax, the more significant is this privilege of tax deferral.

I have here a table showing in the first line of figures the statutory income tax rates imposed by various industrialized countries in Europe. It shows a range of rates from 28½ percent in Belgium to 31 percent in Italy, 51 percent in Germany and 53½ percent in the United Kingdom. If one were to take into account variations in the methods of computing taxable income, the range of effective rates would be somewhat lower, but similar adjustments would have to be made for U.S. tax rates, and for present purposes the statutory rates would seem to be the appropriate ones to use. As you can see, in most of these countries, and particularly those countries which are our more important competitors, the tax rates are substantially at the same level as the U.S. corporation income tax. Tax deferral with respect to profits earned in these countries does not, of course, have any material effect on U.S.-owned firms.

[Table, *Comparison of tax rates applicable to income derived in selected foreign countries under alternative assumptions concerning form of organization*, omitted]

However, to the extent that business operations are conducted in countries with lower tax rates, there is considerable leeway for deferring U.S. tax. With a foreign tax rate of 28½ percent, for example, a company can defer U.S. tax payments equal to 23½ percent of total pretax profits. It thus can through deferral retain nearly an extra dollar out of every four that it earns.

These statutory rates, however, do not give adequate weight to the variety of arrangements that have been made by American firms in their foreign operations which may bring down rather substantially the rates of tax imposed on income from their foreign operations. Thus, an American company operating in West Germany through a German subsidiary will be subject to tax there at the West German income tax rate of 51 percent, and hence it cannot benefit significantly from U.S. tax deferral. However, to the extent that the profits of the German subsidiary can be diverted from the sweep of the German tax system, a lower tax on profits can be attained. And this is precisely what is achieved through a proliferation of corporate entities in tax haven countries, like Switzerland.

The tax haven companies are given the right to license patents developed by their parent organizations or sister corporations. They supply the services of technicians of their corporate affiliates to firms in various other countries. They acquire the distribution rights of products manufactured by their affiliates. The transfer of these various activities to tax haven entities means a transfer of income to them. Since the income taxes in these tax haven countries are very low or nonexistent with respect to income derived outside their own borders, the result of these arrangements is to bring about a substantial reduction in tax on the total income derived from the foreign operations. Switzerland, for example, has a federal income tax ranging from 3 to 8 percent. While local income taxes vary widely, there are opportunities for the negotiation of tax liability to the Cantons. With U.S. tax deferral operating simultaneously, tax payments overall can be and often are very substantially reduced.

If $100 of income of a German subsidiary can be segmented so that $50 is attributed to the entity in Germany and $50 attributed to a selling entity in Switzerland, half the profit would be subject to the 51 percent German tax rate but the other half would be subject to a Swiss national tax of only 8 percent. The overall rate of tax would thus be reduced to less than 30 percent. The Table I last referred to shows on the second line the aggregate income tax in cases where manufacturing subsidiaries are organized in various European countries but which effect their sales through a Swiss sales corporation so that taxable profits are divided equally between the country of manufacture and Switzerland. As a consequence of such arrangements, and taking into account withholding taxes on dividends transferred from the manufacturing company to the Swiss sales company, the resulting tax rates range from about 22 to 33 percent.

The reductions in tax that can be achieved through the use of tax haven operations assume that the incomes attributed to the tax haven companies are fair and reasonable. But the problem is compounded by the fact that incomes are often allocated to tax haven companies which are not economically justifiable. U.S. companies frequently attribute a disproportionate share of profits to the trading, licensing, and servicing companies established in tax haven countries—a practice that is extremely difficult if not impossible for the Internal Revenue Service to police effectively.

This is not simply a question of allocating the profits of foreign operations to tax haven countries. It is a problem that significantly affects U.S. taxation of domestic profits. The technique that is used for diverting profits from one company to another among European affiliates is also used to divert income from U.S. companies to foreign affiliates. Income that would normally be taxable by the United States is thrown into tax haven companies with the object of obtaining tax deferral. This is done, for example, by placing in a Swiss or Panamanian corporation the activities of the export division of a U.S. manufacturing enterprise. A very substantial volume of exports is required merely to offset the loss in foreign exchange which the retention abroad of export profits entails. The recent growth of U.S. subsidiaries in tax haven countries—and Switzerland and Panama are but two examples—suggests that their importance as a means of tax reduction and avoidance will rapidly increase if the deferral privilege is continued. An examination of the public records in Switzerland alone indicates that there are more than 500 firms there which can be identified as being owned by U.S. interests. About 170 of these were created in the year ending March 31, 1961. U.S. officials on the spot are of the opinion that in addition to these firms there are a substantial number of other U.S.-owned firms in Switzerland which cannot be readily identified as such on the basis of the presently available data. Increasingly, U.S. manufacturing subsidiaries operating elsewhere in Europe are being linked to subsidiaries in the tax haven countries. Parenthetically, I might note that the information returns filed by U.S. shareholders or officers of foreign corporations indicate that there are only 92 U.S.-owned corporations in Switzerland all told. There is little doubt that these information returns are inadequate and incomplete. The tightened requirements for filing information returns on new foreign corporations which were adopted by the Congress last year will doubtless give us more accurate information in the future.

PROPOSAL REGARDING ADVANCED COUNTRIES AND TAX HAVEN OPERATIONS

To avoid artificial encouragement to investment in other advanced countries as compared with investment in the United States, we propose that American corporations be fully taxed each year on their current share in the undistributed profits realized by subsidiary corporations organized in economically advanced countries. This change in the method of taxation should be achieved over 2 years, with only half of the profits affected in 1962. Deferral of tax would also be eliminated for individual shareholders controlling closely held foreign corporations in the industrialized countries. The proposed change will not alter the principle that companies may credit income taxes paid abroad against U.S. income tax liability.

In view of the national objective of aiding the development of less-advanced countries, we do not propose the same change in the tax treatment of income from investments in less developed countries. Tax deferral will continue to apply with respect to operations in those areas, except that we propose to eliminate deferral in the case of tax haven companies even in the less industrialized countries. For this purpose, a tax haven company would be defined generally as one receiving more than 20 percent of its gross profit from sources outside the country in which it is created.

This test would reach such typical tax haven activities as export and import companies, licensing companies, and insurance companies. However, the general test would be qualified so as not to affect manufacturing companies operating in less-developed regions which must look to more than one country for their markets. Other possible areas of exception may be considered in the light of forthcoming testimony before this committee.

While it is difficult to estimate quantitatively by how much tax deferral has contributed to the balance-of-payment deficit, it has surely been a significant factor. Particularly when it is enhanced by the resort to tax havens, tax deferral has given artificial encouragement to foreign investment and has acted as a deterrent to the repatriation of dividend income. Deferral thus adversely affects out balance-of-payments position by increasing payments and reducing receipts. For the 4 years 1957 through 1960, the U.S. capital outflow to Western European subsidiaries amounted to $1.7 billion, raising the total investment in these subsidiaries to $6.2 billion at the end of 1960. Earnings from these subsidiaries in the same period were $2.4 billion, of which $1.1 billion were reinvested abroad and $1.3 billion were remitted to the United States in dividends. On balance, the outflow for the 4-year period exceeded dividend remittances by $400 million. Much the same picture applies to Canada. The capital outflow in the same 4 years amounted to

$1.3 billion, bringing our investment there to $9.3 billion. Earnings were $2.4 billion, but $1.3 billion were reinvested and only $1.1 billion were remitted in dividends. Thus, capital outflow exceeded dividend remittances by $200 million.

It is true that deferral causes U.S. assets abroad to rise more rapidly than they would otherwise, so that dividend remittances would also tend to rise over a long span of years. But the time span is apt to be very long. The attached chart shows how the tax deferral privilege can result in a slower remittance of earnings from investment in a foreign subsidiary, as compared with a situation in which the deferral privilege did not exist. Suppose an investment of $1,000 in a foreign subsidiary that yields 20 percent a year before taxes, and that the foreign tax rate is 20 percent. Suppose also that the subsidiary reinvests all of its after-tax earnings for 5 years; and then for the next 15 years reinvests half its profits and remits half its profits to the United States as dividends.

Without the deferral privilege, as the solid line shows, the company would immediately begin to remit funds for U.S. tax payments on its earnings.

With the deferral privilege, as the dotted line shows, the company reinvests the funds it would otherwise have remitted for U.S. tax payments, and it remits nothing for the first 5 years. The greater amount of reinvestment results in a more rapid growth of its net worth, and increases its earnings and remittances, once they begin. Nevertheless, it will be 17 years before cumulative remittances to the United States *equal* those that would have occurred if the deferral privilege had not existed. On the chart this point is reached where the curves cross.

Actually, this is an optimistic example since it assumes that with the deferral privilege the subsidiary will begin remitting *half* of its after-foreign-tax-earnings from the sixth year on. In practice, the existence of the deferral privilege may lead it to remit a considerably lower portion of its profits and thus prolong further the time when the two curves cross.

[Graph, *Cumulative Remittances to U.S. from Net Earnings of a U.S. Foreign Subsidiary*, omitted]

Today, our situation is such that we must look first to the more immediate balance-of-payments results. Last fall, as you know, our balance-of-payments position led to a crisis which threatened the stability of the dollar and therefore jeopardized the economic health of the entire free world. Although returning confidence has given a temporary reprieve, it is important that we act to prevent a recurrence of last fall's situation. We must improve our balance-of-payments position. Eliminating the deferral privilege will help us to do so.

It may be estimated, although very roughly, that the elimination of the deferral privilege for subsidiaries in advanced countries and for tax haven operations in all countries would improve our balance-of-payments position by as much as $390 million per annum. This estimate includes the increase in remittances for U.S. tax payments on foreign earnings, as well as increased dividend remittances and a lower level of capital outflow than would occur if the present privilege were continued.

I have heard it said that elimination of tax deferral such as we propose will not help our balance of payments. Some people even go so far as to claim that it will injure our payments position. In my opinion this view is utterly erroneous. I would cite in support of my opinion that of the responsible financial leaders of Europe. In mid-January, during the height of our balance-of-payments difficulties, the finance ministers of the six Common Market countries met and discussed the U.S. balance-of-payments position. They were good enough to give us the general tenor of their thinking. In particular, the ministers informed us of their unanimous belief that the United States would be justified in discontinuing the fiscal incentives which encouraged the nonremittance of profits made in Europe. This viewpoint from countries which have an interest in attracting and keeping U.S. investment is strong confirmation of our own judgment regarding the adverse impact of the deferral privilege on our balance of payments.

While relief for the balance of payments is an important reason for discontinuing tax deferral, it is not the only one. There exists, in addition, an important issue of equity which has a significant bearing on domestic employment and production, as well as an indirect bearing on our balance-of-payments position. With the present deferral privilege, an American firm contemplating a new investment and finding cost and market conditions comparable at home and abroad is impelled toward the investment opportunity overseas. This is so because it would thereafter be able to finance expansion on the basis of an interest-free loan from the U.S. Treasury, repayable at the option of the borrower. Tax deferral, after all, is just such a loan.

This issue of equity is sometimes presented in reverse; namely, that the withdrawal of the deferral privilege would be unfair because it would change the rules on which companies have already based major investment decisions. This argument seems to me to be very questionable. During the postwar period the promotion of private foreign investment in both advanced and less developed countries was in the public interest. Times have changed, and the need to stimulate investment in advanced countries no longer exists. Hence, there can be no proper claim that preferential treatment should be continued merely to perpetuate a private gain. This change, moreover, cannot severely injure companies already abroad, for a change in the timing of income tax liability will not normally turn a profit into a loss. At most, it may slow the growth of companies abroad or make the financing of growth somewhat more expensive. To alleviate possible problems, our proposal would remove the tax deferral privilege in two steps.

It is sometimes contended that if U.S. firms are to compete successfully abroad they must enjoy as favorable a tax treatment as their foreign competitors. I believe that this argument has been overly stressed. A difference in tax rates, I said before, should not handicap companies producing abroad, although it may slow the rate of expansion. But even if this argument were fully valid, it could not be a decisive objection to our proposal. *As long as the tax systems of various countries differ—and I venture to predict that this will be the case for years to come—we must make a firm choice. Either we tax the foreign income of U.S. companies at U.S. tax rates and credit income taxes paid abroad, thereby eliminating the tax factor in the U.S. investor's choice between domestic and foreign investment; or we permit foreign income to be taxed at the rates applicable abroad, thereby removing the impact, if any, which tax rate differences may have on the competitive position of the American investor abroad. Both types of neutrality cannot be achieved at once. I believe that reasons of tax equity as well as reasons of economic policy clearly dictate that in the case of investment in other industrialized countries we should give priority to tax neutrality in the choice between investment here and investment abroad.*

This does not mean that elimination of the deferral privilege would end U.S. investment in foreign subsidiaries. In many cases, foreign investment opportunities will remain more attractive although the same rates of tax apply to subsidiary earnings as to income from a domestic business. Many U.S. subsidiaries in high tax countries such as the United Kingdom and Germany have not exploited tax haven opportunities and are therefore paying taxes closely comparable to those in the United States. Yet these companies compete effectively. Curtailment of foreign investment which can survive only under the shelter of preferential tax treatment can only be in the U.S. interest and in the interest of the world economy. It will help domestic growth, strengthen our balance-of-payments position and (a matter in which I am not entirely disinterested) substantially increase tax receipts.

* * *

(Emphasis added)

The competing visions of neutrality in the emphasized paragraph are called capital export neutrality (CEN) and capital import neutrality (CIN). CEN refers to the choice that an investor resident in a home country has between investing her savings domestically or in a foreign host country. CEN obtains when home and host country investments that earn the same pretax rates of return also yield the investor the same return after taxes. CEN is violated, for example, if both the home and host countries fail to tax the income from an investment in the host country (while an investment in the home country is taxed). In that case investors would prefer to invest in the host country rather than in the home country even if the pre-tax yield on the domestic investment is higher.

Example: Assume that an investor faces a choice between a home country investment yielding 100 and a host country investment yielding

70. In a tax-free world, the investor would choose the home country investment. Now assume that the home country investment is taxed at 40% while the host country investment is untaxed (e.g., because the host country does not tax investment income earned by non-residents and the home country is unable to enforce its tax jurisdiction on foreign-source income of its residents). In that case the investor faces a choice between a home country investment yielding 60 (100–40 tax) and a host country investment yielding 70 (70–0% tax). The investor would then choose the host country investment even though it yields the lower pretax return.

The economic case against CEN is traditionally made in the name of capital import neutrality (CIN). CIN requires that equal before-tax returns at the margin to competing (domestic and foreign) suppliers of capital to a host country producer translate into equal after-tax earnings. CIN is violated, for example, if foreign investors into a host country are taxed on their investment income at their home country rate (as required by CEN) while the host country does not levy an income tax on investment income. In that case, domestic (host country) investors will have a different net return on their investment in the host country than foreign (home country) investors. The result is that the international allocation of world savings will be distorted.

Example: In terms of the example above, assume that the home country taxes its investors at 40% on foreign as well as domestic investment. In that case, the home country investor prefers the domestic investment (yielding 100 before tax) over the host country investment (yielding 70) because both will subject him to a tax at 40% (so that the after tax yield of the domestic investment is 60 and of the foreign investment is 42). In that case he will have a lower after tax yield (60) than a host country investor in the host country who faces a 0% tax rate (70). After-tax savings will thus be lower in the home country.

The choice between CEN and CIN thus translates into the question what is more responsive to taxation, the choice of investment location (supporting CEN) or the choice whether to save or consume (supporting CIN). What do you think? (Hint: Suppose you know that want to have $1 million at your retirement. If the tax rate on savings is reduced, will you save less or more?)

Because of the above arguments, most economists prefer CEN over CIN. However, there is another consideration involved: The issue of competitiveness. Suppose a U.S. multinational and a German multinational compete to sell widgets through their subsidiaries in Brazil. Brazil has a tax holiday (i.e., a 0% tax rate) in effect for both the subsidiaries, in order to attract investment (this is very common). Germany does not tax the subsidiary of "its" multinational on its Brazilian earnings (because of tax sparing, discussed below in Ch. 9). What would be the effect on the U.S. multinational's ability to compete in the Brazilian market if its subsidiary's earnings were subject to tax at 35%, as proposed by the Kennedy administration?

This is the standard argument for deferral made by U.S. multinationals. To accept it, you need to assume (a) that the welfare or the U.S. is directly correlated with the welfare of "its" multinationals, and (b) that the U.S. multinational will in fact lose market share in Brazil under the conditions stated above. Both propositions are debatable (what do you think?). However, the competitiveness argument has a strong resonance in Congress. That is why Congress in 1961 rejected the Kennedy proposal to end deferral for U.S. multinationals, and instead enacted Subpart F (sections 951–960), which has been described as an "unhappy compromise" between CEN and competitiveness considerations.

b. SUBPART F (SECTIONS 951–960)

Read sections 951–960. In particular, pay attention to

1. The definition of "controlled foreign corporation" (CFC) (section 957(a)), "United States Shareholder" (section 951(b), and "United States person" (section 957(c));

2. The deemed dividend mechanism (sections 951(a) and 959);

3. The definition of "Subpart F income", and in particular "foreign base company income" (section 952(a), 954(a));

4. The principal exceptions (sections 954(b)(3) and (4), 954(c)(2)(A), 954(c)(3), 954(d)(1)(A) [Treas. Reg. § 1.954–3(a)—the so-called manufacturing exception[4] revised in December 2008 with new guidance on "contract manufacturing"], 954(h) and (i)); and

5. The rule for investment of earnings in U.S. property (section 956, especially 956(c)(1)(C)).

Also note the two-thirds rule of Reg. 1.956–2(c)(2), which is of great practical importance in avoiding Subpart F inclusions when a lender requires a security interest in the assets of a U.S. parent, including the stock of CFCs.

(i) DEFINITION OF CFC

The first question of any Subpart F analysis is a question of scope—a foreign corporation is either a CFC. If it is a CFC—the regime applies, but only to taxpayers who are U.S. shareholders of the CFC. The following is an often-cited case clarifying the most important scope definition—that of a CFC.

---

[4]   It is not really an exception, but rather incorporated into the rule itself.

Garlock, Inc. v. Commissioner of Internal Revenue

United States Court of Appeals for the Second Circuit.
489 F.2d 197 (1973).

■ JUDGES: SMITH, MANSFIELD and OAKES, CIRCUIT JUDGES.

This is an appeal from a decision of the Tax Court, *58 T.C. 423 (1972)* determining deficiencies in income tax from the appellant, Garlock, Inc. (Garlock), for its fiscal year ending December 27, 1964, in the sum of $93,335.83, and that ending December 26, 1965, in the sum of $27,061.49. These determinations were made on the basis that Garlock, S.A. (S.A.), a Panamanian corporation and originally a wholly owned subsidiary of appellant, was a "controlled foreign corporation" (CFC) within the meaning of § 957(a) of the Internal Revenue Code of 1954, as amended, and against the claim that § 951 of the Internal Revenue Code of 1954, as amended, is unconstitutional. Section 951, which was enacted in 1962, provides that a United States shareholder of a CFC must include in income its pro rata share of the corporation's "Subpart F income," as defined in § 952, whether or not that income has been distributed to the shareholder. All of S.A.'s income was Subpart F income, and there is no question that appellant is a "United States shareholder" within § 951(b). Thus the primary question before the court is whether S.A. was a CFC during 1964 and 1965 within § 957(a), which provides in pertinent part as follows:

The term "controlled foreign corporation" means any foreign corporation of which *more than 50 percent of the total combined voting power* of all classes of stock entitled to vote *is owned* (within the meaning of § 958(a)), or is considered as owned by applying the rules of ownership of § 958(b), by United States shareholders on any day during the taxable year of such foreign corporation.

(Emphasis added.) While appellant concedes that it owned 50 per cent of the "total combined voting power" of all classes of stock entitled to vote, it contends that it did not own "more than 50 percent" thereof so that S.A. was not a CFC. We disagree and affirm the Tax Court.

Appellant in 1964 and 1965, the tax years in question, was a publicly owned and listed manufacturer of industrial components such as gaskets, packings and seals. In 1958 it had organized S.A. with $50,000 in paid-in capital and for the purpose of marketing appellant's products in Europe and Asia. Through December, 1962, S.A. had one class of common stock issued and outstanding, all of which was owned by appellant. On December 4, 1962, however, the president of appellant submitted a written report to his board of directors proposing a recapitalization of appellant's subsidiary, S.A. That report, quoted in full in the Tax Court opinion, urged that, because the Revenue Act of 1962 contains provisions taxing earnings of CFC's after January 1, 1963, whether or not those earnings were repatriated as dividends, "To avoid this tax result it will be necessary to change the capital stock structure and voting rights in such a way that Garlock, S.A., will no longer be a 'controlled foreign corporation' as defined in the Revenue Act."

The report went on to spell out the proposed revision of the S.A. capital structure: Garlock would retain a $100,000 common stock investment (1,000 shares, $100 par) but S.A. would create a new issue of $100,000 callable, cumulative preferred stock (1,000 shares, $100 par), the preferred shares each to be entitled to one vote along with each common share. The report went on to propose that S.A. would "place this stock [the preferred] with foreign investors who understand our motives and are willing to vote their stock with us in return for an ample dividend rate—probably 8 per cent." It pointed out that Garlock would be "protected from loss of actual control by the following provisions in the preferred stock: a. Stock callable at any time. b. Preferred stock transferrable [sic] only with consent of Garlock, S.A." The report mentioned specifically two foreign investors who had been approached and had said that they "understood the situation," and expressed the belief that one of them would "invest" in the new preferred stock when issued.

The report was approved by Garlock's board of directors at the December, 1962, board meeting and the necessary authority delegated to management; the recapitalization was duly carried out by the directors and shareholders of S.A. under Panamanian law. The same special meeting of S.A. shareholders authorizing the recapitalization and the issuance of voting preference stock also amended the articles of incorporation to provide for the election of directors by a majority vote for terms of from one to five years, the term to depend upon the vote at the time of the respective election, and elected four directors to serve for a term of five years or until their successors were elected and qualified. These four included Garlock's president, vice president, export manager, and assistant secretary.

One of the two specifically mentioned investors in appellant's president's report was Willard International Financial Co., Ltd. (Willard), a Bahamian corporation, which happened to have as counsel the same law firm which was tax counsel to appellant. Willard was the parent corporation of Canadian Camdex Investments, Ltd. (Camdex), a Canadian corporation; Camdex subscribed to the S.A. preferred stock. While the callability provision and absolute restrictions on transferability were not included as terms of the subscription agreement, it was provided that the shares were to be transferable only with the prior written consent of the board of directors of S.A., which consent was not to be "unreasonably withheld." Additional safeguards to the subscriber included: (1) a provision for arbitration in the event of any dispute between the holders of the preferred and common shares as to any corporate matter relating to the business or affairs of S.A. or the rights, obligations or ownership of the preferred stock; (2) a provision to the effect that at all times S.A. was to retain a net current asset or working capital position of at least 200 per cent of the total par value of the preferred stock, i.e., $200,000, in the absence of which any preferred shareholder could demand a purchase at par by S.A.; and (3) a provision giving each preferred shareholder the right after one year from date of issue, on 120 days' written notice, to sell the preferred stock to S.A. at par.

Camdex subscribed for the full $100,000 of S.A. preferred with money from its parent, Willard, and retained 10 per cent of the 1,000 shares it thus received, selling 350 shares in February of 1963 to Nederlandse Overzee Bank, N.V., 350 shares to a nominee company for the Bank of Nova Scotia, and the remaining 200 shares to American African Finance Corp., a corporation organized under the law of French Somaliland. At the time of the issuance of the preferred stock the 8 percent dividend rate it carried exceeded the interest rate prevailing in the foreign market. On October 1, 1963, the board of directors under Panamanian law duly amended S.A.'s bylaws to increase the number of directors from four to five; three Garlock men were retained, but the president of Willard (who was also an officer of Camdex) was added to the board as was the managing director of a Canadian investment banking concern which was the ultimate purchaser of the 350 shares bought for the Bank of Nova Scotia. No meeting of the Shareholders of S.A. was held in 1963, but at an April 1, 1964, shareholders' meeting the five directors elected at the directors' meeting on October 1, 1963, were duly elected for one year or until their successors were elected and qualified. They were similarly re-elected on April 7, 1965. The above are the essential facts, and while the Tax Court opinion covers them in more detail, they will do for our purposes.

Appellant argues principally that § 957(a) makes the CFC test only the simple mechanical one of ownership of more than 50 per cent of the voting stock, regardless of the ownership of the voting power. That is, appellant would read the words of the statute, "more than 50 per cent of the total combined voting power of all classes of stock entitled to vote," with utmost literality. Appellant argues that the Tax Court majority opinion substituted an "actual control" test for the numerical statutory test and thereby ignored the plain meaning of the statute, erroneously interpreted the legislative intent and erroneously applied the doctrine of substance over form.

But, to go to the heart of the matter, the Tax Court opinion relied squarely on Treas. Reg. § 1.957–1(b)(2). This regulation provides, inter alia, that any arrangement to shift formal voting power away from United States shareholders "will not be given effect if in reality voting power is retained." It provides further that "The mere ownership of stock entitled to vote does not by itself mean that the shareholder owning such stock has the voting power of such stock for purposes of section 957." In the very situation of this case, where another class of stock is outstanding, the regulation states that the voting power ostensibly *provided such other class of stock ... will be disregarded [1] if the percentage of voting power ... is substantially greater than its proportionate share of the corporate earnings, [2] if the facts indicate that the shareholders of such other class of stock do not exercise their voting rights independently or fail to exercise such voting rights, and [3] if a principal purpose of the arrangement is to avoid the classification of such foreign corporation as a controlled foreign corporation under section 957.*

(Emphasis added.) Here the Tax Court properly found, on the basis of the original "report" to appellant's board of directors, that a principal purpose of the arrangement was to avoid the classification of S.A. as a CFC; appellant cannot and does not argue to the contrary. While it is suggested that the holders of the preferred could have exercised voting rights independently, in fact there is no indication that they did so, and indeed at all times a majority of the board of directors consisted of appellant's officers. Finally, the percentage of mathematical voting power of the preferred shareholders (50 per cent) was substantially greater than its proportionate share of the corporate earnings: in 1963, 1964 and 1965 S.A.'s net profit was $94,260.61, $173,382.60 and $50,171.20 respectively, but the preferred shareholders received dividends of only $8,000 per year—in other words, in the year 1965 a maximum of 16 per cent. The regulation, in short, applies exactly to the case at hand. Appellant's argument that the preferred shareholders of S.A. did exercise their voting rights independently, Brief at 44, is not seriously pressed. Rather, the appellant claims that the regulation must be held invalid as an arbitrary and unsanctioned extension of the statute, one contrary to the "legislative intent."

We believe, however, that the regulation, as applied to the facts in this case, is proper and within the direct aim and purpose as well as the plain meaning of the statute. The test in the statute is one of ownership of "voting power," a term which, to be sure, is open to at least two different interpretations: appellant's would relate it solely to the record ownership of the number of votes attached to all classes of stock entitled to vote; appellee's interpretation is that ownership of voting power is to be determined after full consideration of legal and equitable aspects of ownership. The statute was enacted to help effectuate "elimination of the tax haven device," as set forth in President Kennedy's recommendations on tax revision, see H.R. Doc. No. 140, 87th Cong., 1st Sess. 7 (1961). The Ways and Means Committee report on the Revenue Act of 1962 stated that "Your committee has also ended tax deferral for American shareholders in certain situations where the multiplicity of foreign tax systems has been taken advantage of by American-controlled businesses to syphon off sales profits from goods manufactured by related parties either in the United States or abroad." H.R. Rep. No. 1447, 87th Cong., 2d Sess. 58 (1962). See also S. Rep. No. 1881, 87th Cong., 2d Sess. 2, 78–80 (1962). In floor debate on the bill Senator Kerr specifically referred to the fact that, if the bill were passed, "It will no longer be possible to flout our tax laws by simply setting up an address company, say in Panama, to sell goods in Europe which did not originate in Panama, which never in fact were in Panama, and which had nothing to do with Panama." 108 Cong. Rec. 17752 (1962). As Secretary of the Treasury Dillon had testified, the Administration's "primary objective in this field . . . [was] to preserve the integrity of the U.S. dollar and to help in the balance of payments. . . ." Hearings Before the House Committee on Ways and Means on the President's 1961 Tax Recommendations, 87th Cong., 1st Sess. 348 (1961). In the light of this legislative history, the appellee's implementation of congressional intent by promulgation of regulations consistent with the statutory design seems to us plainly correct.[1]

Taxpayers generally are fond of quoting Judge Learned Hand's statement that "Any one may so arrange his affairs that his taxes shall be as low as possible; he is not bound to choose that pattern which will best pay the Treasury; there is not even a patriotic duty to increase one's taxes." *Helvering v. Gregory, 69 F.2d 809, 810 (2d Cir.1934), aff'd, 293 U.S. 465, 79 L. Ed. 596, 55 S. Ct. 266 (1935).* It is sometimes forgotten, however, that it was in that very case that Judge Hand's opinion for this court held that a series of transactions which suited the verbal definition of corporate reorganization in the Revenue Act of 1928 nevertheless did not meet the statutory requirements because the transactions lacked a business purpose and the words of the Act made it evident that the aim of Congress was to approve only reorganizations having such a purpose. As Judge Hand said with reference to the tax statute there involved, "the meaning of a sentence may be more than that of the separate words, as a melody is more than the notes, and no degree of particularity can ever obviate recourse to the setting in which all appear, and which all collectively create." *Id. at 810–11.* So too, here, it does not advance the cause a very great deal to say that the "purpose" of Congress or the "intent" of Congress was violated by the regulations adopted. Certainly as the statute indicates, Congress had generally in mind the elimination of the tax avoidance device known as "tax haven" corporations. The language it used is subject to the interpretation—one given to it by the Treasury—that it is "real" voting power and not the mere mechanical number of votes with which Congress was concerned. As Professor Cox reminded us some time ago, "legislative intention" is really simply a metaphor, which "does not state an all-sufficient rule; it enjoins a point of view and sets a goal to which the judge aspires even while he knows it is beyond attainment." Cox, Judge Learned Hand and the Interpretation of Statutes, *60 Harv. L. Rev. 370, 372 (1947).* It is significant here that

---

[1] Appellant argues that the Treasury originally proposed either a voting power or a value of stock test but that since Congress used only the former, there was a "conscious decision to limit the definition of a controlled foreign corporation." Appellant's Brief at 21. This does not mean, however, that the voting power test ultimately adopted was to be applied strictly mechanically, as appellant would have it. Nor does it follow that, because the statute requires that the requisite percentage of voting power be owned only on any one day in the taxable year, Congress was thereby rejecting effective voting control as the test in a case where that effective voting control was vested in the United States shareholder.

the taxpayer sought out parties who understood both its motives and its situation. It is significant also that the terms of the arrangement worked out were such that the preferred shareholders would have no interest in disturbing the taxpayer's continued control. The stock was made attractive by paying a rate in excess of market for the money advanced. The stake of the preferred shareholders was, moreover, quite limited, since the moment the current asset value of S.A., or its working capital was not maintained at a level of at least 200 per cent of the total par value of the preferred, i.e., $200,000, any preferred shareholder could demand a purchase by S.A. at par; indeed, after one year the preferred shareholders had the right on 120 days' written notice to require S.A. to purchase the preferred at par, that is, to have his original investment returned in full.

While the arbitration provision in respect to unresolved matters we might assume to be proper under Panamanian law—without indicating whether indeed Panamanian law was applicable or, if applicable, that the provision would be valid—there is no question but that there would be little or no reason ever to resort to such an unrealistic way of running a corporation in light of the working capital and provisions for the repurchase of the preferred stock above recounted. We say "unrealistic" because the picture of corporate sales, management and other decisions in the fast-moving international trade world of the mid-1960's being made through the process of arbitration under the rules of the International Chamber of Commerce is very nearly risible—the product, perhaps, of an imaginative tax lawyer's drafting contemplation, surely not a working solution to real business needs. Without belaboring the point one is tempted to think of the arbitration provisions of the subscription agreement as sugar coating on the taxpayer's Treasury Department pill.

While in a given case the issuance of a different class of stock with equal voting rights might meet the "voting power" requirement in the statute, quite obviously Congress could not generally have conceived all the ramifications of corporate laws around the world which might cleverly be utilized to make a preferred stock which was rather readily redeemable and carried only a very small percentage of the earnings as interest the equivalent in voting power of common stock held by the United States shareholders.

We agree with the appellee that the preferred shareholders' voting power here was "illusory." We agree also that the regulation is valid and proper as applied to the facts presented. The argument that § 951, which requires an American shareholder to include in income his pro rata share of a CFC's profits, is unconstitutional we think borders on the frivolous in the light of this court's decision in *Eder v. Commissioner, 138 F.2d 27, 28 (1943)*. That case held constitutional the foreign personal holding provisions of the income tax laws upon which Subpart F was patterned, permitting taxation of United States shareholders on the undistributed net income of Colombian corporations even though Colombian law made the taxpayer unable to receive such income in the United States in excess of $1,000 per month. . . .

Affirmed.

NOTES AND QUESTIONS

1. Note the definition of CFC in the current Section 957(a). How would *Garlock* come out under this definition?

2. Do you think the constitutional argument was frivolous?

3. When Subpart F was enacted, it was considered a significant departure from international norms governing jurisdiction to tax. However, most developed jurisdictions have now followed the U.S. in enacting similar rules (see further Chapter 11.4 on treaty override).

4. Given the modern view on jurisdiction, do you think the deemed dividend mechanism is necessary? Note, for example, its effect on loss corporations. What is the alternative? (Hint: consider Section 1504(b)(3)).

5. Note the mix of clearly drawn lines, such as the definition of a U.S. shareholder, and the "softer" voting power definition. What may have been the purpose of this mix? Why vote or value? Would a "control" requirement be better in this context? Note that in some circumstances it is beneficial for taxpayers to be taxed as U.S. shareholders of a CFC.

(ii) THE BASE COMPANY RULE

Subpart F applies exclusively to certain categories of income— Subpart F income. Revisit Sections 952(a) and 954(a). The most important category of Subpart F income is the foreign personal holding company income, primarily passive types of income, such as dividends, interest, royalties and rents, as defined in Section 954(c). There are major exceptions for these rules—the same country exception and active royalties and rents. Why are these types of income considered the most "natural" candidates for deferral disallowance? What are the above two exceptions different? Are these exceptions necessary?

The other "base company" rules are less intuitive, as they involve active income, which is not normally considered easily manipulable. To understand why the base company rule was enacted, re-read Dupont (Ch. 6 above). Is there a need for the base company rule once workable transfer pricing rules are in place? Read the following interesting case/s:

Brown Group, Inc. and Subsidiaries v. Commissioner of Internal Revenue

United States Tax Court.
104 T.C. 105 (1995).

■ Filed JUDGES: HALPERN, HAMBLEN, PARKER, COHEN, SWIFT, PARR, BEGHE, WELLS, RUWE, SWIFT, CHIECHI, JACOBS, CHABOT, LARO.

■ OPINION: HALPERN, JUDGE: Petitioner is the common parent corporation of an affiliated group of corporations making a consolidated return of income (the affiliated group). Respondent determined a deficiency of $388,992.85 in the income tax liability of the affiliated group for its taxable year ended November 1, 1986.

The only issue in dispute is whether Brown Cayman, Ltd.'s (Brown Cayman's) share of partnership income from Brinco, a Cayman Islands partnership, is Subpart F income, includable in the gross income of a member of the affiliated group under section 951(a). We hold that it is.

. . . FINDINGS OF FACT

A trial was held on March 9, 1993. Petitioner called no witnesses. Respondent called one: Theodore Presti. The parties had stipulated certain facts, however, and the facts stipulated are so found. The stipulation of facts and attached exhibits is incorporated herein by this reference. The following summarizes the facts relied on by us in reaching our decision.

Petitioner Brown Group, Inc. (sometimes Brown Group), is a New York corporation. At the time the petition herein was filed, petitioner's principal place of business was in St. Louis, Missouri. . . .

Throughout 1985 and 1986, Brown Group had divisions that sold footwear at the retail and wholesale levels, manufactured footwear, and imported footwear. Brown Group manufactured footwear in the United States and imported footwear from, among other countries, Brazil.

Brown Group International (International), a Delaware corporation, was incorporated in 1985, as a wholly owned subsidiary of Brown Group. Throughout 1985 and 1986, International was a U.S. shareholder of Brown Cayman within the meaning of section 951(b).

Brown Cayman, a Cayman Islands corporation, was incorporated in 1985. Brown Cayman was a controlled foreign corporation within the meaning of section 957(a) at all times relevant to this case.

T.P. Cayman, Ltd. (T.P. Cayman), a Cayman Islands corporation, was incorporated in March 1985.

Pidge, Inc., is a Missouri corporation; the date of its incorporation is not contained in the record.

Brinco, a partnership within the meaning of section 7701, and the regulations thereunder, was formed in the Cayman Islands in March 1985. The partners of Brinco, and their percentage interests in the net profits and losses of Brinco, were Brown Cayman, 88 percent, T.P. Cayman, 10 percent, and an individual, Delcio Birck (Birck), 2 percent.

Prior to the formation of Brinco, Brown Group utilized independent agents to purchase footwear manufactured in Brazil. At that time, Birck, a Brazilian citizen, and Presti, a U.S. citizen, were employed by a company, Michelle Manard, which purchased footwear manufactured in Brazil on behalf of Brown Group and others. Michelle Manard "officially" charged Brown Group a 7-percent commission, although occasionally that rate was greater. Brinco was formed, among other reasons, to attract Presti and Birck to source Brazilian footwear exclusively for the Brown Group companies and to consolidate Brown Group's Brazilian buying power. Brinco was structured as a partnership, among other reasons, because: (1) Presti's salary requirements could not be satisfied within Brown Group's existing payroll structure, (2) it allowed Presti and Birck to have some entrepreneurial interest in Brinco's operations, and (3) it permitted the partners to avoid Brazilian currency controls and currency fluctuations.

During 1985 and 1986, Brinco acted as purchasing agent for International with respect to footwear manufactured in Brazil. The footwear so imported was sold primarily in the United States. Presti was the managing partner of Brinco. As such, he was responsible for the design, manufacture, and quality control of the footwear. He also supervised Brinco's operations within Brazil.

The Brown Group companies paid Brinco a 10-percent commission for acting as their purchasing agent for footwear manufactured in Brazil. The commission was based on the purchase price of the footwear. Brinco's 1985 commission income for acting as purchasing agent for the Brown Group companies was $1,119,970. The Brown Group companies included the commissions paid to Brinco in their costs of goods sold.

Pursuant to negotiations among the Brinco partners, because of the uncertainty of first-year profits, for the 7-month period ending November 2, 1985, T.P. Cayman received guaranteed payments totaling $151,662 ($21,666 a month for 7 months), instead of its share of partnership profits called for in the Brinco partnership agreement. After making guaranteed payments to T.P. Cayman, Brinco's partnership net earnings for 1985 totaled $917,465, which were distributed as follows:

Brown Cayman	98%	$ 897,281
Birck	2%	20,184

In 1986, T.P. Cayman received its share of partnership profits as called for in the Brinco partnership agreement (and no guaranteed payments).

Brinco was dissolved on October 31, 1987. At that time, Presti became executive vice president of International, and Birck, as an independent agent, continued to source footwear for the Brown Group companies on a commission basis.

Respondent determined that Brown Cayman's distributive share of Brinco's earnings is foreign base company sales income, includable as Subpart F income in the gross income of International.

OPINION

I.   Introduction

For all relevant periods, the parties have stipulated that (1) Brown Cayman was a "controlled foreign corporation" (CFC) within the meaning of section 957(a) and (2) International was a "United States shareholder" of Brown Cayman within the meaning of section 951(b). Accordingly, International must include in its gross income its pro rata share (100 percent) of any "Subpart F income" of Brown Cayman. See sec. 951(a). Subpart F income is defined in section 952 to include an item called "foreign base company income". Sec. 952(a)(2). Foreign base company income, in turn, is defined in section 954(a) to include "foreign base company sales income". Sec. 954(a)(2). Foreign base company sales income includes, among other things: "income (whether in the form of profits, commissions, fees, or otherwise) derived in connection with * * * the purchase of personal property from any person on behalf of a related person" where the goods are both produced and sold for use outside the country in which the CFC is incorporated. Sec. 954(d)(1). The term "related person" is defined in section 954(d)(3). It is clear that International was a related person with regard to Brown Cayman. See sec. 954(d)(3) ("such person is a corporation which controls * * * the controlled foreign corporation"). It also is clear that Brinco earned commission income by arranging for the purchase of footwear by International. Brinco was a partnership of which Brown Cayman was a partner. Brown Cayman was entitled to share in the income of Brinco. Pursuant to section 702, Brown Cayman was required to take into account its distributive share of that income. The narrow question we must answer is whether Brown Cayman had income "(whether in the form of profits, commissions, fees, or otherwise) derived in connection with * * * the purchase of personal property from any person on behalf of a related person". See sec. 954(d)(1). We believe that it did.

II.   Arguments of the Parties

A.   Petitioner's Argument

Petitioner argues as follows: under section 954(d)(3), as in effect for the year in issue, Brinco was not a related person with regard to Brown Cayman or International. Absent such a relationship, Brown Cayman's distributive share of Brinco's income cannot be Subpart F income with respect to Brown Cayman or International. Alternatively, the character of the income in question is determined at the partnership (Brinco) level, by treating Brinco as a separate entity. Consequently, the income in question is that of Brinco, not Brown Cayman. Thus, the income cannot be foreign base company sales income of Brown Cayman.

B. Respondent's Argument

Respondent agrees that, under section 954(d)(3), as in effect for the year in issue, Brinco was not a related person with regard to Brown Cayman or International. Respondent's argument is as follows: The aggregate theory of partnerships should apply in this case because that theory furthers the purposes of Subpart F. Under the aggregate theory, Brown Cayman's distributive share of Brinco's income must be treated as foreign base company sales income and, consequently, Subpart F income. International, the U.S. share-holder of Brown Cayman, must include its pro rata share (100 percent) of Brown Cayman's Subpart F income in its gross income under section 951(a). Respondent has not argued that Brinco is a sham.

III. Analysis

A. Introduction

Substantially, we agree with respondent. We believe that a close reading of the regulations under Subpart F, a consideration of the structure and language of subchapter K (the partnership provisions), Congress' purpose in enacting Subpart F, and certain language of section 954(d)(1) compel the result that respondent advocates.

B. Subpart F Regulations

Section 954 deals with the computation of foreign base company income, of which foreign base company sales income is a component. Sec. 954(a)(2). Section 1.954A–1, Income Tax Regs., deals with the computation of foreign base company income for taxable years of a CFC beginning after 1975 and before 1987. See sec. 1.954A–1(a), Income Tax Regs.; sec. 1.954–0T(a)(2), Temporary Income Tax Regs. Section 1.954A–1(c), Income Tax Regs., states in pertinent part:

> For purposes of section 954 and this section, * * * foreign base company sales income as defined in § 1.954–3 * * * shall be taken into account in determining foreign base company income after allowance for deductions properly allocable to such [category] of income. For determination of gross income and deductions for purposes of section 954, see section 952 and the regulations thereunder. * * *

Section 1.952–2(a)(1), Income Tax Regs., states in pertinent part:

> the gross income of a foreign corporation for any taxable year shall, subject to the special rules of paragraph (c) of this section, be determined by treating such foreign corporation as a domestic corporation taxable under section 11 and by applying the principles of section 61 and the regulations thereunder.

Paragraph (c)(1) of section 1.952–2, Income Tax Regs., states that, as a general rule, certain subchapters of chapter 1 of the Code shall not apply. Subchapter K, chapter 1, subtitle A of the Code, sections 701 through 761 (subchapter K), is not among the excluded subchapters. Thus, by implication, subchapter K is applicable.

Section 1.952–3(a), Income Tax Regs., describes the computations that a U.S. shareholder of a CFC must make in connection with the application of section 954 and the subsequent application of section 952. Paragraph (b) of section 1.952–3, Income Tax Regs., states the general rule. That rule is that the U.S. shareholder must determine the Subpart F income of the CFC by, among other things, determining the foreign base company sales income of the CFC.

Section 1.954–3(a)(1)(i), Income Tax Regs., mirroring the statute, states that foreign base company sales income of a CFC includes, among other things, commission income derived in connection with the purchase of personal property from any person on behalf of a related person.

In summary, the cited provisions of the regulations lay out a scheme under which the U.S. shareholder of a CFC must determine the foreign base company sales income of the CFC (including the described commission income) under most of the rules applicable to a domestic corporation determining its tax liability under section 11, including the rules of subchapter K.

C. Subchapter K

Subchapter K deals with the taxation of partners and partnerships.

Section 701 provides that a partnership as such shall not be subject to the income tax. Persons carrying on business as partners are liable for income tax only in their separate or individual capacities.

Section 702(a) provides that, in determining a partner's income tax, each partner must take into account separately the partner's distributive share of items enumerated in section 702(a)(1) through (8). Under section 702(a)(7), a partner must take into account separately those items of income, gain, loss, deduction, or credit prescribed by regulations.

Section 1.702–1(a)(8)(ii), Income Tax Regs., provides that each partner must take into account separately the partner's distributive share of any partnership item that, if separately taken into account by any partner, would result in an income tax liability for that partner different from that which would result if that partner did not take the item into account separately.

Section 702(b) provides that the character of any item included in a partner's distributive share under paragraphs (1) through (7) of section 702(a) is determined as if such item were realized directly from the source from which [it was] realized by the partnership, or incurred in the same manner as incurred by the partnership. Section 1.702–1(b), Income Tax Regs., provides, in pertinent part:

> The character in the hands of a partner of any item of income, gain, loss, deduction, or credit described in section 702(a)(1)

through * * * [7] shall be determined as if such item were realized directly from the source from which realized by the partnership or incurred in the same manner incurred by the partnership. * * *

Section 703(a)(1) provides that a partnership shall separately state the items described in section 702(a) in computing its taxable income.

Brown Cayman, a partner of Brinco, is a foreign corporation and, apparently, has no Federal income tax liability. Nevertheless, International, a U.S. shareholder with respect to Brown Cayman, must take into account its pro rata share of Brown Cayman's Subpart F income. See sec. 951(a). Applying Federal income tax principles, International must compute those items of Brown Cayman's income that constitute Subpart F income. See sec. 1.952–2(a), Income Tax Regs. Unless items that constitute, for instance, foreign base company sales income are separately stated, International will be unable to make that computation. Since, under section 951(a), International is taxed directly on its pro rata share of Brown Cayman's Subpart F income, we must look to International's tax liability to determine whether Brinco must separately state items, such as commission income, that could constitute foreign base company sales income. To give effect to section 702(a)(7) and section 1.702–1(a)(8)(ii), Income Tax Regs., and to avoid frustrating the purpose of Congress in enacting Subpart F, Brinco must separately state its commission income.

D.   Subpart F

1.   Purpose

Subpart F contradicts the general rule that the shareholders of a corporation defer paying a tax on the income earned by the corporation until such income is distributed to them, usually in the form of a dividend. Subpart F was designed to remove the tax deferral benefits of certain offshore operations that Congress considered to be "tax haven" devices; i.e., foreign operations that were artificially structured to take advantage of a low (or zero) rate of foreign tax. S. Rept. 1881, 87th Cong., 2d Sess. (1962), *1962–3 C.B. 707, 784.* (S. Rept. 1881 accompanied H.R. 10650, which became the Revenue Act of 1962, Pub. L. 87–834, 76 Stat. 960, which added Subpart F.)

2.   Conduit Approach

It is important to keep in mind the method that Congress chose to meet its objectives: Subpart F imposes a conduit scheme with regard to Subpart F income. Subpart F income is taxed currently to U.S. shareholders notwithstanding that no distribution of such income is made. See sec. 951. The parallel with subchapter K is obvious. Congress chose to minimize (perhaps even eliminate) the entity character of the CFC in order to tax U.S. shareholders as if they had earned directly the Subpart F income earned by the CFC. It would be ironic, indeed, if one could defeat the clearly expressed intent of Congress to tax the income from the activities involved here by engaging in those activities though a form of doing business that not only is taxed on a conduit basis but whose non-tax-law character often resembles an aggregate of persons doing business together (as mutual agents) rather than an entity.

3. Facts at Hand

The facts of this case show that the formation of Brinco did not significantly change the way Brown Group (through International) imported shoes manufactured in Brazil. Presti and Birck still continued to do the actual commission agent work. They did it, however, as partners (directly or indirectly) in Brinco. Under the prior arrangement, Brown Group had paid a 7-percent commission to Michelle Manard, Presti and Birck's employer. Ostensibly, Brown Group raised its commission rate to 10 percent. However, as the owner, indirectly, of Brown Cayman, a partner in Brinco, Brown Group, was entitled to receive back the bulk of that 10 percent and, apparently, realized a net savings. Had Brown Cayman hired Presti and Birck as employees, or otherwise engaged them as agents, and collected directly from Brown Group or International a commission agent's fee, it would be clear that at least the net amount retained by Brown Cayman would be foreign base company sales income.

The law of partnerships in the Cayman Islands is derived from the law of partnerships in England. See Davies, The Legal System of the Cayman Islands 89, 188–194 (1989). Compare Partnership Law, 1983 (Cayman Islands) with Partnership Act, 1890, 53 & 54 Vic., c. 39 (Eng.). English law lends itself to the view that Brown Cayman, as a partner of Brinco, acting on its own behalf, and through its partners (its agents), did function as a commission agent. The facts seem ripe for the application of Subpart F. A contrary result would lead to just the type of siphoning of profits that Congress was concerned with when it subjected foreign base company sales income to the conduit treatment of Subpart F. But cf. *MCA, Inc. v. United States, 685 F.2d 1099, 1104–1105 (9th Cir. 1982)* (remedy for loophole in Subpart F "lies in new legislation, not judicial improvisation").

E. Aggregate Versus Entity

1. Introduction

To effectuate the purpose of Congress in enacting Subpart F, we will require Brinco to state separately its commission income under section 703. What we are doing might be characterized as emphasizing the "aggregate" or "conduit" nature of Brinco, a partnership, over its "entity" nature. We have pursued a technical road in our analysis, and have avoided framing the issue in terms of aggregate versus entity. Nevertheless, and particularly in light of petitioner's argument that Brinco should be treated as a separate entity, we will address the aggregate versus entity question briefly.

2. Dual Nature

Authorities on partnership taxation have stated that subchapter K does not espouse either the aggregate or the entity theory of partnerships, but rather blends the two theories. 1 McKee Nelson & Whitmire, Federal Taxation of Partnerships and Partners (hereafter McKee et al.), par. 1.02 (2d ed. 1990). We agree. Compare sec. 751 with sec. 741. Moreover, for purposes of interpreting provisions of the Code not contained in subchapter K, a partnership also may be treated either as an aggregate of its partners or as an entity distinct from its partners. Compare *Casel v. Commissioner, 79 T.C. 424, 433–434 (1982)* (aggregate approach of regulations under section 267 appropriate) with *Madison Gas & Elec. Co. v. Commissioner, 72 T.C. 521, 564 (1979),* affd. *633 F.2d 512 (7th Cir.1980)* (business of partnership, a business separate from the business of the partners). The treatment of partnerships in each context must be determined on the basis of the characterization most appropriate for the situation. See H. Conf. Rept. 2543, 83d Cong., 2d Sess. (1954), 1954 U.S.C.C.A.N. 5280. H. Rept. 2543 accompanied H.R. 8300, 83d Cong., 2d Sess., which became the Internal Revenue Code of 1954.

3. Appropriate Emphasis

For the reasons set forth above in our discussion of Subpart F, we believe that, to accomplish the purposes of Congress in enacting Subpart F, the aggregate nature of Brinco as a partnership must be emphasized. We are not here dealing with the computation of Brinco's income but with the consequence to Brinco's partners stemming from their rights under the partnership agreement to share in that income. The relationship between the entity approach to the computation of partnership income found in sections 703 and 706 and the aggregate approach applied to the taxation of that income found in sections 701, 702, and 704 has been described by the Supreme Court as follows:

> For * * * [the purpose of calculating partnership income], the partnership is regarded as an independently recognizable entity apart from the aggregate of its partners. Once its income is ascertained and reported, its existence may be disregarded since each partner must pay a tax on a portion of the total income as if the partnership were merely an agent or conduit through which the income passed. [*United States v. Basye, 410 U.S. 441, 448 (1973);* fn. ref. omitted.]

McKee et al. have characterized the Supreme Court's analysis as follows:

> This analysis of the statute embodies a very clear and sharply defined separation between (1) the treatment of a partnership as a separate entity for purposes of determining its income, and (2) the taxation of partnership income, as so determined, to the partners under the conduit approach. * * * [1 McKee et al., supra par. 9.01[2], at 9–6.]

4. Application of Entity-Aggregate Distinction in Practice

Indeed, an examination of cases requiring an entity (partnership) level determination of income shows that, once such determination is made, the partnership is ignored and the individual partners take account of such income as if they had earned it directly. E.g., *Pleasant Summit Land Corp. v. Commissioner, 863 F.2d 263, 272 (3d Cir.1988)*, affg. in part and revg. in part *T.C. Memo. 1987–469* ("After the partnership's income and deductions are calculated and reported, it is a conduit through which income and deductions are distributed to individual partners."); *Davis v. Commissioner, 74 T.C. 881, 905–906 (1980)*, affd. *746 F.2d 357 (6th Cir.1984)* (capital gains determined at partnership level retain that characterization at partner level).

Notwithstanding such shift in emphasis from an entity view at the partnership level to an aggregate view at the partner level, any characterization of the partnership's activity with regard to an item generally persists. For instance, in *Goodwin v. Commissioner, 75 T.C. 424 (1980)*, affd. without published opinion, *691 F.2d 490 (3d Cir.1982)*, the taxpayer argued that we should inquire as to trade or business activity at his, the partner's, level to characterize certain deductions taken by the partnership. We declined, requiring him to treat his distributive share of the expenses as a non-deductible startup cost associated with the formation of a new (partnership) business. We held: "in the context of section 162, the character of the deductions, i.e., whether they were incurred in the course of a trade or business, must be resolved at the partnership level." *Id. at 437.*

Pertinent to the question at hand, we, and other courts, have attributed to a partner the activities and even the property of a partnership to determine whether, by virtue of such activity or property, the partner had a particular status important for determining some aspect of the partner's Federal income tax status. In *Unger v. Commissioner, 936 F.2d 1316 (D.C.Cir.1991)*, affg. *T.C. Memo. 1990–15*, the question was whether a Canadian resident, a limited partner in a Massachusetts partnership, was taxable on his distributive share of a certain capital gain realized by the partnership. The question turned on whether the partner maintained a "permanent establishment" within the United States. For purposes of the case, the term "permanent establishment" meant an office or other fixed place of business. The court held that, since the partnership maintained a permanent office in Boston, the taxpayer had a permanent establishment in the United States by virtue of his interest in the partnership offices. *Id. at 1320; Donroy, Ltd. v. United States, 301 F.2d 200 (9th Cir.1962)* (similar, but with emphasis on the agency nature of the general partner's relationship to a limited partner); *Johnston v. Commissioner, 24 T.C. 920, 923 (1955)* (permanent place of business in the United States by virtue of partnership interest); *Cantrell & Cochrane, Ltd. v. Commissioner, 19 B.T.A. 16, 24 (1930)* (whether U.K. corporation, a member of a "syndicate" with an office and a place of business in the United States, and engaging in a trade or business in the United States, either itself engaged in a trade or business in the United States or had any office or place of business therein: "In the eye of the law at least it was present here as a party to the conduct of the business of the 'syndicate' through which it established a place of business within the United States for doing a part of its business."). The situation here is analogous. Brown Cayman should be put into the shoes of Brinco for determining whether Brown Cayman was earning commission income on sales by third parties to International.

F.   "[I]n connection with"

Our analysis has relied heavily on the provisions of subchapter K. Indeed, that is the path that the parties have taken, and it is supported by the weight of commentary that the issue has generated. Before addressing one final argument of petitioner, we wish to point out that certain words of section 954(d)(1), as recently interpreted by this Court, lend support to our analysis. As stated earlier, the term "foreign base company sales income" is defined in section 954(d)(1). In pertinent part (with emphasis added), the definition includes:

> income (whether in the form of profits, commissions, fees, or otherwise) derived in connection with * * * the purchase of personal property from any person on behalf of a related person * * *

Recently, we had the opportunity to construe the phrase "in connection with" as used in section 162(k)(1). *Fort Howard Corp. v. Commissioner, 103 T.C. 345, 351 (1994)*. In Fort Howard Corp., we observed that words in a revenue act should be interpreted in their ordinary, everyday sense. *Id. at 351*. We stated that the phrase "in connection with" had been, and should be, interpreted broadly. *Id. at 352*. We said that the phrase means "associated with, or related". Id. We consulted a dictionary, and said: "Events or elements are 'connected' when they are 'logically related' to each other." Id. (quoting Webster's Third New World Dictionary (1986)). That relationship exists here. Brown Cayman was a CFC. Its distributive share of partnership profits was, by design and reality, connected to and dependent on purchases made on behalf of a party related to Brown Cayman.

G.   Brinco as a Related Person

Finally, we wish to dispose of one argument made by petitioner: viz, that, for the year in question, Brinco was not a related person with regard to Brown Cayman or International. That is true; nonetheless, it is irrelevant. Nothing here turns on whether Brinco is a related person with regard to either Brown Cayman or International. We are dealing here with that part of the definition of foreign base company sales income that involves "the purchase of personal property from any person on behalf of a related person". Sec. 954(d)(1). The inquiry is whether Brown Cayman, through Brinco, purchased footwear on behalf of International.

International is the related person, and there is no argument about that. The only possible entity here that can be a controlled foreign corporation is Brown Cayman. As stated, nothing turns on whether Brinco is a related person.

It is true that the definition of related person in section 954(d)(3) was amended in 1986 to include partnerships controlled by or controlling a CFC within the definition of related persons with regard to such CFC. Tax Reform Act of 1986, Pub. L. 99–514, sec. 1221(e)(1), 100 Stat. 2085, 2553–2554. Nevertheless, the relevant definition of what constitutes foreign base company sales income ("income * * * derived in connection with * * * the purchase of personal property from any person on behalf of a related person") was not amended. Sec. 954(d)(1) Nothing here was purchased on behalf of Brinco; indeed, Brinco did the purchasing on behalf of International.

IV. Conclusion

For the reasons stated, we find that Brown Cayman had commission income derived in connection with the purchase of personal property from any person on behalf of International. We hold that such income is foreign base company sales income under section 954(d)(1) and that International must include in its gross income Subpart F income as determined by respondent.

Decision will be entered for respondent.

■ HAMBLEN, PARKER, COHEN, SWIFT, PARR, and BEGHE, JJ., agree with this majority opinion.

■ WELLS, J., did not participate in the consideration of this opinion.

■ CONCUR BY: RUWE; BEGHE; CHIECHI

■ CONCUR: RUWE, J., concurring: I agree with the majority's conclusion that Brown Cayman's distributive share of Brinco's partnership income is Subpart F income. However, I believe that there are technical problems with the majority's reliance on subchapter K and the related aggregate versus entity analysis. These problems can be avoided by simply applying the literal terms of section 954. I will first address the problems and then the solution.

The Problems

1.   Section 702

Section 702 provides that each partner must account separately for certain specifically enumerated types of partnership income, losses, and deductions that are described in section 702(a)(1) through (7). If a partnership item is not described in section 702(a)(1) through (7), section 702(a)(8) provides that a partner is to account for his distributive share as "taxable income or loss" from the partnership "exclusive of items requiring separate computation under other paragraphs of this subsection." Sec. 702(a)(8).

Section 702(b) provides that the character of any item of income that is included in a partner's distributive share under section 702(a)(1) through (7) "shall be determined as if such item were realized directly from the source from which realized by the partnership". Section 702(b)'s character pass-through requirement does not apply to the items covered by section 702(a)(8). The majority uses section 702(b) to characterize Brown Cayman's distributive share of income from Brinco as commissions earned on the purchase of footwear. To do this, Brinco's commission income must be an item described in section 702(a)(1) through (7). Paragraphs (1) through (6) are clearly inapplicable. The majority focuses on paragraph (7) to impute the character of Brinco's commission income to Brown Cayman. Paragraph (7) provides that a partner must separately account for "other items of income * * * to the extent provided by regulations".

The regulation upon which the majority relies is section 1.702–1(a)(8)(ii), Income Tax Regs. Section 1.702–1(a)(8)(ii), Income Tax Regs., provides that "Each partner must take into account separately his distributive share of any partnership item which if separately taken into account by any partner would result in an income tax liability for that partner different from that which would result if that partner did not take the item into account separately."

In order for section 1.702–1(a)(8)(ii), Income Tax Regs., to apply, the tax liability of the "partner" must be affected by whether the partnership item is separately taken into account. The problem with applying this regulation to the facts in the instant case is that Brown Cayman is the partner in question, but it has no tax liability. Even if we treat Brown Cayman as if it were a domestic corporation liable for U.S. tax, its tax liability is in no way affected by separately accounting for and characterizing the partnership income attributable to Brinco's commissions. Brown Cayman's hypothetical tax liability would still be based on the income it derived from its distributive share of partnership income. Sec. 61(a)(13). That distributive share of partnership income would include partnership income attributable to Brinco's purchase of footwear. However, the separate characterization of Brown Cayman's income from Brinco as commission income would have no affect on Brown Cayman's actual or hypothetical tax liability. It follows that section 1.702–1(a)(8)(ii), Income Tax Regs., does not apply, and therefore the result the majority arrives at is not supported by its technical analysis.

2.   Aggregate vs. Entity

While there may be areas in the law of partnership taxation where the aggregate versus entity issue still exists, I do not believe there is any remaining issue with respect to the type of specific partnership income items that must be characterized by individual partners as if they had realized the income directly from the source from which realized by the partnership. Congress has specifically provided statutory rules in section 702(a)(1) through (8) and subsection (b) that answer this question. In section 702(a)(7), Congress also gave the Department of the Treasury broad regulatory authority to specify additional partnership items that must be separately accounted for and characterized at the partner level. As previously explained, nothing in these partnership provisions requires that the character of the commission income that Brinco earned by purchasing footwear on behalf of Brown Group be separately stated and characterized at the partner level as if it had been "realized directly from the source from which realized by the partnership". Sec. 702(b). Brown Cayman's distributive share of partnership income falls under section 702(a)(8), and the separate character of the items making up such income does not pass through to the partners under section 702(b).

The Solution

1.   Section 954(d)

Brown Group International (a U.S. corporation whose stock is wholly owned by Brown Group), Brown Cayman (a Cayman Islands corporation whose stock is wholly owned by Brown Group International), and Brinco (a Cayman Islands partnership in which Brown Cayman held an 88-percent interest) were formed in 1985 to facilitate the purchase of Brazilian footwear on behalf of Brown Group. Brinco earned commission income by acting as purchasing agent for Brown Group International.

The issue is whether Brown Cayman's distributive share of Brinco's income is "Subpart F income". This question can be answered by determining whether Brown Cayman's distributive share of partnership income from Brinco is foreign base company sales income within the meaning of section 954(d)(1).

Section 954(d)(1) provides:

Sec. 954(d). Foreign Base Company Sales Income.—

(1)   In General.—For purposes of subsection (a)(2), the term "foreign base company sales income" means income (whether in the form of profits, commissions, fees, or otherwise) derived in connection with * * * the purchase of personal property from any person on behalf of a related person where—

(A) the property which is purchased * * * is manufactured, produced, grown, or extracted outside the country under the laws of which the controlled foreign corporation is created or organized, and

(B) * * * in the case of property purchased on behalf of a related person, is purchased for use, consumption, or disposition outside such foreign country.

There is no question that Brown Cayman is a controlled foreign corporation or that Brown Group International is a related person within the meaning of section 954(d). There is also no question that the footwear was "manufactured" or "produced" in Brazil, which is "outside the country under the laws of which the controlled foreign corporation is created or organized" (Cayman Islands). Sec. 954(d)(1)(A). Finally, there is no question that the footwear was "purchased for use, consumption, or disposition outside such foreign country." Sec. 954(d)(1)(B). Thus, our only task is to determine whether Brown Cayman's distributive share of Brinco's profits is income of Brown Cayman (the controlled foreign corporation) that was "derived in connection with * * * the purchase of personal property * * * on behalf of a related person" within the meaning of section 954(d)(1).

Brown Cayman's distributive share of Brinco's profits is clearly within the broad term "income (whether in the form of profits, commissions, fees, or otherwise)". Sec. 954(d)(1). Brown Cayman "derived" this income "from" Brinco as part of Brown Cayman's distributive share of Brinco's profits. Under section 61(a), gross income means all income "from whatever source derived, including (but not limited to) the following items: * * * (13) Distributive share of partnership gross income."

The only remaining question is whether Brown Cayman's income from Brinco was "derived in connection with * * * the purchase of personal property * * * on behalf of a related person" within the meaning of section 954(d)(1). Brown Group International, Brown Cayman, and Brinco were organized and operated to purchase footwear for Brown Group. This was done by having Brinco act as the purchasing agent for Brown Group International. The purchase of foot-wear from Brazilian sources (i.e., "from any person") was accomplished by Brinco acting as an agent on behalf of Brown Group International ("a related person"; i.e., related to Brown Cayman). Brinco's purchasing activity as an agent for Brown Group International was the reason why commissions were generated. Those commissions, in turn, produced partnership profits and resulted in Brown Cayman's distributive share of those profits. Brown Cayman's distributive share of profits from Brinco was thus "derived in connection with * * * the purchase of personal property * * * on behalf of a related person." Having met the literal provisions of section 954(d)(1), it becomes unnecessary to attribute the commission-earning activities directly to Brown Cayman through the application of section 702 or the aggregate approach.

2.   Interpretation of "in connection with"

The foregoing analysis relies on a broad reading of the term "in connection with". This phrase has previously been given a broad interpretation. *Snow v. Commissioner, 416 U.S. 500, 502–503 (1974); Huntsman v. Commissioner, 905 F.2d 1182, 1184 (8th Cir.1990); Fort Howard Corp. v. Commissioner, 103 T.C. 345, 351–352 (1994).* In Fort Howard Corp., we said that "in connection with" "means associated with, or related" and that "Events or elements are 'connected' when they are 'logically related' " to each other. *Id. at 351–352.* That relationship exists here. Brown Cayman's distributive share of partnership profits was, by design and in reality, associated with, logically related to, and dependent upon commissions paid to Brinco for acting as a purchasing agent on behalf of a party related to Brown Cayman.

Congress intentionally used the phrase "in connection with" in lieu of more narrow terms such as "from" or "for", and a broad interpretation of the phrase is consistent with the legislative objective of Subpart F. Subpart F was "designed to end tax deferral on 'tax haven' operations by U.S. controlled corporations." S. Rept. 87–1881 (1962), *1962–3 C.B. 707, 785.* Brown Cayman was a U.S. controlled corporation. Its operations consisted of being a partner in Brinco. Had Brown Cayman itself acted as purchasing agent and earned commissions as purchasing agent for Brown Group International, it would be clear that the commissions would be Subpart F income. If we were to accept petitioner's position, Brown Group could circumvent Subpart F and successfully defer a significant amount of U.S. tax simply by establishing and interposing a partnership (Brinco), whose profits would be distributable to Brown Cayman.

During 1985, Brown Group paid commissions to Brinco of $1,119,970. These commissions were added to Brown Group's cost of goods sold. Brinco distributed $897,281 during 1985 to Brown Cayman, its 88-percent partner. As a result, Brown Group reduced its gross profit for U.S. tax purposes by $1,119,970, while at the same time recouping $897,281 of that amount through its controlled foreign corporation without being subject to U.S. tax on the $897,281. Surely, Congress intended Subpart F and the broad language of section 954(d)(1) to apply to this type of situation when it defined foreign base company sales income to include income "derived in connection with * * * the purchase of personal property * * * on behalf of a related person".

■ BEGHE, J., concurring: Having joined the majority opinion, I write separately in an effort to provide some additional support.

I don't disassociate myself from the majority's expansive interpretation and application of section 702 and the regulation thereunder. The rationale of *Rev. Rul. 86–138, 1986–2 C.B. 84* (although revenue rulings are not binding on this Court, see, e.g., *Stark v. Commissioner, 86 T.C. 243, 250–251 (1986)),* properly can be extended to support the majority's conclusion that sections 702(a) and 703(a) should be interpreted to prevent the interposition of an entity that has no U.S. income tax liability from disrupting the conduit regimes of Subpart F and subchapter K.

However, if a literalistic interpretative approach to section 702(a) and section 1.702–1(a)(8)(ii), Income Tax Regs., were to be applied in this case (as the other concurrences and the dissent would do), the operative facts would be outside sections 702 and 703, and there would be no occasion to have recourse to those sections. The preamble of section 702(a) defines the field of coverage of subsections (a) and (b) of section 702 as situations in which a partner is "determining his [here its] income tax". That condition has arguably not been satisfied in this case because, as the concurrences and dissent point out, Brown Cayman has no U.S. income tax liability. Under a consistent application of their interpretative approach, we are therefore forced outside of subchapter K and thrown back to the common law of Federal taxation. It seems to me that the cases cited and summarized at pp. 117–119 of the majority opinion are grounded in longstanding notions of mutual agency that antedate and transcend the argument whether the aggregate or entity theory of partnership is to prevail in a particular tax case that is governed by subchapter K.

If the issue is to be posed in terms of entity vs. aggregate, however, as the parties chose to do, it is appropriate to look to the intention of the applicable statutory provisions outside subchapter K (here, Subpart F) for guidance about which approach is appropriate. See American Law Institute, Federal Income Tax Project, Subchapter K: Proposals on the Taxation of Partners 452, 523–532 (1984); Youngwood & Weiss, "Partners and Partnerships—Aggregate v. Entity Outside of Subchapter K", 48 Tax Law. 39, 40–43 (1994).

The dissent uses inappropriate authorities to support its conclusion that the entity theory must be applied to reach what would properly be characterized as a "bizarre" result under Subpart F. Youngwood & Weiss, supra at 40. Authorities which "determined that partnership level characterization was necessary to ascertain matters such as the existence of a trade or business, the existence of a profit motive and the characterization of gain or loss with regard to partnership property", id. at 57, have no bearing on a case such as this, "where the character of the income must be determined at the level where the income is recognized", id.

It also bears pointing out that *United States v. Basye, 410 U.S. 441, 448 (1973),* quoted by the dissent as adopting the entity theory, does no more than illustrate that "it is not always possible for partnership income to be allocated to specific partners before it is included in income" and that "Any tax system that permitted * * * [an escrow] arrangement to defer the reporting of income would be fatally flawed. Basye simply recognized this principle in the partnership context." American Law Institute, Federal Income Tax Project, Subchapter K: Proposals on the Taxation of Partners 525 (1984).

Finally, in further support of the third leg of the majority opinion: As this writer observed in *Fort Howard Corp. v. Commissioner, 103 T.C. 345, 377 n. 2 (1994)* (Beghe, J., dissenting), the logical relationship that should be focused on to establish the connection is "the 'logic of events' that has to do with cause and effect relationships and necessary connections or outcomes." In the case at hand, all Brinco income was earned commission income, and there is no difficulty in tracing Brown Cayman's distributive share of that income into its hands. There is no competing other kind of income or activity at the Brinco level that displaces to any extent the direct cause and effect relationship between the income-earning activities of Brinco's other partners and the characterization of Brown Cayman's distributive share of Brinco income derived from those activities.

■ SWIFT, J., agrees with this concurring opinion.

■ CHIECHI, J., concurring: Although I agree with the majority's holding that the income in question is foreign base company sales income under section 954(d)(1) and therefore is Subpart F income includable under section 951(a) in the gross income of International, I cannot join in two of the three rationales upon which the majority relies to reach that holding. I concur only in the rationale set forth by the majority under the heading "Aggregate Versus Entity"; that is to say, to effectuate the purpose of Congress in enacting Subpart F, the aggregate nature of Brinco as a partnership must be emphasized in applying section 954(d)(1). That rationale amply supports the majority's conclusion that "Brown Cayman should be put into the shoes of Brinco for [purposes of] determining whether Brown Cayman was earning commission income on sales by third parties to International" (majority op. p. 119).

I cannot join in the ratio decidendi stated by the majority under the heading "Subchapter K" that relies on section 702(a)(7) and section 1.702–1(a)(8)(ii), Income Tax Regs., since, as pointed out by Judge Ruwe in his concurring opinion, that regulation, and therefore that section, does not technically apply because Brown Cayman, as a controlled foreign corporation, has no tax liability. Although Congress may well have intended that section 702(a)(7) apply in the circumstances presented here, that section requires that a partner take into account separately his distributive share of the partnership's other items of income, gain, loss, deduction, or credit only *"to the extent provided by regulations prescribed by the Secretary"* (emphasis added). The regulations prescribed by the Secretary (namely, section 1.702–1(a)(8)(ii), Income Tax Regs.) do not provide that Brown Cayman take such other items into account.

Nor can I join in the third rationale of the majority (and the only rationale in Judge Ruwe's concurring opinion) that is based on the language "in connection with" that appears in section 954(d)(1). To the extent the majority (and Judge Ruwe) suggests that rationale is separate from and independent of the ratio decidendi stated by the majority under the heading "Aggregate Versus Entity", I disagree. It seems to me that Brown Cayman's distributive share of Brinco's profits cannot be characterized as "income * * * derived in connection with * * * the purchase of personal property from any person on behalf of a related person" unless the aggregate approach to Brinco were emphasized in order to give that share of those profits the same character in the hands of Brown Cayman as those profits have in the hands of Brinco, namely, commission income derived from the purchase of personal property on behalf of International. Sec. 954(d)(1). Only after the aggregate approach is applied to pass through to Brown Cayman the character of those profits as such commission income can those profits be considered "derived in connection with * * * the purchase of personal property * * * on behalf of a related person", since Brown Cayman, and not Brinco, is a related person with respect to International. Sec. 954(d)(1); see sec. 954(d)(3). The ratio decidendi stated by the majority under the heading "[I]n connection with" (and by Judge Ruwe in his concurring opinion) cannot, in my opinion, stand alone; it is wholly dependent on and results from the application of the aggregate theory of partnerships to Brinco.

■ JACOBS, J., dissenting: I disagree with the majority's conclusion that Brown Cayman Ltd's. (Brown Cayman's) share of partnership income from Brinco is Subpart F income; therefore, I respectfully dissent.

The majority relies on three reasons to reach the holding that the income in question is Subpart F income: (1) A technical analysis under subchapter K of the Code; (2) application of the aggregate theory of partnerships; and (3) support from the language of section 954(d)(1). Judge Chiechi, in her concurrence, explains the flaw in two of these three reasons, namely, in reasons (1) and (3). In this dissent I explain why the remaining reason, reason (2) (the application of the aggregate theory of partnerships) is flawed.

The controversy involved in this case involves a controlled foreign corporation (Brown Cayman) that was a member of a partnership (Brinco) that earned income by acting as a commission purchasing agent on behalf of the parent (Brown Group International) of the controlled foreign corporation. In reaching its conclusion, the majority would disregard Brinco as an entity and treat Brown Cayman as if it had performed the activities of Brinco. I disagree. In my opinion, the existence of Brinco should be respected, and the commission income Brinco received should be characterized at the partnership level.

"Subpart F income", as defined under section 952(a), is the sum of four specifically defined types of income. Only one type of Subpart F income, specifically "foreign base company income", is involved in this case. "Foreign base company income", as defined under section 954(a), is the sum of five specifically defined types of income. Only one type of foreign base company income, specifically "foreign base company sales income", is involved in this case.

Section 954(d)(1) defines "foreign base company sales income" as follows:

Sec. 954(d). FOREIGN BASE COMPANY SALES INCOME.—

(1) In General.—For purposes of subsection (a)(2), the term "foreign base company sales income" means income (whether in the form of profits, commissions, fees, or otherwise) derived in connection with the purchase of personal property from a related person and its sale to any person, the sale of personal property to any person on behalf of a related person, the purchase of personal property from any person and its sale to

a related person, or the purchase of personal property from any person on behalf of a related person where—

(A) the property which is purchased (or in the case of property sold on behalf of a related person, the property which is sold) is manufactured, produced, grown, or extracted outside the country under the laws of which the controlled foreign corporation is created or organized, and

(B) the property is sold for use, consumption, or disposition outside such foreign country or, in the case of property purchased on behalf of a related person, is purchased for use, consumption, or disposition outside such foreign country.

A "related person" is defined in section 954(d)(3), as in effect for the taxable year in issue, as follows:

(3) RELATED PERSON DEFINED.—For purposes of this section, a person is a related person with respect to a controlled foreign corporation, if—

(A) such person is an individual, partnership, trust, or estate which controls the controlled foreign corporation;

(B) such person is a corporation which controls, or is controlled by, the controlled foreign corporation; or

(C) such person is a corporation which is controlled by the same person or persons which control the controlled foreign corporation.

For purposes of the preceding sentence, control means the ownership, directly or indirectly, of stock possessing more than 50 percent of the total combined voting power of all classes of stock entitled to vote. For purposes of this paragraph, the rules for determining ownership of stock prescribed by section 958 shall apply.

Here, there is no question but that Brown Cayman is a controlled foreign corporation and that Brown Group International is a U.S. shareholder of a controlled foreign corporation. Thus, Brown Group International (and ultimately the affiliated group of which it is a member) must include in income the foreign base company sales income earned by Brown Cayman. But, as hereafter explained, Brown Cayman did not have foreign base company sales income.

In the elaborate detailing of section 954(d)(1), Congress required that, in order for a controlled foreign corporation to have foreign base company sales income, each of the following elements must be present: (1) A purchase or sale, (2) of personal property, (3) from, to, or on behalf of a related person, and (4) such personal property must be manufactured outside the controlled foreign corporation's country of incorporation, and (5) the sale must be for use, consumption, or disposition outside such controlled foreign corporation's country of incorporation. In the instant case four of the five elements are present, namely, the first two and last two elements. But the third element is not present because the purchase of the footwear was not made from, to, or on behalf of a related person.

Rather, the purchase in this case was arranged by Brinco from third parties on behalf of Brown Group International, a party unrelated to Brinco.

As to the third element, the majority does not claim there was a purchase of personal property from or to related parties. Rather, the majority asserts that there was a purchase on behalf of a related person by treating Brown Cayman as if it did the purchasing of footwear, through Brinco, on behalf of Brown Group International. The majority's assertion is erroneous because Brinco is not a sham. In fact, it is undeniable that Brinco was formed and structured as a partnership, at least in part, for substantial business purposes. Further, the form of all of the partnership's (Brinco's) transactions involved reflect their substance.

For tax purposes, there are two different ways of viewing a partnership. A partnership may be viewed as an aggregation of its partners, each of whom directly owns an interest in partnership assets and operations, or as a separate entity, in which separate interests are owned by each of its partners. By disregarding Brinco, the majority uses an aggregate partnership approach. Using the aggregate approach, the majority attributes the partnership's (Brinco's) activities, and not merely the character of the partnership income, to its partner (Brown Cayman).

It is noteworthy that in defining a related person, section 954(d)(3) provides that a partnership that controls a foreign corporation is a related person, and thus the income derived in connection with the purchase or sale of personal property between the two entities (that is, the controlling partnership and controlled foreign corporation) is treated as foreign base company sales income. Had Congress viewed a partnership as an aggregation of its partners (rather than as a separate entity), then there would have been no need to include a partnership in the definition of a related person. Instead, the determination of a related person would be made separately as to each partner depending on whether that partner was related to the entity with whom the partnership purchased or sold personal property.

As stated, I believe the majority's aggregate approach is erroneous. The process of characterizing partnership income, for tax purposes, is a two-part process: First, the partnership is treated as an entity in whose hands the partnership income is characterized, and then the partnership is treated as a conduit (an aggregate concept) through which the income received is passed on to the partners in accord with their distributive shares. Treating the partnership (Brinco) as an entity in whose hands the commission income is to be characterized produces a result that the income in question is not foreign base company sales income, and hence is not Subpart F income.

No court has addressed the issue of whether, in the context of Subpart F of the Code, section 702(b) should be interpreted as determining the character of income at the partner level (aggregate approach) or at the partnership level (entity approach). However, as will be later discussed, regulations issued on December 30, 1994, permit the Internal Revenue Service (Service) to treat, in certain situations, a partnership as an aggregation of its partners, in whole or in part, as appropriate to carry out the provision of the Code or regulations thereunder with respect to transactions that occur on or after December 30, 1994. The transactions involved herein occurred prior to that date.

For the most part, the cases that have directly considered whether partnership items should be characterized at the partner or partnership level have generally concluded that the characterization question should be resolved at the partnership level. See 1 McKee et al., Federal Taxation of Partnerships and Partners, par. 9.01[4][a], at 9–19 (2d ed. 1990) (the authors also note that partnership-level characterization is virtually required by the overall sense of the partnership taxation statutory framework).

The U.S. Supreme Court has stated that, for purposes of calculating partnership income, "the partnership is regarded as an independently recognizable entity apart from the aggregate of the partners". *United States v. Basye, 410 U.S. 441, 448 (1973)*. The Court also noted:

The legislative history indicates, and the commentators agree, that partnerships are entities for purposes of calculating and filing informational returns but that they are conduits through which the taxpaying obligation passes to the individual partners in accord with their distributive shares. [Id. n.8; citations omitted.]

Recent cases cite *United States v. Basye, supra,* in holding that characterization of partnership income derived from the sale of property takes place at the partnership level. For example, in *Pleasant Summit Land Corp. v. Commissioner, 863 F.2d 263 (3d Cir.1988),* affg. in part and revg. in part *T.C. Memo. 1987–469,* the Court of Appeals upheld our factual finding that the sale of real estate held by a partnership was properly characterized as a capital gain. In holding that such characterization takes place at the partnership level, the Court of Appeals quoted Basye and concluded: "we must make our analysis of the investment from the point of view of the partnership". *Id. at 272.*

In *Barham v. United States, 301 F. Supp. 43 (M.D.Ga.1969),* affd. *429 F.2d 40 (5th Cir.1970),* the District Court held that, where the trade or business of a joint venture was the purchase, development, and sale of real estate, the partner-taxpayer's distributive share of income received from the sale of real estate was not entitled to capital gain treatment even though the partner was not engaged in the real estate business. *Id. at 46–49.* The court referred to section 702(b) as the "conduit rule" and stated:

The clear inference to be drawn from the Code sections and the regulation is that, as a general rule, for the purpose of determining the nature of an item of income, deduction, gain, loss or credit * * * the partnership is to be viewed as an entity and such items are to be viewed from the standpoint of the partnership (or joint venture) rather than from the standpoint of each individual member. * * * [*Id. at 46.*]

The court added:

It follows that in section 1221(1) the words "his trade or business" mean the trade or business of the partnership, even though under section 701 partnerships are not liable for income tax. * * * [Id.]

In *McManus v. Commissioner, 583 F.2d 443 (9th Cir.1978),* affg. *65 T.C. 197 (1975),* the Court of Appeals affirmed this Court's holding that a section 1033 election must be made at the partnership level. The Court of Appeals rejected the taxpayer's argument that the partnership was not a taxable entity, stating:

While it is true that a partnership is not liable for tax * * * [it] is required to file returns and the partners are required to conform their individual returns to the partnership returns. If each partner could determine his share of the partnership income separately, confusion would result, confusion which Congress meant to avoid * * * [*Id. at 448;* citation omitted.]

In *Davis v. Commissioner, 74 T.C. 881 (1980),* affd. *746 F.2d 357 (6th Cir.1984),* we held that the special allocation to a partner-taxpayer of royalties paid to the partnership retains its character as a capital gain under section 631(c) in the hands of the taxpayer. We reviewed section 702(b) and stated: "This language has been consistently interpreted to mean that the character of partnership income is determined at the partnership level". *Id. at 905–906* (citing *United States v. Basye, 410 U.S. 441 (1973); Podell v. Commissioner, 55 T.C. 429 (1970); Grove v. Commissioner, 54 T.C. 799 (1970);* sec. 1.702–1(b), Income Tax Regs.).

This Court and several Courts of Appeals have addressed the issue of profit motive, for purposes of section 162, with respect to partnerships. All have held that such characterization is to be made at the partnership level. For example, in *Brannen v. Commissioner, 722 F.2d 695, 704 (11th Cir.1984),* affg. *78 T.C. 471 (1982),* the court held that, in determining whether a partner-taxpayer was entitled to any claimed deductions which were attributable to cash paid by the partnership for a movie, the profit-motive analysis was properly made at the partnership level.

In *Goodwin v. Commissioner, 75 T.C. 424 (1980),* affd. without published opinion *691 F.2d 490 (3d Cir.1982),* this Court also held that profit motive under section 162 is properly applied at the partnership level, and we noted that section 702(b) "has been held to require that the character of the items comprising the partnership income or loss be determined at the partnership level". *Id. at 436* (citing *Davis v. Commissioner, 74 T.C. 881, 905–906 (1980),* affd. *746 F.2d 357 (6th Cir.1984); Miller v. Commissioner, 70 T.C. 448, 455–456 (1978); Podell v. Commissioner, 55 T.C. 429, 432–434 (1970); Grove v. Commissioner, 54 T.C. 799, 803–805 (1970)).* In *Goodwin v. Commissioner, supra at 437,* we then concluded: "that in the context of section 162, the character of the deductions, i.e., whether they were incurred in the course of a trade or business, must be resolved at the partnership level."

In addition, in *Campbell v. United States, 813 F.2d 694 (5th Cir.1987)*, the court held that the attribution of a loss to a trade or business for the purposes of section 172(d)(4) (which allows certain business deductions in calculating a net operating loss) must be made at the partnership level: "We have held that under section 702(b), partnership business deductions may be attributed to the individual partner-taxpayer only if such deductions were incurred in the partnership's trade or business". *Id. at 695–696* (citing *Tallal v. Commissioner, 778 F.2d 275, 276 (5th Cir.1985)*, affg. *T.C. Memo. 1984–486*).

In *Resnik v. Commissioner, 66 T.C. 74, 81 (1976)*, affd. per curiam without published opinion *555 F.2d 634 (7th Cir.1977)*, we concluded that, under section 446(b), we must "first look at the partnership level to ascertain whether the prepayment of interest results in a distortion of income". In so concluding, we reasoned:

The partnership return is more than just an information return. It has consequences that go beyond the mere disclosure to the Commissioner of profits of the enterprise * * * And in computing its net income under the revenue laws, it is generally the partnership, not the individual partner, that exercises the various options open to taxpayers in computing net income under the Code. * * * [*Id. at 80–81* (quoting *Scherf v. Commissioner, 20 T.C. 346, 347–348 (1953))*.]

In *Rev. Rul. 68–79, 1968–1 C.B. 310*, the Service characterized as long-term capital gain a partner's distributive share of capital gain upon the sale of securities because, even though the partner held his partnership interest for less than 6 months, the partnership held the securities longer than the requisite holding period. The ruling stated:

The character of any item of income, gain, loss, deduction, or credit included in a partner's distributive share under paragraphs (1) through (8) of section 702(a) of the Code is determined at the *partnership level*. [*Rev. Rul. 68–79, 1968–1 C.B. at 310;* emphasis added; citation omitted.]

Similarly, the Service has ruled that characterization of ordinary loss under section 1231 must take place at the partnership level. *Rev. Rul. 67–188, 1967–1 C.B. 216*. Likewise, in *Rev. Rul. 77–320, 1977–2 C.B. 78,* the Service expressed the position that section 183 applies to partnerships at the partnership level.

In nearly every context in which the issue of characterization of partnership income is relevant to the facts of this case, this Court and other courts have concluded that the proper level for characterizing an item of income is at the partnership level. Applying the logic of these cases to the determination of foreign base company sales income, I would apply the entity theory of partnership taxation; that is, I would characterize the income involved herein at the partnership (Brinco's) level. As a consequence, I would conclude that the income in question is not Subpart F income.

I recognize that acceptance of my position will result in petitioner's receiving a tax windfall because 100 percent of the commissions paid to Brinco by Brown Group International would be included in its cost of goods sold, whereas 88 percent of the commissions (which ultimately went to Brown Cayman) would not be taxed. But as the Court of Appeals for the Ninth Circuit has stated:

The Government asserts that in enacting Subpart F Congress was more concerned with the nature of the income than the form of the entity generating the income * * *

We find this argument unpersuasive. * * * Congress wrote the statute unambiguously to apply to Subpart F income received from controlled "corporations" only. If the omission of income received from controlled partnerships has indeed created an unjustified loophole in the tax laws, the remedy lies in new legislation, not in judicial improvisation.

[*MCA Inc. v. United States, 685 F.2d 1099, 1104–1105 (9th Cir. 1982).*]

Petitioner may have found a hole in the dike, but the closing of the hole "calls for the application of the Congressional thumb, not the court's." *Fabreeka Prods. Co. v. Commissioner, 294 F.2d 876, 879 (1st Cir. 1961),* vacating and remanding *34 T.C. 290 (1960);* see *Hanover Bank v. Commissioner, 369 U.S. 672, 688 n. 23 (1962).* The Service may have closed the hole in the dike for partnership transactions that occur on and after December 30, 1994, but here, as previously stated, the transactions involved occurred prior to that date.

On December 30, 1994, the Service issued final regulations, section 1.701–2, Income Tax Regs., *60 Fed. Reg. 27* (Jan. 3, 1995), providing for an anti-abuse rule under subchapter K of the Code. The rule permits the Service, in certain instances, to recast partnership transactions that make inappropriate use of the rules of subchapter K. In addition, and more pertinent to this case, section 1.701–2(e), Income Tax Regs., provides that the Service can treat a partnership as an aggregation of its partners in whole or in part as appropriate to carry out the purpose of any provision of the Code or regulations thereunder, except to the extent that: (1) A provision of the Code or regulations prescribes the treatment of the partnership as an entity, and (2) that treatment and the ultimate tax results, taking into account all the relevant facts and circumstances, are clearly contemplated by that provision.

The anti-abuse rule is effective for all transactions involving a partnership that occur on or after May 12, 1994. The provisions permitting the Service to treat a partnership as an aggregation of its partners as appropriate to carry out the purpose of any provision of the Code are effective for all transactions involving a partnership that occur after December 29, 1994. The transactions involved herein occurred prior to November 2, 1986, and Brinco was dissolved on October 31, 1987.

■ CHABOT and LARO, JJ., agree with this dissent.

Brown Group, Inc. and Subsidiaries v. Commissioner of Internal Revenue

United States Court of Appeals for the Eighth Circuit.
77 F.3d 217 (1996).

■ JUDGES: Before FAGG, CIRCUIT JUDGE, GARTH,** SENIOR CIRCUIT JUDGE, WOLLMAN, CIRCUIT JUDGE.

OPINION:

■ GARTH, SENIOR CIRCUIT JUDGE.

This is an appeal from the en banc decision by the United States Tax Court (the "Tax Court"), assessing taxes against appellant, the Brown Group, Inc. ("the Brown Group") and its subsidiaries, on the commission distributions received by the Brown Group's wholly-owned Cayman Islands subsidiary, Brown Cayman, Ltd. ("BCL"), under Subpart F of the Internal Revenue Code (codified at *26 U.S.C. § 951* et seq.).

The issue we address on appeal is whether BCL's distributive share of a foreign partnership's earnings (Brinco partnership) should be taxed to the Brown Group under Subpart F of the Internal Revenue Code. We hold that a foreign partner's distributive share of foreign partnership income cannot be deemed to be "Subpart F income" where the commissions at issue did not constitute "Subpart F income" under the pre-1987 statute, *26 U.S.C. § 954*(d)(3), in that the foreign partnership (Brinco) did not control a controlled foreign corporation such as BCL. Accordingly, we vacate the decision of the Tax Court assessing an income tax deficiency against the Brown Group for the tax year ending November 1, 1986.

. . . II.

A.

Under Subpart F of the Internal Revenue Code, codified at *26 U.S.C. § 951* et seq., a United States shareholder that controls a foreign corporation for an uninterrupted period of thirty or more days must include in its taxable gross income, its pro rata share of the controlled foreign corporation's "Subpart F" income. *26 U.S.C. § 951*(a)(1).

"Subpart F income" is defined as four types of income under section 952(a). The only type of "Subpart F income" involved in this case is "foreign base company income." *26 U.S.C. § 952*(a)(2).

**   Honorable Leonard I. Garth, Senior U.S. Circuit Judge for the United States Court of Appeals for the Third Circuit, sitting by designation.

There are five different types of "foreign base company income," as defined under section 954(a). The only type involved in this case is "foreign base company sales income."

"Foreign base company sales income" is defined in relevant part as:

Income . . . derived in connection with the purchase of personal property from any person and its sale to a related person, or the purchase of personal property from any person on behalf of a related person where—

(A) the property which is purchased . . . is manufactured, produced, grown, or extracted outside the country under the laws of which the controlled foreign corporation is created or organized, and

(B) . . . in the case of property purchased on behalf of a *related person*, is purchased for use, consumption, or disposition outside such foreign country.

26 U.S.C. § 954(d)(1) (emphases added).

Under the version of section 954(d)(3) in effect for the taxable year of 1986, a "related person" is defined as:

(A) an individual, partnership, trust, or estate which controls the controlled foreign corporation; or (B) a corporation which controls, or is controlled by, the controlled foreign corporation; or (C) a corporation which is controlled by the same person(s) which control the controlled foreign corporation.

26 U.S.C. § 954(d)(3) (emphases added). We are concerned here only with section 954(d)(3)(a) which requires that in order to be a "related person," Brinco, a foreign partnership, must control a controlled foreign corporation—in this case, BCL. For purposes of this section, "control" is defined as "the ownership, directly or indirectly, of stock possessing more than fifty percent of the total combined voting power of all classes of stock entitled to vote." Id.

B.

In this case, the parties have stipulated that BGII is a "United States shareholder" and BCL is a "controlled foreign corporation." It is undisputed that Brinco was not a "related person," as defined in *26 U.S.C. § 954*(d)(3), to either BCL or BGII. It is also undisputed that BGII was a "related person" to BCL. The IRS has conceded that Brinco was not a sham partnership.

III.

The present case boils down to a very discrete question of law: whether BCL's distributive share of Brinco's partnership earnings (commissions) constituted "Subpart F income," under *26 U.S.C. § 954*(d)(3), given that the commissions did not constitute "Subpart F income" when earned by Brinco. We exercise de novo review of this question of law. *Jacobson v. Commissioner, 963 F.2d 218, 219 (8th Cir.1992).*

We hold that the Tax Court erred in ignoring the partnership entity in characterizing BCL's earnings as taxable "Subpart F income." Instead, we are persuaded by, and adopt, the reasoning and holding of Judge Jacobs's January 25, 1995 opinion which dissented from the Tax Court's en banc opinion.

It is not disputed that under section 954(d)(3), as that statute existed in 1986, Brinco was not a "related person" to either BGII or BCL. Moreover, this conclusion is supported by the plain language of the statute. Brinco is not a corporation. Hence, the only portion of the "related person" definition that could apply to Brinco is that of a "partnership . . . which controls the controlled foreign corporation." *26 U.S.C. § 954(d)(3)(A).* However Brinco did not control BCL but rather was controlled by BCL. Thus, Brinco was not a "related person" to BGII. It follows therefore that BGII was not a person "related" to Brinco.[5]

Furthermore, even if we were to accept the IRS's broad interpretation of "related person," it is irrelevant to the present inquiry because Brinco is not a controlled foreign corporation, and therefore its income, whether earned on behalf of a "related person" or not, cannot be characterized as Subpart F income.

Because Brinco earned its commission income on behalf of an unrelated person, BGII, that income was not "foreign company sales income" for purposes of Subpart F. Given that partnership income is characterized at the partnership level, the income earned by Brinco retained its character of being not "Subpart F income" when distributed to BCL. Accordingly, BGII (and thus its parent, the Brown Group), under the pre-1987 version of section 954(d)(3), cannot be assessed income tax on Brinco's partnership earnings which were distributed to BCL.

We find this analysis to be consistent with the well-established principle that income is to be characterized at the partnership level and that such income retains its character when distributed to the individual partners.

In *United States v. Basye, 410 U.S. 441, 35 L. Ed. 2d 412, 93 S. Ct. 1080 (1973),* for example, the Supreme Court held that individual partners must include as taxable income, their distributive share of payments made to a retirement trust fund that was compensation to the partnership for services rendered by the partnership. The Court recited a familiar principle of income taxation to the effect that "partners are taxable on their distributive or proportionate shares of current partnership income irrespective of whether that income is actually

---

[5]   At oral argument the IRS argued that BGII is a "related person" because it is related to BCL, and that Brinco was therefore earning its commission income "on behalf of" a "related person." The IRS provides no authority for its conclusion that by "related person," the pre-1987 version of section 954(d)(3) meant to reach persons unrelated to the entity allegedly earning the Subpart F income (Brinco).

distributed to them." Basye, U.S. at 447–48.[6] In the instant case, of course, Brinco's commissions were actually distributed to its partners in the respective proportions to which they were entitled. Hence BCL received 88% of the commissions earned by Brinco.

The Court in Basye further stated that:

While the partnership itself pays no taxes, *26 U.S.C. § 701,* it must report the income it generates and such income must be calculated in largely the same manner as an individual computes his personal income. For this purpose, then, the partnership is regarded as an independently recognizable entity apart from the aggregate of its partners. Once its income is ascertained and reported, its existence may be disregarded since each partner must pay a tax on a portion of the total income as if the partnership were merely an agent or conduit through which the income is passed.

Id. at 448. "The legislative history indicates, and the commentators agree, that partnerships are entities for purposes of calculating and filing informational returns but that they are conduits through which the taxpaying obligation passes to the individual partners in accord with their distributive shares." *Id. at 448 n. 8.* See, e.g., *Pleasant Summit Land Corp. v. Commissioner, 863 F.2d 263, 272 (3d Cir.1988)* (in determining whether individual partners can claim losses from partnership's purchase of property, the analysis must be made of the investment from the point of view of the partnership, not of the individual partners), cert. denied, *493 U.S. 901 (1989); Davis v. Commissioner, 74 T.C. 881, 895 (1980)* (stating that the language of § 702(b) "has been consistently interpreted to mean that the character of partnership income is determined at the partnership level"), aff'd, *746 F.2d 357 (6th Cir.1984).*[7]

Although our holding may result in a tax windfall to the Brown Group due to the particularized definition of "related person" under the pre-1987 version of section 954(d)(3) of the Internal Revenue Code, such a tax loophole is not ours to close but must rather be closed or cured by Congress. *MCA, Inc. v. United States, 685 F.2d 1099, 1104–05 (9th Cir.1982)* (refusing to expand the pre-1987 definition of "related person" to include controlled partnerships). Indeed, Congress has done just that.

---

[6] In Basye, the Court upheld the partnership principle that the partners were required to pay taxes on their distributive shares even in the situation where none of the partners were eligible to receive the amounts in his contingent or tentative account prior to retirement, even though no interest in the account was deemed to vest in a particular beneficiary before retirement, and even though a partner could forfeit his interest in the retirement trust fund under a number of circumstances, such as by taking pre-retirement severance. Id. at 441, 444–45.

[7] Section 702(b) of Subpart K provides that:

The character of any item of income . . . in a partner's distributive share under paragraphs (1) through (7) of subsection (a) shall be determined as if such item were realized directly from the source from which realized by the partnership, or incurred in the same manner as incurred by the partnership.

26 U.S.C. § 702(b) (emphases added).

It closed this loophole the following year, in 1987, when it amended section 954(d)(3) to broaden the definition of "related person" to include not only partnerships that control CFC's but also those that are controlled by CFC's or their parents.

Furthermore, for transactions occurring on and after December 30, 1994, Congress for the first time has apparently permitted, in special circumstances not relevant here, the recasting of partnership income under Subpart F. Treasury Regulation § 1.701–2 was thereafter announced. That Regulation, characterized as the "anti-abuse rule" permitted the IRS to recast partnership transactions that make inappropriate use of Subchapter K rules. In particular § 1.701–2(e) provided that the IRS can treat a partnership as an aggregation of its partners in whole or in part as appropriate to carry out the purpose of any provision of the Code or regulations. However, because section 1.701–2 is effective only for transactions on or after May 12, 1994, and section 1.701–2(e) is effective only for transactions on or after December 29, 1994, those provisions cannot apply to this case. Indeed, as we read the regulations, the IRS does not have the power to recast partnership transactions or apply the aggregate approach for transactions occurring prior to these effective dates.

Because the "loophole" in Subpart F taxable income has been closed, the issue that arises in the present case is unlikely to occur again. Under the pre-1987 law applicable to the instant case, however, the Brown Group cannot be held taxable on BCL's distributive share of Brinco's partnership earnings.[8]

We do not find section 702(b) to shed much light on the present inquiry and, in any event, we conclude that it is unnecessary to reach or address Subpart K in resolving the instant controversy.

IV.

For the foregoing reasons, the Tax Court erred in attributing taxable "Subpart F income" to the Brown Group based on BCL's distributive share of Brinco's earnings. The decision of the Tax Court assessing an income tax deficiency against the Brown Group for the tax year ending November 1, 1986 is vacated and remanded for proceedings consistent with the foregoing opinion.

NOTES AND QUESTIONS

1.   Is there any conceptual difference between the Dupont and Brown Group tax planning?

---

[8]   At oral argument, the IRS invoked the language of 26 U.S.C. § 702(b) of Subpart F of the Internal Revenue Code that states that the character of the partner's income is determined as if the partner directly realized that income from the source from which the partnership realized the income. However that same section also provides that the income "shall be determined as if such item were . . . incurred in the same manner as incurred by the partnership." 26 U.S.C. § 702(b). See n. 8, supra.

2. Try to summarize the various views taken by the judges in this case. Which is the most persuasive? Which is the least persuasive? (Hint: What do you think about the view that ultimately prevailed?) Independent of their substantive positions, the multiple, inconsistent opinions of the various Tax Court judges provide a striking example of the potential value for a litigant in making alternative arguments.

3. Treasury responded to this decision by proposing and then finalizing (August 2002) Treas. Reg. 1.954–1(g). Do you think this was necessary?

4. Why do you think we do not see many copycats of the Brown Group scheme?

5. With globalization, foreign base company services income becomes an increasingly important foreign base company income category. Read section 954(e), and Treas. Reg. 1.954–4(a)–(b)(1) and pay special attention to the *substantial assistance test* elaborated on in Treas. Reg. 1.954–4(b)(2)(ii). Do you think these rules are capable of handling internet-based business? What challenges may such business (e-commerce, internet based call center, etc.) pose to the IRS with respect to these rules?

Notice 2007–13 modified the substantial assistance rules, and can be relied on until regulations are promulgated. The following excerpt from the notice is also a good example for the issues that arise in the context of foreign base company services income.

Notice 2007–13 Excerpt

". . . This notice announces that the Treasury Department and the Internal Revenue Service (the IRS) will amend Treas. Reg. § 1.954–4(b)(1)(iv) and (b)(2)(ii) and the examples thereunder, which provide that substantial assistance rendered by a related person or persons to a controlled foreign corporation ("CFC") is included within the definition of foreign base company services income under section 954(e) of the Internal Revenue Code (Code). These amended regulations will limit the types of activities that constitute substantial assistance to certain assistance rendered, directly or indirectly, by a United States person or persons (as the term is defined in section 957(c) of the Code) to a related CFC. Until regulations reflecting these changes are issued, taxpayers may rely on this notice . . .

Treas. Reg. § 1.954–4(b)(1)(iv) defines "services which are performed for, or on behalf of, a related person" to include substantial assistance contributing to the performance of services by a CFC that has been furnished by a related person or persons. Treas. Reg. § 1.954–4(b)(2)(ii) sets forth the rules for the application of the substantial assistance test. Treas. Reg. § 1.954–4(b)(2)(ii)(a) states, in general, that assistance "shall include, but shall not be limited to, direction, supervision, services, know-how, financial assistance (other than contributions to capital), and equipment, material, or supplies." Treas. Reg. § 1.954–4(b)(2)(ii)(b) and (c) then provide separate tests depending on whether the assistance provided by the related person or persons is in the form of (1) direction, supervision, services or know-how, or (2) financial assistance, equipment, material or supplies.

Treas. Reg. § 1.954–4(b)(2)(ii)(b) provides that assistance in the form of direction, supervision, services or know-how may be substantial under either a subjective or an objective test. Under the subjective test, assistance in the form of direction, supervision, services or know-how will be considered substantial if the assistance provides the CFC with skills which are a principal element in producing the income from the performance of such services by such CFC (the principal element test). For example, a CFC enters into a contract with an unrelated person to drill an oil well. The technical and supervisory personnel who oversee the drilling of the well are employees of M, a person related to CFC. In such an instance, the services performed by CFC for the unrelated party are considered foreign base company services because the services performed by M substantially assist CFC in the performance of the contract and the services performed by M are a principal element in producing the income from the performance of the drilling contract. Cf. Treas. Reg. § 1.954–4(b)(3), Ex. 2.

Alternatively, under the objective test, assistance in the form of direction, supervision, services or know-how may be substantial if the cost to the CFC of the assistance furnished by persons related to the CFC equals 50 percent or more of the total cost to the CFC of performing the services performed by such CFC (the cost test). For these purposes, costs are determined after taking into account adjustments (if any) made under section 482. See Treas. Reg. § 1.954–4(b)(2)(ii)(b).

Treas. Reg. § 1.954–4(b)(2)(ii)(c) states, in general, that financial assistance, equipment, material, or supplies furnished by a person related to the CFC shall be considered assistance only in the amount, after taking into account adjustments (if any) made under section 482, by which the consideration actually paid by the CFC to the related person for the purchase or use of such item is less than the arm's length charge for such purchase or use. The total of all such amounts from all related persons is compared with the profits derived by the CFC from the performance of the services to determine whether the related party's contributions qualify as substantial assistance.

Treas. Reg. § 1.954–4(b)(2)(ii)(d) expands on the tests in Treas. Reg. § 1.954–4(b)(2)(ii)(b) and (c) by providing that, even if assistance furnished by a related person or persons to a CFC is not considered substantial under paragraphs (b) or (c) in isolation, it may nevertheless constitute substantial assistance when taken together or in combination with other assistance furnished by a related person or persons to the CFC. Treas. Reg. § 1.954–4(b)(2)(ii)(e) provides that, in applying Treas. Reg. § 1.954–4(b)(2)(ii)(b) and (d), assistance in the form of direction, supervision, services, or know-how shall not be taken into account, unless the assistance so furnished assists the CFC directly in the performance of the services performed. Treas. Reg. § 1.954–4(b)(3) sets forth examples, including examples addressing the application of the substantial assistance test.

B.   DISCUSSION

The substantial assistance rules were published as final regulations in 1968 (TD 6981). The purpose of the substantial assistance rules is to treat as foreign base company services income, income received by a CFC from rendering services to an unrelated person where in rendering those services a related person substantially contributes to the CFC's performance of such services in a manner that suggests that the CFC, rather than the related party, entered into the contract to obtain a lower rate of tax on the service income. Since the regulations were published in 1968, there has been a substantial expansion in the reach of the global economy, particularly in the provision of global services. As a result, many of the U.S. multinationals that provide services outside of the United States currently have globally integrated businesses with support capabilities for unrelated customer projects in different geographic locations, largely based on factors such as expertise and cost efficiencies.

For example, a CFC may contract with an unrelated person to provide installation and subsequent repair services. A related CFC, however, is the foreign corporation that provides the repair services. Although the foreign related CFC that is providing the support services will continue to have foreign base company services income to the extent that it performs those services outside of its country of incorporation, it does not seem appropriate in the current global economy to continue to treat the profits of the CFC contracting to furnish services to the unrelated person as foreign base company services income because of the support services provided by a related foreign person. If the substantial assistance regulations are not amended to deal with these types of businesses structures, the regulations may cause taxpayers to change the way they do business or structure their operations in light of the substantial assistance rules, even if such a structure would be less efficient from a business perspective by, for example, requiring a taxpayer to duplicate a full service infrastructure in each country.

The Treasury Department and the IRS, however, remain concerned about the ability of related United States persons to shift profits offshore to CFCs organized in low tax jurisdictions in cases where the related United States person or persons provides so much assistance to the CFC that the CFC cannot be said to be providing services on its own account and thus acting as an independent entity. Accordingly, the Treasury Department and the IRS will revise the regulations to eliminate the substantial assistance rules, except in certain limited instances in which a United States person or persons provide sufficient assistance directly or indirectly to a related CFC.

C.   PROPOSED GUIDANCE

The Treasury Department and the IRS will amend Treas. Reg. § 1.954–4(b)(1)(iv) and (b)(2)(ii) and the examples thereunder. Treas. Reg. § 1.954–4(b)(1)(iv) as amended will provide that services performed by a CFC in a case where substantial assistance by a related United States person or persons (as the term is defined in section 957(c) of the Code) contributes to the performance of such service will constitute "services which are performed for, or on behalf of, a related person." Treas. Reg. § 1.954–4(b)(2)(ii) as amended will provide that "substantial assistance" consists of assistance furnished (directly or indirectly) by a related United States person or persons to the CFC if the assistance satisfies an objective cost test. The subjective "principal element" test will no longer apply to determine substantial assistance. For purposes of the objective cost test, the definition of the term "assistance" will include, but will not be limited to, direction, supervision, services, know-how, financial assistance (other than contributions to capital), and equipment, material, or supplies provided directly or indirectly by a related United States person to a CFC.

The cost test will be satisfied if the cost to the CFC of the assistance furnished by the related United States person or persons equals or exceeds 80 percent of the total cost to the CFC of performing the services. The term "cost" will be determined after taking into account adjustments, if any, made under section 482 of the Code. Taxpayers may apply the cost test either by demonstrating that the assistance provided, directly or indirectly, by related United States persons is below the 80 percent cost threshold, or, alternatively, by demonstrating that the cost of the services provided by the CFC itself, and/or by a related CFC, is more than 20 percent of the total cost to the CFC of performing the services. For this purpose, services provided by a CFC itself are not assistance provided "indirectly" by a related United States person (or persons). However, employees, officers, or directors of the CFC who are concurrently employees, officers, or directors of a related United States person during a taxable year of the CFC will be considered employees, officers or directors solely of the related United States person for such taxable year for purposes of this Notice.

The examples under Treas. Reg. § 1.954–4(b)(2)(ii) will be amended to reflect the amendments to the regulations. The application of the proposed cost test is illustrated by the following examples.

Example 1: USP, a U.S. corporation, wholly owns CFC1 and CFC2, each a foreign corporation. CFC1 enters into a contract with FP, an unrelated foreign person, to design a bridge for FP in Country Y, a foreign country that is not CFC1's country of organization. CFC1 incurs a total of $100x of costs to design the bridge for FP. USP performs supervisory services in Country Y for CFC1 with respect to the contract for which CFC1 pays USP a fee. CFC1 directly performs services related to the performance of that contract that cost CFC1 $15x. CFC2 performs centralized support services related to the performance of that contract in Country X, its country of organization, for which CFC1 pays CFC2 $10x. CFC1 is not treated as receiving substantial assistance in the performance of that contract because more than 20% of the cost of that contract is attributable to services furnished directly by CFC1 or a related CFC (CFC2).

Example 2: USP, a U.S. corporation, wholly owns CFC1 and CFC2, each a foreign corporation. CFC2 enters into a contract with FP, an unrelated person, to design a bridge in Country Y, a foreign country that is not CFC2's country of organization. With respect to the contract with FP, USP performs services in Country Y for CFC1 in the form of design and technical services for which CFC1 pays USP $85x. CFC1 contracts with CFC2 to provide those services and others to CFC2 for $90x. CFC2 uses those services together with services it performs itself that cost CFC2 $10x to design the bridge for FP. Pursuant to the cost test, USP provides substantial assistance to CFC2 in the performance of its contract for FP because USP indirectly furnishes assistance to CFC2 (through CFC1) that exceed 80 percent of the total cost to CFC2 for performing the contract.

Example 3: USP, a U.S. corporation, wholly owns CFC1 and CFC2, each a foreign corporation. CFC2 enters into a contract with FP, an unrelated person, to design a bridge in Country Y, a foreign country that is not CFC2's country of organization. With respect to the contract with FP, USP performs services in Country Y for CFC1 in the form of design and technical services for which CFC1 pays USP $60x. CFC1 contracts with CFC2 to provide those services and others to CFC2 for $70x. CFC2 uses those services together with services it performs itself that cost CFC2 $30x to design the bridge for FP. CFC2 is not treated as receiving substantial assistance in the performance of that contract because more than 20% of the cost of that contract is attributable to services furnished directly by CFC2 . . ."

(iii) THE BRANCH RULE (AND CONTRACT MANUFACTURING)

The foreign base company sales income rules evolved in a very controversial manner. Taxpayers attempted to avoid the application of Subpart F by commencing the problematic sales through branches rather than subsidiaries. The following two revenue rulings and Tax Court case are some of the landmarks in the continuous battle between the IRS and taxpayers over these rules.

* * *

Internal Revenue Service (I.R.S.)
Revenue Ruling 75–7.
1975–1 C.B. 244.

FOREIGN BASE COMPANY INCOME; ORE PROCESSED BY UNRELATED FOREIGN CORPORATION

Foreign base company income; ore processed by unrelated foreign corporation. A controlled foreign corporation does not realize foreign base company income within the meaning of section 954(a) of the Code from the sale of a ferroalloy derived from ore concentrate purchased from related persons in the U.S. and Canada, converted for a fee by a controlled process in the plant of a foreign corporation in a country with a lower tax rate, and sold to unrelated foreign persons.

Advice has been requested whether a controlled foreign corporation realizes foreign base company income, within the meaning of section 954(a) of the Internal Revenue Code of 1954, under the circumstances described below.

X, a controlled foreign corporation within the meaning of section 957(a) of the Code, was incorporated in country M. X purchased specific metal ore concentrate in the United States and Canada from related persons, within the meaning of section 954(d)(3).

Conversion of the ore concentrate into a ferroalloy was accomplished by X, pursuant to an arm's length contract, through Y, an unrelated foreign corporation incorporated in country O. The conversion of the ore concentrate required intricate chemical and metallurgical processing involving highly skilled labor working in accordance with scientific controls. Y's plant in country O was one of the few plans in the world equipped to accomplish the conversion.

Y had no present, nor was it contemplated that it would have any future affiliation, directly or indirectly, with X, other than contractual obligations arising under arm's length contracts. Y had no present, nor was it contemplated that it would have any future financial participation in the nature of a joint venture or other risk or profit sharing arrangement in the manufacture of the ferroalloy.

Under the terms of the contract X paid Y a conversion fee. The ore concentrate, before and during processing, and the finished product remained the sole property of X at all times. X alone purchased all raw material and other ingredients necessary in the processing operation and bore the risk of loss at all times in connection with the operation. Complete control of the time and quantity of production was vested in X. Complete control of the quality of the product was also vested in X, and Y was at all times required to use such processes as were directed by X. X could, when the occasion warranted it, send engineers or technicians to Y's plant to inspect, correct, or advise with regard to the processing of the ore concentrate into the finished product.

The negotiation and consummation of the sale of the finished product were solely the responsibility of X. Profits or losses resulting from the sale of the finished product were solely X's. Y's only financial interest in the entire transaction was the fee paid by X for the conversion of the ore. The finished product was sold by X to unrelated parties in foreign countries, other than M, for use, consumption, or disposition in such other foreign countries. The effective tax rate in country M was 46 percent while the effective tax rate in country O was 38.5 percent.

Section 954(a) of the Code provides, in general, that the term "foreign base company income" means the sum of the foreign personal holding company income, the foreign base company sales income, and the foreign base company services income, for the taxable year.

Section 954(d)(1) of the Code provides, in part, that the term "foreign base company sales income" means income derived in connection with the purchase of personal property from a related person and its sale to any person, the sale of personal property to any person on behalf of a related person, or the purchase of personal property from any person on behalf of a related person when the property which is purchased is extracted outside the country under the laws of which the controlled foreign corporation is created or organized, and the property is sold for use or disposition outside such foreign country.

Section 1.954–3(a)(4)(i) of the Income Tax Regulations provides, in part, that foreign base company sales income does not include income of a controlled foreign corporation derived in connection with the sale of personal property manufactured, produced, or constructed by such corporation in whole or in part from personal property which it has purchased. A foreign corporation will be considered, for purposes of section 1.954–3(a)(4)(i), to have manufactured, produced, or constructed personal property which it sells, if the property sold is in effect not the property which it purchased. In the case of the manufacture, production, or construction of personal property, the property sold will be considered, for purposes of section 1.954–3(a)(4)(i), as not being the property which is purchased, if the provisions of section 1.954–3(a)(4)(ii) are satisfied.

Section 1.954–3(a)(4)(ii) of the regulations provides, in part, that if purchased personal property is substantially transformed prior to sale, the property sold will be treated as having been manufactured, produced, or constructed by the selling corporation.

Section 1.954–3(b)(1)(ii) of the regulations provides, in relevant part, that if a controlled foreign corporation carries on manufacturing, producing, constructing, growing, or extracting activities by or through a branch or similar establishment located outside the country under the laws of which such corporation is created or organized and the use of the branch or similar establishment for such activities with respect to personal property purchased or sold by or through the remainder of the controlled foreign corporation has substantially the same tax effect as if the branch or similar establishment were a wholly-owned subsidiary corporation of such controlled foreign corporation, the branch or similar establishment and the remainder of the controlled foreign corporation will be treated as separate corporations for purposes of determining foreign base company sales income of such corporation. See section 954(d)(2) of the Code.

The use of the branch or similar establishment will be considered to have substantially the same tax effect as if it were a wholly-owned subsidiary corporation of the controlled foreign corporation if income allocated to the remainder of the controlled foreign corporation is, by statute, treaty obligation, or otherwise, taxed in the year when earned at an effective rate of tax that is less than 90 percent of, and at least 5 percentage points less than, the effective rate of tax that would apply to such income under the laws of the country in which the branch or similar establishment is located.

Under the contractual arrangement between X and Y, the performance by Y of the operations whereby the ore concentrate is processed into a ferroalloy is considered to be a performance by X. Therefore, X will be treated as having "substantially transformed personal property" within the meaning of section 1.954–3(a)(4) of the regulations.

Furthermore, since X is conducting a manufacturing activity outside country M it will be considered to do so through a branch or similar establishment within the meaning of section 1.954–3(b)(1)(ii) of the regulations. However, since the effective rate of tax in country M is higher than the rate of tax in country O, the manufacturing activity of X conducted in country O will not be considered to have substantially the same tax effect as a wholly-owned subsidiary corporation of X within the meaning of section 1.954–3(b)(1)(ii).

Accordingly, the income derived by X upon the sale of the ferroalloy will not constitute "foreign base company income" within the meaning of section 954(a) of the Code.

* * *

NOTE AND QUESTIONS

1. After reading the next case, *Ashland Oil* consider how the IRS would likely re-evaluate its position in Rev. Rule 75–7. Then continue on to read the IRS new position outlined in Rev. Rule 97–48.

Ashland Oil, Inc. v. Commissioner of Internal Revenue

United States Tax Court.
95 T.C. 348 (1990).

■ JUDGES: NIMS, CHIEF JUDGE.

This case is before the Court on petitioners' motion for summary judgment under Rule 121. (Rule references are to the Tax Court Rules of Practice and Procedure. Unless otherwise noted, section references are to the Internal Revenue Code of 1954 as amended and in effect for the years at issue.)

Petitioner Ashland Oil, Inc., a domestic corporation with its principal office in Ashland, Kentucky, is the parent company of petitioner Ashland Technology, Inc., a domestic corporation with its principal office in Atlanta, Georgia. Respondent determined deficiencies in the Federal income taxes of the subsidiary, Ashland Technology, Inc., as follows:

Year	Deficiency
1975	$ 119,127
1976	1,791,463
1977	2,046,775
1978	1,919,083
1979	2,480,797

Respondent determined the identical deficiencies for the parent, Ashland Oil, Inc., as transferee for the primary liability of Ashland Technology, Inc.

During the years at issue, and prior to its 1981 acquisition by Ashland Oil, Inc., the name of Ashland Technology, Inc., was United States Filter Corp. (U.S. Filter). U.S. Filter and its affiliates timely filed consolidated returns with the Internal Revenue Service at New York, New York, for the years at issue.

The statutory provision here involved is section 954(d)(2), which by its terms applies to a controlled foreign corporation (hereinafter sometimes referred to as a CFC) carrying on activities through a "branch or similar establishment." The substantive issues before us are: (1) Whether section 954(d)(2) applies to a contractual manufacturing arrangement between a CFC and another corporation, which corporation is unrelated to the CFC apart from the contractual arrangement; and, if so, (2) whether section 1.954–3(b)(1)(ii), Income Tax Regs., which treats manufacturing branches as within the scope of section 954(d)(2), is invalid.

Background

A part of the record is a stipulation of facts, to be used only in our consideration of petitioners' motion for summary judgment. Unless otherwise noted, the background facts described below relate to the years at issue, 1975 through 1979.

U.S. Filter was a domestic corporation. Drew Chemical Corp. (Drew Chemical) was a wholly owned domestic subsidiary of U.S. Filter. Drew Ameroid International (Drew Ameroid), a wholly owned foreign subsidiary of Drew Chemical, was organized in 1973 under the laws of Liberia, in large part to save income taxes. Drew Ameroid, with its principal office in Athens, Greece, was a "controlled foreign corporation" of Drew Chemical within the meaning of section 957(a), and Drew Chemical was a "United States shareholder" of Drew Ameroid within the meaning of section 951(b).

Drew Chemical was engaged in the manufacture and sale of industrial and marine chemical products. Drew Ameroid purchased and sold marine chemicals and other personal property, and did not itself manufacture any of the products it sold. The products sold by Drew Ameroid were manufactured or produced outside Liberia, and were also sold for use, consumption, and disposition outside Liberia.

Much of the record concerns the business relationship between Drew Ameroid and Societe Des Produits Tensio-Actifs et Derives, Tensia, S.A. (Tensia).

Tensia was organized in 1950 as a corporation under the laws of Belgium, which was also the location of its principal place of business. Tensia manufactured household and industrial detergents, soaps, and other cleaning products, including marine chemicals. No Tensia stock or other interest was owned, directly or indirectly within the meaning of section 958, by U.S. Filter, Drew Chemical, Drew Ameroid, or any of their affiliates. Similarly, neither Tensia nor any of its affiliates owned, directly or indirectly within the meaning of section 958, any stock or other interest in U.S. Filter, Drew Chemical, Drew Ameroid, or any of their affiliates. Tensia was not a related person with respect to Drew Ameroid within the meaning of section 954(d)(3).

Drew Ameroid and Tensia entered into a manufacturing, license, and supply agreement (the agreement) as of September 15, 1973. Although the agreement was generally subject to termination by either contracting party upon 12 months' written notice, it remained effective and unamended throughout the years at issue.

Under the agreement, Drew Ameroid transferred to Tensia proprietary technical information, trade secrets, specifications, know-how, and other information (including designs, drawings, formulas, methods, techniques, and processes), to be used by Tensia in manufacturing, processing, and/or compounding approximately 25 products for Drew Ameroid. Tensia, for its part, agreed to adhere strictly to production and quality control specifications. The selling price for a product sold by Tensia to Drew Ameroid was the cost of the raw materials and packaging to Tensia plus a "conversion fee," which included labor, overhead, financing, and remuneration (profit) to Tensia. Assuming that Tensia satisfactorily performed its contractual obligations under the agreement, Tensia was guaranteed a profit.

Tensia purchased raw materials, for use in meeting its obligations under the agreement, from several sources. Tensia purchased most of these raw materials, however, from vendors suggested by Drew Ameroid or from Drew Ameroid affiliates functioning as sourcing intermediaries. Tensia, rather than Drew Ameroid, owned the raw materials while they were in that state.

The agreement required Tensia to deliver products within 30 days of the receipt of an order from Drew Ameroid. Tensia delivered the products directly to Drew Ameroid or to whomever Drew Ameroid designated, using labeling and packaging instructions provided by Drew Ameroid. As labeled by Tensia, a given product bore trademarks and tradenames of Drew Ameroid, an affiliate of Drew Ameroid, or a customer of Drew Ameroid.

The negotiation and consummation of the finished product resales were solely the responsibility of Drew Ameroid. As with the raw materials, Tensia owned the finished products until purchased by Drew Ameroid or its affiliates.

The agreement provided that during its term, and for 2 years after its termination, Tensia could not manufacture or sell products similar to those covered by the agreement for distribution to the same customers.

At least one employee of Drew Chemical or Drew Ameroid visited Tensia's manufacturing facilities monthly.

Tensia's gross sales under the agreement never exceeded 8 percent of its total gross sales:

Year	Total gross sales	Under agreement
1974	$ 62.7 million	$ 4.8 million
1975	55.9 million	4.3 million

1976	83.4 million	5.1 million
1977	98.2 million	5.3 million
1978	139.5 million	6.4 million
1979	126.4 million	6.6 million

In contrast, at least 80 percent of Drew Ameroid's income was attributable to the resale of products manufactured by Tensia. Drew Ameroid had overall profits as follows:

Year	Profits
1974	$ 3,556,987
1975	2,804,328
1976	2,750,721
1977	3,867,166
1978	4,058,346
1979	5,082,143

In his notices of deficiency, respondent determined that the manufacture of products by Tensia for Drew Ameroid, and the subsequent sales by Drew Ameroid to unrelated third parties, resulted in foreign base company sales income under the "branch or similar establishment" rule of section 954(d)(2).

Discussion

A U.S. shareholder (Drew Chemical in this case) of a controlled foreign corporation (Drew Ameroid) generally must include in gross income a pro rata share of the CFC's Subpart F income for the taxable year. Sec. 951(a)(1). Subpart F income includes, among other things, foreign base company income. Sec. 952(a)(2). Foreign base company income includes, among other things, foreign base company sales income. Sec. 954(a)(2).

As defined in section 954(d)(1), foreign base company sales income arises from the following transactions in personal property: the purchase from a related person and sale to any person, the purchase from any person and sale to a related person, and the purchase from any person or sale to any person on behalf of a related person. A CFC and another corporation are related persons if one controls the other, through direct or indirect voting stock ownership exceeding 50 percent, or if both are controlled by the same person or persons. Sec. 954(d)(3)(B) and (C). The parties agree that Drew Ameroid and Tensia were not related persons within the meaning of section 954(d)(3).

Generally, in order for income to be considered foreign base company sales income, the property purchased must be manufactured or produced outside the country in which the CFC is organized and must also be sold for use outside that country. Sec. 954(d)(1)(A) and (B). Although the CFC here, Drew Ameroid, was organized in Liberia, the subject property was manufactured in Belgium and sold for use outside Liberia.

Because Drew Ameroid and Tensia were not related persons and respondent does not contend that Drew Ameroid's pertinent sales were made to related persons, the general principles of section 954(d) do not attribute foreign base company sales income to Drew Ameroid. Nonetheless, respondent maintains that foreign base company sales income results from the so-called "branch rule" of section 954(d)(2):

(2) Certain branch income.—For purposes of determining foreign base company sales income in situations in which the carrying on of activities by a controlled foreign corporation through a branch or similar establishment outside the country of incorporation of the controlled foreign corporation has substantially the same effect as if such branch or similar establishment were a wholly owned subsidiary corporation deriving such income, under regulations prescribed by the Secretary the income attributable to the carrying on of such activities of such branch or similar establishment shall be treated as income derived by a wholly owned subsidiary of the controlled foreign corporation and shall constitute foreign base company sales income of the controlled foreign corporation.

The specific disputed issue is whether Tensia is a "branch or similar establishment" under section 954(d)(2). Petitioners argue that Tensia is not a branch within the ordinary meaning of the term and that "similar establishment" cannot be justifiably construed to include Tensia. Respondent appears to use three principal arguments, in various overlapping combinations, in asserting that Tensia is indeed a "branch or similar establishment." The factors most emphasized by respondent are congressional intent, the tax rate disparity between Belgium and Liberia, and the business relationship between Drew Ameroid and Tensia.

Respondent's most general contention is that Congress, in enacting the branch rule of section 954(d)(2), intended it to be a broad "loophole closing" provision. The applicable loophole here, according to respondent, is any arrangement that separates the manufacturing and sales functions so as to avoid or limit tax on the sales. Because the statute does not define "branch or similar establishment," respondent's position necessitates a venture into the legislative history to trace the evolution of the branch rule.

Prior to the Revenue Act of 1962, Pub. L. 87–834, 76 Stat. 960, a foreign corporation controlled by U.S. shareholders was ordinarily not subject to U.S. tax on foreign source income. The income became subject to U.S. tax only when it took the form of dividends distributed to the U.S. shareholders. President Kennedy, in 1961, characterized this tax deferral as undesirable and advocated its elimination in developed countries and in situations involving low-tax jurisdictions known as "tax havens." Tax

Message to Congress of April 20, 1961, H. Doc. 140, 87th Cong., 1st Sess., 107 Cong. Rec. 6377 (1961).

The House Ways and Means Committee conceded that its bill did not go as far as the President's recommendations. H. Rept. 1447, 87th Cong., 2d Sess. (1962), *1962–3 C.B. 405, 461.* The House bill included no provision comparable to the branch rule, but targeted purchase and sale transactions between related persons, defined vaguely in terms of ownership or control, as generating foreign base company sales income. H.R. 10650, 87th Cong., 2d Sess. 112–113 (March 16, 1962). As described in the committee report:

The sales income with which your committee is primarily concerned is income of a selling subsidiary (whether acting as a principal or agent) which has been separated from manufacturing activities of a related corporation merely to obtain a lower rate of tax for the sales income. As a result, this provision is restricted to sales of property to a related person or purchases of property from a related person. * * * [H. Rept. 1447, supra, *1962–3 C.B. at 466.*]

The Secretary of the Treasury, Douglas Dillon, submitted a statutory draft, relating in part to foreign base company sales income, during hearings before the Senate Finance Committee. Hearings on H.R. 10650 Before the Senate Comm. on Finance (Part 11), 87th Cong., 2d Sess. 1 (1962). This draft, which included a proposed section 954(d), reworded the House bill's "ownership or control" related-person standard to a "control" standard defined in terms of stock ownership, and listed individuals, partnerships, trusts, estates, and corporations as persons qualified to be related persons with respect to a CFC. The proposed section 954(d) also included a version of the branch rule, which, like the rest of the proposed section 954(d), does not vary significantly from section 954(d) as eventually enacted. Secretary Dillon described the controlled foreign corporation portion of the draft as consistent with "the more limited tax-haven approach" of the House bill. Hearings on H.R. 10650, supra at III. Secretary Dillon's explanation accompanying the statutory draft mentions the phrase "branch or similar establishment," which appears in the draft, but does not emphasize or define it. Hearings on H.R. 10650, supra at 1–4.

The Senate Finance Committee included the branch rule in its bill, in the form that was later enacted, and retained Secretary Dillon's related-person standard. H.R. 10650, 87th Cong., 2d Sess. 191–192 (Aug. 16, 1962). In comparing its amendments to the House provisions, the committee reported that "In the area of * * * income from sales subsidiary operations, your committee's provision is much the same as the House bill." S. Rept. 1881, 87th Cong., 2d Sess. (1962), *1962–3 C.B. 707, 785.* Although there is a discussion highlighting the "more significant changes" and amendments that "differ considerably" from House provisions, there is no mention of the branch rule in this discussion. S. Rept. 1881, supra, *1962–3 C.B. at 785–786.* The branch rule is instead described later, without any apparent emphasis, in a "general explanation" section:

> Also included in foreign base company sales income are operations handled through a branch (rather than a corporate subsidiary) operating outside of the country in which the controlled foreign corporation is incorporated, if the combined effect of the tax treatment accorded the branch, by the country of incorporation of the controlled foreign corporation and the country of operation of the branch, is to treat the branch substantially the same as if it were a subsidiary corporation organized in the country in which it carries on its trade or business. [S. Rept. 1881, supra, *1962–3 C.B. at 790.*]

The House-Senate Conference Committee report discusses the branch rule only briefly:

> The Senate amendment provides that foreign branches of a controlled foreign corporation shall, under certain circumstances, be treated as wholly owned subsidiary corporations for purposes of determining the foreign base company sales income of the controlled foreign corporation * * *. [H. Rept. 2508 (Conf.), 87th Cong., 2d Sess. (1962), *1962–3 C.B. 1129, 1159.*]

See also Staff of the Comm. on Ways and Means, Comparative Analysis of Differences in House and Senate Versions of H.R. 10650 "The Revenue Act of 1962" 22–23 (Sept. 14, 1962) (describing foreign base company sales income provisions as generally the same, "except * * * [the Senate version] would also apply to branches").

In the absence of a specified technical definition, a statutory term should be given its normal and customary meaning. *Ludwig v. Commissioner, 68 T.C. 979, 984 (1977); First Savings & Loan Association v. Commissioner, 40 T.C. 474, 482 (1963).* Our review of the legislative history, highlighted above, leads us to conclude that Congress did not intend the word "branch" in section 954(d)(2) to take on a meaning other than its ordinary meaning in a business and accounting sense.

Resort to dictionaries is an acceptable means of discerning ordinary usage. *South Jersey Sand Co. v. Commissioner, 30 T.C. 360, 368 (1958),* affd. *267 F.2d 591 (3d Cir. 1959).* Petitioners suggest, as a foundation, a definition from Black's Law Dictionary, 170 (5th ed. 1979): "Division, office, or other unit of business located at a different location from main office or headquarters." A specialized business dictionary cited by petitioners similarly stresses an "office" in a different location than the "parent company."

Respondent rejects petitioners' proposed definition as too narrow, yet offers no alternative that purports to represent normal and customary usage. We find nothing in the legislative history that is inconsistent with petitioners' definition. We recognize, however, that petitioners' proposal, without clarification of the nature of divisions and units, seems to shift the definitional problem rather than resolve it.

Nonetheless, respondent admits that petitioners' definition does not cover Tensia. Regardless of the precise ordinary meaning of "branch," we are confident that such meaning does not encompass Tensia, an unrelated corporation operating under an arm's-length contractual arrangement with Drew Ameroid.

Respondent maintains that the "or similar establishment" language of section 954(d)(2) should be broadly construed to cover Tensia. We read "similar establishment," however, to mean an establishment that bears the typical characteristics of an ordinary-usage branch, yet goes by another name for accounting, financial reporting, local law, or other purposes. Respondent's expansive reading of the term, to include Tensia, is not supported by the legislative history. The Senate Finance Committee and the House-Senate Conference Committee do not even mention the term "similar establishment" in generally describing the branch rule in their respective reports. S. Rept. 1881, supra, *1962–3 C.B. at 790;* H. Rept. 2508 (Conf.), supra, *1962–3 C.B. at 1159.*

Respondent's position on congressional intent would be more persuasive if Congress had granted specific regulatory authority to the Secretary of the Treasury to define "branch or similar establishment." Section 954(d)(2) does grant specific regulatory authority, but, as is apparent from the sentence structure of that section, the authority becomes operative only if a branch or similar establishment is a given. In other words, the Secretary has a specific grant of authority to address certain consequences flowing from the existence of a branch or similar establishment, but does not have such authority to determine what a branch or similar establishment is. The legislative history confirms our reading of the statute:

Paragraph (2) of section 954(d) provides that in situations in which the carrying on of activities by a controlled foreign corporation through a branch or similar establishment * * * has substantially the same effect as if such branch or similar establishment were a wholly owned subsidiary corporation deriving such income, then, under regulations prescribed by the Secretary of the Treasury or his delegate, the income attributable to the carrying on of such activities of such branch or similar establishment shall be treated as income derived by a wholly owned subsidiary * * *. * * * [S. Rept. 1881, supra, *1962–3 C.B. at 950.*]

In sum, we reject respondent's contention that Congress intended the branch rule to apply to "any arrangement" with a specified tax effect.

Respondent's second principal argument also relates to demonstrable tax avoidance, but primarily in the joint context of the statute and regulations. As already noted, the statute and legislative history do not define "branch or similar establishment." The regulations also do not directly define the phrase. Sec. 1.954–3(b)(1), (2), and (3), Income Tax Regs. The illustrations in section 1.954–3(b)(4), Income Tax Regs., invariably assume away the definitional issue by presupposing the existence of branches denoted as "branch B" and "branch C."

Respondent argues, however, that the statute and regulations indirectly define "branch or similar establishment" in that they invoke principles of tax rate disparity between the foreign countries involved. See Fimberg, "The Foreign Base Company Engaged in Selling Activities: A Reappraisal of the Conduct of Foreign Business," 17 Major Tax Plan. 237, 261–262 (1965) (describing branch rule as "self-defining" with reference to tax savings and the regulations); Olsen, "Working With the Branch Rule of Section 954(d)(2)," 27 Tax Law. 105, 107 n. 9 (1973) (branch is "self-defined by the presence of the proscribed tax avoidance"). Petitioners do not challenge respondent's assertion that Belgium had an effective tax rate substantially exceeding that of Liberia during the years at issue.

Respondent's argument draws upon the statutory requirement that the branch have "substantially the same effect as if such branch * * * were a wholly owned subsidiary corporation deriving such income." Sec. 954(d)(2). Because the regulations seemingly implement this provision through a tax rate disparity test, such a disparity between manufacturing and sales locations arguably serves to define a branch or similar establishment.

We find respondent's emphasis on tax rate disparities misplaced for several reasons. Most notably, again with reference to the wording of the statute, the provision respondent draws from the statute merely describes restrictively which branches and similar establishments are subject to the operative provisions of section 954(d)(2). Section 954(d)(2) says, in effect: "Begin with the entire class of the CFC's branches and similar establishments located in other countries. From this group, select those that have 'substantially the same effect' and apply the provisions hereafter." If an establishment is not in the nature of a branch in the first instance, it cannot become so through the application of a restrictive modifying provision.

Furthermore, the legislative history, rather than focusing on tax rate disparities, presents the "substantially the same effect" statutory provision as relating to a different and more straightforward concept: similar foreign tax treatment of branches and corporate subsidiaries. Branch operations are included in foreign base company sales income if—

the combined effect of the tax treatment accorded the branch, by the country of incorporation of the controlled foreign corporation and the country of operation of the branch, is to treat the branch substantially the same as if it were a subsidiary corporation organized in the country in which it carries on its trade or business. [S. Rept. 1881, supra, *1962–3 C.B. at 790.*]

See Staff of the Comm. on Ways and Means, Comparative Analysis of Differences in House and Senate Versions of H.R. 10650 "The Revenue Act of 1962" 22–23 (Sept. 14, 1962) (Senate bill applies to branches "if such branches are, for tax purposes, treated as subsidiaries under foreign law"); Staff of the Comm. on Ways and Means, "The Revenue Act of 1962"

Comparative Analysis of Prior Law and Provisions of Public Law 87–834 (H.R. 10650) 11 (Oct. 19, 1962) (for purposes of foreign base company sales income, "a branch may be treated as a subsidiary if so treated under foreign law"); Fimberg, supra at 260–261; Olsen, supra at 106 n. 7.

Also contrary to the notion that tax rate disparities define branches is *Rev. Rul. 75–7, 1975–1 C.B. 244.* This revenue ruling, cited by respondent, considers an unrelated ore-processing corporation working under an arm's-length contract with the CFC to be a branch or similar establishment under section 954(d)(2).

Revenue rulings represent only the Commissioner's position concerning specific factual situations, rather than substantive authority for deciding a case in this Court. *Stark v. Commissioner, 86 T.C. 243, 250–251 (1986).* Regardless, *Rev. Rul. 75–7* does not support respondent's position on the significance of tax rate disparities to the branch definition issue. *Rev. Rul. 75–7* determines the ore-processing corporation to be a branch or similar establishment despite a tax rate disparity that is backward (in that the manufacturing rate is lower than the sales rate) relative to the perceived abusive situation addressed in the regulations. See sec. 1.954–3(b)(1)(ii)(b), Income Tax Regs.

Respondent's third recurring theme is that the nature of the business relationship between Drew Ameroid and Tensia makes the latter a branch or similar establishment. Respondent likens Tensia to an agent of Drew Ameroid, based on factors that include Drew Ameroid's control over Tensia's manufacturing operations under the agreement, the allocation of risk between the two, and the anticipated lengthy term of the relationship.

We have already indirectly considered this issue in our analysis of respondent's broad "loophole closing" argument. In that context, we determined that Congress intended the term "branch" to have its customary business meaning and the term "similar establishment" to serve a fine-tuning purpose rather than an expansionary one. A separately incorporated manufacturing entity operating pursuant to an arm's-length agreement, with the CFC having no direct or indirect stock interest in that entity (and vice versa), does not fall within any customary meaning of "branch" of which we are aware. In these circumstances, the degree of control exercised by Drew Ameroid over a part of Tensia's manufacturing operations, any disproportionate risk borne by Drew Ameroid relative to Tensia, and the anticipated length of the relationship are irrelevant considerations.

This conclusion does not seem to us to be unjustifiably permissive to taxpayers, primarily because neither Drew Ameroid nor its U.S. shareholder, Drew Chemical, had a claim to any of Tensia's manufacturing income derived under the arm's-length agreement or otherwise.

The significance of Tensia's manufacturing income is apparent when viewed in the context of the tax policy considerations that underlie the Subpart F provisions. The two undesirable concepts emphasized throughout the legislative history are tax deferral and tax havens. Tax deferral refers to a foreign corporation's retention of foreign source earnings, resulting in the deferral of U.S. tax until the foreign corporation distributes dividends to its U.S. shareholders. Tax havens are favorable, low-tax jurisdictions.

A typical situation targeted by section 954(d)(1) is a sales subsidiary in a relatively low-tax jurisdiction, all of the voting stock of which is owned by a manufacturing CFC in a relatively high-tax jurisdiction. In a greatly simplified sense, the U.S. shareholders of this CFC realize income roughly equal to the subsidiary's ultimate sales revenue less the CFC's cost to manufacture the property. Some form of intercorporate pricing, however, splits the income in two, and the sales end is taxed at a lower rate than the manufacturing end. The statute deems this situation unacceptable, presumably because of the tax deferral and tax haven implications, and attributes foreign base company sales income to the CFC, which becomes gross income to the U.S. shareholders.

Tensia's Belgian manufacturing activity for Drew Ameroid bears neither the tax haven nor the tax deferral stigma. Belgium is not the purported tax haven here, Liberia is. Indeed, it is this relative tax rate disparity that provides respondent with the foothold from which to invoke the operative regulations applicable to manufacturing branches. See sec. 1.954–3(b)(1)(ii), Income Tax Regs. Tensia's activities also did not directly give rise to tax deferral, at least as contemplated and described by the President and Congress. Drew Ameroid had no claim to Tensia's manufacturing income and thus had no corresponding distributable amount that it was retaining in lieu of distributing dividends to Drew Chemical in the United States.

These tax policy considerations, we believe, explain why Tensia can be classified differently than a subsidiary or an unincorporated establishment of Drew Ameroid, even though Drew Ameroid had a large measure of control here over the manufacture of the products it sold.

One possible response to this tax policy analysis is that Drew Ameroid's sales operation had both tax deferral and tax haven implications, and Drew Ameroid's activities alone should be enough to support implementation of the branch rule. This position, however, is not consistent with the limits respondent places on the branch rule in his opposition brief:

It must be emphasized that respondent has not applied the manufacturing branch rule to an ordinary purchase of finished goods from a third-party supplier. Respondent agrees that the purchase from an unrelated supplier and resale of goods in the ordinary course by a CFC does not result in foreign base company sales income. * * *

We take this to mean that respondent would not apply the branch rule to a CFC's spontaneous (rather than contracted for) purchase of fungible (rather than custom-made) finished goods. In both respondent's conceded example and the situation before us in this case, there are no substantial tax deferral or tax haven implications attributable to the finished goods supplier. In our view, the applicability of the branch rule should be the same in both situations.

Respondent, in his opposition brief, never concedes that the contractual arrangement here was at arm's length. He also, however, does not expressly question that characterization, which petitioners clearly asserted in their motion. Indeed, respondent argues that "Tensia's receipt of compensation for its manufacturing services is wholly irrelevant to the characterization of the CFC's sales income as foreign base company sales income." There is no factual issue, in a motion for summary judgment, if the nonmoving party fails to point to specific contrary facts. Rule 121(d). Respondent has directed us to no facts that would sufficiently taint the apparent arm's-length nature of this relationship so as to affect our conclusion.

We earlier considered *Rev. Rul. 75–7, 1975–1 C.B. 244,* and briefly discussed how it conflicts with the proposition that tax rate disparities define branches. From a broader perspective, however, the revenue ruling is favorable to respondent because it determines that the arm's-length contract manufacturer therein is a branch or similar establishment. As already noted, revenue rulings are not controlling substantive authority in this Court. Respondent thus takes an indirect route, urging us to invoke the legislative reenactment doctrine.

Respondent's reenactment argument, simply stated, is that because Congress has amended and reenacted Subpart F without rejecting *Rev. Rul. 75–7,* it must approve of that approach. Respondent has not, however, shown that Congress has been even aware of this administrative interpretation, which has not been litigated in a reported decision and has been cited in only a smattering of private letter rulings. Without affirmative indications of congressional awareness and consideration, we decline to cloak this revenue ruling with the aura of legislative approval. See *Commissioner v. Glenshaw Glass Co., 348 U.S. 426, 431 (1955); Interstate Drop Forge Co. v. Commissioner, 326 F.2d 743, 746 (7th Cir.1964),* affg. a Memorandum Opinion of this Court; *Sims v. United States, 252 F.2d 434, 438–439 (4th Cir.1958),* affd. *359 U.S. 108 (1959).*

We find that there is no genuine issue as to any material fact in this case. Rule 121(b). Although, for convenience and clarity, we have considered respondent's intertwined principal arguments separately, there is no favorable synergetic effect from combining them.

We hold that Tensia is not a "branch or similar establishment" of Drew Ameroid within the meaning of section 954(d)(2). In light of this holding, we need not consider petitioners' alternative position that the regulations relating to manufacturing branches are invalid. Petitioners' motion for summary judgment will be granted.

An appropriate order will be issued and decision will be entered under Rule 155.

* * *

Change in Position: Below is the Revenue Ruling previously mentioned, in which the IRS re-evaluated its treatment of contract manufacturing. In Rev. Rul. 97–48, 1997–2 C.B. 89, the Service announced that it would follow the *Ashland Oil* decision and revoked Rev. Rul. 75–7. Do you think this was a wise decision?[5] What are the consequences for Subpart F?

* * *

Internal Revenue Service (I.R.S.)

Revenue Ruling 97–48.
1997–2 C.B. 89.

. . .

This ruling revokes Rev. Rul. 75–7, 1975–1 C.B. 244, and holds that the activities of a contract manufacturer cannot be attributed to a controlled foreign corporation for purposes of either section 954(d)(1) or section 954(d)(2) of the Code to determine whether the income of a controlled foreign corporation is foreign base company sales income. The ruling, however, provides 7805(b) relief for taxable years of a controlled foreign corporation beginning before December 8, 1997.

In Rev. Rul. 75–7, 1975–1 C.B. 244, a controlled foreign corporation entered into an arm's length contract with an unrelated contract manufacturer located outside of its country of incorporation. Under the contract, the unrelated contract manufacturer agreed to perform manufacturing services for the controlled foreign corporation. Under the facts described in Rev. Rul. 75–7, the processing activities of the unrelated contract manufacturer were considered to be performed by the controlled foreign corporation outside its country of incorporation through a branch or similar establishment for purposes of section 954(d)(1) and (2) of the Internal Revenue Code.

In Ashland Oil Co. v. Commissioner, 95 T.C. 348 (1990), the Tax Court held that a manufacturing corporation unrelated to a controlled foreign corporation cannot be a branch or similar establishment of the controlled foreign corporation. See also, *Vetco, Inc. v. Commissioner*, 95 T.C. 579 (1990) (wholly-owned subsidiary of a controlled foreign corporation cannot be a branch or similar establishment of the controlled foreign corporation).

---

[5] Note that in the same year the "check-the-box" regulations were promulgated, and some commentators raised concerns about the abuse potential of the combination of these regulations, extended to cross-border situations, and the concession in the revenue ruling.

The Service will follow the Ashland and Vetco opinions. The activities of a contract manufacturer cannot be attributed to a controlled foreign corporation for purposes of either section 954(d)(1) or section 954(d)(2) of the Code to determine whether the income of a controlled foreign corporation is foreign base company sales income. Accordingly, Rev. Rul. 75–7 is revoked.

Pursuant to the authority of section 7805(b), for taxable years of a controlled foreign corporation beginning before December 8, 1997, the principles of Rev. Rul. 75–7 may be relied upon to attribute the activities of a contract manufacturer in the controlled foreign corporation. A taxpayer that relies on Rev. Rul. 75–7 to attribute the activities of a contract manufacturer to a controlled foreign corporation for purposes of section 954(d)(1), however, must treat the contract manufacturing activities as being performed through a branch or similar establishment of the controlled foreign corporation for purposes of section 954(d)(2). The Service has never been of the view that Rev. Rul. 75–7 allows the activities of a contract manufacturer performed outside the controlled foreign corporation's country of incorporation to be attributed to the controlled foreign corporation without treating those activities as performed through a branch or similar establishment of the controlled foreign corporation.

With the revocation of Rev. Rul. 75–7, the Service's position on the treatment of contract manufacturing for purposes section 954(d) is harmonized with its position on the treatment of contract manufacturing for purposes of section 863(b) (see § 1.863–3(c) of the Income Tax Regulations (production activity limited to activity conducted directly by taxpayer)).

. . .

NOTES AND QUESTIONS

1. What is the "catch" in the Service's position, as revised by Rev. Rul. 97–48? What effect do you think it has on tax planning? Is this revenue ruling in line with the *Ashland Oil* decision?

2. Is the outcome desirable? Think about the increasing importance of contract manufacturing and intellectual property today.

3. In late 2008 and early 2009, the Treasury Department promulgated regulations providing guidance on the treatment of contract manufacturers and manufacturing branches. In general, the regulations require that a CFC make a "substantial contribution" to the manufacturing process in order to qualify for the so-called "manufacturing exception" (Treas. Reg. § 1.954–3(a)(4)).

(iv) THE HYBRID PROBLEM

Notice 98–11

Treatment of Hybrid Arrangements under Subpart F

1998 IRB LEXIS 38; 1998–6 I.R.B. 18; Notice 98–11

February 9, 1998

The Treasury Department and the Internal Revenue Service understand that certain taxpayers are using arrangements involving "hybrid branches" to circumvent the purposes of Subpart F (sections 951–964 of the Internal Revenue Code). These arrangements generally involve the use of deductible payments to reduce the taxable income of a controlled foreign corporation (CFC) under foreign law, thereby reducing the CFC's foreign tax and, also under foreign law, the corresponding creation in another entity of low-taxed, passive income of the type to which Subpart F was intended to apply. Because of the structure of these arrangements, however, this income is not taxed under Subpart F.

The recent entity classification regulations, §§ 301.7701–1 through –3 of the Income Tax Regulations (the "check-the-box" regulations), have facilitated the creation of the hybrid branches used in these arrangements. The preamble to these regulations, in stating that Treasury and the Service would be monitoring the use of partnerships in the international context, indicated a concern that fiscally-transparent entities could be used in a manner inconsistent with the policies and rules of particular Code provisions.

Treasury and the Service have concluded that the use of certain hybrid branch arrangements, such as the ones illustrated below, is contrary to the policies and rules of Subpart F. This notice announces that Treasury and the Service will issue regulations to address such arrangements, and requests public comments with respect to these Subpart F issues.

I. BACKGROUND

Subpart F was enacted by Congress to limit the deferral of U.S. taxation of certain income earned outside the United States by CFCs, which are foreign corporations controlled by United States shareholders. Limited deferral was retained after the enactment of Subpart F to protect the competitiveness of CFCs doing business overseas. This limited deferral allows a CFC engaged in an active business, and located in a foreign country for appropriate economic reasons, to compete in a similar tax environment with non-U.S. owned corporations located in the same country.

Under Subpart F, however, transactions of CFCs that involve related persons frequently give rise to Subpart F income, unless an exception, for example the same country exception, applies. Related person transactions can be more easily manipulated to reduce both United States and foreign taxes. One of the purposes of Subpart F is to prevent CFCs (including those engaged in active businesses) from structuring transactions designed to manipulate the inconsistencies between foreign tax systems to inappropriately generate low-or non-taxed income on which United States tax might be permanently deferred.

U.S. international tax policy seeks to balance the objective of neutrality of taxation as between domestic and foreign business enterprises (seeking neither to encourage nor to discourage one over the other), with the need to keep U.S. business competitive. Subpart F strongly reflects and enforces that balance. These hybrid transactions upset that balance.

II.   ARRANGEMENTS INVOLVING HYBRID BRANCHES

A hybrid branch is one that is viewed under United States tax principles to be part of the CFC (i.e., fiscally transparent), but under the law of the CFC's country of incorporation as an entity separate from the CFC (i.e., non-fiscally transparent). The types of hybrid branch arrangements Treasury and the Service have identified as being inconsistent with the policies and rules of Subpart F may be illustrated by the following examples.

Example 1. CFC1 owns all of the stock of CFC2. CFC1 and CFC2 are both incorporated in Country A. CFC1 also has a branch (BR1) in Country B. The tax laws of Country A and Country B classify CFC1, CFC2 and BR1 as separate, non-fiscally transparent entities. CFC2 earns only non-Subpart F income and uses a substantial part of its assets in a trade or business in Country A. BR1 makes a transfer to CFC2 that the tax laws of both Country A and Country B recognize as a loan from BR1 to CFC2. CFC2 pays interest to BR1. Country A allows CFC2 to deduct the interest from taxable income. Little or no tax is paid by BR1 to Country B on the receipt of interest.

If BR1 is disregarded, then for U.S. tax purposes the loan would be regarded as being made by CFC1 to CFC2 and the interest as being paid by CFC2 to CFC1. While interest received by a CFC is normally Subpart F income under section 954(c) (foreign personal holding company income), in this case, if BR1 is disregarded, the "same country" exception of section 954(c)(3) would apply to exclude the interest from Subpart F income. If BR1 instead were considered to be a CFC, however, this payment would be between two CFCs located in different countries. In that case, Subpart F income would arise because the same-country exception would not apply. Thus, if BR1 is disregarded CFC1 will have lowered its foreign tax on deferred income and created a significant tax incentive to invest abroad rather than in the United States. As this arrangement creates income intended to be Subpart F income which is not subject to Subpart F in this case, the result of the arrangement is inconsistent with the policies and rules of Subpart F.

Example 2. CFC3 is incorporated in Country A. CFC3 has a branch (BR2) in Country B. The tax laws of Country A and Country B classify

CFC3 and BR2 as separate, non-fiscally transparent entities. BR2 makes a transfer to CFC3 that the tax laws of both Country A and Country B recognize as a loan from BR2 to CFC3. CFC3, which earns only non-Subpart F income, pays interest to BR2 that Country A allows as a deduction against taxable income. Little or no tax is paid by BR2 on the receipt of interest.

If BR2 is disregarded, then U.S. tax law would not recognize the income flows (neither the loan nor the interest payment) between the CFC and its branch and, therefore, Subpart F would not apply. If this transaction were between two CFCs, however, the interest would be Subpart F income under section 954(c) and no exception would apply. Thus, if BR2 is disregarded, by use of this arrangement the CFC will have lowered its foreign tax on deferred income in a manner inconsistent with the policies and rules of Subpart F.

Treasury and the Service believe that it is appropriate to prevent taxpayers from using these types of hybrid branch arrangements to reduce foreign tax while avoiding the corresponding creation of Subpart F income. Treasury and the Service will issue regulations to prevent the use of these types of hybrid branch arrangements. Regulations will provide that, when such arrangements are undertaken, the branch and the CFC will be treated as separate corporations for purposes of Subpart F.

III. PARTNERSHIPS AND TRUSTS

Treasury and the Service are aware that the issues under Subpart F raised by hybrid branch arrangements may also be raised by certain partnership or trust arrangements. Treasury and Service intend to address these issues in separate ongoing regulations projects addressing partnerships and trusts.

IV. EFFECTIVE DATE

The regulations on hybrid branch arrangements will apply to all such arrangements entered into (or substantially modified, including, for example, by acceleration of payments or increases in principal) on or after January 16, 1998, the date on which this Notice was issued to the public. In addition, for all hybrid branch arrangements entered into before January 16, 1998, these regulations will apply to all payments (or other transfers) made or accrued after June 30, 1998.

NOTES AND QUESTIONS

1.   Notice 98–11 gave rise to a welter of criticism from U.S. multinationals and from Congress. Can you articulate some of the reasons? (Hint: Whose tax was being avoided?). As a result, Treasury in Notice 98–35 withdrew Notice 98–11 and announced its intention to study all of Subpart F. As for hybrids, Treasury announced that it would not promulgate regulations with an effective date before 2005.

This is an example of the international problems resulting from "check the box." Do you think that rule (reviewed in Ch. 1) should be reconsidered?

2. What about the following situation: a U.S. multinational has a subsidiary earning active income in a jurisdiction that grants a tax holiday to such investments. Do you think Subpart F should apply?

3. The general issue of hybrid entities (and relatedly hybrid instruments) continues to be a matter of significant concern in designing tax rules and tax policy. Action Item 2 of the OECD BEPS project seeks to tackle the issue of hybrids. *See* OECD, *Neutralising the Effects of Hybrid Mismatch Arrangements, Action 2—2015 Final Report.*

7.4   THE OPERATION OF SUBPART F AND OTHER PROVISIONS THAT MAY AFFECT CFCS

a.   SUBPART F INCLUSIONS

Read Section 951(a) and Treas. Reg. § 1.951–1(a)–(b). Note the explicit avoidance of a deemed dividend treatment of Subpart F income. True to its nature as an anti-deferral (not anti-abuse) regime, the provisions of Subpart F do not attempt to penalize taxpayers with such inclusions. Historically, Section 960 allowed a foreign tax credit (by application of Section 902) with respect to such inclusions in the same manner that an actual (rather than deemed) dividend would get. Section 959 completed these "equalization" rules by elimination of future taxation of actual dividends attributable to earnings and profits previously taxed under Subpart F. Section 960 continues to play this role for Subpart F inclusion of a U.S. corporate shareholder even though Section 902 was eliminated as part of the December 2017 tax reform. [Section 902 was removed, as discussed below in 7.5, and further in Chapter 8, because the tax reform introduced a new 100% dividends received deduction, i.e. a participation exemption, for U.S. corporations which are 10% shareholders in a foreign corporation. Thus, these taxpayers no longer need Section 902 to ensure that any dividends reported do not result in unintended additional layers of corporate income taxation.]

b.   COORDINATION WITH PFIC

The elimination of the multiple anti-deferral regimes significantly ameliorated the need to coordinate and provide ordering rules for the application of such regimes. Read Section 951(d). Can a foreign corporation still be both a CFC and a PFIC? Why is it desirable to eliminate application of multiple anti-deferral regimes? Why do you think was this provision drafted this way rather than set a clear definitional boundary between these two regimes?

c. COMPLEMENTARY BACKSTOPS TO DEFERRAL: SECTIONS
    956 & 1248

(i) SECTION 956

Read Section 956. Then read the following case, which focuses on the
use of pledges and guarantees to circumvent Subpart F and the general
rule of 956 Ssection 956(c) mentioned is todaySsection 956(d)]. It is a good
example of the necessity of such a rule, the complexity of the transactions
involved and the difficulty of making determinations under Section 956.

* * *

Daniel K. Ludwig and Gertrude V. Ludwig v. Commissioner

United States Tax Court.
68 T.C. 979 (1977).

. . .

■ FEATHERSTON, JUDGE:

Respondent determined a deficiency in petitioners' Federal income
tax for 1963 in the amount of $4,438,086.75. After various concessions by
the parties, the sole issue remaining for decision is whether a controlled
foreign corporation wholly owned by petitioner Daniel K. Ludwig was a
guarantor, within the meaning of section 956(c) of petitioner's obligations
to a group of lending banks, with the result that income was realized by
petitioner under section 951.

FINDINGS OF FACT

Petitioners Daniel K. Ludwig (hereinafter petitioner) and Gertrude
V. Ludwig, husband and wife, are citizens of the United States, residing
in New York, N.Y. They filed a joint Federal income tax return for 1963
with the Internal Revenue Service, New York, N.Y. Gertrude V. Ludwig
is a party hereto solely by reason of having filed a joint return.

In June 1963, petitioner entered into an agreement with Phillips
Petroleum Co. (hereinafter Phillips), providing for the purchase by
petitioner from Phillips of 1,340,517 shares of stock of Union Oil Co.
(hereinafter Union Oil). These shares represented Phillips' entire holding
in Union Oil, and amounted to approximately 15 percent of Union Oil's
total outstanding stock. The purchase price was $75 per share, or a total
of $100,538,775.

Pursuant to the purchase agreement, the parties were required to
obtain, and they eventually did obtain, (a) the consent of the Antitrust
Division of the U.S. Department of Justice of the sale by Phillips of its
Union Oil stock to petitioner and (b) the consent to the sale by Phillips of
its Union Oil stock to petitioner, pursuant to a preliminary injunction of
January 1961, of the United States District Court for the Southern

District of California in the matter of *United States v. Phillips Petroleum Co.*

In order to pay for the 1,340,517 shares of Union Oil, petitioner arranged to borrow the entire amount of the purchase price from three banks—Chase Manhattan Bank (Chase Manhattan), Chemical Bank New York Trust Co. (Chemical Bank), and Bank of America National Trust & Savings Association (Bank of America). Chase Manhattan served as agent for the lending banks in negotiating the loan agreement with petitioner. All negotiations as to the terms and conditions of the loan agreement (other than those concerning the amount of participation of each of the lending banks) were conducted by Chase Manhattan as agent for the lending banks.

Part of the negotiation of the agreement involved the collateral to be used to secure the loan. Under Regulation U, Federal Reserve Board, 12 C.F.R., Part 221 (1963) (hereinafter Regulation U), a loan of this type (for the purchase of a security listed on a national securities exchange) was required to be secured by collateral having a value of at least twice the amount of the loan. Petitioner offered and the banks accepted as collateral the 1,340,517 shares of Union Oil stock to be acquired by petitioner with the loan proceeds, plus 1,000 shares of Oceanic Tankships, S.A. (Oceanic).

Oceanic was a Panamanian corporation which, during 1963, had 1,000 shares of stock outstanding, all of which were owned by petitioner. During the taxable year 1963, Oceanic's assets consisted primarily of all of the outstanding stock of Universe Tankships, Inc. (Universe), a Liberian corporation engaged principally in the business of owning and operating oceangoing vessels. As of December 31, 1963, Oceanic had accumulated earnings and profits of $5,092,318. At the time Chase Manhattan agreed to accept the stock of Oceanic as collateral for petitioner's loan, it determined that such stock had a value at least equal to its book value of approximately $200 million. Thus, the total collateral for the loan (the Union Oil stock plus the Oceanic stock) was valued by the lending banks at approximately $300 million.

In order to protect the value of the Oceanic stock held as collateral, the banks required of petitioner certain negative covenants restricting his absolute control over the assets and liabilities of Oceanic and Universe during the term of the loan. These restrictions were set forth in the loan agreement and included, in part, the borrower's covenants not to cause Oceanic or Universe to do any of the following without the consent of the lenders:

(1) Borrow money, except in connection with shipping operations;

(2) Pledge assets as collateral, except as to borrowings in connection with shipping operations;

(3)   Guarantee, assume, or become liable on the obligation of another, or invest in or lend funds to another, except to the extent of $40 million total;

(4)   Merge or consolidate with any other corporation;

(5)   Sell or lease (other than in the ordinary course of business) or otherwise dispose of any substantial part of its assets;

(6)   Transfer any shares of any controlled subsidiary;

(7)   Pay or secure any amount owing by Oceanic or Universe to petitioner;

(8)   Pay any dividends, except in such amounts as may be required to make interest or principal payments on petitioner's loan from the lending banks.

The principal purpose of these negative covenants was to protect the lenders against possible actions by petitioner, as the controlling stockholder of Oceanic and (through Oceanic) Universe, which could diminish the value of the Oceanic stock held as collateral. This kind of protection was critical in satisfaction of Regulation U requirements concerning the value of collateral. With the protection of the negative covenants the lending banks could look to the value of the Oceanic stock as their source of recovery in the event of default in repayment by petitioner. In the event of such default the banks expected to be able to sell the pledged Union Oil and/or Oceanic stock to satisfy their claims.

In July 1963, the loan agreement was concluded and petitioner issued personal promissory notes to the lending banks as follows:

Chase Manhattan	$50,269,387.50
Chemical Bank..	40,000,000.00
Bank of America...	10,269,387.50
Total...	100,538,775.00

In that same month, petitioner completed his purchase of the Union Oil stock.

During 1963 through 1965, the board of directors of Oceanic held meetings and kept minutes of these meetings. Such minutes do not reflect any discussion of or reference to petitioner's purchase of Union Oil stock or the loan agreement pursuant to which his Oceanic stock was pledged as collateral.

Subsequent to the execution of the loan agreement, the agreement was amended twice to extend the maturity date of the first installment repayment. The second such amendment extended the maturity date to July 19, 1965. On or about July 20, 1964, petitioner paid from his personal account $2,484,627.26 in interest on the loan. On or about December 23, 1964, petitioner paid from his personal account an additional $2,075,672.63 in interest.

On or about February 17, 1965, petitioner sold all the Union Oil stock purchased on July 19, 1963, to Union Oil for $35.50 per share ($106.50 per share if the price is adjusted for a 3-for-1 stock split which took place in 1964). This resulted in a gain of $45,152,943.87. From the proceeds of this sale, on February 17, 1965, petitioner repaid to the lending banks the loan principal and all remaining interest to date. The gain on the sale was duly reported on petitioners' joint Federal income tax return for 1965. That return showed a tax liability of $11,471,413.78, which was paid.

ULTIMATE FINDING OF FACT

Oceanic was not a guarantor of petitioner's obligations to the lending banks.

OPINION

Under section 951(a)(1)(B), a United States shareholder of a controlled foreign corporation is required to include in gross income his pro rata share of such corporation's increase in earnings invested in United States property during the taxable year. Section 956(a)(1) provides that the amount of the earnings of a controlled foreign corporation invested in United States property for the taxable year is the aggregate amount of such property held, directly or indirectly, at the close of the taxable year but only to the extent that the amount thereof would have constituted a dividend if such amount had been distributed during the year. See sec. 1.956–1(a), Income Tax Regs.

Section 956(b)(1)(C) provides that the term "United States property" includes an obligation of a "United States person." Thus, if a controlled foreign corporation makes a loan to its shareholder, a United States person, the obligation to repay the loan is United States property and the shareholder thereby realizes income under section 951. Section 956(c) goes further and provides that a controlled foreign corporation shall be considered as holding an obligation of a United States person if such corporation is, under regulations issued by the Secretary of the Treasury, a "guarantor" of such obligation.

In the instant case, petitioner was a United States shareholder of a controlled foreign corporation, Oceanic. As of December 31, 1963, that corporation had accumulated earnings and profits of $5,029,318 which, if distributed to petitioner, would have constituted a dividend. In that year, petitioner pledged his Oceanic stock to the lending banks in connection with the Union Oil stock purchase. Respondent contends that Oceanic thereby became a "guarantor," within the meaning of section 956(c), of petitioner's obligation to the lending banks. On this theory, respondent maintains, petitioner realized taxable income under section 951 to the extent of Oceanic's undistributed earnings and profits of $5,029,318.

We do not agree.

Section 956(c), on which respondent relies, is as follows:

For purposes of subsection (a), a controlled foreign corporation shall, under regulations prescribed by the Secretary or his delegate, be considered as holding an obligation of a United States person if such controlled foreign corporation is a pledgor or guarantor of such obligation.

Neither the Code nor the related regulations define the term "guarantor" for purposes of section 956(c). In the absence of any such specific technical definition, the term should be given its normal and customary meaning. *Hanover Bank v. Commissioner,* 369 U.S. 672, 687 (1962), revg. sub nom. *Gourielli's Estate v. Commissioner,* 289 F.2d 69 (2d Cir. 1961), affg. 33 T.C. 357 (1959); *United States Gypsum Co. v. United States,* 253 F.2d 738, 744 (7th Cir. 1958); *First Savings & Loan Assn. v. Commissioner,* 40 T.C. 474, 482 (1963). Black's Law Dictionary defines "guarantor" as one who makes a guaranty, and defines "to guaranty" as follows (Black's Law Dictionary, 833 (rev. 4th ed. 1968)):

> To undertake collaterally to answer for the payment of another's debt or the performance of another's duty, liability, or obligation; to assume the responsibility of a guarantor; to warrant.

This Court had occasion to define the term "guaranty" in Perry v. Commissioner, 47 T.C. 159, 163 (1966), affd. 392 F.2d 458 (8th Cir. 1968), as follows:

> "an undertaking or promise on the part of one person which is collateral to a primary or principal obligation on the part of another, and which binds the obligor to performance in the event of nonperformance by such other, the latter being bound to perform primarily." 24 Am. Jur., Guaranty, sec. 2, p. 873–874.

See also *Underwood v. Commissioner,* 63 T.C. 468, 475 (1975), affd. 535 F.2d 309 (5th Cir. 1976). The term has been similarly defined in the case law of New York, the State in which petitioner's loan agreement was executed, and the loan agreement states that it is governed by New York law. See, e.g., *Pink v. Investors Syndicate Title & Guar. Co.,* 246 App.Div. 172, 285 N.Y.S. 155 (3d Dept. 1936), affd. 273 N.Y. 483, 6 N.E.2d 414 (1936); *Aquavella v. Harvey,* 330 N.Y.S.2d 560, 563 (Monroe County Sup. Ct. affd. 40 App.Div.2d 940, 337 N.Y.S.2d 611 (4th Dept. 1972).

Two essential elements in the nearly uniform definitional language of these cases are (1) an undertaking or promise on the part of the guarantor and (2) a liability of the guarantor to make payment if the primary obligor fails to do so. Both of these critical elements are missing in the instant situation. The alleged guarantor, Oceanic, did not undertake or promise anything. Oceanic took no action whatsoever in connection with petitioner's debt to the lending banks. In the event that petitioner had failed to pay his obligation, Oceanic's pledged stock might have been sold to another, but Oceanic would have had no liability to make any payment. Thus, Oceanic can hardly be considered to have made a guaranty within the usual meaning of that term.

This being the case, section 951 is not applicable, unless the word "guarantor" as used in section 956(c) has a unique meaning and consequence beyond its normal usage. This is, in effect, what respondent would have us hold in this case. Although this issue has not previously been litigated, respondent's position has been spelled out in a revenue ruling which was adopted after the notice of deficiency was issued in the instant case. Rev. Rul. 76–125, 1976–1 C.B. 204, concluded that a stock pledge transaction, almost identical in form to the instant one, had the same effect of indirect repatriation of the controlled foreign corporation's income as if such corporation had itself guarantied the controlling stockholder's obligation. The following language from Rev. Rul. 76–125, supra at 204–205, sets forth the rationale on which respondent relies:

The purpose of section 956 of the Code is to terminate the tax deferment privilege with respect to the earnings of controlled foreign corporations when such earnings are directly or indirectly repatriated. S. Rep. No. 1881, 87th Cong., 2d Sess. 80, 87–88 (1962), 1962–3 C.B. 707 at 794, states, in part, "Generally, earnings brought back to the United States are taxed to the shareholders on the grounds that this is substantially the equivalent of a dividend being paid to them." Consistent with the intent of section 956, section 956(c) is interpreted to hold that use of the assets or credit of a controlled foreign corporation as collateral for an obligation of a United States person shall be considered a repatriation of earnings.

The loan agreement in the instant case indicated it was the intention of the parties that if A (the U.S. controlling stockholder) defaulted on the loan X's (the controlled foreign corporation's) assets * * * would be available to answer for the debt of A. Thus, although the agreement was signed by A for himself only, the net effect of the agreement was the same as a guaranty by X of the loan to A. Under section 956(c) of the Code, X must therefore be considered as holding A's obligation, which is defined as United States property under section 956(b)(1)(C).

The premise of this ruling is that the loan agreement indicated it was the "intention" of the parties that if the controlling United States shareholder defaulted on the loan the foreign corporation's assets would be available to answer for the debt. There is no evidence of any such "intention" in the instant case. To the contrary, the loan agreement gave the lending banks the remedies normally associated with pledge foreclosures. Sale of the pledged asset is the remedy ordinarily followed in case of default and foreclosure. It seems clear that, under usual principles of law applicable to the disposition of collateral for a loan, the banks could not have directly liquidated Oceanic; they would first have had to acquire the Oceanic stock as a purchaser on a foreclosure sale. See footnote 5. We find no basis for questioning the testimony of the officer of Chase Manhattan who negotiated the loan that had the banks foreclosed the pledge they would have sold Oceanic's stock and, further, that to have attempted to liquidate Oceanic and sell its assets would have been impracticable. Thus, this crucial premise on which the ruling is based is lacking in the instant case.

Moreover, Rev. Rul. 76–125, supra at 205, incorrectly reasons that "although the agreement was signed by * * * (the United States shareholder) for himself only, the net effect of the agreement was the same as a guaranty." Had Oceanic guarantied the bank loans in the manner described in section 956(c), it would have subjected itself to a contingent liability to pay the loans if petitioner defaulted. In those circumstances and in case of petitioner's default, the banks could have sued Oceanic for the unpaid balance of the notes and enforced their rights as creditors of Oceanic. Section 956(c) treats such use of the controlled foreign corporation's credit as an indirect repatriation of funds sufficient to trigger the realization of income under section 951.

However, the stock pledge in the instant case had no such current or future effect upon Oceanic's assets and liabilities. Oceanic assumed no liability, contingent or otherwise, to pay petitioner's loans. In case of petitioner's default on the bank loans, the banks might have foreclosed the pledge and sold the Oceanic stock. But the new owner purchasing at the foreclosure sale would have acquired stock with the same value as it would have had if no pledge had occurred. The banks would have had no remedy against Oceanic. Thus, the net effect of the stock pledge was not the same as a guaranty.

That petitioner realized a benefit from owning and pledging his Oceanic stock to secure the bank loans does not mean that Oceanic's earnings were invested in United States property within the meaning of section 951. Neither that section nor section 956(c) reaches every benefit derived from the ownership of stock in a controlled foreign corporation. In a real sense, the owner of such stock gains financially from every increase in its value, including increases attributable to an accumulation of earnings. Such value increases may so enhance his net worth as to enable him to borrow more money than he could have borrowed otherwise. But such an economic benefit does not trigger the realization of income. The owner realizes income under sections 951 and 956(a)(1) only when the controlled foreign corporation's earnings are invested in United States property. Neither a pledge of the controlled foreign corporation's stock to secure a shareholder's loan nor the listing of such stock on a balance sheet as evidence to support a loan, constitutes an investment of earnings in United States property. Only by reason of section 956(c) does the controlled foreign corporation's guaranty of its shareholder's indebtedness constitute such an investment in United States property, and the language of that section does not include a pledge of the controlled corporation's stock.

Respondent attempts to minimize this distinction between a shareholder's pledge of the corporation's stock and the corporation's guaranty of the loan by arguing that the ultimate basis of the lender's security in either case is the underlying assets of the corporation (and, thus, the shareholder-borrower indirectly utilizes these assets). Respondent relies heavily upon the negative covenants (detailed in our Findings) in petitioner's loan agreement in which petitioner is required, as controlling stockholder, to refrain from certain actions with respect to Oceanic's operations and net worth during the term of the loan. Respondent interprets these negative covenants as intended to preserve the assets of the corporation for access by the lenders in the event of petitioner's default.

However, the record amply demonstrates that covenants of this character, restricting the borrowing of funds, the sale of certain assets, or payment of dividends and forbidding gratuitous guaranties, are not at all uncommon. A breach of the restrictions or prohibitions ordinarily constitutes an event of default which permits acceleration of the loan. The Chase Manhattan officer who arranged the loan explained that unless "the loan is so strong that you don't need the protection of the collateral at all, it (inclusion of negative covenants in a loan agreement) is almost a necessity." He further testified that the negative covenants included in the instant loan agreement were less restrictive than those usually found in an agreement of this kind.

The purpose of the negative covenants in the instant case was not, as respondent argues, to enable the lending banks, in the event of petitioner's default, to enforce their claim against Oceanic or its assets. Their purpose was to protect the value of the pledged Oceanic stock as security for the loans. As pointed out in our Findings, the loan was made subject to the provisions of Regulation U which required the banks to make certain at all times that the value of all the pledged security was at least twice the amount of the loan. As discussed above, the recourse of the lenders in the event of petitioner's default would have been to sell the pledged Oceanic stock, not to attempt to recover through direct access to Oceanic's assets.

We think Rev. Rul. 76–125, supra, and respondent's position in this case attempt to stretch the statute and regulations to cover a situation with which they do not deal. True, the legislative history of Subpart F in which sections 951 and 956 appear makes it quite clear that one of its objectives is to tax United States shareholders of controlled foreign corporations on the indirect repatriation of income earned by such corporations but not distributed as dividends (and in many instances, not subjected to tax by the jurisdiction of incorporation). S. Rept. 1881, 87th Cong., 2d Sess. (1962), 1962–3 C.B. 707, 794; H. Rept. 1447, 87th Cong., 2d Sess. (1962), 1962–3 C.B. 405, 462. As noted above, an obvious form of such indirect repatriation would be a loan from the controlled foreign corporation to its controlling stockholder(s). This is dealt with specifically in section 956(b)(1)(C), quoted in footnote 3 supra.

Less directly, the controlling stockholders could derive nearly identical benefits by borrowing funds from another source and having the loan guarantied by the controlled foreign corporation or secured by a pledge of such corporation's assets. Such use of the credit or assets of the controlled foreign corporation indirectly effects a repatriation of available earnings. Section 956(c) was enacted specifically to cover these more subtle forms of indirect repatriation. S. Rept. 1881, supra, 1962–3 C.B. at 956.

But section 956(c) says nothing about pledging the stock of the controlled foreign corporation. Moreover, although that section specifically authorizes the Secretary or his delegate to prescribe regulations for its detailed application, the present regulations do not contain any provisions expanding the guaranty concept to include a pledge of the controlled foreign corporation's stock. Indeed, the regulations dealing with the treatment of pledges and guaranties, in substance, follow the statute. They are cast in terms which assume that "pledgor" and "guarantor" have their normal meaning except that one example explains that the guarantor concept includes an agreement by the controlled foreign corporation to buy the note at maturity if the United States person does not repay the loan. Sec. 1.956–2(c)(1), Income Tax Regs.

Another regulation, defining the term "acquired," provides that property which is an obligation of a United States person "with respect to which a controlled foreign corporation is a pledgor or guarantor" shall be considered acquired when "such corporation assumes liability as a pledgor or guarantor." Sec. 1.956–2(d)(1)(b), Income Tax Regs. A corporation does not assume a liability as pledgor or guarantor unless it is a party to the transaction. Thus, the regulation contemplates that section 956(c) is applicable only where the guarantor—the controlled foreign corporation—is a party to the transaction, not when its stock is merely pledged.

While we are aware that in most cases the value of stock as collateral will be based at least in some part upon the value of the underlying corporate assets (including undistributed income), the extent of the importance of such assets will vary from case to case. In many instances, the going-concern value of the company or the market value of the stock in the public securities market will have more significance than the value of the company's assets. In fact, it is conceivable that stock could be used as collateral in a case where the corporation has no significant tangible assets (or has liabilities substantially offsetting or exceeding the amount of its assets). Thus, the extent to which the stockholder of a controlled foreign corporation derives a benefit from the assets of the corporation is much less certain in the case of a pledge of stock than in the case of a direct commitment of its assets or credit by the corporation. We think that was the rationale followed by the draftsman of section 956 in stopping short of including the stock pledge transaction. Had Congress intended to cover the stock pledge arrangement, it could have, and would have, done so. Boykin v. Commissioner, 260 F.2d 249, 254 (8th Cir. 1958), affg. in part and revg. in part 29 T.C. 813, 817 (1958).

Whether this distinction explains the omission of the stock pledge type of transaction from section 956(c) or whether the omission was an oversight, we can find no basis for respondent's expansive interpretation of that section in the statutory language, its legislative history, or the implementing regulations. If the draftsman's handiwork fell short of fully accomplishing the objectives sought, it must be left to Congress to repair such shortfall. Accordingly, we hold that petitioner did not realize gross income under section 951 by reason of his pledge of his Oceanic stock as collateral for his loan from the lending banks.

To reflect the foregoing. Decision will be entered under Rule 155.

* * *

The IRS has not acquiesced and finally amended Treas. Reg. § 1.956–2(c) in response. Read the regulation. Note that in practice, U.S. multinationals are well-advised to avoid section 956 if possible, so this provision has an effect stronger than just an anti-abuse rule. Is this outcome desirable?

(ii)   SECTION 1248

Read section 1248(a) and the following excerpt from a notice issued subsequently to the 1986 tax reform.

* * *

Notice 87–64

1987–2 C.B. 375

... Section 1248 generally recharacterizes gain recognized by a United States shareholder on the disposition of stock in a controlled foreign corporation (CFC) as a dividend to the extent of earnings attributable to the United States shareholder's ownership interest in the CFC.

Prior to the Act, there were several important consequences of section 1248. Primarily, section 1248 prevented repatriation of income at capital gains rather than ordinary income rates. In addition, because section 1248 recharacterized gain as a dividend, a corporate United States shareholder received an indirect credit for an appropriate portion of foreign taxes paid or accrued by the CFC. After the effective date of the repeal of the capital gains rate differential by sections 301(a) and 311(a) of the Act, the primary consequence of characterizing gain on CFC stock as a dividend will be the receipt of the indirect foreign tax credit that accompanies the deemed dividend.

Section 1248(e), which treats certain dispositions of the stock of a domestic corporation as a disposition of the stock of a foreign corporation, is an anti-abuse provision designed to prevent a United States shareholder from converting what would be ordinary income under section 1248 to capital gain. The repeal of the capital gains rate differential eliminates the need for section 1248(e). Section 631(d)(2) of the Act amended section 1248(e) and (f) of the Code to provide that those provisions would be applicable "Except as provided in regulations prescribed by the Secretary." Pursuant to the grant of regulatory authority in section 631(d)(2) of the Act, regulations under section 1248(e) will be published to suspend the application of section 1248(e) for periods during which capital gains are taxed at the same rates as ordinary income.

Regulations will also be published to restrict the application of section 1248(f). Section 1248(f) prevents a taxpayer from avoiding section 1248 by engaging in certain nonrecognition transactions. The Act, by amending certain sections, including sections 311, 336, 337 and 361(c), expands the number of situations in which gain is recognized on distributions, sales or exchanges of stock in CFCs. In situations in which gain on CFC stock is recognized under the rules of subchapter C as if the CFC stock were sold on the date of the distribution, section 1248(a) shall apply so that the gain recognized under the rules of subchapter C will be characterized as a dividend accompanied by an indirect foreign tax credit. Accordingly, regulations will be published under section 1248(a) and (f) to provide that section 1248(f) will not apply to those distributions in which gain on CFC stock is recognized pursuant to certain sections, including sections 311, 336, and 361(c), as if the CFC stock had been sold at its fair market value at the time of the distribution. In situations in which gain on the CFC's stock is recognized under the rules of subchapter C but the gain is deferred under the consolidated return rules, section 1248(a) will apply at such time as the deferral of gain ends.

Pursuant to the exception contained in section 1248(f)(2), section 1248(f)(1) will not apply to certain distributions of CFC stock to a domestic corporation in which no gain is recognized under new section 337. In addition, regulations under section 1248(f) may limit the application of section 1248(f)(1) in section 355 distributions of CFC stock to situations in which the CFC is no longer a CFC after the distribution or in which one or more of the distributees of the CFC stock are not "United States shareholders" within the meaning of section 951(b) after the distribution. These regulations would also contain provisions to ensure that subsequent to a section 355 distribution that would not be subject to section 1248(f)(1) as stated above, the amount of section 1248 dividend resulting from a subsequent disposition of the CFC stock would include the section 1248 earnings attributable to the CFC stock as of the date of the section 355 distribution. The regulations may require appropriate adjustments to the basis and holding period of the stock of the CFC in the hands of the distributee. The changes to the section 1248(f) regulations would remain in effect regardless of whether a capital gains rate differential exists . . .

* * *

Why wasn't section 1248 repealed in the 1986 tax reform? We will revisit section 1248 in chapter 9 with respect to section 367(b).

d. INVERSIONS

Read new section 7874 and the following excerpt.

* * *

JOINT COMMITTEE ON TAXATION, DESCRIPTION OF THE CHAIRMAN'S MARK FOR THE CONFERENCE COMMITTEE ON H.R. 4520, October 4, 2004.

. . .

U.S. tax treatment of inversion transactions

Under present law, a U.S. corporation may reincorporate in a foreign jurisdiction and thereby replace the U.S. parent corporation of a multinational corporate group with a foreign parent corporation. These transactions are commonly referred to as inversion transactions. Inversion transactions may take many different forms, including stock inversions, asset inversions, and various combinations of and variations on the two. Most of the known transactions to date have been stock inversions. In one example of a stock inversion, a U.S. corporation forms a foreign corporation, which in turn forms a domestic merger subsidiary. The domestic merger subsidiary then merges into the U.S. corporation, with the U.S. corporation surviving, now as a subsidiary of the new foreign corporation. The U.S. corporation's shareholders receive shares of the foreign corporation and are treated as having exchanged their U.S. corporation shares for the foreign corporation shares. An asset inversion reaches a similar result, but through a direct merger of the top-tier U.S. corporation into a new foreign corporation, among other possible forms. An inversion transaction may be accompanied or followed by further restructuring of the corporate group. For example, in the case of a stock inversion, in order to remove income from foreign operations from the U.S. taxing jurisdiction, the U.S. corporation may transfer some or all of its foreign subsidiaries directly to the new foreign parent corporation or other related foreign corporations.

In addition to removing foreign operations from the U.S. taxing jurisdiction, the corporate group may derive further advantage from the inverted structure by reducing U.S. tax on U.S.-source income through various earnings stripping or other transactions. This may include earnings stripping through payment by a U.S. corporation of deductible amounts such as interest, royalties, rents, or management service fees to the new foreign parent or other foreign affiliates. In this respect, the post-inversion structure enables the group to employ the same tax-reduction strategies that are available to other multinational corporate groups with foreign parents and U.S. subsidiaries, subject to the same limitations (e.g., secs. 163(j) and 482).

Inversion transactions may give rise to immediate U.S. tax consequences at the shareholder and/or the corporate level, depending on the type of inversion. . . . The tax on any income recognized as a result of these restructurings may be reduced or eliminated through the use of net operating losses, foreign tax credits, and other tax attributes. . . .

Description of Proposal

The provision defines two different types of corporate inversion transactions and establishes a different set of consequences for each type. Certain partnership transactions also are covered.

Transactions involving at least 80 percent identity of stock ownership

The first type of inversion is a transaction in which, pursuant to a plan or a series of related transactions: (1) a U.S. corporation becomes a subsidiary of a foreign-incorporated entity or otherwise transfers substantially all of its properties to such an entity; (2) the former shareholders of the U.S. corporation hold (by reason of holding stock in the U.S. corporation) 80 percent or more (by vote or value) of the stock of the foreign-incorporated entity after the transaction; and (3) the foreign-incorporated entity, considered together with all companies connected to it by a chain of greater than 50 percent ownership (i.e., the "expanded affiliated group"), does not have substantial business activities in the entity's country of incorporation, compared to the total worldwide business activities of the expanded affiliated group. The provision denies the intended tax benefits of this type of inversion by deeming the top-tier foreign corporation to be a domestic corporation for all purposes of the Code.

In determining whether a transaction meets the definition of an inversion under the proposal, stock held by members of the expanded affiliated group that includes the foreign incorporated entity is disregarded. For example, if the former top-tier U.S. corporation receives stock of the foreign incorporated entity (e.g., so-called "hook" stock), the stock would not be considered in determining whether the transaction meets the definition. Similarly, if a U.S. parent corporation converts an existing wholly owned U.S. subsidiary into a new wholly owned controlled foreign corporation, the stock of the new foreign corporation would be disregarded. Stock sold in a public offering related to the transaction also is disregarded for these purposes.

Transfers of properties or liabilities as part of a plan a principal purpose of which is to avoid the purposes of the proposal are disregarded . . .

Transactions involving at least 60 percent but less than 80 percent identity of stock ownership

The second type of inversion is a transaction that would meet the definition of an inversion transaction described above, except that the 80-percent ownership threshold is not met. In such a case, if at least a 60-percent ownership threshold is met, then a second set of rules applies to the inversion. Under these rules, the inversion transaction is respected (i.e., the foreign corporation is treated as foreign), but any applicable corporate-level "toll charges" for establishing the inverted structure are not offset by tax attributes such as net operating losses or foreign tax credits. . . . These measures generally apply for a 10-year period following the inversion transaction. . . .

The proposal applies to taxable years ending after March 4, 2003.

* * *

The recent so-called anti-inversion legislation followed a hot political debate. Note, however that only very few inversion transactions have been effected to date. Why do you think that is the case? The JCT's description does not mention Subpart F. Nonetheless, it is argued that most inversions are designed primarily to avoid its application. Do you find support for this argument in the above excerpt? Why? Is the new section coordinated in some way with Subpart F? Why are inversions different from other transactions that attempt to avoid Subpart F? How effective/desirable do you think this legislation is?

7.5   THE PARTICIPATION EXEMPTION (SECTION 245A)

The TCJA significantly changed the contours of the outbound regime, converting it in part to an exemption regime and in part to a worldwide regime with a minimum tax. New Section 245A permits an offsetting deduction of 100% for foreign source dividends received by a domestic corporation from a 10% or more owned foreign corporation. This provision is similar to the participation exemption used by most of our trading partners. It means that U.S. corporate shareholders receiving dividends from the non-Subpart F income of CFCs (and other 10% owned foreign corporations) will not be taxed even if that income was not subject to tax at source (e.g., because of a tax holiday) and was not taxable under Section 951A as GILTI (because it falls below the hurdle rate).

However, Section 245A(e) disallows the participation exemption for hybrid dividends that are treated as deductible payments at source. This is consistent with the single tax principle because income that was not taxed at source should be taxed at residence.

NOTES

a.   Why adopt a participation exemption? What are its implications?

    1.   Neutrality (preferring CIN or CON over CEN)

Relief for U.S. Corporations.

2.   Leveling the playing field for U.S. corporations. (although effective tax rates were almost the same).

3.   Encourages import of earned profits to the U.S. for further investments.

4.   Why not?

5.   Instead of "now or later" it's "now or never" with a bigger now.

b.   The DRD concept.

It is a tax law write off that seeks to alleviate the potential consequences of triple or more taxations. The idea is that a corporate tax rate is associated with lower tax rates (usually) or for the benefits of owing a corporation. Under the two, taxing more than one tier is not justified. It was given before TCJA for dividends between two U.S. corporation of per Section 245 to dividend which was distributed by a foreign corporation for the U.S. source income (because you paid taxes on it to the U.S.). U.S. source income is an income which is effectively connected to the U.S.

c.   Situation before TCJA: Deferral.

Foreign source income of a foreign subsidiary is not taxed until it distributes dividends. In the 1960's, the U.S. came up with residence based taxation for CFC's. CFC is any foreign corporation where more than 50% of its voting or value stock are held by large U.S. SHs (each holding at least 10% of the voting power of the FC). For CFC, passive income (and other types of income which are called subpart F) are deemed as dividends for it's pro-rata share. Real dividends are then exempt. However, active business income is eligible for deferral.

Deferral is equivalent to an exemption of the interest on the income that earned on the funds deferred. The economic effect: The more the deferral lasts the larger the exemption of the interest (more money is earned on the working capital). Achieving a stepped-up basis: Another advantage is the opportunity to achieve a "step-up" basis in the shares of the corporation, when the taxpayer dies. Section 1014.

d.   Section 245A.

Section 245A implements a modified territorial tax system. Key feature is deduction for certain US corporations on receipt of dividend from certain foreign corporations (aka participation exemption). Limited to "foreign-source" portion of the dividend . Only applies to foreign corporations that are "specified ten-percent owned foreign corporations" ("STFC"). US corporation must own 10% or more of the STFC (directly or through attribution). Deduction not available for hybrid dividends. No foreign tax credit. Holding period: more than 365 days during 731 day period that began 365 days before the ex-dividend date. Excludes periods where foreign corporation was not STFC or US corporation was not a 10% owner. Excludes period where US corporation had certain contractual arrangements to reduce risk of loss.

e.   Dividends Received by a Partnership.

Conference Committee Report recommended guidance. If a domestic corporation indirectly owns stock of a foreign corporation through a foreign partnership and the domestic corporation would qualify for the participation DRD with respect to dividends from the foreign corporation if the domestic corporation owned such stock directly, the domestic corporation would be allowed a participation DRD with respect to its distributive share of the partnership's dividend from the foreign corporation. Need guidance on attribution from partnership (profits or capital interest?) and holding period (period held partnership interest and partnership held stock).

f.   Deemed Dividends and Section 1059.

TCJA amended Section 1248 and Section 964 to provide that deemed dividends are eligible for deduction under Section 245A (if requirements met). Section 1248: Gain on sale by US person of stock of certain foreign corporations is treated as deemed dividend to extent of E&P attributable to that stock that was earned while the US person held the stock. Why Section 1248 exists? (to prevent taxpayers from changing the character from ordinary income to capital gain. Section 964(e): Gain on sale of stock in a foreign corporation by a CFC is deemed dividend to same extent would have been under Section 1248 if seller was a U.S. person.

TCJA also amended Section 1059 to provide that it applies to Section 245A. Section 1059: If stock is not held more than 2 years before an extraordinary dividend is paid, basis in the stock is reduced by the portion of the dividend that is not subject to tax due to DRD (under Sections 243, 245 or 245A). Extraordinary dividend is a dividend in excess of 10% of basis of common stock (5% for preferred stock).

Example: Deemed dividend

P acquires FC for $200 when it had E&P of $100. FC earns $100. P sells FC for $300 after 1 year.

Section 1248 causes $100 gain (amount of E&P while P held FC) to be deemed dividend; Section 245A applies to deemed dividend.

Example: Section 1059

Goal is to avoid creating artificial losses by reducing basis after an extraordinary dividend. Example: Prior to the enactment of Section 1059, corporation P purchased 50% of the common stock of corporation S for $500. S has undistributed E&P of $1,000. Shortly thereafter, S declares a dividend, with P receiving a $200 dividend distribution. P, upon receipt of the dividend, properly claims an % dividends-received deduction (DRD) under Section 243 The distribution reduces the total fair value of S by the amount of the distribution, thus reducing the fair value of P' s stock in S.

Under the law in effect prior to the passage of Section 1059, P makes no adjustment to the basis in its S stock because the distribution is made out of S' s E&P. When P subsequently sells its devalued S stock for $300 ($500 – $200), P could claim a $200 artificial capital loss ($300 proceeds – $500 basis).

g. Consolidated Group Issues

Need guidance on application of investment adjustment rules to Section 245A (2 different issues). Investment adjustment rules require member of group (M) to increase basis in sub (S) by taxable income and tax-exempt income. Tax-exempt income includes taxable income or gain that is "permanently offset by a deduction or loss that does not reduce, directly or indirectly, the basis of S's assets".

Section 245A gives deduction that offsets income, but unclear whether Section 961(d) is an indirect reduction of basis.

Section 961(d): Where a domestic corporation previously claimed a deduction under Section 245A and sells stock in the STFC at a loss, the basis is reduced by the amount of the deduction previously claimed. Reduction is not below 0. Reduction only for purposes of determining the amount of the loss.

Example: M formed S with $80 and S formed FC with $80. FC earned $20 of non-PTI E&P and distributes $20 to S. (Assume Section 1059 does not apply.) (A distribution of PTI to the US shareholder is not treated as a dividend for US federal income tax purposes). If tax-exempt income, M's basis in S increases to $100. No gain or loss if sold. If not tax-exempt income, M's basis in S remains $80. Would have $20 gain if sold, eliminating benefit of Section 245A deduction. (Because you increase basis of taxable income and decrease it because of a deduction).

Need guidance under either investment adjustment rules or unified loss rules to prevent avoidance of Section 961(d) by consolidated group selling US entity that holds STFC stock instead of selling STFC stock. Section 961(d) only applies to sale of STFC.

Example: M formed S with $80 and S formed FC with $80. FC earned $20 of non-PTI E&P and distributes $20 to S. (Assume Section 1059 does not apply and dividend treated as tax-exempt income.) M's basis in S increased to $100. FC stock depreciates to $70 (without not reason). S sold for $90 ($70 of FC stock and $20 of cash). M recognizes $10 of loss; if S had sold FC, Section 961(d) would have reduced basis to prevent recognition of that $10 loss. Economic loss, but should not allow because could avoid application of Section 961(d) by selling US holding company instead of STFC. Same result if distribution is of pre-acquisition E&P, making loss noneconomic.

Unified loss rules do not resolve the issue. Treas. Reg. 1.1502–36(b) reduces disparity between different blocks of stock. Does not apply because sold all stock held in S. –36(c) reduces disparity between inside and outside basis. Does not apply because both $100—S's basis is $80 in FC stock plus $20 in cash.—36(d) reduces inside basis following sale generally by the amount of the loss to prevent doubling loss (or, at taxpayer's election, basis of stock being sold). Applies here, but only reduces basis in FC stock that already subject to reduction under Section 961(d). Only has impact if FC appreciates by $10 or more before being sold and only prevents doubling of loss. –36(e) contains operating rules that require appropriate adjustments where a prior adjustment to the S stock altered the relationship between inside and outside basis. Does not apply because distribution and Section

245A deduction did not alter this relationship. If M's loss is disallowed under guidance, –36(d) would not apply and Section 961(d) would apply on later sale of FC.

h.   Holding Period Issues.

Need guidance that holding period is not reduced by the period between signing and closing for a sale of STFC. Section 246(c) requires appropriate reduction to the holding period of stock for period when taxpayer is under a contractual obligation to sell. Required holding period is 365 days and begins 365 days before ex-dividend date. Where dispose of stock, no holding period can accrue after the sale. Thus any reduction in the holding period will prevent Section 245A deduction for any dividend after the signing. Applies to both actual dividends of cash or unwanted assets and deemed dividends under Section 1248. Legislative history indicates deduction generally expected to be available for Section 1248 dividends. Why? Because the purpose of holding period was to prevent abusive arbitrage transactions, typically of portfolio stock.

i.   Practice Problem.

Ann holds Parent which is a U.S. corporation that is incorporated in Delaware. Parent holds 50% of FC, a Danish corporation. FC is not a passive foreign corporation.

A.   FC distributed a dividend of 200 in May 2018. It had five deals until the close of the tax year. Sales of inventory with a tax profit of $80 in Indonesia, Sale of a stock in the HK Exchange market with $100 tax profit, Sale of royalties in Denmark $10 (tax profit). Sales of inventory by its U.S. office in Ann Arbor Michigan of $50, and a one-time sale of a machine to a U.S. resident.

What are the tax consequences for Parent? A: 200/250*200= DRD. PerSection 245A(c): Foreign source portion, Section 964(a) (How to calculate E&P), Section 245A(a)(5): Effectively connected) Only office is EC to the U.S.

B.   Will your answer change if FC distributed dividends earlier this year? (no: per Section 245A(c)(2)(B)).

C.   Will your answer change if Parent is an S corp.? What if it is individual? (no: only corp.)

D.   What if Parent is the only partner of a partnership that holds FC? (no, bc disregarded entity)

E.   What if Parent is a partner with another foreign partner. Parent holds 20% of the interests in the partnership?

F.   Same as A but Denmark recognized the dividends as a interest because it was distributed as a special financial instrument. (no, per Section 245(e)).

G.   What if the Indonesian inventory was subject to a low tax rate of 8% because of an Indonesian law that gives a preferred taxation if the corporation invests in a specific area? (is that "tax benefits"?)

H.   Same as G, but the special rate was not given because of a law, but under a special tax planning and was obtained by a tax ruling? What if it was granted under a tax treaty of Indonesia and the Netherlands?

I.   Same as G, but it is not a special low rate, but just a regular rate in Indonesia?

J.   Parent claims for FTC (Foreign Tax Credit) in their returns. Will they receive this FTC? Why?

K.   As a policy matter, would you include a provision that includes distribution by a foreign branch? (As a policy matter, if the purpose of Section 245A is to achieve territoriality, foreign tax income should not be treated differently in any form.) (Currently, branches are consolidated with the parent, and is taxed 21%. Before the tax reform there was unlimited credit to taxes that were paid in a foreign jurisdiction).

7.6   INTEREST LIMITS

New Section 163(j) (which replaces the old earning stripping rule) limits the deduction of net interest expense of a business to 30% of earnings before interest and taxes (EBIT). This limit is necessary to prevent tax sheltering by using borrowed funds to invest in stock of CFCs generating exempt dividends. However, even allowing 30% of the interest deduction can still generate negative tax rates. For example: Corporate taxpayer borrows 100 and invests in a CFC that distributes a dividend of 10. Interest payments are 10 and 3 are deductible under Section 163(j). Before tax this results in a return of 10–10=0. After tax, since the dividend is exempt and 3 of interest are deductible against other income, the return is negative 3.

NOTES

a.   House vs. Senate provision (EBITDA vs. EBIT respectively). EBITDA is a lower number, and the interest deduction would be more constrained. (Thirty percent of a smaller number is a smaller number.) In addition, if a taxpayer increases its investment, its depreciation rises, and the limit becomes tighter. The act of investment may cost a firm a portion of its interest deduction. (The more investment you have the more depreciation you have). Moreover, this might happen even if the new investment is done with cash from current sales, or repatriated profits from abroad, or proceeds from new share issues, without any new borrowing (because the depreciation increases and so is the limitation). It would penalize past investment funded by old debt. Last, it undercuts the investment incentive of the expensing and bonus depreciation provision

b.   The problem of negative tax rates: There are two consistent ways to treat interest in an economically optimal tax system, one that does not discriminate against saving and investment. Either the interest should be deducted by the borrower and taxed to the lender, or the interest should not deductible by the borrower and not taxable income for the lender. In either case, a portion of the returns on an investment that is financed with borrowed money is subject to one layer of tax, paid by either the borrower or the lender but not both. Taxing the interest portion of the investment return on the borrower's tax form by disallowing the deduction, and taxing it again when the lender receives it, is double taxation. This is akin to the double tax imposed on dividends or retained earnings of C corporations. This double taxation of C corporations is one of the biases in the income tax against saving and investment. Removing the deduction for interest would eliminate the distinction between debt and equity finance for C corporations. However, it would introduce a new distortion between debt financing and financing with a business's own income for the entire pass-through sector (They will prefer using their own capital). If a business can expense its capital costs, the tax rate on the investment is zero. If the business can also deduct interest, it is paying a negative tax on that investment; this constitutes an investment subsidy from the government. (Since you get a benefit of the time value of money that you are not taxed on, but you get to deduct it).The expense is spread economically throughout the life of the property (as if it was a lease).

Example: If the cost of a machine is 100, and the return is 100, then the tax rate is zero. If a taxpayer deducts more than the cost—it is a negative tax rate. The cost of a machine includes interest paid. Assumption—the taxpayer took a loan to fund this expense. (Cost goes up by 10). When the taxpayer expenses the amount paid for the machine, it can deduct more income, and invest this money. It has a benefit of time value of money. That makes sense because the expense is spread for the period of life of the asset. (Cost goes down by 10). Now, the benefit and the interest offset each other (Cost is 100). If you get to deduct the interest, you get to deduct 110 which is more than your cost: Negative tax rates.

However:

A. Minimizing the incentive for investment only applies to C corp.

B. Producers (Someone who creates and supplies goods or services) with a particular edge will always earn outsized profits (called "quasi-rents"). A new and better product will yield unusually high returns (more than the cost) until the competition can catch up.

C. It ignores the tax paid by the lender. The lender receives some of the return on the asset in the form of interest and pays tax on that portion. The borrower pays tax on the rest.

D. What about tax exempt lenders?

c. TCJA changes:

Increased Section 179 expensing;

Reductions in ADS lives of certain real property;

The elimination of categories of qualified leasehold improvements; and

Expansion of bonus depreciation to include used property and increase in bonus-eligibility to 100% for certain property.

Cost Recovery, although is not necessarily an international tax provision (except 168(g), can be considered to be a capital import provision, and thus, very important for cross-border transactions.

d.   Pre TCJA Depreciation: Way back in the 20th century: improvements were depreciated over the full amount of years of the underlying property. Since then, various types of incentives were added: Section 168(e)(3)(E) grants three classes of leasehold improvements which provides 15-year depreciation period:1. Qualified Leasehold Improvements. (lease of unrelated parties; interior portion of a non-residential; and more than three years than first started). 2. Qualified Retail Improvement Property (interior portion of non-residential; used in retail t/b of selling tangibles to the public; more than three years) and 3. Qualified Restaurant Property (a Building or improvement; more than 50% is devoted to preparing or selling meals). In 2015 fourth category was added: Qualified Improvements Property—Not pursuant to a lease or on a three years old building. Just an interior improvement made that was placed in service after the date of that the building was set. Instead of the 15-year life depreciation, it was eligible for 50% bonus depreciation and depreciated for 39 years (at that time the bonus depreciation was 50%), the same as the underlying real estate. (The other 50% is depreciated over 39 years).

TCJA eliminated the different categories on leasehold property.

e.   Bonus Depreciation: Since 2001, Section 168(k) has provided taxpayers the ability to immediately deduct a percentage of the acquisition cost of qualifying assets as "bonus depreciation." To take bonus depreciation, the property must either: A. have a regular depreciation life of 20 years or less, B. be computer software, C. be water utility property, or D. be qualified improvement property. (Remember, this needed to be added separately to the list of bonus-eligible assets because the previous version of qualified improvement property had a 39-year regular depreciation life, and thus would not have generally been eligible for bonus depreciation.) Importantly, the original use of the property had to start with the taxpayer claiming the bonus depreciation; thus, used property did not qualify. It becomes crucial for M&A. Finally, bonus depreciation was not permitted on any asset that was required to be depreciated using the ADS method.

f.   Perhaps the most impactful change in all of the Tax Cuts and Jobs Act was to provide for 100% expensing of certain assets. Full bonus depreciation is phased down by 20 percent each year for property placed in service after Dec. 31, 2022, and before Jan. 1, 2027. Retroactive (it's a benefit) from Sep. 27th. The reference for Qualified Improvements Property was removed since it is now has a 15-year period recovery. Used property will now qualify for the Bonus Depreciation. Intangibles amortization remains deductible over a 15-year period without bonus depreciation.

g.   Alternative Depreciation System: Old Law: Under Section 168(g), certain assets (include assets that are used internationally) must be depreciated using the "alternative depreciation system" (ADS). In general, ADS depreciation requires use of the straight-line method over a longer life, meaning a taxpayer will recover the cost of an ADS asset at a slower rate than it would a "regular" MACRS asset. For example, under Section 168(g)(2)(C), both residential (27.5 year regular life) and nonresidential real property (39 years) have an ADS life of 30 and 40 years respectively. In addition, under the table provided at Section 168(g)(3)(B), qualified leasehold, restaurant and retail improvements (15 year life) are granted an ADS life of 39 years. Importantly, any asset that is required to be depreciated using the ADS is NOT eligible for bonus depreciation.

New Law: ADS for Qualified Improvement Property is 20 years (or 15 year recovery period for non ADS Qualified Improvement Property). RE T/B with Qualified Improvement Property can elect out of interest deductions limitation rule but then have to depreciate the property under ADS and no Bonus Depreciation under 168(k).

h. Section 179: Depreciation Order: Section 179—Bonus Depreciation— Regular Depreciation. Unlike bonus depreciation, which requires a taxpayer to first capitalize and then depreciate an acquired asset, Section 179 allows a taxpayer to elect to simply expense the cost of an asset without capitalizing it at all (the difference between 100% bonus depreciation: no basis after expense and less than 100% Bonus depreciation if you sell within the tax year). The benefit is limited, however, to $510,000 in 2017, with that maximum deduction reduced dollar for dollar as total qualifying assets placed in service exceed $2,030,000. The deduction is further limited to the taxable income derived from that business, with any deduction in excess of the limitation carried forward to the next year. The Section 179 limitation will be increased to $1,000,000 for tax years beginning after 2017, with the phase-out beginning at $2,500,000 of qualifying assets placed in service. In addition, the references to qualified leasehold, restaurant and retail improvements among qualifying Section 179 property have been removed, replaced by a reference to Section 168(e)(6), which gives birth to the now-condensed class of qualified improvement property. As a result, all leasehold improvements—provided they are made to the interior portion of nonresidential rental property AFTER the building has been placed in service—will be eligible for immediate Section 179 expensing.

7.7 GILTI

TCJA and new Sections 951A and 250 provide that a U.S. shareholder of any CFC must include in gross income for a taxable year its GILTI (Global Intangible Low-Taxed Income) in a manner generally similar to inclusions of subpart F income. GILTI means, with respect to any U.S. shareholder for the shareholder's taxable year, the excess (if any) of the shareholder's net "CFC tested income" over the shareholder's "net deemed tangible income return." The shareholder's "net deemed tangible income return" is an amount equal to 10 percent of the aggregate of the shareholder's pro rata share of the qualified business asset investment ("QBAI") of each CFC with respect to which it is a U.S. shareholder. "Net CFC tested income" means, with respect to any U.S. shareholder, the excess of the aggregate of its pro rata share of the tested income of each CFC over the aggregate of its pro rata share of the tested loss of each CFC. The tested income of a CFC means the excess of the gross income of the corporation determined without regard to certain exceptions (including the current active finance exception and the CFC look-through rule) over deductions (including taxes) properly allocable to such gross income. QBAI means, with respect to any CFC for a taxable year, the average of the aggregate of its adjusted bases, determined as of the close of each quarter of the taxable year, in specified tangible property used in the production of tested income in its trade or business and of a type with respect to which a deduction is generally allowable under Section 167.

The tax rate of future GILTI is determined by taking the US tax rate (21%) and allowing a deduction of 50%, for a net rate of 10.5%. This rate can be partially offset by foreign tax credits, but in a separate basket (but with cross-averaging within the basket). The section is effective for taxable years of foreign corporations beginning after December 31, 2017.

What this means in plain English is that Amazon, Apple, Facebook, Google, Netflix, and their ilk will have to pay tax at 10.5% on future GILTI because they have CFCs that produce "tested income" (and no loss) in excess of 10% over their basis in offshore tangible assets, which is zero or close to it (since they derive almost all of their income from intangibles). Other MNEs (e.g., GE or Intel) will pay less because they have more tangible assets offshore. This creates an obvious incentive to move jobs (not just profits) offshore. In addition, the proposal standing on its own would also induce profit shifting because of the combination of the participation exemption and the lower rate (10.5% is less /than 21%). It may also cause inversions to avoid the minimum tax on GILTI.

NOTES

a.   Situation before TCJA: Foreign source income of a foreign subsidiary is not taxed until it distributes dividends. In the 1960's, the U.S. came up with residence based taxation for CFC's. CFC was any foreign corporation where more than 50% of its voting or value stock are held by large U.S. SHs (each holding at least 10% of the voting power of the FC). For CFC, passive income (and other types of income which are called subpart F) are deemed as dividends for it's pro-rata share. Real dividends are then exempt. However, active business income is eligible for deferral. Deferral is equivalent to an exemption of the interest on the income that earned on the funds deferred. The economic effect: The more the deferral lasts the larger the exemption of the interest (more money is earned on the working capital). Achieving a stepped-up basis: Another advantage is the opportunity to achieve a "step-up" basis in the shares of the corporation, when the taxpayer dies.

b.   GILTI: Contains elements of a flat-rate minimum tax on foreign income. GILTI is an add-on to the existing rules for foreign source income. It disincentivizes shifting profits abroad and shift it back tax free with Section 245A.

c.   General Rule: Section 951A requires each U.S. SH of CFC to include in its gross income each year its share of "Global Intangible Low-Taxed Income" for the year. Calculated on a U.S. SH-by-U.S. SH basis. GILTI=Net Tested Income—Net Deemed Tangible Income Return (NTDIR). GILTI>=0. Calculated on a yearly basis (but NTDIR is calculated for depreciation quarterly). If the U.S. SH is a domestic corporation that elects to receive the benefit of FTC's for a taxable year, 100% of the foreign taxes attributable to GILTI are included in the gross income under Section 78 (GILTI Inclusion).

d.   Net CFC Tested Income: It is based on "Tested Income" or "Tested Loss" of each CFC (Related CFC). NET CFC Tested Income=Aggregate of U.S. SH's pro rata share of the tested income of each Related CFC with positive tested income—U.S. SH's pro rats share of the tested loss of each Related CFC with a tested loss. NET CFC Tested Income>=0. What's CFC? (More than 50% owned (by vote or value) by US shareholders. For this purpose, stock owned directly, indirectly and (enhanced)constructively is taken into account. Under the Tax Act, a U.S. person can be a U.S. shareholder if it owns either 10 percent of the voting power or 10 percent of the value of a CFC).

e.   Tested Income: Tested Income of a CFC=CFC's gross income (with certain exceptions)—deductions properly allocable to such gross income (under Section 954(b)(5)). Specified exceptions to Income:

   1.   Effectively connected income—not foreign and is taxed under the inbound provisions.

   2.   Gross income taken into account in determining the subpart F income of the CFC. (It is taxed under other provisions of Subpart F)

   3.   Gross income excluded from foreign base company or insurance company subpart F by reason of High Tax exception in Section 954(b)(4). (if Elected out. Can elect out if 90%—18.9 now) Although there other operating high-taxed income that is included).

   4.   Dividends received from a related person (As if it received DRD—not to tax a lot of tiers on the same income).

   5.   Foreign oil and gas extraction. Tested loss is the excess of deductions. Accordingly, a CFC cannot have a loss and profit, but a taxpayer can have a profit and loss from different CFC's.

f.   NTDIR: Multi-step process.

   1.   For each Related CFC with positive tested, its "specified tangible property is its tangible property used in the production of tested income. And its "qualified business asset investment" ("QBAI") is the aggregate adjusted tax basis of its specified tangible property that is used in a t/b and subject to an allowance of depreciation. (That means, if a Related CFC doesn't have positive tested income for a year, none of its tangible property for the year is taken into account and it has no QBAI). (remember ADS depreciation and Section 338?)

   2.   A U.S. SH aggregates its pro rata share of the QBAI for all of the Related CFCs.

3.   This aggregate QBAI is multiplied by 10%, which is considered a deemed return on the tangible assets that should not be subject to U.S. tax. (QBAI Return)

4.   This deemed return is reduced by any interest expense taken into account in calculating the SH's net CFC tested income for this year, except to the extent interest income attributable to that interest expense was also taken into account in determining the SH's net CFC tested income. (Equivalent to disallow the interest: as if added back to the tested income). Also, the reduction applies even if it is not the same Related CFC as is the QBAI.

5.   The result is NTDIR. Note that gross interest expense of a CFC (unless paid to a related CFC of the same U.S. SH) reduces the U.S. SH's NDTIR, even if the CFC has offsetting interest income from an unrelated party.

6.   Incentivize offshores purchase of assets to increase QBAI NTDIR is treated is an exempt return. It's trade or business tangible income in a foreign country—usually active, therefore-foreign source income—benefits. Only 10%, Tax Basis? Tax Basis is $0 but all is tangible.

g.   Calculating GILTI: It is very important to distinguish calculations that are done at the CFC level and calculations that are done at the U.S. SH's level. Tested income is purely a CFC level concept, and NTDIR is purely a SH level concept. Each CFC with positive tested income has its own QBAI, but the calculation of the exempt return on QBAI is done at the at the SH's level by aggregating QBAI of all Related CFCs and multiplying the total by 10%. Likewise, each CFC has its own interest expense allocable to its own tested income, but the total of such interest expenses of all Related CFCs of a U.S. SH (except if paid to another Related CFC of the same U.S. SH) is aggregated at the SH's level in calculating the reduction to NTDIR.

h.   The GILTI gross income inclusion is the U.S. SH's share of: (1) The aggregate net tested income, if positive, of all Related CFCs with limited exceptions such as subpart F income, minus (2) 10% of the tax basis of the tangible depreciable assets of those Related CFCs with positive tested income; (3) However, any gross interest expense (not paid to a Related CFC of the same U.S. SH) will reduce the size of item (1) and automatically reduce the size of (2), so such interest expense does not reduce the GILTI gross income inclusion except to the extent it exceeds the size of item (2). Why it is structured like this? (intangibles like goodwill, avoidance by recharacterize royalties or consolidate them). What type of principles in tax law and international tax it is supposed to achieve?

i.   *Example*: Erica, a U.S. SH, holds 20% of CFC1 and 100% of CFC2. CFC1 has $200 gross income which includes: a. $20 effectively connected income to the U.S. (should not be included in the tested income); b.$30 interest expense (should be reduced at the corporate level), but no interest income allocated to that expense; and c. $80 dividends received from a related person. The depreciable property is a machine that is used for trade or business, which was purchased 5 years ago for $100 and was fully depreciated. CFC1 also had a factory that was deemed as purchased under Section 338 for $500, a week ago. This factory was fully depreciable before the purchase. CFC 2 had $15 loss that includes $10 interest expense. It recently purchased a lot of machinery that have current tax basis of $1000.

Answer: First: both are probably CFC and Erica is a U.S. SH. CFC1 has a tested income of $200–$20–$80=$100. CFC2 has a tested loss of $15. We take pro rata shares, and it is $100*20%=$20 for CFC1, and the whole tested loss of $15. There is a net tested income of $5.Now we need to calculate NTDIR. CFC1 has $0 on the machine and $500 (if Section 338 gets a step up basis for purposes of QBAI). It is pro-rata then it is $500*20%=$100. CFC2 has a loss, therefor, no QBAI. Now deem the return of 10% of $100=$10. Interest deductions of$40 reduce NTDIR to $0, but not less. Section 951A Inclusion is $5–$0=$5.

j.   Relation to FDII: A domestic corporation is entitled to a deduction equal to the sum of (A) 37.5% of its "foreign-derived intangible income", (B) 50% of the section 951A inclusion and (c) 50% of the Section 78 amount of included in its income and attributable to GILTI. Together: Section 250 Deduction. Only corporation; unless an individual elects treatment under section 962 as a corporate SH. (Individuals will be taxed again on the same GILTI when distributed unlike corp.).

Example: U.S. SH with no FDII has $100 of Section 951A inclusion solely from a CFC with no foreign taxes. The Section 250 deduction is $50, resulting in $50 of taxable income. The income is taxed at 21% to a corporate U.S. SH, for an effective tax rate of 10.5% on GILTI. (50% of 21%). From a policy perspective, section 250 deduction is not a deduction for a corporate expenditure, but rather a mechanism to reduce the tax rate. If calculated as % of income, why not lowering the rate of income instead of deductions? (Losses?—no because it cannot be if it's part of the income, it is for the carve-back mechanism)

k.   Carve Back: Under section 250(a)(2), if the sum of the U.S. SH's FDII and Section 951A (and possibly Section 78) inclusions exceeds its taxable income (not taking into account the Section 250 deduction), then, solely for purposes of calculating the Section 250 deduction, those inclusions are reduced pro rata by the excess (the "carve-back"). In addition, the Section 250 deduction is disallowed in calculating a net operating loss. The carve-back comes into effect if the U.S. SH has current losses or loss carryovers to the year in question, and those losses exceed the non-GILTI, non-FDII income of the corporation. In that cases, the carve-back requires that these losses be used to offset FDII and GILTI eligible for the Section 250 deduction, and the deduction is calculated by reference to the FDII and GILTI that remain (if any) after the losses have been used. As a result, the excess losses might be absorbed in the year but provide the U.S. SH with a tax benefit of only fraction of the usual tax benefit of a loss.

l.   *Example 1*: U.S. SH has $100 of operating income and $100 of section 951A inclusion. If the SH has no other income or loss, the Section 250 deduction is $50, taxable income is $150, and the tax is $31.50. If the SH instead has a $100 NOL carryforward to the year, the pre-section 250 taxable income and Section 951A inclusion for the year are both $100, so there is no carve-back. The Section 250(a)(1) deduction is $50, the taxable income is $50, and the tax is $10.50. The tax savings from the NOL is ($100*21%) $21, as would be expected. (The NOL is first used on the taxable income).

m.   *Example 2*: Same facts as Example 1, except NOL is $150. Now, taxable income before Section 250 is $50 ($200 taxable income—$150 NOL), and the carve-back limits the Section 250 deduction to 50% of that (50 of Excess(100–50)/100 of GILTI), or $25. Taxable income is $25, and the tax liability is $5.25, a rate of savings of $10.5. The NOL is applied before the deduction in the case of excess.

n.   Purposes of GILTI: Like a world-wide system, a significant amount of income of a U.S. shareholder that is earned through CFCs is subject to immediate U.S. tax if the foreign tax rate is insufficient. Moreover, gains on a sale of CFC stock are taxable if they exceed previously taxed income in the CFC. the GILTI regime taxes GILTI income at a significantly lower rate than domestic income. NDTIR is permanently exempt from U.S. tax, and dividends from foreign subsidiaries are exempt from U.S. tax.

o.   To the extent that GILTI is a world-wide tax system, it results in yet another hybrid between: (1) a flat minimum domestic and foreign tax rate on a U.S. shareholder's non-NDTIR GILTI inclusions earned through CFCs (the "flat-rate theory"), and (2) the imperfect adding of the GILTI regime onto the existing tax regime for foreign source income, particularly Subpart F income (the "add-on theory").

Flat Rate Theory: The strongest evidence that Congress intended the flat-rate theory is that the Conference Report arguably contemplates no GILTI tax if the foreign tax rate is at least 13.125%. Moreover, the flat rate theory is arguably more consistent with the tax rate on FDII. Other Factors that are consistent with this theory (although with the Add-On theory also) are: 1. The ability to offset tested income of some CFCs with tested losses of other CFCs; 2. The fact that the GILTI FTC limitation is determined on a world-wide basis rather than a country-by-country basis.

Add-on Theory: Other elements of the GILTI regime support the add-on theory because they can cause a much higher tax rate on the net world-wide income of the CFCs owned by a U.S. shareholder. Under this view, the add-on theory is in effect a "minimum tax theory", namely that Congress intended the world-wide effective tax rate on GILTI to be no less than 10.5%, but U.S. tax could apply even if the foreign rate is more than 13.125%. For example, a tested loss in a CFC can cause a loss of FTCs and NDTIR exclusion, and neither unused tested losses nor unused FTCs can be carried over. All interest expense of a shareholder's CFCs not reflected in tested income of a Related CFC is in substance first allocated to tax-exempt NDTIR, rather than being allocated between taxable income and exempt NDTIR. The Section 250 deduction of the U.S. shareholder is limited to its taxable income. Tax Credits—Add-on or flat rate?

p.   GILTI and consolidated groups: Under Sections 951A and 78, each U.S. corporation must calculate its own GILTI inclusion based on its own Related CFCs. However, a consolidated group is treated as a single entity for many purposes of the Code, and in a typical group there will be more than one, and perhaps many, members that are U.S. shareholders of CFCs. It is important for guidance to state the extent to which a consolidated group is to be treated as a single corporation for purposes of the various GILTI calculations. The statute, and the legislative history suggest similarity between Subpart F income and GILTI, and consolidation principles do not apply to calculating Subpart F inclusions. However, there are differences.

The issue is whether the limitation under Section 250(a)(2)(ii) of the deduction to the taxable income "of the domestic corporation" refers to a single member of the group or to the taxable income of the group as a whole. Reasons for a group limitation: resources of IRS to police and trace deductions, prevent increased tax rates of unwary TPs, easy to avoid by the carve-back, no matter how big the loss of the group, consistency with the idea that it is irrelevant to track losses in a consolidated group (even when members leave since losses cannot be carried forward). It can be allocated to one member with no other items of income or deduction, and then avoid the carve back to other members.

The issue is whether the amount of GILTI inclusion should be aggregated or should not be aggregated. The aggregation approach can be either beneficial or harmful to taxpayers, depending on the situation. The reason is that aggregating or not aggregating particular CFCs with other CFCs in calculating GILTI can have a significant effect in determining the benefits that the group will receive from tested losses, QBAI return, and FTCs. *Examples*: The examples that follow illustrate these situations. In the examples, CFC1 is owned by group member M1, and CFC2 is owned by group member M2. If aggregation applies, M1 and M2 are together referred to as M. Unless otherwise indicated, there is no FTC or QBAI return.

Example 1: Tested income can be offset by tested loss of another CFC. Absent FTCs or QBAI return, aggregation is generally better for taxpayers when CFC1 has tested income and CFC2 has a tested loss. This is because tested income and tested loss can offset each other when they are included in a single GILTI calculation. *Example*: Assume CFC1 has $100 of tested income, and CFC2 has $100 of tested loss. Under aggregation, M has a $0 Section 951A inclusion. Under non-aggregation, M1 has $100 of tested income and Section 951A inclusion, and M2 obtains no benefit from the tested loss of CFC2. The group is better off under aggregation. However, if there is interest expense in a CFC with tested losses and QBAI return in a CFC with tested income, nonaggregation may be better for the taxpayer. CFC1 has $100 of tested income and $100 of QBAI return. CFC2 has $100 of interest expense and $50 of tested loss. Under nonaggregation, neither M1 nor M2 has any Section 951A inclusion. Under aggregation, the CFC2 interest expense of $100 offsets M's NDTIR from CFC1 (since interest is allocated with respect to QBAI), so M has a section 951A inclusion of $50 (100–50).

Example 2: If a Related CFC has QBAI return in excess of its tested income, such excess will reduce the Section 951A inclusion of its shareholder arising from other Related CFCs. This provides a benefit of aggregation. Example: Assume CFC1 has $100 of tested income and no QBAI return, and CFC2 has $10 of tested income and $100 of QBAI return. Absent aggregation, M1 has a Section 951A inclusion of $100, and M2 has no inclusion. With aggregation, M has a Section 951A inclusion of $10.

Example 3: As illustrated in the first example, a tested loss of one CFC has the benefit of offsetting tested income of other CFCs in the same aggregation group. However, a tested loss also reduces the inclusion percentage for FTCs paid by other CFCs in the same aggregation group. Example (base case with aggregation: tested loss offsets high- and low-taxed tested income): Assume (1) CFC1 has $100 of tested income net of foreign taxes and a foreign tax rate of 13.125%, (2) CFC2 has $100 of tested income and foreign tax of $0, and (3) the group also owns CFC3 with a $100 tested loss. With aggregation, the Section 951A inclusion is $100 and the inclusion percentage is 50%, regardless of who owns CFC3. Calculation: The Section 951A inclusion is equal to CFC1's $100 of tested income, plus CFC2's $100 of tested income, minus CFC3's $100 of tested loss, or $100. The inclusion percentage is the $100 Section 951A inclusion, divided by the sum of CFC1's $100 of tested income and CFC2's $100 of tested income, or 50%. A portion of CFC1's foreign taxes is available to M for use as a FTC because the inclusion percentage is 50%. (No aggregation, tested loss only offsets high-taxed income; result is worse for taxpayers than aggregation).

Same facts as Example 8(a), but assume CFC3 is owned by M1. Absent aggregation of M1 and M2, M1 has no Section 951A inclusion and an inclusion percentage of 0%. M2 has a Section 951A inclusion of $100 and no FTC. The result is worse than under aggregation because the tested loss of CFC3 is "wasted" when used against high-taxed income in CFC1. (No aggregation, tested loss only offsets low-taxed income; result is better for taxpayers than under aggregation).

Same facts, but assume CFC3 is owned by M2. Then, M1 has a section 951A inclusion of $100 and a 100% inclusion percentage, so no tax is due (because the taxes paid is enough to cover U.S. liability). M2 has no inclusion, and no tax. Full use has been obtained for both the tested loss in one GILTI group, and the FTC in a different GILTI group.

Example 4: When NDTIR reduces the section 951A inclusion, the result is a pro rata cutback of FTCs based on the reduction of the section 951A inclusion, without regard to which CFC had QBAI return. If one CFC has QBAI return and the other does not, and tax rates on the CFCs are different, the single calculation of the inclusion percentage under aggregation can be better or worse for taxpayers than the separate calculations of the inclusion percentage under nonaggregation.

Example 4(1): (base case with aggregation; NDTIR reduces inclusion percentage). Assume (1) CFC1 has $100 of tested income net of foreign taxes, and no QBAI return, and (2) CFC2 has $100 of tested income net of foreign taxes, and $100 of QBAI return. Also assume that either CFC1 or CFC2 has a foreign tax rate of 13.125%, and the other has a 0% rate. Under aggregation, M has $200 of tested income, a Section 951A inclusion of $100 ($200 minus $100 of NDTIR), and an inclusion percentage of 50%.

Example 4(2): (no aggregation; lower foreign tax on QBAI return; result is taxpayer-favorable compared to aggregation). Assume the same facts as

Example 9(a), but with the foreign taxes being imposed on CFC1. Under nonaggregation, M1 has a section 951A inclusion of $100 and an inclusion percentage of 100%, while M2 has a section 951A inclusion of $0. This allows for full usage of FTC on the non-exempt income in CFC1, while aggregation "wastes" half of the FTC on the QBAI return in CFC2.

Example 4(3): (no aggregation; higher foreign tax on QBAI return; result is taxpayer-unfavorable compared to aggregation). Same facts as in Example 9(a), but the foreign taxes are imposed on CFC2. Under nonaggregation, M1 has a $100 section 951A inclusion, with no FTC offset, and M2 has no section 951A inclusion. This is worse for taxpayers than the aggregation case because the FTC in CFC2 is totally "wasted".

q. Interest expense: Gross interest expense of a CFC reduces NDTIR of the U.S. shareholder unless the corresponding interest income is taken into account in determining the U.S. shareholder's net CFC tested income. This can make aggregation or nonaggregation more favorable depending on the facts.

Example 1: Suppose CFC1 has interest expense to a third party and no QBAI return, and CFC2 has no interest expense but has QBAI return. Under aggregation, the interest expense of CFC1 will reduce M's NDTIR. Without aggregation, there will be no reduction in M2's NDTIR, so aggregation is worse for the group.

Example 2: Alternatively, suppose CFC1 has QBAI return and pays interest to CFC2. With aggregation, the interest will have no effect on the group's net CFC tested income or NDTIR. Without aggregation, the interest will reduce M1's NDTIR and net CFC tested income, and increase M2's net CFC tested income. Total net CFC tested income is the same in both cases, but aggregation avoids the reduction in NDTIR and is better for the group in this fact pattern.

r. Tax liabilities through Sections 351 and 332 tax free re-organizations. As a policy, aggregation makes sense since economically the SH is the same entity. On the other hand, the GILTI calculation for a single member of the group already involves considerable aggregation of the tax attributes of the Related CFCs of that member, and it is a logical extension of that procedure to extend the aggregation to CFCs owned by all group members. Proposed Reg. chose to: The consolidated group is not treated as a single entity, for purposes of Section 951A, under the proposed regs. Aggregation of certain GILTI items: Tested Loss, QBAI, Tested interest income, Tested income expense. Allocation: In proportion to such member's pro-rata share of tested income to the total tested income of the group. GILTI inclusion, however, occur on a member-by-member basis.

s. The Issue: Assume that all the gross income of a CFC is included in tested income. The threshold question is which expenses of a CFC should be allowed as a deduction in calculating tested income. The statute provides that tested income is "gross income" determined without regard to certain specified items, less deductions (including taxes) "properly allocable to such gross income under rules similar to the rules of section 954(b)(5) (or to which such deductions would be allocable if there were such gross income)". Section

954(b)(5) contains the same reference to deductions "properly allocable" to Subpart F income. However, it refers to the method to allocate known deductions to different categories of income, not the method to determine whether an expense is properly counted as a deduction. There is no guidance from either the statute or legislative history.

There are a couple of methods whether an expense should properly count as a deduction for purposes of GILTI, and the choice of method could produce different outcomes. There are considerations regarding what type of deductions should be allowed such as: 1. the purpose of GILTI (disallowance of some deduction can cause an increase in the tax rate); 2. coherence with other GILTI provisions, similarities to Subpart F (not a deemed dividend so no necessarily relates to E&P); 3. avoidance of other provisions (such as 163(j): interest can be shifted to CFCs if it's allowed there—although TPs will get a bit of tax); 4. burden on TPs

Under any of the foregoing methods of determining tested income, the question arises as to whether losses can be carried forward. Consider a U.S. shareholder with a single CFC that has no QBAI return, a tested loss in year 1, an equal amount of tested income in year 2, and no foreign tax liability. Absent a loss carryover, the shareholder would have a net GILTI inclusion and resulting tax liability in year 2, in the absence of any economic income over the two year period. This result is inconsistent with the flat-rate theory of GILTI, assuming the flat-rate theory is intended to apply over time as opposed to only in years with profits. The case before—NOLs were not allowed in counting Subpart F income. However, it was determined through E&P—that might have the same results.

t. If allowed there are two suggested ways to carryover losses: (1) at the CFC level, or (2) at the U.S SH level: CFC Level: Under the existing rules, if a Related CFC has a tested loss, all or part of that tested loss is available to shelter tested income of the U.S. shareholder from Related CFCs. First, rules would need to address how to determine which tested losses allocable to a particular U.S. shareholder are used to offset tested income of that shareholder. In that case are some tested losses from Related CFCs not utilized to offset tested income of other Related CFCs, the net tested loss at the shareholder level should logically be allocated to the various Related CFCs with tested losses in proportion to the tested loss of each Related CFC. This calculation would be done separately for each U.S. shareholder of a CFC with a tested loss. Third, suppose some but not all U.S. shareholders of a CFC can use their share of a tested loss in year 1. The non-users would include, for example, all U.S. persons that are not U.S. shareholders of the CFC, all U.S. shareholders that do not have tested income from other CFCs, and all non-U.S. individual and corporate shareholders that directly hold stock in the CFC. The unused portion of the tested loss is the portion allocable to the shareholders.

Example 1: Whether the new limitation 80% should apply. A U.S. shareholder owns 100% of a single CFC, and the CFC has a tested loss of $100 in year 1. In year 2, the CFC has $100 of tested income, of which $20 is QBAI return. Absent the loss carryover, the shareholder would have a section 951A inclusion of $80. If the loss carryover is allowed in the amount of 80% of the year 2 tested income, the shareholder's net CFC tested income will be $100 minus $80, or $20, and its Section 951A inclusion will be $20 of net CFC tested income minus $20 of NDTIR, or $0. Thus, the loss carryover eliminates 100% of the Section 951A inclusion. Another elimination of 100% of the income with NOL is: In year 1, CFC1 has a tested loss of $100 that is not used by its 100% U.S. shareholder. In year 2, CFC1 has tested income of $100, and the U.S. shareholder also owns CFC2 that has a tested loss of $20. Assume there is no NDTIR. The section 951A inclusion aside from the loss carryover is $80. The elimination of 100% of the Section 951A inclusion for year 2 is arguably inconsistent with the purpose of the 80% limitation for domestic corporations. That rule does not allow a carryover to year 2 to eliminate 100% of the taxable income in year 2. Under this theory, the carryover should be limited to 80% of the section 951A inclusion in Year 2.

The allowance of the loss carryover equal to 80% of tested income in year 2, without regard to QBAI return, is helpful to the taxpayer in Example 10(a). However, it can also be very adverse to taxpayers. Same facts as the last example, but in year 2, the CFC has $100 of tested income, of which all $100 is QBAI return. Even without the loss carryover, the Section 951A inclusion is $0. If $80 of the loss carryover is allowed in year 2, it has been absorbed with no tax benefit to the U.S. shareholder. The avoidance of the 80% limitation in Example 10(a), and the wasting of loss carryovers in Example 10(b), would not arise if the loss carryover is limited to 80% of the excess of tested income over QBAI return in the carryover year. In that case (i) the carryover utilized in Example 10(a) will be 80% of ($100 minus $20), or $64, (ii) tested income and net CFC tested income will be $36, (iii) the Section 951A inclusion will be $36 minus $20, or $16, and (iv) $36 of the $100 of tested loss from year 1 will be carried forward to year 3.

u. Carryover at the U.S. SH level: As a reminder, tested losses of a CFC are taken into account in reducing the U.S. shareholder's income inclusion under section 951A(a). A U.S. shareholder's section 951A inclusion is the excess (if any) of the shareholder's net CFC tested income for the year over its NDTIR for the year. The question is how the tested losses that move up to the shareholder are "absorbed" in the current year and affect the amount of the carryover to future years (or are absorbed in future years and unavailable for further carryover). The following example illustrates two methods for calculating carryovers. Assume a U.S. shareholder has two CFCs ("CFC1" and "CFC2"), CFC1 has $100 of tested income and $150 of QBAI return. CFC2 has $100 of tested loss. Under the statute, the U.S. shareholder has $0 tested income and $150 of NDTIR. As will be seen below, the two approaches give carryovers from year 1 of $0 and $150. Under one approach (the "tested loss carryover approach"), $100 of tested losses would be absorbed by the $100 of tested income, and there would be no carryover of tested loss. More generally, the carryover amount would be the "net CFC tested loss", which would be defined in the same manner as net CFC tested income, except tested losses of some CFCs could exceed tested income of other CFCs.

The alternative approach (the "shareholder calculation carryover approach") applies the entire calculation at the shareholder level. If the

Section 951A formula for inclusion would result in a negative number, aside from the prohibition of a negative result, that amount could be carried over, just like any excess of taxable expenses over taxable income. In the example, the Section 951A formula would result in minus $150 in year 1 (net tested income of $0 and NDTIR of $150), and this could be carried over. This approach allows NDTIR not only to offset net CFC tested income, but also allows NDTIR to create its own carryover if it exceeds net CFC tested income. Specifically, the carryover of the negative amount in the GILTI formula is equal to net CFC tested income minus NDTIR, to the extent this number is negative and without regard to whether it exceeds aggregate tested losses of loss CFCs for the year. This approach in effect treats NDTIR as exempt income earned on tangible assets, whether or not that is true in fact. It assumes that, say, a CFC with $100 of tested income and $150 of QBAI return really had a $50 tested loss on intangible assets and $150 of income on tangible assets, whether or not that is true as a factual matter. The shareholder obtains "credit" for the deemed $50 loss on intangible assets by being allowed a loss carryover of $50.

Other issues under both methods of U.S. SH level: Ordering of use of carryover losses between GILTI and Non-GILTI losses. Should they be subject to the 80% rule?The question is whether each type of carryover should be limited to offsetting 80% of its respective income type. For example, if there was $100 of GILTI inclusion and $100 of non-GILTI income and sufficient carryovers of both types, the net result could be either (1) $20 of GILTI inclusion and $20 of non-GILTI income, or (2) $0 of GILTI inclusion and $40 of non-GILTI income.

v.   Section 163(j): First issue is whether Section 163(j) applies to CFC. If it applies, the second issue is whether the carryover also applies. Is there a difference between a situation where the interest deduction where the interest is allowed and then there is a reduction in tested income that creates a loss and can be carried forward or disallowed and carried forward. Moreover, absent a carryover rule, a CFC could have plenty of tested income over a period of two or more years, but because the income is bunched into a few of the years, interest deductions would be permanently disallowed. Phantom income: a carryover is necessary to mitigate the consequences of "phantom income" or "phantom tested income" that can arise from a Section 163(j) disallowance for interest paid between related parties. Suppose a CFC ("CFC1") pays interest to a related CFC ("CFC2") and the interest deduction is disallowed under Section 163(j). Then, CFC2 has an increase in tested income from the receipt of the interest payment, but CFC1 does not have a reduction in tested income. The group has net positive tested income, which may result in a Section 951A inclusion, without any cash profit.

Also, As in the case of the 80% limit for NOL carryovers, there is a question as to how the 30% limit on Section 163(j) carryovers should apply to the tested income of the CFC that also has QBAI return in the carryover year. A U.S. shareholder owns 100% of a single CFC, and the CFC has an excess Section 163(j) deduction of $100 in year 1. In year 2, the CFC has $100 of tested income, of which $30 is QBAI return. Absent the loss carryover, the shareholder would have a Section 951A inclusion of $70.If the carryover is limited to 30% of tested income, or $30, then tested income is reduced to $70. Then, the U.S. shareholder's NDTIR is reduced by the $30 of allowed interest, namely to $0, since interest expense first reduces NDTIR until NDTIR is reduced to $0.100 As a result, the U.S. shareholder's Section 951A inclusion is still $70, and the $30 interest carryover is absorbed but provides no tax benefit.

Arguably the allowed carryover should be increased by $21, to $51, to reduce the Section 951A inclusion by 30%, to $49. However, if the interest expense of $100 had actually been incurred in year 2, $30 would be allowed under section 163(j), tested income would be $70, NDTIR would be $0, and the Section 951A inclusion would be $70. Under section 163(j)(2), a carryover is to be treated the same as, not better than, interest actually incurred in year 2 similar to that raised in NOLs. Specifically, with tested loss in another CFC offset tested income.

Example: In year 1, CFC1 has a Section 163(j) carryover of $100 to year 2. In year 2, CFC1 has tested income of $100, and the U.S. shareholder also owns CFC2 that has a tested loss of $70. The Section 951A inclusion aside from the carryover is $30. If the carryover to year 2 is allowed to the extent of 30% of the $100 of tested income of CFC1 in year 2, then tested income of CFC1 will be $70 and the Section 951A inclusion will be $0. The reduction in Section 951A inclusion from $30 to $0 is arguably not consistent with the intent of the 30% limitation in Section 163(j) because under this theory, the carryover is limited to 30% of the Section 951A inclusion of $30, so the allowed carryover is $9, net tested income of CFC1 is $91, and the Section 951A inclusion is $91 less $70, or $21.

7.8   FDII

To address the problem of shifting income from the US to CFCs, new Section 250 applies a reduced 13.125% to "foreign derived intangible income" (FDII) which is defined as the amount which bears the same ratio to the corporation's "deemed intangible income" as its "foreign-derived deduction eligible income" bears to its "deduction eligible income."

Deemed intangible income is the excess of a domestic corporation's deduction eligible income (gross income without regard to subpart F income, GILTI, and other enumerated categories) over its deemed tangible income return (10% of its QBAI).

The "foreign-derived deduction eligible income" is defined as income derived in connection with (1) property that is sold by the taxpayer to any foreign person for a foreign use or (2) services to any foreign person or with respect to foreign property. In other words, this category comprises exports for property and services, including royalties from the licensing of intangibles.

Deduction eligible income is essentially the domestic corporation's modified gross income calculated without regard to subpart F and GILTI (as well as a few other enumerated categories). So a U.S. company's foreign derived intangible income, which gets the 13.125% rate, is the amount that bears the same ratio to the deemed intangible income as the U.S. company's exports bear to its modified gross income.

This "remedy" may be effective in partially addressing the shifting problem (although 13.125% is higher than 10.5%), but the FDII provision has an obvious WTO problem: It is a subsidy contingent on export performance, which is explicitly banned by the Subsidies and Countervailing Measures (SCM) agreement. This was precisely the type of export subsidy struck down in the FSC and ETI cases in the WTO, resulting in massive potential sanctions and forcing the US to repeal the subsidy. A WTO challenge to FDII is likely.

NOTES

a. New Section 250 is a rare taxpayer favorable international provision in the TCJA that relates to in particular GILTI and BEAT. Focus is on export sales (including licenses, leases, etc.) and exported services by U.S. corporations. Apparently the provision is applied on a U.S. "consolidated return" basis (but one of many areas of needed guidance). General intention is to incentivize U.S. corporations to bring intangibles (and manufacturing) back to the United States by generating a significant deduction on certain inbound payments (sales proceeds, rents, royalties, etc.).

b. FDII does in some ways bring to mind "patent box" regimes adopted by certain foreign jurisdictions where certain income associated with certain intangibles (patents, trademarks, etc.) may qualify for a reduced tax rate. In general FDII is now eligible for a 37.5% deduction (3/8). On $100 of FDII, there is $62.50 of net income taxed at 21%, for tax of $13.125 (a 13.125% effective tax rate). For years starting after 12/31/25, the deduction declines to 21.875%, for an effective tax rate of 16.41% ($16.41 tax assuming same 21% rate). As discussed below, basic approach to determine income that is eligible for the FDII deduction is (1) determine the excess of the non-routine, deemed intangible income of a U.S. corporation (or group) over the deemed routine, "tangible" property income and (2) determine the portion of #1 that is treated as "foreign" for FDII purposes (and therefore eligible for the deduction).

c. "Foreign" portion above generally relates to income of a U.S. corporation (or group) in connection with property that the US Corp (or group) sells, leases, licenses, etc. to a non-U.S. person and for use, consumption outside of the United States OR Services provided by the US Corp (or group) to persons "located" outside the United States or with respect to property "located" outside the United States. Significant issues relating to allocation of expenses to this foreign income, impact of NOLs and NOL carryforwards of U.S. taxpayer, etc. Also rules relating to intermediaries. Can apply to sales and services provided to related or unrelated foreign persons (if related foreign person must have ultimate unrelated party foreign use, etc.)

d. Relationship to GILTI: GILTI, BEAT, and the Transition Tax have gotten considerably more attention than FDII. GILTI and FDII in particular are distinct but related in many ways. GILTI is covered by new Section 951A generally applicable to tax years beginning after 12/31/17. Focus primarily on certain income of controlled foreign corporations (CFCs). In general, non-Subpart F income of a CFC in excess of deemed routine "tangible" property income is subject to U.S. tax for certain U.S. shareholders at an effective tax rate of 10.5% (21% base rate less 50% GILTI deduction) enormously complex provision with significant complications for expense allocations, impacts of NOLs, availability of foreign tax credits, etc.

"Computational" Treasury Regulations issued on September 13, 2018 with more forthcoming. GILTI and FDII each seek to carve out from gross income deemed routine "tangible" returns from deemed non-routine "intangible" returns. Rules for neither are truly tied or traced to actual tangible or intangible income (just loose reference to the mechanical allocation process).

Both regimes work off same deemed "tangible" base—"qualified business asset investments" or "QBAI" looking generally to tax basis of QBAI (tangible depreciable property); 10% of QBAI is income base. Recent proposed GILTI regulations (Sept. 13, 2018) address, among other things, some basic provisions regarding QBAI that also apply to FDII (including certain anti-abuse rules). However, impact of QBAI is completely different under each regime (really mirror images of each other).

GILTI effectively subjects the excess over 10% of QBAI each year to current U.S. taxation (subject to U.S. 50% deduction and haircut of foreign tax credits)—"punishes" for IP being offshore! FDII does the opposite—the excess over 10% of QBAI each year is potentially eligible for the FDII 37.5% deduction, provided that and to the extent that such excess is allocable to foreign use, consumption, etc.—benefit for IP being onshore! Odd dichotomy of incentives—(1) GILTI incentivizes CFCs and their U.S. shareholders to invest in tangible assets and income offshore in order to reduce GILTI, while (2) FDII incentivizes for US corp. to divest domestic tangible assets and income to increase FDII.

e. FDII Mechanics: FDII mechanics involve a series of complex computations and determinations

FDII = Foreign Derived Intangible Income

FDII = Deemed Intangible Income (DII)* (Foreign Derived Deduction Eligible Income (FDDEI)/Deduction Eligible Income (DEI))

This ratio encapsulates the foreign portion allocation discussed above

DII = DEI minus Deemed Tangible Income (DTI)

DTI = 10% of Qualified Business Asset Investment (QBAI)—discussed above

FDDEI (amount potentially eligible for 37.5% deduction) = DEI derived from "foreign sales and services"

DEI = Total Net Income of US corporation (or group) excluding specific categories (Subpart F, GILTI, Foreign Branch Income, Financial Services Income, CFC dividends)

f.   Example 1—

USCo has $1000 of net income, $1000 of Qualified Business Asset Investment, 10% of QBAI is $100, and $500 of net income from foreign sales

FDII = ($1000–$100) * ($500/$1000) = $450 (37.5% of which is deductible)

Example 2—

USCo has $1100 of net income, $1000 of Qualified Business Asset Investment, 10% of QBAII is $100, and $600 of net income from foreign sales

FDII = ($1100–$100) * ($600/$1100) = $545.45

The additional $100 of net income from foreign sales only generated ~$95 of additional FDII.

Key Observation: An additional dollar of FDDEI does not generate an additional dollar of FDII

g.   What Counts as Foreign?

Direct Third-Party Sales

Goods must be sold to non-United States person for use, consumption, disposition outside of the United States

Direct Third-Party Services

Services must be provided to any person "located outside" of the United States

Related Party Sales or License with Third-Party Sales

Goods or IP must be used in connection with sale of goods to an unrelated non-United States person for use, consumption, disposition outside of the United States

Related Party Sales or Licenses with Third-Party Services

Goods or IP must be used in connection with provision of services to a non-United States person

Related Party Services with Third-Party Sales

No special related-party rule; service must be provided to any person located outside of the United States

Related-Party Services with Third-Party Services

Not FDII eligible if related-foreign person provides any "substantially similar service" to persons located in the United States (conduit round tripping concept)

Note that there is a potential cliff effect—disallowance is not limited "to the extent" of similar services

"Round tripping" safeguards for sales/services going outbound but returned to the United States—can lose deduction.

h. Interaction of FDII and GILTI:

GILTI and FDII deductions are reduced where FDII and GILTI exceed taxable income

Example—

FDII = $75; GILTI = $100; Total Taxable Income = $100

FDII + GILTI – Taxable Income = $75

FDII Reduction = $75 * ($75 / $175) = $32.14

GILTI Reduction = $75 – $32.14 = $42.86

FDII = $75 – $32.14 = $42.86; FDII Deduction = $42.86 * 37.5% = $16.1

GILTI = $100 – $42.86 = $57.14; GILTI Deduction = $57.14 * 50% = $28.57

Taxable Income = $100 – $16.1 – $28.57 = $55.3

Tax = $55.2 * 21% = $11.6

Absent haircut

FDII + GILTI Deduction = $75 * 37.5% + $100 * 50% = $78.125

Taxable Income = $21.875

Tax = $4.6

i. Need for guidance: Like many TCJA provisions there is a real need for guidance to fill in holes of what were in many case provisions that were rushed through the legislative process

FDII is no exception

Been overshadowed by other provisions and so extent of benefit from FDII is unclear; but pursuit of FDII benefit can require operational, accounting, and other business changes that are tougher to undertake given uncertainty and lack of guidance

Selected areas of uncertainty/need for guidance

Whether FDII applies to U.S. corporations on a consolidated group basis

Interaction of FDII with U.S. transfer pricing principles and BEPS principles (routine versus nonroutine returns, etc.)

Coordination with GILTI (note some addressed on QBAI in recent proposed GILTI regulations)

Treatment of allocable expenses to reduce FDII

Impact of NOLs and NOL carryforwards

Foreign use or consumption generally

Treatment of "bundled" transactions involving both sales (and licenses) and services (different rules)

Treatment of related and unrelated "intermediaries"

Scope and mechanics of the QBAI base (issue for GILTI as well)

Addressed to some extent in recent proposed GILTI regulations

For services, the "location" point—"location of person outside the U.S." (as opposed to non-U.S. person) and "location of property outside the U.S."

Guidance on hybrid rules and FDII

j.   WTO Issues: Under the WTO's SCM agreement, the non-collection or forgiveness of taxes otherwise due is considered a subsidy for the purposes of the SCM agreement (Art. 1)

The SCM distinguishes 2 types of subsidies:

Prohibited subsidies

Actionable subsidies

The SCM agreement does not apply to services. While services are excluded from the SCM, the FDII provision clearly applies a lower rate (13.125% instead of 21%) to a domestic US corporation's sales of goods to any foreign person for a foreign use.

FDII clearly involves the non-collection or forgiveness of taxes otherwise due, i.e., a subsidy under the SCM, and the subsidy is likewise clearly contingent in law and in fact upon export performance.

Thus, there is little doubt that the FDII provision is prohibited subsidy in violation of the SCM that entitles trading partners to impose sanctions (unilaterally or after receiving approval from the WTO's Dispute Resolution Body).

k.   The problems of FDII: FDII discourages domestic manufacturing because it taxes tangible investments at 21% up to a 10% return, while a domestic corporation that has no US activities and just imports goods and re-exports them benefits from the lower 13.125% rate.

Unlike former Section 199, Section 250 is a blatant violation of the SCM, and will certainly be struck down if challenged, because it is de jure as well as de facto contingent on export performance.

Section 250 has not so far encouraged inbound FDI. See: Foreign Direct Investment in the United States, Preliminary 1st Quarter 2018 (2018), https://ofii.org/report/foreign-direct-investment-in-the-united-states-preliminary-1st-quarter-2018.

The reason may be that it is too risky to move intangibles into the US, because it may be a Hotel California situation ("you can check in, but you cannot check out") if the law is changed, and then the intangibles are trapped in the US because of the enhanced Sections 367 and 482.

Ironically, this may also be why FDII has not been challenged in WTO.

7.9   REVIEW PROBLEMS—CHAPTER 7

1. A, a U.S. citizen, invested $1,000 in FC (in 2016), an F country technology company founded by her friend, a foreign citizen and resident. She owns 1,000 of FC's 100,000 common shares. FC has no other classes of shares or other U.S. persons as shareholders. Its activities take place solely in F. In 2016 and 2017, FC suffered large losses (more than $1m in each). In 2016–2018 it also earned $10 of interest (annually) short-term deposits with a local bank. In 2018 it barely broke even, but in 2019 began to earn significant royalties from licensing some of its technologies (assume $5m annually), and interest and capital gains on other investments it made.

    a. What are the U.S. tax consequences to A from this investment if she undertook no tax planning apart from the facts described above?

    b. Would you advise A to engage in a different tax strategy? Assume that she would have made the investment regardless.

    c. Would your answers to the above questions change if FC's business strategy has always been limited to licensing its technology rather than engage in production. Assume similar incomes/losses.

    d. Alternatively, would A be better off selling the stock back to FC?

    e. Would your answers to the above questions change if A owned 50% of FC? Alternatively, if B, a U.S. citizen unrelated to A owned 50% of FC?

2. Assume now that FC is owned: (1) 30% by Z, a nonresident alien friend of A, (2) 10% by A; and (3) 60% by a Cayman corporation, C, which is owned 70% by USA CO., a U.S. corporation, and 30% by KoreaCO, a Korean corporation. In year 1 (apply post-2017 law), FC's income included $100,000 of business profits in F—its country of organization, $10,000 of dividends subject to 10% withholding tax in the dividends' source country (not the U.S.) and $100,000 of royalties paid by an unrelated tax haven corporation. FC did not distribute, or pay any foreign taxes in year 1 (all income covered by prior losses in its organization country). A's sole item of income (ignore deductions) for the year was $50,000 of domestic wages. What was A's U.S. tax liability for the year (assume a flat 20% U.S. tax)?

3. Assume, instead, that FC had $100,000 of domestic active income subject to 50% tax, and $100,000 of income from selling its product in Asia through Y, a wholly-owned Singapore subsidiary.

    a. Assume, instead, that FC contracts with an unrelated Panamanian company to manufacture its product. FC's Panamanian wholly-owned subsidiary, P, supervises the manufacturer and ships the final product to the customers in Japan and China. The sale is concluded and the proceeds received by P in Panama and deposited

there on behalf of FC. Assume the same $100,000 of income from
these sales.

CHAPTER 8

THE FOREIGN TAX CREDIT

8.1   INTRODUCTION

The United States was the first country in the world to adopt a generally applicable foreign tax credit in 1918. Other countries with global tax systems, such as the U.K., only granted deductions for taxes paid to other countries (the U.K. did, however, grant credits for taxes paid to other jurisdictions within the British Empire).

The foreign tax credit was largely the brainchild of T.S. Adams, a Yale economist who was the principal adviser to the Treasury on tax matters in the formative years of the income tax. Adams believed in source based taxation, for both normative and practical reasons. From a normative perspective, Adams wrote that "[a] large part of the cost of government is traceable to the necessity of maintaining a suitable business environment"; these costs justify imposing a tax as compensation to the government bearing them. From a practical perspective, the source jurisdiction gets the "first bite at the apple": "Every state insists upon taxing the non-resident alien who derives income from sources within that country, and rightly so, at least inevitably so."

Accepting the legitimacy and inevitability of source-based taxation raises the specter of double taxation if the residence jurisdiction of the taxpayer also sought to tax the same income. The solution adopted by some European countries was to exempt foreign source income altogether. Adams refused to adopt this solution because it posed the risk of some income going untaxed altogether: "the state which with a fine regard for the rights of the taxpayer takes pains to relieve double taxation, may fairly take measures to ensure that the person or property pay at least one tax."

The solution was the foreign tax credit: The residence jurisdiction taxes the foreign source income but grants a credit for source-based taxes. In that way, double taxation is avoided but a residual tax is paid to the residence jurisdiction if there is no source-based tax or the source-based tax rate is lower than the rate applicable in the residence jurisdiction.

The foreign tax credit is granted by Sections 901–909. Note that the credit is elective (Section 901(a)). However, for most taxpayers, a credit will usually be preferable to the alternative deduction (under Section 164):

	Credit	Deduction
Foreign income	100	100
Foreign tax	21	21
U.S. gross income	100	100
U.S. net income	100	79
U.S. tax @(35%)	21	16.59
For. tax credit	(21)	0
After-tax income	79	62.41

Note also that the credit is available to U.S. taxpayers unilaterally, i.e., without depending on a tax treaty.[1] Other countries grant only a deduction in the absence of a treaty. Why? Which solution is preferable? What is the impact on other countries' desire to enter into treaties with the U.S.?

Note, finally, that the OECD model tax treaty presents an option between the credit (Art. 23B) and the exemption (Art. 23A) methods. Which method would be chosen by a credit and exemption countries wishing to conclude a bilateral tax treaty? Revisit your answer to the former question.

8.2   THE THREE HOOPS

In order to obtain the foreign tax credit, the taxpayer must first pass through three "hoops" set by the Code and regulations. The taxpayer must show that (a) a tax was paid to a foreign jurisdiction, (b) the tax was paid by the taxpayer seeking the credit, and (c) the tax paid was a creditable tax. Each of these "hoops" raises its own set of issues.

a.   WAS A TAX PAID?

Read Treas. Reg. 1.905–2, and then the following case:

Continental Illinois Corporation v. Commissioner of Internal Revenue

United States Court of Appeals for the Seventh Circuit.
998 F.2d 513 (1993).

■ JUDGES: Before POSNER and COFFEY, CIRCUIT JUDGES, and WILLIAMS, SENIOR DISTRICT JUDGE.*

■ POSNER, CIRCUIT JUDGE. The Internal Revenue Service assessed substantial deficiencies against the Continental Illinois National Bank for the years 1975 through 1979. Continental challenged these deficiencies in the Tax Court, which conducted several trials that have

---

[1]   There are other restrictions.

*   Hon. Spencer M. Williams of the Northern District of California, sitting by designation.

produced the rulings, some in favor of Continental, some in favor of the IRS, that the parties have brought before us on this appeal and cross-appeal. *55 T.C.M. (CCH) 1325 (1988); 58 T.C.M. (CCH) 790 (1989); 61 T.C.M. (CCH) 1916 (1991).* The parties and the amici have favored us with more than two hundred pages of briefs, rich in detail that we can ignore. The issues are straightforward. They concern just two types of loan: "net loans" made to foreign borrowers, and "CAP loans."

"Net loans" are loans net of any tax that the borrower's country imposes on the interest. In a gross loan, the parties agree to an interest rate, and the interest is paid to the lender subject to any obligation that local law imposes on the borrower to withhold the tax that the lender owes on the interest. Thus, if the agreed rate of interest is 12 percent and the withholding rate 25 percent, the borrower remits only 9 percent interest to the lender and pays the rest to the local taxing authority. In a net loan, the parties agree upon the interest that the lender will be entitled to receive net of any local tax on it; this protects the [lender?] against an unexpected increase in the tax rate. Determination of the tax due on the interest for such a loan generally requires computing a grossed-up interest income figure (which we'll call x) that will generate the same amount of tax that would have been due had the form of the loan not been changed from gross to net. To compute x requires first computing what we will call r, the rate that, after subtraction of (in our example) 25 percent of the rate, equals the agreed-upon after-tax interest rate. So: r minus .25r equals 9 percent; r equals 12 percent. The grossed-up income (x) is simply r times the amount of the loan. What we are calling x and r will nowhere be specified in the loan contract. They are artifacts created in order to make sure that net lending will not be used to reduce the lender's tax liability to the foreign country. In both the gross and the net loan the lender receives (in our example) 9 percent on his money after tax. The difference is that in the gross loan a change in the tax rate will raise or lower the amount of money the lender can take out of the country because his entitlement is to interest before the tax on it is computed or paid, and a change in the tax rate will therefore change what he can take out, while in a net loan a change in the tax rate will not affect the amount of money that he can take out of the country because the contract for such a loan entitles him to a fixed amount of interest over and above the local tax, whatever that tax may be.

The Internal Revenue Code allows a taxpayer to credit against the federal income tax that he must pay on income earned in a foreign country any income tax that he paid to that country on the same income. *26 U.S.C. § 901.* In our example of a gross loan, the lender can thus set off the 3 percent interest that is withheld from his foreign interest income and paid over to the foreign taxing authority against his federal tax obligations. In the case of a net loan, however, for a long time either the IRS took the position, or Continental believed it was the IRS's position, that the only taxable income received by the lender was the agreed-upon after-foreign-tax rate; since no foreign tax had been taken out of that income, no foreign tax credit was available. In 1976 Continental learned that it was the IRS's position that the lender's taxable income was x, the grossed-up amount, and that any foreign tax paid on x could be taken as a foreign tax credit. Continental launched a study of all its net loans to determine how much foreign tax had been withheld, and it attempted to credit the amounts withheld against its federal income tax, restating its taxable income to include those amounts. In terms of our example, it reported x as taxable income and claimed a foreign tax credit of .25x. We shall see that this restatement promised Continental a net tax savings.

The first issue is whether Continental's inability to produce tax receipts for the amounts withheld is fatal to its claiming those amounts as foreign tax credits. Continental makes two arguments that it is not, one that the Tax Court correctly rejected, the other that it erroneously accepted. The first argument is that the foreign tax credit attaches irrevocably when the borrower (or other foreign debtor of the U.S. taxpayer) "withholds" for taxes moneys that would otherwise go to the lender (or other U.S. creditor), even if those moneys are never paid over to the foreign taxing authority. We disagree. Put aside the awkwardness that the "withholding" involves no subtraction from what would be due the lender were there no foreign tax, because the lender's entitlement is net of that tax. The important point is that it is a foreign tax credit that the Internal Revenue Code allows, not a foreign fraud credit. If Continental's position prevailed, American businessmen would have strong incentives to collude with foreign businessmen in overwithholding foreign taxes, since such overwithholding would generate foreign tax credits for the American at no cost to the foreigner. It is true that if the foreigner withholds more than is actually due (or collectable), pocketing the difference, the American will have a higher taxable income. But every extra dollar of taxable income will be creditable against U.S. income tax, and the result will be a net tax benefit. Suppose the American is in the 30 percent bracket. Then the phantom additional dollar of foreign income will create a $30 tax liability and a $1 tax benefit, for a net benefit of 70.

This is reason enough why the IRS insists that the foreign tax not merely be withheld, but paid to the lawful taxing authority. And it is an insistence grounded in the language of the Internal Revenue Code. The amount allowed as a foreign tax credit is the amount of any foreign tax "paid or accrued," and if accrued taxes when paid differ from the amount of the credit taken that amount must be readjusted accordingly. *26 U.S.C. §§ 901*(b)(1), 905(c).

Continental presented letters from its borrowers stating that they had indeed paid the taxes they withheld on Continental's net loans. These letters are the basis of its second argument, which the Tax Court accepted, that even if the foreign tax credit does not attach at the moment of "withholding," actual payment was adequately proved. The regulations require that the taxpayer submit "the receipt for each such tax payment," or in lieu thereof "a photostatic copy of the check, draft, or other medium of payment showing the amount and date thereof, with certification identifying it with the tax claimed to have been paid, together with evidence establishing that the tax was paid for taxpayer's account as his own tax on his own income." Treas. Reg. §§ 1.905–2(a)(2), 2(b)(1). The borrowers' letters did not comply with these straightforward requirements. We cannot imagine on what basis the requirements might be thought an abuse of the Internal Revenue Service's necessarily broad power to prescribe the methods of proving entitlement to lucrative tax benefits. Continental complains that the enforcement of the requirements against it is "unfair," because, had it only realized before 1976 that net loans could generate foreign tax credits, it would have required its borrowers to furnish it with tax receipts. But that is tantamount to arguing that the IRS was under a judicially enforceable obligation, when it changed its position on the foreign tax credit status of net loans (if it changed its position—which is unclear, but also on the view we take of the case unnecessary to clear up), to relax its normal rules for proving payment of foreign taxes so that taxpayers could take maximum advantage of the new position. In effect, by not relaxing its rules on proof, the IRS changed its position on the foreign tax credit status of net loans prospectively. Continental insists on full retroactivity. There is no basis in law, public policy, natural justice, or any other source of norms for such an insistence with respect to so artificial an entitlement as the foreign tax credit. Continental's argument is even weaker if there was no change in the IRS's position in 1976—if Continental just awakened then to the possibility of obtaining foreign tax credits for interest income on net loans. It would be remarkable for a corporate taxpayer to seek to shift to the Internal Revenue Service the burden of its own lack of diligence in exploiting opportunities for tax savings.

But Continental is on solid ground in arguing that if it is not entitled to the foreign tax credits, its taxable income on the net loans should be restated from (in our example) 12 to 9 percent. Had it not learned in 1976 that it could obtain foreign tax credits on the interest income generated by its net loans, it would have reported as taxable income merely the agreed-upon net interest rate. In 1976 it saw an opportunity to make money by increasing its reported income to the grossed-up level (x) and taking the difference as a foreign tax credit, since, as we have pointed out, reporting an extra dollar of income confers a net benefit on a taxpayer who can simultaneously claim an extra dollar of foreign tax credit. The attempt to take advantage of a lawful opportunity to save taxes failed because of difficulties of proof, and the logical, practical, and legal consequence is to return to square one, where Continental's taxable income is the interest it actually received. The tax years about which the parties are wrangling are "open," meaning that no final determination of Continental's tax liability for those years has been made; and there is no suggestion that a restatement of its interest income for those years would confer a windfall on Continental. It would be the tax equivalent of entrapment for the IRS, having in effect invited Continental to restate its net loan income in a form that would permit the bank to claim foreign tax credits, now to insist on taxing the bank on a phantom income figure—the x rate that would have benefited Continental had its claim of foreign tax credits been accepted but that confers no benefit now that the claim has been rejected.

The IRS's argument that Continental has failed to prove that the foreign taxes were not paid (for if they were paid, then Continental's income really was x) is barred by the doctrine of judicial estoppel, which forbids a litigant to repudiate a legal position on which it has prevailed. It is true that the doctrine is usually applied to successive suits, *Astor Chauffeured Limousine Co. v. Runnfeldt Investment Corp.*, 910 F.2d 1540, 1547–48 (7th Cir.1990), but it is not so limited. *Witham v. Whiting Corp.*, 975 F.2d 1342, 1345 (7th Cir.1992). A party can argue inconsistent positions in the alternative, but once it has sold one to the court it cannot turn around and repudiate it in order to have a second victory, which is what the IRS is seeking here. Having persuaded us to reject Continental's effort to show that the taxes were paid, the IRS may not argue against a restatement of income on the ground that they really were paid. Either they were or they weren't. If they were, Continental is entitled to a foreign tax credit, and if they weren't, it is entitled to restate its income to take the foreign taxes out.

The IRS argues in the alternative (!) that if the taxes were not paid, Continental's only remedy is to claim a bad-debt deduction against income in the year in which the borrower reneged on its implied obligation to pay the local tax on interest income earned by Continental. Such an implied obligation would arise if, should the borrower fail to pay the tax, Continental would be liable to the foreign taxing authorities, for if so the borrower is obligated to Continental to pay the local tax due on the interest income generated by the loan. But there is no indication that any such obligation either existed or was violated. The taxes may have been paid after all, or may never have been due, or, what the IRS itself treats as the same thing (Technical Advice Memorandum 86003 (Dec. 30, 1985)), the tax law of the foreign country might not be enforced, or Continental may have borne no residual liability for the tax (the case in Brazil, as we are about to see). Judicial estoppel prevents our considering the first possibility; the others are ones in which there was (either de jure or de facto—and we have noted that the IRS treats these the same) no obligation to the foreign authorities, hence no implied obligation to Continental, hence no debt to go bad. We conclude that Continental is entitled to restate its income to take out the foreign taxes on which foreign tax credits were disallowed.

Net loans that Continental made to Brazilian borrowers raise a separate issue. Here Continental was able to satisfy the IRS that the local taxes really had been paid by the borrowers, but the IRS still refused to allow foreign tax credits, and this on two grounds. The first, which the Tax Court correctly rejected, is that under Brazilian law the tax is not on the lender at all, but, although called a withholding tax and computed on the basis of the lender's Brazilian income, on the borrower. The argument is semantic. Brazilian law makes the borrower exclusively responsible for paying the tax only in the sense that there is no remedy against the lender if the borrower fails to pay, whereas in some other countries the taxing authorities can go after the taxpayer himself if the employer or other withholder absconds. This is a distinction without a difference as far as foreign lenders to Brazilian borrowers are concerned. The Brazilian banking authorities will not allow a Brazilian borrower to buy foreign currency with which to pay interest to an American lender unless the borrower establishes that he has withheld and remitted the proper amount of taxes.

Naturally the Brazilian and American tax systems are not identical, but the differences between them with respect to withholding are too minor to justify a conclusion that Brazil is "really" taxing the borrower and not the lender. The essential similarity is that the tax is based on the income received by the lender. Such a tax is an income tax. Actually it is a gross-receipts tax rather than an income tax, because the cost of lending is not netted out of the interest received by the lender. But the IRS treats it as an income tax, and the correct characterization is not important to this case. See Private Letter Rul. 76–1123–9900A (Nov. 23, 1976); 1 Joseph Isenbergh, International Taxation PP 18.4–18.7, 18.26–18.29, at pp. 497–502, 526–29 (1990). At all events, the tax is "paid" by the lender even if the borrower operates as his agent for payment and even if the tax enforcement guns are trained on the agent rather than on the principal. *Citizens & Southern Corp. v. Commissioner, 919 F.2d 1492 (11th Cir.1990),* affirming without opinion *Continental Illinois Corp. v. Commissioner, 55 T.C.M. (CCH) 1325, 1330 (1988); Nissho Iwai American Corp. v. Commissioner, 89 T.C. 765, 773–74 (1987).*

The second ground for rejecting foreign tax credits on the Brazilian net loans, the ground the Tax Court correctly in our view accepted, is that beginning in 1975 the Brazilian government rebated most of the withheld taxes. (The part not rebated is entitled to foreign tax credit.) The year before, in an effort to stimulate foreign investment, the Brazilian government had slashed the tax rate on interest on foreign loans from 25 percent to 5 percent. This was fine for net loans, but had a boomerang effect on gross loans, though they were a distinct minority of all foreign loans. The tax cut increased the amount of foreign currency that the borrower had to buy to pay interest on a gross loan. Before on a 12 percent gross loan the borrower had paid 9 percent in foreign currency to the lender and the rest to the government in cruzeiros; now the borrower paid 11.4 percent (.12–.05(.12)) in foreign currency to the lender. So the following year Brazil passed a law restoring the 25 percent tax rate but rebating 20 percent to the borrowers, leaving the latter with a 5 percent effective tax rate. Continental claims to be entitled to treat the full 25 percent as a foreign tax that it can credit against its U.S. tax liability. The IRS argues that the 25 percent must be reduced by the rebate, so that the creditable tax rate is only 5 percent.

The IRS has two grounds, both accepted by the Tax Court, only one unsound. The unsound one is based on the principle of substance over form: an arrangement that has no rationale other than to beat taxes can be disregarded. *Yosha v. Commissioner, 861 F.2d 494 (7th Cir. 1988); Bramblett v. Commissioner, 960 F.2d 526, 533 (5th Cir.1992)*. To rebate local taxes merely to generate foreign tax credits for a U.S. taxpayer to the ultimate benefit of the locals who do business with that taxpayer would qualify for the application of this principle. But as Continental points out, there is no evidence that this was the purpose of the rebate or the only effect. Brazil did want to preserve its stimulus for foreign investment yet stem a foreign-currency hemorrhage, and it chose a method of doing so that it might have chosen were there no U.S. foreign tax credit, for the rebate lowered the costs of Brazilian borrowers from foreign banks without increasing the amount of foreign currency that had to be paid those banks in the short run.

The other ground for knocking down the foreign tax credit to the post-rebate tax rate is Temp. Treas. Reg. § 4.901–2(f)(3), *45 Fed. Reg. 7563* (Nov. 17, 1980), 26 C.F.R. § 4.901–2(f)(3) (1981) (and, for Continental's 1978 taxable year, a revenue ruling to the same effect, *II Rev. Rul. 78–258, 1978–1 Cum. Bull. 239)*, which disallows foreign tax credit to the extent that the tax is used to subsidize the taxpayer. The temporary regulation is defunct, but its principle, and indeed virtually its exact words, have now been incorporated into the Internal Revenue Code. *26 U.S.C. § 901*(i).

"Subsidy" is a tricky concept. It is by no means clear that the Brazilian tax rebate subsidized, in the sense of conferring an actual benefit upon, American net lenders like Continental. Joseph Isenbergh, "The Foreign Tax Credit: Royalties, Subsidies, and Creditable Taxes," *39 Tax L. Rev. 227, 244–47 (1984)*; 1 Isenbergh, supra, P 18.10.2 at pp. 507–08. Indeed, insofar as the interest rate had been fixed in the loan contract before the rebate was instituted, only the borrowers benefited; for we noted at the outset that the difference between a net and a gross loan is that a net loan allocates the risk and benefit of any change in the tax rate to the borrower because the lender's return is specified net of tax. Even if not frozen by the contract the interest rate might not rise by the amount of the subsidy. It is true that the subsidy would make the borrowers more eager to take out foreign loans and that an increase in demand usually results in an increase in price, but the increase in demand need not be proportionally equal to the increase in price and it would be tempered here by competition among the foreign lenders; also, Brazil imposed ceilings on interest rates. Figuring out who gets how much of the benefit of a subsidy is like figuring out who really pays a tax, since the nominal taxpayer has an incentive to shift it as best he can forward or backward. It all depends on contract terms and on conditions of demand and supply.

The IRS regulation (now codified by Congress, as we noted) elides a difficult factual inquiry by deeming the taxpayer subsidized if the country subsidizes a person with whom the taxpayer "engages in a business transaction," provided the subsidy "is determined directly or indirectly by reference to the amount of income tax . . . imposed by the country on [that] person with respect to such transaction." Temp. Treas. Reg. § 4.901–2(f)(3)(ii)(B). That description fits this case to a t. The borrower gets the subsidy, he engages in a business transaction with the U.S. taxpayer (the loan), and the subsidy is measured by the local tax on the U.S. lender's local income; it is 80 percent of that tax (20 percent vs. 25 percent). The regulation is clear as a bell, and its validity cannot seriously be questioned, even if we disregard its later codification by Congress. Just as the IRS must be given leeway in deciding what proof to require that a tax has actually been paid, so it must be given leeway in deciding when a rebate to a foreign business partner of a U.S. taxpayer should be deemed a subsidy to the taxpayer, disentitling him to a foreign tax credit. The IRS can hardly be faulted for having chosen a bright-line approach in preference to interminable investigation of the mysteries of public finance, much as the latter approach might appeal to the legal, accounting, and economic-consulting communities. The Supreme Court has chosen a similar bright-line approach for resolving the analytically identical problem posed by the passing-on of price increases by antitrust plaintiffs. *Illinois Brick Co. v. Illinois, 431 U.S. 720, 52 L. Ed. 2d 707, 97 S. Ct. 2061 (1977).* See also *McKesson Corp. v. Division of Alcoholic Beverages & Tobacco, 496 U.S. 18, 46–47, 110 L. Ed. 2d 17, 110 S. Ct. 2238 (1990).*

We need not discuss separately the so-called "repass" loans, where the subsidy was paid not to the borrowers but to local banks with which Continental transacted—but the banks were required to pass the subsidy on to the borrowers. These loans fell within the letter as well as the spirit of the subsidy regulation. The statutory codification eliminates all possible doubt for the future. *26 U.S.C. § 901*(i)(1).

The last issue we discuss is whether the Tax Court was correct to require Continental to report as income[,] interest that the bank received subject to a contingent obligation to rebate it to the borrower. Beginning in 1972 Continental offered what it called "CAP" loans to some of its corporate borrowers. These loans usually had a fixed term of five to ten years. Interest, rather than being fixed in advance, was computed as a percentage of or over the prime rate. This floating rate was capped by a fixed rate specified in the loan contract, and Continental agreed that if at the expiration of the loan the borrower had neither defaulted on nor prepaid the loan Continental would refund any interest that it had received above the cap rate. When Continental received an interest payment that exceeded the cap rate (because the floating rate had floated above it), it reported only the cap rate as income. The excess it carried on its books "as interest collected but not earned." If it received an interest payment that was below the cap rate because the floating rate was below it, it would treat the payment as income, and if there was a balance in the borrower's "interest collected but not earned" account it would add to the interest payment that it had received so much of the balance in the account as necessary to equal the cap rate, and it would treat the sum an income, debiting the borrower's excess-interest account.

When Continental instituted its CAP loan program it thought the cap rate would on average exceed the floating rate; it was offering the borrowers insurance rather than a lower expected price of money. But because of the unexpectedly steep inflation during the 1970s, the floating rate regularly pierced the cap, requiring Continental to make substantial refunds to its borrowers. It claims not to be required to treat any interest it received above the cap rate during the life of the loan as income, since such receipts were subject to a contractual obligation to be refunded at the expiration of the loan.

Not every receipt is income. A deposit, for example, is not. *Commissioner v. Indianapolis Power & Light Co., 493 U.S. 203, 107 L. Ed. 2d 591, 110 S. Ct. 589 (1990); Illinois Power Co. v. Commissioner, 792 F.2d 683, 689–90 (7th Cir.1986).* The recipient—bank, landlord, electric utility, whatever—holds the money under obligation (albeit defeasible) to return it. On the other hand income does not cease to be such because there is some likelihood that the recipient may have to give it back. For there is always some likelihood of that. The income that a seller receives from the sale of goods may have to be refunded because the goods were defective or the seller broke the contract of sale in some other way—and some sellers offer to take goods back and refund the buyer's money with no questions asked. A seller who offers a discount for customers who buy a minimum amount in the course of a year receives income from those customers subject to a contingent obligation to repay a portion to those customers who reach the minimum. Such contingencies have never been thought to entitle a seller to delay recognizing income until the time during which the contingencies could have materialized is past.

Ours is an intermediate case. The seller (here the lender) is not merely holding the money that he receives from the sale of his goods (or here the rent of his money) in the account of the buyer (borrower), as if it were a deposit; but the likelihood that he will have to repay much or even all of this "income" to the customers is substantial. There is no bright line that can be used for classifying such a case, and much therefore must be left to the Internal Revenue Service's discretion, *Thor Power Tool Co. v. Commissioner, 439 U.S. 522, 532–33, 58 L. Ed. 2d 785, 99 S. Ct. 773 (1979),* not here abused. When Continental embarked upon its CAP loan program it expected to be able to keep the interest generated by the floating rate. The cap was for insurance. It was like a guarantee, specifically like a seller's promise to rebate a portion of the purchase price if the customer establishes that he could have bought the same good from another seller at a lower price. Guarantees of this sort resemble warranties against defective goods. They reduce the certainty of the seller's income stream but do not convert income into the equivalent of a deposit or a bailment.

No other issues need be discussed. The judgment of the Tax Court is affirmed in part and reversed in part, as indicated in this opinion, and the case is remanded to that court for such further proceedings as may be appropriate in light of this opinion.

NOTES AND QUESTIONS

1. What do you think of the receipt requirement? Is this a realistic demand by the IRS?

2. Why is it important to have both the date and amount of tax payment stated on the receipt?

3. What happens if a tax was duly paid, but then refunded to the taxpayer in a subsequent year due to a statutory change in the foreign country? See Treas. Reg. § 1.901–2(e)(2).

4. What is the problem with taxes used to provide subsidies? See section 901(i). Is this definition clear? How would you clarify it? See Treas. Reg. § 1.901–2(e)(3).

5. Read Treas. Reg. §§ 1.901–2(c) & 1.903–1, and then the following Revenue Ruling:

* * *

Rev. Rul. 2003–8

ISSUE

[1] Are the withholding taxes specified in Article 61 of the Costa Rican Income Tax Law creditable taxes under sections 901 and 903 of the Internal Revenue Code of 1986?

FACTS

[2] Costa Rica's income tax law imposes a withholding tax on various types of income paid to persons operating or residing outside of Costa Rica at rates specified in Costa Rican Income Tax Law Article 59. The Costa Rican Tax Administration has authority to grant a total or partial exemption from liability for withholding taxes on profits, dividends, social participation, interest, commissions, financial expenses, patents, royalties, reinsurance, consolidation and insurance premiums of all types referred to in Article 59. Costa Rican Income Tax Law art. 61. The exemption can be given if the persons who act as withholding or receiving agents, or the interested parties, prove, to the satisfaction of the Costa Rican Tax Administration, that the recipient of such income is not granted in the country in which it operates or resides any credit against its tax liability for the withholding tax that was paid to Costa Rica. *Id*. In order to claim an exemption under Article 61, the

Costa Rican Tax Administration requires the foreign recipient or its withholding agent to provide certification from the tax authorities of the country in which the recipient operates or resides verifying that the tax is not creditable in that country. Costa Rican Income Tax Regulation art. 65.

LAW AND ANALYSIS

[3] Section 901 of the Code allows a credit against United States income tax for the amount of any income, war profits, and excess profits taxes paid or accrued to any foreign country. Section 1.901–2(a)(1) of the Income Tax Regulations provides that a foreign levy is an income tax only if it is a tax, and if the predominant character of that tax is an income tax in the United States sense. Section 1.901–2(a)(3)(ii) provides that the predominant character of a foreign tax is that of an income tax in the United States sense only to the extent that liability for the tax is not dependent, by its terms or otherwise, on the availability of a credit for the tax against income tax liability to another country. Section 1.901–2(c)(1) provides that liability for foreign tax is dependent on the availability of a credit for the foreign tax against income tax liability to another country only if and to the extent that the foreign tax would not be imposed on the taxpayer but for the availability of such a credit.

[4] Section 903 of the Code allows a credit against United States income tax for an amount of tax paid or accrued "in lieu of" an income, war profits or excess profits tax otherwise generally imposed by any foreign country. Section 1.903–1(a) of the regulations provides that a foreign levy is a tax in lieu of an income tax only if it is a tax, and it meets the "substitution requirement" of section 1.903–1(b). Section 1.903–1(b)(2) provides that a foreign tax meets the substitution requirement only to the extent that the liability for the foreign tax is not dependent (by its terms or otherwise) on the availability of a credit for the foreign tax against the income tax liability to another country.

[5] Therefore, if a foreign country imposes a withholding tax only in the event that a credit for the tax is available from the recipient's country of domicile, the tax is not creditable under section 901 or 903.

HOLDING

[6] The withholding taxes referred to in Article 61 of the Costa Rican Income Tax Law are not creditable taxes under section 901 or 903 of the Code since they are imposed only in the event that a credit for the tax is available from the country in which the recipient operates or resides. This ruling is an official confirmation by the Internal Revenue Service that the withholding taxes referred to in Article 61 are not creditable in the United States."

What seems to be the reason for the adoption of the Costa Rican tax? Note that the tax applies regardless of the method of relief employed by the residence country of the investor.

6. In many foreign tax systems, the corporate tax is treated as an advance payment of the shareholder's tax liability, which is then credited to the shareholder upon receipt of a dividend. Does this raise a subsidy issue?

7. Note that 2007 proposed regulations and 2008 proposed, temporary and final regulations (amending the proposed regulations in part) expand (or clarify) the "tax paid" requirement for a foreign tax credit by reinforcing Treas. Reg. § 1.901–2(e)(5) that defines noncompulsory payment of taxes to include certain transactions intended to provide (or inflate) foreign tax credits inappropriately (the so-called foreign tax credit generator transactions). Final regulations were issued in 2013.

b. WAS A TAX PAID BY THE TAXPAYER?

The second hoop that the taxpayer seeking the credit is required to pass through is the requirement that she (and not somebody else) was the one who actually paid the foreign tax. This raises the question what type of payment is exactly required? Does it need to be direct or whether the economic burden of the tax matters? The Supreme Court began to settle this issue in the following case.

Biddle v. Commissioner of Internal Revenue

Supreme Court of the United States.
302 U.S. 573 (1938).

■ OPINION: MR. JUSTICE STONE delivered the opinion of the Court.

In their British income tax returns, stockholders in British corporations are required to report as income, in addition to the amount of dividends actually received, amounts which reflect their respective proportions of the tax paid by the corporation on its own profits. The principal question raised by these petitions is whether these amounts constitute "income . . . taxes paid or accrued during the taxable year to [a] foreign country" so as to entitle the stockholders, if they are citizens of the United States, to credits of those amounts upon their United States income tax, by virtue of § 131(a)(1) of the Revenue Act of 1928. A further question is whether any of the amounts not so available as a credit may be deducted from gross income under § 23(c)(2) of the Act for the purpose of ascertaining the net income subject to tax.

Petitioner in No. 55 and respondent in No. 505, hereafter called the taxpayers, received cash dividends during the taxable years 1929 and 1931, respectively, on their stock in three British corporations. Each of the corporations having itself paid or become liable to pay the British tax on the profits thus distributed, no further exaction at the "standard" (normal) rate was due the British government on account of the distribution from either the stockholders or the corporation.[1] Only in the case of individuals whose income exceeds a stated amount is a surtax levied. In these circumstances the corporations are directed to certify to shareholders, at the time of sending out warrants for the dividends, the gross amount from which the income tax "appropriate thereto" is deducted, the rate and amount of the income tax appropriate to the gross amount, and the net amount actually paid.[2]

The tax "appropriate" to the dividend is computed by applying the standard rate for the year of distribution, to the value of the money or other property distributed.[3] The amount so computed will equal the tax paid at the standard rate by the corporation on its profits if, but only if, the tax rate is the same in the year when the profits are earned as in the year when they are distributed.

One of the companies availed itself of the statutory permission[4] to declare a gross dividend, from which it deducted the tax before actual distribution, certifying to the taxpayers that the dividend would be paid "less" income tax. The other two companies declared the dividend in the amount distributed to stockholders and certified that it was "free of tax." The certificates of the latter did not purport to show any deduction of tax from a gross dividend, but did indicate the amount of the tax appropriate to the dividend and showed the same net return to stockholders as if the tax had been deducted from a computed gross dividend.

In their returns transmitted to the Department of Inland Revenue of the British government, the taxpayers reported as income subject to surtax the amount of income taxes appropriate to their dividends, in addition to the money actually received, and paid surtaxes on that total sum. In their United States income tax returns for those years, the taxpayers included in gross income the entire sums so reported in the British returns. Up to the limit set by § 131(b), they claimed as credits against the tax payable to the United States the amount of British tax appropriate to the dividends as well as the amount of surtax paid. A deduction from gross income was claimed under § 23(c)(2) for the amount by which the limit was exceeded.

---

[1] British Income Tax Act 1918, 8 and 9 Geo. V, c. 40, as amended by § 38, Finance Act of 1927, 17 and 18 Geo. V, c. 10. General Rule 1 of the 1918 Act provides, "Every body of persons shall be chargeable to tax in like manner as any person is chargeable under the provisions of this Act." By § 237 of the 1918 Act "body of persons" includes "any company . . . whether corporate or not corporate."

[2] Section 33, Finance Act of 1924, 14 and 15 Geo. V, c. 21.

[3] The Act of 1918 prescribes general rules for the assessment and collection of taxes "on profits from property, trade or business." By General Rule 20 it is provided that the tax is to be paid on the "full amount" of the profit "before any dividend thereof is made in respect of any share . . . and the body of persons paying such dividend shall be entitled to deduct the tax appropriate thereto." The tax "appropriate" to a dividend payment is the standard rate of tax for the year in which the dividend is declared, regardless of the rate at which the amount distributed was in fact taxed when it was received by the company. Hamilton v. Commissioners of Inland Revenue, 16 British Tax Cases, 213, 229, 234; Neumann v. Commissioners of Inland Revenue, 18 British Tax Cases, 332, 359, 361.

[4] General Rule 20, Income Tax of 1918.

Deficiency assessments of the taxpayers were brought to the Board of Tax Appeals for review. There the issues were narrowed to the questions now before us, whether the taxpayers, after adding to gross income the amounts included in the British returns as taxes appropriate to the dividends received, were then entitled to deduct those amounts from the tax as computed, to the extent permitted by § 131(b), and whether the excess was a permissible deduction from gross income.

The board held that the sums in dispute should not have been included in gross income, because they represented neither property received by the taxpayers nor the discharge of any taxes owed by them to the British government. It held further that § 131(a)(1) of the Revenue Act of 1928, which directs that the income tax be credited with "the amount of any income . . . taxes paid or accrued during the taxable year to any foreign country . . ." is inapplicable because the United Kingdom fails to tax dividends at the normal rate, and hence the taxes appropriate to dividends were paid by the corporations rather than the taxpayer stockholders.

In No. 55 the Court of Appeals for the Second Circuit affirmed the determination of the board, *86 F.2d 718,* since followed by that circuit in *F. W. Woolworth Co. v. United States, 91 F.2d 973*, and the Court of Appeals for the Third Circuit, in No. 505, reversed, *91 F.2d 534,* following a decision of the Court of Appeals for the First Circuit in *United Shoe Machinery Corp. v. White, 89 F.2d 363.* We granted certiorari to resolve this conflict of decision, and because of the importance of the question in the administration of the revenue laws. At the outset it is to be observed that decision must turn on the precise meaning of the words in the statute which grants to the citizen taxpayer a credit for foreign "income taxes paid." The power to tax and to grant the credit resides in Congress, and it is the will of Congress which controls the application of the provisions for credit. The expression of its will in legislation must be taken to conform to its own criteria unless the statute, by express language or necessary implication, makes the meaning of the phrase "paid or accrued," and hence the operation of the statute in which it occurs, depend upon its characterization by the foreign statutes and by decisions under them. Cf. *Crew Levick Co. v. Pennsylvania*, 245 U.S. 292, 294; *Weiss v. Weiner*, 279 U.S. 333, 337; *Burnet v. Harmel*, 287 U.S. 103, 110.

Section 131 does not say that the meaning of its words is to be determined by foreign taxing statutes and decisions, and there is nothing in its language to suggest that in allowing the credit for foreign tax payments, a shifting standard was adopted by reference to foreign characterizations and classifications of tax legislation. The phrase "income taxes paid," as used in our own revenue laws, has for most practical purposes a well understood meaning to be derived from an examination of the statutes which provide for the laying and collection of income taxes. It is that meaning which must be attributed to it as used in § 131.

Hence the board's finding, supported as it is by much expert testimony, that "the stockholder receiving the dividend is regarded in the English income tax acts as having paid 'by deduction or otherwise' the tax 'appropriate' to the dividend" is not conclusive. At most it is but a factor to be considered in deciding whether the stockholder pays the tax within the meaning of our own statute. That must ultimately be determined by ascertaining from an examination of the manner in which the British tax is laid and collected what the stockholder has done in conformity to British law and whether it is the substantial equivalent of payment of the tax as those terms are used in our own statute.

We are here concerned only with the "standard" or normal tax. The scheme of the British legislation is to impose on corporate earnings only one standard tax, at the source, and to avoid the "double" taxation of the corporate income as it passes to the hands of its stockholders, except as they are subject to surtax which the corporation does not pay. The corporation pays the standard tax and against it the remedies for non-payment run. It has been intimated that the shareholder may be held to payment of the tax in the event of the corporation's default, *Hamilton v. Commissioners of Inland Revenue*, 16 British Tax Cases, 213, 236, but the contrary view finds more support in judicial opinion, id. at 230; *Dalgety & Co., Ltd. v. Commissioners of Inland Revenue*, 15 British Tax Cases, 216, 238; *Neumann v. Commissioners of Inland Revenue*, 18 British Tax Cases, 341, 345, 358, 362–363, 368, and was adopted by the taxpayers' expert.

Although the corporation, in the United Kingdom as here, pays the tax and is bound to pay it, the tax burden in point of substance is passed on to the stockholders in the same way that it is passed on under our own taxing acts where the tax on the corporate income is charged as an expense before any part of the resulting net profit is distributed to stockholders. See Magill, Taxable Income, 24 et seq. Whether the tax is deducted from gross profits before a dividend is declared, or after, when the deduction is taken from the gross dividend, the net amount received by the stockholder is the same. Under either system, if no dividend is declared no tax is paid by the stockholder.[5] If a dividend is declared it must be paid, however the deduction is made, from what is left after the corporation has paid taxes upon its earnings. The differences in the two methods of deduction are to be found only in the formal bookkeeping data which, in the British system, are communicated to the stockholders, not for the purpose of laying or collecting the tax which the corporation has already paid or must pay, but to aid the stockholders in computing their surtax and in securing the benefit of any refund of the tax.

---

[5]   Cf. *Dalgety & Co., Ltd. v. Commissioners of Inland Revenue*, 15 British Tax Cases 216, 238; *Neumann v. Commissioners of Inland Revenue*, 18 British Tax Cases 341, 345, 358, 362–363, 368.

The stockholders' surtax is computed upon the gross dividend, the dividend which he actually receives plus the tax deducted.[6] If the stockholder's income is exempt or less than the minimum amount subject to the tax, refund is made to him of the proportionate share of the tax paid by the corporation.[7] It is upon these features of the British system that the taxpayers chiefly rely to support their argument that the stockholder pays the tax. For these limited purposes, which do not affect the assessment and payment of the tax, it is true that the British acts treat the stockholder as though he were the taxpayer. But with respect to the surtax the stockholder pays it and the taxpayers here have received for its payment the credit which our statute allows. Inclusion of the deducted amount in the base on which surtax is calculated, together with the provisions for refund of the tax to the stockholder who, in any event, bears its economic burden, are logical recognitions of the British conception that the standard tax paid by the corporation is passed on to the stockholders.

Our revenue laws give no recognition to that conception. Although the tax burden of the corporation is passed on to its stockholders with substantially the same results to them as under the British system, our statutes take no account of that fact in establishing the rights and obligations of taxpayers. Until recently they have not laid a tax, except surtax, on dividends, but they have never treated the stockholder for any purpose as paying the tax collected from the corporation. Nor have they treated as taxpayers those upon whom no legal duty to pay the tax is laid. Measured by these standards our statutes afford no scope for saying that the stockholder of a British corporation pays the tax which is laid upon and collected from the corporation, and no basis for a decision that § 131 extends to such a stockholder a credit for a tax paid by the corporation— a privilege not granted to stockholders in our own corporations. It can hardly be said that a tax paid to the Crown by a British corporation subject to United States income tax is not a tax paid within the meaning of § 23(c) (2), of the 1928 Act, which allows a deduction from gross income for taxes paid to a foreign country, cf. *Welch v. St. Helens Petroleum Co., 78 F.2d 631,* or that its stockholders could take credit under § 131 for their share of the tax on the theory that they also had paid it. The taxpayers urge that departmental rulings sustaining credits or deductions by stockholders of British corporations, S. M. 3040, IV-1 C. B. 198; S. M. 5363, V-1 C. B. 89; I. T. 2401, VII-1 C. B. 126; G. C. M. 3179, VII-1 C. B. 240, have taken on the force of law by virtue of the reenactment of the deduction and credit provisions carried into §§ 23 and 131 of the 1928 Act. Laying aside the fact that departmental rulings not promulgated by the Secretary are of little aid in interpreting a tax statute, *Helvering v. New York Trust Co., 292 U.S. 455, 467–468,* these

---

[6]   Hamilton v. Commissioners of Inland Revenue, 16 British Tax Cases 213, 229, 234; Neumann v. Commissioners of Inland Revenue, 18 British Tax Cases 332, 345, 358–360, 361.

[7]   Income Tax Act of 1918, §§ 29(1), 55(1), 211(1) as amended by Finance Act, 1920, § 27(1).

rulings rest for their conclusions as to the application of § 131 upon their interpretation of the nature and effect of the British legislation. The presumption that Congress, in reenacting a statute, can ascertain the course of administrative interpretation and, knowing its own intent, will correct the administrative ruling if mistaken, cannot apply to rulings upon the intent of other legislative bodies. So far as the rulings with which we are now concerned sought to state the force and effect of British law they can have no more binding effect on courts than in the case of any determination of fact which calls into operation the taxing statutes. So far as they have construed our own statute as adopting the British characterization, they plainly misinterpret an unambiguous provision. Where the law is plain the subsequent reenactment of a statute does not constitute adoption of its administrative construction. *Iselin v. United States, 270 U.S. 245; Louisville & N. R. Co. v. United States, 282 U.S. 740; Helvering v. New York Trust Co., supra.*

What we have said is decisive of the second question, whether any of the amounts not available for credit under § 131 may be deducted from gross income for the purpose of arriving at taxable net income. By § 23(c)(2) of the 1928 Act the deductions of "income . . . taxes imposed by the authority of any foreign country" are limited to taxes paid or accrued. Since we have held that the taxpayer has not paid or become subject to the foreign tax here in question, the section by its terms is inapplicable.

* * *

NOTES AND QUESTIONS

1. Was it reasonable not to grant a credit under these circumstances? What is the result in terms of the incentive to invest in U.K. vs. U.S. corporations?

2. Section 302(a) of the Jobs and Growth Tax Relief Reconciliation Act of 2003 ("JGTRRA") (Pub. L. 108–27) amended IRC Section 1(h) by adding a new section 1(h)(11), which extended capital gains' treatment (15% flat rate) to the "qualified dividend income." Section 1(h)(11)(C)(iv) provides that rules similar to Section 904(b)(2)(B) (adjustment of the foreign tax credit limitations to the preferential capital gains' tax rate) apply with respect to this dividend rate differential. Note that since foreign tax credits are allowed only against foreign source income, the application of Section 904(b)(2)(B) has been uncommon as long as it applied solely to capital gains; the abundance of foreign source dividends should make its application ubiquitous now.

3. What if the taxpayers were corporations and held over 10% of the stock of the U.K. corporations? Note that Section 902 (discussed below) has been repealed. What has effectively replaced for these corporate, 10% shareholders? See Section 245A.

4. An interesting development in regard to the issue of "who is the taxpayer" is the *Guardian Industries* case (infra, page 441), which was affirmed on appeal (infra, note 3, page 444). Note that the scheme in this case and similar schemes follow the logic of the *Biddle* decision, and the government's position is conceptually reverse to its position that generated the technical taxpayer rule originally. Of course, this may be justified as necessary on anti-abuse grounds. Note also the particular role that "check-the-box" plays in this scheme. Similar tax planning is possible even without using "check-the-box," but, as some say, "check-the-box" just made it (much) easier. Read also Treas. Reg. § 1.901–2(f), revised in 2012. Tax reform discussions have frequently included the possibility of changes to the check-the-box rules because of their role in international tax planning. But as yet, tax reform since 1996 (when the check-the-box regulations were issued) has left these rules untouched.

5.   Note the emphasis on the person responsible under foreign law to pay the tax. This means that the actual incidence or burden of the tax is not relevant (see *Continental Illinois*, above). This is called the "technical taxpayer rule" (read Treas. Reg. § 1.901–2(f)), and it has caused its own problems (think about the planning opportunities that a technical rule, which applies to a reality that may realistically be different the economic reality, presents), discussed below. It has also given rise to the phenomenon of foreign countries hiring U.S. tax counsel to write their tax laws to make sure taxes are creditable although the taxpayer does not bear the burden of the tax. The third hoop, discussed next, is designed to fight this phenomenon.

c.   WAS THE TAX A CREDITABLE TAX?

Inland Steel Company v. United States

United States Court of Claims.
230 Ct.Cl. 314, 677 F.2d 72 (1982).

■ OPINION BY: PER CURIAM*

The court adopts the trial judge's findings of fact, with the changes indicated in the order entered this day, but the findings are not reproduced with this opinion. Any findings contained in this opinion that are not also embodied in the formal findings shall likewise be considered part of the court's findings.

Opinion: Inland Steel Company, an integrated steel manufacturer, claimed refunds for taxes paid for calendar years 1964 and 1965 on four issues, two of which have been compromised and dismissed. Two issues, the deductibility of certain accruals in Inland's Supplemental Unemployment Benefit plan (SUB) and credit for taxes paid pursuant to the Ontario Mining Tax Act (OMT), have been tried and are disposed of in this opinion, in Parts I and II respectively.

. . .

---

*   This opinion has its basis in that of Trial Judge Harkins, with several modifications, deletions, additions, and rearrangements. We reach the same results.

II

Ontario Mining Tax

Plaintiff conducted an iron ore mining operation in Atikokan, Ontario, in 1964 and 1965 through a wholly-owned subsidiary, Caland Ore Company, Limited (Caland). Development of the open pit iron ore mine began in approximately 1952 or 1953 on property leased from Steep Rock Iron Ore Mine Company, a privately-owned company; commercial production started in 1960 or 1961. From the start of operations, and during 1964, Caland sold unprocessed ore that was shipped directly from the mine site as soon as it was mined. Caland did not maintain an inventory of unsold ore at year-end. In 1965, Caland sold both iron ore and pellets produced in a processing operation that commenced that year. In 1965, at year-end Caland had an unsold inventory of unprocessed ore at the mine site.

Caland paid taxes on its mining operation under the Ontario Mining Tax Act[13] (OMT) which were claimed as an I.R.C. § 901 foreign tax credit on plaintiff's consolidated United States federal income tax return. In the relevant years, the Internal Revenue Service required the OMT payments to be reported as deductions under I.R.C. § 164. Calands' 1964 OMT payment of $947,537 was based solely on sales of unprocessed iron ore. Caland's 1965 OMT payment, as finally approved by the Ontario mine assessor, was based solely on the proceeds of sales of unprocessed iron ore and processed pellets, and the 1965 OMT return did not include a valuation for Caland's inventory of unsold ore. Caland's 1965 OMT tax payment was $365,412; Caland claims a total of $1,006,906 as available for carryover and carryback to 1965. The sum of all OMT amounts in issue is $2,589,855.

In addition to its OMT tax payments, in 1964 and 1965, Caland was subject to and paid income taxes to Canada, under the Income Tax Act of Canada, and to Ontario under the Ontario Corporation Tax Act. Plaintiff has obtained I.R.C. § 901 foreign tax credit for the amounts paid pursuant to those income tax laws.[14]

The tax credit in I.R.C. § 901[15] is a device designed to eliminate double taxation on income generated in a "foreign country," which the Treasury Regulations define to include any foreign state or political subdivision.[16] Whether a foreign tax is an income tax under I.R.C. § 901(b)(1) is to be decided under criteria established by United States revenue laws and court decisions. To be creditable, the foreign tax must

---

[13] Ont. Rev. Stat. c. 242 (1960).

[14] Plaintiff's petition also sought credit under I.R.C. § 903 for the OMT payments. This issue has not been pursued and is considered to be abandoned.

[15] *26 U.S.C. § 901*(b)(1) (1976) provides a credit to United States income taxpayers for the "amount of any income, war profits and excess profits taxes paid or accrued during the taxable year to any foreign country. . . ."

[16] Treas. Reg. § 1.901–2(b) (1960).

[handwritten margin note: creditable credits standard.]

be the substantial equivalent of an income tax as that term is understood in the United States.[17]

I.R.C. § 901(b)(1) provides an exemption from taxation to the extent of the tax paid to the foreign country. It is a privilege extended by legislative grace, and the exemption must be strictly construed.[18] The purpose of the foreign tax credit is to encourage domestic corporations to do business abroad without having to operate through a foreign corporation.[19] The primary objective of the foreign tax credit, however, is to prevent double taxation; encouragement of American foreign trade is a secondary objective.[20]

A.   The test. In *Bank of America*,[21] this court has distilled the authorities and articulated the applicable test. To qualify as an income tax in the United States sense, the foreign country must have made an attempt always to reach some net gain in the normal circumstances in which the tax applies. Taxes plainly on subjects other than income, even though measured to some extent by income, are not income taxes. The label and form of the foreign tax is not determinative. In *Bank of America*, where the court had before it taxes on gross income from the banking business, the test was stated as follows:[22]

[handwritten margin note: Test.]

This review of the pertinent judicial decisions and Internal Revenue Service rulings, as well as of comparable gross income levies in the federal income tax system, persuades us that the term "income tax" in § 901(b)(1) covers all foreign income taxes designed to fall on some net gain or profit, and includes a gross income tax if, but only if, that impost is almost sure, or very likely, to reach some net gain because costs or expenses will not be so high as to offset the net profit.

In that case, the special banking levies did not qualify for the credit because no provision was made to account for the costs or expenses of producing the income. The tax would fall on banks that were successful as well as those that were unsuccessful. Failure to take into account operating expenses normal to an active business indicated the governments involved had not designed the taxes to "nip" net profit.

The court's analysis in *Bank of America* shows that it is important, for the foreign tax credit, to determine the expenses of which the foreign tax takes account, in order to see whether taxation of net gain is the

---

[17] *Biddle v. Commissioner, 302 U.S. 573 (1938); Missouri Pacific R.R. v. United States, 183 Ct. Cl. 168, 175, 392 F.2d 592, 597 (1968); Allstate Ins. Co. v. United States, 190 Ct. Cl. 19, 27, 419 F.2d 409, 413–14 (1969).*

[18] *Keasbey & Mattison Co. v. Rothensies, 133 F.2d 894, 898* (3d Cir.), cert. denied, *320 U.S. 739* (1943).

[19] *New York & Honduras Rosario Mining Co. v. Commissioner, 168 F.2d 745, 749 (2d Cir.1948).*

[20] *Commissioner v. American Metal Co., 221 F.2d 134, 137 (2d Cir.),* cert. denied, *350 U.S. 829* (1955).

[21] *Bank of America Nat'l Trust & Sav. Ass'n v. United States, 198 Ct. Cl. 263, 459 F.2d 513,* cert. denied, *409 U.S. 949* (1972).

[22] *Id. at 281, 459 F.2d at 523.*

ultimate objective or effect of that tax. For instance, a gross income tax on mining royalties was creditable when the taxpayer did not operate the mine and retained only a royalty right under its contract with the operator. In such a situation, no costs or expenses of the taxpayer to obtain the royalties would over balance them and the taxpayer would not suffer a deficit on the royalty transaction even if the mining operations went badly. Similarly, a Mexican tax on receipts in the form of interest or rents was creditable because such interest and rents, taxed at the source, are rarely, if ever, wholly offset by the taxpayer's costs or expenses of obtaining that type of income; a Brazilian tax on gross earnings from interest and dividends was creditable because that type of passive investment income involved few or no expenses of production.[23]

On the other hand, when the income came from an active asbestos quarry, a tax that restricted allowable deductions to costs incurred in mining operations only, with no deductions for expenses incident to the general conduct of the business, was not creditable.[24] Similarly, in Bank of America, the foreign taxes were not creditable because no provision was made to reach the net gain realized after an accounting for costs normally incident to the banking business.

Problems of that type are what we have to consider here. Caland's income subject to the OMT is generated in the conduct of an iron ore mining business. Creditability of the OMT under I.R.C. § 901 requires a determination that the deductions normally or essentially incident to the general conduct of that business are available in computation of the OMT liability so as to assure that the tax applies only to the net gain produced by the business.

B.   Operation of OMT. Unlike the Canadian federal and provincial income taxes, which are administered by their respective revenue departments, the OMT is administered by ministries concerned with mining and natural resource regulation.[25] Structurally, the OMT in the relevant years was organized to provide a graduated rate of tax on net profits above $10,000, as determined by the statutory formula, from the taxpayer's mineral extraction activity.

The OMT profit is determined by deducting specified mining expenses from the gross revenue from production. The mine assessor considered the mining operation to end, under the OMT, when the ore passed through the primary crusher, even if the crusher were located underground.

---

[23] Bank of America Nat'l Trust & Sav. Ass'n v. United States, supra, 198 Ct. Cl. at 276, 459 F.2d at 520, analyzing Santa Eulalia Mining Co. v. Commissioner, 2 T.C. 241 (1943); and 198 Ct. Cl. at 279, 459 F.2d at 522, analyzing I.T. 2620, 11–1 Cum. Bull. 44 (1932) and I.T. 4013, 1950–1 Cum. Bull. 65.

[24] Keasbey & Mattison Co. v. Rothensies, supra, 133 F.2d at 897–98.

[25] The Canadian income tax is administered by the Canadian Department of National Revenue; the Ontario income tax is administered by the Ontario Ministry of Revenue; the OMT in 1964 and 1965 was administered by the Ontario Department of Mines and, at the time of trial by the Ministry for Natural Resources, Mineral Resources Branch.

The OMT provides three methods to compute gross revenue from mine production: (1) when unprocessed ore is shipped from the mine site, the gross revenue is the amount received from sales; (2) if the ore is processed at the mine, the gross revenue is "the amount of the actual market value of the output at the pit's mouth"; (3) if the ore is processed at the mine, and there is no means of ascertaining such actual market value, the gross revenue is the "amount at which the mine assessor appraises such output."

The computation authorized in method No. 2 was an administrative shortcut that in practice was utilized by the mine assessor only for the mining of gypsum and gold. This method allowed inventory produced and processed, but unsold at year-end, to be valued and the OMT profit therefrom to be taxed, even though the income was not yet "realized" under United States standards.

Caland's gross revenue reported on its 1964 OMT return was computed as authorized by method No. 1; its gross revenue for 1965, when it produced both unprocessed and processed ore, was calculated as permitted in method No. 3. Caland's original 1965 OMT return included a valuation for unsold ore in inventory. On review, the mine assessor required the return to be amended to eliminate that value. The administrative procedure to appraise the value of output at pit's mouth in method No. 3 followed by the mine assessor's office included in gross revenue only the proceeds of ore and pellets actually sold during the year. No valuation was placed on ore in inventory but unsold at year-end.

The mine assessor generally followed a standard procedure in a method No. 3 appraisal of the value of output at the pit's mouth. This procedure involved deduction from the sale price of the processed product of: (1) costs of processing and marketing; (2) a portion of head office expenses allocable to processing; (3) an allowance for depreciation of processing plant; and (4) an allowance for a processing profit. The processing profit allowance was an arbitrary 8 percent of original cost of processing assets, but not less than 15 percent or more than 65 percent of the profits of the combined mining and processing operations before deduction of the allowance itself.[26]

The OMT lists ten categories of expenses and allowances that may be deducted from the proceeds attributable to the extraction activity. These deductions include transportation costs, working expenses (including office overhead) directly connected with the mining operation, depreciation of mining plant, and certain exploration and development costs incurred anywhere in Ontario following commencement of production.

Not all expenses directly identified with the general conduct of the mining activity were allowable deductions. The mine assessor excluded

---

[26] Caland's 1965 processing allowance on its amended return was 15 percent of the combined profits allowed for its mining and processing operations.

15 categories of business and administrative expenses that were not considered to be directly related to the extraction of ore. These included: costs of acquiring land (including legal fees, purchase price, option payments, rent, miner's license fee, recording fees and royalties other than to the Crown), taxes of all kinds, municipal, provincial and federal (except sales and excise taxes on purchases of goods and equipment), cost of annual meetings, and 50 percent of director's fees and expenses.

In addition to mine operating expenses excluded by the mine assessor, the OMT specifically did not permit to be used in the computation of OMT profit: a deduction for interest or dividends on capital, royalty payments to private parties, depletion of mineral resources, and certain preproduction exploration and development expenses. Caland incurred preproduction exploration and development expenses, at its Atikokan mine from the inception of development, of approximately $30.8 million (Can.), of which $7.3 million (Can.) were eligible for deduction. Caland's royalty payment to Steep Rock Iron Ore Company of $3,448,376 (Can.) in 1964 and $4,172,673 (Can.) in 1965, were not included in the computation of OMT profits for those years. Caland's interest expenses of $1,842,293 (Can.) in 1964 and $1,831,836 (Can.) in 1965 for financing the mining venture were not included in the computation of OMT profit for those years. Caland's 1964 and 1965 computation of OMT profits did not include an allowance for the physical depletion of its mineral resource.

C.   History and purpose of OMT. The OMT is a formulary tax that nominally and structurally is designed to reach a particular type of net profit derived from a statutorily circumscribed business activity—the extractive phase of a mining operation. The tax is a hybrid type of tax, with both income tax and property tax features. It is structured and administered to allow a formulary profit that is designed to overcome Canadian constitutional limitations and to simplify administration of collection burdens. The historical development of the OMT, and its present position in the Canadian tax structure, support the conclusion that the OMT is a tax on the privilege of mining in Ontario. Notwithstanding its nominal objective to reach a defined net profit, the OMT was not intended to reach a concept of net gain in the United States tax sense, even when restricted to the limited business activity to which it applies.

In the Canadian system, the federal government is authorized to raise money by any mode or system of tax, and may levy both direct and indirect taxes. Provincial governments derive their taxing powers from the 1867 British North American Act, and are empowered to levy only direct taxes within the province in order to raise revenue for provincial purposes.[27]

---

[27]   The British North American Act, 1867, section 92, provides:

"In each Province the Legislature may exclusively make Laws in relation to Matters coming within the Classes of Subject next herein-after enumerated; that is to say,—

In a purely economic analysis, the distinction between a direct and an indirect tax is blurred. Every traditionally indirect tax would have some persons who are the first and final payers, and, conversely, every direct tax may on occasion be shifted to another. The Canadian courts, however, in order to have a concept of general application, have abandoned a strict economic analysis and have applied a simplified expression of the classical definition. The judicial test is that a direct tax is intended to be borne by the person on whom imposed and the payer of an indirect tax is supposed to indemnify himself at the expense of another.[28]

Before confederation, the Province of Ontario imposed a royalty, an indirect tax, on the value of ores raised or mined. In 1907, Ontario introduced a tax on profits derived from the extraction of ore, which with minor amendments was embodied in the Mining Tax Act of 1914. The revision was made so that the OMT would be a direct tax that would be constitutional under Canadian law. Constitutional validity of the OMT has been considered, and the Ontario Court of Appeals has held the OMT to be a "direct tax" in the Canadian sense. In its opinion, the court stated that the OMT is not a tax on gross profit but a tax on "what might very reasonably, I think, be described as net profit."[29] This characterization is not unimportant, but at the same time it is not decisive, nor is it necessarily to be taken as referring to "net profit" in the sense known to the United States.

The "net profit" that is reached by the OMT is based exclusively on the mining activity and is an artificial concept utilized to satisfy the requirements of Canada's tax system. An official report by the Ontario Committee on Taxation in 1967 (the Smith report), noted the hybrid nature of the OMT and the omission of various elements that normally enter a calculation of profit. According to the Smith report, "[o]ne fundamental criticism" of the OMT is that its nature is not clear. "It is neither a tax on actual profits, because of the severe limitation on deductions, nor a royalty. The present position seems to have been

---

. . .

"2. Direct Taxation within the Province in order to the raising of a Revenue for Provincial Purposes."

[28] Nickel Rim Mines, Ltd. v. Attorney General for Ontario, 53 D.L.R. 2d 290, 294 (1965), citing and quoting *Bank of Toronto v. Lambe, 12 App. Cas. 575 (1887).* The definition, by John Stuart Mill, quoted with approval was:

"Taxes are either direct or indirect. A direct tax is one which is demanded from the very persons who it is intended or desired should pay it. Indirect taxes are those which are demanded from one person in the expectation and intention that he shall indemnify himself at the expense of another; such are the excise or customs.

"The producer or importer of a commodity is called upon to pay a tax on it, not with the intention to levy a peculiar contribution upon him, but to tax through him the consumers of the commodity, from whom it is supposed that he will recover the amount by means of an advance in price."

[29] Id. at 292.

reached by a process of arbitrary decision-making rather than as a logical result of basic principles."[30]

The Smith report notes that Ontario had adopted a profits tax to assure classification as a "direct tax" on the operator, because a province is constitutionally unable to impose a royalty on mineral production on private land. The OMT was distinguished from a royalty reserved to the Crown. The report concluded: "In order to impose a constitutionally valid royalty on mineral production, the whole basis of land tenure for mining companies in Ontario would have to be changed." The Smith report accepted the concept of a profits tax because it is "probably better suited than a royalty to obtain a revenue from a high-risk industry, inasmuch as, unlike a royalty, it does not tend to convert a marginally successful mine into a loser."[31] Incidence of the OMT is broadly similar to that of the corporation income tax. Ontario iron mines are operated either by Ontario steel corporations or companies affiliated with United States steel manufacturers. Competitive conditions existing in the steel industry, the report concludes, prevent the shifting of the OMT tax burden in the short run.[32]

B.C. Lee, Comptroller and Mine Assessor, Ontario Department of Mines, and responsible for the administration of the OMT in 1964 and 1965, was of the opinion that the OMT "is levied on the mine much the same as a property tax is levied on the assessed value of a building and its land." He concluded that the OMT was not in fact an income tax "although a certain artificial profit is arrived at to determine the tax base."[33]

D.   Application of the test to OMT. As we have held in Part II, C, supra, the OMT was not actually intended to parallel a United States income tax. The question then is: did it nevertheless have the effect of falling on some net gain? In calculating it, significant costs were not taken into account, but taxpayer contends that these omissions fail to show that net gain was very unlikely to be reached.

Plaintiff first claims the OMT is a creditable foreign income tax because it is restricted to income from a particular source—mining—and a full array of deductions for expenses incident to the general conduct of that specialized activity assures that the tax falls only on net income. In

---

[30] The Ontario Committee on Taxation, (1967), c. 32, para. 37.

[31] Smith report, c. 32, paras. 6, 38, and 39.

[32] The Smith report states in para. 47:

"The major amount of Ontario's iron ore production is thus used for steel-making by the mine operator, the United States parent or some other affiliate of the mine operator, and so the burden of the mining profits tax falls at least initially upon the steel manufacturer either directly as the mine operator or indirectly as the shareholder of the mine operator. Because of the competitive conditions existing in the steel industry there can be no shifting in the short run, and since the proportion of the total requirements of U.S. mills filled from Ontario ore is so small it is doubtful that the tax would have any significant effect upon the price of steel in the United States, even in the long run."

[33] Speech of B.C. Lee, "Provincial Taxation," Canadian Tax Foundation Eighteenth Annual Tax Conference 89, Nov. 23–25, 1964.

plaintiff's view, deductions for interest, depletion and royalty payments to private parties would not be appropriate and are not allowed in the OMT because they are not expenses incurred in earning the particular class of income intended to be taxed. Such financial items, plaintiff claims, relate to a division of income among participants in the mining venture; they are not expenses of the particular mining activity. Deductions for preproduction exploration and development expenses were not allowed because they were taken into account in the original low tax rate, were not normally significant, and were not thought to be proper deductions in computation of net income.

Plaintiff compares the OMT to the "schedular" taxes utilized in some foreign countries. In such taxes, income from different sources or activities is segregated into different "schedules" and taxed under separate rules and rate tables. Plaintiff also points to the United States withholding taxes in I.R.C. §§ 871 and 881 as a direct parallel with the OMT. Withholding taxes, according to plaintiff, are creditable and are comparable to the OMT in that a particular type of income is taxed after deduction of operating expenses but without restriction for the financial items—interest, royalties, depletion—that represent a distribution of operating income.

In Bank of America, this court discussed domestic withholding taxes in I.R.C. §§ 871 and 881 in its consideration of taxes analogous to taxes on gross income.[34] The analogy was there rejected on the ground that it seemed clear that costs and expenses affecting production of the income being taxed in this country would not wipe out net gain. Nonresident alien taxpayers not engaging in business would not be likely to have expenses that would wipe out gains; foreign corporations with income from investment sources in this country are taxed in I.R.C. § 881(a) on gross income "only to the extent the amount so received is not effectively connected with the conduct of a trade or business within the United States"; and a foreign corporation connected with United States business, which in some years might experience losses, is taxed in I.R.C. § 882 only after charitable deductions and deductions related to the United States activities. Plaintiff's withholding tax analogy is not persuasive—the OMT is quite different from those taxes.

The class of income taxed by the OMT is likewise not comparable to the schedular type of classification or to the income reached by the withholding taxes. The OMT is a tax imposed on an active business operation that is measured by a particularized and artificial computation of net profit. The key to creditability is not that a particular class of net profit, reached by an accounting procedure that may be acceptable or justified for other considerations, is taxed; to be creditable, the net profit subject to foreign tax must be analogous to the type of net profit reached by the United States income tax. In view of the large-scale omission from

---

[34] *Bank of America Nat'l Trust & Sav. Ass'n v. United States, supra,* 198 Ct. Cl. at 280–81, 459 F.2d at 523.

the OMT of significant costs of the mining business, it cannot be said that the net gain of that business is sure, or very likely, to be reached by the tax. For instance, the nondeductibility of land expenses, rent, and private royalties—all or a large part of each of which mirror important costs of mining production—remove from the consideration of the OMT crucial expenses that are normally incurred in the mining business, significant expenses which may well offset any gain the company could make from mining. The same is true of other exploration, development, and pre-production costs.

Plaintiff's comment on the court's analysis of Santa Eulalia[35] is similarly defective. Plaintiff asserts the OMT reaches the same net profit as the gross income tax on mining royalties held creditable in Santa Eulalia because the royalty was itself a distribution of net profit, determined after all operating expenses had been deducted. In Santa Eulalia, however, the taxpayer was the royalty collector, who was not involved with mine operations; it was the taxpayer's expenses in obtaining the royalties that the court noted were unlikely to balance his gain so as to suffer a deficit on the royalty transaction. Caland is not in such a position. Caland is a taxpayer that is the active mine operator; whether it in fact has a net profit is dependent on the relationship of its expenses, operating and general, to its income from that business operation.

In the same connection, plaintiff strongly urges that the expenses disallowed as deductions in the OMT—e.g., interest, royalties, depletion—are not pertinent to the particular class of income that is subject to the OMT. They do not need to be deductible, it is claimed, because they do not affect the profits of the mine as a separate business activity. Plaintiff would define profit of a mining activity as the excess of the sales revenue over operating costs required to produce the salable mineral product. The profit thus defined would be shared by the three classes of participants in the mining enterprise—creditors, mineral owners and equity owners. Plaintiff would separate the accounting for interest to creditors, and royalties and depletion to the mineral owners, from the profit of the mine as a particular class of activity. Deductions for these items would not be included in mining expenses, it is argued, because they affect only the manner that profit is distributed among the several investors in the mine. Taxpayer also emphasizes periods in the history of the United States income tax when deductions were not permitted for interest, depletion, royalty payments, and other expenses. Plaintiff contends, correctly, that "net income" has not been a fixed concept during the development of the United States income tax system. Accounting treatment of concepts as elusive as depletion, mineral

---

[35] *Bank of America Nat'l Trust & Sav. Ass'n v. United States, supra, 198 Ct. Cl. at 276, 459 F.2d at 520,* commenting on *Santa Eulalia Mining Co. v. Commissioner, 2 T.C. 241 (1943),* appeal dismissed, *142 F.2d 450 (9th Cir.1944).*

royalties, and interest on capital investments, may vary with the objectives of the analysis.

The answer, in our view, is that, even if these observations might be true for some of the individual items, taken singly, that Ontario holds to be nondeductible, when the mass of the omitted items in the OMT are considered together and in combination as applied to plaintiff's mining business, it is clear to us that that tax does not seek to reach, or necessarily reach, any concept of net gain from the mining business which would be recognized as such in this country. It is as if a very large chunk of the outlays of that business had been shaved off, and only a fraction left, out of which "net gain" is to be found. The exclusions are far too widespread and important to permit the conclusion that some net gain is sure to be reached.

It may be (as we are told by one witness) that every company paying the tax had some true net gain, but that fact does not necessarily prove that companies not required to pay the OMT tax failed to have a net gain. Conversely, there was expert testimony that a taxpayer could show a loss under the Canadian federal and provincial income tax laws while, at the same time, be subject to tax under the OMT. We can see, in short, no real connection between "net profit" under the OMT and the general concept of net gain known to the United States (and to the regular Canadian income tax laws).

This disharmony is quite understandable. Where, as in the OMT, such essentials as land and rental expenses are omitted,[36] it is hard to believe that some net gain from mining is always made, or very likely so; it is as if wages (which can be considered in one aspect as an allocation of "profits") and production costs were wholly nondeductible and disregarded in calculating net gain. Nor is it appropriate, in the United States tax sense, to consider all such expenses as merely an allocation of profits. They are part of the expenses of the mining business, not too different from labor and production costs.

Moreover, plaintiff's attempt to separate mine operating costs from financing expense draws too fine a line. A separate corporation whose sole business was the operation of a single mine could not compute a net profit if it did not include all of its expenses relevant to its business. As a unit in a diversified and complex corporate structure, direct costs for Caland's particular mining activity can be separated conveniently from financing expenses relevant to that activity. Unlike the situation in a single business activity, the mining expenses plaintiff labels "financing" or "profit-sharing," rather than being general operating expenses of Caland's business, can be shifted to some other phase of plaintiff's corporate operations. Plaintiff's corporate interrelationships permit accounting flexibility but they are not determinative of whether Caland's operations in Canada produced profit for purposes of an I.R.C. § 901

---

[36] Including land and rent expenses not centered on the ore itself.

credit. Allocation of amounts for corporate general overhead and expenses is the bane of all corporate managers because of the effect the allocations have on performance of the profit centers for which they are responsible.

Finally, there is the problem of the taxation of unsold inventory. Plaintiff concedes that § 3–(3)(b) of the OMT allows the mine assessor to tax unsold gold and gypsum held in inventory, but would have the creditability issue determined by the administrative practice applicable to iron ore and all other minerals. The mine assessor, except for gold and gypsum, imposed the tax only on OMT profits that resulted from actual sales. Plaintiff labels the gold and gypsum treatment a de minimis variation of the mine assessor's consistent practice, which, in the normal case computed a profit number from the value of ore that had actually been sold.[37]

Resort to the administrative practice of the mine assessor is not necessary or controlling. The OMT in § 3–(3)(b) expressly provides a method for the mine assessor to value processed minerals that are "not sold" at the actual market value of the output at the pit's mouth. Under this authority, for ores which "had an actual market value" the mine assessor was empowered to impose a tax on OMT profits from any type of production that had been placed in inventory and was not sold. This authority, in fact, was used for gold and gypsum, minerals that account for 10 percent of Ontario's total production in the review years. The OMT in its structure and express provisions thus permits the tax to be imposed on unrealized income, a generally impermissible result for an income tax in the United States sense.

The sum of it is that, from several viewpoints and in several aspects, taxpayer has failed to show that the OMT fits our concept of an income tax, or the concept spelled out in *Bank of America, supra*. The foreign tax credit under I.R.C. § 901 is therefore not allowable. This failure to permit a credit for payments made by Caland under the OMT will not result in double taxation because the OMT profit is not "net gain" of the type sought by the United States income tax. Rather, taxes paid to the Province of Ontario under the OMT seem to be taxes on the privilege to conduct mining operations in Ontario.

CONCLUSION OF LAW

Upon the findings and the foregoing opinion, the plaintiff is entitled to deductions in 1964 and 1965 for all amounts of Contingent Liability accrued in those years under its Supplemental Unemployment Benefit

---

[37] Plaintiff points to the court's remarks in *Bank of America (supra, 198 Ct. Cl. at 273, 459 F.2d at 519)* that reference should be made to the "actual system historically utilized by Congress in imposing domestic income taxes" to support its contention that administrative practice should control rather than theoretical construction. Plaintiff's reference is not apposite because the court did not refer to an administrative interpretation of statutory authority. The court gave preference to actual Congressional enactments over theoretical and potential tax schemes that were constitutionally permissible but which Congress had declined to use.

plan, and judgment is entered to that effect. Plaintiff is not entitled to foreign tax credits in those years for payments under the Ontario Mining Tax Act. Plaintiff's claim on the Ontario Mining Tax Act issue is dismissed and the remainder of the case is remanded to the Trial Division for further proceedings under Rule 131(c) to determine the amount of refund due.

Order September 10, 1982 entered judgment for plaintiff for $1,423,122 in taxes, plus $748,208 in assessed interest plus statutory interest.

NOTES AND QUESTIONS

1.   Read Treas. Reg. § 1.901–2(b)(4)—the net income requirement for creditability of a foreign tax. This requirement was revisited in *Texasgulf, Inc. v. Commissioner*, 107 T.C. 51 (1996), when the Tax Court held that the OMT was creditable because of the changes made to Treas. Reg. § 1.901–2 in 1983, replacing the "substantial equivalence" test of *Inland Steel* with the requirement that the "predominant character" of the tax would be that of an income tax in the U.S. sense. This allowed the taxpayer to demonstrate that the processing allowance "effectively compensated" for the disallowed deductions. Do you think this was right? Consider also the inflexible interpretation of the *Texasgulf* court, emphasizing that the tax "either is or is not an income tax, in its entirety, for all persons subject to the tax."

2.   Two other tests for creditability of a foreign tax are the realization test, which is not normally concerning in practice, and the gross receipts test, which may produce problematic results. Consider, e.g. the following: In the early 1990s, Bolivia tried to install a corporate cash flow tax, in which all expenses could be deducted (rather than capitalized). This type of tax has two versions, one in which all financial receipts and payments are ignored, the other in which loans are included in income and both interest and principal are deductible. The two versions are generally equivalent from a present value perspective. The IRS rejected the first version because it disallowed the interest deduction, the second because it included loan principal in income. This led Bolivia to abandon the proposal. What do you think?

3.   The Bolivian cash flow tax is the same as the proposed "flat tax" in the U.S. Some commentators have argued that because of this the flat tax would not be creditable; others have disagreed. What do you think?

4.   Interestingly, a 2008 Mexican Flat Tax (that serves a similar role to an alternative minimum tax) has raised the question of creditability most recently—yet possibly with a different outcome. The tax is generally, though not exclusively, calculated on a cash flow basis. The IRS issued Notice 2008–3 which protects taxpayers from creditability challenges, subject to some restrictions, until the IRS establishes a final position on the matter.

5.   Should foreign taxes be subject to this hoop? Why? At least one commentator has argued that all taxes that were paid and not rebated should be creditable. Do you agree?

6. Read again question 5 in section 8.2.a. above. What is the relationship between soak-up taxes and taxes in lieu of income taxes—how can one distinguish between them? What may be the implication for U.S. international tax policy?

8.3   THE FOREIGN TAX CREDIT LIMITATION

From its enactment in 1918 to 1921, the foreign tax credit was not subject to any limitation. This could lead to a reduction of U.S. tax on U.S. source income, as illustrated by the following example of a U.S. corporation earning 100 of U.S. source income and 100 of foreign source income:

	U.S.	Foreign
Taxable income	100	100
Foreign tax	0	35
Tentative U.S. tax	21	21
Foreign tax credit	(14)	(21)
Net U.S. tax	7	0
Net after-tax	93	65

In addition, suppose the foreign country in this example, being aware of the U.S. foreign tax credit, raises its tax rate to 42%. The result would be as follows:

	U.S.	Foreign
Taxable income	100	100
Foreign tax	0	42
Tentative U.S. tax	21	21
Foreign tax credit	(21[2])	(21)
Net U.S. tax	0	0
Net after-tax	100	58

Note that the taxpayer has the same after tax income (158) in both situations, but that in the first case he pays 35 to the foreign country and 7 to the U.S., while in the second case he pays 42 to the foreign country and 0 to the U.S. The taxpayer is indifferent, but the foreign country has succeeded in transferring 7 from the U.S. fisc to its own.

Because of these two reasons (unwillingness to reduce U.S. tax rates on U.S. source income, and unwillingness to allow foreign countries to raise taxes at the expense of the U.S. Treasury) the foreign tax credit has,

---

[2] This hypothetical envisions a world in which the foreign taxes paid on the $100 of foreign source income are first used as a credit to reduce U.S. income tax on that foreign source income and then any remaining credit (i.e. to the extent the foreign tax on the foreign source income exceeds the U.S. income tax on the foreign source income) is permitted to reduce (i.e. serve as a credit against) U.S. income tax on the U.S. source income.

since 1921, been limited. Note, however, that any limitation on the foreign tax credit violates CEN (discussed in Ch. 7 above) when the foreign tax rate is higher than the U.S. rate. This can most easily be seen if one considers a refundable credit (which has the same effect as allowing foreign taxes to offset tax on U.S. source income). With a refundable credit, an investor is neutral between investing in the U.S. with a 21% tax rate, and investing in a foreign country with a 35% tax rate, because in the latter case she would get a refund of 14% from the U.S. Treasury. This preserves CEN, but no country with foreign tax credits has been willing to go that far.

The basic foreign tax credit limitation is set out in Section 904(a). The Section 904(a) formula is:

$$\text{FTC limitation} = \text{U.S. tax rate} \times \text{world-wide income} \times \frac{\text{Foreign source income}}{\text{World wide income}}$$

For U.S. taxpayers, increasing foreign source income is generally good because it increases their foreign tax credit limitation (see Ch. 2). Taxpayers with more foreign taxes than allowed by the limitation can carry such credits back two years and forward five years (sec. 904(c)).[34] Such taxpayers are said to be in an "excess credit" position. Taxpayers with less foreign taxes than allowed by the limitation are said to be in an "excess limitation" position. Such taxpayers can bear additional foreign taxes without increasing their tax burden (because such taxes merely substitute for U.S. taxes).

After the 1986 tax reform, many U.S. corporate taxpayers were in an excess credit position because of the reduction of the corporate tax rate from 46% to 34%, both because foreign rates were higher and because of the changes to the interest allocation rules (see Ch. 3) which decreased their foreign source income. However, by 1997 most U.S. taxpayers were able to credit all their foreign taxes (i.e., were in an excess limitation position or indifferent). This was in part the result of reductions in foreign tax rates, and in part the result of foreign tax minimization strategies such as those described in Notice 98–11 (Ch. 7 above). The December 2017 tax reform reduction of the corporate tax rate to 21% (effective 2018) may lead to U.S. taxpayer's with unused (excess) foreign tax credits, depending on foreign tax rates.

A general limitation such as the one imposed by Section 904(a) can have different effects on the incentives to invest in the U.S. or abroad, depending on whether the taxpayer is in an excess credit or an excess limitation position. Consider the two following examples:

---

[34] One year carryback for foreign taxes that may be carried to tax years beginning after October 22, 2004, and ten years carryforward for foreign taxes that may be carried to tax years ending after October 22, 2004, which is the date of enactment of AJCA. Sec. 417, amending IRC sec. 905(c).

Excess credit:	Foreign Country A
Taxable income	100
Foreign tax	42
U.S. tentative tax	21
FTC limitation	21 (21% × 100)
Foreign tax credit	(21)
Net U.S. tax	0
Total tax	42
After-tax income	58
Excess credit	21

Taxpayer now can choose between investing to earn an additional 100 in the U.S. or in foreign country B, which has no income tax. If she invests in the U.S., the result will be:

Excess credit:	Foreign Country A	U.S.
Taxable income	100	100
Foreign tax	42	0
U.S. tentative tax	21	21
FTC limitation	21 (21% × 100)	0
Foreign tax credit	(21)	0
Net U.S. tax	0	21
Total tax	42	21
After-tax income	58	79
Excess credit	21	

If she instead her additional funds invests in foreign country B to earn that additional $100, the result will be:

Excess credit:	Foreign Country A	Foreign Country B
Taxable income	100	100
Foreign tax	42	0
U.S. tentative tax	21	21
FTC limitation	42 (21% × 200)	70
Foreign tax credit	(42) but only 21 used	0 from Country B, but 2 remaining from A to use now
Net U.S. tax	0	0
Total tax	42	0
After-tax income	58	100

Excess credit	21 to be now used in next column with U.S. tax on Country B income

Thus, in this case the taxpayer has an incentive to invest in country B and not in the U.S., which violates CEN.

However, consider now a taxpayer in excess limitation:

Excess Limitation:	Foreign Country B
Taxable income	100
Foreign tax	0
U.S. tentative tax	21
FTC limitation	21 (21% × 100)
Foreign tax credit	0
Net U.S. tax	21
Total tax	21
After-tax income	79
Excess limitation	21

Taxpayer now can choose between investing to earn an additional 100 in the U.S. or in foreign country A, which has an income tax at 40%. If she invests in the U.S., the result will be:

Excess limitation:	Foreign Country B	U.S.
Taxable income	100	100
Foreign tax	0	0
U.S. tentative tax	21	21
FTC limitation	21 (21% × 100)	0
Foreign tax credit	0	0
Net U.S. tax	21	21
Total tax	21	21
After-tax income	79	79
Excess limitation	21	

If she invests in foreign country A, the result will be:

Excess limitation:	Foreign Country B	Foreign Country A
Taxable income	100	100
Foreign tax	0	40
U.S. tentative tax	21	21

FTC limitation	42 (21% × 200)	70
Foreign tax credit	0	(40)
Net U.S. tax	21 but then use 19 of credit from Country A tax to bring to 0	0 with excess credit of 19 to use against U.S. tax on Country B income
Total tax	2	40
After-tax income	98	60
Excess limitation	2	

So that in this case the taxpayer is indifferent between investing in the U.S. and in foreign country A. However, the U.S. Treasury is not indifferent, because investing in the U.S. in this case results in an additional 21 of U.S. tax that are not paid in the case of an investment in foreign country A.

Because of these incentive effects, the Code had for a long time additional limitations on the foreign tax credit. One version of these limitations was a per country limitation, which would have prevented the taxpayer from averaging the taxes of countries A and B in the above example (by imposing the FTC limit separately for each country).

The current version is to impose the limitation separately by category of income (or "basket"), and for tax years beginning after December 31, 2006, only two separate limitation categories exist: (1) General income basket, and (2) Passive income basket.[39] Read section 904(d). In general, the idea here is to segregate income subject to high taxes (active income) from income subject to low taxes (passive income), even if they come from the same country. Note, however, that it is still possible for a taxpayer in an excess credit position to average her position with income of the same kind that is subject to a different rate of tax. The key is to reduce the average foreign tax rate below the U.S. rate (21% for corporations). This ability to "cross-credit" is another reason why few U.S. taxpayers are now in an excess credit position.

Under the TCJA, two additional baskets were created, for GILTI income and for foreign branch income, which are discussed below. Cross-crediting is allowed within those baskets.

NOTES AND QUESTIONS

1. Do you think the basket system is justified? Remember that any limitation on the foreign tax credit violates CEN. Is the additional complexity worth the effort, especially if most taxpayers are in an excess limitation position?

---

[39] AJCA sec. 404, amending IRC sec. 904(d). In prior years there have been multiple "baskets" that were costly to administer and comply with, and created significant complexity with little payoff. They were therefore collapsed into the two existing baskets.

2. The basket system was enacted in 1986. The original Treasury proposal was to superimpose the baskets over the per-country limitation. This was rejected as too complex. What do you think?

3. For an excellent defense of the basket system in all it complexity, see Kingson, The Foreign Tax Credit and Its Critics, American J. Tax Policy (1991).

The effect of losses can significantly complicate the computation of foreign tax credits. Read Section 904(f). Note that in this case the U.S. permits reduction of U.S. tax on U.S. source income (compare to the text above regarding the general (Section 904(a)) limitation), but requires recapture of such reduction as soon as possible. The general premise of Section 904(f) is to allow temporary use of foreign losses outside their "baskets," but require that such use be reversed on a multiple-year basis, resulting in losses reducing only income in their appropriate basket. Read Treas. Reg. 1.904(f)–2(c)(5) for simple illustrations of the basic rule. Note that AJCA introduced new Section 904(g) (applicable to losses for tax years beginning after Dec. 31, 2006), which purpose is to equalize the treatment of domestic losses to that of foreign losses under Section 904(f).

4. A domestic Corporation X, subject to a flat 321%, had the following items of income (foreign taxes born in brackets—assume all in USD)

U.S. source income	For source business income	For source interest income
2015 100	100(40)	100(10)
2015 100	(100) + 100 (15)	100(10)
2017 0	(200)	100(10)
2018 1000	(100) + 200(50)	100(10)
2019 (100)	100(15) + 200(60)	100(10)

Calculate X's U.S. tax liability for the above years. What planning techniques can you identify in X's earning pattern above? What difficulties are not addressed by X? How could you solve this difficulty?

8.4   THE INDIRECT CREDIT

The indirect credit of Section 902 has been abolished by the TCJA because of the participation exemption. However, section 960 provides for credits on the underlying income in the same way as former Section 902, so the following case, which explains the origins of the formula provided for in Section 960, is still relevant:

American Chicle Co. v. United States

Supreme Court of the United States.
316 U.S. 450, 62 S.Ct. 1144, 86 L.Ed. 1591 (1942).

■ OPINION: MR. JUSTICE ROBERTS delivered the opinion of the Court.

This case involves the application of § 131(f) of the Revenue Acts of 1936 and 1938,[1] which allows a tax credit to domestic corporations in respect of income received from foreign subsidiaries.

During the taxable years 1936, 1937, and 1938, the petitioner, a domestic corporation, received dividends from foreign subsidiaries of which it was sole stockholder. The subsidiaries paid taxes upon their earnings to the countries of their domicile. In its income tax returns, the petitioner claimed the credit allowed by § 131 for the foreign taxes so paid. The Commissioner of Internal Revenue computed the credit at a less sum than that the petitioner claimed. The petitioner paid the resultant taxes, and presented claims for refund, which were rejected. This action was brought in the Court of Claims for asserted overpayments. The sole matter in controversy is the proper method of arriving at the credit granted by § 131. That section permits a domestic corporation to credit against its tax the amount of income, war-profits, and excess-profits taxes paid or accrued during the taxable year to any foreign country, with certain limits set by subsections (b)(1) and (2). The purpose of the provision, like that of its predecessor, § 238 of the Revenue Act of 1921,[2] is to obviate double taxation.[3]

Section 131(f), dealing with taxes of a foreign subsidiary,[4] provides that, for the purpose of the section, a domestic corporation receiving dividends from such a subsidiary "in any taxable year shall be deemed to have paid the same proportion of any income, war-profits, or excess-profits taxes paid" by the subsidiary to a foreign country, "upon or with respect to the accumulated profits" of the subsidiary "from which such dividends were paid, which the amount of such dividends bears to the amount of such accumulated profits." "Accumulated profits" of the subsidiary are defined as "the amount of its gains, profits, or income in excess of the income, war-profits, and excess-profits taxes imposed upon or with respect to such profits or income."

The parties are in agreement as to the fraction to be used in calculating the proportion. The numerator is the dividends received by the parent. The denominator is the "accumulated profits" of the subsidiary. The dispute relates to the multiplicand to which the fraction is to be applied. The petitioner says it is the total foreign taxes paid by the subsidiary. The respondent says it is the taxes paid upon or with respect to the accumulated profits of the subsidiary; i.e., so much of the

---

[1]   49 Stat. 1648, 1696; 52 Stat. 447, 506; 26 U. S. C. § 131.

[2]   42 Stat. 227, 258.

[3]   *Burnet v. Chicago Portrait Co.*, 285 U.S. 1.

[4]   A foreign corporation of whose voting stock the taxpayer owns a majority.

taxes as is properly attributed to the accumulated profits, or the same proportion of the total taxes which the accumulated profits bear to the total profits. The Court of Claims so held.[5] Since several decisions have gone the other way,[6] we granted certiorari.

If the language of the Revenue Act is to be given effect, the Government's view seems correct. The statute does not purport to allow a credit for a stated proportion of the total foreign taxes paid or the foreign taxes paid "upon or with respect to" total foreign profits, but for taxes paid "upon or with respect to" the subsidiary's "accumulated profits," which, by definition, are its total taxable profits less taxes paid.

If, as is admitted, the purpose is to avoid double taxation, the statute, as written, accomplishes that result: The parent receives dividends. Such dividends, not its subsidiary's profits, constitute its income to be returned for taxation. The subsidiary pays tax on, or in respect of, its entire profits; but, since the parent receives distributions out of what is left after payment of the foreign tax,—that is, out of what the statute calls "accumulated profits," it should receive a credit only for so much of the foreign tax paid as relates to or, as the Act says, is paid upon, or with respect to, the accumulated profits.

Hence we think that, under the plain terms of the Act, the Commissioner and the court below were right in limiting the credit by the use as multiplicand of a proportion of the tax paid abroad appropriately reflecting the relation of accumulated profits to total profits of the subsidiary. But the petitioner insists that the legislative history and a long indulged administrative construction require us, in effect, to elide the phrase "upon or with respect to the accumulated profits" of the foreign subsidiary.

Section 240(c) of the Revenue Act of 1918[7] allowed the domestic parent receiving dividends from a foreign subsidiary a credit for the same proportion of the taxes paid by the foreign corporation during the taxable year to any foreign country which the amount of the dividends received by the parent during the taxable year bore to the total taxable income of the subsidiary upon or with respect to which such taxes were paid.

This provision had the same object as § 131 of the Revenue Acts of 1936 and 1938; that is, to avoid double taxation. The difficulty with it was that it did not relate the credit to the accumulated profits or surplus of the subsidiary out of which the dividends were paid. Thus, if dividends were paid out of surplus earned in prior years, and it happened that the subsidiary paid no tax to the foreign country in the taxable year in

---

[5]   94 Ct. Cls. 699, 41 F.Supp. 537.

[6]   *F. W. Woolworth Co. v. United States*, 91 F.2d 973; *International Milling Co. v. United States*, 89 Ct. Cls. 128, 27 F.Supp. 592; *Aluminum Co. of America v. United States*, 123 F.2d 615.

[7]   c. 18, 40 Stat. 1057, 1082.

question, the parent could claim no credit whatever. There were other eccentric results flowing from the provision of the Act of 1918.

In the Revenue Act of 1921, § 238(e)[8] was the analogous section. The draftsman of the section stated to the Senate Committee in charge of the measure: "I rewrote the old provision, safeguarding it from some abuses which it was open to and closing up some of the gaps that were in the old provision." Section 238(e) is substantially the same as § 131(f). The alterations of § 240(c) of the Act of 1918 were made to permit identification of the accumulated profits of each taxable year out of which the dividends might have been paid and to give credit for a proportion of the subsidiary's taxes attributable to such accumulated profits.

The Chairman of the Senate Finance Committee indicated that the calculation of the proportion of foreign tax paid would be exactly the same as it had been under the 1918 Act. But this would be true only if the dividends were paid in a given year out of the prior year's earnings and taxes were paid in the same year in respect of the same prior year's earnings. The petitioner seeks in this case to apply the proportion provided by the 1918 Act; but this is to ignore the alterations made in that Act in 1921 which have ever since been retained. In Committee hearings and in Congressional Reports with respect to the purpose and effect of the changes wrought by the 1921 Act, there were statements indicating an understanding that the credit was to be proportioned to the dividends made available to the parent in this country. The Treasury made no regulation applicable to § 238(e) of the Revenue Act of 1921. It provided a form for reporting the tax, which sanctioned the petitioner's method of computing the credit; and, from 1921 to 1930, the Commissioner calculated credits for foreign subsidiaries' taxes by that method. In 1930, however, the Treasury promulgated a new form which required the credit to be computed in the way the Commissioner did in the present case; and promulgated Regulations 77 under the Revenue Act of 1932, which, in Article 698, required the computation of the credit in the same manner. The regulations have since remained unchanged: See Regulations 103 §§ 19.131–3 and 19.131–8. Although the regulations definitely govern this case, and were made prior to the years in controversy, the petitioner insists that the antecedent administrative interpretation long in force renders it impossible for the Commissioner to promulgate a regulation changing for the future the earlier practice, even though the new regulation comports with the plain meaning of the statute. We think the contention cannot be sustained.[9]

The judgment is: Affirmed.

---

[8]   c. 136, 42 Stat. 227, 259.

[9]   *Helvering v. Wilshire Oil Co., 308 U.S. 90; Helvering v. Reynolds, 313 U.S. 428; White v. Winchester Country Club, 315 U.S. 32.*

QUESTION

What would have been the result under the taxpayer's view if its subsidiary earned $100, paid $21 in foreign tax, and remitted a $79 dividend to the parent? See Section 78.

United States v. Goodyear Tire & Rubber Company and Affiliates

Supreme Court of the United States.
493 U.S. 132, 110 S.Ct. 462, 107 L.Ed.2d 449 (1989).

■ JUDGES: MARSHALL, J., delivered the opinion for a unanimous Court. REHNQUIST, BRENNAN, WHITE, BLACKMUN, STEVENS, O'CONNOR, SCALIA, KENNEDY.

■ OPINION: JUSTICE MARSHALL delivered the opinion of the Court. In this case, we must decide whether "accumulated profits" in the indirect tax credit provision of the Internal Revenue Code of 1954, *26 U.S.C. § 902* (1970 ed.), are to be measured in accordance with United States or foreign tax principles. We conclude that "accumulated profits" are to be measured in accordance with United States principles.

I

Goodyear Tire and Rubber Company (Great Britain) Limited (Goodyear G. B.) is a wholly owned subsidiary of Goodyear Tire and Rubber Company (Goodyear), a domestic corporation. Goodyear brought this suit seeking a refund of federal income taxes collected for the years 1970 and 1971. During those years, Goodyear G. B. filed income tax returns in, and paid taxes to, the United Kingdom and the Republic of Ireland. Goodyear G. B. also distributed dividends to Goodyear, its sole shareholder. Goodyear reported these dividends on its federal tax return, as required by *26 U.S.C. §§ 301,* 316 (1970 ed.). Goodyear thereafter sought credit for a portion of the foreign taxes paid by Goodyear G. B. in the amount specified in § 902.[1]

Section 902 provides a parent of a foreign subsidiary with an "indirect" or "deemed paid" credit on its domestic income tax return to reflect foreign taxes paid by its subsidiary. The credit protects domestic corporations that operate through foreign subsidiaries from double

---

[1]   Section 902(a) provides:

"For purposes of this subpart, a domestic corporation which owns at least 10 percent of the voting stock of a foreign corporation from which it receives dividends in any taxable year shall—

"(1) to the extent such dividends are paid by such foreign corporation out of accumulated profits (as defined in subsection (c)(1)(A)) of a year for which such foreign corporation is not a less developed country corporation, be deemed to have paid the same proportion of any income, war profits, or excess profits taxes paid or deemed to be paid by such foreign corporation to any foreign country or to any possession of the United States on or with respect to such accumulated profits, which the amount of such dividends (determined without regard to section 78) bears to the amount of such accumulated profits in excess of such income, war profits, and excess profits taxes (other than those deemed paid). . . ." *26 U.S.C. § 902* (1970 ed.).

taxation of the same income: taxation first by the foreign jurisdiction, when the income is earned by the subsidiary, and second by the United States, when the income is received as a dividend by the parent. In some circumstances, a foreign subsidiary may choose to distribute only a portion of its available profit as a dividend to its domestic parent. For that reason, a domestic parent cannot automatically claim credit for all foreign taxes paid by its subsidiary: § 902 limits a domestic parent's credit to the amount of tax paid by the subsidiary attributable to the dividend issued. The foreign tax deemed paid by the domestic parent is calculated by multiplying the total foreign tax paid (T) by that portion of the subsidiary's after-tax accumulated profits (AP-T) that is actually issued to the domestic parent in the form of a taxable dividend (D).[2]

In 1973, Goodyear G. B. reported a net loss on its British tax return and carried back that loss to offset substantial portions of its 1970 and 1971 income. Based on the 1973 carried-back losses, British taxing authorities recalculated Goodyear G. B.'s income and tax liability for the years 1970 and 1971. Goodyear G. B. thereafter received a refund of a substantial portion of its 1970 and 1971 foreign tax payments.

In response to the refunds, and pursuant to § 905(c) of the Code which permits redetermination of the foreign tax credit whenever "any tax paid is refunded in whole or in part," the Commissioner of Internal Revenue recalculated the indirect tax credit available to Goodyear for the tax years 1970 and 1971. The Commissioner lowered the foreign taxes paid (T) to reflect the refund. He refused, however, to lower accumulated profits (AP) for those years to reflect British tax authorities' redetermination of Goodyear G. B.'s income. The deductions that created, for British tax purposes, the 1973 loss would not have been allowable in the computation of United States income tax if Goodyear G. B. had been a United States corporation filing a United States return. See App. 19–29 (Stipulation of Facts). In the Commissioner's view, accumulated profits are to be calculated in accordance with United States tax principles; accordingly, the Commissioner regarded Goodyear G. B.'s 1970 and 1971 accumulated profits as unaffected by the deductions allowed under British law.

In view of the reduced amount of Goodyear's tax deemed paid, the Commissioner assessed substantial tax deficiencies for the tax years 1970 and 1971. Goodyear paid the deficiencies and, following the IRS' denial of its administrative refund claim, brought this action in the United States Claims Court, averring that foreign tax law principles govern the calculation of "accumulated profits" in § 902's tax credit. Calculating "accumulated profits" in accordance with British tax law principles, Goodyear maintained that Goodyear G. B.'s after-tax accumulated profits for 1970 and 1971 were insufficient to cover the

---

[2]　The formula for calculating the § 902 credit is as follows:

Credit = Foreign Taxes Paid (T) × (Dividends (D)/Accumulated Profits (AP) minus Foreign Taxes (T)).

dividends paid in those years. In such a circumstance, § 902 requires that, for the purpose of computing the indirect credit, the excess of the dividend be deemed paid out of the after-tax accumulated profits of the preceding year. If in that year the remaining portion of the dividend exceeds the after-tax accumulated profits, the remainder of the dividend is allocated or "sourced" to the next most recent year, until the dividend is exhausted.[3] Thus, Goodyear argued that the dividends it received from Goodyear G. B. in 1970 and 1971 should have been sourced to prior tax years, 1968 and 1969, until Goodyear G. B.'s after-tax accumulated profits covered the dividends. Through this sourcing mechanism, Goodyear would, in computing its domestic tax liability for the dividends issued by Goodyear G. B., receive credit for a portion of the foreign taxes paid by Goodyear G. B. in 1968 and 1969. Because Goodyear G. B. paid substantial foreign taxes in those tax years, allocation of the dividend to those years would yield a tax deemed paid by Goodyear in excess of L 1 million, over four times greater than the tax the Commissioner deemed paid. If the term "accumulated profits" is defined in accordance with domestic tax principles, as the Commissioner advocated, the dividends issued in 1970 and 1971 are fully exhausted by the accumulated profits of those years, resulting in a tax deemed paid of L 247,124.

The Claims Court rejected Goodyear's claim. *14 Cl. Ct. 23 (1987).* Viewing the statutory definition of "accumulated profits" in § 902(c)(1)(A) as inconclusive, *id., at 28–29,* the court turned to the purposes underlying § 902 and found that they favored calculation of "accumulated profits" in accordance with United States tax concepts, *id., at 29–31.* The Court of Appeals for the Federal Circuit reversed. *856 F. 2d 170 (1988).* The court held that the "plain meaning" of § 902 "requires [accumulated profits] to be determined under foreign law." *Id., at 172.* The court also held that the fundamental congressional purpose underlying § 902, " 'elimination of international double taxation,' " ibid. (quoting *H. H. Robertson Co. v. Commissioner, 59 T. C. 53, 74 (1972),* aff'd, *500 F.2d 1399 (C.A.3 1974)),* would be defeated if the taxes paid by a foreign subsidiary, but not its accumulated profits, were calculated in terms of foreign law. *856 F.2d, at 172.*

The Court of Appeals' decision has important consequences for the calculation of the indirect tax credit of domestic parents that have received dividends from their subsidiaries abroad. To clarify the operation of the § 902 credit in the tax years to which it applies,[4] we granted certiorari, *490 U.S. 1045 (1989),* and now reverse.

---

[3] The operation of this sourcing principle is described in *General Foods Corp. v. Commissioner, 4 T. C. 209, 215 (1944).*

[4] Calculation of the indirect credit for tax years beginning after 1986 is governed by the amended version of § 902 established by the Tax Reform Act of 1986, 100 Stat. 2528, *26 U.S.C. § 902* (1982 ed., Supp. V). The amended version substantially overhauls the method of calculating the credit and removes the controversy regarding the definition of "accumulated profits." The current version of § 902(c)(1) replaces "accumulated profits" with "undistributed earnings," which are defined as the "earnings and profits of the foreign corporation (computed in accordance with sections 964 and 986)." Section 964(a) in turn provides that "the earnings

Our starting point, as in all cases involving statutory interpretation, "must be the language employed by Congress." *Reiter v. Sonotone Corp., 442 U.S. 330, 337 (1979)*. We find that the text of § 902 does not resolve whether "accumulated profits" are to be calculated in accordance with foreign or domestic tax concepts.

It is true, as the Court of Appeals emphasized, that §§ 902(a)(1) and 902(c)(1)(A) link "accumulated profits" to the foreign tax imposed on the subsidiary. The link is forged by describing the foreign tax as that tax imposed "on or with respect to" accumulated profits. The provisions also, however, link "accumulated profits" to "dividends" by describing "accumulated profits" as the pool from which the "dividends" are issued. Section 316(a), in turn, makes clear that domestic principles control whether a payment is a "dividend" subject to domestic tax. On the basis of this link, a leading treatise has concluded that "accumulated profits of the foreign corporation . . . are, in general, equated with earnings and profits of the foreign corporation and are determined in accordance with domestic law principles." B. Bittker & J. Eustice, Federal Income Taxation of Corporations and Shareholders P17.11, para. 17–44 (5th ed. 1987) ("Adoption of these principles has the virtue of correlating the denominator of the § 902 computation with the definition of dividends (the numerator), thus avoiding the possible distortions that could arise if different definitional approaches were used for the numerator and denominator of the § 902 fraction"). Because § 902 relates "accumulated profits" both to the foreign tax paid by the subsidiary, calculated in accordance with foreign law, and to the dividend issued by the subsidiary, calculated in accordance with domestic law, we are unpersuaded that the statutory language is dispositive. We must therefore look beyond the statute's language to the legislative history, purposes, and operation of the indirect tax credit.

III

A.   The history of the indirect credit clearly demonstrates that the credit was intended to protect a domestic parent from double taxation of its income. Congress first established the indirect tax credit in § 240(c) of the Revenue Act of 1918, 40 Stat. 1082, permitting a domestic parent to receive a credit for a portion of the foreign taxes paid by its subsidiary during the year in which the subsidiary issued a dividend to the parent. This Court subsequently described the purpose of § 240(c) as protection against double taxation. *American Chicle Co. v. United States, 316 U.S. 450, 452 (1942);* see also Bittker & Eustice, supra, at para. 17.11, p. 17–40.

The legislative history of the indirect credit also clearly reflects an intent to equalize treatment between domestic corporations that operate through foreign subsidiaries and those that operate through

---

and profits of any foreign corporation . . . shall be determined according to rules substantially similar to those applicable to domestic corporations." *26 U.S.C. § 964*(a) (1982 ed.).

unincorporated foreign branches. In § 238(e) of the Revenue Act of 1921, 42 Stat. 259, Congress amended § 240(c) to permit a domestic corporation to claim credit for taxes its subsidiary paid in years other than those in which the dividend was issued. Prior to the amendment, a domestic corporation could not receive credit for foreign taxes paid on distributed income if its subsidiary issued the dividend out of income earned in prior years, see *316 U.S., at 453*, because § 240(c) limited the credit to taxes paid by the subsidiary "during the taxable year" in which the dividend was issued. The amendment corrected this deficiency by relating the credit to the accumulated profits out of which the dividends were paid.

In defending the amended version of the indirect credit, one sponsor described the purpose of the credit as securing, for domestic corporations that receive income in the form of dividends from foreign subsidiaries, the same sort of deduction available to domestic corporations that receive income from foreign branches. 61 Cong. Rec. 7184 (1921).[5] This goal of equalized treatment is reflected as well in testimony regarding the amendment before the Senate Committee on Finance, in which a spokesperson for the Department of the Treasury described the proposal as intended "to give this American corporation about the same credit as if conducting a branch." Hearings on H. R. 8245 before the Senate Committee on Finance, 67th Cong., 1st Sess., pt. 2, p. 389 (1921). More recently, the Senate Report on the 1962 amendments to the indirect credit confirms Congress' intent to treat foreign branches and foreign subsidiaries alike in terms of the tax credits they generate for their domestic companies. See S. Rep. No. 1881, 87th Cong., 2d Sess., 66–67 (1962).[6]

B. Given these purposes, we now turn to the operation of the indirect tax credit. Goodyear contends that the failure to calculate accumulated profits in terms of foreign law subjects domestic corporations that receive dividends from their foreign subsidiaries to

---

[5] Senator Smoot stated:

"[A] foreign subsidiary is much like a foreign branch of an American corporation. If the American corporation owned a foreign branch, it would include the earnings or profits of such branch in its total income, but it would also be entitled to deduct from the tax based upon such income any income or profits taxes paid to foreign countries by the branch in question. Without special legislation, however, no credit can be obtained where the branch is incorporated under foreign laws."

[6] The 1962 amendment addresses a tax preference that results if a domestic parent is credited with foreign taxes paid on subsidiary income that is used to satisfy the subsidiary's foreign tax obligations. In such circumstance, the parent receives credit for taxes paid on undistributed income. This Court sought to eliminate this tax advantage in *American Chicle Co. v. United States, 316 U.S. 450, 452 (1942)*, by including in the § 902 credit only those taxes paid on a subsidiary's after-tax income. The 1962 amendment addressed the problem differently, permitting a domestic parent to include all foreign taxes paid in its § 902 calculation but also requiring the parent to treat such taxes as a deemed dividend from its subsidiary. The amendment thus requires domestic parents to "gross up" the dividend income they receive by the amount of the foreign taxes attributable to such income. See S. Rep. No. 1881, 87th Cong., 2d Sess., 69 (1962). The Senate Report, describing the purpose of the amendment as removing an "unjustified tax advantage" for domestic parents, illustrates how foreign subsidiaries and foreign branches are treated unequally absent the "grossing up" requirement, even under the American Chicle rule. S. Rep. No. 1881, supra, at 66–67.

double taxation. This undesirable result occurs, in Goodyear's view, because calculation of accumulated profits in accordance with domestic principles may disconnect the relationship in § 902's formula between accumulated profits and the foreign tax paid by the subsidiary. A subsidiary incurs foreign tax liability in proportion to its foreign defined income. To recover foreign taxes paid by its subsidiary, a domestic parent's dividend must be allocated or sourced to years in which its subsidiary paid foreign tax. If, however, accumulated profits are defined in domestic terms, the dividends of a domestic parent may be allocated to years in which the subsidiary paid little or no tax. In such a scenario, the parent may not be credited with foreign taxes paid by its subsidiary. To avoid this mismatching of accumulated profits and foreign tax, Goodyear contends that accumulated profits should be determined in accordance with the same principles that govern the imposition of the tax: those found in foreign law.

The Government contests Goodyear's characterization of this case as one of "double taxation." In the Government's view, the dividends received by Goodyear should not be allocated to prior years because to do so would permit Goodyear to avoid taxation altogether on domestically defined income that its subsidiary earned in 1970 and 1971. Under domestic rules, Goodyear G. B. earned sufficient income in 1970 and 1971 to cover the dividends it issued to Goodyear in those years. That British taxing authorities recognized little income in those years should not, in the Government's view, prevent the United States from recognizing the substantial income attributable to those years under domestic rules. According to the Government, the foreign tax paid in 1968 and 1969 by Goodyear G. B.—the years to which Goodyear seeks to source its dividends—relates to income that Goodyear G. B. chose not to distribute during those years as dividends to Goodyear. To credit Goodyear with taxes paid on undistributed income, the Government concludes, would be inequitable because it would provide domestic parents that operate through foreign subsidiaries favorable treatment vis-a-vis domestic corporations that use foreign branches.

Goodyear attempts to avoid the force of the Government's analysis by exploring hypothetical situations in which the calculation of accumulated profits in accordance with domestic rules presents a more plausible claim of double taxation than does this case. For example, if a subsidiary earns an equal amount of income under foreign and domestic rules, but those rules regard the income as being earned in different years, the domestic parent would be credited with a lower portion of the tax paid by the subsidiary if domestic timing rules govern. This result appears anomalous because the same credit should be available where foreign and domestic tax principles recognize equal amounts of income and the amount of tax paid remains constant. The effect of the divergence in foreign and domestic tax principles is particularly clear when a subsidiary pays a substantial foreign tax in a given year and the amount of income recognized under domestic rules in that year is zero. In such a circumstance, none of the tax paid by the subsidiary can be credited to the parent because a dividend cannot be sourced to a year in which there are no accumulated profits. Goodyear's hypotheticals persuade us that if accumulated profits are calculated according to domestic tax principles, situations can arise in which § 902's statutory goal of avoiding double taxation will be disserved. Equally persuasive, however, is the Government's claim that defining accumulated profits in terms of foreign tax principles can unfairly advantage domestic parents that operate through foreign subsidiaries over companies operating through unincorporated branches. Thus, no definitional approach to "accumulated profits" uniformly and unqualifiedly satisfies the dual purposes underlying the indirect credit.

C. We nonetheless believe that the Government's interpretation of "accumulated profits" is more faithful to congressional intent. Our view is informed first and most significantly by our assessment that the risk of double taxation outlined by Goodyear is less substantial than the risk of unequal treatment cited by the Government. Defining "accumulated profits" in accordance with domestic tax concepts results in double taxation only when a dividend is sourced to a year in which domestic tax concepts recognize little or no income and yet a subsidiary pays substantial foreign tax. Goodyear offers no basis for the suggestion that such mismatching commonly occurs.

Goodyear's approach, on the other hand, leads to unequal tax treatment of subsidiaries and branches whenever the foreign taxing authority calculates income more or less generously than the United States. A domestic corporation must pay tax on all income of a foreign branch that is recognized under domestic law. Under Goodyear's interpretation, a domestic corporation may in some cases receive credit for taxes paid on income that, under domestic rules, the parent never received. This result is difficult to square with the express congressional purpose of ensuring tax parity between domestic corporations that operate through foreign subsidiaries and those that operate through foreign branches.

The Government's approach is also supported by administrative interpretations of § 902. In defining the credits available against foreign tax under the predecessor to § 902, the Commissioner stated that "it is important in establishing the amount of the accumulated profits that it be based as a fundamental principle upon all income of the foreign corporation available for distribution to its shareholders *whether such profits be taxable by the foreign country or not.*" I. T. 2676, XII-1 Cum. Bull. 48, 50 (1933) (emphasis added). The Commissioner's approach requires a domestic assessment of income for the purposes of calculating accumulated profits. The Commissioner's position is reflected as well in a formal regulation promulgated by the Treasury in 1965, Treas. Reg. § 1.902–3(c)(1), 26 CFR § 1.902–3(c)(1) (1972), which defines "accumulated profits" under § 902(a)(1) as "the sum of the earnings and profits of [the foreign subsidiary] for such year, and the foreign income taxes imposed on or with respect to the gains, profits, and income to which such earnings and profits are attributable." Defining a subsidiary's "accumulated profits" as its "earnings and profits" reflects an intent to calculate accumulated profits according to domestic principles, because "earnings and profits" in this context is a domestic tax concept.

Lastly, we find support for the Government's position in the statutory canon adopted in *Biddle v. Commissioner, 302 U.S. 573, 578 (1938),* that tax provisions should generally be read to incorporate domestic tax concepts absent a clear congressional expression that foreign concepts control. This canon has particularly strong application here where a contrary interpretation would leave an important statutory goal regarding equal tax treatment of foreign subsidiaries and foreign branches to the varying tax policies of foreign tax authorities.

IV

"Accumulated profits," as that term appears in § 902's indirect tax credit, should be calculated in accordance with domestic tax principles. The judgment of the Court of Appeals is therefore reversed, and the case is remanded for further proceedings consistent with this opinion.

It is so ordered.

NOTES AND QUESTIONS

1. What is the problem with defining accumulated profits differently than the foreign jurisdiction does, while foreign taxes are set by the foreign jurisdiction? Do you agree with the Court's response?

2. What is the general logic in requiring American standards of calculations to apply in a rule, which sole purpose is to calculate an appropriate foreign tax amount? Isn't it possible that the insistence of the court on applying American standards will result in a competitive advantage to foreigners in this context? Does it matter that the U.S. grants the foreign tax credit unilaterally, rather than through reciprocal treaties?

Vulcan Materials Company and Subsidiaries v. Commissioner of Internal Revenue

United States Tax Court.
96 T.C. 410 (1991).

■ OPINION BY: TANNENWALD

OPINION:

Respondent determined a deficiency in petitioner's 1984 Federal income tax in the amount of $133,679. The sole issue for decision is the amount of Saudi Arabian taxes that petitioner should be deemed to have paid under section 902[1] for the purpose of determining its foreign tax credit.

All of the facts have been stipulated, and the stipulation of facts and attached exhibits are incorporated herein by reference.

Petitioner is a domestic corporation with its principal corporate offices in Birmingham, Alabama, which, along with certain of its subsidiaries, filed a consolidated return for its 1984 taxable year. For all relevant years, petitioner kept its books and records and filed its Federal corporate income tax returns using the accrual method of accounting and on the basis of a calendar year.

Petitioner was a member of a Saudi Arabian partnership (Saudi partnership) which began operations in Saudi Arabia in 1976. The other original partners in the Saudi partnership included Trading & Development Co. (Tradco), a Saudi Arabian company; Shepherd Construction Co., Inc. (Shepherd); Fred Weber, Inc. (Weber); and Dalton Rock Products Co. (Dalton). Shepherd, Weber, and Dalton were U.S. corporations unrelated to Vulcan or Tradco by ownership through 1984. Tradco was wholly owned by a Saudi Arabian national at all times from 1976 through, and including, 1984. Weber withdrew from the partnership in 1977.

The Saudi partnership's operations consisted of the production of construction materials under a contract with the Arabian American Oil Co. (Aramco) and the operation of a Saudi Arabian quarry under a contract with Tradco. For the taxable year ending December 31, 1978, each partner's share in the Saudi partnership's income and tax attributable thereto was as follows:

Partners	Ownership Percentage
Vulcan	48%
Dalton	10
Shepherd	10
Tradco	32

Petitioner reported its share of the Saudi partnership's income on its 1978 Federal corporate income tax return, and pursuant to section 702(a)(6), claimed a section 901 direct paid credit for the Saudi Arabian income tax attributable to its share of the Saudi partnership's income.[2]

In 1979, the business and assets of the Saudi partnership were transferred to Tradco-Vulcan Co., Ltd. (TVCL), a corporation organized and existing under the laws of Saudi Arabia, in exchange for shares in

---

[1] All statutory references are to the Internal Revenue Code as amended and in effect for the year in issue. The provisions of sec. 902 have been substantially revised since 1984.

[2] The parties have also stipulated that this treatment was not challenged by respondent, an element which we consider irrelevant.

TVCL. The shares of TVCL were issued to the partners in the Saudi partnership in proportion to their partnership interests. TVCL's shareholders and their interests at the time of its initial organization and through the years in issue were as follows:

	Percentage
Shareholder	Interest
Vulcan	48%
Shepherd	10
Dalton	10
Tradco	32

At all relevant times since its formation, TVCL has continued to carry on the same lines of business as the partnership.

Saudi Arabia Royal Decree No. 17/2/28/3321 (1950), as amended, contains the income tax laws of Saudi Arabia. The Saudi Arabian income tax laws are not applicable to the income of Saudi Arabian nationals and Saudi Arabian corporations wholly owned by Saudi Arabian nationals. Rather, such Saudi Arabian nationals and corporations are required by Islamic law, the Shari'ah, to pay a tax called the Zakat. In the case of a Saudi Arabian corporation wholly owned by Saudi Arabian nationals, the Zakat was calculated in 1984 and for all relevant prior years as a flat-rate percentage of the net equity of the corporation less its net fixed assets; for 1984, the Zakat percentage was 1.25.

Saudi Arabian income tax laws impose an income tax on a "mixed corporation" (i.e., a Saudi Arabian corporation owned in part by Saudi Arabian nationals and in part by non-Saudi Arabian nationals) with respect to that portion of the corporation's net profits attributable to the ownership interest of non-Saudi Arabian shareholders. The portion of the net profits attributable to the non-Saudi Arabian shareholders is determined by reference to the percentage ownership interests of the non-Saudi Arabian shareholders as reflected by their stock ownership. The requirements of the Shari'ah are satisfied by imposing the Zakat on the Saudi Arabian shareholders' interests in the net equity of the corporation less its net fixed assets. Dividends paid by Saudi Arabian corporations, whether to Saudi Arabian or non-Saudi Arabian shareholders, are not subject to any further Saudi Arabian tax.

TVCL has always maintained profit accounts and paid dividends from those accounts to its shareholders. TVCL allocated and distributed its profits to a particular shareholder as follows:

The pre-Saudi Arabian tax profits of such corporation are allocated to each shareholder, both Saudi Arabian and non-Saudi Arabian, on the basis of each shareholder's proportionate share interest in the corporation. Each shareholder's share of profits is then reduced by the Saudi Arabian tax. In the case of the Saudi Arabian shareholder, its share of the pre-corporate income tax profits is reduced by the Zakat tax paid on the basis of its shareholder interest. In the case of the non-Saudi Arabian shareholders, each such shareholder's share of pre-corporate income tax profits is reduced by its proportionate share of the Saudi Arabian corporate income tax paid on the basis of that non-Saudi Arabian shareholder's interest. As a result of the above calculation, there is a profit account for each shareholder. Each profit account is further reduced by the dividends paid to each shareholder.

The above profit accounts indicated an allocation to Tradco of 32 percent of the pre-tax profits of TVCL reduced by the Zakat and by previous distributions to Tradco, and an allocation to the three U.S. shareholders of their respective shares of TVCL's pre-tax profits (i.e., petitioner—48 percent, Shepherd—10 percent, and Dalton—10 percent) reduced by the Saudi Arabian income taxes and by previous distributions to such shareholders. All dividends through 1984 were in proportion to the balances in the shareholders' profit accounts at the end of the month preceding the declaration of the dividend.

In 1984, TVCL, which used the calendar year as its taxable year, paid dividends to petitioner aggregating 1,327,405 riyals, of which 557,924 riyals were paid in the first 60 days of 1984 and, under section 902(c)(1), were considered as paid out of the 1983 profits of TVCL, and 769,481 riyals were paid later in the year out of its 1984 profits. TVCL's pre-income-tax profits for 1983 and 1984, calculated pursuant to U.S. tax principles but stated in Saudi Arabian currency, were 20,902,753 and 10,436,790 riyals, respectively. TVCL credited 68 percent of such pretax amounts (i.e., 14,213,872 and 7,097,017 riyals, respectively) to the profit accounts of its U.S. shareholders in proportion to their ownership interests, and the balance thereof to the profit account of Tradco. TVCL's Saudi Arabian corporate income taxes for the 2 years were 6,883,191 and 4,267,909 riyals, respectively, all of which TVCL charged against the profit accounts of the U.S. shareholders in proportion to their relative share interests. The applicable conversion rates for Saudi Arabian income taxes paid for the 2 years were 3.46 and 3.53 riyals to the dollar, respectively.

On its 1984 Federal corporate income tax return, petitioner claimed a section 902 deemed paid credit for Saudi Arabian income taxes for each of the 2 years 1983 and 1984 by using a fraction, the numerator of which was the amount of the dividends paid to petitioner out of the profits of such year and the denominator of which was the portion of TVCL's pre-tax profits for the year that was allocated to the U.S. shareholders, reduced by TVCL's Saudi Arabian income taxes for each year, as follows (expressed in riyals):

1983

Saudi tax	6,883,191
Dividend	557,924
Pre-tax profits allocated to U.S. shareholders	14,213,872

Computation of allowable section 902 credit:

6,883,191   ×   557,924   /   14,213,872 − 6,883,191   =   523,866

1984

Saudi tax	4,267,909
Dividend	769,481
Pre-tax profits allocated to U.S. shareholders	7,097,017

Computation of allowable section 902 credit:

4,267,909   ×   769,481   /   7,097,017 − 4,267,909   =   1,160,816

In his notice of deficiency, respondent calculated petitioner's deemed paid credit for Saudi Arabian taxes paid by TVCL in the same manner as petitioner had on its 1984 return, except in one major aspect. In the denominators of the fractions, respondent included all of TVCL's pre-income-tax profits for the year, including amounts allocated by it to Tradco. Thus, respondent's calculations were as follows (expressed in riyals):

1983

Saudi tax	6,883,191
Dividend	557,924
Pre-tax profits allocated to U.S. shareholders	20,902,753

Computation of allowable section 902 credit:

6,883,191   ×   557,924   /   20,902,753 − 6,883,191   =   273,924

1984

Saudi tax	4,267,909
Dividend	769,481
Pre-tax profits allocated to U.S. shareholders	10,436,790

Computation of allowable section 902 credit:

4,267,909   ×   769,481   /   10,436,790 − 4,267,909   =   532,362

On its 1984 Federal corporate income tax return, petitioner claimed that $477,533 of the Saudi Arabian income taxes paid by TVCL with respect to its 1983 and 1984 profits was allowable as a deemed paid credit using the previously described calculation. On the other hand, respondent, using his own calculation, determined that $229,980 was the deemed paid credit allowable to petitioner and disallowed $247,553 in foreign tax credits claimed by petitioner. As a collateral adjustment, pursuant to section 78, respondent decreased petitioner's income by the same amount.

Section 902 provides:

Sec. 902(a). Treatment of Taxes Paid by Foreign Corporation.—For purposes of this subpart, a domestic corporation which owns at least 10 percent of the voting stock of a foreign corporation from which it receives dividends in any taxable year shall be deemed to have paid the same proportion of any income, war profits, or excess profits taxes paid or deemed to be paid by such foreign corporation to any foreign country or to any possession of the United States, on or with respect to the accumulated profits of such foreign corporation from which such dividends were paid, which the amount of such dividends (determined without regard to section 78) bears to the amount of such accumulated profits in excess of such income, war profits, and excess profits taxes (other than those deemed paid).

      * * *

(c)   Applicable Rules.—

(1)   Accumulated profits defined.—For purposes of this section, the term "accumulated profits" means, with respect to any foreign corporation, *the amount of its gains, profits, or income computed without reduction by the amount of the income, war profits, and excess profits taxes imposed on or with respect to such profits or income by any foreign country or by any possession of the United States.* The Secretary shall have full power to determine from the accumulated profits of what year or years such dividends were paid, treating dividends paid in the first 60 days of any year as having been paid from the accumulated profits of the preceding year or years (unless to his satisfaction shown otherwise), and in other respects treating dividends as having been paid from the most recently accumulated gains, profits, or earnings.

[Emphasis added.]

Thus, petitioner's credit for the income taxes paid by TVCL is determined by application of the following formula:

Foreign income taxes deemed paid	=	Foreign income taxes paid	×	Dividends received by petitioner from TVCL /
		Accumulated profits of TVCL minus foreign income taxes paid by TVCL		

The parties are in agreement as to the amount of the foreign taxes paid and of the dividends received. Their dispute centers on the meaning of the term "accumulated profits." Petitioner contends that the proper figure is the amount of the profits of TVCL upon which the Saudi Arabian income tax was imposed, i.e., 68 percent of the total accumulated profits of TVCL, the portion of the profits allocable to all U.S. shareholders. Respondent contends that the proper figure is the total accumulated profits of TVCL. For the reasons hereinafter set forth, we agree with petitioner.

Initially, we need to dispose of the applicability of *United States v. Goodyear Tire & Rubber Co., 493 U.S. 132 (1989),* in which the Supreme Court determined that "accumulated profits" were to be determined in accordance with U.S. rather than foreign tax rules. Applying that standard, the Supreme Court refused to permit the taxpayer to take into account a loss of its British subsidiary attributable to deductions which were allowed under British tax law but would not have been allowed under U.S. law. Compare *Champion International Corp. v. Commissioner, 81 T.C. 424, 447 (1983).*

Respondent contends that Goodyear precludes us from taking into account the fact that under Saudi Arabian law the income taxes were imposed only on a portion of TVCL's accumulated profits. We think respondent misconceives the scope of Goodyear. There is no question that, under Goodyear, the determination of TVCL's accumulated profits turns upon the application of U.S. tax rules, and petitioner does not contend otherwise. The question before us is not how TVCL's accumulated profits are to be determined but whether, pursuant to section 902, all or only a pro rata portion of such profits so determined are to be included in the denominator of the formula.

The fact that the Supreme Court in Goodyear put its stamp of approval on the position of respondent set forth in I.T. 2676, XII-1 C.B. 48, 50 (1933), see 110 S.Ct. at 470, does not, as respondent argues, support his view of Goodyear. In that ruling, respondent stated:

> It is important in establishing the amount of the accumulated profits that it be based as a fundamental principle upon all income of the foreign corporation available for distribution to its shareholders, whether such profits be taxable by a foreign country or not. [I.T. 2676, XII-1 C.B. at 50.]

> It is clear, however, that respondent's ruling was directed at the methodology for calculating "income" for purposes of the deemed foreign tax credit and, in fact, the Supreme Court itself described respondent's statement precisely that way. United States v. Goodyear Tire & Rubber Co., 110 S.Ct. at 470.

Turning to the question before us, we start out by examining the applicable statutory provisions because, if they are unambiguous, we are not permitted, except in rare and unusual situations, to depart from the statutory language. See *Cal-Maine Foods, Inc. v. Commissioner, 93 T.C. 181, 208–209 (1989).* See also *Demarest v. Manspeaker*, 498 U.S. 184 (1991). Respondent contends that the language of section 902 mandates that the total accumulated profits of TVCL be used. We are not convinced such is the case. The phraseology of section 902(a) and (c)(1), which we have italicized, see supra pp. 453–454 relates the taxes paid to "the accumulated profits of such foreign corporation from which such dividends were paid" (sec. 902(a)) and specifies that "accumulated profits" should be determined without reduction by the taxes "imposed on or with respect to such profits" (sec. 902(c)(1)). Similarly, we are not persuaded that the terminology of section 1.902–1(e)(1), Income Tax Regs., requires us to conclude that the statutory provisions are as all-encompassing as respondent maintains. That terminology states that, in determining the accumulated profits of a foreign corporation, there shall be included "The earnings and profits of such corporation for such year." The use of the word "The" is not necessarily equivalent of "the entire" or "all." We recognize that respondent has ruled in accordance with the position he takes herein. *Rev. Rul. 87–14, 1987–1 C.B. 181.* However, the ruling is devoid of any analysis; it simply announces its conclusion and cites the pertinent statutory provisions and regulations. Moreover, we note that the position taken in this ruling is inconsistent with the approach respondent adopted in explaining the methodology to be used in calculating the foreign tax credit under the United States-United Kingdom Income Tax Convention, December 31, 1975, 31 U.S.T. (Part 6) 5668, T.I.A.S. 9682, *1980–1 C.B. 394.* See infra p. 455 Granted that the interpretation of a treaty is not equivalent to the interpretation of a statutory provision, we think that there is sufficient commonality involved to cause us not to give particular weight to respondent's ruling, which clearly is not binding upon us. *Stubbs, Overbeck & Associates, Inc. v. United States, 445 F.2d 1142, 1146–1147 (5th Cir.1971).*

In short, we think that the statutory and regulatory provisions are sufficiently unclear to permit us to examine the objectives of the foreign tax credit. See *Fehlhaber v. Commissioner, 94 T.C. 863, 865–866 (1990).* Those objectives, so recently articulated in United States v. Goodyear Tire & Rubber Co., supra, have, since the inception of the foreign tax credit in 1918, been avoiding double taxation and affording a U.S. corporation operating through a foreign subsidiary the same credits as if it were conducting a branch operation in the foreign country. See 110 S.Ct. at 467–468. In terms of those objectives, we are satisfied that petitioner should prevail.

There can be no question that if TVCL had been conducted as a branch, only petitioner's share of the profits would have been taken into account, and that it would have received a direct credit for the foreign taxes paid, and respondent does not contend otherwise. Similarly, if accumulated profits are not limited to the profits which were the subject of the Saudi Arabian income tax and in which petitioner shared, petitioner will not be entitled to the full credit for the Saudi Arabian taxes imposed on its share of those profits and, to that extent, double taxation will result. Indeed, the logical result of respondent's position is that if the share of TVCL's profits allocable to U.S. shareholders were not subject to any Saudi Arabian income tax but only the share allocated to the Saudi Arabian shareholders were the base for imposing such tax, the U.S. shareholders would be entitled to a foreign tax credit under section 902 even though they suffered no economic burden from such income tax. Such a result would be bizarre to say the least, as respondent himself has recognized in setting forth examples of situations which he claims would be abusive by permitting the U.S. tax burden to be manipulated through the establishment of separate shareholder accounts for accumulated profits, and the foreign income taxes attributable thereto, simply to suit the U.S. shareholders' purpose. But the situation here is not simply the result of the establishment of separate accounts by the parties in interest; it is founded on the stipulated structure of the Saudi Arabian tax law.

Respondent also seeks to counteract petitioner's position by an analysis which aggregates the Saudi Arabian income tax and the Zakat tax (which is a noncreditable type of tax) and then allocating the resulting tax burden among TVCL's shareholders, in order to sustain his claim that petitioner is not really exposed to a double tax burden under respondent's approach. This analysis mixes apples and pears. In *United Dyewood Corp. v. Bowers, 44 F.2d 399 (S.D.N.Y.1930),* affd. per curiam *56 F.2d 603 (2d Cir.1932),* a British subsidiary of the taxpayer was subject to British income tax on the average of 3 years of taxable income and to an excess profits tax on the current year's taxable income. Respondent maintained that both amounts of taxable income and both amounts of British taxes should be aggregated for the purpose of computing the taxpayer's deemed foreign tax credit. That position was rejected, and respondent was required separately to compute the credits for each of the taxes.

The sourcing of accumulated profits has been utilized in various other contexts. Thus, *Rev. Rul. 69–440, 1969–2 C.B. 46,* uses the sourcing method of earnings and profits to allocate distributions among various classes of stock in order to determine what portion should constitute dividends under section 316 in respect of each class. The determination of "dividends" under section 316 is applicable to a comparable determination under section 902(a), see sec. 1.902–1(a)(6), Income Tax Regs., and has been applied to source accumulated profits to the appropriate taxable year for the purpose of calculating the foreign tax credit. See *Champion International Corp. v. Commissioner, 81 T.C. at 431–432.* Additionally, in providing the U.S. Senate with an explanation of the operation of the deemed foreign tax credit in respect of United Kingdom taxes, respondent utilized the separate proportionate interest approach utilized by petitioner herein. See Technical Explanation of the United States-United Kingdom Income Tax Convention, *1980–1 C.B.*

455, 472–476. See also *Xerox Corp. v. United States, 14 Cl. Ct. 455 (1988).* Respondent is, of course, correct that this explanation was not an interpretation of section 902 as such but was presented in the specific context of a negotiated agreement. Admittedly, the foregoing examples of sourcing are distinguishable, but we believe they provide useful analogies in resolving the issue before us. In this connection, we note that, while the economic burden of the foreign income tax is irrelevant for determining who is liable for such tax, see, e.g., *Biddle v. Commissioner, 302 U.S. 573 (1938),* it is an important element in determining how that liability should be apportioned under section 902 among the parties in interest.

The long and short of the matter is that "no definitional approach to 'accumulated profits' uniformly and unqualifiedly satisfies the dual purposes underlying the indirect credit." See *United States v. Goodyear Tire & Rubber Co.,* 110 S.Ct. at 469. Such being the case, the question before us is which interpretation of that term as discussed by the parties herein "is more faithful to congressional intent." 110 S.Ct. at 469. Our view is that petitioner's interpretation of the phrase "accumulated profits," rather than that of respondent, best carries out that intent. We so hold.

Decision will be entered for the petitioner.

NOTES AND QUESTIONS

1.   What do you think of the government's position?

2.   Do you think that the court's decision created significant tax avoidance opportunities? Why wouldn't countries change their tax systems to adjust to the *Vulcan* distinction of *Goodyear*?

3.   Are you persuaded by the court's method of distinguishing *Goodyear*? If not, do you think *Goodyear* should be reconsidered?

4.   Revisit question 7 in section 8.3. Assume in addition to the facts there that X has a 15%-owned subsidiary in country Y, with the following items of income (foreign taxes born in brackets—assume all in USD) and dividend distributions to X:

	Business Income	**Dividend distribution**
2000	100(40)	0
2001	0	100(10)
2002	100(40)	100(10)
2003	(100)	100(0)
2004	100(35)	100(15)

Recalculate X's U.S. tax liability for the above years. How may these new facts affect X's tax planning? What would you advise X to do in order to reduce its U.S. tax liability? Does the fact that the taxpayer can decide to distribute dividend at will matter in this context?

8.5　FOREIGN TAX CREDIT "ABUSE"

The following case is a good example of the relatively recent surge of the so-called corporate tax shelter industry, where tax advisers targeted certain tax law constructs which—if implemented by the right taxpayers—could result in profits above and beyond the normal economic profits from the transactions between the engaged taxpayers. Foreign tax credits could be particularly lucrative in this context, inter alia, due to the multiple limitations on their use and the ability to engage in these schemes parties who are not U.S. taxpayers.

Compaq Computer Corporation and Subsidiaries v. Commissioner of Internal Revenue

United States Tax Court.
113 T.C. 214 (1999).

■ OPINION: COHEN, CHIEF JUDGE: The issues addressed in this opinion are whether petitioner's purchase and resale of American Depository Receipts (ADR's) in 1992 lacked economic substance and whether petitioner is liable for an accuracy-related penalty pursuant to section 6662(a). (In a separate opinion, *Compaq Computer Corp. & Subs. v. Commissioner, T.C. Memo. 1999–220,* we held that income relating to printed circuit assemblies should not be reallocated under section 482 to petitioner from its Singapore subsidiary for its 1991 and 1992 fiscal years. Petitioner has also filed a Motion for Summary Judgment on the issue of whether petitioner is entitled to foreign tax credits for certain United Kingdom Advance Corporation Tax payments.) Unless otherwise indicated, all section references are to the Internal Revenue Code in effect for the years in issue, and all Rule references are to the Tax Court Rules of Practice and Procedure.

FINDINGS OF FACT

Some of the facts have been stipulated, and the stipulated facts are incorporated in our findings by this reference. Since 1982, petitioner has been engaged in the business of designing, manufacturing, and selling personal computers. Details concerning petitioner's business operations are set forth in *T.C. Memo 1999–220* and are not repeated here.

Petitioner occasionally invested in the stock of other computer companies. In 1992, petitioner held stock in Conner Peripherals, Inc. (Conner Peripherals), a publicly traded, nonaffiliated computer company. Petitioner sold the Conner Peripherals stock in July 1992, recognizing a long-term capital gain of $231,682,881.

Twenty-First Securities Corporation (Twenty-First), an investment firm specializing in arbitrage transactions, learned of petitioner's long-term capital gain from the sale of Conner Peripherals, and on August 13, 1992, Steven F. Jacoby (Jacoby), a broker and account executive with Twenty-First, mailed a letter to petitioner soliciting petitioner's business.

The letter stated that Twenty-First "has uncovered a number of strategies that take advantage of a capital gain", including a Dividend Reinvestment Arbitrage Program (DRIP) and a "proprietary variation on the DRIP", the ADR arbitrage transaction (ADR transaction).

An ADR (American Depository Receipt) is a trading unit issued by a trust, which represents ownership of stock in a foreign corporation that is deposited with the trust. ADR's are the customary form of trading foreign stocks on U.S. stock exchanges, including the New York Stock Exchange (NYSE). The ADR transaction involves the purchase of ADR's "cum dividend", followed by the immediate resale of the same ADR's "ex dividend". "Cum dividend" refers to a purchase or sale of a share of stock or an ADR share with the purchaser entitled to a declared dividend (settlement taking place on or before the record date of the dividend). "Ex dividend" refers to the purchase or sale of stock or an ADR share without the entitlement to a declared dividend (settlement taking place after the record date).

James J. Tempesta (Tempesta) was an assistant treasurer in petitioner's treasury department in 1992. He received his undergraduate degree in philosophy and government from Georgetown University and his master's degree in finance and accounting from the University of Texas. Tempesta's responsibilities in petitioner's treasury department included the day-to-day investment of petitioner's cash reserves, including the evaluation of investment proposals from investment bankers and other institutions. He was also responsible for writing petitioner's investment policies that were in effect during September 1992. Petitioner's treasury department primarily focused on capital preservation, typically investing in overnight deposits, Eurodollars, commercial paper, and tax-exempt obligations.

On September 15, 1992, Tempesta and petitioner's treasurer, John M. Foster (Foster), met with Jacoby and Robert N. Gordon (Gordon), president of Twenty-First, to discuss the strategies proposed in the August 13, 1992, letter from Twenty-First. In a meeting that lasted approximately an hour, Jacoby and Gordon presented the DRIP strategy and the ADR transaction. Following the meeting, Tempesta and Foster discussed the transactions with Darryl White (White), petitioner's chief financial officer. They decided not to engage in the DRIP investment but chose to go forward with the ADR transaction, relying primarily on Tempesta's recommendation. Tempesta notified Twenty-First of this decision on September 16, 1992.

Although cash-flow was generally important to petitioner's investment decisions, Tempesta did not perform a cash-flow analysis before agreeing to take part in the ADR transaction. Rather, Tempesta's investigation of Twenty-First and the ADR transaction, in general, was limited to telephoning a reference provided by Twenty-First and reviewing a spreadsheet provided by Jacoby that analyzed the transaction. Tempesta shredded the spreadsheet a year after the transaction.

Joseph Leo (Leo) of Twenty-First was responsible for arranging the execution of the purchase and resale trades of ADR's for petitioner. Bear Stearns & Co., Inc. (Bear Stearns), was used as the clearing broker for petitioner's trades, and the securities selected for the transaction were ADR shares of Royal Dutch Petroleum Company (Royal Dutch). Royal Dutch ordinary capital shares were trading in 21 organized markets throughout the world in 1992, but primarily on the NYSE in the United States as ADR's. Before agreeing to enter into the transaction, petitioner had no specific knowledge of Royal Dutch, and Tempesta's research of Royal Dutch was limited to reading in the Wall Street Journal that Royal Dutch declared a dividend and to observing the various market prices of Royal Dutch ADR's.

In preparation for the trades, Leo determined the number of Royal Dutch ADR's to be included in each purchase and resale trade. He also selected the market prices to be paid, varying the prices in different trades so the blended price per share equaled the actual market price plus the net dividend. Leo did not, however, discuss the size of the trades or the prices selected for the trades with any employee or representative of petitioner. Leo also chose to purchase the Royal Dutch ADR's from Arthur J. Gallagher and Company (Gallagher). Gallagher had been a client of Twenty-First since 1985 and participated in various investment strategies developed by Twenty-First over the years. During 1991, Gallagher participated in several ADR transaction trades as the purchaser of the ADR's. Tempesta had no knowledge of the identity of the seller of ADR's. He only knew that the seller was a client of Twenty-First.

On September 16, 1992, Leo instructed ABD-N.Y., Inc. (ABD), to purchase 10 million Royal Dutch ADR's on petitioner's behalf from Gallagher on the floor of the NYSE. He also instructed ABD to resell the 10 million Royal Dutch ADR's to Gallagher immediately following the purchase trades. The purchase trades were made in 23 separate cross-trades of approximately 450,000 ADR's each with special "next day" settlement terms pursuant to NYSE rule 64. The aggregate purchase price was $887,577,129, cum dividend.

ABD executed the 23 sale trades, selling the Royal Dutch ADR's back to Gallagher, immediately following the related purchase trade. Accordingly, each purchase trade and its related sale trade were completed before commencing the next purchase trade. The sales transactions, however, had regular settlement terms of 5 days, and the aggregate sales price was $868,412,129, ex dividend. The 23 corresponding purchase and resale trades were completed in about an hour between approximately 2:58 p.m. and 4:00 p.m.

Leo had instructed the ABD floor brokers to execute the trades only if the prices selected were within the range of the current market prices.

Thus, when, between the sixth and seventh trades, the market price changed, Leo modified the price for subsequent trades to compensate for the change. In addition, NYSE rule 76 required an open outcry for each cross-trade, and NYSE rule 72 allowed other traders on the floor or the "specialist" responsible for making the cross-trades to break up the transaction by taking all or part of the trade. However, for cross-trades priced at the market price, there was no incentive to break up the transaction.

Pursuant to the "next day" settlement rules, the purchase cross-trades were settled between petitioner and Gallagher on September 17, 1992. On that date, Gallagher's account with Bear Stearns was credited $887,547,543 for the purchase trades, including a reduction for Securities and Exchange Commission fees (SEC fees) of $29,586. Gallagher was subsequently reimbursed for the SEC fees. Also on September 17, 1992, petitioner transferred $20,651,996 to Bear Stearns, opening a margin account.

On September 18, 1992, at 10:47 a.m., petitioner complied with the applicable margin requirements, transferring $16,866,571 to its margin account with Bear Stearns. The margin requirement for purchase and sale transactions completed on the same day was 50 percent of the purchase price of the largest trade executed on that day. It was not necessary to make payments for each completed trade. Accordingly, this wire transfer was made by petitioner to demonstrate its financial ability to pay under the applicable margin rules. The $16,866,571 was transferred back to petitioner that same day at 1:39 p.m.

Pursuant to the regular settlement rules, the resale cross-trades were settled between petitioner and Gallagher on September 21, 1992. The total selling price credited to petitioner's account with Bear Stearns was $868,412,129 (before commissions and fees). Expenses incurred by petitioner with respect to the purchase and resale trades included: SEC fees of $28,947, interest of $457,846, a margin writeoff of $37, and commissions of $998,929. Petitioner had originally agreed to pay Twenty-First commissions of $1,000,000, but Twenty-First adjusted its commissions by $1,070.55 to offset computational errors in calculating some of the purchase trades.

Due to the different settlement dates, petitioner was the shareholder of record of 10 million Royal Dutch ADR's on the dividend record date and was therefore entitled to a dividend of $22,545,800. On October 2, 1992, Royal Dutch paid the declared dividend to shareholders of record as of September 18, 1992, including petitioner. Contemporaneously with the dividend, a corresponding payment was made to the Netherlands Government representing withholding amounts for dividends paid to U.S. residents within the meaning of the United States-Netherlands Tax Treaty, Convention With Respect to Taxes on Income and Certain Other Taxes, Apr. 29, 1948, U.S.-Neth., art. VII, para. 1, 62 Stat. 1757, 1761. The withholding payment equaled 15 percent of the declared dividend,

$3,381,870. Accordingly, a net dividend of $19,163,930 was deposited into petitioner's margin account at Bear Stearns and wired to petitioner on October 2, 1992.

On its 1992 Federal income tax return, petitioner reported the loss on the purchase and resale of Royal Dutch ADR's as a short-term capital loss in the amount of $20,652,816, calculated as follows:

Adjusted basis	$888,535,869
Amount realized	867,883,053
Capital loss	$20,652,816

Petitioner also reported dividend income in the amount of $22,546,800 and claimed a foreign tax credit of $3,382,050 for the income tax withheld and paid to the Netherlands Government with respect to the dividend.

ULTIMATE FINDINGS OF FACT

Every aspect of petitioner's ADR transaction was deliberately predetermined and designed by petitioner and Twenty-First to yield a specific result and to eliminate all economic risks and influences from outside market forces on the purchases and sales in the ADR transaction.

Petitioner had no reasonable possibility of a profit from the ADR transaction without the anticipated Federal income tax consequences.

Petitioner had no business purpose for the purchase and sale of Royal Dutch ADR's apart from obtaining a Federal income tax benefit in the form of a foreign tax credit while offsetting the previously recognized capital gain.

OPINION

Respondent argues that petitioner is not entitled to the foreign tax credit because petitioner's ADR transaction had no objective economic consequences or business purpose other than reduction of taxes. Petitioner argues that it is entitled to the foreign tax credit because it complied with the applicable statutes and regulations, that the transaction had economic substance, and that, in any event, the economic substance doctrine should not be applied to deny a foreign tax credit.

In *Frank Lyon Co. v. United States, 435 U.S. 561, 583–584, 55 L. Ed. 2d 550, 98 S. Ct. 1291 (1978),* the Supreme Court stated that "a genuine multiple-party transaction with economic substance * * * compelled or encouraged by business or regulatory realities, * * * imbued with tax-independent considerations, and * * * not shaped solely by tax-avoidance features" should be respected for tax purposes. Innumerable cases demonstrate the difference between (1) closing out a real economic loss in order to minimize taxes or arranging a contemplated business transaction in a tax-advantaged manner and (2) entering into a prearranged loss transaction designed solely for the reduction of taxes on unrelated income. In the former category are *Cottage Sav. Association v. Commissioner, 499 U.S. 554, 113 L. Ed. 2d 589, 111 S. Ct. 1503 (1991);* and *Esmark, Inc. & Affiliated Cos. v. Commissioner, 90 T.C. 171 (1988),* affd. without published opinion *886 F.2d 1318 (7th Cir.1989).* In the latter category are *ACM Partnership v. Commissioner, 157 F.3d 231 (3d Cir.1998),* affg. in part *T.C. Memo 1997–115; Goldstein v. Commissioner, 364 F.2d 734 (2d Cir.1966);* and *Friendship Dairies, Inc. v. Commissioner, 90 T.C. 1054 (1988).* Referring to tax shelter transactions in which a taxpayer seeks to use a minimal commitment of funds to secure a disproportionate tax benefit, the Court of Appeals for the Seventh Circuit stated, in *Saviano v. Commissioner, 765 F.2d 643, 654 (7th Cir.1985),* affg. *80 T.C. 955 (1983):*

> The freedom to arrange one's affairs to minimize taxes does not include the right to engage in financial fantasies with the expectation that the Internal Revenue Service and the courts will play along. The Commissioner and the courts are empowered, and in fact duty-bound, to look beyond the contrived forms of transactions to their economic substance and to apply the tax laws accordingly. * * *

Petitioner repeatedly argues, and asks the Court to find, that it could not have had a tax savings or tax benefit purpose in entering into the ADR transaction because:

> In this case, a tax savings or tax benefit purpose cannot be attributed to Compaq because Compaq did not enjoy any tax reduction or other tax benefit from the transaction. Compaq's taxable income INCREASED by approximately $1.9 million as a result of the Royal Dutch ADR arbitrage. Compaq's worldwide tax liability INCREASED by more than $640,000 as a direct result of the Royal ADR arbitrage. The reason for this increase in income taxes is obvious—Compaq realized a net profit with respect to the Royal Dutch ADR arbitrage. That net profit, appropriately, was subject to tax.

Petitioner's calculation of its alleged profit is as follows:

ADR transaction:

ADR purchase trades	($887,577,129)	
ADR sale trades	868,412,129	
Net cash from ADR transaction		($19,165,000)
Royal Dutch dividend		22,545,800
Transaction costs		(1,485,685)
PRETAX PROFIT		$1,895,115

[*17]

Petitioner asserts:

Stated differently, the reduction in income tax received by the United States was not the result of a reduction in income tax paid by Compaq. Each dollar of income tax paid to the Netherlands was just as real, and was the same detriment to Compaq, as each dollar of income tax paid to the United States. Even Respondent's expert acknowledged this detriment, and that Compaq's worldwide income tax increased as a result of the Royal Dutch ADR arbitrage. A "tax benefit" can be divined from the transaction only if the income tax paid to the Netherlands with respect to Royal Dutch dividend is ignored for purposes of computing income taxes paid, but is included as a credit in computing Compaq's U.S. income tax liability. Such a result is antithetical to the foreign tax credit regime fashioned by Congress.

In the complete absence of any reduction in income tax, it is readily apparent that Compaq could not have engaged in the transaction solely for the purpose of achieving such an income tax reduction.

Petitioner's rationale is that it paid $3,381,870 to the Netherlands through the withheld tax and paid approximately $640,000 in U.S. income tax on a reported "pretax profit" of approximately $1.9 million. (The $640,000 amount is petitioner's approximation of U.S. income tax on $1.9 million in income.) If we follow petitioner's logic, however, we would conclude that petitioner paid approximately $4 million in worldwide income taxes on that $1.9 million in profit.

Petitioner cites several cases, including *Levy v. Commissioner, 91 T.C. 838, 859 (1988); Gefen v. Commissioner, 87 T.C. 1471, 1492 (1986); Pearlstein v. Commissioner, T.C. Memo. 1989–621;* and *Rubin v. Commissioner, T.C. Memo. 1989–484,* that conclude that the respective transactions had economic substance because there was a reasonable opportunity for a "pretax profit". These cases, however, merely use "pretax profit" as a shorthand reference to profit independent of tax savings, i.e., economic profit. They do not involve situations, such as we have in this case, where petitioner used tax reporting strategies to give the illusion of profit, while simultaneously claiming a tax credit in an amount (nearly $3.4 million) that far exceeds the U.S. tax (of $640,000) attributed to the alleged profit, and thus is available to offset tax on unrelated transactions. Petitioner's tax reporting strategy was an integrated package, designed to produce an economic gain when—and only when—the foreign tax credit was claimed. By reporting the gross amount of the dividend, when only the net amount was received, petitioner created a fictional $1.9 million profit as a predicate for a $3.4 million tax credit.

While asserting that it made a "real" payment to the Netherlands in the form of the $3,381,870 withheld tax, petitioner contends that that withholding tax should be disregarded in determining the U.S. tax effect of the transaction and the economic substance of the transaction. Respondent, however, persuasively demonstrates that petitioner would incur a prearranged economic loss from the transaction but for the foreign tax credit.

The following cash-flow analysis demonstrates the inevitable economic detriment to petitioner from engaging in the ADR transaction:

Cash-flow from ADR transaction:

ADR purchase trades [*20]	($887,577,129)
ADR sale trades	868,412,129
Net cash from ADR transaction	($19,165,000)

Cash-flow from dividend:

Gross dividend	22,545,800
Netherlands withholding tax	(3,381,870)
Net cash from dividend	19,163,930
OFFSETTING CASH-FLOW RESIDUAL	(1,070)

Cash-flow from transaction costs:

Commissions	(1,000,000)	
Less: Adjustment	1,071	
SEC fees	(28,947)	
Margin writeoff	37	
Interest	(457,846)	
Net cash from transaction costs	(1,485,685)	
NET ECONOMIC LOSS	($1,486,755)	

The cash-flow deficit arising from the transaction, prior to use of the foreign tax credit, was predetermined by the careful and tightly controlled arrangements made between petitioner and Twenty-First. The scenario was to "capture" a foreign tax credit by timed acquisition and sale of ADR's over a 5-day period in which petitioner bought ADR's cum dividend from Gallagher and resold them ex dividend to Gallagher. Petitioner was acquiring a foreign tax credit, not substantive ownership of Royal Dutch ADR's. See *Friendship Dairies, Inc. v. Commissioner, supra at 1067.*

Petitioner argues that there were risks associated with the ADR transaction, but neither Tempesta nor any other representative of petitioner conducted an analysis or investigation regarding these alleged concerns. Transactions that involve no market risks are not economically substantial transactions; they are mere tax artifices. See *Yosha v. Commissioner, 861 F.2d 494, 500–501 (7th Cir. 1988),* affg. *Glass v. Commissioner, 87 T.C. 1087 (1986).* Tax-motivated trading patterns generally indicate a lack of economic substance. See *Sheldon v. Commissioner, 94 T.C. 738, 766, 769 (1990).* The purchase and resale prices were predetermined by Leo, and the executing floor brokers did not have authority to deviate from the predetermined prices even if a price change occurred. In addition, the ADR transaction was divided into 23 corresponding purchase and resale cross-trades that were executed in succession, almost simultaneously, and within an hour on the floor of the NYSE. Thus, there was virtually no risk of price fluctuation. Special next-day settlement terms and large blocks of ADR's were also used to minimize the risk of third parties breaking up the cross-trades, and, because the cross-trades were at the market price, there was no risk of other traders breaking up the trades. None of the outgoing cash-flow resulted from risks. Accordingly, we have found that this transaction was deliberately predetermined and designed by petitioner and Twenty-First to yield a specific result and to eliminate all market risks.

To satisfy the business purpose requirement of the economic substance inquiry, "the transaction must be rationally related to a useful nontax purpose that is plausible in light of the taxpayer's conduct and * * * economic situation." *AMC Partnership v. Commissioner, T.C. Memo. 1997–115,* affd. in part, revd. in part, and remanded *157 F.3d 231 (3d Cir.1998);* see also *Levy v. Commissioner, supra at 854.* This inquiry takes into account whether the taxpayer conducts itself in a realistic and legitimate business fashion, thoroughly considering and analyzing the ramifications of a questionable transaction, before proceeding with the transaction. See *UPS of Am. v. Commissioner, T.C. Memo. 1999–268.*

Petitioner contends that it entered into the ADR transaction as a short-term investment to make a profit apart from tax savings, but the objective facts belie petitioner's assertions. The ADR transaction was marketed to petitioner by Twenty-First for the purpose of partially shielding a capital gain previously realized on the sale of Conner Peripherals stock. Petitioner's evaluation of the proposed transaction was less than businesslike with Tempesta, a well-educated, experienced, and financially sophisticated businessman, committing petitioner to this multimillion-dollar transaction based on one meeting with Twenty-First and on his call to a Twenty-First reference. As a whole, the record indicates and we conclude that petitioner was motivated by the expected tax benefits of the ADR transaction, and no other business purpose existed.

Petitioner also contends that the ADR transaction does not warrant the application of the economic substance doctrine because the foreign tax credit regime completely sets forth Congress' intent as to allowable foreign tax credits. Petitioner argues that an additional economic substance requirement was not intended by Congress and should not be applied in this case.

Congress creates deductions and credits to encourage certain types of activities, and the taxpayers who engage in those activities are entitled to the attendant benefits. See, e.g., *Leahy v. Commissioner, 87 T.C. 56, 72 (1986); Fox v. Commissioner, 82 T.C. 1001, 1021 (1984)*. The foreign tax credit serves to prevent double taxation and to facilitate international business transactions. No bona fide business is implicated here, and we are not persuaded that Congress intended to encourage or permit a transaction such as the ADR transaction, which is merely a manipulation of the foreign tax credit to achieve U.S. tax savings.

Finally, petitioner asserts that the enactment of section 901(k) by the Taxpayer Relief Act of 1997, Pub. L. 105–34, sec. 1053(a), 111 Stat. 941, also indicates that Congress did not intend for the economic substance doctrine to apply under the facts of this case. Section 901(k)(1) provides that a taxpayer must hold stock (or an ADR) for at least 16 days of a prescribed 30-day period including the dividend record date, in order to claim a foreign tax credit with respect to foreign taxes withheld at the source on foreign dividends. If the taxpayer does not meet these holding requirements, the taxpayer may claim a deduction for the foreign taxes paid if certain other requirements are met.

Section 901(k) does not change our conclusion in this case. That provision was passed in 1997 and was effective for dividends paid or accrued after September 4, 1997. The report of the Senate Finance Committee indicates that "No inference is intended as to the treatment under present law of tax-motivated transactions intended to transfer foreign tax credit benefits." S. Rept. 105–33, 175, 177 (1997). A transaction does not avoid economic substance scrutiny because the transaction predates a statute targeting the specific abuse. See, e.g., *Krumhorn v. Commissioner, 103 T.C. 29, 48–50 (1994); Fox v. Commissioner, supra 82 T.C. at 1026–1027*. Accordingly, section 901(k), enacted 5 years after the transaction at issue, has no effect on the outcome of this case.

ACCURACY-RELATED PENALTY

Respondent determined that petitioner is liable for the section 6662(a) penalty for 1992. Section 6662(a) imposes a penalty in an amount equal to 20 percent of the underpayment of tax attributable to one or more of the items set forth in section 6662(b). Respondent asserts that the underpayment attributable to the ADR transaction was due to negligence. See sec. 6662(b)(1). "Negligence" includes a failure to make a reasonable attempt to comply with provisions of the internal revenue laws or failure to do what a reasonable and ordinarily prudent person would do under the same circumstances. See sec. 6662(c); *Marcello v. Commissioner, 380 F.2d 499, 506 (5th Cir.1967)*, affg. on this issue *43 T.C. 168 (1964)*; sec. 1.6662–3(b)(1), Income Tax Regs. Petitioner bears the burden of proving that respondent's determinations are erroneous.

See Rule 142(a); *Freytag v. Commissioner, 904 F.2d 1011, 1017 (5th Cir.1990), affg. 89 T.C. 849, 887 (1987), affd. 501 U.S. 868, 115 L. Ed. 2d 764, 111 S. Ct. 2631 (1991).*

The accuracy-related penalty does not apply with respect to any portion of an underpayment if it is shown that there was reasonable cause for such portion of an underpayment and that the taxpayer acted in good faith with respect to such portion. See sec. 6664(c)(1). The determination of whether the taxpayer acted with reasonable cause and in good faith depends upon the pertinent facts and circumstances. See sec. 1.6664–4(b)(1), Income Tax Regs. The most important factor is the extent of the taxpayer's effort to assess the proper tax liability for the year. See id.

Respondent argues that petitioner is liable for the accuracy-related penalty because petitioner negligently disregarded the economic substance of the ADR transaction; petitioner failed to meet its burden of proving that the underpayment was not due to negligence; and petitioner failed to offer evidence that there was reasonable cause for its return position for the ADR transaction or that it acted in good faith with respect to such item. Petitioner argues that there is no basis for a negligence penalty because the return position was reasonable, application of the economic substance doctrine to the ADR transaction is "inherently imprecise", and application of the economic substance doctrine to disregard a foreign tax credit raises an issue of first impression. We agree with respondent.

In this case, Tempesta, Foster, and White were sophisticated professionals with investment experience and should have been alerted to the questionable economic nature of the ADR transaction. They, however, failed to take even the most rudimentary steps to investigate the bona fide economic aspects of the ADR transaction. See *Freytag v. Commissioner, supra*. As set forth in the findings of fact, petitioner did not investigate the details of the transaction, the entity it was investing in, the parties it was doing business with, or the cash-flow implications of the transaction. Petitioner offered no evidence that it satisfied the "reasonable and ordinarily prudent person" standard or relied on the advice of its tax department or counsel. If any communications occurred in which consideration was given to the correctness of petitioner's tax return position when the return was prepared and filed, petitioner has chosen not to disclose those communications. We conclude that petitioner was negligent, and the section 6662(a) penalty is appropriately applied.

Our holding in this opinion will be incorporated into the decision to be entered in this case when all other issues are resolved.

NOTES AND QUESTIONS

1. Compare the amount paid by the taxpayer for the ADRs, the dividend amount, and the amount received by the taxpayer upon sale. What is the implication regarding who bore the burden of the tax?

2. Given the technical taxpayer rule, do you think the court was correct?

3. What is the relationship of this case to Notice 98–5 (later in this chapter)? To Section 901(k)?

4. In IES Industries, Inc. v. United States, 253 F.3d 350 (8th Cir.2001), the court held for the taxpayer on facts substantially identical to *Compaq* (the case involved the same tax shelter marketed by the same promoter). The court held that:

> We reject the government's argument and agree with IES that the law supports our contrary conclusion: the economic benefit to IES was the amount of the gross dividend, before the foreign taxes were paid. IES was the legal owner of the ADRs on the record date. As such, it was legally entitled to retain the benefits of ownership, that is, the dividends due on the record date. While it received only 85% in cash, 100% of the amount of the dividends was income to IES. . . . In this case, income was realized by the payment of IES's foreign tax obligation by a third party. . . . Because the entire amount of the ADR dividends was income to IES, the ADR transactions resulted in a profit, an economic benefit to IES.

The court then goes on to discuss the risk of loss issue, noting that "IES likewise bore the risk that the dividend would not be paid . . . The risk may have been minimal, but that was in part because IES did its homework before engaging in the transactions" (noting that IES officials met twice with the promoter and consulted IES' accountants and lawyers, distinguishing *Compaq* on this ground).

What do you think?

5. In late 2001, the U.S. Court of Appeals (5th. Cir.) reversed the above *Compaq* case in a highly criticized decision (the opinion follows this note).[3] The 5th Circuit held that the transaction in *Compaq* was not a complete sham and therefore allowed Compaq its foreign tax credits. In the meantime, there is a lively policy debate about the economic substance doctrine, and its content and scope. To some extent, The Health Care and Education Reconciliation Act of 2010 codified economic substance. See new Section 7701(*o*).

---

[3] Compaq Computer Corp. v. Commissioner, 277 F.3d 778 (5th Cir. 2001). For critique, see Daniel N. Shaviro and David A. Weisbach, The U.S. Fifth Circuit Gets It Wrong in Compaq v. Commissioner, 26 Tax Notes Int'l 191 (Apr. 15, 2002).

Compaq Computer Corporation and Subsidiaries, Petitioner-Appellant v. Commissioner of Internal Revenue

United States Court of Appeals, Fifth Circuit.
277 F.3d 778 (2001).

■ EDITH H. JONES, CIRCUIT JUDGE:

. . . "[W]here . . . there is a genuine multiple-party transaction with economic substance which is compelled or encouraged by business or regulatory realities, is imbued with tax-independent considerations, and is not shaped solely by tax-avoidance features that have meaningless labels attached, the Government should honor the allocation of rights and duties effectuated by the parties." *Frank Lyon Co., 435 U.S. at 583–84, 98 S.Ct. at 1303–04.* See *Holladay v. Comm'r, 649 F.2d 1176, 1179 (5th Cir. Unit B Jul.1981)* ("[T]he existence of a tax benefit resulting from a transaction does not automatically make it a sham as long as the transaction is imbued with tax-independent considerations."), cited in *Merryman v. Comm'r, 873 F.2d 879, 881 (5th Cir.1989).* The Government has stipulated that aside from its contention that the Royal Dutch transaction lacked economic substance, it has no objection to how Compaq chose to report its tax benefits and liabilities concerning the transaction.

In *Rice's Toyota World, Inc. v. Comm'r, 752 F.2d 89 (4th Cir.1985)*, the court held that after Frank Lyon Co., it is appropriate for a court to engage in a two-part inquiry to determine whether a transaction has economic substance or is a sham that should not be recognized for income tax purposes. "To treat a transaction as a sham, the court must find that the taxpayer was motivated by no business purposes other than obtaining tax benefits in entering the transaction, and that the transaction has no economic substance because no reasonable possibility of a profit exists." Id. at 91 (emphasis added). See id. ("[S]uch a test properly gives effect to the mandate of the Court in Frank Lyon that a transaction cannot be treated as a sham unless the transaction is shaped solely by tax avoidance considerations.") (emphasis added). Other courts have said that business purpose and reasonable possibility of profit are merely factors to be considered in determining whether a transaction is a sham. See, e.g., *ACM Partnership v. Comm'r, 157 F.3d 231, 247 (3d Cir.1998)* ("[T]hese distinct aspects of the economic sham inquiry do not constitute discrete prongs of a 'rigid two-step analysis,' but rather represent related factors both of which inform the analysis of whether the transaction had sufficient substance, apart from its tax consequences, to be respected for tax purposes.") (citation omitted); *James v. Comm'r, 899 F.2d 905, 908–09 (10th Cir.1990).* Because we conclude that the ADR transaction in this case had both economic substance and a business purpose, we do not need to decide today which of these views to adopt.

The Tax Court reasoned that Compaq's ADR transaction had neither economic substance nor a non-tax business purpose. The court first concluded that Compaq had no reasonable opportunity for profit apart from the income tax consequences of the transaction. The court reached this conclusion by employing a curious method of calculation: in computing what it called Compaq's net "cash flow" from the transaction, the court assessed neither the transaction's pre-tax profitability nor its post-tax profitability. Instead, the court assessed profitability by looking at the transaction after Netherlands tax had been imposed but before considering U.S. income tax consequences. The court subtracted Compaq's $20.7 million in capital losses, not from the $22.5 million gross dividend, but from the $19.2 million net dividend. The court then ignored the $3.4 million U.S. foreign tax credit that Compaq claimed corresponding to the $3.4 million Netherlands tax. Put otherwise, in determining whether the ADR transaction was profitable, the court treated the Netherlands tax as a cost of the transaction, but did not treat the corresponding U.S. tax credit as a benefit of the transaction. The result of this half pre-tax, half after-tax calculation was a net loss figure of roughly $1.5 million.

The court rejected Compaq's argument that it had a profit prior to the assessment of tax. [Compaq] used tax reporting strategies to give the illusion of profit, while simultaneously claiming a tax credit in an amount (nearly $3.4 million) that far exceeds the U.S. tax (of $640,000) attributed to the alleged profit, and thus is available to offset tax on unrelated transactions. . . . By reporting the gross amount of the dividend, when only the net amount was received, petitioner created a fictional $1.9 million profit as a predicate for a $3.4 million tax credit. As for Compaq's business purpose, the Tax Court concluded that Compaq was motivated only by the expected tax benefits of the ADR transaction. Among other things, the court said, Compaq had not engaged in a businesslike evaluation of the transaction. See *id. at 224–25.*

The Tax Court's decision is in conflict with *IES Indus., Inc. v. United States, 253 F.3d 350 (8th Cir.2001). In IES, the court held as a matter of law that an ADR transaction identical to this one was not a sham transaction for income tax purposes. Undertaking the two-part inquiry set out in* Rice's Toyota World, *752 F.2d at 91–92, the court declined to decide whether a transaction would be a sham if either economic substance or business purpose, but not both, was present. See* IES, 253 F.3d at 353–54. *Instead, the court concluded that both economic substance and business purpose were present in the transaction before it.*

. . . Turning first to economic substance, the court rejected the argument that the taxpayer purchased only the right to the net dividend, not the gross dividend. "[T]he economic benefit to IES was the amount of the gross dividend, before the foreign taxes were paid. IES was the legal owner of the ADRs on the record date. As such, it was legally entitled to retain the benefits of ownership, that is, the dividends due on the record date." Id. at 354. The court said that the part of the gross dividend withheld as taxes by the Dutch government was as much income to the taxpayer as the net dividend remaining after taxes. The court relied on the venerable principle, articulated in *Old Colony Trust Co. v. Comm'r, 279 U.S. 716, 729, 49 S.Ct. 499, 504, 73 L.Ed. 918 (1929),* that "[t]he discharge by a third person of an obligation to him is equivalent to receipt by the person taxed." In Old Colony Trust Co., the Supreme Court held that when an employer pays an employee's income taxes, the payment of the taxes constitutes income to the employee. Similarly, in *Diedrich v. Comm'r, 457 U.S. 191, 199–200, 102 S.Ct. 2414, 2420, 72 L.Ed.2d 777 (1982),* the Court held that when a donor of a gift of property conditions the gift on the donee's paying the gift tax owed by the donor on the gift, the donee's payment of the donor's gift tax obligation constituted income to the donor.

The IES court saw no reason why the Old Colony Trust Co. principle should not apply to the payment of foreign tax by withholding. "The foreign corporation's withholding and payment of the tax on IES's behalf is no different from an employer['s] withholding and paying to the government income taxes for an employee: the full amount before taxes are paid is considered income to the employee." *IES, 253 F.3d at 354.* When the full amount of the gross dividend was counted as income to the taxpayer, the transaction resulted in a profit to the taxpayer. See id.

As for business purpose, the court said that "[a] taxpayer's subjective intent to avoid taxes . . . will not by itself determine whether there was a business purpose to a transaction." Id. at 355. Compare *Holladay, 649 F.2d at 1179.* The court rejected the Government's argument that because the ADR transaction carried no risk of loss, it was a sham. The court noted that some risk, minimal though it may have been, attended the transaction. That the taxpayer had tried to reduce the risks did not make it a sham. "We are not prepared to say that a transaction should be tagged a sham for tax purposes merely because it does not involve excessive risk. IES's disinclination to accept any more risk than necessary in these circumstances strikes us as an exercise of good business judgment consistent with a subjective intent to treat the ADR trades as money-making transactions." *IES, 253 F.3d at 355.*

The court further noted that the ADR transactions had not been conducted by alter egos or by straw entities created by the taxpayer simply for the purpose of facilitating the transactions. Instead, "[a]ll of the parties involved . . . were entities separate and apart from IES, doing legitimate business before IES started trading ADRs and (as far as we know) continuing such legitimate business after that time." Id. Each individual ADR trade was an arm's-length transaction. See id. at 356.

We agree with the IES court and conclude that the Tax Court erred as a matter of law by disregarding the gross amount of the Royal Dutch dividend and thus ignoring Compaq's pre-tax profit on the ADR transaction. We add the following comments.

. . . First, as to economic substance: the Commissioner does not explain why the Old Colony Trust Co. principle does not apply here. That the tax was imposed by the Netherlands rather than by the United States, or that it was withheld rather than paid at the end of the tax year, is irrelevant to how the part of the dividend corresponding to the tax should be treated for U.S. income tax purposes. Pre-tax income is pre-tax income regardless of the timing or origin of the tax. See *Old Colony Trust Co., 279 U.S. at 729, 49 S.Ct. at 504* ("It is . . . immaterial that the taxes were directly paid over to the government [by the taxpayer's employer, rather than by the taxpayer]."); *Riggs Nat'l Corp. v. Comm'r, 163 F.3d 1363, 1365 (D.C.Cir.1999)* ("In calculating his United States tax liability, the lender must include in gross income the interest payment he receives from the borrower and the Brazilian tax paid (on his behalf) by the borrower to the Brazilian tax collector."); *Reading & Bates Corp. v. United States, 40 Fed. Cl. 737, 750 (1998)* ("The indemnification agreement at issue results in taxable income to plaintiff because it contractually discharges plaintiff's Egyptian tax obligation."). Because Compaq was entitled to payment of the dividend as of the record date, Compaq was liable for payment of tax on the dividend; accordingly, the payment of Compaq's Netherlands tax obligation by Royal Dutch was income to *Compaq. See 113 T.C. at 219* ($3.4 million payment to Netherlands "represent[ed] withholding amounts for dividends paid to U.S. residents" under treaty between *U.S. and Netherlands); IES, 253 F.3d at 351–52, 354; Treas. Reg. § 1.901–2(f)(1)* ("The person by whom tax is considered paid for purposes of [the foreign tax credit provisions of the Revenue Code] is the person on whom foreign law imposes legal liability for such tax, even if another person (e.g., a withholding agent) remits such tax."); *Treas. Reg. § 1.901–2(f)(2)(i)* ("Tax is considered paid by the taxpayer even if another party to a direct or indirect transaction with the taxpayer agrees, as a part of the transaction, to assume the taxpayer's foreign tax liability."). Indeed, the Commissioner admitted in this case that according to generally accepted accounting principles, the entire amount of Compaq's gross dividend must be reported as income. If the $3.4 million had been paid to the United States (whether by withholding or at the end of the tax year) instead of the Netherlands, there would have been no argument that this money was not income to Compaq. It follows that the gross Royal Dutch dividend, not the dividend net of Netherlands tax, should have been used to compute Compaq's pre-tax profit.

The Tax Court also erred by failing to include Compaq's $3.4 million U.S. tax credit when it calculated Compaq's after-tax profit. *113 T.C. at 223*. This omission taints the court's conclusion that the "net economic loss" from the transaction after tax was about $1.5 million. If the effects of tax law, domestic or foreign, are to be accounted for when they subtract from a transaction's net cash flow, tax law effects should be counted when they add to cash flow. To be consistent, the analysis should either count all tax law effects or not count any of them. To count them only when they subtract from cash flow is to stack the deck against finding the transaction profitable. During this litigation, the I.R.S. has consciously chosen to try to stack the deck this way. See *I.R.S. Notice 98–5, 1998–1 C.B. 334, 1997 WL 786882* ("In general, reasonably expected economic profit will be determined by taking into account foreign tax consequences (but not U.S. tax consequences) [of transactions]. . . . In general, expected economic profit will be determined by taking into account expenses associated with an arrangement, without regard to whether such expenses are deductible in determining taxable income. For example, in determining economic profit, foreign taxes will be treated as an expense."). The Commissioner, however, has provided no reason to endorse its approach and ignore Old Colony Trust Co. That the Government would get more money from taxpayers does not suffice.

. . . To un-stack the deck and include the foreign tax credit in calculating Compaq's after-tax profit from the Royal Dutch transaction does not give Compaq a windfall. The purpose of the Revenue Code's foreign tax credit provisions is to reduce international double taxation. See, e.g., *Norwest Corp. v. Comm'r, 69 F.3d 1404, 1407 (8th Cir.1995)*. Compaq reported its gross Royal Dutch dividend income to both the United States and the Netherlands. Without the tax credit, Compaq would be required to pay tax twice—first to the Netherlands through withholding on the gross dividend, and then to the United States—on the same dividend income. Taking the tax credit into account, Compaq owed roughly $644,000 more in worldwide income tax liability as a result of the transaction than it would have owed had the transaction not occurred. Although the United States lost $2.7 million in tax revenues as a result of the transaction, that is only because the Netherlands gained $3.4 million in tax revenues.

If the effects of the transaction are computed consistently, Compaq made both a pre-tax profit and an after-tax profit from the ADR transaction. Subtracting Compaq's capital losses from the gross dividend rather than the net dividend results in a net pre-tax profit of about $1.894 million. Compaq's U.S. tax on that net pre-tax profit was roughly $644,000. Subtracting $644,000 from the $1.894 million results in an after-tax profit of about $1.25 million. The transaction had economic substance.

Second, as to business purpose: even assuming that Compaq sought primarily to get otherwise unavailable tax benefits in order to offset unrelated tax liabilities and unrelated capital gains, this need not invalidate the transaction. See *Frank Lyon Co., 435 U.S. at 580, 98 S.Ct. at 1302* ("The fact that favorable tax consequences were taken into account by Lyon on entering into the transaction is no reason for disallowing those consequences. We cannot ignore the reality that the tax laws affect the shape of nearly every business transaction.") (footnote omitted); *Holladay, 649 F.2d at 1179; ACM Partnership, 157 F.3d at 248 n. 31* ("[W]here a transaction objectively affects the taxpayer's net economic position, legal relations, or non-tax business interests, it will not be disregarded merely because it was motivated by tax considerations."); *Helvering v. Gregory, 69 F.2d 809, 810 (2d Cir.1934)* (Hand, J. Learned) ("Any one may so arrange his affairs that his taxes shall be as low as possible; he is not bound to choose that pattern which will best pay the Treasury; there is not even a patriotic duty to increase one's taxes."), aff'd, *293 U.S. 465, 55 S.Ct. 266, 79 L.Ed. 596 (1935)*. Yet the evidence in the record does not show that Compaq's choice to engage in the ADR transaction was solely motivated by the tax consequences of the transaction. Instead, the evidence shows that Compaq actually and legitimately also sought the (pre-tax) $1.9 million profit it would get from the Royal Dutch dividend of approximately $22.5 million less the $20.7 million or so in capital losses that Compaq would incur from the sale of the ADRs ex dividend.

According to the Commissioner, tax-exempt organizations with no use for U.S. income tax credits have an incentive to loan out their ADRs to non-tax-exempt persons in transactions of the kind at issue in this case. The non-exempt persons can use the capital losses and tax credits resulting from ADR transactions to offset unrelated capital gains and tax liabilities. The fact that the differing tax attributes of investors make ADRs more valuable for some investors than for others does not deprive ADR transactions of economic substance for purposes of the tax laws. The possible benefits from ADR transactions for investors with unrelated capital gains and tax liabilities are analogous to the benefits that taxpaying investors (especially investors with high incomes), but not tax-exempt persons, get from the purchase of tax-exempt bonds with lower yields than the pre-tax yields available from non-exempt bonds. See Yin, supra, at 222–23. In both instances the benefits would not exist were it not for the investors' individual tax attributes.

Although, as the Tax Court found, the parties attempted to minimize the risks incident to the transaction, those risks did exist and were not by any means insignificant. The transaction occurred on a public market, not in an environment controlled by Compaq or its agents. The market prices of the ADRs could have changed during the course of the transaction (they in fact did change, *113 T.C. at 218);* any of the individual trades could have been broken up or, for that matter, could have been executed incorrectly; and the dividend might not have been paid or might have been paid in an amount different from that anticipated by Compaq. See *IES, 253 F.3d at 355*. The absence of risk that can legitimately be eliminated does not make a transaction a sham, see id.; but in this case risk was present. In light of what we have said about the nature of Compaq's profit, both pre-tax and post-tax, we conclude that the transaction had a sufficient business purpose independent of tax considerations.

Because the Royal Dutch ADR transaction had both economic substance and a non-tax business purpose, it should have been recognized as valid for U.S. income tax purposes. This court's decisions applying the economic substance doctrine to disregard various transactions are not to the contrary. Without enumerating all of the decisions, we mention some to give a flavor of the differences between the facts at issue in the decisions and in this case. In *Freytag v. Comm'r, 904 F.2d 1011 (5th Cir.1990),* aff'd on other grounds, *501 U.S. 868, 111 S.Ct. 2631, 115 L.Ed.2d 764 (1991),* this court affirmed a Tax Court decision disallowing losses allegedly incurred as a result of investments in a commodity straddle program. The taxpayers' investment agent had "absolute authority over the pricing and timing of the transactions" at issue, which "occurred in [a] self-contained market of its own making." 904 F.2d at 1016. In Merryman, a business partnership was disregarded for tax purposes because "the formation and role of the partnership served no other purpose except tax avoidance;" a number of facts found by the Tax Court indicated that the partnership lacked economic reality and was a mere formality. See id. at 881–83. In Killingsworth, this court affirmed a Tax Court decision concluding that a scheme of option hedge or option straddle transactions lacked economic substance. We relied on Revenue Code section 108, a provision that is not relevant to this case, and noted that the transactions "appear[ed] to be devoid of profit making potential." *864 F.2d at 1218.* In Holladay, this court affirmed the Tax Court's decision to disallow half of certain tax benefits that an agreement between two joint venturers allocated to only one of the venturers. The allocation had no valid non-tax business purpose. *649 F.2d at 1180.* Compare *Boynton v. Comm'r, 649 F.2d 1168, 1173–74 (5th Cir. Unit B Jul.1981).*

In this case, by contrast, the ADR transaction had both a reasonable possibility of profit attended by a real risk of loss and an adequate non-tax business purpose. The transaction was not a mere formality or artifice but occurred in a real market subject to real risks. And, as has been discussed, the transaction gave rise to a real profit whether one looks at the transaction prior to the imposition of tax or afterwards.

For the foregoing reasons, the Tax Court erred as a matter of law in disallowing Compaq's identification of gross dividend income, a foreign tax credit, and capital losses associated with the Royal Dutch ADR arbitrage transaction. It is unnecessary to reach the alternative arguments for reversal offered by Compaq: first, that the statutory foreign tax credit regime implicitly displaces the economic substance doctrine; and second, that a 1997 amendment to the foreign tax credit scheme, which added what is now *Internal Revenue Code § 901(k),* implies that ADR transactions that took place before the amendment are to be recognized for tax purposes. Because we reverse the Tax Court's decision concerning the underlying transaction, it follows that the court erred in imposing the negligence penalty and that the court's holding that Compaq was not entitled to deduct its out of pocket losses becomes superfluous.

The decision of the Tax Court is REVERSED.

NOTES AND QUESTIONS

1. Revisit your answer to question 2 for the Tax Court's case. What do you think now?

2. Do you think that the court's decision is in line with the purpose of the foreign tax credit rules?

3. How do you view the threat of the "economic substance" doctrine to tax planning after this decision?

4. After reading the two *Compaq* cases, what is your opinion regarding a proposal to allow the trade in tax attributes, such as these credits? (in your answer do not forget to factor in compliance and enforcement costs)

      * * *

This following notice represents the most ambitious action by the government in its battle against foreign tax credit abuse—think about it when you read the notice. Nonetheless, as you shall see below, it was later withdrawn. What is the underlying policy motivating this Notice? Should the IRS have withdrawn it?

Notice 98–5

Foreign Tax Credit Abuse

1998 IRB LEXIS 15; 1998–3 I.R.B. 49; Notice 98–5

January 20, 1998

Treasury and the Internal Revenue Service understand that certain U.S. taxpayers (primarily multinational corporations) have entered into or may be considering a variety of abusive tax-motivated transactions with a purpose of acquiring or generating foreign tax credits that can be used to shelter low-taxed foreign-source income from residual U.S. tax. These transactions generally are structured to yield little or no economic profit relative to the expected U.S. tax benefits, and typically involve either: (1) the acquisition of an asset that generates an income stream subject to foreign withholding tax, or (2) effective duplication of tax benefits through the use of certain structures designed to exploit inconsistencies between U.S. and foreign tax laws. This notice announces that Treasury and the Service will address these transactions through the issuance of regulations as well as by application of other principles of existing law, and requests public comment with respect to these and related foreign tax credit issues.

I.   BACKGROUND

United States persons are subject to U.S. income tax on foreign-source as well as U.S.-source income. Subject to applicable limitations, U.S. persons with foreign-source income may credit income taxes imposed by foreign jurisdictions against their U.S. income tax liability on foreign-source income.

Worldwide taxation of U.S. persons coupled with the allowance of a foreign tax credit establishes general tax neutrality between foreign and domestic investment by U.S. taxpayers. A tax system that simply exempts foreign-source income from taxation creates an incentive for citizens and residents to invest overseas in low-taxed jurisdictions. On the other hand, worldwide taxation without a foreign tax credit creates double taxation that distorts investment decisions by inhibiting foreign investment or business activities. The foreign tax credit provisions of the Code, principally sections 901 through 907 and 960, effectuate Congress's intent to provide relief from double taxation and alleviate these distortions. *American Chicle Co. v. United States, 316 U.S. 450 (1942); Burnet v. Chicago Portrait Co., 285 U.S. 1 (1932).*

In contrast to certain tax credits that are intended to create an incentive for taxpayers to invest in certain activities, such as the research credit under section 41 or the low-income housing credit under section 42, the foreign tax credit is designed to reduce the disincentive for taxpayers to invest abroad that would be caused by double taxation. In other words, the foreign tax credit is intended to preserve neutrality between U.S. and foreign investment and to minimize the effect of tax consequences on taxpayers' decisions about where to invest and conduct business.

Relief from double taxation generally is not calculated separately with respect to each dollar of foreign-source income and tax. The foreign tax credit limitation or "basket" regime of section 904(d) permits, to a limited extent, a credit for foreign tax imposed with respect to income taxed at a rate in excess of the applicable U.S. rate to shelter from U.S. tax income from other, similar investments and activities that are subject to a relatively low rate of tax (the "cross-crediting regime"). Accordingly, the foreign tax credit provisions do not limit credits on an item-by-item basis. Rather, subject to certain restrictions, the provisions permit cross-crediting of foreign taxes imposed with respect to specified groups or types of income as consistent with the interrelated quality of multinational operations of U.S. persons.

Multinational corporations that are subject to relatively low rates of tax on their foreign-source income may be in an excess limitation position. Generally, such taxpayers may properly use credits for foreign taxes imposed on high-taxed foreign income to offset residual U.S. tax on their low-taxed foreign income. Treasury and the Service are concerned, however, that such taxpayers may enter into foreign tax credit-generating schemes designed to abuse the cross-crediting regime and effectively transform the U.S. worldwide system of taxation into a system exempting foreign-source income from residual U.S. tax.

This result is clearly incompatible with the existence of the detailed foreign tax credit provisions and cross-crediting limitations enacted by Congress. No statutory purpose is served by permitting credits for taxes generated in abusive transactions designed to reduce residual U.S. tax on low-taxed foreign-source income. The foreign tax credit benefits derived from such transactions represent subsidies from the U.S. Treasury to taxpayers that operate and earn income in low-tax or zero-tax jurisdictions. The effect is economically equivalent to the tax sparing benefits for U.S. taxpayers that Congress and the Treasury have consistently opposed in the tax treaty context because such benefits are inconsistent with U.S. tax principles and sound tax policy.

II. ABUSIVE ARRANGEMENTS

Treasury and the Service have identified two classes of transactions that create potential for foreign tax credit abuse. The first class consists of transactions involving transfers of tax liability through the acquisition of an asset that generates an income stream subject to foreign gross basis taxes such as withholding taxes. Transactions described in this class may include acquisitions of income streams through securities loans and similar arrangements and acquisitions in combination with total return swaps. In abusive arrangements involving such transactions, foreign tax credits are effectively purchased by a U.S. taxpayer in an arrangement where the expected economic profit from the arrangement is insubstantial compared to the foreign tax credits generated.

The second class of transactions consists of cross-border tax arbitrage transactions that permit effective duplication of tax benefits. Duplicate benefits result when the U.S. grants benefits and, in addition, a foreign country grants benefits (including benefits from a full or partial imputation or exemption system, or a preferential rate for certain income) to separate persons with respect to the same taxes or income. These duplicate benefits generally can result where the U.S. and a foreign country treat all or part of a transaction or amount differently under their respective tax systems. In abusive arrangements involving such transactions, the U.S. taxpayer exploits these inconsistencies where the expected economic profit is insubstantial compared to the foreign tax credits generated.

The following are examples of abusive arrangements within the scope of this notice.

Example 1

On June 29, 1998, US, a domestic corporation, purchases all rights to a copyright for $75.00. The copyright will expire shortly and the only income expected to be received with respect to the copyright is a royalty payable June 30, 1998. The gross amount of the royalty is expected to be $100.00. The royalty payment is subject to a 30-percent Country X withholding tax. On June 30, 1998, U.S. receives the $100.00 royalty payment, less the $30.00 withholding tax. U.S. reasonably expects to incur a $5.00 economic loss (having paid $75.00 for the right to receive a $70.00 net royalty payment), but expects to acquire a $30.00 foreign tax liability. In this example, U.S. has effectively purchased foreign tax credits in a transaction that was reasonably expected to result in an economic loss.

Example 2

On June 29, 1998, US, a domestic corporation, purchases a foreign bond for $1096.00 (including accrued interest). The foreign bond provides for annual interest payments of $100.00 payable June 30 of each year. The interest payments are subject to a 4.9-percent Country X withholding tax. On June 30, 1998, U.S. receives a $95.10 interest payment on the bond (net of a $4.90 Country X withholding tax). On July 4, 1998, U.S. sells the bond for $1001.05. Because the value of the bond is not reasonably expected to appreciate due to market factors, U.S. reasonably can expect only a $0.15 economic profit (the $1001.05 sales price and the $95.10 net interest coupon, less the $1096.00 purchase price) and expects to acquire a $4.90 foreign tax liability. In this example, U.S. has effectively purchased foreign tax credits in a transaction with respect to which the reasonably expected economic profit is insubstantial in relation to expected U.S. foreign tax credits. No implication is intended as to whether the interest described in this example will constitute high withholding tax interest under section 904(d)(2)(B).

Example 3

F, an entity that does not receive a tax benefit from foreign tax credits, wishes to acquire a foreign bond with a value of $1000.00 that provides for annual interest payments of $100.00. The interest payments are subject to a 4.9-percent Country X withholding tax. Instead of purchasing the bond, F invests its $1000.00 elsewhere and enters into a three-year notional principal contract (NPC) with US, an unrelated domestic corporation. Under the terms of the NPC, U.S. agrees to make an annual payment to F equal to $96.00 and F agrees to make an annual payment to U.S. equal to the product of $1000.00 and a rate calculated based on LIBOR. In addition, the parties agree that, upon termination of the NPC, U.S. will make a payment to F based on the appreciation, if any, in the value of the foreign bond, and F will make a payment to U.S. based on the depreciation, if any, in the value of the foreign bond. In order to hedge its obligations under the NPC, U.S. purchases the bond for $1000.00. Assume that, in connection with the purchase of the foreign bond, U.S. incurs or maintains an additional $1000.00 of borrowing at an interest rate equal to the LIBOR-based rate provided for in the NPC.

At the time U.S. enters into this arrangement, U.S. reasonably expects to incur an annual $0.90 economic loss each year under the arrangement (the $95.10 net interest payment on the bond plus the LIBOR-based amount received from F under the NPC, less the sum of the $96.00 payment to F under the NPC and the LIBOR-based amount associated with the $1000.00 borrowing incurred or maintained in order to acquire the foreign bond). In this example, U.S. has effectively purchased foreign tax credits in a transaction that was reasonably expected to result in an economic loss.

Example 4

US, a domestic corporation, forms N, a Country X corporation, by contributing $10.00 to the capital of N in exchange for the only share of N common stock. N borrows $90.00 from F, a Country X individual unrelated to US, at an annual interest rate of 7.5 percent, and N purchases preferred stock of an unrelated party with a par value of $100.00 or a bond with a face amount of $100.00. U.S. reasonably expects the preferred stock or bond to pay dividends or interest at an annual rate of 10 percent. Alternatively, rather than purchasing preferred stock or the bond, N lends $100.00 to U.S. at an annual interest rate of 10 percent.

Country X treats the F loan as an equity investment and does not allow a deduction for N's interest expense. Country X imposes an individual income tax and a corporate income tax of 30 percent. Country X thus is expected to impose a $3.00 corporate income tax each year on N. Country X has an imputation system, under which dividends from Country X corporations are excluded from the gross income of Country X individuals. (A similar result could be achieved if the dividends are wholly or partially exempt from Country X tax due to a consolidated return or group relief regime, a dividend-received deduction, or an imputation credit.)

At the time U.S. enters into this arrangement, U.S. reasonably expects that N will have annual earnings and profits of $0.25 ($10.00 dividend or interest income from the preferred stock or bond (or $10.00 interest income from the loan to US), less $6.75 interest expense and $3.00 foreign tax liability). U.S. expects that each year N will pay a $0.25 dividend to U.S. and U.S. will claim a $3.00 foreign tax credit for taxes deemed paid under section 902. In this example, U.S. has entered into an arrangement to exploit the inconsistency between U.S. and Country X tax laws in order to generate foreign tax credits in a transaction with respect to which the reasonably expected economic profit is insubstantial in relation to expected U.S. foreign tax credits.

Example 5

US, a domestic corporation, forms N, a Country X entity. U.S. contributes $100.00 to the capital of N in exchange for a 100-percent ownership interest. N borrows $900.00 from F, an unrelated Country X corporation, at an annual interest rate of 8 percent, and N purchases preferred stock of an unrelated party with a par value of $1000.00 that U.S. reasonably expects to pay dividends at an annual rate of 10 percent. The dividends are subject to a Country Y 25-percent withholding tax.

Country X treats the F loan as an equity investment in N and treats N as a partnership. Consequently, F claims a foreign tax credit in Country X for 90 percent of the withholding tax paid by N. Under U.S. law, the F loan is respected as debt, and N is disregarded as a separate entity (a partnership with only one partner). See Reg. § 301.7701–3(a) and § 301.7701–3(b)(2)(C). Thus, U.S. claims a U.S. foreign tax credit for the taxes paid by N and the tax benefit of the foreign taxes paid by N are effectively duplicated.

At the time U.S. enters into this arrangement, U.S. reasonably expects an annual profit of $3.00 ($100.00 dividend income, less $72.00 interest expense and $25.00 foreign tax liability) and an annual foreign tax credit of $25. In this example, U.S. has entered into an arrangement to exploit the inconsistency between U.S. and Country X tax laws in order to generate foreign tax credits in a transaction with respect to which the reasonably expected economic profit is insubstantial in relation to expected U.S. foreign tax credits.

III. REGULATIONS TO BE ISSUED PURSUANT TO THIS NOTICE

Regulations will be issued to disallow foreign tax credits for taxes generated in abusive arrangements such as those described in Part II above. These regulations will be issued under the authority of some or all of the following sections of the Internal Revenue Code of 1986: section 901, section 901(k) (4), section 904, section 864(e)(7), section 7701(1), and section 7805(a).

In general, these regulations will disallow foreign tax credits in an arrangement such as those described in Part II above from which the reasonably expected economic profit is insubstantial compared to the value of the foreign tax credits expected to be obtained as a result of the arrangement. The regulations will emphasize an objective approach to calculating expected economic profit and credits, and will require that the determination of expected economic profit reflect the likelihood of realizing both potential gain and potential loss (including loss in excess of the taxpayer's investment). Thus, under the regulations, expected economic profit will be determined without regard to executory financial contracts (e.g., a notional principal contract, forward contract, or similar instrument) that do not represent a real economic investment or potential for profit or that are not properly treated as part of the arrangement. Further, the regulations will require that expected economic profit be determined over the term of the arrangement, properly discounted to present value.

It is expected that the regulations in general and any test relying on a comparison of economic profit and credits in particular would be applied to discrete arrangements. The utility of a test comparing profits and credits depends upon the proper delineation of the arrangement to be tested. If necessary to effectuate the purposes of the regulations, a series of related transactions or investments may be treated as a single arrangement or portions of a single transaction or investment may be treated as separate arrangements. The proper grouping of transactions and investments into arrangements will depend on all relevant facts and circumstances.

For example, a series of transactions involving a purchase and resale might be treated as a single arrangement. Similarly, an investment together with related hedging and financing transactions, e.g., a borrowing, an investment, and an asset swap designed to limit the taxpayer's economic exposure with respect to the investment, might be treated as a single arrangement. In addition, if a controlled foreign corporation, as part of its business, enters into a buy-sell transaction involving a debt instrument, that buy-sell transaction could be treated as a separate arrangement.

In general, reasonably expected economic profit will be determined by taking into account foreign tax consequences (but not U.S. tax consequences). However, it is inappropriate in the context of the U.S. foreign tax credit system to allow foreign tax credits with respect to abusive arrangements simply because the arrangements generate substantial foreign tax savings. Accordingly, the regulations will provide that the calculation of expected economic profit will not include expected foreign tax savings attributable to a tax credit or similar benefit allowed by a foreign country with respect to a tax paid to another foreign country.

In general, expected economic profit will be determined by taking into account expenses associated with an arrangement, without regard to whether such expenses are deductible in determining taxable income. For example, in determining economic profit, foreign taxes will be treated as an expense. In addition, interest expense (and similar amounts, including borrowing fees, "in lieu of" payments, forward contract payments, and notional principal contract payments) generally will be taken into account in determining expected economic profit only to the extent that the indebtedness or contract giving rise to the expense is part of the arrangement.

In addition, the regulations will provide special rules that will operate to deny credits for foreign taxes generated in abusive arrangements involving asset swaps or other hedging devices (including rules that allocate interest expense to an arrangement in certain cases other than pursuant to a tracing approach). For example, an arrangement involving a purchase of a foreign security coupled with an asset swap that is designed to hedge substantially all of the taxpayer's risk of loss with respect to the security for the duration of the arrangement generally will constitute an abusive foreign tax credit arrangement even if the taxpayer has not incurred indebtedness for the specific purpose of acquiring the asset. However, the regulations will not treat arrangements involving debt instruments as abusive solely because the taxpayer diminishes its risk of interest rate or currency fluctuations, unless the taxpayer also diminishes its risk of loss with respect to other risks (e.g., creditor risk) for a significant portion of the taxpayer's holding period. See Part VI of this notice for additional rules for portfolio hedging strategies and partial hedges.

Under the foregoing principles, the regulations will not disallow foreign tax credits merely because income from the arrangement is subject to a high foreign tax rate. Treasury and the Service anticipate that credits for taxes paid to a high-tax jurisdiction will not be subject to disallowance under the regulations absent other indicia of abuse.

The regulations generally will not disallow a credit for withholding taxes on dividends if the holding period requirement of section 901(k) is satisfied. However, the regulations will operate to determine whether foreign tax credits with respect to cross-border tax arbitrage arrangements (as described in Part II, above) will be disallowed, even if such credits arise with respect to withholding taxes on dividends and the section 901(k) holding period is satisfied. In addition, the regulations generally will apply to determine whether credits should be disallowed with respect to qualified taxes (as defined in section 901(k)(4)(B)) that are not subject to the general section 901(k) holding period rule. For example, the regulations may disallow credits with respect to gross basis taxes paid or accrued with respect to certain arrangements involving equity swaps and equity buy-sell transactions entered into by securities dealers even if such credits would not have been disallowed under section 901(k) pursuant to section 901(k)(4). See section 901(k)(4)(C).

IV.   EFFECTIVE DATE OF REGULATIONS ISSUED PURSUANT TO THIS NOTICE

The regulations to be issued with respect to arrangements of the kind described in Part II above generally will be effective with respect to taxes paid or accrued on or after December 23, 1997, the date this notice was issued to the public. The effective date of the regulations issued pursuant to this notice, however, will not limit the application of other principles of existing law to determine the proper tax consequences of the structures or transactions addressed in the regulations.

V.   IRS COORDINATION PROCEDURES

The Service intends to carefully examine foreign tax credits claimed in arrangements of the type described in Part II to determine whether such credits should be disallowed under existing law even without application of the regulations to be issued pursuant to this notice. The Service plans to establish early coordination procedures utilizing foreign tax credit experts in the National Office and the International Field Assistance Specialization Program to assist examining agents in analyzing these transactions. These coordination procedures will continue in effect following issuance of the regulations to ensure uniform and appropriate application of the regulations by examining agents.

VI.   OTHER FOREIGN TAX CREDIT GUIDANCE

Treasury and the Service are considering issuing other guidance to ensure that foreign tax credits are allowed to U.S. taxpayers in a manner consistent with the overall structure of the Code and the intent of Congress in enacting the credit. For example, Treasury and the Service are considering issuing additional regulations under section 904(d)(2)(B)(iii) to address abusive transactions involving high withholding taxes. Treasury and the Service are also considering whether additional approaches may be necessary to identify abuses in the case of foreign gross basis taxes generally.

In addition, Treasury and the Service are considering various approaches to address structures (including hybrid entity structures) and transactions intended to create a significant mismatch between the time foreign taxes are paid or accrued and the time the foreign-source income giving rise to the relevant foreign tax liability is recognized for U.S. tax purposes. For such structures and transactions, Treasury and the Service are considering either deferring the tax credits until the taxpayer recognizes the income, or accelerating the income recognition to the time at which the credits are allowed (e.g., by allocating the credits or the income under section 482).

Finally, Treasury and the Service are concerned about credits claimed in transactions described in Part II above, with respect to assets or income streams that are hedged pursuant to portfolio hedging strategies and with respect to hedges entered into with respect to assets or income streams that the taxpayer holds without diminished risk of loss for a significant period of time.

In general, regulations addressing these other foreign tax credit issues will be effective no earlier than the date on which proposed regulations (or other guidance such as a notice) describing the tax consequences of the arrangements are issued to the public. The effective date of any such regulations will not, however, affect the application of other principles of existing law to determine the proper tax consequences of the structures or transactions addressed in the regulations. . . .

NOTES AND QUESTIONS

1.   Do you think this is justified? Why? What about the emphasis on profit potential?

2.   What is the relationship of this notice to the technical taxpayer rule?

3.   What is the relationship of this notice to sSections 901(k)–(*l*)?

4.   How would *Compaq* and *IES* come out under the notice? Under new Section 901(*l*)?

5.   As mentioned, Notice 98–5 was withdrawn on February 17, 2004, by Notice 2004–19. Nevertheless, AJCA, sec. 832, added a new Section 901(*l*) [old Section 901(*l*) was redesignated Section 901(m)], which extends the minimum holding periods currently required by Section 901(k) as a condition for the creditability of withholding taxes on dividend income to all other types of income. Note that despite its different scope, the new Section 901(*l*) addressed some of the concerns of Notice 98–5.

    * * *

Finally, read the following case:

Guardian Industries Corp. and Subsidiaries v. U.S.

United States Court of Federal Claims.
65 Fed. Cl. 50 (2005).

. . .

■ MEROW, SENIOR JUDGE.

Plaintiff seeks to recover a $2,724,752 refund from the corporate income tax payment(s) it made to the Internal Revenue Service ("IRS") for 2001, based upon asserted entitlement to a foreign tax credit under 26 U.S.C. § 901(b)(1). Both parties have moved for summary judgment. For the reasons discussed below, it is determined that plaintiff is entitled to the credit sought.

Facts

Guardian Industries Corp., a Delaware Corporation with principal corporate offices located in Auburn Hills, Michigan, is the parent company of a group of subsidiaries in the United States, referred to collectively as "Guardian." Guardian comprises a consolidated group for United States income tax purposes. Guardian, together with its affiliates throughout the world, is a leading manufacturer of glass products for commercial and residential applications. Interguard Holding Corp. ("IHC"), a Delaware corporation, is a wholly-owned subsidiary of Guardian, and is a member of the Guardian U.S. Consolidated Group.

Within Europe, Guardian and its affiliates conduct glass manufacturing and distribution operations in various countries, including the Grand Duchy of Luxembourg ("Luxembourg"), where some 1,200 persons are employed and 3 manufacturing facilities operated, representing a capital investment of more than $200,000,000.

Effective January 1, 2001, for the purpose of payment of Luxembourg corporate income taxes (Loi de l'impot sur le revenue ("LIR")), the Luxembourg tax authorities approved the taxation of the income derived from Guardian's operation of a fiscal unitary group of Luxembourg companies on a consolidated basis pursuant to Article 164bis of the LIR.

Guardian owns its Luxembourg operations through IHC which is the sole shareholder of Guardian Industries Europe, S.a.r.l. ("GIE"), a company organized under the laws of Luxembourg as a Société à responsabilité limitée. GIE, in turn, holds the requisite controlling interests in the following Luxembourg companies: Guardian Europe, S.A.; Guardian Luxcoating, S.A.; Guardian Germany Investments, S.A.; Guardian Glass, S.A.; Guardian Luxembourg, S.A.; Guardian Luxguard I, S.A.; Guardian Luxguard II, S.A.; Guardian Automotive Europe Development & Services, S.A.; Guardian Brazil Investments, S.A. Collectively, these companies comprise the "Guardian Luxembourg

Group" for consolidated taxation purposes under Article 164bis of the LIR, with GIE operating as the parent company.

On January 8, 2001, GIE filed Form 8832 with the IRS electing, effective January 1, 2001, as a foreign eligible entity with a single owner, to be disregarded as an entity separate from IHC. By a Notice, dated March 12, 2001, IRS notified GIE that the election had been approved, effective January 1, 2001. *See Dover Corp. and Subsidiaries v. Commissioner*, 122 T.C. 324 (2004).

During 2001, GIE (IHC) made or accrued advance payments to Luxembourg for 2001 LIR taxes in the amount of 3,429,074 Euros for the Guardian Luxembourg Group.

On June 4, 2002, Guardian filed its 2001 consolidated U.S. Corporation Income Tax Return (Form 1120) with the IRS. In this return Guardian treated the Luxembourg tax as allocable pro rata to the various members of the Guardian Luxembourg Group. On June 18, 2002, Guardian filed an Amended U.S. Corporation Income Tax Return for 2001 (Form 1120X) claiming a refund of $2,855,214. In its Disclosure Statement (Form 8275) filed with this Amended Return, plaintiff explained its position concerning a credit for taxes paid to Luxembourg as follows:

> 1. Foreign Tax Credit—Luxembourg Fiscal Unitary Group Income Tax. Guardian Industries Europe, S.a.r.l. (hereinafter GIE) timely filed Form 8832, Entity Classification Election, making its election in accordance with Reg § 1.301.7701–3 to be "a foreign eligible entity with a single owner electing to be disregarded as a separate entity" effective January 1, 2001. On or about March 12, 2001, the Internal Revenue Service gave its acknowledgement to GIE via written notice that GIE would be treated as a disregarded entity. As such, in accordance with Reg § 1.301.7701–2(a), for U.S. tax purposes GIE is treated in the same manner as that of a branch of IHC. GIE owns shares directly and indirectly of several Luxembourg corporations engaged in, or related to active manufacturing operations in Luxembourg. This Luxembourg group of corporations (fiscal unitary group, hereafter FUG) files a consolidated income tax return in accordance with Luxembourg law for determining the FUG's consolidated income tax liability, paying of that liability, and reporting of the corporate income tax (Impot sur la revenu and related surcharges). In accordance with Luxembourglaw [sic], GIE was liable for, and paid or accrued the FUG corporate income taxes for all FUG members. Taxpayer has determined that pursuant to Luxembourg law, the FUG members other than the parent, GIE do not have any liability (joint, several, or otherwise) for the FUG consolidated corporate income taxes and Reg § 1.901–2(f)(3) therefore does not apply. Accordingly, in this amended return, no portion of the FUG consolidated corporate

income taxes paid or accrued by GIE have been allocated to the other members of the FUG. Instead, in accordance with Reg § 1.901–2(f)(1), the consolidated corporate income tax of the Luxembourg FUG is properly treated as paid or accrued by GIE. Given GIE's status as a branch of IHC, in this amended tax return, Taxpayer has reported the Luxembourg FUG consolidated corporate income taxes as paid or accrued by IHC.

On October 16, 2002, Guardian filed with the IRS a second Form 1120X for 2001, reflecting an adjustment concerning Indian Income taxes unrelated to the issues involved in this litigation. In this second Form 1120X for 2001, a net overpayment of $2,724,752 is claimed.

No action having been obtained on the refund claims by the IRS, on December 23, 2002, plaintiff timely filed its Complaint, seeking a refund judgment in this matter. Jurisdiction is present pursuant to 28 U.S.C. § 1491.

Discussion

The issue presented by this litigation is whether Guardian is entitled, pursuant to section 901 of the Internal Revenue Code and the applicable Treasury Regulations, to a direct foreign tax credit for the 2001 LIR tax paid or accrued by GIE (IHC) with respect to the taxable income of the Guardian Luxembourg Group.

Defendant opposes the direct foreign tax credit plaintiff claims asserting that Luxembourg law does not render GIE (IHC) solely liable for the LIR tax paid or accrued with respect to the Guardian Luxembourg Group, that each member of the Group becomes jointly and severally liable for the Group's aggregate tax liability, and that Treas. Reg. § 1.901–2(f)(3) allocates the foreign tax among them regardless of who actually remits the tax.2

Treasury Regulations and case law establish that the person on whom foreign law imposes legal liability for the foreign income tax is the person by whom the tax is considered paid, for Section 901 purposes. Treas. Reg. § 1.901–2(f)(1); *Biddle v. Commissioner*, 302 U.S. 573, 580–581 (1938); *Norwest Corp. v. Commissioner*, 69 F.3d 1404, 1407 (8th Cir. 1995).

Plaintiff asserts that under Luxembourg law GIE (IHC) alone was legally liable for the 2001 LIR tax, not the other Group members, and Guardian is thereby entitled to a direct foreign tax credit under Code Section 901.

In order to resolve this conflict, a ruling on Luxembourg law is required. Pursuant to RCFC 44.1, in determining foreign law, the court "may consider any relevant material or source, including testimony, whether or not submitted by a party or admissible under the Federal Rules of Evidence." By Order, filed March 9, 2004, the parties were requested to "explore all possibilities and procedures, if any, for obtaining evidence from an appropriate Luxembourg official(s) or tribunal (advisory opinion) with respect to the Luxembourg law issues involved in this matter. . . ." *See United States v. Schultz*, 333 F.3d 393, 400–401 (2nd Cir. 2003) cert. denied, 540 U.S. 1106 (2004) (testimony by government officials); *Sidali v. INS*, 107 F.3d 191, 197–8 (3rd Cir. 1997) (diplomatic note). The usual method for presenting foreign law is expert testimony accompanied by extracts from foreign legal materials. *Jinro Am. Inc. v. Secure Inv., Inc.*, 266 F.3d 993, 1000 (9th Cir. 2001).

The parties have presented reports from experts in Luxembourg law. Plaintiff has submitted reports from: Professor Doctor Alain Steichen, a partner in the Luxembourg law firm of Bonn Schmitt Steichen, a Professor of tax law at Centre Universitaire de Luxembourg, and the author of numerous publications concerning Luxembourg tax law; Roger Molitor, an international tax partner in the accounting firm of KPMG, Managing Partner of the KPMG Tax Advisers, Luxembourg, who has practiced as a professional, specializing in Luxembourg tax matters for the last 25 years; Carlo Mack, Deputy Tax Director, Luxembourg Administration des Contributions Directes responding to a letter, dated March 22, 2004, from Roger Molitor and Patrick Goldschmidt, KPMG Tax Advisors. Defendant has presented reports from André Elvinger, an Avocat à la Cour, admitted to practice in the Grand-Duchy of Luxembourg in all courts, including the administrative courts dealing with tax matters. Maitre Elvinger was admitted to the Luxembourg bar in 1953 and served as President of the Bar in 1986 and 1987. He has published numerous articles in the field of tax law and is a member of the International Fiscal Association since 1958. Maitre Elvinger is a founder and partner in Elvinger, Hoss & Prussen, one of the leading law firms in Luxembourg, and has represented the Luxembourg Government and Luxembourg tax payers in tax litigation. Defendant also presents a response by Monsieur Carlo Mack to a letter dated April 21, 2004, from Mr. Rick Smith, Deputy Tax Attaché, Department of the Treasury, American Embassy, Paris, France and to matters discussed during a telephone conference on May 12, 2004, with IRS and Department of Justice officials.

As noted previously, all parties agree that Article 164bis of the LIR forms the statutory basis for the consolidated taxation involved in this litigation. This Article does not address joint and several liability of the Group members. In relevant part, for 2001 Article 164bis provided (in translation): "A fully-taxable resident company, the share capital of which is at least 99%-held, either directly or indirectly, by another fully-taxable resident company and which is economically and organizationally integrated into the latter may, upon approval by the Ministry of Finance, be assimilated for corporate income tax purposes to a permanent establishment of the parent company." Article 164bis also provided that "(5) A Grand-ducal decree shall determine the terms and conditions for the above-mentioned special regime."

The Grand-ducal decree, dated July 1, 1981, adopted pursuant to Article 164bis, paragraph 5 provides, in relevant part (translated):

Article 1

(1) Should a tax consolidation regime apply for a group of companies, the parent company and the subsidiary companies that are assimilated to permanent establishments of the parent company must have the same opening and closing dates for their respective fiscal years. Each entity of the group has to determine its own annual tax result and has to file a tax return as if it would not be a part of the group. The parent company must furthermore file a tax return including the taxable income of the group obtained by adding or compensating the fiscal results of companies members of the group and by deducting from this amount special allowable expenses incurred by these companies. If the tax consolidation regime leads to a double taxation or a double deduction, this effect has to be neutralized by an appropriate adjustment to the group global result.

. . .

(4) The parent company is liable for corporate income tax corresponding to taxable income of the group, computed in accordance with above-mentioned rules. It is also liable, in accordance with Article 135 Income Tax Law, to pay corporate income tax advances computed on the basis of above-mentioned taxable income.

Defendant's expert, Maitre Elvinger, opines that, while Article 164bis does not contain any provision regarding joint or several liability to tax, paragraph 7 StAnpG3 applies and results in joint and several liability of the parent and subsidiaries. In translation, paragraph 7 reads as follows:

(1) Persons who owe the same tax law obligation or who are liable separately for the same tax obligation, are jointly and severally liable.

(2) Persons who are to be assessed together or who are jointly to be made subject to a tax, are jointly and severally liable. This applies even where one or more of these persons would have been free of tax if they had been assessed separately or made subject to tax separately.

Plaintiff's expert, Professor Steichen, responds that in order for StAnpG § 7 to apply there must exist "a specified provision of tax law determining that, in a given particular situation, two or more taxpayers 'owe/are liable for the same tax obligation' or are 'assessed together' or 'jointly made subject to a tax,' i.e., that one of the conditions precedent is met." Professor Steichen cites several examples where a Luxembourg tax law has requisite language, such as that for the municipal business tax, Abgabenordnung § 114, "haftet sie für diejenigen Steuern" (it is liable for the same taxes). By contrast, Professor Steichen notes that no provision of Article 164bis or the Grand-ducal decree state that parent and subsidiary owe/are liable for the same tax obligation or are assessed together, or are jointly made subject to the tax. Professor Steichen therefor "confirms that there can be no joint and several liability between parent and subsidiary for corporate income tax on group income, because none of the conditions required by StAnpG § 7 is met."

Professor Steichen's conclusion that only the parent company is liable for the group income tax is shared by the Deputy Director of the Luxembourg Administration des Contributions Directes, Carlo Mack. The court is appreciative of Monsieur Mack's cooperation in responding to inquiries presented by both parties concerning Luxembourg tax matters. Monsieur Mack noted his agreement with the proposition that "the parent company (head of the tax grouping) is the sole debtor of the corporate income tax of the group,. . . ." Monsieur Mack also answered defendant's inquiry as to a computation of the portion of consolidated taxable income attributable to each member by responding, "The Luxembourg tax law requires determination of separate and individual taxable income of all companies that are members of the group, but it doesn't provide a determination to the separate tax liability that is only attributable to the parent company, sole debtor pursuant to the Grand-ducal Decree of 1981."

The manner in which the regime under Article 164bis is administered by the Luxembourg tax authorities is also consistent with the parent company having sole liability for the consolidated group corporate income tax. While individual member of the group file tax returns, the income or losses of the members are attributed to the parent who files a consolidated return and receives the notice of assessment for the LIR tax and the members each receive an assessment notice indicating zero taxable income.

Conclusion

There are no material facts at issue which would preclude reaching a decision on the excellent briefing presented by the parties in this matter. The reports submitted by the experts are comprehensive and helpful. Upon careful analysis of the materials presented it is concluded that under Luxembourg Law GIE (IHC) was solely liable for the 2001 LIR payments or accruals made for the consolidated taxable income of the Guardian Luxembourg Group and that there exists no joint or several liability on behalf of the member of this Group. As the liability under foreign law is imposed solely upon GIE (IHC), this entity is entitled to a direct credit pursuant to Code Section 901(b)(1). Accordingly, it is ORDERED:

(1) That plaintiff's Motion for Summary Judgment, filed May 13, 2003, shall be GRANTED;

(2) Defendant's Cross-motion for Summary Judgment, filed January 7, 2004, shall be DENIED;

(3) Counsel shall confer to reach agreement as to the refund amount resulting from the application of the tax credit for 2001 LIR payments or accruals;

(4) Absent prior agreement, on or before May 3, 2005, counsel shall file a status report(s) indicating the further proceedings, if any, required in this matter in order to obtain a final resolution as to the amount of recovery.

■ JAMES F. MEROW, SENIOR JUDGE.

NOTES AND QUESTIONS

1. Why did the IRS litigate this case? How is it different from *Compaq*? Was it important that the scrutinized scheme was located in Luxemburg?

2. Luxembourg's law provided a particularly convenient setting for Guardian's tax planning, but the basic scheme could be replicated also in other jurisdictions. What is the importance of the check-the-box rules for these schemes?

3. The U.S. Court of Appeals for the Federal Circuit affirmed the *Guardian* decision, noting "We reject the government's argument. There is no indication that the applicable Treas. Reg. § 1.901–2(f)(1) contemplates an inquiry into which party earns the income under foreign law. Also, contrary to the government's argument, the British and Brazilian cases discussed above do not hold that entitlement to the credit depends on which entity "earned" the income but rather on which entity bore the imposition of the tax. The Treasury has the ability to draft a regulation that specifically calls for such a regime, and it has not done so here." In light of the court's comments here, again review the proposed regulations amending Treas. Reg. § 1.901–2(f) and consider what they seek to accomplish.

4. How would the *Guardian* decision affect foreign governments attempting to introduce or revise their fiscal unity regimes? Should this effect bother the U.S.?

5. What is the effect of this case on the "technical taxpayer rule"?

Statutory Response: On August 10, 2010 Congress enacted legislation limiting the availability of the foreign tax credit in an effort to combat perceived cases of abuse, including those symbolized by the transactions in *Guardian*. Among the changes enacted in August, were the following:

> **(1) New Section 909**—This provision, effective for taxable years beginning after December 31, 2010, adopts a matching rule to prevent the foreign tax credits from being separated from the underlying foreign income. If the credit is split from the income in a "foreign tax credit splitting event", the tax is not taken into account when determining the foreign tax credit under Section 902 or Section 960. [That tax can be later taken into account for purposes of calculating foreign tax credits, when the appropriate domestic (or Section 902 corporation) takes the related income into account for its own taxation under Chapter

1 of the code.] Note that this new statutory provision take a different approach as compared to the proposed technical taxpayer regulations issued in 2006. How would the transaction in *Guardian* be treated under new Section 909?

(2) New Section 901(m)—responds to concerns over the elections and transactions that taxpayers can pursue which have the effect of increasing basis domestically for assets without a corresponding increase in basis abroad. These elections and transactions include certain stock purchases with a Section 338(g) or Section 338(h)(10) election, certain cross border check the box elections, and certain acquisitions of partnership interests where the partnership holds foreign assets. Although the details of the new Section 901(m) require an understanding of these other provisions (e.g., Section 338)—the core idea implemented by Section 901(m) is that if a taxpayer makes an asset acquisition covered by Section 901(m), a portion of the taxpayer's foreign tax credit is permanently disallowed (although permitted as a deduction). The new provision is generally applicable for acquisitions after December 31, 2010, although some exceptions apply.

(3) New Section 960(c)—seeks to stop taxpayer's affirmative use of Section 956. Taxpayers previously sought to trigger current inclusion of underlying foreign income of a lower tier subsidiary (along with its foreign tax credits) under section 956 so as to bring the income and the credits directly onto the U.S. return without running the payments up through the chain of intermediary CFCs. Now, under new Section 960(c) the taxpayer essentially must go through the analysis and figure out what would happen if the payment went up the chain. In comparison to Section 901(m), the new Section 960(c) has the "advantage" of not requiring permanent loss of credits. Rather any used credits stay in the pool. However, application of Section 960(c) cannot be used to increase a taxpayer's foreign tax credit—it can only decrease the credit that would have been available under Section 960. Section 960(c) applies to acquisition of U.S. property made after December 31, 2010.

8.6   THE TCJA CHANGES

The TCJA abolishes the indirect credit (Section 902)[4] and limits the availability of the direct credit (Section 901) on dividends that qualify for the participation exemption (i.e. the 100% dividends received deduction). However, indirect credits under Section 960 are retained for GILTI,

---

[4]   Bear in mind that U.S. corporate 10% shareholders of foreign corporations, who would previously have relied on Section 902 to secure relief from multiple layers of corporate income taxation on receipt of a dividend from the foreign corporation now benefit from the Section 245A 100% dividends received deduction.

except that only 80% of the foreign tax may be credited, and for other Subpart F income (with no 80% limitation). This results in a full offset of the 10.5% minimum tax on GILTI if the foreign rate is 13.125%. As noted above, new foreign tax credit baskets apply to GILTI and to income from foreign branches.

Cross crediting within the GILTI basket is permitted, which creates an incentive to invest in high tax foreign jurisdictions. Assume a US taxpayer with 100 income from a low tax foreign jurisdiction that exceeds the GILTI hurdle rate. If the taxpayer derives another 100 from the US, it will pay 21 on the US income and 10.5 on GILTI for a total of 31.5. But if it earns 100 from a foreign jurisdiction with a tax rate of 26.25, then it will only pay 26.25 because it will have foreign tax credits of 26.25x80%=21 to eliminate its US tax on GILTI (10.5%x200).

NOTES

a. Foreign tax credits are given for taxes paid in a foreign jurisdiction (under certain circumstances). As domestic FTCs they reduce the tax liability after the rate calculation. FTCs are separated by baskets. GILTI is a separate basket, with no carrybacks or carryforwards. Any income that is GILTI is not general category income. If a domestic corporation includes GILTI in income, and elects to credit foreign taxes, it is treated as having a "deemed paid" FTC equal to the product of (1) 80% of the aggregate "tested foreign income taxes" paid or accrued by the Related CFC's, and (2) the domestic corporation's "inclusion percentage".

b. Tested Foreign Income Taxes are foreign income taxes paid or accrued by a Related CFC that are "properly allocable" to the tested income of the CFC taken into account by U.S. SH in calculating GILTI. Accordingly, foreign taxes include (among other income) taxes attributable to QBAI return, since tested income is not reduced by QBAI return. However, if a particular CFC does not have positive tested income for a year, foreign taxes paid by that CFC for that year do not give rise to tested foreign income taxes for the year.

c. A domestic's corporation's "Inclusion Percentage" is a fraction of: the numerator of which is its Section 951A inclusion and the denominator of which is the aggregate of its share of the tested incomes of all Related CFCs with positive tested income. Remember: corporation's Section 951A inclusion is the tested income of a Related CFCs with positive tested income, reduced by (1) tested loss of Related CFCs with tested loss, and (2) NTDIR based on QBAI of Related CFCs with positive tested income. These items reduce the numerator but not the denominator. That decreases the paid taxes on QBAI.

d. Example: U.S. SH owns (1) CFC1 with tested income of $100 after foreign taxes, foreign taxes of $15, and QBAI return of $20, and (2) CFC2 with tested loss of $30 after foreign taxes and foreign taxes of $10. The section 951A inclusion is $100 (tested income of CFC1) minus $20 (NTDIR) minus $30 (tested loss of CFC2), or $50, and the tested foreign income taxes are $15. The inclusion percentage is $50 (the Section 951A inclusion) divided by $100 (the positive tested income of CFC1), or 50%. The allowed FTC is therefore 80% times 50% time $15, or $6.

e.   Taxpayers have the annual option of deducting foreign income taxes in lieu of taking FTC, but cannot both deduct foreign income taxes and take an FTC. It is generally more advantageous for taxpayers to take the FTC, as it reduces the taxpayer's tax liability dollar for dollar. When a taxpayer claims an FTC on its income tax return, it must also add back the amount of the FTC to its Tested Income.

f.   Section 78 gross-up requires that inclusion of indirect FTC be "grossed up" by the amount of the deemed paid FTC, i.e., such indirect FTC is treated as a dividend. 100% of the foreign taxes deemed paid by the domestic corporation are counted in the deemed dividend, or "Section 78 Amount". The Section 250 deduction is allowed against the full grossed-up amount. (Why? Because it represent reduction of tax rate and not a real corporate deduction).

g.   Example on Section 78 inclusion: same as the last example, the TP's section 78 inclusion is the same as the allowed FTC, but without the 20% cutback, so it is 50% times $15, or $7.5. The total GILTI inclusion is $50+$7.5= $57.5. Now let's apply section 78. Consider the simple case where the U.S. shareholder owns a single CFC with $100 of pre-tax tested income, no QBAI return, and $13.125 of foreign taxes. The tested income and section 951A inclusion are $86.875 ($100–$13.125). The inclusion percentage is 100% (86.875/86.875), so it does not reduce the foreign tax credit of $13.125. The credit results in a Section 78 inclusion of $13.125. The GILTI inclusion is $100 and the allowed foreign tax credit is 80% of $13.125, or $10.50. If the full section 250 deduction of $50 is allowed (after the gross up), taxable income will be $50 and the tentative U.S. tax liability is $10.50. If no expenses are allocated to GILTI income the FTC will exactly offset the U.S. tax.

h.   In general, a taxpayer's FTC for a year is limited to (1) the taxpayer's foreign source taxable income for the year, multiplied by (2) the effective U.S. tax rate on the taxpayer's worldwide taxable income for the year. (Section 904(a)). Mathematically, this is equivalent to the rule that the allowed FTC cannot exceed (1) total U.S. tax liability, multiplied by (2) foreign source taxable income, with the product divided by (3) worldwide taxable income. Since (1) divided by (3) is the effective U.S. tax rate on worldwide taxable income, the formula is equivalent to that in the text. This determination is made separately for each FTC basket, including the GILTI basket. (Section 904(d)). This requires separation of gross income.

i.   Under preexisting law, deductions that are "definitely related" to gross income are generally allocated and apportioned to that gross income, and other deductions are generally ratably allocated and apportioned. Following the TCJA, interest deductions are generally allocated and apportioned on the basis of the tax basis of assets, rather than the value of assets or income.

j.   Examples: U.S. source income is $0, foreign source income (after Section 250 deduction) is $50, U.S. tax before FTC is $10.50, and effective U.S. tax rate is 21% ($10.50/$50). The Section 904 limit is $50 (foreign source income) multiplied by 21% (effective U.S. tax rate), or $10.50, so the full credit is allowable.

Same facts but CFC QBAI's is 0, and U.S. shareholder also has U.S. source business income of $10 (before interest deductions) and $10 of interest deductions. Assume the interest deductions are all treated as U.S. source deductions. The result will be the same since no QBAI in the foreign jurisdiction, the entire interest deduction is allocated to the U.S., and U.S. source income is still 0 ($10–$10).

Same facts as the last example except $5 of the interest deductions are allocable to the foreign source GILTI inclusion. Then, nothing changes except the FTC limit under Section 904(a). That limit is now $45 (foreign source GILTI inclusion of $50 minus interest expense of $5) times the effective U.S. tax rate of 21%, or $9.45. Thus, only $9.45 of FTC is allowed. Compare: FTC without regards to interest $10.50 minus $9.45, or $1.05. Note that this loss of credits has the same tax cost ($1.05) as would the allowance of the full FTC and the disallowance of the $5 of foreign source interest deductions. (5$*0.21) The same result would arise for any other deductions allocable to the GILTI inclusion—but remember that interest is fungible.

k. Members of an affiliated group, whether or not they file a consolidated return, must allocate and apportion interest expense of each member as if all members of the group were a single corporation. A similar rule applies for purposes of allocating and apportioning certain other expenses that are not directly allocable or apportioned to any specific income producing activity. For affiliated groups filing a consolidated return, all foreign taxes paid by group members are aggregated, and a single Section 904 limit is calculated for the group.

8.7   REVIEW QUESTIONS—CHAPTER 8

1. USCO, a Delaware corporation, manufactures widgets in the U.S. (assume a flat 21% domestic corporate tax). USCO has distribution operations and offices in two additional countries—T, a country with a flat 40% tax, and B, a country with a flat 10% tax. USCO also wholly owns a country Y (33.33% flat tax) subsidiary—S.

    a. In year 1, USCO had $500 of U.S. source income, $300 of income in T and $200 in B (assume that both are foreign source income). S had $1,500 of income in country Y, and distributed $1,000 to USCO. The distribution was subject to a 5% withholding tax in Y. What is USCO's U.S. tax liability for the year?

    b. Does your answer change if all of USCO's income is derived from the sale of purchased inventory widgets and the terms of the sales contract are always that title passes to the final customer from USCO only after on-site installation and testing (on the customer's premises)?

    c. Assume now, in (a), that country B increases its taxes to 20%. How would USCO's tax position change?

    d.   Could USCO "remedy" its excess credit position by investing in a tax haven—an investment that would generate (zero taxed) foreign source interest income of $100?

2.   P, a domestic corporation owns 10% of F, a manufacturing foreign corporation that is not a CFC. In 2019, F pays a $1,000 dividend ($100 to P), subject to 15% withholding tax. F has $10,000 of undistributed earnings (assume all accounts are post-86) and $5,000 foreign income taxes at the start of 2019 and earned no income in 2019. The corporate income tax rate in its country of incorporation is 40%. What are the U.S. tax consequences of the dividend to P?

    a.   What if F earned $1,000 in 2019 subject to 50% income tax in country F?

    b.   Now assume that P earned in 2019 $1,000 of rental income subject to 30% income tax in country F (except for the dividend), and that exactly half of F's income over the years comes from rents (F hires an unrelated management company to manage its properties in order to concentrate on its manufacturing operations) and the rest from its manufacturing activity. What is P's U.S. tax liability for 2019?

    c.   Would your answer change in (b) if F were a CFC and the $100 a Subpart F inclusion (otherwise all operations are the same)?

    d.   Assume, alternatively, that P owned 50% of F's stock, F owned 50% of F1, a corporation organized in the same country as F, and F1 owned 40% of the stock of F2, a neighboring country (foreign) corporation. None of the above is a CFC. In 2019 F2 earned $1,000 subject to 10% income tax. It has no undistributed earnings or foreign income tax accounts in the beginning of the year. It pays a $900 (proportional) dividend to its shareholders. F1 earned $1,000 other than the dividend in 2019. It pays 20% tax on its aggregate income. It also has no undistributed earnings or foreign income tax accounts in the beginning of the year. F1 paid a $600 (proportional) dividend to its shareholders in 2019. Assume no withholding taxes or foreign tax credit in the foreign countries.

PART E

THE U.S. AND THE INTERNATIONAL TAX REGIME

CHAPTER 9

SECTION 367 AND CROSS-BORDER TRANSFERS OF PROPERTY

9.1   IN GENERAL

Some of the most important subchapter C provisions provide for exceptions to the general rule of taxability (realization & recognition) of gains from property transactions. Sections 332, 351, 354, 355, 356 and 361 provide for such exceptions, allowing certain taxpayers not to recognize their realized gains or losses and, by that, to defer taxation of these gains (or losses). Section 367 provides an exception to these important exceptions in certain international (not purely domestic) transactions. It contains several anti-avoidance rules, aimed at certain potential abuses of the generous deferral opportunities mentioned above. Skim Section 367 and pay attention to the loose connection between its subsections. Section 367 was first adopted by the Revenue Act of 1932. Read the following Congressional report regarding its adoption and note the original concern which drove Congress to enact Section 367—not allowing taxpayers to escape U.S. taxation (particularly realized but not recognized gains) by transferring property across borders:

* * *

Report-Ways and Means Committee (72d Cong., 1st Sess., H. Rept. 708)—sec. 112(k) added by the Revenue Act of 1932.[1]

"Property may be transferred to foreign corporations without recognition of gain under the exchange and reorganization sections of the existing law. This constitutes a serious loophole for avoidance of taxes. Taxpayers having large unrealized profits in securities may transfer such securities to corporations organized in countries imposing no tax upon the sale of capital assets. Then, by subsequent sale of these assets in the foreign country, the entire tax upon the capital gain is avoided. For example, A, an American citizen, owns 100,000 shares of stock in corporation X, a domestic corporation, which originally cost him $1,000,000 but now has a market value of $10,000,000. Instead of selling the stock outright A organizes a corporation under the laws of Canada to which he transfers the 100,000 shares of stock in exchange for the entire capital stock of the Canadian company. This transaction is a nontaxable exchange. The Canadian corporation sells the stock of corporation X for $10,000,000 in cash. The latter transaction is exempt from tax under the

---

[1]   Taken from *Seidman's Legislative History of Federal Income Tax Laws 1938–1861*, (3d. ed., Prentice-all, Inc. 2003).

Canadian law and is not taxable as United States income under the present law. The Canadian corporation organizes corporation Y under the laws of the United States and transfers the $10,000,000 cash received upon the sale of corporation X's stock in exchange for the entire capital stock of Y. The Canadian corporation then distributes the stock of Y to A in connection with a reorganization. By this series of transactions, A has had the stock of X converted into cash and now has it in complete control.

While it is probable that the courts will not hold all transactions of this nature to be tax-free exchanges, the committee is convinced that the existing law may afford opportunity for substantial tax avoidance. To prevent this avoidance the proposed amendment withdraws the transaction from the operation of the nonrecognition sections where a foreign corporation is a party to the transaction, unless prior to the exchange the commissioner is satisfied that the transaction does not have as one of its principal purposes the avoidance of taxes. It will be noted that under this provision a taxpayer acting in good faith can ascertain prior to the transaction, by submitting his plan to the commissioner, that it will not be taxable if carried out in accordance with the plan. Of course, if the reorganization of the transfer is not carried out in accordance with the plan the commissioner's approval will not render the transaction tax free. (p.20)"

* * *

The basic concerns of Section 367 have not changed much in the last 70-plus years since its adoption. It has gone, however, through several major amendments, which focused on its operation—how to identify the potentially abusive transactions? How to "fine-tune" its impact? How to make sure that it applies to the truly (potentially) abusive transactions and not apply to similar, clearly-not-abusive transactions? The following two "blue book" excerpts, explaining the two major reforms of Section 367 over the years, demonstrates these concerns of Congress.

* * *

GENERAL EXPLANATION OF THE TAX REFORM ACT OF 1976(H.R. 10612, 94th CONGRESS, PUBLIC LAW 94–455); JCS–33–76; (Part 17 of 28 Parts) LEXIS [excerpt]

. . .

Prior law

Certain types of exchanges relating to the organization, reorganization, and liquidation of a corporation can be made without recognition of gain to the corporation involved or to its shareholders. Under prior law, however, when a foreign corporation was involved in certain of these types of exchanges, tax-free treatment was not available unless prior to the transaction the Internal Revenue Service had made a determination that the exchange did not have as one of its principal purposes the avoidance of federal income taxes. Under prior practice this determination was made by issuing a separate ruling for each transaction. The required determination had to be obtained before the transaction began in all cases unless the transaction involved only a change in the form of organization of a second (or lower) tier foreign subsidiary with no change in ownership . . . there was no effective way a taxpayer could appeal an adverse decision by the Commissioner to the courts because the statute required the Commissioner's, not the court's, satisfaction.

In 1968, the Internal Revenue Service issued guidelines (Rev. Proc. 68–23, 1968–1 Cum. Bull. 821) as to when favorable rulings "ordinarily" would be issued. As a condition of obtaining a favorable ruling with respect to certain transactions, the section 367 guidelines required the taxpayer to agree to include certain items in income (the amount to be included was called the section 367 toll charge). For example, if a domestic corporation transferred property to a foreign subsidiary (a transaction otherwise accorded tax-free treatment under section 351), the transaction was given a favorable ruling only if the domestic corporation agreed to include in its gross income for its taxable year in which the transfer occurred an appropriate amount to reflect realization of income or gain with respect to certain types of assets (*e.g.*, inventory, accounts receivable, and certain stock or securities) transferred to the foreign corporation as part of the transfer. If the transaction involved the liquidation of a foreign corporation into a domestic parent, a favorable ruling was issued if the domestic parent agreed to include in its income as a dividend for the taxable year in which the liquidation occurred the portion of the accumulated earnings and profits of the foreign corporation which were properly attributable to the domestic corporation's stock interest in the foreign corporation. These two cases illustrate that the statutory standard for determining that a transaction did not have as one of its principal purposes tax avoidance had evolved through administrative interpretation into a requirement generally that tax-free treatment would be permitted only if the U.S. tax on accumulated earnings and profits (in the case of transfers into the United States by a foreign corporation) or the U.S. tax on the potential earnings from liquid or passive investment assets (in the case of transfers of property outside the United States) was paid or was preserved for future payment. . . .

Reasons for change

Several problems developed insofar as section 367 and the related provisions of section 1248 were concerned. First, the advance ruling requirement often resulted in an undue delay for taxpayers attempting to consummate perfectly proper business transactions. Second, a number of cases had arisen where a foreign corporation was involved in an exchange within the scope of the section 367 guidelines without the knowledge of its U.S. shareholders, and thus no request for prior approval had been made. In a case of this type, an otherwise tax-free transaction became a taxable transaction, and if a second or lower tier foreign subsidiary was involved, the U.S. shareholders of the controlled foreign corporation might have been taxed under the Subpart F rules. This could have occurred under the Service's section 367 guidelines despite the fact that a favorable ruling would clearly have been issued by the Internal Revenue Service had it been requested prior to the transaction.

The third area of difficulty in the administration of section 367 under prior law concerned situations where the IRS required a U.S. shareholder to include certain amounts in income as a toll charge even though there was no present tax avoidance purpose but, rather, only the existence of a potential for future tax avoidance. . . .

The fourth problem concerned the fact that since the law required the satisfaction of the Commissioner, a taxpayer was unable to go through with a transaction and litigate in the courts the question of whether tax avoidance was one of the purposes of the transaction. While the Congress generally approves the standard applied by the IRS, there may have been cases where these standards were inappropriate or were not being correctly applied. Congress believes it is fair to permit taxpayers to litigate these questions in the courts.

The Congress further believes that the interpretation of the rules governing exchanges described in section 367 should not be done in individual rulings but should be provided by clear and certain regulations. While it is recognized that the prior rules were necessarily highly technical and largely procedural and while it is essential to protect against tax avoidance in transfers to foreign corporations and upon the repatriation of previously untaxed foreign earnings, unnecessary barriers to justifiable and legitimate business transactions should be avoided. The Congress believes that U.S. taxpayers participating in certain types of transactions involving foreign corporations should be able to determine the tax effects of the transaction from the statute and accompanying regulations rather than being required to apply to the Internal Revenue Service for a determination in advance of the transaction. Only in those types of transactions where the amount of tax, if any, which must be paid to protect against tax avoidance can only be determined by judging the specific facts of the case should the taxpayer be required to obtain a determination from the Internal Revenue Service. Moreover, in cases where such a ruling is to be required, taxpayers should be permitted to obtain the ruling within some limited time after the transaction has begun.

. . .

Explanation of provisions

The Act approaches the problems outlined above first by amending section 367 to establish separate rules for two different groups of transactions: (i) transfers of property from the United States, and (ii) other transfers (this latter group including transfers into the United States and those which are exclusively foreign). Transactions in the first group generally include those transactions where the statutory aim is to prevent the removal of appreciated assets or inventory from U.S. tax jurisdiction prior to their sale, while transactions in the second group include those where the statutory purpose in most cases is to prepare for taxation the accumulated profits of controlled foreign corporations.

Transfers from the United States.—With respect to the first group (sec. 367(a)), it is provided that if in connection with an exchange described in section 332, 351, 354, 355, 356, or 361, there is a transfer of property (other than stock or securities of a foreign corporation which is a party to the exchange) by a U.S. person to a foreign corporation, the foreign corporation will not be considered a corporation (for purposes of determining gain) unless, pursuant to a request filed not later than the close of the 183rd day after the beginning of the transfer, the taxpayer establishes to the satisfaction of the Internal Revenue Service that the exchange did not have as one of its principal purposes the avoidance of Federal income taxes. . . .

The Act thus provides that for transfers of property out of the United States the requirement of an advance ruling is replaced by a requirement that the taxpayer file a request for clearance with the Internal Revenue Service within 183 days after the beginning of the transfer. Even this post-transaction clearance from the Internal Revenue Service may not be required in certain clear cut situations involving outbound transfers where significant tax avoidance possibilities do not exist or where the amount of any section 367 toll charge can be ascertained without a ruling request. The Act provides that the Secretary is to designate by regulations those transactions which for these reasons do not require the filing of a ruling request. For transactions designated by the regulations, taxpayers may go ahead with the transaction without a ruling but are subject to any section 367 toll charge prescribed by the regulations. For example, if a section 351 transfer to a foreign corporation involves only the transfer of cash and inventory property, the Secretary may by regulations designate the transaction as one which does not require the filing of a request, although the regulations would require the inventory to be taken into income.

. . .

Other transfers.—The Act establishes separate treatment under section 367(b) for a second group of transfers which consists of exchanges described in sections 332, 351, 354, 355, 356, and 361 that are not treated as transfers out of the United States (under section 367(a)) under the rules described above. With respect to these other transactions, a ruling is not required. Instead, a foreign corporation will not be treated as a corporation to the extent that the Secretary of the Treasury provides in regulations that are necessary or appropriate to prevent the avoidance of Federal income taxes. . . .

Transfers covered in these regulations are to include transfers constituting a repatriation of foreign earnings. Also included are transfers that involve solely foreign corporations and shareholders (and involve a U.S. tax liability of U.S. shareholders only to the extent of determining the amount of any deemed distribution under the Subpart F rules). It is anticipated that in this latter group of exchanges, the regulations will not provide for any immediate U.S. tax liability but will maintain the potential tax liability of the U.S. shareholder.

. . .

Examples of transfers into the United States which are to be treated within this group (sec. 367(b)(1)) include: (i) the liquidation of a foreign corporation into a domestic parent; (ii) the acquisition of assets of a foreign corporation by a domestic corporation in a type "C" or "D" reorganization; and (iii) the acquisition of stock in a foreign corporation by a domestic corporation in a type "B" reorganization. With respect to transfers which exclusively involve foreign parties (i.e., where no U.S. persons are parties to the exchange), examples of situations coming within section 367(b)(1) include: (i) the acquisition of stock of a controlled foreign corporation by another foreign corporation; (ii) the acquisition of stock of a controlled foreign corporation by another foreign corporation which is controlled by the same U.S. shareholders as the acquired corporation; (iii) the acquisition of the assets of a controlled foreign corporation by another foreign corporation; (iv) the mere recapitalization of a foreign corporation (type "E" reorganization); and (v) a transfer of property by one controlled foreign corporation to its foreign subsidiary. For these exclusively foreign transactions, it is anticipated that regulations will provide for no immediate U.S. tax liability.

The Secretary's authority to prescribe regulations relating to the sale or exchange of stock in a foreign corporation includes authority to establish rules pursuant to which an exchange of stock in a second tier foreign corporation for other stock in a similar foreign corporation will result in a deferral of the toll charge which otherwise would be imposed based on accumulated earnings and profits. This deferral could be accomplished by designating the stock received as stock with a deferred tax potential in a manner similar to section 1248 without reference to the December 31, 1962, date; the amount includable as foreign source dividend income upon the subsequent disposition of the stock in question results in dividend income only to the extent of the gain realized on the subsequent sale or exchange. In addition, if a second tier foreign subsidiary is liquidated into a first tier foreign subsidiary, the regulations may provide that the tax which would otherwise be due in the absence of a ruling is deferred until the disposition of the stock in the first tier foreign subsidiary.

* * *

GENERAL EXPLANATION OF THE REVENUE PROVISIONS OF THE DEFICIT REDUCTION ACT OF 1984

[JOINT COMMITTEE PRINT]; (H.R. 4170, 98th CONGRESS; PUBLIC LAW 98–369); JCS–41–84; (Part 12 of 81 Parts)

LEXIS [excerpt]

. . .

Prior Law

. . .

Transfers for use in a trade or business

In the case of an exchange involving the transfer of property (other than certain "tainted assets" described below) to a foreign corporation controlled by the transferor after the transfer (a "section 351 exchange"), a favorable ruling ordinarily was issued when the transferred property was to be devoted by the foreign corporation to the active conduct of a trade or business in a foreign country. The guidelines contemplated that the foreign corporation, in addition to devoting the property to the active conduct of a trade or business, would have need for a substantial investment in fixed assets in such business or would be engaged in the purchase and sale abroad of manufactured goods.

Tainted assets

Where property falling within any of several categories of "tainted assets" was transferred to a foreign corporation, the IRS generally issued a favorable ruling only if the transferor agreed to pay a toll charge that reflected the realization of income or gain with respect to the tainted assets, regardless of whether the transfer was made for use in an active trade or business. The character of the toll charge and any basis adjustments were determined as though the tainted assets had been transferred in a taxable exchange. The categories of tainted assets included:

(1) Inventory, certain copyrights, and other property described in section 1221(1) and (3);

(2) Accounts receivable, installment obligations, and similar property with respect to which income had been earned, unless the income had been or would be included in the transferor's gross income;

(3) Property transferred under circumstances that made it reasonable to believe that its subsequent disposition by the transferee was one of the principal purposes of the transfer;

(4) Property leased or licensed by the transferor to a user (other than the transferee) at the time of the transfer;

(5) Property transferred under circumstances that made it reasonable to believe that the property would be leased or licensed by the transferee after the transfer; however, in the

case of tangible property, a favorable ruling ordinarily was issued if the leasing of the property was part of the active conduct of a trade or business by the transferee in the foreign country, the transferee had a need for substantial investment in fixed assets in such business, and the lessee did not use the property in the United States (See Rev. Proc. 80–14, 1980–1 C.B. 617);

(6) Certain U.S. and foreign patents, trademarks, and similar intangibles (discussed in more detail below); and

(7) With a limited exception, stock and securities.

Treatment of stock or securities

Under the "same country exception," a favorable ruling was issued when (1) the stock was in a foreign corporation organized under the laws of the same foreign country as the transferee, (2) immediately after the exchange the foreign corporation was 80-percent owned (within the meaning of section 368(c) of the Code) by the transferee and had a substantial part of its business assets in the country in which the transferee was organized, and (3) the transferee was 50-percent owned (as defined in section 954(d)(3) of the Code) by persons who, immediately before the exchange, controlled the transferor.

A favorable ruling was also issued where stock of a domestic corporation was acquired in exchange for stock of a foreign corporation if, immediately after the exchange, the shareholders of the acquired domestic corporation did not own (directly or indirectly) more than 50 percent of the total combined voting power of the acquiring foreign corporation. A favorable ruling was not issued, however, if the assets of the acquired domestic corporation consisted principally of stock or securities.

The case of *Kaiser Aluminum Chemical Corp. v. Commissioner*, 76 T.C. 325 (1981), acq., 1982–2 C.B. 1, illustrated the difficulties encountered by taxpayers who sought favorable rulings on stock transfers that were made in circumstances not addressed by the guidelines. In that case, the Tax Court overturned an IRS ruling that treated stock as a tainted asset, noting that the transferred stock was closely akin to operating assets, the taxpayer's stock interest was related to its manufacturing operations as a source of supply, the stock was not liquid or readily marketable, and the stock was not a portfolio investment providing a passive return on assets.

. . .

Treatment of partnerships

Proposed Treasury regulations provided for the treatment of a transfer of property by a partnership to a foreign corporation as an indirect transfer of the property by the partners (Prop. Treas. reg. sec. 1.367(a)–1(b)(3)). The proposed regulations did not distinguish between limited and general partnerships and did not provide rules for the transfer by partners of their partnership interests.

Transfers of intangible assets

Under the guidelines, a toll charge had to be paid to obtain a favorable ruling with respect to a transfer to a foreign corporation of a U.S. patent, trademark, or other intangible for use in connection with manufacturing for sale or consumption in the United States, or in connection with a U.S. trade or business. Thus, the transfer of U.S.-developed know-how to a tax-haven subsidiary for use in manufacturing goods for the U.S. market was subject to tax. Similarly, the U.S. holder of a trademark could not transfer it tax-free to a foreign subsidiary (which could then charge the U.S. transferor a license fee for the trademark's use in connection with a U.S. trade or business).

Under the guidelines, transfers of foreign patents, trademarks, and similar intangibles for use in connection with the sale of goods manufactured in the United States were subject to a toll charge. By implication, transfers of intangibles for use in connection with a foreign trade or business for consumption outside the United States generally were not treated as taxable. Thus, U.S. persons who took advantage of tax incentives for research could transfer the fruits of that research (intangibles) to foreign corporations that could then use the intangibles free of any U.S. tax. In addition, some taxpayers took the position that the transfer of foreign patents or know-how for use in foreign manufacturing for the U.S. market was not subject to tax under the guidelines.

. . .

Use of closing agreements

Under prior law, the IRS was authorized to issue a favorable ruling under section 367 if a transferor was willing to enter into a closing agreement that obligated the transferor to pay tax on any gain from a subsequent disposition of the transferred assets by the transferee within a certain number of years after the transfer. The IRS declined to exercise this authority because of the perceived administrative burden of concluding such agreements and possible difficulties in enforcing them.

In the Kaiser case, the Tax Court noted the unwillingness of the Service to propose a closing agreement that specified terms and conditions for a transfer of stock subject to section 367. The court indicated that an agreement by the transferor to pay tax on a subsequent disposition of the stock by the transferee would have obviated the issue of whether the taxpayer's principal purpose was tax avoidance.

Incorporation of foreign loss branches

The transfer of the assets of a foreign branch of a U.S. taxpayer to a foreign corporation, which otherwise qualified as a tax-free contribution to the capital of the foreign corporation or as a tax-free organization, was treated as an outbound transfer. Thus, corporate status was denied to the foreign transferee unless the IRS determined that the transfer did not have the avoidance of Federal income taxes as one of its principal purposes.

Where a U.S. taxpayer operates through a foreign branch, losses incurred by the branch prior to its incorporation reduce the amount of the taxpayer's worldwide income that is subject to Federal income tax. After the branch is incorporated, generally, future income from the activity is not taken into account by the taxpayer until it receives dividends from the foreign corporation. Therefore, the guidelines required the recognition of gain on the transfer of the assets of a foreign branch to a foreign corporation, to the extent of previously deducted losses. See Rev. Rul. 78–201, 1978–1 C.B. 91. If the losses of the foreign branch contributed to an overall foreign loss that reduced U.S.-source income, a statutory provision could apply to require not only recognition of gain but also recharacterization of the gain as U.S.-source income (sec. 904(f)). In the case of an overall foreign loss, the amount of gain required to be recognized under the guidelines was reduced by the amount of income required to be recognized by the statutory rule.

The Tax Court, however, held that the transfer of the assets of a foreign branch to a foreign corporation did not have a tax avoidance purpose. *Hershey Foods Corp. v. Commissioner*, 76 T.C. 312 (1981), gov't appeal dismissed, No. 81–2096 (3d. Cir. 1981). In that case the court rejected the application of a tax benefit theory on the ground that there had been no recovery of an amount that was once the subject of a deduction. But see *United States v. Bliss Dairy Inc.*, 460 U.S. 370, 103 S.Ct. 1134, 75 L.Ed.2d 130 (1983), rev'g 645 F.2d 19 (9th Cir. 1981) (holding that the tax benefit rule may be invoked regardless of whether an actual recovery of an amount previously deducted exists).

. . .

Judicial interpretation of the principal purpose test

The Tax Court interpreted the statute's principal purpose test to allow tax-free transfers of appreciated property to foreign corporations unless the avoidance of Federal income taxes was a purpose that was first in importance. Dittler Bros. v. Commissioner, 72 T.C. 896, 915 (1979), aff'd mem., 642 F.2d 1211 (5th Cir. 1981). In Dittler Bros., a U.S. corporation owned know-how for the production of rub-off lottery tickets. It transferred that know-how for 50 percent of the stock of a corporation organized in the Netherlands Antilles. The Netherlands Antilles corporation, which operated through a subsidiary, was to use that know-how in connection with foreign manufacturing for foreign markets. The other 50 percent belonged to a United Kingdom corporation that contributed marketing intangibles. Related parties were to do the manufacturing and marketing of lottery tickets for the Netherlands Antilles corporation. The Netherlands Antilles corporation operated through independent contractors and had very little in the way of fixed assets.

The IRS denied the U.S. transferor's request for a ruling that the transfer of know-how did not have as one of its principal purposes the avoidance of Federal income tax. The IRS based its denial on the failure to satisfy the guideline requirement that the transferee devote the assets to the active conduct of a trade or business and have need for fixed assets in that business. The Service's factual grounds for that denial included (1) the Netherlands Antilles corporation would not engage in any active business; rather, its income would arise from the know-how and other intangibles and rights that it received from related parties; and, (2) the arrangement created a potential for tax avoidance in that income from exploitation of the know-how was diverted to a passive recipient in a foreign tax-haven country.

Despite the active trade or business standard in the guidelines, the Tax Court held that the taxpayer was free to establish that a favorable ruling should be issued based on all the facts and circumstances. The Tax Court concluded that the transfer did not have tax avoidance as a principal purpose, based on several factors, including that (1) the U.S.'s transferor's U.K. co-owner demanded the Antilles location and the form of the transaction, and (2) there was a business reason for retention of up to 25 percent of the transferee's profits. The court did not reach the question whether transacting business through independent contractors constitutes an active trade or business.

Treatment of liquidating distributions by a domestic corporation

A liquidating distribution of appreciated property by an 80-percent-owned domestic subsidiary into its foreign parent corporation (under section 332) was treated as an outbound transfer, subject to the ruling requirement that was generally applicable to transfers of appreciated property to foreign corporations. The only statutory sanction for the failure to obtain the required ruling was the denial of the exception to the recapture rules (for depreciation, investment credits, and other items) that otherwise would be available.

Reasons for Change

The Congress originally enacted the special rules for nonrecognition transactions involving foreign corporations specifically to prevent avoidance of U.S. tax by transferring appreciated property outside the United States. Although this provision generally worked well over the years, a series of Tax Court cases threatened to weaken it.

The prior-law provisions in section 367(a) applied only to transfers pursuant to "a plan having as one of its principal purposes the avoidance of Federal income taxes." Interpreting this provision in Dittler Bros., the Tax Court required that a tax avoidance purpose for a transfer be greater in importance than any business purpose before section 367(a) was applied to prevent a tax-free outbound transfer of property. This narrow interpretation by the Tax Court caused the IRS difficulty in administering section 367(a). The IRS was prevented from restricting tax avoidance transfers that the provisions of that section were intended to combat.

Transfers of intangibles

In addition to the general problems associated with judicial interpretations of the principal purpose test of section 367(a), specific and unique problems existed with respect to applying section 367(a) to the transfer by U.S. persons of manufacturing intangibles to foreign corporations. Under its published ruling guidelines, the IRS generally issued favorable rulings for transfers of patents and similar intangibles for use in an active trade or business of the foreign transferee corporation. The only exceptions were transfers of certain intangibles used in connection with a U.S. trade or business or in connection with goods to be manufactured, sold or consumed in the United States. In light of this favorable ruling policy, a number of U.S. companies adopted a practice of developing patents or similar intangibles at their facilities in the United States, with a view towards using the intangibles in foreign operations. When these intangibles were ready for profitable exploitation, they were transferred to a manufacturing subsidiary incorporated in a low-tax foreign jurisdiction (or in a high-tax jurisdiction that offered a tax holiday for specified local manufacturing operations). By engaging in such practices, the transferor U.S. companies hoped to reduce their U.S. taxable income by deducting substantial research and experimentation expenses associated with the development of the transferred intangible and, by transferring the intangible to a foreign corporation at the point of profitability, to ensure deferral of U.S. tax on the profits generated by the intangible. By incorporating the transferee in a low-tax jurisdiction, the U.S. companies also avoided any significant foreign tax on such profits.

Tainted assets

The Congress generally approved of the prior-law administrative practice of denying tax-free treatment to exchanges involving outbound transfers of liquid or passive investment assets unless the U.S. tax on the potential earnings from such assets was paid or preserved for future payment.

The Act generally codifies the tainted asset categories described in the IRS guidelines; however, the Act liberalizes the treatment of stock and securities. Stock will be considered as transferred for use in an active trade or business when transferred under circumstances similar to those of the Kaiser case (where the stock was akin to a direct interest in producing assets) or under certain other limited circumstances identified in regulations.

Transfers of appreciated foreign currency by U.S. businesses have increased significantly in recent years due to the increased activities of

U.S. businesses in foreign countries and the substitution of floating for fixed exchange rates in 1971. Because of the obvious liquidity of foreign currency, it can easily be disposed of by a foreign transferee.

Incorporation of foreign loss branches

In certain cases, a U.S. taxpayer's foreign branch incurred losses prior to its incorporation that reduced the amount of the U.S. taxpayer's worldwide income subject to U.S. income tax. As a result of the incorporation, the income produced by these operations did not increase the amount of the U.S. taxpayer's worldwide income that was subject to U.S. income tax. The Congress concluded that the IRS position on this issue, as expressed in Rev. Rul. 78–201 and as modified by subsequent rulings, was correct. Because the Tax Court took the contrary view, the Congress believed that it was important to clarify the law to prevent future tax avoidance.

Goodwill and certain similar intangibles

Except in the case of an incorporation of a foreign loss branch, the Congress did not believe that transfers of goodwill, going concern value, or certain marketing intangibles should be subject to tax. Goodwill and going concern value are generated by earning income, not by incurring deductions. Thus, ordinarily, the transfer of these (or similar) intangibles does not result in avoidance of Federal income taxes.

Ruling requirement and declaratory judgment procedure

Standards for the issuance of rulings were well-defined through continuing administrative interpretation and practice. The development of such standards imparted a substantial degree of regularity to the ruling process. Given certain facts, taxpayers were able to predict whether the IRS would issue a favorable or an adverse ruling. Many taxpayers considered the ruling requirement burdensome, and the requirement placed a steadily increasing demand on IRS resources as outbound transfers increased in number.

The Congress believed that the elimination of the principal purpose test rendered the ruling requirement unnecessary. Accordingly, taxpayers will now be able to proceed freely with exchanges involving outbound transfers without advance or post-transaction clearance. The exchanges either will be tax-free or will involve the payment of an appropriate toll charge, in accordance with the substantive rules set forth in section 367, as amended by the Act. Taxpayers planning a transfer subject to section 367 who seek the certainty of tax treatment that a ruling provides may request a discretionary ruling regarding the tax treatment of the transfer.

The special declaratory judgment procedure of prior law was enacted because a taxpayer who received an adverse ruling could not proceed with the transaction at issue (unless the taxpayer was willing to comply with the ruling and treat the transaction as fully taxable or pay a toll charge). The Congress believed that the declaratory judgment procedure was no longer necessary in light of the elimination of the ruling requirement.

With the elimination of the ruling requirement and the declaratory judgment procedure, there was also eliminated an unintended advantage conferred on taxpayers: full control over the nature of the factual evidence upon which an IRS determination or a declaratory judgment determination under section 367 was based. Under the new discretionary ruling procedure, the IRS will decline to rule if the taxpayer does not present facts that the IRS deems sufficient to issue a ruling. Moreover, judicial review of a section 367 determination will involve a trial and full development of a factual record. That factual record will be independent of the existing administrative record; it might include information about the manner in which the exchange at issue was actually carried out (as distinguished from information about the plan for the exchange) and information about how the transferred property was used and whether the transferee disposed of it after the transfer.

So that the IRS will continue to be informed of outbound transfers of property, the Act establishes a notification requirement and a set of penalties for failure to comply with the requirement. Without a mechanism for apprising the IRS of outbound transfers, the IRS generally would have to depend on audits to detect outbound transfers of property subject to section 367 and any instances of failure to pay tax due on such transfers. Because of the complexity of many corporate income tax returns and certain exchanges that corporations carry out, the audit process is not a reliable means of isolating exchanges subject to section 367.

Explanation of Provision. . .

Special rule for transfers of intangibles

Except as provided in regulations, a transfer described in section 351 of intangible property to a controlled corporation or in certain corporate reorganizations described in section 361 is treated as a sale. Intangible property is defined as any (i) patent, invention, formula, process, design, pattern, or know-how, (ii) copyright, literary, musical, or artistic composition, (iii) trademark, trade name, or brand name, (iv) franchise, license, or contract, (v) method, program, 433 system, procedure, campaign, survey, study, forecast, estimate, customer list, or technical data, or (vi) any similar item which property has substantial value independent of the services of any individual. Intangible property is ineligible for the active trade or business exception.

On the transfer of intangible property, the transferor is treated as receiving amounts that reasonably reflect the amounts the would have been received under an agreement providing for payments contingent on productivity, use, or disposition of the property. Amounts are treated as received over the useful life of the intangible property on an annual basis. Earnings and profits of the transferee foreign corporation are reduced by the amount of income required to be included in income by the transferor. Any amounts included in gross income by reason of this special rule are treated as ordinary income from sources within the United States.

These special rules (including the sourcing rule) apply only to situations involving a transfer of the intangible property to a foreign corporation. See generally *E.I. Dupont de Nemours & Co. v. United States*, 471 F.2d 1211 (Ct. Cl. 1973) (holding that the grant of a no non-exclusive license with respect to a patent constituted a "transfer of property" within the meaning of section 351). in any case in which the IRS determines that an adjustment under section 482 (relating to the allocation of income and deductions among taxpayers) is a appropriate because a foreign corporation obtained the use of the intangible property without sufficient compensation therefore, the special rule for transfers of intangibles will have no application of amounts included in the income of a U.S. taxpayer pursuant to such an adjustment. Thus, for example, the source of any adjustment to the income of a U.S. taxpayer under section 482 would be determined without regard to the sourcing rule in the Act. In addition, the special rule for intangibles will have no application to bona fide cost-sharing arrangements (under which research and development expenditures are shared by affiliates as or before the they are incurred, instead of being recouped by licensing or selling the intangible after successful development). See generally Treas. rev. sec. 1.482–2(d)(4) (relating to the application of section 482 where a member of a group of controlled entities acquires an interest in intangible property, as a participating party in a bona fide cost-sharing arrangement with respect to the development of such property). It is recognized that the Treasury Department may find it appropriate to elaborate on the current rules relating to cost-sharing arrangements, to adequately address arrangements with respect to intangibles.

The disposition of (1) the transferred intangible by a transferee corporation, or (2) the transferor's interest in the transferee corporation will result in recognition of U.S.-source ordinary income to the original transferor. The amount of U.S.-source ordinary income will depend on the value of the intangible at the time of the second transfer.

Incorporation of foreign loss branch

The active trade or business exception is inapplicable to the transfer of the assets of a foreign branch of a U.S. person to a foreign corporation in an exchange described in section 332, 351, 354, 434 355, 356, or 361. The Act requires the recognition of gain equal to the lesser of (1) the excess of pre-incorporation losses incurred by the foreign branch with respect to which a deduction was allowed to the taxpayer over the amount of any income required to be recognized by section 904(f)(3) in the current taxable year (but not amounts that were simply recharacterized as U.S.-source income under section 904(f)(1)), or (2) the gain on the transfer. In computing the tax imposed under this rule, gain on transfers of goodwill, going concern value, and marketing intangibles developed by a foreign branch will be included.

In applying the rule requiring gain recognition, a pre-incorporation loss is reduced by taxable income derived by the foreign branch in a taxable year after the taxable year in which the loss was incurred and before the close of the taxable year of the transfer. The Act provides for the characterization of the recognized gain (as ordinary income or capital gain) by reference to the character of the previously incurred losses. For example, if a branch incurred a capital loss or a foreign oil extraction loss in an earlier year, its later incorporation would yield capital gain or foreign oil extraction income, as the case may be.

On incorporation of a loss branch with appreciated intangibles, the transfer of intangibles will be subject to the special rule for intangibles, not the loss branch rule, except that gain on transfers of goodwill, going concern value, or marketing intangibles will be taxable under the loss branch rule to the extent that transfers of such property are excepted in regulations relating to the special rule for intangibles and the rule for tainted assets. In all other respects, the provision for transfers of foreign loss branches are to apply in a manner consistent with the IRS's published rulings under prior law. Thus, for example, losses that result in gain recognition on incorporation include expenses directly related to a branch's property that was not transferred but abandoned as worthless. See Rev. Rul. 78–201, 1978–1 C.B. 91.

Example

A taxpayer's branch in country A incurred a $100 loss in year one; that loss offset $100 of U.S. source income in year one. In year two, the taxpayer's branch in country B earned $200 of foreign source income; the taxpayer treated $100 of that income as U.S. source income pursuant to section 904(f)(1). In year three, the taxpayer incorporates the country A branch; that incorporation involves the transfer to a new country A corporation of assets with an excess of fair market value over basis of $85. In year three, none of the gain on the incorporation is required to be recognized by section 904(f)(3) as U.S. source income (because of the previous recharacterization in year two under section 904(f)(1)). Therefore, the taxpayer includes in income $85 (the lesser of the gain ($85) or the excess of the previously deducted losses ($100) over amounts subject to section 904(f)(3) ($0 in this case)) as ordinary income from sources without the United States.

. . .

Goodwill and certain similar intangibles

The Act contemplates that, ordinarily, no gain will be recognized on the transfer of goodwill, going concern value, or marketing intangibles (such as trademarks or trade names) developed by a foreign branch to a foreign corporation (regardless of whether the foreign corporation is newly organized). Thus, where appropriate, it is expected that regulations relating to tainted assets and the special rule for intangibles will provide exceptions for this type of property. As noted above, however, no such exception will be provided under the loss branch rule. In addition, as under prior law, gain will be recognized on transfers of marketing intangibles for use in connection with a U.S. trade or business, or in connection with goods to be manufactured, sold, or consumed in the United States.

. . .

Notification requirement

The Act establishes a notification requirement for certain transfers to foreign persons and a set of penalties for failure to comply with the requirement. A U.S. person who transfers property to a foreign corporation in an exchange subject to section 367, or a domestic corporation that makes a liquidating distribution described in section 336 to a foreign person, is required to furnish to the Secretary such information with respect to the exchange as the Secretary may require, at the time and in the manner provided in regulations. If a U.S. person fails to comply with the notification requirement, there is imposed a penalty equal to 25 percent of the amount of the gain realized on the exchange, unless the failure was due to reasonable cause and not to willful neglect. In addition, the Act extends the general three-year limitation on assessment and collection of any tax imposed on an exchange with respect to which a taxpayer fails to give the required notice. In such a case, the time for assessment of the tax imposed does not expire before the date three years after the date the Secretary is notified. Thus, if a taxpayer fails to notify the Secretary of an exchange subject to section 367, the time for assessment of any tax imposed on the exchange by reason of section 367(a) or (d) continues indefinitely.

* * *

NOTES AND QUESTIONS

1. In 2006, Treasury revised the definition of a statutory merger under section 368(a)(1)(A) to now include certain foreign mergers (Treas. Reg. § 1.368–2(b)). Correspondingly, the regulations under section 367 were amended to except such transactions from the application of this section (Treas. Reg. § 1.367(a)–3).

2. Basic problem: Corporation X, a Delaware corporation with a New York City headquarters owns three major assets—A New York City plant (and the land on which it is located) with an adjusted basis of $1m and a fair market value of $10m, manufacturing equipment with an adjusted basis of $0 and fair market value of $500,000 and a patented manufacturing process with an adjusted basis of $0, which was presented to potential investors as having a value of $100m. It also wholly owns a foreign subsidiary, S, which distributes X's products in Europe. Assume minimal gain or loss in the X stock.

X is contemplating the following options:

A.   Transferring all of X's assets and liabilities to a Foreign corporation F (which is X's main competitor in Europe) in exchange for voting stock, and the subsequent liquidation of the target corporation (X). F's tender is conditioned on S being merged with X first.

B.   Merger of F into S (F's shareholders receive X stock).

C.   Inversion of X to a Barbados corporation (no capital gains or losses expected) and consequently acquisition of F in a stock-for-stock transaction.

Think about the challenges that these optional transactions present in the context of Section 367.

3.   The TCJA expanded the reach of Section 367(a) in two notable ways. First, it repealed Section 367(a)(3), which previously allowed an exception to Section 367 (and thus allowed deferral provisions to apply) for the transfer of assets to a foreign corporation where those assets would be used in the foreign corporation's foreign trade or business. Consider how this statutory change might impact your analysis of the example in Note 2 above. Second, the TCJA broadened the definition of intangibles covered by Section 367(d) to include goodwill, going concern value, and workforce in place as well as any other item the value of which is not attributable to tangible property or the services of any individual.

9.2   INCORPORATION OF A LOSS BRANCH

A classic example of tax abuse in general and the abuse potential leading to Section 367 in particular is the case of incorporation of a loss branch. The natural progression of most businesses is expected to start with a few years of losses, when the initial investment and market penetration take place, to break-even and, if successful, to profit making years. Therefore, it is just logical, absent any anti-abuse rules, to expect businesses to organize in a branch form, which allows the shareholders to currently reduce their tax liabilities by the initial start-up losses, and incorporate the business once it breaks even and defer taxation of profits other than at the new subsidiary level. Failed businesses just never reach the point of incorporation, allowing the investors at least to currently use all the losses in such businesses—losses which could be difficult to use if incurred by an incorporated business (subsidiary). This basic planning model is particularly beneficial if the new business is foreign, since once incorporated deferral allows such a business to never repatriate its profits (unless certain anti-deferral regimes described in Chapter 7 apply), and avoid U.S. taxation of such profits. It is possible, hence to imagine a scenario where a business' losses reduce U.S. revenue, without taxation of its profits, once made. The following excerpts from a revenue ruling and a Tax Court case demonstrate the difficulty created by this tax planning opportunity/abuse.

. . .

1978–1 C.B. 91; 1978 IRB LEXIS 495,

Rev. Rul. 78–201

. . . Advice has been requested whether the transaction described below is one for which a favorable ruling will be issued under section 367 of the Internal Revenue Code of 1954.

P is a domestic corporation that is engaged in the manufacture and sale of plastic components for the radio and television industries in the United States. In 1975 P commenced business operations in country A. For various business reasons these operations were carried on by a branch that P established in country A by the transfer of cash and newly purchased assets with a value of $100x.

Beginning in 1975, deductions were taken by P under section 167 and certain other sections of the Code for expenses incurred by the branch operations. The income and losses of P and its country A branch for the years 1975, 1976, and 1977, were as follows:

	U.S. Source Income	Country A Branch Income
Taxable Income in 1975	$1,000x	($50x)
Taxable Income in 1976	$1,200x	($30x)
Taxable Income in 1977	$1,000x	($10x)

During each of the three years P's other foreign branches received income in excess of the losses of the branch in country A.

In late 1977, P transferred the assets of branch A to a corporation newly created under the laws of country A solely in exchange for its stock. The foreign transferee was not to be engaged in a trade or business in the United States within the meaning of section 864 of the Code and was to have no income from sources within the United States within the meaning of section 861. The transfer of assets in exchange for stock would have fulfilled all the requirements of section 351 had the transferee been a domestic corporation. Furthermore, the transfer met the requirements of section 3.02(1) of Rev. Proc. 68–23, 1968–1 C.B. 821. Within 183 days of the beginning of the transfer P requested a ruling from the Internal Revenue Service that the transaction was not in pursuance of a plan of tax avoidance within the meaning of section 367.

Section 351 of the Code provides that no gain or loss shall be recognized if property is transferred to a corporation by one or more persons solely in exchange for stock or securities in such corporation and immediately after the exchange such person or persons are in control (as defined in section 368(c)) of the corporation.

Section 358 of the Code provides that in the case of an exchange to which section 351 applies, the basis of the property permitted to be received under such section without the recognition of gain or loss shall be the same as that of the property exchanged (A) decreased by (i) the fair market value of any other property (except money) received by the taxpayer; (ii) the amount of any money received by the taxpayer; and (iii) the amount of loss to the taxpayer that was recognized on such exchange, and (B) increased by the amount of gain to the taxpayer that was recognized on such exchange (not including any portion of such gain that was treated as a dividend).

Section 362(a) of the Code provides that if property was acquired on or after June 22, 1954, by a corporation in connection with a transaction to which section 351 applies, then the basis shall be the same as it would be in the hands of the transferor, increased in the amount of gain recognized to the transferor on such transfer.

Section 367(a)(1) of the Code provides that if, in connection with any exchange described in section 351, there is a transfer of property (other than stock or securities of a foreign corporation that is a party to the reorganization) by a United States person to a foreign corporation, for purposes of determining the extent to which gain shall be recognized on such transfer, a foreign corporation shall not be considered to be a corporation unless, pursuant to a request filed not later than the close of the 183rd day after the beginning of such transfer (and filed in such form and manner as may be prescribed by regulations by the Secretary), it is established to the satisfaction of the Secretary that such exchange is not in pursuance of a plan having as one of its principal purposes the avoidance of Federal income taxes.

Rev. Proc. 68–23 sets forth guidelines for taxpayers and their representatives in connection with requests for rulings required under section 367 of the Code in respect of certain types of transactions involving foreign corporations. Section 3.02(1) of Rev. Proc. 68–23 relates to transfers to foreign corporations controlled by domestic transferors and provides that such a transfer of property will ordinarily receive favorable consideration where the transferred property is to be devoted by the transferee foreign corporation to the active conduct, in any foreign country, of a trade or business. It is contemplated that the transferee foreign corporation, in addition to the active conduct of a trade or business, will have need for a substantial investment in fixed assets in such business.

Section 2.02 of Rev. Proc. 68–23 provides however, that in reviewing each request for ruling to determine whether a favorable section 367 ruling should be issued under the guidelines, the Service reserves the right to issue an adverse ruling if, based on all the facts and circumstances of a case, it is determined that the taxpayer has not established that tax avoidance is not one of the principal purposes of the transaction.

The losses incurred by the foreign branch operations prior to its incorporation were taken into account by P and reduced the amount of P's worldwide income subject to Federal income tax. However, as a result of the incorporation of the foreign branch operations, the income to be produced by these operations will not be taken into account by P and, thus, will not increase the amount of P's worldwide income subject to Federal income tax. Therefore, the transfer by P of the assets of the branch to the foreign corporation will be deemed to be in pursuance of a plan having as one of its principal purposes the avoidance of Federal income taxes within the meaning of section 367 of the Code. Accordingly, the transfer by P of the assets of branch A to the foreign corporation will be deemed not to be in pursuance of a plan having as one of its principal purposes the avoidance of Federal income taxes, within the meaning of section 367 of the Code, only if the transferor, P, recognizes as gain on the transfer an amount of ordinary foreign source income equal to the sum of the Country A branch losses previously incurred (that is, $90x). This income must be recognized as ordinary income by P for its taxable year in which the transfer occurred.

In addition, because the transaction qualifies as an exchange to which section 351 of the Code applies, pursuant to section 362(a) the basis of the assets transferred will be the same as the basis of such assets in the hands of P immediately prior to the exchange, increased by the amount of gain recognized to P on the transfer. Pursuant to section 358(a)(1), the basis of the stock of the foreign subsidiary received by P will be the same as the basis of the assets transferred in exchange therefore increased by the amount of gain recognized to P on the transfer.

. . .

HERSHEY FOODS CORPORATION v. COMMISSIONER OF INTERNAL REVENUE

76 T.C. 312 (1981)

. . . FAY, *Judge*:

Respondent determined petitioner is not entitled to a favorable ruling under section 367 unless petitioner agrees to include certain amounts in income. Having exhausted its administrative remedies as required by section 7477(b)(2), petitioner has timely invoked the jurisdiction of this Court for a declaratory judgment pursuant to section 7477(a). The issue is whether respondent's determination is reasonable. . . .

Avoidance of Federal income taxes is not defined by section 367 or by any other section using the phrase. See, e.g., secs. 269 and 1502. To give taxpayers some guidance in this area, respondent issued Rev. Proc. 68–23, 1968–1 C.B. 821, which sets forth transactions which will usually receive favorable consideration under section 367. In the case of a foreign incorporation under section 351, Rev. Proc. 68–23, *supra*, provides that, if the foreign corporate transferee will devote the transferred property to the active conduct of a trade or business and either will need a substantial investment in fixed assets in such business or will be engaged in the purchase and sale abroad of manufactured goods, a favorable ruling will ordinarily be issued. Sec. 3.01(1), Rev. Proc. 68–23, *supra*. HC, the Canadian corporate transferee in this case, clearly meets the requirements necessary for Hershey to receive a favorable ruling under that provision. However, respondent contends this is not the usual situation and points to section 2.02, Rev. Proc. 68–23, *supra*, which provides, in part: In reviewing each request for ruling to determine whether a favorable section 367 ruling should be issued under the guidelines, the Service reserves the right to issue an adverse ruling if, based on all the facts and circumstances of a case, it is determined that the taxpayer has not established that tax avoidance is not one of the principal purposes of the transaction. Similarly, a taxpayer shall be free to establish that based on all the facts and circumstances of the taxpayer's case a favorable ruling under section 367 of the Code should be issued, notwithstanding a contrary statement or implication contained in the guidelines. . . .

The fact which troubles respondent in this case is that Hershey's Canadian branch, which will be transferred to HC, has suffered a series of losses in the past which reduced Hershey's worldwide income subject to Federal income tax. He reasons that transferring the historically unprofitable branch to a foreign corporation results in a presumption of tax avoidance since Hershey's future Canadian income will not be subject to Federal income tax. Respondent perceives a mismatching of loss and income and contends Hershey's income will not be reflected clearly as a result. That argument parallels Rev. Rul. 78–201, 1978–1 C.B. 91, which held that foreign incorporation of a branch operation when the branch could be expected to turn from a loss operation to a profit operation raises a presumption of tax avoidance.

Petitioner maintains that Rev. Rul. 78–201 is unsupportable, and that, even if correct, it does not apply in this case. Petitioner argues that no tax avoidance potential exists because Hershey's income has been and will be clearly reflected and because section 904(f) preemptively covers foreign loss recaptures in connection with foreign incorporations. We agree with petitioner for the reasons below.

We are admittedly puzzled by respondent's reliance on any clear reflection of income doctrine in this case. If his position were correct, we would be forced to view the Hershey Canadian branch's entire history as one event in determining whether income was clearly reflected. But that is not how the clear reflection of income doctrine is applied.

Federal income taxes are computed on an annual basis, not on a transactional basis. . . . Each year stands on its own. A transactional approach under which we would wait to see the end result of an entire business venture before determining the proper tax consequences might be thought by some to be more equitable, but that is not the approach used in our system of income taxation. Thus, it is within the framework of annual taxation that the clear reflection of income doctrine operates.

Accordingly, what that doctrine requires is that a taxpayer's income be clearly reflected *each* year, not that a taxpayer's lifetime income or even his income in relation to a specific ongoing transaction be reflected clearly when viewed as a whole. There is no evidence or any contention by respondent that Hershey's income has not been clearly reflected in each of the years it suffered losses from the operation of the Canadian branch, and we do not see how foreign incorporation of Hershey's Canadian branch causes a failure to reflect income clearly.

Only if the Canadian branch becomes profitable after foreign incorporation and its entire historical existence is then viewed as one occurrence for tax purposes under a transactional approach would income fail to be reflected clearly. But, as noted above, annual taxation not transactional taxation is the American rule. If the branch were not incorporated and eventually produced income, that income would not be affected by the earlier losses. The only result of foreign incorporation is that income in future years will not be subject to Federal income tax. Essentially the same result would obtain if Hershey ceased to operate its Canadian branch, or if the branch had been profitable in the past.

In essence, respondent is espousing a tax benefit theory of taxation. There are two basic ways in which deductions taken in one year are included as income in another year—by application of a statutory recapture section (see, e.g., secs. 1245, 1250, 904(f)(3), and 617(a)(1)) or by application of the tax benefit rule—neither of which applies in this case.

Under the tax benefit rule, an amount properly deducted from gross income in determining one year's tax liability is includable in gross income when it is recovered in a subsequent year. *Davis v. Commissioner*, 74 T.C. 881 (1980). *Estate of Munter v. Commissioner*, 63 T.C. 663 (1975). The keys to tax benefit income are a prior benefit and "recovery of *property* that was once the subject of an income tax deduction." See *Alice Phelan Sullivan Corp. v. United States*, 180 Ct.Cl. 659, 663, 381 F.2d 399, 401 (1967). (Emphasis added.) There has been no recovery by petitioner, and none is envisaged. See generally *Nash v. United States*, 398 U.S. 1 (1970). Therefore, the tax benefit rule does not apply in this case.

Nor can we find any other basis for respondent's determination of a tax-avoidance purpose. His position in this case represents an unreasonable use of the power conferred upon him by section 367. The United States taxes U.S. entities operating abroad but cannot and does not tax foreign entities on their foreign operations. Thus, every foreign incorporation of a U.S. business operating abroad takes the future profits involved outside of U.S. tax jurisdiction. We fail to perceive any crucial difference between a domestic corporation's foreign incorporation of a foreign loss branch and its foreign incorporation of a foreign profit branch. In both cases, only future, currently unearned, operating income is being removed from the clutches of Federal income taxation.

Moreover, we note that respondent's position in this case represents an extension of section 367's historical application. By 1976 "the statutory standard for determining that a transaction did not have as one of its principal purposes tax avoidance had evolved through administrative interpretation into a requirement generally that tax-free treatment would be permitted only if * * * the U.S. tax on the potential earnings from liquid or passive investment assets (in the case of transfers of property outside the United States) was paid or was preserved for future payment." Joint Committee on Taxation, 94th Cong., 2d Sess., General Explanation of the Tax Reform Act of 1976, at 257, 1976–3 C.B. (Vol. 2) 1, 269. Thus, in a section 351 setting, section 367 operated with respect to the *type* of assets being transferred, e.g., inventory, know-how, or stock, that might carry passive income which could just as easily be earned or realized in the United States or income which had essentially already been earned. In contrast, Rev. Rul. 78–201, *supra*, looks to currently unearned, future operating (not passive) income as the income upon which tax is being avoided.

We are fortified in our conclusion that no tax-avoidance potential exists in this case by the fact that Congress, in 1976, dealt comprehensively with the tax treatment of foreign losses. Basically, Congress took three major steps—(1) repeal of the per country method of calculating available foreign tax credits; (2) recharacterization of certain foreign source income as U.S. source income to account for foreign losses in excess of foreign income; and (3) enactment of section 904(f)(3) which requires the recapture of excess foreign losses upon disposition of foreign branch assets. See generally Joint Committee on Taxation, 94th Cong., 2d Sess., General Explanation of the Tax Reform Act of 1976, at 236, 1976–3 C.B. (Vol. 2) 1, 248. As we will explain below, the net effect of those congressional actions combined with approval of respondent's argument in this case would result in double counting of Hershey's Canadian branch losses against Hershey.

Before the 1976 congressional action, available foreign tax credits could be claimed under either of two methods—the per country method or the overall method. In the case of a taxpayer suffering both foreign losses and foreign profits, the per country method could produce a lower Federal income tax liability since a loss in one country would not reduce the income from another country and concomitantly would not reduce the foreign tax credits available with respect to the foreign country operation producing income. See S. Rept. 94–938, p. 236, 1976–3 C.B. (Vol. 3) 248, 274. On the other hand, use of the overall method requires netting of all foreign losses and income regardless of the country in which they originate. Thus, a loss in one country will reduce the income in another country resulting in less foreign tax credits being available with respect to the foreign operations producing income. See S. Rept. 94–938, *supra*. By repealing the per country method, Congress ensured that all foreign losses will be matched against some foreign income in the year the losses are deducted unless losses exceeded income.

If foreign losses exceed foreign income, no foreign tax credits are available and excess losses serve to reduce U.S. source income. In that case, Congress felt that additional measures were necessary to ensure that U.S. source income bore its full share of Federal income tax. . . .

Accordingly, Congress enacted section 904(f)(1) which provides in essence that, when any excess foreign loss reduces U.S. source income otherwise subject to tax, future foreign source income equal in amount to the excess loss will be treated as U.S. source income. That will reduce the amount of foreign tax credits available since the amount of foreign source income will be reduced. Thus, when the year(s) of excess loss and the year(s) of recharacterization are viewed together, U.S. source income will bear its full tax share.

Congress also addressed itself to the possibility that foreign branch assets might be disposed of before full excess foreign loss recapture via recharacterization of foreign source income could be accomplished. Section 904(f)(3) accelerates the recapture process upon such disposition by requiring recognition at the time of disposition of an amount of income equal to the lesser of the gain realized or the amount of any previously unrecaptured excess foreign loss.

The combined effect of the three above-stated steps is to ensure, in the long run, that foreign losses only reduce foreign income—any foreign loss matched against U.S. source income either will cause a recharacterization of later foreign source income as U.S. income or will itself be recognized upon a disposition of foreign branch assets. Thus, the objective of Congress, that U.S. income bear its Federal income tax share, is met. See generally *Theo. H. Davies & Co. v. Commissioner*, 75 T.C. 443 (1980).

Respondent maintains that even though section 904(f)(3) requires recapture of excess foreign losses upon foreign incorporation of a foreign branch, it does not preclude foreign loss recapture as a toll charge under section 367. In the case of a taxpayer who would have the same losses recaptured under both section 904(f)(3) and section 367, the result would be absurd. With that statement, respondent agrees. See Rev. Rul. 80–246, 1980–37 I.R.B. 8. Nevertheless, respondent contends that, when section 904(f)(3) does not apply because no excess loss which has reduced U.S. source income is present, section 367 may be used to recapture past foreign losses. We disagree.

Since only the overall method of calculating available foreign tax credits is permitted, foreign losses must first be matched against foreign income thereby reducing foreign tax credits. Any foreign loss used to reduce United States source income will be recaptured. If we were to sustain respondent's position we would be counting Hershey's Canadian branch losses against it twice—first, to reduce other foreign income and thus reduce foreign tax credits and, second, as additional foreign source income. In effect, we would undermine the whole rationale behind the foreign tax credit system—the prevention of double taxation. . . .

While we are generally hesitant to hold that one Code section precludes application of another Code section to the same situation, we find such result warranted in this case. See *Abegg v. Commissioner*, 429 F.2d 1209 (2d Cir. 1970), affg. 50 T.C. 145 (1968), cert. denied 400 U.S. 1008, 91 S.Ct. 566, 27 L.Ed.2d 621 (1971). Congress carefully studied the tax consequences of foreign losses and enacted comprehensive legislation to prevent any tax benefits previously allowed which Congress felt were unwarranted. From that, we infer that Congress never intended section 367 to be used to recapture past losses when a branch is incorporated in a foreign country. . . .

For the above-stated reasons we find respondent's determination, that the proposed transaction has as one of its principal purposes the avoidance of Federal income taxes unless Hershey agrees to recognize certain prior losses as income, unreasonable. . . .

     * * *

NOTES AND QUESTIONS

1. Does the court's conclusion that Congress never intended section 367 to be used to recapture past losses when a branch is incorporated in a foreign country makes sense? Is it true that the Commissioner's position would have led to double taxation in this case?

2. In response to *Hershey,* Section 367(a)(3)(C) was enacted, disallowing application of nonrecognition provisions when a domestic corporation transferred assets of its foreign branch to a foreign subsidiary—to the extent the foreign branch had prior net losses. Note that this was an exception to the general exception in Section 367(a)(3) discussed earlier, which permitted the transfer of business assets to foreign subsidiaries to retain the benefits of nonrecognition]. Although the Section 367(a)(3) general business assets exception was repealed in TCJA, tax reform added new Section 91 to explicitly recapture branch losses. Section 91 provides that if a domestic corporation transfers "substantially all of the assets of a foreign branch" to its 10% owned foreign corporation, then the domestic corporation must include in gross income in the year of the transfer an amount equal to the prior foreign branch losses deducted by the domestic corporation.

     * * *

9.3   THE OPERATION OF SECTION 367

1. Read section 367(a) and the relevant parts of the bluebook excerpts in Section 9.1. above. Note the simplicity and crudeness of this measure. Naturally, the exceptions and the detailed regulations shape the actual scope of this rule. Note particularly the exception for property used in an active conduct of trade or business (Treas. Reg. Section 1.367(a)–2T), the

special rules regarding transfers of stock or securities to a foreign corporation (Section 367(a)(2) & Treas. Reg. Section 1.367(a)–3). Note the specific distinction between transfers of property and stock or securities (the rules applying to transfers of intellectual property are also different—see the next subsection). Revisit the note on inversion transactions in Chapter 7.4.D—how could these transactions be tax-efficient in light of these rules?

2.   Read Section 367(d), Treas. Reg. 1.367(d)–1T(a)–(c), (g)(4)–(6), and then reread the section on outbound transfers of intellectual property in the 1984 blue book excerpt, supra, in Chapter 9.1.A. What is special about intangibles that require such a deviation from the regular outbound Section 367(a) rule. Why not recharacterize the income as royalty rather than sale proceeds income? Read again the notes on inversion transactions (chapter 7) and the cost-sharing regulations (chapter 6)—how could these techniques be used to avoid application of Section 367(d)? Do you expect to see more or fewer inversion-type transactions involving intangibles than other types of property? Why would a U.S. inventor incorporate her idea in the U.S. at all? Why is the transfer of intangibles particularly problematic in this context?

3.   Read again the relevant sections in the 1976 and 1984 blue book excerpts, supra, in Chapter 9.1.A., Sections 367(b) and 1248, and Treas. Reg. Section 1.367(b)–1, –2(a)–(d), –3(a)–(b)(3)(i). Note that this set of rules apply to both inbound and "other," including foreign-to-foreign transactions. Note the loose connection between these rules and the rules of Section 367(a). What is the primary role of Section 367(b)? What do you think about the application of these rules to transactions that take place entirely outside the U.S.?

4.   Section 367(e) provides a special rule for cross-border liquidations. What is the purpose of a separate rule, different from the regular inbound and outbound rules?

5.   For the requirement of a gain recognition agreement ("GRA"), read Treas. Reg. 1.367(a)–8.

6.   The following excerpt demonstrates a typical application of some of the above rules:

        * * *

PLR–112485–04 (Excerpt)

        . . . This is in response to your letter, dated February 2, 2004, requesting a private letter ruling that based on your representations, the proposed merger of a wholly owned domestic subsidiary of Acquirer, a foreign corporation, with and into Target, a domestic corporation will qualify for an exception to the general rule of section 367(a)(1) of the Internal Revenue Code of 1986, as amended (the Code). Additional information was submitted in letters dated February 19, 2004, April 8, 2004, April 21, 2004, May 5, 2004, and May 7, 2004. . . .

Acquirer is engaged in Business A. Acquirer is a publicly traded company, which has a non-US government as its indirect majority shareholder. Acquirer was incorporated in Year 1 in Country A and began operations in Year 2.

Target is engaged in the same business as Acquirer. Target is a publicly traded company, which has one class of stock issued and outstanding. Target was incorporated in State A in Year 3.

On Date 1, Acquirer and Target entered into an agreement whereby U.S. Sub, a wholly owned domestic subsidiary of Acquirer, will merge with and into Target with Target surviving the merger (the "Merger"). Holders of Target stock, in exchange for their Target shares, will receive American Depository Shares ("ADS") in Acquirer. Acquirer and Target represent that the Merger will qualify as a reorganization within the meaning of section 368(a) of the Code.

The exchange of Target shares by U.S. persons is subject to section 367(a) of the Code, which provides that where no exception applies, the transfer of appreciated property (including stock) by a U.S. person to a foreign corporation in a transaction that would otherwise qualify as a reorganization exchange is treated as a taxable transfer. In the case of a section 367(a) transaction in which a U.S. person transfers stock to a foreign corporation, the U.S. transferor will qualify for nonrecognition treatment only if the requirements of Treas. Reg. Section 1.367(a)–3(c)(1) are satisfied.

Among the requirements of Treas. Reg. Section 1.367(a)–3(c)(1) is the requirement that the U.S. target company must satisfy the reporting requirements of Treas. Reg. Section 1.367(a)–3(c)(6). Target represents that it will comply with the reporting requirements of Treas. Reg. Section 1.367(a)–3(c)(6). Additionally, a transfer by a U.S. transferor that is a five-percent shareholder of the transferee foreign corporation immediately after the transfer will only qualify for the exception in Treas. Reg. § 1.367(a)–3(c) if the transferor enters into a five-year gain recognition agreement as provided in Treas. Reg. Section 1.367(a)–8.

Among the remaining requirements under Treas. Reg. Section 1.367(a)–3(c)(1) is the requirement that U.S. persons transferring U.S. target stock must receive, in the aggregate, 50 percent or less of both the total voting power and total value of the stock in the transferee foreign corporation (taking into account the attribution rules under section 318 of the Code, as modified by the rules of section 958(b) of the Code). The Taxpayers represent that U.S. transferors of Target stock will receive, in the aggregate, actually or constructively, 50-percent or less of both the total voting power and total value of all shares of Acquirer stock outstanding after the merger. Another requirement is that U.S. persons who are officers or directors of the U.S. target corporation, or who are 5-percent shareholders of the U.S. target corporation, must own in the aggregate, 50-percent or less of each of the total voting power and total value of the stock in the transferee foreign corporation (taking into account the attribution rules of section 318 of the Code, as modified by the rules of section 958(b) of the Code). The Taxpayers represent that U.S. persons who are officers, directors or 5-percent target shareholders (as defined in Treas. Reg. Section 1.367(a)–3(c)(5)(iii)) of Target will own, in the aggregate, actually or constructively, 50percent or less of each of the total voting power and total value of all shares of Acquirer immediately after the Merger.

The active trade or business test of Treas. Reg. Section 1.367(a)–3(c)(3) must be satisfied. The active trade or business test consists of three elements. The first element provides that the transferee foreign corporation (or any qualified subsidiary or qualified partnership as defined under Treas. Reg. Section 1.367(a)–3(c)(5)(vii) and (viii)) must have been engaged in the active conduct of a trade or business outside of the United States, within the meaning of Treas. Reg. Sections 1.367(a)–2T(b)(2) and (3), for the entire 36-month period immediately preceding the exchange of U.S. target stock. Acquirer represents that it or one or more of its "qualified subsidiaries" (as defined in Treas. Reg. Section 1.367(a)–3(c)(5)(vii)) will have been engaged in the active conduct of a trade or business outside the United States (the "Acquiring Business"), within the meaning of Treas. Reg. Sections 1.367(a)–2T(b)(2) and (3), for the entire 36-month period immediately preceding the Merger.

The second element of the active trade or business test provides that at the time of the exchange, neither the transferors nor the transferee foreign corporation (or any qualified subsidiary or qualified partnership engaged in the active trade or business) will have the intention to substantially dispose of or discontinue such trade or business. Target represents that at the time of the Merger, no shareholders of Target (to the knowledge of Target) have any intention to substantially dispose of, or discontinue, the Acquiring Business. Acquiring represents that at the time of the Merger, Acquiring (including its qualified subsidiaries) does not have any intention to substantially dispose of, or discontinue, the Acquiring Business.

The third element of the active trade or business test is the substantiality test as defined in Treas. Reg. Section 1.367(a)–3(c)(3)(iii). Under the substantiality test, the transferee foreign corporation must be equal to or greater in value than the U.S. target corporation at the time of the U.S. target stock exchange (see Treas. Reg. Section 1.367(a)–3(c)(3)(iii)(A)). Pursuant to Treas. Reg. Section 1.367(a)–3(c)(iii)(B)(1) the value of the transferee foreign corporation is reduced by the amount of any asset acquired outside the ordinary course of business by such corporation or any of its qualified subsidiaries or qualified partnerships within the 36-month period preceding the exchange to the extent that (i) at the time of the exchange such asset produces or is held for the production of passive income, as defined in section 1297(b) or (ii) such asset was acquired for the principal purpose of satisfying the substantiality test (commonly referred to as the "stuffing" rule). In addition, pursuant to Treas. Reg. Section 1.367(a)–3(c)(iii)(B)(3) the value of the transferee foreign corporation is reduced by the value of assets received within the 36-month period prior to the acquisition if such assets were owned by the U.S. target company or an affiliate. Acquirer represents that it did not undertake any debt issuance, acquisition, merger or restructuring with the 36 months preceding the Merger for any purpose related to satisfying the substantiality test.

During the 36 months preceding the Merger, Acquirer (i) purchased X% of the stock of FX, a foreign corporation and that ownership interest in FX is worth $Y; (ii) issued $Z worth of convertible notes; (iii) issued $AA worth of ordinary shares; and (iv) and the employees of Acquirer exercised compensatory options for Acquirer ordinary shares worth $BB.

FX is engaged in the same business as Acquirer and is treated as an integrated element of Acquirer's business and not a passive investment. Acquirer purchased the FX shares in the ordinary course of business in order to expand its global presence in Business A.

During the prior 36-month period, Acquirer's capital expenditures exceeded its cash flow from operations by $CC. Acquirer's issuances of equity and convertible notes were necessary to fund Acquirer's net capital expenditures, plus its working capital requirements and other commitments during the most recent 36 months and for Acquirer to maintain enough capital to fund future expenditures and/or acquisitions.

Acquirer issued convertible notes, which are convertible to Acquirer ordinary shares subject to certain limitations. The convertible notes were out-of-the-money when issued, have been out-of-the-money at all times since issuance, and are currently out-of-the-money. None of the convertible notes have been converted to equity. Acquirer also represents that as a result of the Merger, none of Acquirer's currently outstanding debt will be required to be converted.

It is further represented that the compensatory options (both currently outstanding and those exercised between Date 2 and Date 3) were issued to Acquirer's employees for valid business reasons and in the ordinary course of business.

Based solely on the information submitted and on the representations set forth above, and provided the convertible notes constitute debt not equity, and subject to the caveats below, it is held as follows:

1.   The transfer of Target shares by U.S. persons who are not 5-percent transferee shareholders (as defined in Treas. Reg. Section 1.367(a)–3(c)(5)(ii)) for ADS of Acquiring will qualify for an exception to section 367(a)(1) under Treas. Reg. Section 1.367(a)–3(c)(1) and (9).

2.   Any U.S. person transferring Target shares who is a 5-percent transferee shareholder (as defined in Treas. Reg. Section 1.367(a)–3(c)(5)(ii)) will qualify for the exception to section 367(a) only upon

entering into a 5-year gain recognition agreement pursuant to Treas. Reg. section 1.367(a)–8. . . .

9.4　REVIEW QUESTIONS—CHAPTER 9

1.　X, a domestic corporation transfers manufacturing equipment worth $100,000 with a basis of $10,000 to S, a (newly organized) foreign corporation, in exchange for all of its stock. X was and will continue to manufacture widgets in the U.S. and S will manufacture widgets in foreign country S for local sale. Does X recognize gain in this transaction?

2.　Assume now that X transferred laboratory equipment rather than manufacturing equipment, plus the rights to an idea that came up in the ordinary course of X's business in the U.S. and X thought had good prospects for exploitation worldwide. X relocated the employee that came up with the idea to manage S and the research activities conducted by S. What are the tax consequences of such a transfer?

3.　D, a domestic corporation, has a wholly-owned foreign subsidiary S, which has $100 of E&P includable in the Section 1248 amount. X, another domestic corporation, has a wholly-owned foreign subsidiary F, which has $200 of E&P includable in the section 1248 amount. D transferred all of S' stock to F in exchange for 40% of F's stock. Assume that the transaction qualifies as a type B reorganization if Section 367 does not apply. What is the effect of Section 367 on this transaction?

CHAPTER 10

FOREIGN CURRENCY

10.1 INTRODUCTION

Consider the following scenarios:

(1) Pet Palace Inc., a U.S. corporation providing a full range of pet care products, has a U.K. branch that operates a store in London. The U.K. store's receipts and expenses are all in British pounds.

(2) Great Books, Inc., a U.S. corporation engaged in the publishing and sale of paperbacks, has a wholly owned subsidiary in Mexico which paid 1.2 million pesos in income taxes to Mexico. Great Books, Inc. seeks to credit these foreign taxes against its U.S. taxes due (as an indirect foreign tax credit upon receipt of a dividend from its subsidiary).

(3) ScreenMakers, Inc., a U.S. corporation engaged in developing and manufacturing computer screens, has a South Korean branch that borrowed 5,000,000 won on January 1, 2019 when the exchange rate was 1000 won=1$. Repayment was made on September 1, 2019 when the exchange rate was 1000 won=.75$.

(4) CitySide, Inc., a U.S. corporation, purchased 800,000 yen on March 15, 2019 for $8,000. On October 1, 2019, CitySide sold all of the yen for $7,000.

(5) Magni-Lock Co., a U.S. corporation engaged in the manufacture of high quality locking devices, uses a special chemical in the production of its locks. This chemical is primarily available from a foreign supplier in Japan. At the beginning of the year, Magni-Lock Co. enters into a forward contract (i.e. an agreement to buy a specific quantity of an item, on a specific future date, for a specific price) with its foreign supplier to acquire 400,000 gallons of this chemical for 5,000,000 ¥, on June 1. At the time the forward contract is entered into, 100¥ =1$. However, on June 1, when the forward contract is completed (and the yens exchanged for gallons of chemicals), 100¥ =.75 $. Effectively, Magni-Lock will now have to pay out fewer dollars (converted to yen) to acquire the chemicals than it anticipated when it entered the forward contract.

What do these examples have in common? A U.S. taxpayer engaged in transactions that directly or indirectly involve foreign currency. What is the problem? Well, U.S. tax reporting is conducted in U.S. dollars— and these transactions are not—thus, they raise currency translation questions (ex. 1 and 2) and potential currency gain/loss questions (ex. 3, 4, and 5). More specifically, how should Pet Palace report the branch's earnings (which were originally calculated in pounds) on its U.S. tax return? How does Great Books calculate its indirect foreign tax credit in dollars on a 1.2 million peso income tax paid to Mexico? Does

ScreenMakers ability to repay its won denominated debt with effectively fewer dollars produce taxable gain? When CitySide buys and sells yen like bushels of wheat, does it generate taxable gain and loss? When Magni-Lock's forward purchase of the chemical turns out to be a good deal because of movements in the currency rates, is there taxable gain?

The answers to these common questions are important, especially with the growing quantity of cross border commercial activity. However, until 1986, little guidance was available in the U.S. tax law for foreign currency transactions. Congress remedied this gap with the passage of a special foreign currency regime (Sections 985–989) in the Tax Reform Act of 1986. The central operating provision is Section 988. The new regime details specific rules governing the character, source and timing of gain and loss from certain foreign currency transactions, and the translation of certain foreign currency items (e.g., foreign taxes paid) into U.S. dollars. This chapter introduces the basic theory behind the foreign currency regime and the operation of its key provisions. Despite the comprehensive nature of this regime, however, it does not cover every transaction that involves a foreign currency. For a transaction to be covered, it must fall within the enumerated list of transactions, as discussed later in this chapter.

10.2   ORIGIN AND OVERVIEW OF THE REGIME

Legislative History: General Explanation of the Tax Reform
Act of 1986 (Section 1261 of the Act, new sec. 985–989
of the Code) (Bluebook)

Prior Law

Background

When a U.S. taxpayer uses foreign currency, gain or loss (referred to as "exchange gain or loss") may arise from fluctuations in the value of the foreign currency relative to the U.S. dollar. Gain or loss results because foreign currency, unlike the U.S. dollar, is treated as property for Federal income tax purposes.

The principal issues presented by foreign currency transactions relate to the timing of recognition, the character (capital or ordinary), and the geographic source or allocation (domestic or foreign) of exchange gains or losses. Another area of concern is the treatment of a U.S. taxpayer that operates abroad through a branch or subsidiary corporation that keeps its books and records in a foreign currency; here, the issues relate to the method used to translate results recorded in a foreign currency into U.S. dollars.

Foreign currency transactions

Most of the rules for determining the Federal income tax consequences of foreign currency transactions were embodied in a series of court cases and revenue rulings issued by the Internal Revenue Service

('IRS'). Additional rules of limited application were provided by Treasury regulations and, in a few instances, statutory provisions.

Foreign exchange gain or loss could arise in the course of a trade or business or in connection with an investment transaction. Exchange gain or loss could also arise where foreign currency was acquired for personal use.

Reasons for Change

Prior law was unclear regarding the character, the timing of recognition, and the source of gain or loss due to fluctuations in the exchange rate of foreign currency. Further, no rules were prescribed for determining when the results of a foreign operation could be recorded in a foreign currency, and taxpayers were permitted to use a method of translating foreign currency results into U.S. dollars that was inconsistent with general Federal income tax principles. The result of prior law was uncertainty of tax treatment for many legitimate business transactions, as well as opportunities for tax-motivated transactions. The Congress determined that a comprehensive set of rules should be provided for the U.S. tax treatment of transactions involving foreign currency.

Functional currency

The financial accounting concept of functional currency provides a reasonable basis for determining the amount and the timing of recognition of exchange gain or loss. The Act reflects the principle that income or loss should be measured in the currency of a taxpayer's primary economic environment. Under this approach, the U.S. dollar will be the functional currency of most U.S. persons. The Congress recognized, however, that there are circumstances in which it is appropriate to measure the results of a U.S. person's foreign operation in a foreign currency so that a taxpayer is not required to recognize exchange gain or loss on currency that is not repatriated but is used to pay ordinary and necessary expenses.

Foreign currency transactions

The lack of a coherent set of rules for the treatment of foreign currency transactions resulted in uncertainty. The courts addressed several issues by referring to general Federal income tax rules that produced anomalous results when applied to exchange gain or loss. . . . Further, the IRS and the courts took contrary positions with respect to certain issues (e.g., whether a debtor's exchange gain or loss on repayment of a loan is capital or ordinary in nature). . . .

Explanation of Provisions

1. Overview

The Act sets forth a comprehensive set of rules for the treatment of foreign currency denominated transactions, in new Subpart J. The tax treatment of a foreign currency denominated transaction turns on the identity of the taxpayer's functional currency. Exchange gain or loss is recognized on a transaction-by-transaction basis only in the case of transactions involving certain financial assets or liabilities (referred to as "section 988 transactions") that are denominated in a nonfunctional currency. In the case of section 988 transactions, exchange gain or loss generally is treated as ordinary income or loss. To the extent provided in regulations, exchange gain or loss on certain hedging instruments is characterized and sourced in a manner that is consistent with the related exposure, and a portion of the unrealized exchange gain or loss on section 988 transactions is accrued currently.

A uniform set of criteria is provided for determining the currency in which the results of a foreign operation should be recorded. Business entities using a functional currency other than the U.S. dollar generally are required to use a profit and loss translation method. Exchange gain or loss on a remittance from a branch is treated as ordinary income or loss, and sourced or allocated by reference to the income giving rise to post-1986 accumulated earnings. A consistent set of rules applies to the translation of foreign taxes and adjustments thereto. . . .

NOTES AND QUESTIONS

As suggested by the legislative history, the new regime seeks to anticipate the array of circumstances in which foreign currency issues can arise. In addition to those noted in the text, try to identify others. Think of the kinds of activities and transactions in which taxpayers engage, the kinds of payments they make and receive, and the potential currency implications.

10.3   QUALIFIED BUSINESS UNITS, FUNCTIONAL CURRENCY AND THE CALCULATION OF INCOME AND LOSS

a.   QUALIFIED BUSINESS UNITS AND THEIR CURRENCY

The first step in applying the foreign currency regime is the determination of the taxpayer's "functional" currency (because only transactions in "nonfunctional" currencies can generate foreign currency gain, loss or translation issues for a taxpayer). Currency is only "foreign" if it is not your functional, i.e. operating, currency. Section 985. The question of what is the taxpayer's functional currency depends on who the taxpayer is, and what activities it pursues. If a corporation conducts most of its activities in one currency (e.g., operates a restaurant in the United States), then the functional currency of that taxpayer would be the U.S. dollar. Transactions involving other currencies, such as the purchase and sale of Australian dollars could generate currency gain or loss for that taxpayer. Similarly, if a business operates a movie theatre in Japan its functional currency is likely to be the yen, and transactions in currencies other than the yen (such as the U.S. dollar or the British pound) could generate foreign currency gain or loss.

In reality, however, many businesses with cross border activities have a substantial presence in multiple countries and thus a taxpayer may seem to have more than one functional currency. For example consider the following expansion of the Pet Palace scenario outlined at the beginning of the chapter:

> Pet Palace not only has a branch in the U.K. that operates a London store, but also has a branch in Japan and a subsidiary in Peru. Pet Palace thus seems to have four functional currencies: the store and business activities in the United States would likely have the U.S. dollar as its functional currency; the U.K. branch would have the British pound; the Japanese branch would have the yen, and the Peruvian subsidiary, the nuevo sol.

How do the tax rules handle this common situation?

The answer is that functional currency is not determined exclusively at the single taxpayer level (e.g., corporation), but rather at the level of "qualified business units" (QBUs). Section 989. A QBU is any "separate and clearly identified unit of a trade or business of a taxpayer which maintains separate books and records." Section 989(a). Certainly a corporation can constitute a QBU. Treas. Reg. 1.989(a)–1(b)(2)(i). But a branch can also qualify if it maintains separate books and records (as might be expected of a branch located in a different country and using a different currency from the home office on a regular basis). The identification of functional currency is made for each QBU, although there are certain presumptions.[1] Section 985(b)(1)(B). Returning to the Pet Palace example, Pet Palace has four QBUs, and each can (and under the above facts likely does) have a different functional currency.

The election of a functional currency is treated as a method of accounting by the tax system.[2] Once the taxpayer adopts a functional currency, that election applies going forward unless the Commissioner grants permission to change.[3] Generally a substantial change must occur in the QBU's economic operating environment before a change will be permitted.[4]

---

[1] A number of QBUs are required to treat the U.S. dollar as their functional currency, including one that (1) conducts its activities primarily in dollars, (2) has its residence in the United States, or (3) does not keep books in records in the currency of any of the economic environments in which it conducts its primary activities. Sections 985(b)(1)(B), (b)(2); Treas. Reg. 1.985–1.

[2] Treas. Reg. 1.985–4(a); 1.985–1(c)(6).

[3] Treas. Reg. 1.985–4(a).

[4] Treas. Reg. 1.985–4(b).

b. CALCULATION OF INCOME/LOSS FOR TAXPAYER WITH MORE THAN ONE QBU

Three basic steps allow a taxpayer with multiple QBUs, each with different functional currencies, to calculate a unified taxable income:[5]

(1) Each QBU calculates its own taxable income or loss in its own functional currency;

(2) Each QBU's income (or loss) calculated in step 1 is translated to the taxpayer's general functional currency at the appropriate exchange rate (usually the average exchange rate). Sections 987(2), 989(b)(4); and

(3) Adjustments are made for certain transactions between QBUs with different functional currencies. Section 987.[6]

Returning again to Pet Palace, the corporation's U.K. and Japanese branches would calculate their respective income and loss in their own functional currency, and then translate that amount to U.S. dollars (the functional currency of Pet Palace overall). The income/loss of the subsidiary (calculated in Peruvian nuevo sol) does not immediately appear on Pet Palace's U.S. return. That information becomes necessary if and when a Subpart F situation arises, or a dividend[7] occurs.

Although the statute and regulations provide a great deal more detail regarding translation of items paid, incurred, or received by QBUs of different functional currencies under a wide range of circumstances, the above overview captures the essence of the translation problem and the statutory solution.

The second issue tackled by the foreign currency regime concerns transactions in a nonfunctional currency (such as the purchase and sale of a nonfunctional currency). The next section outlines the approach for these transactions.

---

[5] Section 987.

[6] Note that as a basic rule, the tax system does not recognize transactions "within" a single taxpayer. Thus, a transaction between Pet Palace's British and Japanese branches would have no tax effect. Where, however, each branch (QBU) has a different functional currency, special rules allow exchange gain or loss to be recognized on such intra-taxpayer transactions. Treas. Reg. 1.988–1(a)(10)(ii). The next section discusses how taxpayers (and QBUs) can generate gain or loss on transactions involving nonfunctional currencies. The purpose of the regulation just cited regarding intra-taxpayer transactions is to permit the exchange gain and loss rules to be applied in that intra-taxpayer context where no "taxable" transaction would otherwise be acknowledged.

[7] Dividends paid by the foreign subsidiary to its U.S. parent are usually translated into dollars at the spot rate on the date the dividend is paid. Sections 986(b)(2), 989(b)(1). To determine the amount of any Section 902 indirect credit available with the dividend, the foreign taxes paid by the subsidiary (e.g., Pet Palace's Peruvian subsidiary) are translated into dollars at the average exchange rate for the year (assuming an accrual basis taxpayer). Sections 986(a)(1), 986(a)(2).

10.4   SECTION 988 FOREIGN CURRENCY TRANSACTIONS

Transactions in a taxpayer's functional currency can never generate currency gain or loss. For example, if a taxpayer's functional currency is the U.S. dollar, then using dollars to purchase an asset does not generate gain or loss. This intuitive observation rests on our understanding of money, or more specifically, our functional currency, as NOT being property. However, sometimes a taxpayer may engage in transactions involving another currency. How should they be treated? Do they generate a special currency gain or loss?

Section 988 defines a set of transactions, often known as "section 988 transactions" for which special currency gain or loss rules apply. If the transaction in question is not on the list, the rules do not apply. The first question is what transactions are covered? The second question is what are the tax implications of qualifying?

a.   COVERED TRANSACTIONS

The statute defines a Section 988 transaction as one that satisfies two requirements:[8]

First, the transaction must be:

(1)   "The acquisition of a debt instrument or becoming the obligor under a debt instrument;"[9]

(2)   "Accruing (or otherwise taking into account) . . . any item of expense or gross income or receipt which is to be paid or received after the date on which so accrued or taken into account;"[10]

(3)   "Entering into or acquiring any forward contract, futures contract, option or similar financial instrument."[11]

---

[8]   Section 988(c)(1).

[9]   Section 988(c)(1)(B)(I). The term "debt instrument" includes a "bond, debenture, note, certificate or other evidence of indebtedness" and where provided in the regulations, preferred stock. Section 988(c)(4).

[10]   Section 988(c)(1)(B)(ii).

[11]   Section 988(c)(1)(B)(iii). What if a transaction seemingly within the ambit of Section 988 is also covered by Section 1256 and its mark to market rules? The statute explicitly answers this question. Generally, if regulated futures contracts or nonequity options are covered by Section 1256 (with special mark to market rules, and special capital gains rules) they do not qualify as Section 988 transactions. Section 988(c)(1)(D)(I); Treas. Reg. 1.988–1a(7)(I). A taxpayer may elect out of this result—and treat its otherwise Section 1256 contracts as section 988 transactions. The election may make sense for taxpayers using such contracts to hedge other section 988 transactions. (Special hedging rules govern Section 988 transactions. Section 988(d)). The election, once made, can be revoked only with permission of the Secretary. Section 988(c)(1)(D)(ii). In a case of first impression, the Tax Court followed the IRS' narrow view of financial contracts to which the Section 1256 mark-to-market rules apply. In Summitt v. Commissioner, 134 T.C. No. 12 (May 20, 2010), the court ruled that the taxpayer's foreign currency option contracts were not Section 1256 contracts and thus no loss on the contracts could be recognized under Section 1256. Somewhat surprisingly to observers, the 6th Circuit ruled instead in 2016 that over-the-counter currency option contracts constitute "foreign currency contracts" under sSection 1256(g)(2)(A) and thus are subject to the mark-to-market rules of Section 1256. Wright v. Commissioner 809 F.3d 877 (6th Cir. 2016).

Second, the transaction must be one in which the amount to be paid or received by the taxpayer is: (1) "denominated in terms of a nonfunctional currency"[12] or (2) "is determined by reference to the value of 1 or more nonfunctional currencies."[13]

How do these requirements apply to real transactions? The debt category is relatively clear—if a U.S. corporation with the dollar as its functional currency borrows yen, that obligation is a Section 988 transaction for the U.S. corporation. The second category is similarly straightforward. If the same U.S. corporation with the dollar as its functional currency agrees to pay a foreign consultant 20,000 for services, and accrues that expense on its books on January 5, 2010, but does not pay it until October 1, 2010 the transaction is a Section 988 transaction.

The third set of transactions (forwards, futures, etc.) is more complex, if only because the transactions may be less familiar and themselves can be detailed. For example, if the same U.S. corporation enters into a forward contract to purchase yen, that transaction is a section 988 transaction. However, if the U.S. corporation enters into a forward contract (denominated in a nonfunctional currency) to purchase oil, the contract would not constitute a Section 988 transaction.[14] Why not? Although part of the gain or loss on the oil contract would be attributable to exchange movements from the time the contract was entered into to the time of performance, Section 988, by its terms, does not apply. Section 988 provides that in the case of forwards, futures, and similar contracts, a transaction is covered only if "the underlying property to which the instrument ultimately relates is money (e.g., functional currency), nonfunctional currency, or property the value of which is determined by reference to an interest rate."[15] The underlying property in the above example was oil—which is not a form of money. Thus, in the case of the forward contract for oil, there would be no currency gain or loss to calculate; it would simply be the acquisition under a forward contract of oil at a certain price (translated into dollars on the date of the actual purchase).

Despite these limitations, the regime does reach Section 988 transactions that are imbedded in transactions not otherwise within its scope. For example, if the same U.S. corporation purchases Saudi riyal on February 1, 2019 and later uses them to purchase oil under the forward contract on August 15, 2019, the U.S. corporation has a Section 988 transaction regarding the actual disposition of the Saudi riyal. Under Section 988, "any disposition of any nonfunctional currency . . . shall be treated as a Section 988 transaction." Thus, gain or loss would be

---

[12]   Section 988(c)(1)(A)(i).

[13]   Section 988(c)(A)(ii).

[14]   Treas. Reg. 1.988–1(a)(2)(iii)(A).

[15]   Treas. Reg. 1.988–1(a)(2)(iii)(B)(2).

calculated based on the change in exchange rates from the acquisition of the Saudi riyal to the date of disposition in August.

b. MEASURING AND CALCULATING EXCHANGE GAIN AND LOSS

What *is* exchange gain or loss? It is gain or loss realized as a result of a change in the exchange rates between the "booking" date (i.e. the acquisition date, date of becoming an obligor on a debt, or the date on which an item is taken into account) and the "payment" date (the date that payment is made or received, or the rights under the contract are terminated, as in an option). Thus, when nonfunctional currency is acquired and disposed of, the exchange gain or loss is calculated as: Amount Realized on sale/disposition minus the Adjusted Basis in the currency.[16]

> Ex: U.S. Co. (a U.S. dollar functional currency taxpayer) buys 1,000 Swiss francs when 1SF=1$. U.S. Co. now has a basis in the SF of $1,000. Later, U.S. Co. sells the 1,000 SF for $1,333 at a time when .75SF=1$. U.S. Co. has section 988 gain on the transaction equal to $333 (AR$1,333 minus AB$1,000).

> Ex: On March 1, 2019, U.S. Co. (a U.S. dollar functional currency taxpayer) enters into a forward contract to acquire 10,000SF on July 15, 2019. On May 1, U.S. Co. assigns the contract to another party for $2,000. U.S. Co. realizes exchange gain of $2,000 at this time (AR$2,000 minus AB$0 in the contract).

If a taxpayer is purchasing property using nonfunctional currency, the transaction is separated into two steps to calculate sSection 988 gain or loss. Step 1: Taxpayer is treated as disposing of the nonfunctional currency for functional currency at the spot rate on the date the property is purchased. Step 2: The taxpayer is treated as purchasing the property using dollars. Treas. Reg. 1.988–2(a)(2)(ii)(B). The first step constitutes a Section 988 transaction the second does not. Treas. Reg. 1.988–2(a)(ii)(c). This two step process isolates the gain or loss due to movements in exchange rates for taxation under the Section 988 regime.

> Ex: On February 15, 2019, U.S. Co. (a U.S. dollar functional currency taxpayer) buys 20,000£ when 1£=.5$. On March 15, 2019, U.S. Co. enters into a forward contract to purchase a compressor for 20,000£ on July 15, 2019. On July 15, when the exchange rate was 1£=1$, U.S. Co. takes delivery under the forward contract and the pays 20,000£ price using the pounds acquired on February 15. The forward contract is **not** a Section 988 transaction because the underlying property (a compressor) is not a Section 988 transaction.[17] The disposition of the pounds

---

[16]   Treas. Reg. 1.988–(2)(a)(2).
[17]   Treas. Reg. 1.988–1(a)(2)(iii)(A).

is, however, and the foreign currency gain or loss is calculated under the two step method. First U.S. Co. is treated as selling the pounds for dollars on July 15, generating $10,000 in foreign currency gain (AR$20,000 [value of pounds on July 15] minus AB$10,000 [cost of pounds on February 15]). Second, U.S. Co. is treated as acquiring the compressor for $20,000 thus creating a basis of that amount in the compressor.

Special "netting" rules determine the amount of Section 988 gain or loss realized on a debt instrument. The amount of currency gain or loss on a debt cannot exceed the total gain or loss realized. Treas. Reg. 1.988–2(b)(8). Effectively, currency gain or loss will be netted against gain or loss due to price movements in the debt instrument itself.

> Ex: U.S. Co. (a U.S. dollar functional currency taxpayer) buys a 16,000£ bond when 1£=1U.S. Later, U.S. Co. sells the bond for 8,000£ when 1£=2$. In economic terms U.S. Co. has no gain or loss: it paid $16,000 for the bond and received $16,000 on the sale. U.S. Co. has offsetting currency gain of $8,000 and market loss on the bond of $8,000, but realizes neither because of the netting rule.

c.   TAXATION OF SECTION 988 TRANSACTIONS

Turning now to the second major question, what is the impact of being a section 988 transaction? The statute provides rules for character, source and timing, and for special situations.

i.   *Character*—Section 988 exchange gain or loss is generally characterized as ordinary income or loss.[18] When congress enacted the regime in 1986, the relationship between currency gains/losses and interest was recognized. However, the drafters of the regime rejected an explicit interest characterization of section 988 gains and losses, and instead adopted an ordinary[19] (but non-interest) treatment.[20]

ii.   *Source*—The exchange gain or loss from a Section 988 transaction is generally sourced to the residence of the taxpayer.[21] Section 988(a)(3). For example, U.S. Co. buys a U.K. corporation's pound bond for 200,000£, when 1£=1$. Later, the U.S. Co. sells the bond for 200,000£ when 1£=.5$ Thus, U.S. Co. realizes a currency loss of $100,000 (AR$100,000 [200,00£ at 1£=.5$] minus AB$200,000 [200,000£ at 1£=1$].) This loss is domestic source; it is not allocated and apportioned. It does not reduce foreign source income.

---

[18]   Treas. Reg. 1.988–3(a).

[19]   A limited exception to the ordinary treatment is available for certain forwards, futures, and options contracts. If a taxpayer elects, and the contract meets several requirements, then capital treatment will apply. Treas. Reg. 1.988–3(b).

[20]   S. Rep. No. 313, 99th Cong., 2d Sess. (1986) 451–452, 460–461.

[21]   Although the Code typically allocates and apportions losses, section 988 explicitly provides a source rule for these currency losses. Section 988(a)(3)(A).

Two important exceptions apply to the source rule regarding QBUs and nonresidents' U.S. trade or businesses. A QBU (e.g., a foreign branch of a U.S. corporation) is resident in the country of the QBU's principal place of business. Thus, section S88 gain or loss of Pet Palace's U.K. branch would be U.K. source. Treas. Reg. 1.988–4(b). With respect to nonresidents, although the Section 988 gain or loss of a foreign corporation is generally foreign source, a special rule applies to a U.S. trade or business's section 988 gain and loss. Any Section 988 gain or loss that is effectively connected to a nonresident's U.S. trade or business will be treated as U.S. source. Treas. Reg. 1.988–4(c).

iii. *Timing*—Section 988 generally relies on the basic provisions of the Code to govern the timing of gain and loss for covered transactions (implicit in the examples in this chapter).[22] In the case of a Section 988 forward, futures or option contract, however, currency gain or loss is triggered on the delivery date.[23] For example, on January 2, 2019, U.S. Co. enters into a forward contract when the exchange rate is 100¥=1$, to purchase 10,000¥ on June 2, 2019. On June 2, when the U.S. corporation takes delivery, and the exchange rate is 100 ¥ =.75$, the corporation recognizes $25 of exchange gain as if it had sold the forward contract on June 2 [value of the 10,000¥ on June 2 ($100) minus the cost of the 10,000¥ on January 2 under the forward contract ($75)].

iv. *Special Rules*

Section 988 addresses additional issues likely to arise when taxpayers use nonfunctional currency. Section 988(d) provides special hedging treatment. If a taxpayer has a Section 988 transaction that "is part of a 988 hedging transaction . . . [all of the transactions] shall be integrated and treated as a single transaction. . . ." Section 988(d)(1). Generally, currency hedging transactions are used by taxpayers to hedge the risk of currency fluctuations (for assets or liabilities). Essentially, the hedging rules (detailed in the regulations),[24] allow the hedge and hedged item to be "integrated" and treated as a single synthetic instrument, thereby eliminating potential tax mismatches, and permitting the tax treatment to mirror the economic effect more closely. Treas. Reg. 1.988–5. For example, in Letter Ruling 200813026, the IRS permitted a U.S. parent engaged in the manufacture of highly sophisticated technology devices to use the integrated hedging treatment of Treas. Reg. 1.988–5 for its executory contracts to purchase specialized equipment in foreign currency and the corresponding foreign currency hedges into which the U.S. parent entered.

---

[22] "Except as otherwise provided . . . the recognition of exchange gain or loss upon the sale or other disposition of nonfunctional currency shall be governed by the recognition provisions . . . which apply to the sale or disposition of property (*e.g.*, section 1001 or, to the extent provided in regulations, section 1092)." Treas. Reg. 1.988–2(a)(1)(i).

[23] Treas. Reg. 1.988–2(d)(4)(ii).

[24] Treas. Reg. 1.988–5.

The Section 988 regime also provides special rules for debt instruments and deposits denominated in hyperinflationary currencies.[25] Treas. Reg. 1.988–2(b)(15). Hyperinflationary currency means a "currency of a country in which there is cumulative inflation during the base period of at least 100 percent." Treas. Reg. 1.985–1(b)(2)(ii)(D). The rapid and significant change in exchange rates due to severe inflation requires more frequent calculation of currency gain or loss.

10.5   RETURN TO ORIGINAL HYPOTHETICALS

Having examined the fundamental structure of the Section 988 regime, we now return to the hypotheticals we considered at the beginning of the chapter and complete our review of their treatment:

(1) Pet Palace: as discussed throughout this chapter, Pet Palace has four QBUs, each with a different functional currency. Each branch QBU will calculate gain/loss in its own functional currency and then translate that into dollars at the average exchange rate for the year to be included on Pet Palace's U.S. return. Section 989(b)(4). Although the foreign subsidiary's income is not currently reported on Pet Palace's return, any dividends must be translated to dollars at the "spot rate on the date . . . [it] is included in income." Section 989(b)(1). To obtain the indirect foreign tax credit, the foreign taxes paid (to Mexico) must be translated to dollars at the average exchange rate for the taxable year. Section 986(a)(1).

(2) Great Books: This scenario concerns the indirect foreign tax credit explicitly (See chapter 8). The 1.2 million pesos paid by the subsidiary to Mexico must be translated to dollars at the average exchange rate for the year. Section 986(a)(1).

(3) Screenmakers: The nonfunctional currency debt generates Section 988 gain of $250 (difference between value of the won received at the time of borrowing $1,000 and the value of the won at the time of repayment, $750).

(4) Cityside: The purchase and sale of yen produces Section 988 gain of $1,000.

(5) Magni-Locks: The forward contract (denominated in yen) to acquire the special chemical is not a section 988 transaction. However, Magni-Locks's (presumed) purchase of yen to complete the deal and the actual disposition of yen in the purchase under the forward contract is itself a Section 988 transaction. Gain or loss is calculated as if Magni-Lock sold its 5,000,000¥ on July 1 when 100¥=.75$. The AR would be $37,500 and the AB would be the cost of the yen on the date of

---

[25] Treas. Reg. 1.988–1(f), 1.985–1(b)(2)(ii)(D).

their purchase. Magni-Lock would then take a basis in the 400,000 gallons of chemical of $37,500.

10.6   REVIEW QUESTIONS—CHAPTER 10

1. X, a domestic corporation, wholly-owns F, a company organized in a foreign country F that checked-the-box to be taxed as a branch for U.S. tax purposes. The functional currencies of the above corporations are: X—USD, F—FC.

     a.   X has no income in 2018. X organized F on Jan. 1, 2018, with $1000 equity, when 1FC was worth $1. F finished 2018 with a business loss of 200 FC. The average exchange rate for 2018 was 1.5FC=$1 and the spot rate for Dec. 31, 2018 was 1.2FC=$1. How does F's loss affect X?

     b.   In 2019 X has no income other than 200 FC of net profit made by F from business done solely in country F. What are X's tax consequences for the year (The average exchange rate for 2019 was 1.2FC=$1 and the spot rate for Dec. 31, 2018 was 1.5FC=$1)?

     c.   Now add the fact that F paid 10% (20 FC) in income taxes to country F on this income.

     d.   How would your answer change if F did not check-the-box, but distributed all of its after-tax earnings in 2019 to X on Dec. 31 as a dividend?

2. X, a domestic corporation that uses the USD as its functional currency, purchases material from F, a foreign country F company with FC as its functional currency, for 100 FC. It agrees to pay F 50 FC (bought previously by X for $50) at the time of the purchase (spot rate 1FC=$1.5) and furnish a 50 FC note that was paid, as promised, one year later, including 5 FC of interest (on this date one year later X purchased the 55 FC needed, for $50). What are the tax consequences of the above transactions?

CHAPTER 11

THE ROLE OF TREATIES

11.1 THE U.S. MODEL

In 2016 the Treasury Department had issued new versions of the U.S. Model income Tax Convention and Model Technical Explanation. Here is a(n almost) complete copy of this new Model:

UNITED STATES MODEL INCOME TAX CONVENTION

CONVENTION BETWEEN THE GOVERNMENT OF THE UNITED STATES OF AMERICA AND THE GOVERNMENT OF _____ FOR THE AVOIDANCE OF DOUBLE TAXATION AND THE PREVENTION OF TAX EVASION WITH RESPECT TO TAXES ON INCOME

The Government of the United States of America and the Government of _____, intending to conclude a Convention for the elimination of double taxation with respect to taxes on income without creating opportunities for non-taxation or reduced taxation through tax evasion or avoidance (including through treaty-shopping arrangements aimed at obtaining reliefs provided in this Convention for the indirect benefit of residents of third states), have agreed as follows:

Article 1

GENERAL SCOPE

1.   This Convention shall apply only to persons who are residents of one or both of the Contracting States, except as otherwise provided in this Convention.

2.   This Convention shall not restrict in any manner any benefit now or hereafter accorded:

a)   by the laws of either Contracting State; or

b)   by any other agreement to which both Contracting States are parties.

3.   a)   Notwithstanding the provisions of subparagraph (b) of paragraph 2 of this Article:

i)   for purposes of paragraph 3 of Article XXII (Consultation) of the General Agreement on Trade in Services, the Contracting States agree that any question arising as to the interpretation or application of this Convention and, in particular, whether a taxation measure is within the scope of this Convention, shall be determined exclusively in accordance with the provisions of Article 25 (Mutual Agreement Procedure) of this Convention; and

ii) the provisions of Article XVII (National Treatment) of the General Agreement on Trade in Services shall not apply to a taxation measure unless the competent authorities agree that the measure is not within the scope of Article 24 (Non-Discrimination) of this Convention.

b) For the purposes of this paragraph, a "measure" is a law, regulation, rule, procedure, decision, administrative action or any similar provision or action.

4. Except to the extent provided in paragraph 5 of this Article, this Convention shall not affect the taxation by a Contracting State of its residents (as determined under Article 4 (Resident)) and its citizens. Notwithstanding the other provisions of this Convention, a former citizen or former long-term resident of a Contracting State may be taxed in accordance with the laws of that Contracting State.

5. The provisions of paragraph 4 of this Article shall not affect:

a) the benefits conferred by a Contracting State under paragraph 3 of Article 7 (Business Profits), paragraph 2 of Article 9 (Associated Enterprises), paragraph 7 of Article 13 (Gains), subparagraph (b) of paragraph 1, paragraphs 2, 3 and 6 of Article 17 (Pensions, Social Security, Annuities, Alimony and Child Support), paragraph 3 of Article 18 (Pension Funds), and Articles 23 (Relief From Double Taxation), 24 (Non-Discrimination) and 25 (Mutual Agreement Procedure); and

b) the benefits conferred by a Contracting State under paragraph 1 of Article 18 (Pension Funds), and Articles 19 (Government Service), 20 (Students and Trainees) and 27 (Members of Diplomatic Missions and Consular Posts), upon individuals who are neither citizens of, nor have been admitted for permanent residence in, that Contracting State.

6. For the purposes of this Convention, an item of income, profit or gain derived by or through an entity that is treated as wholly or partly fiscally transparent under the taxation laws of either Contracting State shall be considered to be derived by a resident of a Contracting State, but only to the extent that the item is treated for purposes of the taxation laws of such Contracting State as the income, profit or gain of a resident.

7. Where an item of income, profit or gain arising in one of the Contracting States otherwise would be entitled to the benefits of this Convention in that Contracting State and, under the law of the other Contracting State, a person's tax in respect of such item is determined by reference to the amount thereof that is remitted to or received in that other Contracting State and not by reference to the full amount thereof, then the relief to be allowed under this Convention in the first-mentioned Contracting State shall apply only to so much of the amount as is taxed in the other Contracting State.

8.   Where an enterprise of a Contracting State derives income from the other Contracting State, and the first-mentioned Contracting State treats that income as attributable to a permanent establishment situated outside of that Contracting State, the benefits of this Convention shall not apply to that income if:

> a)   the profits that are treated as attributable to the permanent establishment are subject to a combined aggregate effective rate of tax in the first-mentioned Contracting State and the state in which the permanent establishment is situated that is less than the lesser of (i) 15 percent or (ii) 60 percent of the general statutory rate of company tax applicable in the first-mentioned Contracting State; or

> b)   the permanent establishment is situated in a third state that does not have a comprehensive convention for the avoidance of double taxation in force with the Contracting State from which the benefits of this Convention are being claimed, unless the first-mentioned Contracting State includes the income treated as attributable to the permanent establishment in its tax base.

However, if a resident of a Contracting State is denied the benefits of this Convention pursuant to this paragraph, the competent authority of the other Contracting State may, nevertheless, grant the benefits of this Convention with respect to a specific item of income if such competent authority determines that such grant of benefits is justified in light of the reasons such resident did not satisfy the requirements of this paragraph (such as the existence of losses). The competent authority of the Contracting State to which the request has been made shall consult with the competent authority of the other Contracting State before either granting or denying a request made under this paragraph by a resident of that other Contracting State.

Article 2
TAXES COVERED

1.   This Convention shall apply to taxes on income imposed on behalf of a Contracting State irrespective of the manner in which they are levied.

2.   There shall be regarded as taxes on income all taxes imposed on total income, or on elements of income, including taxes on gains from the alienation of property.

3.   The existing taxes to which this Convention shall apply are:

> a)   in the case of _____:

> b)   in the case of the United States: the Federal income taxes imposed by the Internal Revenue Code (which do not include social security and unemployment taxes) and the Federal taxes imposed on the investment income of foreign private foundations.

4.   This Convention also shall apply to any identical or substantially similar taxes that are imposed after the date of signature of this Convention in addition to, or in place of, the existing taxes. The

competent authorities of the Contracting States shall notify each other of any significant changes that have been made in their taxation laws or other laws that relate to the application of this Convention.

Article 3
GENERAL DEFINITIONS

1.   For the purposes of this Convention, unless the context otherwise requires:

a)   the term "person" includes an individual, an estate, a trust, a partnership, a company, and any other body of persons;

b)   the term "company" means any body corporate or any entity that is treated as a body corporate for tax purposes according to the laws of the Contracting State in which it is resident;

c)   the terms "enterprise of a Contracting State" and "enterprise of the other Contracting State" mean, respectively, an enterprise carried on by a resident of a Contracting State, and an enterprise carried on by a resident of the other Contracting State; the terms also include an enterprise carried on by a resident of a Contracting State through an entity that is treated as fiscally transparent in that Contracting State;

d)   the term "enterprise" applies to the carrying on of any business;

e)   the term "business" includes the performance of professional services and of other activities of an independent character;

f)   the term "international traffic" means any transport by a ship or aircraft, except when such transport is solely between places in a Contracting State;

g)   the term "competent authority" means:

i)   in _____: _____; and

ii)   in the United States: the Secretary of the Treasury or his delegate;

h)   the term "_____:" means _____;

i)   the term "United States" means the United States of America, and includes the states thereof and the District of Columbia; such term also includes the territorial sea thereof and the sea bed and subsoil of the submarine areas adjacent to that territorial sea, over which the United States exercises sovereign rights in accordance with international law; the term, however, does not include Puerto Rico, the Virgin Islands, Guam or any other United States possession or territory;

j)   the term "national" of a Contracting State means:

i)   any individual possessing the nationality or citizenship of that Contracting State; and

ii) any legal person, partnership or association deriving its status as such from the laws in force in that Contracting State;

k) the term "pension fund" means any person established in a Contracting State that is:

i) generally exempt from income taxation in that Contracting State; and

ii) operated exclusively or almost exclusively:

A) to administer or provide pension or retirement benefits; or

B) to earn income for the benefit of one or more persons established in the same Contracting State that are generally exempt from income taxation in that Contracting State and that are operated exclusively or almost exclusively to administer or provide pension or retirement benefits;

l) the term "special tax regime" means any statute, regulation or administrative practice in a Contracting State with respect to a tax described in Article 2 (Taxes Covered) that meets all of the following conditions:

i) results in one or more of the following:

A) a preferential rate of taxation for interest, royalties, guarantee fees or any combination thereof, as compared to income from sales of goods or services;

B) a permanent reduction in the tax base with respect to interest, royalties, guarantee fees or any combination thereof, without a comparable reduction for income from sales of goods or services, by allowing:

1) an exclusion from gross receipts;

2) a deduction without regard to any corresponding payment or obligation to make a payment;

3) a deduction for dividends paid or accrued; or

4) taxation that is inconsistent with the principles of Article 7 (Business Profits) or Article 9 (Associated Enterprises); or

C) a preferential rate of taxation or a permanent reduction in the tax base of the type described in part (1), (2), (3) or (4) of subclause (B) of this clause with respect to substantially all of a company's income or substantially all of a company's foreign source income, for companies that do not engage in the active conduct of a trade or business in that Contracting State;

ii) in the case of any preferential rate of taxation or permanent reduction in the tax base for royalties, does not condition such benefits on the extent of research and development activities that take place in the Contracting State;

iii) is generally expected to result in a rate of taxation[1] that is less than the lesser of either:

A) 15 percent; or

B) 60 percent of the general statutory rate of company tax applicable in the other Contracting State;

iv) does not apply principally to:

A) pension funds;

B) organizations that are established and maintained exclusively for religious, charitable, scientific, artistic, cultural or educational purposes;

C) persons the taxation of which achieves a single level of taxation either in the hands of the person or the person's shareholders (with at most one year of deferral), that hold a diversified portfolio of securities, that are subject to investor-protection regulation in the Contracting State and the interests in which are marketed primarily to retail investors; or

D) persons the taxation of which achieves a single level of taxation either in the hands of the person or the person's shareholders (with at most one year of deferral) and that hold predominantly real estate assets; and

v) after consultation with the first-mentioned Contracting State, has been identified by the other Contracting State through diplomatic channels to the first-mentioned Contracting State as satisfying clauses (i) through (iv) of this subparagraph.

No statute, regulation or administrative practice shall be treated as a special tax regime until 30 days after the date when the other Contracting State issues a written public notification identifying the regime as satisfying clauses (i) through (v) of this subparagraph; and

---

[1] For inclusion in an instrument reflecting an agreed interpretation: Except as provided below, the rate of taxation shall be determined based on the income tax principles of the Contracting State that has implemented the regime in question. Therefore, in the case of a regime that provides only for a preferential rate of taxation, the generally expected rate of taxation under the regime will equal such preferential rate. In the case of a regime that provides only for a permanent reduction in the tax base, the rate of taxation will equal the statutory rate of company tax generally applicable in the Contracting State to companies subject to the regime in question less the product of such rate and the percentage reduction in the tax base (with the baseline tax base determined under the principles of the Contracting State, but without regard to any permanent reductions in the tax base described in subparagraph (l)(i)(B)) that the regime is generally expected to provide. Therefore, a regime that generally provides for a 20 percent permanent reduction in a company's tax base would have a rate of taxation equal to the applicable statutory rate of company tax reduced by 20 percent of such statutory rate. In the case of a regime that provides for both a preferential rate of taxation and a permanent reduction in the tax base, the rate of taxation would be based on the preferential rate of taxation reduced by the product of such rate and the percentage reduction in the tax base.

m)   two persons shall be "connected persons" if one owns, directly or indirectly, at least 50 percent of the beneficial interest in the other (or, in the case of a company, at least 50 percent of the aggregate vote and value of the company's shares) or another person owns, directly or indirectly, at least 50 percent of the beneficial interest (or, in the case of a company, at least 50 percent of the aggregate vote and value of the company's shares) in each person. In any case, a person shall be connected to another if, based on all the relevant facts and circumstances, one has control of the other or both are under the control of the same person or persons.

2.   As regards the application of this Convention at any time by a Contracting State, any term not defined herein shall, unless the context otherwise requires, or the competent authorities agree to a common meaning pursuant to the provisions of Article 25 (Mutual Agreement Procedure), have the meaning that it has at that time under the law of that Contracting State for the purposes of the taxes to which this Convention applies, any meaning under the applicable tax laws of that Contracting State prevailing over a meaning given to the term under other laws of that Contracting State.

Article 4
RESIDENT

1.   For the purposes of this Convention, the term "resident of a Contracting State" means any person who, under the laws of that Contracting State, is liable to tax therein by reason of his domicile, residence, citizenship, place of management, place of incorporation, or any other criterion of a similar nature, and also includes that Contracting State and any political subdivision or local authority thereof. This term does not include any person whose tax is determined in that Contracting State on a fixed-fee, "forfait" or similar basis, or who is liable to tax in respect only of income from sources in that Contracting State or of profits attributable to a permanent establishment in that Contracting State.

2.   The term "resident of a Contracting State" includes:

a)   a pension fund established in that Contracting State; and

b)   an organization that is established and maintained in that Contracting State exclusively for religious, charitable, scientific, artistic, cultural, or educational purposes; notwithstanding that all or part of its income or gains may be exempt from tax under the domestic law of that Contracting State.

3.   Where, by reason of the provisions of paragraph 1 of this Article, an individual is a resident of both Contracting States, then his status shall be determined as follows:

a)   he shall be deemed to be a resident only of the Contracting State in which he has a permanent home available to him; if he has a permanent home available to him in both Contracting States, he shall be deemed to be a resident only of the Contracting State with which his personal and economic relations are closer (center of vital interests);

b)   if the Contracting State in which he has his center of vital interests cannot be determined, or if he does not have a permanent home available to him in either Contracting State, he shall be deemed to be a resident only of the Contracting State in which he has a habitual abode;

c)   if he has a habitual abode in both Contracting States or in neither of them, he shall be deemed to be a resident only of the Contracting State of which he is a national;

d)   if he is a national of both Contracting States or of neither of them, the competent authorities of the Contracting States shall endeavor to settle the question by mutual agreement.

4.   Where by reason of the provisions of paragraph 1 of this Article a company is a resident of both Contracting States, such company shall not be treated as a resident of either Contracting State for purposes of its claiming the benefits provided by this Convention.

5.   Where by reason of the provisions of paragraph 1 of this Article a person other than an individual or a company is a resident of both Contracting States, the competent authorities of the Contracting States shall by mutual agreement endeavor to determine the mode of application of this Convention to that person.

Article 5

PERMANENT ESTABLISHMENT

1.   For the purposes of this Convention, the term "permanent establishment" means a fixed place of business through which the business of an enterprise is wholly or partly carried on.

2.   The term "permanent establishment" includes especially:

a)   a place of management;

b)   a branch;

c)   an office;

d)   a factory;

e)   a workshop; and

f)   a mine, an oil or gas well, a quarry, or any other place of extraction of natural resources.

3.   A building site or construction or installation project, or an installation or drilling rig or ship used for the exploration or exploitation of the sea bed and its subsoil and their natural resources, situated in one of the Contracting States constitutes a permanent establishment only if it lasts, or the activities of the rig or ship lasts, for more than twelve

months. For the sole purpose of determining whether the twelve-month period referred to in this paragraph has been exceeded:

a)   where an enterprise of a Contracting State carries on activities in the other Contracting State at a place that constitutes a building site or construction or installation project and these activities are carried on during periods of time that in the aggregate do not last more than twelve months; and

b)   connected activities are carried on at the same building site or construction or installation project during different periods of time, each exceeding thirty days, by one or more enterprises that are connected persons with respect to the first-mentioned enterprise, these different periods of time shall be added to the periods of time during which the first-mentioned enterprise has carried on activities at that building site or construction or installation project.

4.   Notwithstanding the preceding provisions of this Article, the term "permanent establishment" shall be deemed not to include:

a)   the use of facilities solely for the purpose of storage, display or delivery of goods or merchandise belonging to the enterprise;

b)   the maintenance of a stock of goods or merchandise belonging to the enterprise solely for the purpose of storage, display or delivery;

c)   the maintenance of a stock of goods or merchandise belonging to the enterprise solely for the purpose of processing by another enterprise;

d)   the maintenance of a fixed place of business solely for the purpose of purchasing goods or merchandise, or of collecting information, for the enterprise;

e)   the maintenance of a fixed place of business solely for the purpose of carrying on, for the enterprise, any other activity of a preparatory or auxiliary character;

f)   the maintenance of a fixed place of business solely for any combination of the activities mentioned in subparagraphs (a) through (e) of this paragraph, provided that the overall activity of the fixed place of business resulting from this combination is of a preparatory or auxiliary character.

5.   Notwithstanding the provisions of paragraphs 1 and 2 of this Article, where a person—other than an agent of an independent status to whom paragraph 6 of this Article applies—is acting on behalf of an enterprise and has and habitually exercises in a Contracting State an authority to conclude contracts that are binding on the enterprise, that enterprise shall be deemed to have a permanent establishment in that Contracting State in respect of any activities that the person undertakes for the enterprise, unless the activities of such person are limited to those mentioned in paragraph 4 that, if exercised through a fixed place of

business, would not make this fixed place of business a permanent establishment under the provisions of that paragraph.

6.   An enterprise shall not be deemed to have a permanent establishment in a Contracting State merely because it carries on business in that Contracting State through a broker, general commission agent, or any other agent of an independent status, provided that such persons are acting in the ordinary course of their business as independent agents.

7.   The fact that a company that is a resident of a Contracting State controls or is controlled by a company that is a resident of the other Contracting State, or that carries on business in that other Contracting State (whether through a permanent establishment or otherwise), shall not be taken into account in determining whether either company has a permanent establishment in that other Contracting State.

Article 6
INCOME FROM REAL PROPERTY
(IMMOVABLE PROPERTY)

1.   Income derived by a resident of a Contracting State from real property (immovable property), including income from agriculture or forestry, situated in the other Contracting State may be taxed in that other Contracting State.

2.   The term "real property" or "immovable property" shall have the meaning which it has under the law of the Contracting State in which the property in question is situated. The term shall in any case include property accessory to real property (immovable property), livestock and equipment used in agriculture and forestry, rights to which the provisions of general law respecting landed property apply, usufruct of real property (immovable property) and rights to variable or fixed payments as consideration for the working of, or the right to work, mineral deposits, sources and other natural resources. Ships and aircraft shall not be regarded as real property (immovable property).

3.   The provisions of paragraph 1 of this Article shall apply to income derived from the direct use, letting, or use in any other form of real property (immovable property).

4.   The provisions of paragraphs 1 and 3 of this Article shall also apply to the income from real property (immovable property) of an enterprise.

5.   A resident of a Contracting State that is liable to tax in the other Contracting State on income from real property (immovable property) situated in the other Contracting State may elect for any taxable year to compute the tax on such income on a net basis as if such income were business profits attributable to a permanent establishment in such other Contracting State. Any such election shall be binding for the taxable year of the election and all subsequent taxable years unless the competent

authority of the Contracting State in which the property is situated agrees to terminate the election.

Article 7

BUSINESS PROFITS

1.   Profits of an enterprise of a Contracting State shall be taxable only in that Contracting State unless the enterprise carries on business in the other Contracting State through a permanent establishment situated therein. If the enterprise carries on business as aforesaid, the profits that are attributable to the permanent establishment in accordance with the provisions of paragraph 2 of this Article may be taxed in that other Contracting State.

2.   For the purposes of this Article, the profits that are attributable in each Contracting State to the permanent establishment referred to in paragraph 1 of this Article are the profits it might be expected to make, in particular in its dealings with other parts of the enterprise, if it were a separate and independent enterprise engaged in the same or similar activities under the same or similar conditions, taking into account the functions performed, assets used and risks assumed by the enterprise through the permanent establishment and through the other parts of the enterprise.

3.   Where, in accordance with paragraph 2 of this Article, a Contracting State adjusts the profits that are attributable to a permanent establishment of an enterprise of one of the Contracting States and taxes accordingly profits of the enterprise that have been charged to tax in the other Contracting State, the other Contracting State shall, to the extent necessary to eliminate double taxation, make an appropriate adjustment if it agrees with the adjustment made by the first-mentioned Contracting State; if the other Contracting State does not so agree, the Contracting States shall eliminate any double taxation resulting therefrom by mutual agreement.

4.   Where profits include items of income that are dealt with separately in other Articles of this Convention, then the provisions of those Articles shall not be affected by the provisions of this Article.

5.   In applying this Article, paragraph 8 of Article 10 (Dividends), paragraph 5 of Article 11 (Interest), paragraph 5 of Article 12 (Royalties), paragraph 3 of Article 13 (Gains) and paragraph 3 of Article 21 (Other Income), any income, profit or gain attributable to a permanent establishment during its existence is taxable in the Contracting State where such permanent establishment is situated even if the payments are deferred until such permanent establishment has ceased to exist.

Article 8
SHIPPING AND AIR TRANSPORT

1.   Profits of an enterprise of a Contracting State from the operation of ships or aircraft in international traffic shall be taxable only in that Contracting State.

2.   For purposes of this Article, profits from the operation of ships or aircraft include, but are not limited to:

    a)   profits from the rental of ships or aircraft on a full (time or voyage) basis;

    b)   profits from the rental on a bareboat basis of ships or aircraft if the rental income is incidental to profits from the operation of ships or aircraft in international traffic; and

    c)   profits from the rental on a bareboat basis of ships or aircraft if such ships or aircraft are operated in international traffic by the lessee.

Profits derived by an enterprise from the inland transport of property or passengers within either Contracting State shall be treated as profits from the operation of ships or aircraft in international traffic if such transport is undertaken as part of international traffic.

3.   Profits of an enterprise of a Contracting State from the use, maintenance, or rental of containers (including trailers, barges, and related equipment for the transport of containers) shall be taxable only in that Contracting State, except to the extent that those containers are used for transport solely between places within the other Contracting State.

4.   The provisions of paragraphs 1 and 3 of this Article shall also apply to profits from participation in a pool, a joint business, or an international operating agency.

Article 9
ASSOCIATED ENTERPRISES

1.   Where:

    a)   an enterprise of a Contracting State participates directly or indirectly in the management, control or capital of an enterprise of the other Contracting State; or

    b)   the same persons participate directly or indirectly in the management, control, or capital of an enterprise of a Contracting State and an enterprise of the other Contracting State; and in either case conditions are made or imposed between the two enterprises in their commercial or financial relations that differ from those that would be made between independent enterprises, then any profits that, but for those conditions, would have accrued to one of the enterprises, but by reason of those conditions have not so accrued, may be included in the profits of that enterprise and taxed accordingly.

2.   Where a Contracting State includes in the profits of an enterprise of that Contracting State, and taxes accordingly, profits on which an enterprise of the other Contracting State has been charged to tax in that other Contracting State, and the other Contracting State agrees that the profits so included are profits that would have accrued to the enterprise of the first-mentioned Contracting State if the conditions made between the two enterprises had been those that would have been made between independent enterprises, then that other Contracting State shall make an appropriate adjustment to the amount of the tax charged therein on those profits. In determining such adjustment, due regard shall be had to the other provisions of this Convention and the competent authorities of the Contracting States shall if necessary consult each other.

Article 10
DIVIDENDS

1.   Dividends paid by a company that is a resident of a Contracting State to a resident of the other Contracting State may be taxed in that other Contracting State.

2.   However, such dividends may also be taxed in the Contracting State of which the company paying the dividends is a resident and according to the laws of that Contracting State, but if the beneficial owner of the dividends is a resident of the other Contracting State, except as otherwise provided, the tax so charged shall not exceed:

   a)   5 percent of the gross amount of the dividends if, for the twelve-month period ending on the date on which the entitlement to the dividends is determined:

      i)   the beneficial owner has been a company that was a resident of the other Contracting State or of a qualifying third state. The term "qualifying third state" means a state that has in effect a comprehensive convention for the avoidance of double taxation with the Contracting State of the company paying the dividends that would have allowed the beneficial owner to benefit from a rate of tax on dividends that is less than or equal to 5 percent; and

      ii)   at least 10 percent of the aggregate vote and value of the shares of the payor of the dividends was owned directly by the beneficial owner or a qualifying predecessor owner. The term "qualifying predecessor owner" means a company from which the beneficial owner acquired the shares of the payor of the dividends, but only if such company was, at the time the shares were acquired, a connected person with respect to the beneficial owner of the dividend, and a resident of a state that has in effect a comprehensive convention for the avoidance of double taxation with the Contracting State of the company paying the dividends that would have allowed such company to benefit from a rate of tax on dividends that is less than or equal to 5 percent. For this purpose, a company that is a resident of a Contracting State shall be considered to own directly the shares owned by an entity that:

> A)   is considered fiscally transparent under the laws of that Contracting State; and

> B)   is not a resident of the other Contracting State of which the company paying the dividends is a resident; in proportion to the company's ownership interest in that entity; and

b)   15 percent of the gross amount of the dividends in all other cases.

This paragraph shall not affect the taxation of the company in respect of the profits out of which the dividends are paid.

3.   Notwithstanding the provisions of paragraph 2 of this Article, dividends shall not be taxed in the Contracting State of which the company paying the dividends is a resident if:

a)   the beneficial owner of the dividends is a pension fund that is a resident of the other Contracting State; and

b)   such dividends are not derived from the carrying on of a trade or business by the pension fund or through a person that is a connected person with respect to the pension fund.

4.   a)   Subparagraph (a) of paragraph 2 of this Article shall not apply in the case of dividends paid by a U.S. Regulated Investment Company (RIC) or a U.S. Real Estate Investment Trust (REIT). In the case of dividends paid by a RIC, subparagraph (b) of paragraph 2 and paragraph 3 of this Article shall apply. In the case of dividends paid by a REIT, subparagraph (b) of paragraph 2 and paragraph 3 of this Article shall apply only if:

> i)   the beneficial owner of the dividends is an individual or pension fund, in either case holding an interest of not more than 10 percent in the REIT;

> ii)   the dividends are paid with respect to a class of shares that is publicly traded and the beneficial owner of the dividends is a person holding an interest of not more than 5 percent of any class of the REIT's shares; or

> iii)   the beneficial owner of the dividends is a person holding an interest of not more than 10 percent in the REIT and the REIT is diversified.

b)   For purposes of this paragraph, a REIT shall be "diversified" if the value of no single interest in real property (immovable property) exceeds 10 percent of its total interests in real property (immovable property). For the purposes of this rule, foreclosure property shall not be considered an interest in real property (immovable property). Where a REIT holds an interest in a partnership, it shall be treated as owning directly a proportion of the partnership's interests in real property (immovable property) corresponding to its interest in the partnership.

5. In the case of the United States, notwithstanding the provisions of paragraph 2 of this Article, dividends paid by an expatriated entity and beneficially owned by a company resident in _____ that is a connected person with respect to such expatriated entity may be taxed in accordance with the law of the United States for a period of ten years beginning on the date on which the acquisition of the domestic entity is completed. For purposes of applying this paragraph:

   a) no effect shall be given to any amendment to section 7874 of the Internal Revenue Code after the date of signature of this Convention; and

   b) no entity shall be treated as an expatriated entity that:

   i) is a connected person with respect to the domestic entity immediately after the date on which the acquisition of the domestic entity is completed; and

   ii) prior to that date, was never a connected person with respect to the domestic entity.

However, an entity described in the preceding sentence shall become an expatriated entity if, subsequent to the date on which the acquisition of the domestic entity is completed, the entity joins in filing a U.S. consolidated return with either the domestic entity or another entity that was a connected person with respect to the domestic entity immediately prior to the date on which the acquisition of the domestic entity was completed.

6. Notwithstanding the provisions of paragraphs 1 and 2 of this Article, in the case of a company seeking to satisfy the requirements of paragraph 4 of Article 22 (Limitation on Benefits) regarding a dividend, if such company fails to satisfy the criteria of that paragraph solely by reason of:

   a) the requirement in subclause (B) of clause (i) of subparagraph (e) of paragraph 7 of Article 22 (Limitation on Benefits) of this Convention; or

   b) the requirement in clause (ii) of subparagraph (e) of paragraph 7 of Article 22 (Limitation on Benefits) that a person entitled to benefits under paragraph 5 of Article 22 (Limitation on Benefits) would be entitled to a rate of tax with respect to the dividend that is less than or equal to the rate applicable under paragraph 2 of this Article; such company may be taxed in the Contracting State of which the company paying the dividends is a resident and according to the laws of that Contracting State. In these cases, however, the tax so charged shall not exceed the highest rate among the rates of tax to which persons described in subparagraph (e) of paragraph 7 of Article 22 (Limitation on Benefits) of this Convention (notwithstanding the requirements referred to in subparagraphs (a) and (b) of this paragraph) would have been entitled if such persons had received the dividend directly. For purposes of this paragraph, (i) such persons' indirect ownership of the shares of the company paying the dividends shall be treated as direct ownership, and (ii) a person described in clause (iii) of subparagraph (e) of paragraph 7 of Article 22 (Limitation on Benefits) shall be treated as entitled to the limitation of tax to which such person would be entitled if such person were a resident of the same Contracting State as the company receiving the dividends.

7.   For purposes of this Article, the term "dividends" means income from shares or other rights, not being debt-claims, participating in profits, as well as income that is subject to the same taxation treatment as income from shares under the laws of the Contracting State of which the company making the distribution is a resident. The term does not include distributions that are treated as gain under the laws of the Contracting State of which the company making the distribution is a resident. In such case, the provisions of Article 13 (Gains) shall apply.

8.   The provisions of paragraphs 1 through 6 of this Article shall not apply if the beneficial owner of the dividends, being a resident of a Contracting State, carries on business in the other Contracting State, of which the company paying the dividends is a resident, through a permanent establishment situated therein, and the holding in respect of which the dividends are paid is effectively connected with such permanent establishment. In such case the provisions of Article 7 (Business Profits) shall apply.

9.   A Contracting State may not impose any tax on dividends paid by a resident of the other Contracting State, except insofar as the dividends are paid to a resident of the first-mentioned Contracting State or the dividends are attributable to a permanent establishment situated therein, nor may it impose tax on a corporation's undistributed profits, except as provided in paragraph 10 of this Article, even if the dividends paid or the undistributed profits consist wholly or partly of profits or income arising in that Contracting State.

10. a)   A company that is a resident of one of the Contracting States and that has a permanent establishment in the other Contracting State or that is subject to tax in the other Contracting State on a net basis on its income that may be taxed in the other Contracting State under Article 6 (Income from Real Property (Immovable Property)) or under paragraph 1 of Article 13 (Gains) may be subject in that other Contracting State to a tax in addition to the tax allowable under the other provisions of this Convention.

b)   Such tax, however, may be imposed:

i) on only the portion of the business profits of the company attributable to the permanent establishment and the portion of the income referred to in subparagraph (a) of this paragraph that is subject to tax under Article 6 (Income from Real Property (Immovable Property)) or under paragraph 1 of Article 13 (Gains) that, in the case of the United States, represents the dividend equivalent amount of such profits or income and, in the case of _____, is an amount that is analogous to the dividend equivalent amount; and

ii)   at a rate not in excess of the rate specified in subparagraph (a) of paragraph 2 or paragraph 6 of this Article, but only if for the twelve-month period ending on the date on which the entitlement to the dividend equivalent amount is determined, the company has been a resident of the other Contracting State or of a qualifying third state. The term "qualifying third state" has the same meaning as in clause (i) of subparagraph (a) of paragraph 2 of this Article.

Article 11
INTEREST

1.   Interest arising in a Contracting State and beneficially owned by a resident of the other Contracting State shall be taxable only in that other Contracting State.

2.   Notwithstanding the provisions of paragraph 1 of this Article:

a)   interest arising in _____ that is determined with reference to receipts, sales, income, profits or other cash flow of the debtor or a connected person with respect to the debtor, to any change in the value of any property of the debtor or a connected person with respect to the debtor or to any dividend, partnership distribution or similar payment made by the debtor or a connected person with respect to the debtor may be taxed in _____, and according to the laws of _____, but if the beneficial owner is a resident of the United States, the interest may be taxed at a rate not exceeding 15 percent of the gross amount of the interest;

b)   interest arising in the United States that is contingent interest of a type that does not qualify as portfolio interest under the law of the United States may be taxed by the United States, but if the beneficial owner is a resident of _____, the interest may be taxed at a rate not exceeding 15 percent of the gross amount of the interest;

c)   interest arising in a Contracting State and beneficially owned by a resident of the other Contracting State that is a connected person with respect to the payor of the interest may be taxed in the first-mentioned Contracting State in accordance with domestic law if such resident benefits from a special tax regime with respect to such interest in its Contracting State of residence;

d)   in the case of the United States, interest paid by an expatriated entity and beneficially owned by a company resident in _____ that is a connected person with respect to such expatriated entity may be taxed in accordance with the law of the United States for a period of ten years beginning on the date on which the acquisition of the domestic entity is completed. For purposes of applying this paragraph:

   i)   no effect shall be given to any amendment to section 7874 of the Internal Revenue Code after the date of signature of this Convention; and

   ii)   no entity shall be treated as an expatriated entity that:

      A)   is a connected person with respect to the domestic entity immediately after the date on which the acquisition of the domestic entity is completed; and

      B)   prior to that date, was never a connected person with respect to the domestic entity.

However, an entity described in the preceding sentence shall become an expatriated entity if, subsequent to the date on which the acquisition of the domestic entity is completed, the entity joins in filing a U.S. consolidated return with either the domestic entity or another entity that was a connected person with respect to the domestic entity immediately prior to the date on which the acquisition of the domestic entity was completed;

e)   interest arising in a Contracting State and beneficially owned by a resident of the other Contracting State that is a connected person with respect to the payor of the interest may be taxed in the first-mentioned Contracting State in accordance with domestic law if such resident benefits, at any time during the taxable year in which the interest is paid, from notional deductions with respect to amounts that the Contracting State of which the beneficial owner is resident treats as equity;

f)   interest arising in a Contracting State and beneficially owned by a resident of the other Contracting State that is entitled to the benefits of this Article only by reason of paragraph 5 of Article 22 (Limitation on Benefits) may be taxed in the first-mentioned Contracting State, but the tax so charged shall not exceed 10 percent of the gross amount of the interest; and

g)   interest that is an excess inclusion with respect to a residual interest in a real estate mortgage investment conduit may be taxed by each Contracting State in accordance with its domestic law.

3.   Notwithstanding the provisions of paragraph 1 of this Article, in the case of a company seeking to satisfy the requirements of paragraph 4 of

Article 22 (Limitation on Benefits) of this Convention regarding a payment of interest, if such company fails to satisfy the criteria of that paragraph solely by reason of:

a)   the requirement in subclause (B) of clause (i) of subparagraph (e) of paragraph 7 of Article 22 (Limitation on Benefits) of this Convention; or

b)   the requirement in clause (ii) of subparagraph (e) of paragraph 7 of Article 22 (Limitation on Benefits) that a person entitled to benefits under paragraph 5 of Article 22 (Limitation on Benefits) would be entitled to a rate of tax with respect to the interest that is less than or equal to the rate applicable under paragraph 2 of this Article; such company may be taxed by the Contracting State in which the interest arises according to the laws of that Contracting State. In these cases, however, the tax so charged shall not exceed the highest rate among the rates of tax to which persons described in subparagraph (e) of paragraph 7 of Article 22 (Limitation on Benefits) of this Convention (notwithstanding the requirements referred to in subparagraphs (a) and (b) of this paragraph) would have been entitled if such persons had received the interest directly. For purposes of this paragraph, a person described in clause (iii) of subparagraph (e) of paragraph 7 of Article 22 (Limitation on Benefits) shall be treated as entitled to the limitation of tax to which such person would be entitled if such person were a resident of the same Contracting State as the company receiving the interest.

4.   The term "interest" as used in this Article means income from debt-claims of every kind, whether or not secured by mortgage, and whether or not carrying a right to participate in the debtor's profits, and in particular, income from government securities and income from bonds or debentures, including premiums or prizes attaching to such securities, bonds or debentures, and all other income that is subjected to the same taxation treatment as income from money lent under the law of the Contracting State in which the income arises. Income dealt with in Article 10 (Dividends) and penalty charges for late payment shall not be regarded as interest for the purposes of this Convention.

5.   The provisions of paragraphs 1 through 3 of this Article shall not apply if the beneficial owner of the interest, being a resident of a Contracting State, carries on business in the other Contracting State in which the interest arises through a permanent establishment situated therein, and the debt-claim in respect of which the interest is paid is effectively connected with such permanent establishment. In such case the provisions of Article 7 (Business Profits) shall apply.

6.   For purposes of this Article, interest shall be deemed to arise in a Contracting State when the payor is a resident of that Contracting State. Where, however, the person paying the interest, whether a resident of a Contracting State or not, has in a Contracting State a permanent establishment or derives profits that are taxable on a net basis in a

Contracting State under paragraph 5 of Article 6 (Income from Real Property (Immovable Property)) or paragraph 1 of Article 13 (Gains), and such interest is borne by such permanent establishment or allocable to such profits, then such interest shall be deemed to arise in the Contracting State in which the permanent establishment is situated or from which such profits are derived.

7. The excess, if any, of the amount of interest allocable to the profits of a company resident in a Contracting State that are:

a) attributable to a permanent establishment in the other Contracting State (including gains under paragraph 3 of Article 13 (Gains)); or

b) subject to tax in the other Contracting State under Article 6 (Income from Real Property (Immovable Property)) or paragraph 1 of Article 13 (Gains); over the interest paid by that permanent establishment, or in the case of profits subject to tax under Article 6 (Income from Real Property (Immovable Property)) or paragraph 1 of Article 13 (Gains), over the interest paid by that company, shall be deemed to arise in that other Contracting State and to be beneficially owned by a resident of the first-mentioned Contracting State. The tax imposed under this Article on such interest shall not exceed the rates provided in paragraphs 1 through 3 of this Article.

8. Where, by reason of a special relationship between the payor and the beneficial owner or between both of them and some other person, the amount of the interest, having regard to the debt-claim for which it is paid, exceeds the amount that would have been agreed upon by the payor and the beneficial owner in the absence of such relationship, the provisions of this Article shall apply only to the last-mentioned amount. In such case the excess part of the payments shall remain taxable according to the laws of each Contracting State, due regard being had to the other provisions of this Convention.

Article 12

ROYALTIES

1. Royalties arising in a Contracting State and beneficially owned by a resident of the other Contracting State shall be taxable only in that other Contracting State.

2. Notwithstanding the provisions of paragraph 1 of this Article:

a) a royalty arising in a Contracting State and beneficially owned by a resident of the other Contracting State that is a connected person with respect to the payor of the royalty may be taxed in the first-mentioned Contracting State in accordance with domestic law if such resident benefits from a special tax regime with respect to the royalty in its Contracting State of residence; and

b) in the case of the United States, royalties paid by an expatriated entity and beneficially owned by a company resident in _____ that is a connected person with respect to such expatriated entity may be taxed in accordance with the law of the United States for a period of ten years beginning on the date on which the acquisition of the domestic entity is completed. For purposes of applying this paragraph:

   i)   no effect shall be given to any amendment to section 7874 of the Internal Revenue Code after the date of signature of this Convention; and

   ii) no entity shall be treated as an expatriated entity that:

      A)   is a connected person with respect to the domestic entity immediately after the date on which the acquisition of the domestic entity is completed; and

      B)   prior to that date, was never a connected person with respect to the domestic entity.

However, an entity described in the preceding sentence shall become an expatriated entity if, subsequent to the date on which the acquisition of the domestic entity is completed, the entity joins in filing a U.S. consolidated return with either the domestic entity or another entity that was a connected person with respect to the domestic entity immediately prior to the date on which the acquisition of the domestic entity was completed.

3.   Notwithstanding the provisions of paragraph 1 of this Article, in the case of a company seeking to satisfy the requirements of paragraph 4 of Article 22 (Limitation on Benefits) of this Convention regarding a royalty, if such company fails to satisfy the criteria of that paragraph

solely by reason of the requirement in subclause (B) of clause (i) of subparagraph (e) of paragraph 7 of Article 22 (Limitation on Benefits) of this Convention, such company may be taxed in the Contracting State of which the royalty arises and according to the laws of that Contracting State, except that the tax so charged shall not exceed the highest rate among the rates of tax to which persons described in subparagraph (e) of paragraph 7 of Article 22 (Limitation on Benefits) of this Convention (notwithstanding the requirement of subclause (B) of clause (i) of subparagraph (e) of paragraph 7 of Article 22 (Limitation on Benefits)) would have been entitled if such persons had received the royalty directly. For purposes of this paragraph, a person described in clause (iii) of subparagraph (e) of paragraph 7 of Article 22 (Limitation on Benefits) shall be treated as entitled to the limitation of tax to which such person would be entitled if such person were a resident of the same Contracting State as the company receiving the royalties.

4.   The term "royalty" as used in this Article means payments of any kind received as consideration for the use of, or the right to use, any copyright of literary, artistic, scientific or other work (including cinematographic films); any patent, trademark, design or model, plan,

secret formula or process; or for information concerning industrial, commercial or scientific experience.

5.   The provisions of paragraphs 1 through 3 of this Article shall not apply if the beneficial owner of the royalties, being a resident of a Contracting State, carries on business in the other Contracting State in which the royalties arise through a permanent establishment situated therein and the right or property in respect of which the royalties are paid is effectively connected with such permanent establishment. In such case the provisions of Article 7 (Business Profits) shall apply.

6.   Royalties shall be deemed to arise in a Contracting State when they are in consideration for the use of, or the right to use, property, information or experience in that Contracting State.

7.   Where, by reason of a special relationship between the payor and the beneficial owner or between both of them and some other person, the amount of the royalties, having regard to the use, right, or information for which they are paid, exceeds the amount that would have been agreed upon by the payor and the beneficial owner in the absence of such relationship, the provisions of this Article shall apply only to the last-mentioned amount. In such case the excess part of the payments shall remain taxable according to the laws of each Contracting State, due regard being had to the other provisions of this Convention.

Article 13

GAINS

1.   Gains derived by a resident of a Contracting State from the alienation of real property (immovable property) situated in the other Contracting State may be taxed in that other Contracting State.

2.   For the purposes of this Article the term "real property (immovable property) situated in the other Contracting State" shall include:

a)   real property (immovable property) referred to in Article 6 (Income from Real Property (Immovable Property));

b)   where that other Contracting State is the United States, a United States real property interest; and

c)   where that other Contracting State is _____,

i)   shares, including rights to acquire shares, other than shares in which there is regular trading on a stock exchange, deriving 50 percent or more of their value directly or indirectly from real property referred to in subparagraph (a) of this paragraph situated in _____; and

ii)   an interest in a partnership or trust to the extent that the assets of the partnership or trust consist of real property situated in _____, or of shares referred to in clause (i) of this subparagraph.

3.   Gains from the alienation of movable property forming part of the business property of a permanent establishment that an enterprise of a Contracting State has in the other Contracting State, including such gains from the alienation of such a permanent establishment (alone or with the whole enterprise), may be taxed in that other Contracting State.

4.   Gains derived by an enterprise of a Contracting State from the alienation of ships or aircraft operated or used in international traffic or personal property pertaining to the operation or use of such ships or aircraft shall be taxable only in that Contracting State.

5.   Gains derived by an enterprise of a Contracting State from the alienation of containers (including trailers, barges and related equipment for the transport of containers) used for the transport of goods or merchandise shall be taxable only in that Contracting State, unless those containers are used for transport solely between places within the other Contracting State.

6.   Gains from the alienation of any property other than property referred to in paragraphs 1 through 5 of this Article shall be taxable only in the Contracting State of which the alienator is a resident.

7.   Where an individual who, upon ceasing to be a resident (as determined under paragraph 1 of Article 4 (Resident)) of one of the Contracting States, is treated under the taxation law of that Contracting State as having alienated property for its fair market value and is taxed in that Contracting State by reason thereof, the individual may elect to be treated for purposes of taxation in the other Contracting State as if the individual had, immediately before ceasing to be a resident of the first-mentioned Contracting State, alienated and reacquired such property for an amount equal to its fair market value at such time.

Article 14

INCOME FROM EMPLOYMENT

1.   Subject to the provisions of Articles 15 (Directors' Fees), 17 (Pensions, Social Security, Annuities, Alimony, and Child Support) and 19 (Government Service), salaries, wages and other similar remuneration derived by a resident of a Contracting State in respect of an employment shall be taxable only in that Contracting State unless the employment is exercised in the other Contracting State. If the employment is so exercised, such remuneration as is derived therefrom may be taxed in that other Contracting State.

2.   Notwithstanding the provisions of paragraph 1 of this Article, remuneration derived by a resident of a Contracting State in respect of an employment exercised in the other Contracting State shall be taxable only in the first-mentioned Contracting State if:

   a)   the recipient is present in the other Contracting State for a period or periods not exceeding in the aggregate 183 days for all twelve-month periods commencing or ending in the taxable year concerned;

b)   the remuneration is paid by, or on behalf of, an employer who is not a resident of the other Contracting State; and

c)   the remuneration is not borne by a permanent establishment that the employer has in the other Contracting State.

3.   Notwithstanding the preceding provisions of this Article, remuneration described in paragraph 1 of this Article that is derived by a resident of a Contracting State in respect of an employment as a member of the regular complement of a ship or aircraft operated in international traffic shall be taxable only in that Contracting State.

. . . .

Article 21

OTHER INCOME

1.   Items of income beneficially owned by a resident of a Contracting State, wherever arising, not dealt with in the foregoing Articles of this Convention shall be taxable only in that Contracting State.

2.   Notwithstanding paragraph 1 of this Article:

a)   a guarantee fee arising in a Contracting State and characterized as other income by that Contracting State and beneficially owned by a resident of the other Contracting State that is a connected person with respect to the payor of the guarantee fee may be taxed in the first-mentioned Contracting State in accordance with domestic law if such resident benefits from a special tax regime with respect to the guarantee fee in its Contracting State of residence; and

b)   in the case of the United States, a guarantee fee characterized as other income paid by an expatriated entity and beneficially owned by a company resident in _____ that is a connected person with respect to such expatriated entity may be taxed in accordance with the law of the United States for a period of ten years beginning on the date on which the acquisition of the domestic entity is completed. For purposes of applying this paragraph:

i)   no effect shall be given to any amendment to section 7874 of the Internal Revenue Code after the date of signature of this Convention; and

ii)   no entity shall be treated as an expatriated entity that:

A)   is a connected person with respect to the domestic entity immediately after the date on which the acquisition of the domestic entity is completed; and

B)   prior to that date, was never a connected person with respect to the domestic entity.

However, an entity described in the preceding sentence shall become an expatriated entity if, subsequent to the date on which the acquisition of the domestic entity is completed, the entity joins in filing a U.S. consolidated return with either the domestic entity or another entity that was a connected person with respect to the domestic entity immediately prior to the date on which the acquisition of the domestic entity was completed.

3.   The provisions of paragraphs 1 and 2 of this Article shall not apply to income, other than income from real property (immovable property) as defined in paragraph 2 of Article 6 (Income from Real Property (Immovable Property)), if the beneficial owner of the income, being a resident of a Contracting State, carries on business in the other Contracting State through a permanent establishment situated therein and the right or property in respect of which the income is paid is effectively connected with such permanent establishment. In such case the provisions of Article 7 (Business Profits) shall apply.

Article 22

LIMITATION ON BENEFITS

1.   Except as otherwise provided in this Article and in paragraph 6 of Article 10 (Dividends), paragraph 3 of Article 11 (Interest) and paragraph 3 of Article 12 (Royalties), a resident of a Contracting State shall not be entitled to the benefits of this Convention otherwise accorded to residents of a Contracting State unless such resident is a "qualified person" as defined in paragraph 2 of this Article at the time when the benefit would be accorded.

2.   A resident of a Contracting State shall be a qualified person at the time when a benefit otherwise would be accorded by this Convention if, at that time and, with respect to clause (i) of subparagraph (f) of this paragraph, on at least half of the days of any twelve-month period that includes the date when the benefit otherwise would be accorded, the resident is:

a)   an individual;

b)   a Contracting State, political subdivision or local authority thereof, or any agency or instrumentality of any such Contracting State, political subdivision or local authority;

c)   a company, if the principal class of its shares (and any disproportionate class of shares) is regularly traded on one or more recognized stock exchanges, and either:

i)   its principal class of shares is primarily traded on one or more recognized stock exchanges located in the Contracting State of which the company is a resident; or

ii)   the company's primary place of management and control is in the Contracting State of which it is a resident;

d)   a company, if:

    i)   at least 50 percent of the aggregate vote and value of the shares (and at least 50 percent of the aggregate vote and value of any disproportionate class of shares) in the company is owned directly or indirectly by five or fewer companies entitled to benefits under subparagraph (c) of this paragraph, provided that, in the case of indirect ownership, each intermediate owner is a resident of the Contracting State from which a benefit under this Convention is being sought or is a qualifying intermediate owner; and

    ii) with respect to benefits under this Convention other than under Article 10 (Dividends), less than 50 percent of the company's gross income, and less than 50 percent of the tested group's gross income, is paid or accrued, directly or indirectly, in the form of payments that are deductible for purposes of the taxes covered by this Convention in the company's Contracting State of residence (but not including arm's length payments in the ordinary course of business for services or tangible property, and in the case of a tested group, not including intra-group transactions): (A) to persons that are not residents of either Contracting State entitled to the benefits of this Convention under subparagraph (a), (b), (c) or (e) of this paragraph; (B) to persons that are connected persons with respect to the company described in this subparagraph and that benefit from a special tax regime with respect to the deductible payment; or (C) with respect to a payment of interest, to persons that are connected persons with respect to the company described in this subparagraph and that benefit from notional deductions described in subparagraph (e) of paragraph 2 of Article 11 (Interest);

e)   a person described in paragraph 2 of Article 4 (Resident) of this Convention, provided that:

    i)   in the case of a person described in subclause (A) of clause (ii) of subparagraph (k) of paragraph 1 of Article 3 (General Definitions), more than 50 percent of the person's beneficiaries, members or participants are individuals resident in either Contracting State; and

    ii) in the case of a person described in subclause (B) of clause (ii) of subparagraph (k) of paragraph 1 of Article 3 (General Definitions), the earnings of such person benefit exclusively, or almost exclusively, pension funds that satisfy the requirements of clause (i) of this subparagraph; or

f)   a person other than an individual, if:

    i)   persons that are residents of that Contracting State entitled to the benefits of this Convention under subparagraph (a), (b), (c) or (e) of this paragraph own, directly or indirectly, shares or other beneficial interests representing at least 50 percent of the aggregate vote and value (and at least 50 percent of the aggregate vote and value of any disproportionate class of shares) of the shares or other beneficial interests of such person, provided that, in the case of indirect ownership, each intermediate owner is a qualifying intermediate owner; and

ii) less than 50 percent of the person's gross income, and less than 50 percent of the tested group's gross income, is paid or accrued, directly or indirectly, in the form of payments that are deductible for purposes of the taxes covered by this Convention in the person's Contracting State of residence (but not including arm's length payments in the ordinary course of business for services or tangible property, and in the case of a tested group, not including intra-group transactions): (A) to persons that are not residents of either Contracting State entitled to the benefits of this Convention under subparagraph (a), (b), (c) or (e) of this paragraph; (B) to persons that are connected persons with respect to the person described in this subparagraph and that benefit from a special tax regime with respect to the deductible payment; or (C) with respect to a payment of interest, to persons that are connected persons with respect to the person described in this subparagraph and that benefit from notional deductions described in subparagraph (e) of paragraph 2 of Article 11 (Interest).

3.   a)   A resident of a Contracting State shall be entitled to benefits under this Convention with respect to an item of income derived from the other Contracting State, regardless of whether the resident is a qualified person, if the resident is engaged in the active conduct of a trade or business in the first-mentioned Contracting State, and the income derived from the other Contracting State emanates from, or is incidental to, that trade or business. For purposes of this Article, the term "active conduct of a trade or business" shall not include the following activities or any combination thereof:

i)   operating as a holding company;

ii)   providing overall supervision or administration of a group of companies;

iii)   providing group financing (including cash pooling); or

iv)   making or managing investments, unless these activities are carried on by a bank, insurance company or registered securities dealer in the ordinary course of its business as such.

b)   If a resident of a Contracting State derives an item of income from a trade or business activity conducted by that resident in the other Contracting State, or derives an item of income arising in the other Contracting State from a connected person, the conditions described in subparagraph (a) of this paragraph shall be considered to be satisfied with respect to such item only if the trade or business activity conducted by the resident in the first-mentioned Contracting State to which the item is related is substantial in relation to the same or complementary trade or business activity carried on by the resident or such connected person in the other Contracting State. Whether a trade or business activity is substantial for the purposes of this paragraph shall be determined based on all the facts and circumstances.

c)   For purposes of applying this paragraph, activities conducted by persons connected to a resident of a Contracting State shall be deemed to be conducted by such resident.

4.   A company that is a resident of a Contracting State shall be entitled to a benefit under this Convention, regardless of whether the resident is a qualified person if, at the time when the benefit would be accorded, and on at least half of the days of a twelve-month period commencing or ending on the date when the benefit otherwise would be accorded:

a)   at least 95 percent of the aggregate vote and value of its shares (and at least 50 percent of any disproportionate class of shares) is owned, directly or indirectly, by seven or fewer persons that are equivalent beneficiaries, provided that, in the case of indirect ownership, each intermediate owner is a qualifying intermediate owner; and

b)   less than 50 percent of the company's gross income, and less than 50 percent of the tested group's gross income, is paid or accrued, directly or indirectly, in the form of payments that are deductible for purposes of the taxes covered by this Convention in the company's Contracting State of residence (but not including arm's length payments in the ordinary course of business for services or tangible property, and in the case of a tested group, not including intra-group transactions): (i) to persons that are not equivalent beneficiaries; (ii) to persons that are equivalent beneficiaries only by reason of paragraph 5 of this Article or of a substantially similar provision in the relevant comprehensive convention for the avoidance of double taxation; (iii) to persons that are equivalent beneficiaries that are connected persons with respect to the company described in this paragraph and that benefit from a special tax regime with respect to the deductible payment, provided that if the relevant comprehensive convention for the avoidance of double taxation does not contain a definition of a special tax regime analogous to the definition in subparagraph (l) of paragraph 1 of Article 3 (General Definitions), the principles of the definition provided in this Convention shall apply, but without regard to the requirement in clause (v) of that definition; or (iv) with respect to a payment of interest, to persons that are equivalent beneficiaries that are connected persons with respect to the company described in this paragraph and that benefit from notional deductions of the type described in subparagraph (e) of paragraph 2 of Article 11 (Interest).

5.   A company that is a resident of a Contracting State that functions as a headquarters company for a multinational corporate group consisting of such company and its direct and indirect subsidiaries shall be entitled to benefits under this Convention with respect to dividends and interest paid by members of its multinational corporate group. A company shall be considered a headquarters company for this purpose only if:

a)   such company's primary place of management and control is in the Contracting State of which it is a resident;

b)   the multinational corporate group consists of companies resident in, and engaged in the active conduct of a trade or business in, at least four countries, and the trades or businesses carried on in each of the four countries (or four groupings of countries) generate at least 10 percent of the gross income of the group;

c)   the trades or businesses of the multinational corporate group that are carried on in any one state other than the Contracting State of residence of such company generate less than 50 percent of the gross income of the group;

d)   no more than 25 percent of such company's gross income is derived from the other Contracting State;

e)   such company is subject to the same income taxation rules in its Contracting State of residence as persons described in paragraph 3 of this Article; and

f)   less than 50 percent of such company's gross income, and less than 50 percent of the tested group's gross income, is paid or accrued, directly or indirectly, in the form of payments that are deductible for purposes of the taxes covered by this Convention in the company's Contracting State of residence (but not including arm's length payments in the ordinary course of business for services or tangible property or payments in respect of financial obligations to a bank that is not a connected person with respect to such company, and in the case of a tested group, not including intra-group transactions): (i) to persons that are not residents of either Contracting State entitled to the benefits of this Convention under subparagraph (a), (b), (c) or (e) of paragraph 2 of this Article; (ii) to persons that are connected persons with respect to such company and that benefit from a special tax regime with respect to the deductible payment; or (iii) with respect to a payment of interest, to persons that are connected persons with respect to such company and that benefit from notional deductions described in subparagraph (e) of paragraph 2 of Article 11 (Interest).

If the requirements of subparagraph (b), (c) or (d) of this paragraph are not fulfilled for the relevant taxable year, they shall be deemed to be fulfilled if the required ratios are met when averaging the gross income of the preceding four taxable years.

6.   If a resident of a Contracting State is neither a qualified person pursuant to the provisions of paragraph 2 of this Article, nor entitled to benefits under paragraph 3, 4 or 5 of this Article, the competent authority of the other Contracting State may, nevertheless, grant the benefits of this Convention, or benefits with respect to a specific item of income, taking into account the object and purpose of this Convention, but only if such resident demonstrates to the satisfaction of such competent authority a substantial nontax nexus to its Contracting State of residence and that neither its establishment, acquisition or maintenance, nor the conduct of its operations had as one of its principal purposes the obtaining of benefits under this Convention. The competent authority of the Contracting State to which the request has been made shall consult with the competent authority of the other Contracting State before either granting or denying a request made under this paragraph by a resident of that other Contracting State.

7.   For the purposes of this Article:

   a)   the term "recognized stock exchange" means:

      i)   any stock exchange registered with the U.S. Securities and Exchange Commission as a national securities exchange under the U.S. Securities Exchange Act of 1934;

      ii)   the _____ Stock Exchange; and

      iii)   any other stock exchange agreed upon by the competent authorities of the Contracting States;

   b)   the term "principal class of shares" means the ordinary or common shares of the company, provided that such class of shares represents the majority of the aggregate vote and value of the company. If no single class of ordinary or common shares represents the majority of the aggregate vote and value of the company, the "principal class of shares" are those classes that in the aggregate represent a majority of the aggregate vote and value of the company;

   c)   the term "disproportionate class of shares" means any class of shares of a company, or in the case of a trust, any class of beneficial interests in such trust, resident in one of the Contracting States that entitles the shareholder or interest holder to disproportionately higher participation, through dividends, redemption payments or otherwise, in the earnings generated in the other Contracting State;

   d)   a company's "primary place of management and control" is in the Contracting State of which it is a resident only if:

      i)   the executive officers and senior management employees of the company exercise day-to-day responsibility for more of the strategic, financial and operational policy decision-making for the company and its direct and indirect subsidiaries in that

Contracting State, and the staff of such persons conduct more of the day-to-day activities necessary for preparing and making those decisions in that Contracting State, than in any other state; and

ii) such executive officers and senior management employees exercise responsibility for more of the strategic, financial and operational policy decision-making for the company and its direct and indirect subsidiaries, and the staff of such persons conduct more of the day-to-day activities necessary for preparing and making those decisions, than the officers or employees of any other company;

e)   the term "equivalent beneficiary" means:

     i)   a resident of any state, provided that:

A) the resident is entitled to all the benefits of a comprehensive convention for the avoidance of double taxation between that state and the Contracting State from which the benefits of this Convention are sought, under provisions substantially similar to subparagraph (a), (b), (c) or (e) of paragraph 2 of this Article or, when the benefit being sought is with respect to interest or dividends paid by a member of the resident's multinational corporate group, the resident is entitled to benefits under provisions substantially similar to paragraph 5 of this Article, provided that, if such convention does not contain a comprehensive limitation on benefits article, the resident would be entitled to the benefits of this Convention by reason of subparagraph (a), (b), (c) or (e) of paragraph 2 of this Article if such resident were a resident of one of the Contracting States under Article 4 (Resident) of this Convention. Notwithstanding the preceding sentence, an individual who is (1) liable to tax in his or her state of residence with respect to foreign source income or gains only on a remittance or similar basis, or (2) whose tax is determined in that Contracting State on a fixed-fee, "forfait" or similar basis, shall not be considered an equivalent beneficiary; and

B)   1)   with respect to income referred to in Article 10 (Dividends), 11 (Interest) or 12 (Royalties) of this Convention, if the resident had received such income directly, the resident would be entitled under such convention, a provision of domestic law or any other international agreement, to a rate of tax with respect to such income for which benefits are being sought under this Convention that is less than or equal to the rate applicable under this Convention. Regarding a company seeking benefits under paragraph 4 of this Article with respect to dividends, for purposes of this subclause:

> I)   if the resident is an individual, and the company is engaged in the active conduct of a trade or business in its Contracting State of residence that is substantial in relation, and similar or complementary, to the trade or business that generated the earnings from which the dividend is paid, such individual shall be treated as if he or she were a company. Activities conducted by a person that is a connected person with respect to the company seeking benefits shall be deemed to be conducted by such company. Whether a trade or business activity is substantial shall be determined based on all the facts and circumstances; and

> II) if the resident is a company (including an individual treated as a company), to determine whether the resident is entitled to a rate of tax that is less than or equal to the rate applicable under this Convention, the resident's indirect ownership of the shares of the company paying the dividends shall be treated as direct ownership; or

2)   with respect to an item of income, profit or gain referred to in Article 7 (Business Profits), 13 (Gains) or 21 (Other Income) of this Convention, the resident is entitled to benefits under such convention that are at least as favorable as the benefits that are being sought under this Convention; and

C)   notwithstanding that a resident may satisfy the requirements of subclauses (A) and (B) of this clause, where the item of income, profit or gain has been derived through an entity that is treated as fiscally transparent under the laws of the Contracting State of the company seeking benefits, if the item of income, profit or gain would not be treated as the income, profit or gain of the resident under a provision analogous to paragraph 6 of Article 1 (General Scope) of this Convention had the resident, and not the company seeking benefits under paragraph 4 of this Article, itself owned the entity through which the income, profit or gain was derived by the company, such resident shall not be considered an equivalent beneficiary with respect to the item of income; and

ii)   a resident of the same Contracting State as the company seeking benefits under paragraph 4 of this Article that is entitled to all the benefits of this Convention by reason of subparagraph (a), (b), (c) or (e) of paragraph 2 of this Article or, when the benefit being sought is with respect to interest or dividends paid by a member of the resident's multinational corporate group, the resident is entitled to benefits under paragraph 5 of this Article, provided that, in the case of a resident described in paragraph 5 of this Article, if the resident had received such interest or dividends directly, the resident would be entitled to a rate of tax with respect to such income that is less than or equal to the rate applicable under this Convention to the company seeking benefits under paragraph 4 of this Article; or

iii) a resident of the Contracting State from which the benefits of this Convention are sought that is entitled to all the benefits of this Convention by reason of subparagraph (a), (b), (c) or (e) of paragraph 2 of this Article, provided that all such residents' ownership of the aggregate vote and value of the shares (and any disproportionate class of shares) of the company seeking benefits under paragraph 4 of this Article does not exceed 25 percent of the total vote and value of the shares (and any disproportionate class of shares) of the company.

f) the term "qualifying intermediate owner" means an intermediate owner that is either:

i) a resident of a state that has in effect with the Contracting State from which a benefit under this Convention is being sought a comprehensive convention for the avoidance of double taxation that includes provisions addressing special tax regimes and notional deductions analogous to subparagraph (*l*) of paragraph 1 of Article 3 (General Definitions) and subparagraph (e) of paragraph 2 of Article 11 (Interest), respectively; or

ii) a resident of the same Contracting State as the company applying the test under subparagraph (d) or (f) of paragraph 2 or paragraph 4 of this Article to determine whether it is eligible for benefits under the Convention;

g) the term "tested group" means the resident of a Contracting State that is applying the test under subparagraph (d) or (f) of paragraph 2 of this Article or paragraph 4 or 5 of this Article to determine whether it is eligible for benefits under the Convention (the "tested resident"), and any company that:

i) participates as a member with the tested resident in a tax consolidation, fiscal unity or similar regime that requires members of the group to share profits or losses; or

ii) shares losses with the tested resident pursuant to a group relief or other loss sharing regime in the taxable year; and

h)   the term "gross income" means gross receipts as determined in the person's Contracting State of residence for the taxable year that includes the time when the benefit would be accorded, except that where a person is engaged in a business that includes the manufacture, production or sale of goods, "gross income" means such gross receipts reduced by the cost of goods sold, and where a person is engaged in a business of providing non-financial services, "gross income" means such gross receipts reduced by the direct costs of generating such receipts, provided that:

i)   except when relevant for determining benefits under Article 10 (Dividends) of this Convention, gross income shall not include the portion of any dividends that are effectively exempt from tax in the person's Contracting State of residence, whether through deductions or otherwise; and

ii)   except with respect to the portion of any dividend that is taxable, a tested group's gross income shall not take into account transactions between companies within the tested group.

Article 23

RELIEF FROM DOUBLE TAXATION

1.   In the case of _____, double taxation will be relieved as follows:

2.   In accordance with the provisions and subject to the limitations of the law of the United States (as it may be amended from time to time without changing the general principle hereof), the United States shall allow to a resident or citizen of the United States as a credit against the United States tax on income applicable to residents and citizens:

a)   the income tax paid or accrued to _____ by or on behalf of such resident or citizen; and

b)   in the case of a United States company owning at least 10 percent of the voting stock of a company that is a resident of _____ and from which the United States company receives dividends, the income tax paid or accrued to _____ by or on behalf of the payor with respect to the profits out of which the dividends are paid.

For the purposes of this paragraph, the taxes referred to in subparagraph (a) of paragraph 3 and paragraph 4 of Article 2 (Taxes Covered) shall be considered income taxes.

3.   For the purposes of applying paragraph 2 of this Article, an item of gross income, as determined under the law of the United States, derived by a resident of the United States that, under this Convention, may be taxed in _____ shall be deemed to be income from sources in _____.

4.   Where a United States citizen is a resident of _____:

a)   with respect to items of income, profit or gain that under the provisions of this Convention are exempt from United States tax or that are subject to a reduced rate of United States tax when derived by a resident of _____ who is not a United States citizen, _____ shall allow as a credit against _____ tax only the tax paid, if any, that the United States may impose under the provisions of this Convention other than taxes that may be imposed solely by reason of citizenship under paragraph 4 of Article 1 (General Scope);

b)   for purposes of applying paragraph 2 to compute United States tax on those items of income, profit or gain referred to in subparagraph (a) of this paragraph, the United States shall allow as a credit against United States tax the income tax paid to _____ after the credit referred to in subparagraph (a) of this paragraph; the credit so allowed shall not reduce the portion of the United States tax that is creditable against the _____ tax in accordance with subparagraph (a) of this paragraph; and

c)   for the exclusive purpose of relieving double taxation in the United States under subparagraph (b) of this paragraph, items of income, profit or gain referred to in subparagraph (a) of this paragraph shall be deemed to arise in _____ to the extent necessary to avoid double taxation of such income under subparagraph (b) of this paragraph.

Article 24

NON-DISCRIMINATION

1.   Nationals of a Contracting State shall not be subjected in the other Contracting State to any taxation or any requirement connected therewith that is more burdensome than the taxation and connected requirements to which nationals of that other Contracting State in the same circumstances, in particular with respect to residence, are or may be subjected. This provision shall also apply to persons who are not residents of one or both of the Contracting States. However, for the purposes of United States taxation, United States nationals who are subject to tax on a worldwide basis are not in the same circumstances as nationals of _____ who are not residents of the United States.

2.   The taxation on a permanent establishment that an enterprise of a Contracting State has in the other Contracting State shall not be less favorably levied in that other Contracting State than the taxation levied on enterprises of that other Contracting State carrying on the same activities.

3.   The provisions of paragraphs 1 and 2 of this Article shall not be construed as obliging a Contracting State to grant to residents of the other Contracting State any personal allowances, reliefs, and reductions for taxation purposes on account of civil status or family responsibilities that it grants to its own residents.

4.   Except where the provisions of paragraph 1 of Article 9 (Associated Enterprises), paragraph 8 of Article 11 (Interest), or paragraph 7 of Article 12 (Royalties) apply, interest, royalties, and other disbursements paid by an enterprise of a Contracting State to a resident of the other Contracting State shall, for the purpose of determining the taxable profits of such enterprise, be deductible under the same conditions as if they had been paid to a resident of the first-mentioned Contracting State. Similarly, any debts of an enterprise of a Contracting State to a resident of the other Contracting State shall, for the purpose of determining the taxable capital of the first-mentioned resident, be deductible under the same conditions as if they had been contracted to a resident of the first-mentioned Contracting State.

5.   Enterprises of a Contracting State, the capital of which is wholly or partly owned or controlled, directly or indirectly, by one or more residents of the other Contracting State, shall not be subjected in the first-mentioned Contracting State to any taxation or any requirement connected therewith that is more burdensome than the taxation and connected requirements to which other similar enterprises of the first-mentioned Contracting State are or may be subjected.

6.   Nothing in this Article shall be construed as preventing either Contracting State from imposing a tax as described in paragraph 10 of Article 10 (Dividends) or paragraph 7 of Article 11 (Interest).

7.   The provisions of this Article shall, notwithstanding the provisions of Article 2 (Taxes Covered), apply to taxes of every kind and description.

Article 25

MUTUAL AGREEMENT PROCEDURE

1.   Where a person considers that the actions of one or both of the Contracting States result or will result for such person in taxation not in accordance with the provisions of this Convention, it may, irrespective of the remedies provided by the domestic law of those Contracting States, and the time limits prescribed in such laws for presenting claims for refund, present its case to the competent authority of one or both of the Contracting States.

2.   The competent authority shall endeavor, if the objection appears to it to be justified and if it is not itself able to arrive at a satisfactory solution, to resolve the case by mutual agreement with the competent authority of the other Contracting State, with a view to the avoidance of taxation that is not in accordance with this Convention. Any agreement reached shall be implemented notwithstanding any time limits or other procedural limitations in the domestic law of the Contracting States. Assessment and collection procedures shall be suspended during the period that any mutual agreement proceeding is pending.

3.   The competent authorities of the Contracting States shall endeavor to resolve by mutual agreement any difficulties or doubts arising as to the interpretation or application of this Convention. They also may

consult together for the elimination of double taxation in cases not provided for in this Convention. In particular the competent authorities of the Contracting States may agree:

a)   to the same attribution of income, deductions, credits, or allowances of an enterprise of a Contracting State to its permanent establishment situated in the other Contracting State;

b)   to the same allocation of income, deductions, credits, or allowances between persons;

c)   to the settlement of conflicting applications of this Convention, including conflicts regarding:

   i)   the characterization of particular items of income;

   ii)   the characterization of persons;

   iii) the application of source rules with respect to particular items of income;

   iv)   the meaning of any term used in this Convention;

   v)   the timing of particular items of income;

d)   to advance pricing arrangements; and

e)   to the application of the provisions of domestic law regarding penalties, fines, and interest in a manner consistent with the purposes of this Convention.

4.   The competent authorities of the Contracting States may agree to increase any specific monetary amounts referred to in this Convention to reflect economic or monetary developments.

5.   The competent authorities of the Contracting States may communicate with each other directly, including through a joint commission, for the purpose of reaching an agreement in the sense of the preceding paragraphs.

6.   Where a person has presented a case to the competent authority of one or both of the Contracting States either:

a)   pursuant to paragraph 1 of this Article on the basis that the actions of one or both of the Contracting States resulted or will result for that person in taxation not in accordance with the provisions of this Convention; or

b)   on a taxpayer-specific case regarding a matter described in paragraph 3 of this Article; and the competent authorities are unable to reach agreement to resolve that case, and the conditions described in paragraph 7 of this Article are met, the case shall be resolved through arbitration conducted in the manner prescribed by paragraphs 7 through 9 of this Article and according to any rules or procedures agreed upon by the competent authorities of the Contracting States pursuant to paragraph 10 of this Article.

7.   A case shall be submitted to arbitration on the earliest date on which all of the following conditions have been satisfied:

a)   tax returns have been filed with at least one of the Contracting States with respect to the taxable years at issue in the case;

b)   at least two years have passed since the commencement date of such case, unless the competent authorities of the Contracting States have agreed to a different date and notified the presenter of the case of such agreement;

c)   the presenter of the case has submitted a written request to the competent authority to which the case was presented for a resolution of the case through arbitration; and

d)   all concerned persons and their authorized representatives or agents have submitted to the competent authorities of both Contracting States written agreements not to disclose to any other person any information received during the course of the arbitration proceeding from either Contracting State or the arbitration panel, other than the determination of the panel.

A case shall not, however, be submitted to arbitration if a decision with respect to such case has already been rendered by a court or administrative tribunal of either Contracting State, or if the competent authorities of the Contracting States have agreed prior to the date on which the arbitration otherwise would be submitted that the particular case is not suitable for resolution through arbitration.

8.   For the purposes of this Article, the following definitions shall apply:

a)   the term "presenter" means the person that has presented a case to the competent authority of one or both of the Contracting States either:

i)   pursuant to paragraph 1 of this Article on the basis that the actions of one or both of the Contracting States result or will result for that person in taxation not in accordance with the provisions of this Convention; or

ii)   on a taxpayer-specific case regarding a matter described in paragraph 3 of this Article;

b)   the term "concerned person" means the presenter and all other persons, if any, whose tax liability to either Contracting State may be directly affected by a mutual agreement to resolve a case submitted to arbitration pursuant to paragraph 7 of this Article; and

c)   the "commencement date" for a case means the earliest date on which the information necessary to undertake substantive consideration for a mutual agreement has been received by both competent authorities.

9.   For the purposes of arbitrations under this Article, the following rules shall apply:

a)   The arbitration panel shall consist of three individual members. The competent authority of each Contracting State shall select one member of the arbitration panel. In the event that the competent authority of a Contracting State fails to select a member for the arbitration panel in the manner and within the time periods agreed by the competent authorities of the Contracting States pursuant to paragraph 10 of this Article, the competent authority of the other Contracting State shall select a second member. The two members of the arbitration panel who have been selected shall select the third member, who shall serve as Chair of the arbitration panel. If the two initial members of the arbitration panel fail to select the Chair in the manner and within the time periods agreed by the competent authorities of the Contracting States pursuant to paragraph 10 of this Article, these members shall be dismissed, and each competent authority of the Contracting States shall select a new member of the arbitration panel. The Chair shall not be a national or lawful permanent resident of either Contracting State. The members appointed shall not be employees, nor have been employees within the twelve-month period prior to the date on which a case is submitted to arbitration, of the tax administration or the treasury department of the Contracting State that identified them. Furthermore, the members appointed shall not have any prior involvement with the specific matters at issue in the arbitration proceeding for which they are being considered as arbitrators.

b)   The members of the arbitration panel and their staff shall be considered to be "persons or authorities" to whom information may be disclosed under Article 26 (Exchange of Information and Administrative Assistance) of this Convention.

c)   All material received by a competent authority of a Contracting State in the course of, or relating to, an arbitration proceeding (including the arbitration panel's determination) shall be considered to be information exchanged between the Contracting States. Accordingly, no such information relating to an arbitration proceeding may be disclosed by the competent authorities of the Contracting States, except as permitted under Article 26 (Exchange of Information and Administrative Assistance). The competent authorities of the Contracting States shall ensure that members of the arbitration panel and their staff agree in writing to treat any information relating to the arbitration proceeding consistent with the confidentiality and nondisclosure provisions of Article 26 (Exchange of Information and Administrative Assistance) of this Convention and the applicable domestic laws of the Contracting States.

d)   If at any time before the arbitration panel delivers a determination to the competent authorities of the Contracting States:

i)   the competent authorities of the Contracting States reach a mutual agreement to resolve the case pursuant to this Article;

ii)   the presenter of the case withdraws the request for arbitration;

iii)   a decision concerning the case is rendered by a court or administrative tribunal of one of the Contracting States during the arbitration proceeding; or

iv)   if any concerned person or their authorized representatives or agents violates the written nondisclosure statement required by subparagraph (d) of paragraph 7 of this Article, and the competent authorities of both Contracting States agree that such violation should result in the termination of the arbitration proceeding; the mutual agreement procedure, including the arbitration proceeding, with respect to the case shall terminate.

e)   After a case is submitted to arbitration, the presenter shall be permitted to submit to the competent authorities of both Contracting States for submission to the arbitration panel a paper setting forth the presenter's analysis and views of the case for consideration by the arbitration panel. Such submission must be submitted before the date on which the competent authorities of the Contracting States are required to submit their position papers to the arbitration panel, and shall not include any information not previously provided to the competent authorities before the case was submitted to arbitration.

f)   After a case is submitted to arbitration, the competent authority of each of the Contracting States shall be permitted to submit to the arbitration panel a position paper with a proposed resolution addressing each adjustment or similar issue raised in the case, and shall simultaneously provide a copy of such position paper to the other competent authority. Such proposed resolution shall be a resolution of the entire case and shall reflect all agreements previously reached between the competent authorities of the Contracting States with respect to any adjustment or similar issue raised in the case. Such proposed resolution shall be limited to a disposition of specific monetary amounts (for example, of income, profit, gain or expense) or, where specified, the maximum rate of tax charged pursuant to the Convention for each adjustment or similar issue in the case. The competent authority of each of the Contracting States shall also be permitted to submit additional supporting papers for consideration by the arbitration panel, and shall simultaneously provide a copy of such supporting papers to the other competent authority.

g)   Notwithstanding the provisions of subparagraph (e) of this paragraph, it is understood that, in the case of an arbitration proceeding concerning:

i) the tax liability of an individual for which the competent authorities have been unable to reach agreement with respect to the individual's Contracting State of residence;

ii) the taxation of the business profits of an enterprise with respect to which the competent authorities have been unable to reach an agreement on whether a permanent establishment exists; or

iii) such other issues the determination of which are contingent on resolution of similar threshold questions; the position paper may include positions regarding clause (i), (ii) or (iii) of this subparagraph, in addition to proposed resolutions limited to specific monetary amounts (for example, of income, profit, gain or expense) or, where specified, the maximum rate of tax charged pursuant to this Convention due as a consequence of the arbitration panel's determination regarding residency, the existence of a permanent establishment or other threshold questions.

h) Where an arbitration proceeding concerns a case comprising multiple adjustments or issues each requiring a disposition of specific monetary amounts of income, profit, gain or expense or, where specified, the maximum rate of tax charged pursuant to this Convention, the position paper may propose a separate disposition for each adjustment or similar issue.

i) Each competent authority shall be permitted to submit a reply to any position paper submitted to the arbitration panel, and shall simultaneously provide the other competent authority with a copy of any such reply submitted to the arbitration panel.

j) The arbitration panel shall deliver a determination in writing to the competent authorities of the Contracting States. The determination reached by the arbitration panel in the arbitration proceeding shall be limited to one of the proposed resolutions for the case submitted by one of the competent authorities of the Contracting States for each adjustment or similar issue and any threshold questions, and shall not include a rationale or any other explanation of the determination. The determination of the arbitration panel shall have no precedential value with respect to the application of this Convention in any other case.

k) The determination of the arbitration panel with respect to a case submitted to arbitration shall constitute a resolution by mutual agreement under this Article and shall be binding on the Contracting States if it is accepted by all of the concerned persons. Unless the competent authorities of both Contracting States agree to a longer time period, the concerned persons shall have 45 days from the date they receive the determination of the arbitration panel to notify, in writing, the competent authority of the Contracting

State to whom the case was presented of their acceptance of determination. In the event the case is pending in litigation, each concerned person that is a party to such litigation must also advise, within the same time frame, the relevant court of its acceptance of the determination of the arbitration panel and its intention to withdraw from the consideration of the court the issues resolved through the proceeding. If any concerned person fails to so advise the relevant competent authority and relevant court within this time frame, the determination of the arbitration panel shall be considered not to have been accepted by the concerned persons. Where the determination of the arbitration panel is not accepted, the case shall not be eligible for any subsequent further consideration by the competent authorities.

l)   The fees and expenses of the members of the arbitration panel, as well as any costs incurred in connection with the proceeding by the Contracting States, shall be borne equitably by the competent authorities of the Contracting States.

10. The competent authorities of the Contracting States shall agree in writing, before the first case is submitted to arbitration, on time periods and procedures that are consistent with paragraphs 6 through 9 of this Article for:

a)   establishing when information necessary to undertake substantive consideration for a mutual agreement has been received by both competent authorities for purposes of determining the commencement date, and for notifying each other when such requirement has been satisfied;

b)   notifying the presenter of any agreements that a case is not suitable for resolution through arbitration, or to change the date on which a case shall be submitted to arbitration;

c)   the appropriate application of arbitration in the context of a request for an advanced pricing agreement, including rules concerning the date on which a case may be submitted to arbitration;

d)   obtaining the agreements of all concerned persons and their authorized representatives or agents not to disclose any information received during the course of the arbitration proceeding from the competent authority of either Contracting State or the arbitration panel, other than the determination of such panel pursuant to subparagraph (d) of paragraph 7 of this Article, and the agreements of the members of the arbitration panel and their staff to treat any information relating to the arbitration proceeding consistent with the confidentiality and nondisclosure provisions of Article 26 (Exchange of Information and Administrative Assistance), as required by subparagraph (c) of paragraph 9 of this Article;

e)   the appointment of the members of the arbitration panel;

f)   the submission of position papers, supporting papers and reply submissions by the competent authorities of the Contracting States to the arbitration panel;

g)   the submission to the competent authorities of both Contracting States by the presenter of a paper setting forth the presenter's views and analysis of the case for consideration by the arbitration panel;

h)   the delivery by the arbitration panel of its determination to the competent authorities of the Contracting States;

i)   the acceptance or rejection by the concerned persons of the determination of the arbitration panel; and

j)   the adoption by the arbitration panel of any additional procedures necessary for the conduct of its business.

The competent authorities of the Contracting States may mutually agree in writing to modify their agreement concerning these time periods and procedures, as needed, and may further agree in writing on such other rules, time periods and procedures as may be necessary for the effective and timely implementation of an arbitration proceeding.

Article 26
EXCHANGE OF INFORMATION AND
ADMINISTRATIVE ASSISTANCE

1.   The competent authorities of the Contracting States shall exchange such information as is foreseeably relevant for carrying out the provisions of this Convention or the domestic laws of the Contracting States concerning taxes of every kind imposed by a Contracting State to the extent that the taxation thereunder is not contrary to the Convention, including information relating to the assessment or collection, or administration of, the enforcement or prosecution in respect of, or the determination of appeals in relation to, such taxes. The exchange of information is not restricted by paragraph 1 of Article 1 (General Scope) or Article 2 (Taxes Covered).

2.   Any information received under this Article by a Contracting State shall be treated as secret in the same manner as information obtained under the domestic law of that Contracting State and shall be disclosed only to persons or authorities (including courts and administrative bodies) involved in the assessment, collection, or administration of, the enforcement or prosecution in respect of, or the determination of appeals in relation to, the taxes referred to in paragraph 1 of this Article, or the oversight of such functions. Such persons or authorities shall use the information only for such purposes. They may disclose the information in public court proceedings or in judicial decisions. Notwithstanding the preceding sentences of this paragraph, the competent authority of the Contracting State that receives information under the provisions of this Article may, with the written consent of the Contracting State that provided the information, also make available that information for other

purposes allowed under the provisions of a mutual legal assistance treaty in force between the Contracting States that allows for the exchange of tax information.

3.   In no case shall the provisions of paragraphs 1 and 2 of this Article be construed so as to impose on a Contracting State the obligation:

a)   to carry out administrative measures at variance with the laws and administrative practice of that or of the other Contracting State;

b)   to supply information that is not obtainable under the laws or in the normal course of the administration of that or of the other Contracting State; or

c)   to supply information that would disclose any trade, business, industrial, commercial, or professional secret or trade process, or information the disclosure of which would be contrary to public policy.

4.   If information is requested by a Contracting State in accordance with this Article, the other Contracting State shall use its information gathering measures to obtain the requested information, even though that other Contracting State may not need such information for its own tax purposes. The obligation contained in the preceding sentence is subject to the limitations of paragraph 3 of this Article but in no case shall such limitations be construed to permit a Contracting State to decline to supply information solely because it has no domestic interest in such information.

5.   In no case shall the provisions of paragraph 3 of this Article be construed to permit a Contracting State to decline to supply information solely because the information is held by a bank, other financial institution, nominee or person acting in an agency or a fiduciary capacity or because it relates to ownership interests in a person.

6.   If specifically requested by the competent authority of a Contracting State, the competent authority of the other Contracting State shall provide information under this Article in the form of depositions of witnesses and authenticated copies of unedited original documents (including books, papers, statements, records, accounts, and writings).

7.   Each of the Contracting States shall endeavor to collect on behalf of the other Contracting State such amounts as may be necessary to ensure that relief granted by the Convention from taxation imposed by that other Contracting State does not inure to the benefit of persons not entitled thereto. This paragraph shall not impose upon either of the Contracting States the obligation to carry out administrative measures that would be contrary to its sovereignty, security, or public policy.

8.   The requested Contracting State shall allow representatives of the requesting Contracting State to interview individuals and examine books and records in the requested Contracting State with the consent of the persons subject to examination.

9.   The competent authorities of the Contracting States may develop an agreement upon the mode of application of this Article, including agreement to ensure comparable levels of assistance to each of the Contracting States, but in no case will the lack of such agreement relieve a Contracting State of its obligations under this Article.

Article 27

MEMBERS OF DIPLOMATIC MISSIONS AND CONSULAR POSTS

Nothing in this Convention shall affect the fiscal privileges of members of diplomatic missions or consular posts under the general rules of international law or under the provisions of special agreements.

Article 28

SUBSEQUENT CHANGES IN LAW

1.   If at any time after the signing of this Convention, a Contracting State reduces the general statutory rate of company tax that applies with respect to substantially all of the income of resident companies with the result that such rate falls below the lesser of either (a) 15 percent or (b) 60 percent of the general statutory rate of company tax applicable in the other Contracting State, or the first-mentioned Contracting State provides an exemption from taxation to resident companies for substantially all foreign source income (including interest and royalties), the Contracting States shall consult with a view to amending this Convention to restore an appropriate allocation of taxing rights between the Contracting States. If such consultations do not progress, the other Contracting State may notify the first-mentioned Contracting State through diplomatic channels that it shall cease to apply the provisions of Articles 10 (Dividends), 11 (Interest), 12 (Royalties) and 21 (Other Income). In such case, the provisions of such Articles shall cease to have effect in both Contracting States with respect to payments to resident companies six months after the date that the other Contracting State issues a written public notification stating that it shall cease to apply the provisions of Articles 10 (Dividends), 11 (Interest), 12 (Royalties) and 21 (Other Income).

2.   For the purposes of determining the general statutory rate of company tax:

   a)   the allowance of generally available deductions based on a percentage of what otherwise would be taxable income, and other similar mechanisms to achieve a reduction in the overall rate of tax, shall be taken into account; and

   b)   a tax that applies to a company only upon a distribution by such company, or that applies to shareholders, shall not be taken into account.

Article 29
ENTRY INTO FORCE

1.   This Convention shall be subject to ratification in accordance with the applicable procedures of each Contracting State. The Contracting States shall notify each other in writing, through diplomatic channels when their respective applicable procedures have been satisfied.

2.   This Convention shall enter into force on the date of the later of the notifications referred to in paragraph 1 of this Article. The provisions of this Convention shall have effect:

   a)   in respect of taxes withheld at source, for amounts paid or credited on or after the first day of the second month next following the date on which this Convention enters into force;

   b)   in respect of other taxes, for taxable years beginning on or after the first day of January next following the date on which this Convention enters into force.

3.   Notwithstanding paragraph 2 of this Article:

   a)   the provisions of paragraphs 6 through 10 of Article 25 (Mutual Agreement Procedure) of this Convention shall have effect with respect to:

      i)   cases that are under consideration by the competent authorities as of the date on which this Convention enters into force. For such cases, the commencement date shall be the date on which this Convention enters into force; and

      ii)   cases that come under consideration after the date on which this Convention enters into force; and

   b)   the provisions of Article 26 (Exchange of Information and Administrative Assistance) shall have effect from the date of entry into force of this Convention, without regard to the taxable year to which the matter relates.

Article 30
TERMINATION

This Convention shall remain in force until terminated by a Contracting State. Either Contracting State may terminate the Convention by giving notice of termination to the other Contracting State through diplomatic channels. In such event, the Convention shall terminate on the date of such notification. Notwithstanding such termination, this Convention shall cease to have effect:

   a)   in respect of taxes withheld at source, for amounts paid or credited after the expiration of the six-month period beginning on the date on which notice of termination was given; and

   b)   in respect of other taxes, for taxable years beginning on or after the expiration of the six-month period beginning on the date on which notice of termination was given.

IN WITNESS WHEREOF, the undersigned, being duly authorized thereto by their respective Governments, have signed this Convention.

DONE at in duplicate, in the English and languages, both texts being equally authentic, this day of, 20__.

FOR THE GOVERNMENT OF FOR THE GOVERNMENT OF THE UNITED STATES OF AMERICA: _____

NOTES AND QUESTIONS

1. Note the structure of the convention. This structure, including the specific order of the paragraphs, is identical in every tax convention (there are over 3,000 of them), and is based in general on the two basic model conventions, the OECD model (from 2017, with constant updates) and the UN model (from 2017, with recent updates). Because of the underlying similarity of all bilateral tax conventions, it is possible to speak of an international tax regime built from these conventions that in general has binding force as customary international law. In practical terms, it is hard to envision a tax convention that does not follow this model or the general rules contained therein.

2. The basic framework of tax conventions may be described as a compromise between residence and source jurisdictions in which the residence jurisdiction, in general, retains exclusive rights to tax passive income (dividends, interest, royalties etc.), except for some residual taxation of dividends at source. Active income ("business profits") and income attributable to a "permanent establishment" is taxable primarily by the source country and the residence country must provide a credit for such taxes against its own tax liability. How does the U.S. model fit this general framework?

3. Besides preventing double taxation, the other aim of tax conventions is to prevent fiscal evasion through exchange of information. In general, countries enter into tax treaties both to obtain the benefits of reduced withholding taxes on investments by their residents, and to obtain the benefits of information exchange for their own residence based taxation. The latter may be particularly important in the future, since withholding taxes frequently are waived on a unilateral basis (see Ch. 4 above).

4. How is the definition of permanent establishment geared to U.S. interests? If you were drafting a model treaty for a developing country, how would you draft this provision?

5. Is the definition of a permanent establishment adequate for today's economy? See the discussion of *Wayfair* in Ch. 5 above.

6. Why does the U.S. avoid source based taxation on interest, royalties and rents? Is this in the U.S.' interest given the level of capital it imports? How does this relate, as a matter of the U.S. bargaining posture, to the portfolio interest exemption? What would be an appropriate posture for a developing country?

7. Note that the provisions of Art. 23 do not allow for "tax sparing", i.e., granting credits for taxes a foreign country would have levied but for a tax holiday. What is the practical effect of this U.S. position? (Hint: remember the ability to average active foreign source income in the general basket).

8.   Does the U.S. need the elaborate provisions of Art. 22, given the existence of Code Sections 163(j) and 7701(*l*)?

9.   Some have questioned whether bilateral tax treaties are necessary—and whether instead, the relevant goals instead could be achieved through domestic law. What do you think? Which provision and goals of the treaty could (and perhaps often are) accomplished through domestic legislation? For which goals is a treaty likely essential? For which goals might the existence of a treaty improve and streamline both cross border commerce and taxation?

10.   The mutual agreement procedure of Art. 25 is the treaty's dispute settlement mechanism. Taxpayers and policy makers struggled over the years with its slow, expensive and uncertain characteristics. Recently, countries, led by the OECD, have concentrated an attempt to address changes to this mechanism. The OECD is now promoting binding arbitration as a possible advancement. The U.S. has agreed to just such provisions in some recent treaties. See, e.g., Germany (Announcement 2008–124), and Belgium (Announcements 2009–43, 2009–44). A few recent revenue procedures provide some relevant guidance for taxpayers. Rev. Proc. 2006–54 contains the most recent changes to the general U.S. competent authority procedures; Rev. Proc. 2006–44 contains procedures for seeking binding arbitration in appeals; Rev. Proc. 2002–44 contains the rules for mediation in appeals.

11.   Exchange of information (Art. 26) has become a highly debated issue in recent years because of the banking scandals involving a number of European banks, including the Swiss bank, UBS. The banks actively assisted U.S. taxpayers in hiding income subject to U.S. taxation. When the U.S. sought information on these taxpayers from UBS in 2008 and 2009—the bank and the Swiss government resisted the surrender of any information on the grounds of Swiss domestic laws governing bank secrecy. One of the long standing problems with exchange of information treaty provisions (the U.S. had a version of an exchange of information provision in its 1951 treaty with Switzerland) has been the circumstances under which information will be provided—and the degree to which a treaty partner may rely on its own domestic law to refuse to provide information. During 2009, the U.S. signed agreements with UBS and with Switzerland to provide for certain exchange of information in the UBS case, however, the execution of the agreement as well as its broader effects continue to generate debate and legal challenges. This has led to the enactment of FATCA and the evolution of a automatic exchange of information under a Common Reporting Standard (CRS) among countries (but not including the US).

11.2   THE RELATIONSHIP BETWEEN TREATIES AND THE CODE

TECHNICAL CORRECTIONS ACT OF 1988

SENATE, REPORT 100–445; 100TH Congress
2d Session; S. 2238

TITLE I.—TECHNICAL CORRECTIONS TO
THE TAX REFORM ACT OF 1986

XII. FOREIGN TAX PROVISIONS (SEC. 112 OF THE BILL)

H.   Miscellaneous Foreign Provisions

1.   Relationship with treaties (sec. 112(aa) of the bill, Title VII and Title XII of the Reform Act, and sec. 7852 of the Code)

Present Law

Relationship of statutes and treaties in general

Under the Constitution, "Laws of the United States which shall be made in Pursuance thereof; and all Treaties made, or which shall be made, under the Authority of the United States, shall be the supreme Law of the Land." U.S. Const. art. VI, cl. 2. When two particular statutes or a statute and a treaty conflict, both cannot be supreme; one must give way. If two statutes conflict the one adopted later controls. A later law abrogates a prior contrary law. 1 W. Blackstone, Commentaries. For purposes of applying this principle, treaties are on the same footing as statutes. Thus, when a statute and a treaty provision conflict, generally the one adopted later controls. "An Act of Congress, which must comply with the Constitution, is on a full parity with a treaty, and . . . when a statute which is subsequent in time is inconsistent with a treaty, the statute to the extent of conflict renders the treaty null." *Reid v. Covert*, 354 U.S. 1, 18, 77 S.Ct. 1222, 1 L.Ed.2d 1148 (1957). Whether the issue concerns the interaction of two statutes or a statute and a treaty, "[t]he duty of the courts is to construe and give effect to the latest expression of the sovereign will." *Whitney v. Robertson*, 124 U.S. 190, 195, 8 S.Ct. 456, 31 L.Ed. 386 (1888).

One difficulty in trying to interpret the relationship of either earlier and later statutes, or an earlier treaty provision and a later statute, is in determining whether there is an actual conflict between the two: that is, whether it is impossible to give effect to both provisions, properly construed. Hence a body of interpretative guidelines has been articulated by the courts, addressing both treaty-statute relationships and inter-statutory relationships, to explain how they resolve such issues. Of these guidelines, one of the most important is the initial presumption of harmony between earlier and later pronouncements. In the case of two statutes, "[t]he cardinal rule is that repeals by implication are not favored. Where there are two acts upon the same subject, effect should be given to both if possible. . . . [T]he intention of the legislature to repeal must be clear and manifest." *Posadas v. National City Bank*, 296 U.S. 497, 503, 56 S.Ct. 349, 80 L.Ed. 351 (1936). The same principle applies in the case of a treaty and a later statute: "When the two relate to the same subject, the courts will always endeavor to construe them so as to give effect to both, if that can be done without violating the language of either." *Whitney v. Robertson*, 124 U.S. at 194. "A treaty will not be deemed to have been abrogated or modified by a later statute unless such purpose on the part of Congress has been clearly expressed." *Cook v. United States*, 288 U.S. 102, 120, 53 S.Ct. 305, 77 L.Ed. 641 (1933).

It is a proper function of the courts to carry out the process of harmonization, that is, to construe earlier and later provisions in a way that is consistent with the intent of each and that results in an absence of conflict between the two. For example, courts may harmonize two provisions by resort to the principle that as between a generally applicable and a specifically applicable provision, the specifically applicable provision prevails. In the case of treaties with, and statutes concerning, Native Americans, courts may find that a fiduciary relationship justifies an expansive reading of one statute or treaty and a narrow reading of the other. They may resort to the principle that a previously existing statutory rule, reenacted verbatim, continues to operate in the same fashion post-reenactment. Courts may find convincing evidence that the purpose of the later statute was completely unrelated to the earlier provision purported to be repealed, and that therefore the earlier provision continues to apply without change.

Prior judicial efforts to find consistency between earlier and later statutes and treaties illustrate the difficulties of determining when application of the general later-in-time rule should result in giving effect only to the later provision; however, these difficulties cannot be permitted to obscure the fact that if an actual conflict does exist concerning a matter within the scope of both an earlier treaty and a later statute, as properly construed, the later statute prevails.

Relationship of the Internal Revenue Code and treaties

When Congress enacted the Internal Revenue Code of 1954, it included in that Code (sec. 7852(d)) a statement that no provision of the Internal Revenue title, i.e., the Internal Revenue Code, was to apply in any case where its application would be contrary to any treaty obligation of the United States in effect on the date of enactment of the 1954 Code (August 16, 1954). The intent of that provision was to ensure that the substitution of the 1954 Code for the preexisting 1939 Code did not operate to override then-existing treaty provisions. A House bill provision amending Code section 7852(d) to reflect that intent—namely, to ensure that post-1954 statutory changes not yield to pre-1954 treaties—was inadvertently dropped in the 1986 Tax Reform Act.

In a number of respects, the 1986 Act (and its legislative history) did not specifically address its interaction with U.S. treaties. Many recent tax Acts, by contrast, have specifically addressed interaction with treaties. "[I]n the interest of forestalling any possible litigation," the Revenue Act of 1962 expressly provided that it took precedence over any prior treaty obligation (H.R. Rep. No. 1447, 87th Cong., 2d Sess. 96 (1962); Pub. L. No. 87–834, sec. 31). One major conflict between that Act and treaties, not identified in the legislative history of that Act, was the conflict between the Act's separate foreign tax credit limitation for interest income and treaties that (at least literally) required the United States to retain the foreign tax credit limitation rules that it used at some earlier date. The Foreign Investors Tax Act of 1966 took the opposite approach. Although that Act reduced the burdens on foreign investors and thus no treaty violations were found, the Act (sec. 110) specifically provided that it did not apply in any case where its application would be contrary to any U.S. treaty obligation.

In more recent years, Congress has specifically indicated that it intended the later-in-time rule to operate so that tax Acts prevail over treaties in the case of conflicts. Congress took this approach with respect to the foreign tax credit changes in the Tax Reform Act of 1976 (H.R. Rep. No. 94–658, 94th Cong., 2d Sess. 237 (1976)) and with respect to the Crude Oil Windfall Profit Tax Act of 1980 (H.R. Rep. No. 96–817, 96th Cong., 2d Sess. 106 (1980) (conference report)). In connection with the Deficit Reduction Act of 1984, Congress in 1986 resolved certain conflicts in favor of treaties but indicated that, in the event of unidentified treaty conflicts, the later-in-time rule was to operate and the legislation was to prevail (see description of technical corrections made to the 1984 Act by the 1986 Act, H.R. Rep. No. 99–426, 99th Cong. 1st Sess. 917 (1985); S. Rep. No. 99–313, 99th Cong., 2d Sess. 935 (1986)).

Explanation of Provision

In general

The bill modifies the 1954 transition rule (embodied in sec. 7852(d)) governing the relationship between treaties and the Code to clarify that it does not prevent application of the general rule providing that the later in time of a statute or a treaty controls (sec. 7852(d)). The bill provides that no provision of the Internal Revenue title that was in effect on August 16, 1954, shall apply in any case where its application would be contrary to any treaty obligation of the United States in effect on the date of enactment of the 1954 Code (August 16, 1954). This provision makes it clear that treaty provisions that were in effect in 1954 and that conflict with the 1954 Code as originally enacted are to prevail over then-existing Code provisions but not over later amendments to the Code.

In addition, the bill clarifies the interaction between the 1986 Act, this bill, and provisions of U.S. treaties, identifying and clarifying known interactions where possible, and providing guidance for the future interpretation of now-unknown interactions.

Identified interactions between statutes and treaties

The bill provides that the following provisions of the 1986 Act will not apply to the extent that their application would be contrary to any income tax treaty obligation of the United States in effect on the date of enactment of the 1986 Act (October 22, 1986): section 123 of the Act (imposing tax on certain scholarship and fellowship grants); subsections (b) and (c) of section 1212 of the Act (imposing a 4-percent gross withholding tax on certain transportation income earned by foreign persons and amending the rules that allow a reciprocal exemption for certain transportation income earned by foreign persons); section 1247 of the Act (relating to the exemption that the United States provides to foreign governments in some cases); and section 1242 of the Act insofar as it relates to new Code section 864(c)(7) (treating gain from sale of assets used in a U.S. trade or business as effectively connected income after cessation of the trade or business in certain cases). In addition, in the event of conflict with an income tax treaty, the source rules of section 1212(a) of the Act (governing the source of certain transportation income) and of section 1214 of the Act (governing the source of payments from 80/20 companies) will not apply except for purposes of the foreign tax credit limitation. Further, the provisions of section 1241 of the Act that relate to new Code section 884(f)(1)(A) (to the extent that that provision treats interest paid in excess of interest deducted as U.S. source) and to Code section 861(a)(2)(B) (reducing the fraction of U.S. income that exposes a foreign corporation to U.S. withholding tax on dividend payments it makes) will not apply in the event of a treaty conflict. In addition, in the event of conflict with an income tax treaty, the source rules of section 1211 of the Act (determining the source of income from certain sales of personal property) will not apply to individuals treated as residents of a treaty country under a U.S. treaty.

Moreover, to the extent that the source rule of Code section 865(e)(2) conflicts with a U.S. income tax treaty, the bill provides that the treaty will prevail. A conflict may arise with this source rule because, under the Act, income derived by a foreign person from the sale of inventory property that is attributable to a U.S. office is U.S. source. This result occurs even though the sale may occur outside the United States and a foreign country may tax the sale on a source basis. By contrast, a U.S. resident who sells inventory property outside the United States may not pay any U.S. tax on the income because the income is considered foreign source. Thus, the nonresident may incur more burdensome taxation than a similarly situated U.S. resident. If this occurs, the bill allows a nonresident with nondiscrimination protection to treat this income as foreign source.

Finally, the bill provides that the Act's imposition of tax in certain cases on "excess interest" (i.e., the amount of a foreign corporation's U.S. interest deduction in excess of the amount of interest its U.S. trade or business has paid) will not apply in the event of a treaty conflict.

The bill's amendments to Act section 1211, described in Part XII.B.1., above, provide a coordination rule for cases where sales of stock and certain intangibles yield foreign source income tax treaty and U.S. source income under new Code section 865.

The bill codifies application of the later-in-time rule with respect to the following provisions of the 1986 Act, notwithstanding any treaty provision in effect on the date of enactment of the 1986 Act (October 22, 1986): section 1201 of the Act, amending the foreign tax credit limitation, and section 701 of the Act (as it relates to the limitation on the use of foreign tax credits against minimum tax liability).

Except for cases that have been identified in the bill or in the Act, the committee is not now aware of any other cases where a harmonious reading of the Act and U.S. treaties is not possible. Congress intended harmonious construction of the Act and U.S. income tax treaties to the extent possible. Thus, in some cases, despite the existence of arguments alleging the existence of a conflict, the committee does not believe that any nondiscrimination provision of any U.S. treaty bars the application of reasonable collection mechanisms designed to ensure the collection of a tax, the imposition of which is permitted by the treaty. The committee believes that the Act's partnership withholding provision and the bill's replacement provision (new Code sec. 1446), which allow for refunds in appropriate cases, constitute such a reasonable collection mechanism, and thus are fully consistent with existing U.S. treaty obligations.

Similarly, the committee believes that the Act's imposition of tax on installment gains received after a foreign person ceases a U.S. trade or business (Act section 1242) is fully consistent with existing U.S. treaty obligations. Some treaties prevent imposition of U.S. tax on business profits of a foreign person unless those profits are attributable to a permanent establishment through which the foreign person carries on business in the United States. The committee believes that these treaties do not prevent imposition of U.S. tax on income that was, when realized, attributable to a permanent establishment, even though that income is recognized after the permanent establishment no longer exists. Under a similar analysis, the committee understands that the Act creates no conflict with treaties in taxing amounts earned for personal services in the United States which are paid after the person earning the income no longer maintains a U.S. presence.

Other Act provisions that the committee believes are fully consistent with U.S. treaty obligations include the Act's dual residence company provisions (Act sec. 1249), and the provisions requiring that payments with respect to intangibles be commensurate with the income attributable to the intangible (Act sec. 1231).

Similarly, the committee does not believe that requiring recognition of gain by a domestic corporation that is liquidating into a foreign parent corporation or engaging in a tax-free reorganization where the domestic corporation's assets are being removed from U.S. taxing jurisdiction violates any nondiscrimination clause. In some cases, provisions based on capital ownership prohibit imposition of more burdensome taxes on foreign-owned U.S. enterprises than on similar U.S.-owned U.S. enterprises. For this purpose, however, a U.S. enterprise transferring assets to a shareholder who will bear U.S. corporate level tax on the income generated by those assets is not similar to a U.S. enterprise transferring assets to a shareholder who will not bear U.S. corporate level tax on the income generated by those assets. Thus, the Act's provision recognizing gain in these cases (sec. 631(d)), and the bill's provision making modifications thereto, are fully consistent with U.S. treaty obligations in the committee's view. Nonetheless, in view of an Internal Revenue Service announcement (subsequently withdrawn) indicating that certain liquidations were treaty-protected, the bill provides that the Reform Act's amendments to Code section 367(e)(2) do not apply in the case of a corporation completely liquidated into a treaty-country parent before June 10, 1987, the date of the bill's original introduction.

As another example, the committee believes that the Act's inclusion of book income in the alternative minimum tax base for certain taxable years (and of adjusted current earnings for other, future taxable years) does not conflict with existing treaty provisions exempting foreign residents from U.S. tax on business profits not attributable to a permanent establishment in the United States. In this case a foreign corporation with U.S. effectively connected book income that is not attributable to a U.S. permanent establishment remains exempt from U.S. minimum tax after the 1986 Act, if a pre-Act business profits treaty provision similar to Article 7 of the OECD Model Treaty applies to that corporation. (See Treas. Reg. sec. 1.56–1T(b)(6)(ii)(B).) The reason for this result is that a change in measuring the amount of effectively connected income subject to tax (here, the 1986 enactment of the book income preference) can properly be viewed as consistent with the continued exemption by existing treaty of U.S. tax on effectively connected income not attributable to a permanent establishment. Similarly, a foreign corporation with U.S. effectively connected book income that is attributable to a U.S. permanent establishment will now be subject to minimum tax on the tax preference items for book income or adjusted current earnings, as the case may be, even if a pre-Act treaty provision like Article 7 of the OECD Model Treaty applies to that corporation. Again, the committee believes that this change in measuring the amount of effectively connected income subject to tax is properly viewed as consistent with the continued application of the existing treaty.

If, in any of the cases described above where conflicts are understood not to exist, any treaty is somehow read so that it would bar operation of the Act, the committee intends that the Act is to be effective notwithstanding the treaty.

Treaty-statute interactions in other cases

Notwithstanding Congress' intent that the Act and income tax treaties be construed harmoniously to the extent possible, conflicts other than those addressed in this bill or in the Act ultimately may be found or alleged to exist. Similarly, conflicts between treaties and other acts of Congress affecting revenue are likely to be found or alleged to exist in the future, either with respect to existing or future treaties and statutes. The bill provides that for purpose of determining the relationship between a provision of a treaty and any law of the United States affecting revenue, neither the treaty nor the law shall have preferential status by reason of its being a treaty or a law. In adopting this rule, the committee intends to permanently codify (with respect to tax-related provisions) present law to the effect that canons of construction applied by the courts to the interaction of two statutes enacted at different times apply also in construing the interactions of revenue statutes and treaties enacted and entered into at different times. The committee does not intend this codification to alter the initial presumption of harmony between, for example, earlier treaties and later statutes. Thus, for example, the bill continues to allow an earlier ratified treaty provision to continue in effect where there is not an actual conflict between that treaty provision and a subsequent revenue statute (i.e., where it is consistent with the intent of each provision to interpret them in a way that gives effect to both). Nor does the committee intend that this codification blunt in any way the superiority of the latest expression of the sovereign will in cases involving actual conflicts, where that expression appears in a treaty or a statute.

In the interest of bringing issues to light expeditiously and apprising the IRS in a timely manner of treaty claims whose merit is not now known, the bill further provides that any treaty-based position taken by a taxpayer that overrules or otherwise modifies the operation of a statute enacted after the treaty entered into force shall be disclosed on the taxpayer's return (or by such other means as the Secretary may provide, if no return is required to be filed) in such manner as the Secretary may prescribe. The committee intends this provision to apply in any case where the taxpayer takes a position in reliance on a treaty and that position is contrary to the result that a later-enacted statute would have dictated had the treaty not existed.

. . .

Although the committee believes that the bill's provision regarding the equal status of treaties and statutes merely codifies present law, the committee believes that this provision, and the bill's disclosure provision, are necessary technical corrections to the Act for several reasons. The committee is concerned that the relationship of the tax laws and treaties is misunderstood. The internal tax laws of most countries provide some sort of regime for taxing either the foreign income of domestic persons, the domestic income of foreign persons, or both. Either type of income, then, is potentially subject to two autonomous tax systems each of which is at best designed to mesh with other tax systems only in broad general terms. Double taxation of the same income, or taxation of certain income by neither system, can potentially result. Income tax treaties, in the committee's view, are agreements that provide the mechanism for coordinating two identified tax systems by reference to their particular provisions and the particular tax policies they reflect, and which have as their primary objectives is a desirable goal that serves to improve the long term environment for commercial and financial dealings between residents of the treaty partners.

Treaties only help.

The committee believes that when a treaty partner's internal tax laws and policies change, treaty provisions designed and bargained to coordinate the predecessor laws and policies must be reviewed for purposes of determining how those provisions apply under the changed circumstances. The committee recognizes that there are cases where giving continued effect to a particular treaty provision does not conflict with the policy of a particular statutory change. In certain other cases, however, a mismatch between an existing treaty provision and a newly-enacted law may exist, in which case the continued effect of the treaty provision may frustrate the policy of the new internal law. In some cases the continued effect of the existing treaty provision would be to give an unbargained-for benefit to taxpayers or one of the treaty partners. At that point, the treaty provision in question may no longer eliminate double taxation or prevent fiscal evasion; if not, its intended purpose would no longer be served.

The committee recognizes that some would prefer that existing treaties be conformed to changing U.S. tax policy solely by treaty renegotiation. However, the committee notes that in recent years, U.S. tax laws have been constantly changing. Moreover, once U.S. tax policy has changed, the existence of an unbargained-for benefit created by the change would have the effect of making renegotiation to reflect current U.S. tax policy extremely difficult, because the other country may have little or no incentive to remove an unbargained-for benefit whose cost is borne by the United States.

The committee recognizes that the parties to the treaty can differ as to whether the continued effect of a treaty provision in light of a particular statutory change provides such an unbargained-for benefit or otherwise frustrates the basic objectives of tax treaties. Remedies may be available in the case of what one party views as a breach of international law. However, the committee believes that under the constitutional system of government of the United States, where tax laws must be passed by both Houses of Congress and signed by the President, and where it is the role of the courts to decide the constitutionality of the laws and what the laws mean, it is not the role of taxpayers, the Judicial branch, or the Executive branch to determine that constitutionally valid statutes that actually conflict with earlier treaties ought not to be given effect either because of views of international law or for any other reason.

The committee is concerned that there are some who assert that treaties receive preferential treatment in their interaction with statutes. The committee is further concerned that whatever support is found for this view is based on misinterpretations of authoritative pronouncements on the subject. For example, before original introduction of this technical corrections legislation, the Internal Revenue Service announced that new Code section 367(e)(2), discussed above, which imposes corporate-level tax in certain liquidations, would not apply where it "would violate a treaty non-discrimination provision" (Notice 87–5, 1987–1 C.B. 416). Eventually, the Internal Revenue Service withdrew its notice on a prospective basis, and concluded that no treaty conflict existed (Notice 87–66, 1987–2 C.B. 376). The committee is concerned that the language used in the original notice may have suggested an erroneous inference that, had section 367(e)(2) actually created a conflict in a particular case, it would have been given no effect under the terms of the original Notice. Normal application of the later-in-time rule would not permit this result.

Other examples exist where the committee is troubled with erroneous inferences that have apparently been drawn from language used by the Executive branch. For example, in Revenue Ruling 80–223, 1980–2 C.B. 217, the Service considered the issue of whether foreign tax credit provisions enacted in the Tax Reduction Act of 1975 (sections 901(f) and 907) prevailed over conflicting provisions in earlier treaties that provide for foreign tax credits determined pursuant to the foreign tax credit provisions of the Code in effect as of dates specified in such treaties. The analysis stated the following:

In *Cook v. United States*, 288 U.S. 102, 53 S.Ct. 305, 77 L.Ed. 641 (1933), subsequent inconsistent legislation was held not to supersede an earlier treaty provision because neither the committee reports nor the debates on the subsequent legislation mentioned the earlier treaty. It is, therefore, necessary to examine the legislative history underlying the enactment of sections 901(f) and 907 of the Code for a clear indication from Congress as to whether it intended these sections to supersede any provision of treaties entered into prior to the enactment of these sections.

The committee believes it would be erroneous to assert that the absence of legislative history mentioning a treaty was sufficient to reach the result in Cook. That case dealt with the question of how to construe an anti-bootlegger provision (section 581) of (the Tariff Act of 1930) that first became law in an act (the Tariff Act of 1922) passed early on during Prohibition. Section 581 of the 1930 Act was a verbatim reenactment of section 581 of the Tariff Act of 1922. The scope of section 581 of the 1922 Act had been limited by a U.S.-Great Britain treaty made in 1924. The case came before the Supreme Court as Prohibition was in the last stages of being written out of the Constitution. The Court reached its conclusion on the stated ground that the treaty limit continued to apply under the 1930 Act, because section 581, "with its scope narrowed by the Treaty, remained in force after its re-enactment in the Act of 1930." 288 U.S. at

120. Properly construed, therefore, the committee believes that Cook stands not for the proposition that Congress must specifically advert to treaties to have later statutes given effect, but that for purposes of interpreting a reenacted statute, it may be appropriate for some purposes to treat the statute as if its effect was continuous and unbroken from the date of its original enactment.

Similarly the committee believes it would be erroneous to assert that an income tax statute such as the Tax Reduction Act of 1975 prevails over treaties only if treaty interactions are mentioned in the statute or legislative history. On the other hand, the committee believes that any such mention, if made, would be dispositive.

In view of what the committee believes is the correct treatment of treaty-statute interactions, then, the committee finds it disturbing that some assert that a treaty prevails over later enacted conflicting legislation in the absence of an explicit statement of congressional intent to override the treaty; that it is treaties, not legislation, which will prevail in the event of a conflict absent an explicit and specific legislative override. The committee does not believe this view has any foundation in present law. Moreover, the committee believes that it is not possible to insert an explicit statement addressing each specific conflict arising from a particular act in the act or its legislative history; for in the committee's view, it is not possible for Congress to assure itself that all conflicts, actual or potential, between existing treaties and proposed legislation have been identified during the legislative process of enacting a particular amendment to the tax laws. In the absence of a clear statement that legislation prevails over prior treaties, dubious tax avoidance schemes, in the committee's view, have been suggested. See, e.g., Tax Notes, March 9, 1987, at 1004, improperly suggesting that the failure to clarify the relationship between the Subchapter S Revision Act of 1982 and earlier treaties allows foreigners to own and operate U.S. business tax-free.

The committee believes that a basic problem that gives rise to the need for a clarification of the equality of statutes and treaties is the complexity arising from the interaction of the Code, treaties, and foreign laws taken as a whole. The committee notes that the United States has over 35 income tax treaties, some of extreme complexity, plus additional treaties bearing on income tax issues. In addition, the application of United States tax law to complex business transactions exacerbates these complexities. The committee does not believe that Congress can either actually or theoretically know in advance all of the implications for each treaty, or the treaty system, of changes in domestic law, and therefore Congress cannot at the time it passes each tax bill address all potential treaty conflict issues raised by that bill. This complexity, and the resulting necessary gaps in Congressional foreknowledge about treaty conflicts, make it difficult for the committee to be assured that its tax legislative policies are given effect unless it is confident that where they conflict with existing treaties, they will nevertheless prevail.

The committee further believes that codification of this rule, together with the disclosure requirements in the bill, will lead to the early discovery of now-unknown treaty conflicts and to their appropriate resolution. If any case actually arises in which proper application of the canons of construction ultimately reveals an actual conflict, the committee expects that full legislative consideration of that conflict will take place to determine whether application of the general later-in-time rule is consistent with the spirit of the treaty (namely, to prevent double taxation by an agreed division of taxing jurisdiction, and to prevent fiscal evasion) and the proper expectations of the treaty partners.

. . .

NOTES AND QUESTIONS

1. Why do you think the courts and the IRS have been reluctant to apply the later in time rule, thus necessitating the amendment to Section 7852? How is the fact that tax statutes must originate in the House and be passed by both House and Senate, while treaties are negotiated by the Executive and ratified by the Senate alone, relevant to this issue?

2. In most countries, treaties take precedence to statutes because they represent a bilateral bargain. How do you think our treaty partners feel about treaty overrides? In some newer treaties, there are specific provisions for cutting back on some treaty benefits in case of an override. What does this imply for the U.S. ability to negotiate treaties? The TCJA raised the specter of treaty overrides in the U.S. again. In particular, some observers have argued that new Section 59A (BEAT) may be a treaty override. At the time of the 2017 tax reform, the Congressional Research Service prepared an overview of treaty overrides for Congress. See "What Happens if H.R. 1 Conflicts with U.S. Tax Treaties?" Erika K. Lunder, Legislative Attorney (December 19, 2017), Congressional Research Service 7–5700, IS40318.

3. Read Section 894(c). This section was inspired by a transaction in which a Canadian corporation formed a US LLC that was treated as a subsidiary by Canada but as a branch by the US. Payments from the LLC to the Canadian corporation were treated as exempt dividends in Canada but as deductible interest subject to reduced withholding under the treaty in the US. After enactment, the Canada-US treaty was amended to eliminate this transaction. Do you think this override was justified? See the discussion of this and other recent overrides in 11.4 below.

11.3 JUDICIAL INTERPRETATION OF TREATIES

Xerox Corporation v. United States

United States Court of Appeals for the Federal Circuit.
41 F.3d 647 (1994).

. . .

OPINION:

■ NEWMAN, CIRCUIT JUDGE.

This tax appeal has its origins in the United Kingdom system of corporate and shareholder taxation that was adopted in the Finance Act of 1972. The ensuing changes of tax structure in the United Kingdom resulted in renegotiation of the tax treaty between the United Kingdom and the United States, in order to obtain for United States shareholders the avoidance of double taxation on dividends. This benefit had been made available to United Kingdom shareholders through a method of "imputation," enacted in the 1972 law.

The issue is whether Xerox Corporation is entitled, by virtue of the tax treaty, to an indirect foreign tax credit for tax year 1974 for certain Advance Corporation Tax ("ACT") that was paid in the United Kingdom by its affiliated company Rank Xerox Ltd. ("RXL"), on dividends that RXL paid to Xerox Corporation in 1974.

We conclude that the tax treaty and revenue code allow the tax credit to Xerox for the tax year in which the ACT was paid or accrued in the United Kingdom, whether or not the ACT was offset against mainstream corporation tax in the United Kingdom, or was otherwise used or surrendered by RXL in accordance with United Kingdom law.

BACKGROUND

Xerox, a New York corporation, owned directly and indirectly the majority of the voting shares of RXL, a corporation of the United Kingdom. RXL had various subsidiary companies in the United Kingdom, including Rank Xerox Management Limited, Rank Xerox U.K. Limited, and Rank Xerox Ireland Limited. In 1974, the tax year here at issue, RXL paid a dividend distribution to Xerox and paid the requisite ACT in the United Kingdom on the distribution.

A portion of that ACT was set off in 1974 against RXL's mainstream corporation tax in the United Kingdom, as permitted by British law; the foreign tax credit for that portion of the 1974 ACT is not in dispute. However, a portion of the ACT was not used to offset RXL's mainstream tax. In 1980 this unused ACT was surrendered by RXL to its United Kingdom subsidiaries, again as permitted by British law. The United States Internal Revenue Service ("IRS") then withdrew the foreign tax credit for this portion of the ACT, credit that had been allowed to Xerox in 1974, and required payment of the corresponding income tax on the dividends received by Xerox in 1974. Xerox paid the tax and brought suit for refund in the Claims Court. Recovery was denied. Xerox Corp. v. United States, 14 Cl. Ct. 455 (1988). Final Judgment was entered on Nov. 5, 1992. Xerox states that it has been allowed no foreign tax credit for this ACT, and that the same profits have thereby been taxed twice.

A.   The United Kingdom Finance Act of 1972

The system of corporate taxation that was instituted by the United Kingdom Finance Act of 1972 was designed, inter alia, to eliminate double taxation of the same profits, at both the corporate and shareholder levels. This was achieved by "imputation" to resident shareholders of the tax paid by the corporation on distributions to the shareholders. In accordance with the Finance Act of 1972 a United Kingdom corporation must pay 1) mainstream corporation tax, which is a tax on corporate income, and 2) advance corporation tax (ACT), a tax on any qualifying distribution to shareholders. Section 85 of the Finance Act of 1972 provides that ACT payments can be used by a United Kingdom corporation to offset its mainstream corporation tax (the "Section 85 offset"). However, the ACT must be paid by the United Kingdom corporation when the shareholder distribution is made, regardless of the corporation's mainstream tax liability or offset opportunity.

The ACT is payable whether or not the corporation has any profits. ACT is not refundable, whether or not it is used as a Section 85 offset by the United Kingdom corporation that paid the tax. Unused Section 85 offset can be carried back to the two preceding taxable periods or carried forward indefinitely.

Section 92 of the Finance Act of 1972 permits the distributing corporation that paid the ACT to surrender, at any time, all or part of its Section 85 offset to a United Kingdom subsidiary that is 51% or more owned by the distributing corporation. The subsidiary can then use the surrendered offset against its own mainstream corporation tax. The right to carry forward or surrender Section 85 offset to subsidiaries is useful, for example, when the United Kingdom parent corporation has excess foreign tax credits, because those credits must be used in the year they are earned.

Section 86 of the Finance Act of 1972 provides that a United Kingdom resident shareholder is entitled to a tax credit for the ACT paid by the corporation. This is called the "Section 86 credit":

86(1) [Entitlement to Credit] Where a company resident in the United Kingdom makes a qualifying distribution after 5th April 1973 and the person receiving the distribution is another such company or a resident in the United Kingdom, not being a company, the recipient of the distribution shall be entitled to a tax credit under this section. . . .

86(2) [Purpose and amount of tax credit] The tax credit in respect of a distribution shall be available for the purposes specified in the section and the subsequent provisions of this

Act, and shall be equal to such proportion of the amount or value of the distribution as corresponds to the rate of advance corporation tax in force for the financial year in which the distribution is made.

In this way double taxation on dividends is alleviated for United Kingdom residents. The Section 86 credit can not be withdrawn or withheld by the United Kingdom tax authorities.

The resident shareholder receives the Section 86 credit when the dividend is received. However, the Finance Act of 1972 excluded non-resident shareholders from this benefit. In a document entitled Reform of Corporation Tax Presented to the Parliament by the Chancellor of the Exchequer by Command of her Majesty, April 1972, at p. 11 P32, it was stated that one of the reasons for denying non-resident shareholders the Section 86 credit was to require tax treaty partners to renegotiate the treaty terms, whereby the British government hoped to obtain balancing concessions.

B.   The Renegotiated Tax Treaty

On enactment of the Finance Act of 1972, the United States requested renegotiation of the existing tax treaty. The purpose was to obtain the benefit of the shareholder tax credit for United States investors who receive dividends from United Kingdom companies, thereby avoiding double taxation of the same profits. See S. Exec. Rep. No. 95–18, 95th Cong., 2nd Sess., 22–24, 32–37 (1978), reprinted in 1980–1 C.B. 411, 420–21, 426–29; Statement of Assistant Secretary of the Treasury Laurence N. Woodworth, July 19, 1977, before the Senate Foreign Relations Committee, id. at 86, 89–90, reprinted in 1980–1 C.B. at 433, 435–36.

The renegotiated tax treaty was signed on December 31, 1975, and amended by diplomatic notes on April 13, 1976, First Protocol of August 26, 1976, Second Protocol of March 31, 1977, and Third Protocol of March 15, 1979, together comprising the Convention Between the Government of the United States of America and the Government of the United Kingdom of Great Britain and Northern Ireland for the Avoidance of Double Taxation and the Prevention of Fiscal Evasion with Respect to Taxes on Income and Capital Gains, 31 U.S.T. 5668 (hereinafter the "Treaty"), reprinted in 1980–81 C.B. at 394. As was explained to the Senate during the ratification proceedings, Articles 10 and 23 of the Treaty were "designed to resolve the problems presented by the interaction of the U.S. system of corporate taxation and the new hybrid system adopted by the United Kingdom in 1973 [the Finance Act of 1972] which in part integrates corporate and shareholder taxation." S. Exec. Rep. No. 95–18 at 4, reprinted in 1980–81 C.B. at 413.

Treaty Article 10 is retroactive only to April 6, 1975, and thus does not apply to the ACT paid on Xerox's 1974 dividends. However, it is a guide to the purpose of the Treaty and the intent of its terms. The relevant portion is:

Article 10—Dividends

    * * *

(2)(a) In the case of dividends paid by a corporation which is a resident of the United Kingdom:

(i) to a United States corporation which either alone or together with one or more associated corporations controls, directly or indirectly, at least 10 percent of the voting stock of the corporation which is a resident of the United Kingdom paying the dividend, the United States corporation shall be entitled to a payment from the United Kingdom of a tax credit equal to one half of the tax credit to which an individual resident in the United Kingdom would have been entitled had he received the dividend, subject to the deduction withheld from such payment and according to the laws of the United Kingdom of an amount not exceeding 5 per cent of the aggregate-gate of the amount or value of the dividend and the amount of the tax credit paid to such corporation;

The tax credit in Article 10 is paid to the United States corporate shareholder for the tax period in which the ACT is paid or accrued by the United Kingdom corporation on the dividend distribution; that is, the period in which the United Kingdom shareholder would have received a credit under Section 86. This credit is not defeasible by subsequent events concerning how the United Kingdom corporation uses its Section 85 offset, as the government asserts for the tax credit in Article 23.

Treaty Article 23 is retroactive to April 1, 1973. With only Article 23 in force in 1974, it was agreed that a 1974 tax credit for the ACT paid by RXL in 1974 on the dividends to Xerox, if the credit were held to be available to Xerox, would apply to all the ACT at issue.

Article 23—Elimination of Double Taxation

23(1) In accordance with the provisions and subject to the limitations of the law of the United States (as it may be amended from time to time without changing the general principles hereof), the United States shall allow to a resident or national of the United States as a credit against the United States tax the appropriate amount of tax paid to the United Kingdom; and, in the case of a United States corporation owning at least 10 per cent of the voting stock of a corporation which is a resident of the United Kingdom from which it receives dividends in any taxable year, the United States shall allow credit for the appropriate amount of tax paid to the United Kingdom by that corporation with respect to the profits out of which such dividends are paid. Such appropriate amount shall be based upon the amount of tax paid to the United Kingdom, but the credit shall not exceed the limitations (for the purpose of limiting the credit to the United States tax on income from sources outside of the United States) provided by United States law for the taxable year. For the purposes of applying the United States credit in relation to tax paid to the United Kingdom:

(a) the taxes referred to in paragraphs (2)(b) and (3) of Article 2 (Taxes Covered) shall be considered to be income taxes;

(b) the amount of 5 or 15 per cent, as the case may be, withheld under paragraph (2)(a)(i) or (ii) of Article 10 (Dividends) from the tax credit paid by the United Kingdom shall be treated as an income tax imposed on the recipient of the dividend; and

(c) that amount of tax credit referred to in paragraph (2)(a)(i) of Article 10 (Dividends) which is not paid to the United States corporation but to which an individual resident in the United Kingdom would have been entitled had he received the dividend shall be treated as an income tax imposed on the United Kingdom corporation paying the dividend.

Thus for dividends distributed to a United States shareholder corporation, Article 10 provides that half of the ACT paid in the United Kingdom is repaid as a tax credit by the United Kingdom, and Article 23 provides that the remainder is allowed as a United States tax credit as if the ACT were an income tax in the United Kingdom.

The government's position is that the Article 23 tax credit for ACT paid is not available to a United States shareholder corporation until or unless the Section 85 offset has been used in the United Kingdom to offset mainstream corporation tax; that is, that the tax credit provided in Article 23(1)(c) is an interim or provisional credit, which in Xerox's case was withdrawn when RXL surrendered its Section 85 offset to its subsidiaries. The Court of Federal Claims so held.

DISCUSSION

In construing a treaty, the terms thereof are given their ordinary meaning in the context of the treaty and are interpreted, in accordance with that meaning, in the way that best fulfills the purposes of the treaty. See *United States v. Stuart*, 489 U.S. 353, 365–66, 103 L. Ed. 2d 388, 109 S. Ct. 1183 (1989) (interpreting a treaty to carry out the intent or expectations of the signatories); *Kolovrat v. Oregon*, 366 U.S. 187, 193–94, 6 L. Ed. 2d 218, 81 S. Ct. 922 (1961) (a treaty should be interpreted to carry out its purpose). As discussed in *Sumitomo Shoji America, Inc. v. Avagliano*, 457 U.S. 176, 185, 72 L. Ed. 2d 765, 102 S. Ct. 2374 (1982), the court's role is "limited to giving effect to the intent of the Treaty parties." See generally Restatement (Third) of Foreign Relations Law of the United States, Part III, Introductory Note at 144–145 (1987). The judicial obligation is to satisfy the intention of both of the signatory parties, in construing the terms of a treaty. *Valentine v. United States*, 299 U.S. 5, 11, 81 L. Ed. 5, 57 S. Ct. 100 (1936) ("it is our duty to interpret [the treaty] according to its terms. These must be fairly construed, but we cannot add or detract from them.").

Unless the treaty terms are unclear on their face, or unclear as applied to the situation that has arisen, it should rarely be necessary to rely on extrinsic evidence in order to construe a treaty, for it is rarely possible to reconstruct all of the considerations and compromises that led the signatories to the final document. However, extrinsic material is often helpful in understanding the treaty and its purposes, thus providing an enlightened framework for reviewing its terms. See *Air France v. Saks*, 470 U.S. 392, 400, 84 L. Ed. 2d 289, 105 S. Ct. 1338 (1985) ("In interpreting a treaty it is proper, of course, to refer to the records of its drafting and negotiation.") However, "the ultimate question remains what was intended when the language actually employed . . . was chosen, imperfect as that language may be." *Great-West Life Assurance Co. v. United States*, 230 Ct. Cl. 477, 678 F.2d 180, 188 (Ct. Cl. 1982). In this context we have reviewed the evidence as well as the arguments proffered by both sides.

A. The Purpose of the Treaty

The stated purpose of the renegotiation, and the stated purpose of Article 23, is the elimination of double taxation of United Kingdom corporate distributions of dividends to United States shareholders. As explained by Paul W. Oosterhuis, an attorney for the Senate Joint Committee on Taxation, "generally favorable tax credit rules is an important concession to the United Kingdom which will make U.S. direct investment in the United Kingdom more attractive." (quoted in *Snap-On Tools, Inc. v. United States*, 26 Cl. Ct. 1045, 1069 (1992), aff'd, 26 F.3d 137 (Fed.Cir.1994) (Table)). It is not disputed that the ACT on the dividends paid by RXL to Xerox in 1974 is subject to Article 23 of the Treaty.

Article 23 provides that "the United States shall allow credit for the appropriate amount of tax paid to the United Kingdom." It was stipulated in the Claims Court that Article 23(1)(c) provides a tax credit to the United States shareholder for ACT paid by the United Kingdom corporation, by treating the ACT as an income tax imposed on the United Kingdom corporation paying the dividend. The government's position, as we have stated, is that the Treaty permits the United States to reverse that tax credit unless or until the ACT is set off against mainstream corporation tax in the United Kingdom.

The Treaty does not mention such a condition on the allowance of foreign tax credit in the United States for ACT paid in the United Kingdom. Xerox argues that this omission is strong evidence that this restrictive condition was not intended by the signatories, for so dramatic a change in the effect of the Treaty—in this case defeating the purpose of avoiding double taxation on profits—should not be inferred by silence. Xerox argues that if the downstream disposition of the Section 85 offset were controlling of the availability of the benefit for which the Treaty was renegotiated, the Treaty could not have omitted stating this condition explicitly. Xerox states that the plain meaning of the Treaty, in the context of its purpose, does not permit its interpretation to require this modification.

Article 10 is relevant to understanding the plain meaning of the Treaty, as we have mentioned, because its provision, whereby the United Kingdom pays half of the tax credit for the ACT directly to the United States shareholder, is not dependent on whether or when the United Kingdom corporation or its United Kingdom subsidiaries uses the Section 85 offset against mainstream corporation tax. Indeed, no such dependency has been suggested by the government for Article 10.

United Kingdom shareholders receive the ACT credit whether or not the ACT offset is used, surrendered, or saved by the British payor of the dividend. Stipulated Fact 30 in the Claims Court record is that a United Kingdom shareholder "is entitled to the benefit of the U.K. shareholder credit in respect to the period in which the qualifying distribution is made," without regard to whether or how the U.K. company uses the ACT "in that accounting period or in any other accounting period." This weighs against the government's argument that the Article 23 credit must be interpreted as not available to the United States shareholder until the occurrence of some subsequent event in the United Kingdom.

The government states that the United States always intended to restrict the availability of the ACT credit to United States taxpayers on the basis here asserted, and that this position was known to and was accepted by both signatories. In support, the government relies on the Treasury's Technical Explanation issued in 1977 and Revenue Procedure 80–18, documents we shall discuss post. In opposition, Xerox relies on the plain language of the treaty itself, its ratification history, and testimony of the chief negotiators for the United States and the United Kingdom. The 1986 Competent Authority Agreement is relevant, as are the provisions of the United States tax code with respect to foreign tax credits.

B.   The Negotiation History

The Senate Report that accompanied the Treaty when it was presented for ratification in 1978 stated that "the United States agrees that it will continue to allow its U.S. citizens and residents to claim . . . the indirect foreign tax credit (Code sec. 902)." S. Exec. Rep. No. 95–18 at 32, reprinted in 1980–81 C.B. at 426. The Report explained that a reason for renegotiation of the existing treaty was to ensure that the ACT would be credited by the IRS:

There is, therefore, a reasonable possibility that the ACT would not be viewed by the IRS as a creditable tax in the absence of the proposed treaty.

S. Exec. Rep. No. 95–18 at 34, reprinted in 1980–81 C.B. at 427. The Report explained that in the absence of the new treaty provisions, the ACT that was paid by the foreign corporation might not be creditable to the United States taxpayer until some later year in which United Kingdom mainstream tax liability was offset by the ACT:

However, notwithstanding these technical difficulties [that ACT did not fit the IRS criteria for a creditable foreign tax], the ACT could be treated as a creditable income tax to the extent that it is allowed as an offset against the U.K. "mainstream" corporate tax, which is a creditable income tax. Under this treatment, in situations where the ACT is offset against a mainstream tax accruing in years subsequent to the dividend payment, no foreign tax credit would be allowed in the absence of the treaty until that later year in which the mainstream liability is offset.

S. Exec. Rep. No. 95–18 at 34, reprinted in 1980–81 C.B. at 427. Thus the position here taken by the government against Xerox was foreseen as occurring "in the absence of the proposed treaty," id., and its remedy was a stated purpose of the Treaty.

Affidavits of negotiators for both sides were in accord with each other and with this purpose. Robert J. Patrick, Jr., International Tax Counsel for the Treasury and a principal negotiator for the United States, averred that the assumption during the negotiations was that under the Treaty "the U.S. foreign tax credit [for ACT paid to the U.K.] resulted in the resulting U.S. tax credits going to the U.S. corporate shareholders in the year the dividend was paid, rather than revenues going to the U.S. Treasury." He and David S. Foster of the Treasury, who succeeded Patrick as International Tax Counsel, and Paul W. Oosterhuis of the Senate Joint Committee on Taxation, averred that Article 23 was not viewed during the negotiations as providing a "provisional" or "interim" credit for ACT: the theory on which the IRS withdrew, in 1980, the ACT credit it had allowed in 1974. Mr. Patrick averred that "to the best of my knowledge, this interpretation of the Treaty has never previously been set forth by the United States, the United Kingdom, or anyone else." Mr. Oosterhuis averred that "to the best of my recollection, the Treasury Department never presented to the Senate in its ratification procedure any explanation that the ACT is creditable under Article 23(1)(a) or that the credit for ACT under Article 23(1)(c) is an interim credit."

These statements are consistent with the clear text of the treaty and its purpose of avoiding double taxation of dividends. A provisional or interim credit, defeasible by actions of the distributing corporation six years later inside the United Kingdom, is in bold conflict with that plain meaning.

The negotiators for the United Kingdom testified to similar effect, and responded to the government's statements in the Claims Court that they had accepted the proposed interpretation. Lord Rees, the responsible Minister of the United Kingdom Government for this Treaty and the Minister of State at the British Treasury from 1979 to 1981, averred:

As I stated in comments delivered to the House of Commons in January 1977 and again on 18th February 1980, a fair balance had to be struck between United States and United Kingdom portfolio and direct investors. . . . Developing a fair balance for the United States direct investor was more difficult but was eventually accomplished by the United Kingdom giving an immediate 50 percent refund (subject to a 5 percent withholding tax which was currently creditable against United States tax liability) and the United States giving an indirect foreign tax credit for the other 50 percent under Article 23(1)(c). To strike the intended fair balance with United Kingdom shareholders, this indirect foreign tax credit had to be currently creditable. Therefore, to the extent that the United States Treasury Technical Explanation denies a current indirect foreign tax credit, it frustrates the policy underlying these provisions of the Treaty. Consequently, had the United States Government interpretation of Article 23(1) been brought to my attention as the responsible Minister of the United Kingdom Government, I would have raised objections to its inter-pretation of the Treaty as being in conflict with the policy underlying the Treaty.

(Emphases added, citations to exhibits omitted.) The affidavit of the Rt. Hon. Denzil Davies, Minister of State at the Treasury from 1975 to 1979, was to the same effect, and equally strongly stated.

The government argues that there is "no reason to give any weight" to affidavits that were drafted after the Treaty entered into force. It is correct that post facto statements of legislators interpreting a statute are usually not accorded much weight, see Consumer Product Safety Commission v. GTE Sylvania, Inc., 447 U.S. 102, 116–118 & n. 13, 64 L. Ed. 2d 766, 100 S. Ct. 2051 (1980), for it is seldom easy to reconstruct all of the legislative interests. Similar reasoning well applies to treaties. However, one need not ignore the identity and stature of the affiants, or the nature of their involvement, particularly when the affiants simply but strongly reinforce the plain meaning of the text of the treaty. When the recollections of the persons principally involved are fully consistent with the clear text of the treaty, and when no substantial contrary evidence has been proffered, these affidavits add weight to the wisdom expressed in Rocca v. Thompson, 223 U.S. 317, 332, 56 L. Ed. 453, 32 S. Ct. 207 (1912), that had the signatories intended the purpose now urged, "it would have been very easy to have declared that purpose in unmistakable terms."

C.   The Technical Explanation

In 1977, in connection with the Senate ratification proceedings, the Treasury issued a Technical Explanation that stated, inter alia, that the United States foreign tax credit for ACT depended on when the ACT was used to offset mainstream tax in the United Kingdom, and that any credit previously given would be reduced accordingly:

1.   ACT paid with respect to a distribution shall be treated as attributable to the accumulated profits (determined under U.S. principles) of the year of distribution, except in two circumstances:

a)   to the extent the ACT reduces mainstream tax for a prior or subsequent year; and

b)   if, after attribution of ACT which does not reduce mainstream tax, accumulated profits would not exceed corporate taxes for the year.

ACT which reduces mainstream tax in any year or years shall be attributable to any accumulated profits of the year or years for which the mainstream tax is reduced. Where ACT is used to offset mainstream tax, the offset will be viewed as a refund of the ACT initially allowed as a credit and as a tax paid in respect of the year for which the ACT is applied as an offset. Consequently, a reduction in the foreign tax credit for the year from which the ACT is carried must be made in accordance with section 905(c) of the Code. . . .

Technical Explanation of the Convention between the Government of the United States of America and the Government of the United Kingdom of Great Britain and Northern Ireland for the Avoidance of Double Taxation and the Prevention of Fiscal Evasion with Respect to Taxes on Income and Capital Gains Signed at London, on December 31, 1975, as Amended by the Notes Exchanged at London on April 13, 1976, the Protocol Signed at London on August 26, 1976, and the Second Protocol signed at London on March 31, 1977 (herein "Technical Explanation"), submitted to the Senate Foreign Relations Committee at hearings held on July 19–20, 1977, reprinted in 1980–81 C.B. at 473–74.

This approach was referred to and criticized in general terms in the Senate Executive Report, as quoted supra. Referring specifically to the Technical Explanation, the Report mentioned the "difficult and complex issues" raised, and declined to "adopt or reject" the "amplifications" in the Technical Explanation:

The Treasury's technical explanation also set forth a complex set of rules and examples intended to be used for purposes of determining the earnings to which ACT payments by a U.K. corporation are to be attributed for purposes of computing the indirect foreign tax credit. . . .

The ACT refunds, the withholding tax, and the unrefunded portion of the ACT are treated for U.S. foreign tax credit purposes in a manner which is generally favorable to U.S. shareholders. These rules raise difficult and complex issues. In recommending the ratification of the proposed treaty, the Committee does not intend that these rules necessarily serve as a model for future treaties. Further, in recommending the ratification of the treaty, the Committee does not intend to adopt or reject the amplifications of the foreign tax credit rules contained in the Treasury technical explanation. Consequently, Treasury would not be foreclosed by the ratification of the treaty from modifying those administrative interpretations in the future should it deem it advisable to do so. Of course, the rules contained in the treaty also do not limit any legislative action in this area; the computation of the foreign tax credit for unrefunded ACT may be subject to any generally applicable changes in the U.S. foreign tax credit rules which may subsequently be enacted.

S. Exec. Rep. No. 95–18 at 36–37, reprinted in 1980–81 C.B. at 429. One may debate the meaning of this cool treatment of the Technical Explanation. What is clear, however, is that the Treasury's position was not embraced by the Senate. That this position is absent from the text of the Treaty is not surprising for, as the negotiators and the Senate recognized, it defeats the stated purpose of avoiding double taxation of the same profits.

A treaty must be construed in accordance with the intent of both signatories. Both of the United Kingdom's Ministers for the Treasury averred that they did not accept, or even know of, the position taken in the Technical Explanation:

I can say categorically that I was not at any time as Minister or as a Member of the House of Commons shown the Technical Explanation, or briefed on the Technical Explanation or the point at issue in the case. Since I was the responsible Government Minister speaking for the Government in the debates before the House of Commons, I would be the only person to bring any such material before the House of Commons or authorize it to be deposited in the library of the House of Commons.

* * *

The United Kingdom Government did not accept this United States Treasury Technical Explanation of Article 23 either explicitly or implicitly.

* * *

When the House of Commons approved the Order in Council giving effect to the Treaty as a matter of U.K. domestic law in February 1980, neither it nor I as the Minister responsible had any knowledge, express or implied, of the Technical Explanation. In these circumstances, it is not surprising that the United Kingdom voiced no objection to the Technical Explanation.

Affidavit of Lord Rees at 5–8. The Rt. Hon. Denzil Davies averred:

I can state from my own knowledge that during the whole of the period when I was a Minister of State responsible for the Treaty, I had no knowledge of and never saw the United States Treasury Technical Explanation of the Treaty in any form

* * *

The United Kingdom Government of which I was a member and on whose behalf I was the responsible Minister in this matter did not accept the United States Treasury's Technical Explanation either explicitly or implicitly.

Affidavit of Rt. Hon. Denzil Davies at 5–6

The government refers to the affidavit of a Treasury employee and member of the United States negotiating team, Steven P. Hannes, who stated that "copies of the Technical Explanation would have been sent to the U.K. negotiators." No evidence of such "sending" was provided, and it must be assumed that the Treasury's files contained no such support. On this extremely one-sided record, it would violate any reasonable canon of construction to infer mutual assent by the signatories to the position taken by the Treasury.

D. The Revenue Procedure

On the effective date, after the Treaty was ratified by both signatories, the Treasury issued Revenue Procedure 80–18, which introduced a different theory on which to deny the Article 23 credit for ACT, depending on whether the United Kingdom corporation surrendered the Section 85 offset to subsidiaries in the United Kingdom:

> For U.S. foreign tax credit purposes and pursuant to Article 23, the parent corporation has not paid or accrued the unrefunded ACT [Section 85] offset against the subsidiary's mainstream tax and has contributed to the capital of the subsidiary an amount equal to the unrefunded ACT offset.

Rev. Proc. 80–18, § 3.05, reprinted in 1980–1 C.B. at 625. That is, if the British corporation that paid the ACT later surrenders the Section 85 offset to its subsidiaries, Revenue Procedure 80–18 treats that surrender as a contribution to the capital of the subsidiary, and reverses the tax credit previously granted pursuant to Article 23(1)(c). Thereafter, the government argues, ACT is creditable only under Article 23(1)(a). As we shall discuss, this interpretation strains the plain meaning of the treaty. It would also defeat the Treaty purpose of avoiding double taxation.

Revenue Procedures "do not have the force and effect of Treasury Department Regulations." 1980–81 C. B. at v. See Helvering v. New York Trust Co., 292 U.S. 455, 468, 78 L. Ed. 1361, 54 S. Ct. 806 (1934) (revenue rulings cited by the Commissioner "have none of the force or effect of Treasury Decisions and do not commit the Department to any interpretation of law"); Spang Industries, Inc. v. United States, 791 F.2d 906, 913 (Fed.Cir.1986) ("a revenue ruling is entitled to some weight as reflecting the Commissioner's interpretation of the regulation, but does not have the same force as a regulation"); State Bank of Albany v. United States, 209 Ct. Cl. 13, 530 F.2d 1379, 1382 (Ct. Cl. 1976) ("It may be helpful in interpreting a statute, but it is not binding on . . . the courts.") Thus although the Revenue Procedure warrants fair consideration as reflecting the Treasury's position, it is not insulated from inquiry.

The new theory offered in Procedure 80–18 leads to the faulty conclusion that Xerox's credit for the ACT that was paid by RXL on the dividends received by Xerox can be rescinded based on downstream activity within the United Kingdom. The internal disposition of ACT in any of the ways authorized by the Finance Act of 1972 is not relevant to the Section 23 credit. A foreign country's internal procedures do not determine United States tax credit rules, other than as encompassed within a Treaty. *United States v. Goodyear Tire & Rubber Co.*, 493 U.S. 132, 107 L. Ed. 2d 449, 110 S. Ct. 462 (1989). A Revenue Procedure can not change the terms and purpose of a treaty. Procedure 80–18, n3 insofar as it would reverse Xerox's entitlement to the Article 23 credit for the ACT that was paid by RXL on the dividends paid to Xerox, is declared void.

E.   The Competent Authority Agreement

A dispute, ambiguity, or uncertainty concerning a treaty is ideally resolved by the signatories themselves. Such a process can provide useful clarification, short of substantive change which would require ratification. The Treaty's Article 25 provides for such a "Mutual Agreement Procedure." This procedure was invoked in 1986 at the initiative of the United States with the approval of the Claims Court, while this case was pending.

After a period of discussion, an agreed letter from the United States Competent Authority (by delegation of the Secretary of the Treasury, the Competent Authority was the Associate Commissioner (Operations) of the Internal Revenue Service), to the United Kingdom Competent Authority, was issued on December 18, 1986 and accepted on December 23, 1986. The Agreement states, in substantial part:

1.   It is agreed that Article 23(1)(c) provides a mechanism by which a U.S. foreign tax credit may be obtained for that part of the U.K. tax credit referred to in Article 10(2)(a)(I) which is not paid to a U.S. corporation but to which an individual resident in the United Kingdom would have been entitled had he received the dividend.

2.   It is agreed that Article 23(1)(c) was included in the Convention for the purpose of ensuring that in accordance with Article 23(1)(a) the Advance Corporation Tax ("ACT") payment which generally underlies the U.K. tax credit referred to in paragraph 1 would be treated as an income tax paid to the United Kingdom by the U.K. corporation paying the dividend, because the United States questioned to what extent, in the absence of the Convention, payments of ACT would be treated as payments of a creditable corporate income tax for U.S. foreign tax credit purposes.

3.   It is agreed that, pursuant to Article 23(1), the Article 23(1)(c) mechanism must be applied in accordance with the provisions and subject to the limitations of the law of the United States and that a credit is to be given under Article 23(1)(c) only for the appropriate amount of tax paid to the United Kingdom.

4.   It is agreed that Article 23(1) of the convention was not intended to provide two U.S. foreign tax credits for a single payment of ACT to the United Kingdom or U.S. foreign tax credits in excess of the amount of corporation tax (including both ACT and mainstream corporation tax) paid to the United Kingdom in respect of the profits out which a dividend is paid.

5. It is agreed that under the language of Article 23(1) which provides that the Article 23(1)(c) credit must be allowed in accordance with the provisions and subject to the limitations of the law of the United States, the timing of the credit is to be determined as a matter of U.S. law.

We discern no substantive change from the Treaty provisions. The Agreement summarizes the Treaty purpose and its implementation as applied to the ACT, deplores the taking of double credit in the United States, and confirms that United States law applies to the timing of the credit. Xerox points out that this Agreement did not treat the important aspects of the Treasury's litigation position, such as that the Article 23 credit is only provisional, or that downstream surrender of the Section 85 offset in the United Kingdom permits or requires revocation of the Article 23 credit.

The Treasury states that paragraph 5 of the Agreement is important because it provides that United States law determines the timing of the credit, and that revenue Procedure 80–18 "elaborates" United States law and thus controls this case. As we have discussed supra, a Revenue Procedure is neither law nor regulation, and is not binding on the courts. The Competent Authority Agreement is silent on the Section 85 offset and the effect of when and how that offset is used in the United Kingdom. This was the main issue in dispute, then and now. The omission from the Agreement of the positions taken in this Revenue Procedure and the earlier Technical Explanation appears to us to emphasize the weaknesses in the government's argument.

The Agreement's affirmation that the timing of the tax credit is governed by United States law directs us to the Internal Revenue Code. As we next discuss, the Code allows the United States taxpayer an indirect foreign tax credit for, inter alia, income taxes paid by the foreign corporation on dividends to the United States shareholder, the credit to be taken when the foreign tax is paid or accrued.

Finally, there is no issue here of double tax credit in the United States. Although the government devotes a significant portion of its brief to this spectre, it is undisputed that this taxpayer has not received single tax credit, and has made no claim that is suspect on this ground.

F.   The Internal Revenue Code Provisions

A treaty, when ratified, supersedes prior domestic law to the contrary, United States v. Lee Yen Tai, 185 U.S. 213, 220–22, 46 L. Ed. 878, 22 S. Ct. 629 (1902), and is equivalent to an act of Congress. However, tacit abrogation of prior law will not be presumed and, unless it is impossible to do so, treaty and law must stand together in harmony. In this case there is easy harmony between the Treaty and the United States law governing foreign tax credits, §§ 901–906 of the Internal Revenue Code of 1954.

In construing the tax law, as for any statute, the starting point is the words of the statute, Bread Political Action Committee v. Federal

Election Commission, 455 U.S. 577, 580, 71 L. Ed. 2d 432, 102 S. Ct. 1235 (1982), taking the words in their ordinary meaning in the field of interest, Perrin v. United States, 444 U.S. 37, 42, 62 L. Ed. 2d 199, 100 S. Ct. 311 (1979), and giving full effect to "every word Congress used." Reiter v. Sonotone Corp., 442 U.S. 330, 339, 60 L. Ed. 2d 931, 99 S. Ct. 2326 (1979). As a special rule in tax cases, "if doubt exists as to the construction of a taxing statute, the doubt should be resolved in favor of the taxpayer." Hassett v. Welch, 303 U.S. 303, 314, 82 L. Ed. 858, 58 S. Ct. 559 (1938); Auto-Ordnance Corp. v. United States, 822 F.2d 1566, 1571 (Fed.Cir.1987).

26 U.S.C. § 902

Revenue Code § 902 authorizes, inter alia, a tax credit under 26 U.S.C. § 901 for income taxes paid to a foreign government when a domestic corporation owns at least 10 percent of the voting stock of a foreign corporation from which it receives dividends in any taxable year. The Treaty, by defining ACT as an income tax, brought ACT within the purview of § 902. In accordance with § 902(a), the domestic corporation shall "be deemed to have paid the same proportion of any income ... taxes paid or deemed to be paid by such foreign corporation to any foreign country ... on or with respect to such accumulated profits." Section 902 also includes provisions relating to second and third tier foreign corporations that pay dividends through their parent corporation to the United States corporation.

Each party states that § 902 supports its position. The government states that since § 902 permits a tax credit involving second tier foreign corporations, credit for the ACT paid by RXL in 1974 was properly reversed when RXL surrendered the Section 85 offset to its subsidiaries. The government's position is that credit for this ACT can not be allowed to Xerox until "each foreign subsidiary up the line distributes dividends to its parent."

We do not share this reasoning. The ACT here at issue was for dividends that were paid to Xerox in 1974; the ACT on those dividends was paid by RXL in the United Kingdom in 1974, and was not refundable or reversible. The second-tier RXL subsidiaries did not pay, and had no obligation to pay, the ACT on those dividends. The ACT obligation by RXL was completed in 1974, and was not defeasible by whether, when, or how RXL used its offset rights under United Kingdom law, including whether and when the offset was surrendered to RXL's subsidiaries in the United Kingdom.

In accordance with § 901 and 902, Xerox was entitled to the credit when the dividends were distributed to Xerox and the ACT thereon was paid or accrued by RXL, see § 905. The straightforward reading of the Code provisions firmly links the foreign tax credit to the payment to the United States shareholder of dividends on which foreign income tax was paid. In United States v. Goodyear the Court reaffirmed that under § 902 the dividends received by the United States parent must be sourced to the year in which the foreign subsidiary paid the foreign tax, citing "§ 902's statutory goal of avoiding double taxation." Goodyear, 493 U.S. at 144. That principle is not served by the government's theory.

In view of our conclusion that the conditions now imposed on ACT credits have no support in § 902 and are contrary thereto, we do not reach Xerox's alternative argument that in accordance with § 902 Xerox is entitled to the tax credit even without recourse to the Treaty.

26 U.S.C. § 905

The government also relies on Code Section 905, which relates to adjustments to and accounting periods for indirect foreign tax credits. Section 905(a) allows the foreign tax credit to be taken in the year in which the foreign tax accrues, and requires consistency in accounting:

§ 905(a) Year in which credit taken.

The credits provided in this subpart may, at the option of the taxpayer and irrespective of the method of accounting employed in keeping his books, be taken in the year in which the taxes of the foreign country or the possession of the United States accrued, subject, however, to the conditions prescribed in subsection (c). If the taxpayer elects to take such credits in the year in which the taxes of the foreign country or the possession of the United States accrued, the credits for all subsequent years shall be taken on the same basis, and no portion of any such taxes shall be allowed as a deduction in the same or any succeeding year.

Section 905(c) does not determine entitlement, but authorizes recalculation of the tax credit if the amount of foreign tax is refunded or adjusted after the credit is taken.

§ 905(c) Adjustments on payment of accrued taxes.

If accrued taxes when paid differ from the amounts claimed as credits by the taxpayer, or if any tax paid is refunded in whole or in part, the taxpayer shall notify the Secretary or his delegate, who shall redetermine the amount of tax for the year or years affected. The amount of tax due on such redetermination, if any, shall be [paid or credited]. . . . In such redetermination by the Secretary or his delegate of the amount of tax due from the taxpayer for the year or years affected by a refund, the amount of the taxes refunded for which credit has been allowed under this section shall be reduced by the amount of any tax described in section 901 imposed by the foreign country or possession of the United States with respect to such refund; but no credit under this subpart, and no deduction under section 164 (relating to deduction for taxes) shall be allowed for any taxable year with respect to such tax imposed on the refund. . . .

The Court of Federal Claims erred in its reliance on § 905(c) as substantive basis for the withdrawal of credit upon the 1980 surrender by RXL of the Section 85 offset. Section 905(c) indeed permits redetermination of the foreign tax credit when any foreign tax is refunded or adjusted. However, the ACT paid in 1974 was not refunded or adjusted in 1980. The movement of the Section 85 offset from British parent to subsidiary is not a refund or adjustment of the ACT. This tax obligation in the United Kingdom was fixed and paid in 1974, when the dividends were paid to Xerox. It is not refundable, and no adjustment of the 1974 United States tax credit is warranted. Neither § 902 nor § 905 supports the reversal or postponement of credit for the ACT paid by RXL in 1974.

CONCLUSION

Review of the evidence and arguments persuades us that the Treaty's meaning on this issue is plain and unambiguous, and that it should not be construed contrary to its clear purpose of avoidance of double taxation. It is inappropriate for courts to depart from the purpose and import of a treaty, "particularly [when] there is no indication that application of the words of the treaty according to their obvious meaning effects a result inconsistent with the intent or expectations of its signatories." Maximov v. United States, 373 U.S. 49, 54, 10 L. Ed. 2d 184, 83 S. Ct. 1054 (1963).

The ACT is a separate tax, and is not properly viewed as a prepayment or interim credit or estimated tax of mainstream corporate tax. The ACT does not become provisional by virtue of the offset procedures available under United Kingdom law. The Treaty requires that the unrepaid (under Article 10) portion of the ACT be "treated as an income tax," Article 23(c), thus accommodating § 901 et seq. of the Revenue Code.

We conclude that the ACT is creditable in the United States, in accordance with § 902, in the year it is paid or accrued in the United Kingdom. RXL's subsequent disposition of its offset rights under the Finance Act of 1972 did not defeat the foreign tax credit for ACT, which vested in Xerox when the tax and dividends were paid

The decision of the Court of Federal Claims is reversed. Payment of the claimed refund is ordered, calculated in accordance with law.

COSTS

Costs in favor of Xerox.

REVERSED

NOTES AND QUESTIONS

1. Why was the ACT not creditable, absent the Treaty? Does the court understand this?

2. What was the point of the competent authorities' agreement? Why did the U.S. believe it settled the question?

3. What was the double credit issue? What happens when the RXL subsidiaries pay a dividend to Xerox?

4.   Note the various sources used by the court to interpret the treaty. Should the testimony of the negotiators be accepted? Do you think it likely that the U.K. was unaware of the Technical Explanation? Is there a discrepancy between the testimony of the U.S. and U.K. negotiators? Why? See further discussion in 11.4 below.

11.4   INTERNATIONAL TAX AS INTERNATIONAL LAW

The following text explores the relationship between international tax law (as embodied in treaties and in domestic law) and (public and private) international law.

Avi-Yonah, International Tax as International Law
57 Tax L. Rev. 483 (2004).

1.   Introduction: Is International Tax Law Part of International Law?

To an international lawyer, the question posed above probably seems ridiculous. *Of course* international tax law is part of international law, just like tax treaties are treaties. But to an international *tax* lawyer, the question probably seems less obvious, because most international tax lawyers do not think of themselves primarily as international lawyers (public or private), but rather as tax lawyers who happen to deal with cross-border transactions. And indeed, once we delve into the details, it becomes clear that in some ways international tax law is different from "regular" international law. For example, international tax lawyers talk about residence and source jurisdiction, not nationality and territoriality-and as we shall see, the different names also carry different content. And while tax treaties are indeed treaties, they are concluded differently than other treaties (e.g., they are negotiated by the Treasury, not the State Department), are subject to different modes of interpretation (the Vienna Convention on the Law of Treaties ("VCLT"), the "Bible" of the international lawyer, is rarely invoked), and in the United States are subject to a rather peculiar mode of unilateral change, the treaty override.

The purpose of this essay is to introduce to the international lawyer the somewhat different set of categories employed by international tax lawyers, and explain the reasons for some of the differences. At the same time, I hope to persuade practicing international tax lawyers and international tax academics that their field is indeed part of international law, and that it would help them to think of it this way. For example, I believe that knowledge of the VCLT would help international tax lawyers in interpreting tax treaties, and avoid some common mistakes.

This essay is divided into five parts. After this introduction, Part 2 discusses international jurisdiction to tax and how it differs from traditional international law concepts of jurisdiction. The issues addressed in this Part are familiar to international tax lawyers but may be new and interesting for international lawyers. Part 3 discusses tax treaties and how they differ from regular treaties in both interpretation and modification. Here, international tax lawyers can learn from international lawyers, but also vice versa. Part 4 discusses the difficult and much debated question whether there exists an international customary tax law. In this context it is international tax lawyers who have most to gain by listening to international lawyers. Part 5 concludes by returning to the question posed above, answering in the affirmative, and then summarizing the ways international tax lawyers and international lawyers can learn from each other.

2. Jurisdiction to Tax.

The traditional grounds of jurisdiction to prescribe in international law are *nationality* ("the activities, interest, status or relations of [a state's] nationals outside as well as within its territory") and *territoriality* ("conduct that, wholly or in substantial part, takes place within [a state's] territory"). Territoriality is expanded to cover conduct outside a state's territory that has, or is intended to have, a "substantial effect" within its territory. As we shall see, international tax law modifies both concepts to a significant extent, resulting primarily in expanding the scope of nationality jurisdiction.

a. Individuals: Redefinition of Nationality Jurisdiction as Residence.

Nationality is usually understood as equivalent to citizenship. However, except for the United States, almost no other country in the world claims the right to tax its citizens on foreign source income when they live permanently in another country. The United States insists on the right to tax its citizens on worldwide income no matter where they live. This was upheld by the Supreme Court in *Cook v. Tait* because of the benefits the U.S. provides its citizens even if they live overseas. But the opinion is weak, its underlying rationale is doubtful (are these benefits really so great?) and almost no other country follows the rule. Thus, although international law seems to sanction the U.S. practice (and the U.S. has written it into all its tax treaties), it seems a dubious rule to follow, and it has been criticized by academics.

Instead, every country in the world (including the United States) has adopted a definition of nationality for tax purposes that is much broader than how nationality is commonly understood. That definition is residence, which usually implies mere physical presence in the country for a minimum number of days. In the U.S., physical presence for 183 days in a given year is generally sufficient to subject an individual to taxing jurisdiction on her world-wide income for that year. Even fewer days suffice if added to days spent in the U.S. in the previous two years. Other countries follow a similar rule, although they sometimes supplement it with a "fiscal domicile" test that looks to less bright line factors such as location of principal abode, family ties, and the like. The two tests (physical presence and fiscal domicile) are also incorporated into tax treaties.

This definition is a remarkable expansion of the concept of nationality. I doubt there is another substantive area of international law in which nationality jurisdiction for individuals rests on so flimsy a ground as mere physical presence. In fact, because of this expansive view, it is easy to be subject to residence-based taxation by a country in one year and not in the next, and it is also easy for individuals to have dual tax residency. Elaborate rules are needed to address situations in which individuals move in and out of resident status from year to year (e.g., rules on deemed sales of their property when they leave), and to avoid dual residence double taxation.

Why has nationality based jurisdiction been so expanded in tax law? The reason is easy to see if one considers the implications of the relative ease of acquiring a tax haven nationality. If tax law followed the general international law rule and imposed world-wide taxation only on citizens, then a lot of U.S. citizens would abandon their citizenship in exchange for that of some Caribbean tax haven jurisdiction, and thereby avoid taxation on their foreign source income while living permanently in the United States. In general, living in a country for over half a year is considered a sufficient ground for world-wide taxation because of the presumed benefits derived from that country.

The residence rule is so widely followed and incorporated into so many treaties that it can be considered part of customary international law, even though it seems contrary to widely shared understandings of nationality (see part 4 below). It is thus appropriate for the United States to follow this rule. It is doubtful, however, whether the U.S. should continue to insist on taxing its citizens living overseas, especially since because of a combination of exemptions and credits (and enforcement difficulties) it collects little tax from them.

b.   Corporations: Expansion of Nationality Jurisdiction to CFCs.

The nationality of corporations is a thorny issue, which comes up in other areas of the law as well. In general, corporations are considered nationals based either on the country in which they are incorporated (the U.S. approach), or the country from which they are managed and controlled (the U.K. approach), or both. Each approach has its advantages and disadvantages; the U.S. approach is the easiest to administer but also the most manipulable, as shown recently by so-called "inversion" transactions in which corporations shifted their nominal country of incorporation to Bermuda while retaining all of their headquarters and management in the United States. The U.K. approach is less easily manipulated but requires more administrative resources to police.

The interesting aspect of nationality jurisdiction for corporations in tax law is the gradual adoption of a rule that permits countries to tax "controlled foreign corporations" (CFCs), i.e., corporations controlled by nationals, as if they were nationals themselves. This rule originated with the United States. Because the definition of corporate nationality in the U.S. is formal (country of incorporation), it is easy for U.S. nationals (residents) who have foreign source income to avoid taxation on such income by shifting it to a corporation incorporated in another country, preferably a tax haven, where it can accumulate tax free. For example, Jacob Schick, the inventor of the Schick disposable razor, transferred his patent to it to a Bermuda corporation which accumulated the royalties; Schick later proceeded to retire to Bermuda, gave up his U.S. citizenship, and lived on the accumulated tax-free profits.

To address this problem, the U.S. adopted in 1937 a rule which taxed shareholders in "foreign personal holding corporations" (FPHCs). FPHC was defined as a foreign corporation controlled (over 50% by vote) by five or fewer U.S. resident individuals, and whose income was over 60% passive (since passive income was considered easier to shift than active income). Interestingly, at the time, the U.S. considered it a breach of international law to tax a FPHC (a foreign national) directly on foreign source income; instead, it adopted a rule that taxed the U.S. shareholders on a deemed dividend of the accumulated passive income of the FPHC. This rule can be compared to the personal holding company (PHC) regime adopted at the same time, which applied to domestic corporations and taxed them directly on their accumulated income at the shareholder rate (PHCs were used by shareholders to shelter U.S. source income from the higher individual rate by earning the income through a corporation subject to tax at a lower rate).

The deemed dividend rule was upheld by Judge Frank of the Second Circuit without paying any attention to its international law implications. And yet, it clearly represented a major expansion of U.S. residence taxing jurisdiction, since taxing a deemed dividend is economically equivalent to taxing a foreign corporation directly on foreign source income. It could certainly be argued in 1943 that this rule was a breach of international law, just like Judge Hand's *Alcoa* antitrust decision (1945), which invented the effects doctrine, was likewise arguably a breach of international law.

The impact of the deemed dividend rule was greatly expanded when the Kennedy administration decided in 1961 to propose applying the same rule to all income of corporations that are over 50% controlled by large (10% by vote each) U.S. shareholders, i.e., to subsidiaries of U.S. multinationals (CFCs). Ultimately, this resulted in the enactment in 1962 of "Subpart F" which applied the deemed dividend rule to certain types of income (mostly passive income) of all CFCs.

Again, there was no international law challenge to the deemed dividend rule. Instead, other countries began to copy the CFC regime:

Germany (1972), Canada (1975), Japan (1978), France (1980), the U.K. (1984). Currently, there are 23 countries with CFC rules (mostly developed ones), and the number is likely to increase. Thus, it would seem that the CFC concept has arguably become part of customary international law, just like the expansion of territorial jurisdiction over international waters rapidly changed international law from the 1970s onward.

Even more striking is the fact that many of the countries adopting the CFC rule abandoned the deemed dividend idea, which can lead to significant difficulties in practice, in favor of direct taxation of the CFC's shareholders on its earnings on a pass-through basis. Thus, the jurisdictional rule has been changing and no longer seems to require a deemed dividend, and may even permit direct taxation of a CFC on its foreign source income because it is controlled by residents. Indeed, the IRS itself has adopted this view, because it now believes that both the PHC regime, as well as the older accumulated earnings tax regime, apply directly to foreign corporations even though their effect is to tax the corporation on foreign source income. This is particularly striking for PHCs, because it was so clear in 1937 that the U.S. had no jurisdiction to tax foreign corporations on foreign source income that Congress did not bother to specify that a PHC could not be a foreign corporation (while at the same time adopting the parallel FPHC regime explicitly for foreign corporations). Now this oversight enables the IRS to argue that under the new understanding of jurisdictional limits, the PHC rules as well as the FPHC rules apply to foreign corporations.

Claiming that nationality jurisdiction applies to foreign corporations just because they are controlled by nationals is a striking departure from ordinary international law. Compare, for example, the oft recurring disputes about the extraterritorial application of international sanctions. In both the Fruehauf (1965) and Sensor (1982) cases, the foreign courts explicitly rejected U.S. claims to require foreign subsidiaries of U.S. multinationals to obey U.S. sanctions aimed at China and the USSR, respectively. In Sensor, the Dutch court went through all the possible grounds for jurisdiction and explicitly found that none applied. It was clear that nationality jurisdiction did not apply even though the subsidiary was controlled from the United States.

What, then, enables the United States and other countries to expand nationality jurisdiction to subsidiaries in the tax area? The explanation is the "first bite at the apple rule", adopted by the League of Nations in 1923. Under that rule, the source (territorial) jurisdiction has the primary right to tax income arising within it, and the residence (nationality) jurisdiction is obligated to prevent double taxation by granting an exemption or a credit. Thus, permitting the expansion of residence jurisdiction to CFCs does not harm the right of source jurisdictions to tax them first; residence (nationality) jurisdiction only applies as a residual matter when the source jurisdiction abstains from taxing. This still leads sometimes to complaints by source jurisdictions that the residence jurisdiction is taking away their right to effectively grant tax holidays to foreign investors, but even that is mitigated by the restricted application of CFC rules to passive income.

In general, I believe this story is a good illustration of the growth of customary international law in the tax area. In the 1930–1960s period, there was a clear rule of customary international law that prohibited taxing foreign corporations on foreign source income. That rule was universally observed and was considered binding, as illustrated by the U.S. avoiding an outright breach through the deemed dividend mechanism. However, once a lot of countries changed the rule by taxing shareholders directly on CFC income, the U.S. did not consider it binding any more, as indicated by applying the PHC regime to foreign corporations. The next step for the U.S. would be to abolish the obsolete deemed dividend rule and replace it by a direct tax on the CFCs.

c.   The Problem of Territorial Jurisdiction (Source).

The right of countries to tax income arising in their territory is well established in international law. In fact, some countries (e.g., France) begin with the assumption that the only income they have the right to tax is domestic source income, although France and other territorial jurisdictions have long since begun to tax some income of nationals from foreign sources. And even countries that begin with worldwide taxation of nationals, like the U.S. and the U.K., in practice do not tax as heavily foreign source income.

The special problem of territoriality in the tax area is that the source of income is very difficult to define. In fact, most public finance economists would deny that it is a meaningful concept in the majority of cases. Think of a law firm in country A that provides advice on the legal implications of a merger of two multinationals whose parents are in countries A and B and whose operations are in twenty countries around the globe. What is the economic source of the law firm's income?

Ideally, one could imagine a world in which all countries tax only on a nationality (residence) basis, and the only problem would be assigning residence to individuals (not too hard) and to corporations (quite difficult). But in practice, as long as countries desire to tax non-residents on domestic source income, as they have every right to do under international law, the problem of defining source would persist.

To some extent the problem has been solved by arbitrary rules embodied in tax treaties (and that in my view may form part of customary international law) that define the source of various categories of income. For example, income from services is sourced where the services are provided (and not where they are consumed); dividend and interest income are sourced by the residence of the payor; capital gains are sourced by the residence of the seller; and so on. The difficulty then becomes deciding which category income falls into, which is sometimes very hard (consider for example how to distinguish between sales, services and royalty income when downloading software off the internet, buying it in a store, or receiving it in a pre-installed package on a PC).

In the case of multinationals, the sourcing issue becomes even harder because taxing them requires allocating the income of a controlled group of corporations among taxing jurisdictions. If tax authorities merely followed the form (regarding which subsidiary nominally earned the income from inter-group transactions), all income of multinationals would be booked in tax haven subsidiaries. A whole branch of tax law called transfer pricing is devoted to resolving this problem. In Part 4, I will return to this point, because it provides a good illustration of customary international tax law.

The main point here is simply that territoriality, which is a relatively easy concept to define in international law in general, becomes very hard when tax law is concerned. And it may be a pity that international law makes it so easy to tax foreigners on a territoriality basis, although as long as we want to tax corporations, I suspect that source-based taxation is inevitable (since the residence of corporations is inherently more manipulable and less meaningful than the residence of individuals).

3.   Tax Treaties.

a.   Treaty Interpretation and the VCLT.

Tax treaties are, of course, treaties: They are considered by the Senate Foreign Relations Committee (and not the Finance Committee) and ratified by the Senate just like any other treaty. But they are also unlike other treaties. First, they are negotiated by the International Tax Counsel in the Treasury's Office of Tax Policy, not by the State Department. Second, their interpretation is governed primarily by the Technical Explanation, which is likewise drafted by the Treasury and not by State. And finally, the ways tax treaties are interpreted differ markedly from the interpretation of other treaties.

The biggest difference relates to the role of the VCLT. Bederman writes that "[t]he VCLT is, quite literally, a treaty on treaties. Almost every question of treaty law is settled in that document, and it is an essential bit of reading for every international lawyer." But not for the international *tax* lawyer. A search of the tax cases database in LEXIS revealed among hundreds of treaty interpretation cases only one quite recent case in which a court discussed the potential application of the VCLT.

It is true, of course, that the United States signed but never ratified the VCLT; but this does not prevent American international lawyers from relying on it in non-tax contests as embodying customary international law (in fact, having signed the VCLT, the U.S. is supposed not to act contrary to it, VCLT Art. 18). Rather, the lack of reference to the VCLT in tax treaty cases simply results from the fact that most tax lawyers have never heard of it. Instead, they rely for example on the

OECD commentary on the OECD model tax treaty, which is frequently cited in treaty interpretation cases.

This can sometimes lead to unfortunate, even bizarre, results. For example, VCLT Art. 31 states a general rule that treaties should be interpreted "in good faith in accordance with the ordinary meaning to be given to the terms of the treaty in their context and in light of its object and purpose". "Context" for this purpose includes any subsequent protocols and contemporaneous instruments relating to the treaty, and subsequent practice relating to implementation. VCLT Art. 32 states that as supplementary sources recourse may be had to "preparatory work of the treaty and the circumstances of its conclusion", but only "to confirm the meaning resulting from the application of article 31" or to "determine the meaning when interpretation according to article 31 (a) leaves the meaning ambiguous or obscure; or (b) leads to a result which is manifestly absurd or unreasonable."

Now consider the case of *Xerox Corporation v. United States.* That case involved a highly technical question on the interpretation of the 1975 U.S.-U.K. tax treaty. As the Court of Claims saw it, the IRS view of the matter was supported by (a) the language of the treaty itself, (b) the contemporaneous technical explanation, (c) IRS practice as evidenced by a Revenue Procedure, and (d) a subsequent agreement between the competent authorities designed to settle the matter. Instead, the Court of Appeals chose to ignore all of those sources and rely instead on affidavits submitted to it by the treaty negotiators as to what they meant. It is hard to imagine such a result under the VCLT, since all the Art. 31 sources supported the IRS and the affidavits (at best Art. 32, and therefore inferior, sources) were not even contemporaneous with the treaty but executed years later when the affiants were in private practice and had no stake in protecting the fisc. Not surprisingly, it is hard to defend the result in *Xerox* from a pure tax perspective either; the general consensus is that the corporation "got away with murder".

My point here is simply that it would be a good idea for international tax lawyers to study the VCLT. A lot of hard thinking went into that treaty, and it should not lightly be ignored.

b.   Treaty Overrides.

The most notorious difference between tax treaties and other U.S. treaties is the frequency of treaty overrides (other treaties are overridden, but much less frequently). Under international law, *pacta sunt servanda*; "Every treaty in force is binding upon the parties and must be performed by them in good faith" (VCLT Art. 26). "A party may not invoke the provisions of its internal law as justification for its failure to perform a treaty". VCLT Art. 27.

Under U.S. law, however, treaties are under the Supremacy Clause of the constitution equal in standing to regular laws. Therefore, at least as interpreted by the Supreme Court, the general rule of later in time controls. In the tax context this rule has been embodied in IRC 7852(d), which states that "[f]or purposes of determining the relationship between a provision of a treaty and any law of the United States affecting revenue, neither the treaty nor the law shall have preferential status by reason of its being a treaty or law."

Of course, this unique U.S. interpretation applies to all U.S. treaties, not just to tax treaties. But at least in recent years, its clearest manifestation has been in the tax area. The reason that tax is particularly sensitive in this context is first, that tax law changes all the time while treaties are slow to renegotiate, and second, that the U.S. House of Representatives has a special role to play in the tax area (all revenue measures must originate with it), but is excluded from involvement with treaties, and therefore insists on its right to change tax treaties through legislation even though this clearly violates customary international law as embodied in the VCLT.

But the interesting question is, when does the U.S. resort to treaty overrides? The answer is rarely, and that when it does so deliberately, an argument can be made that it is justified in doing so. Consider three recent cases from the period 1986–1997: the branch profits tax, the earnings stripping rule, and the reverse hybrid rule.

The branch profits tax (BPT) was enacted in 1986 to equalize the position of foreign investors who operate in the U.S. through a subsidiary and through a branch. Before 1986, investors who operated through a subsidiary were subject to tax on the subsidiary's income and also to a withholding tax on dividends, whereas investors who operated through a branch were only subject to a tax on the branch income because distributions from the branch were not a dividend and not subject to withholding tax. Under the branch profit tax, distributions from a branch were made subject to withholding tax. But a problem arose: Many US tax treaties forbad taxing distributions from foreign corporations resident in a treaty country to their foreign shareholders even if the distribution came out of earnings of a U.S. branch, and arguably the branch profits tax violated the spirit of this rule (although not its letter). So did the U.S. resort to treaty override? It did not. Instead, it announced that the BPT will not apply to residents of those treaty countries until the treaties were renegotiated to permit the BPT. In fact, by now most U.S. treaties have been so renegotiated, and other countries have adopted the BPT in their own laws.

But this left the U.S. in a difficult position, because while treaties were slowly renegotiated, it could collect the BPT on some branches but not on others. At the time, there were no limitation on benefits provisions in U.S. treaties, leading to a concern that there would be widespread treaty shopping (i.e., setting up a corporation in a treaty jurisdiction just to benefit from the treaty). So the U.S. inserted a limitation on benefits provision into the BPT rule in the Code and made that an explicit treaty override. Was it justified? I believe that an underlying assumption of treaties is that they are only intended to benefit bona fide residents (otherwise, any treaty becomes a "treaty with the world"). Thus, I think the override was justified because it is consistent with the underlying purpose of the treaties. But countries like the Netherlands that later negotiated much longer limitation on benefits provisions that were full of loopholes may have had reason to be miffed, because they derive revenue by letting their treaties be used for treaty shopping.

Next, consider the earnings stripping rule, adopted in 1989. That rule is a "thin capitalization" provision, i.e., it is intended to prevent foreign parents from eliminating the tax base of their U.S. subsidiaries (or branches) through interest deductions by capitalizing them mostly with debt rather than equity. When the rule was adopted the U.S. was very worried it will appear to be a violation of the non-discrimination provision in tax treaties if it applied only to foreign related parties. Thus, to avoid even the appearance of a treaty override, the U.S. instead applied the rule to all "tax exempt related parties", i.e., to domestic tax exempts as well as foreigners. But this was an obvious ruse, since no domestic tax exempts are ever related (i.e., control over 50%) to domestic taxable subsidiaries. Nor do I believe the ruse was necessary, because in fact most countries have a thin capitalization rule and apply it explicitly to foreigners. I thus believe thin capitalization is an accepted customary international law exception to non-discrimination, which is necessary because the source country has the primary right to tax active business income and without thin capitalization that base can easily disappear. What is striking, though, is how reluctant the U.S. was to override treaties.

Finally, consider the reverse hybrid rule, adopted by the U.S. as a treaty override in 1997. The rule was adopted in response to a transaction in which a Canadian parent set up a limited liability company (LLC) in the U.S. and capitalized it with what was for Canadian purposes equity but for U.S. purposes was treated as debt. The LLC was treated as a branch by the U.S. but as a subsidiary by Canada. The result was that from a U.S. perspective the tax on the branch was offset by interest deductions on the debt with a reduced rate of withholding tax under the treaty, but from a Canadian perspective the income was treated as exempt dividends from a controlled subsidiary. Hence double non-taxation. The U.S. could have (and indeed later did) renegotiate the treaty, but this takes time, and a lot of revenue was being lost. Hence the treaty override, which Canada did not object to, which denied treaty benefits to such a "reverse hybrid". Fundamentally, I believe the override was justified because the purpose of tax treaties is to prevent double taxation and not enable double non-taxation; reductions of tax at source should be premised on taxation by the residence jurisdiction.

So in all of these cases I think an override was justified. The reality is that tax law and practice change too fast to wait for treaties to be renegotiated. Still, overrides should be used sparingly and only when consistent with the underlying purpose of the treaty. And there are unjustified overrides, such as the provision of the alternative minimum tax (AMT) that limits the foreign tax credit to 90%.[1] That leads directly to double taxation and is not justifiable in the treaty context, but courts (including recently the *Kappus* court) have accepted it as a valid override (even though Congress did not explicitly designate it as such).

4. Is There A Customary International Tax Law?

Customary international law is law that "results from a general and consistent practice of states followed by them from a sense of legal obligation." "International agreements create law for states parties thereto and may lead to the creation of customary international law when such agreements are intended for adherence by states generally and are in fact widely accepted."

There clearly are international tax practices that are widely followed, such as for example avoiding double taxation by granting an exemption for foreign source income or a credit for foreign taxes. Moreover, there are over 2,000 bilateral tax treaties in existence, and they all follow one of two widely accepted models (the OECD and UN model treaties), which themselves are quite similar to each other and are "intended for adherence by states generally." Is this enough to create a customary international tax law?

This question is hotly debated among international tax lawyers, although it is not usually couched in these terms. Instead, the debate is about whether countries are bound by an "international tax regime" or "international tax system", or whether international tax is only about the law adopted by each country and the treaties it binds itself with. Specifically, the debate is about international tax arbitrage, i.e., transactions that utilize differences between tax laws to achieve double non-taxation. On the one side are those who argue that there is nothing wrong with tax arbitrage since there is no "international tax regime" and each country is free to do as it likes, so taxpayers are also free to exploit differences. On the other hand are those who argue that countries are not so free and that a coherent international tax regime does exist. The debate is in part about specific provisions in U.S. law that are designed to prevent double non-taxation, such as the dual consolidated loss rules (which prevent taxpayers from claiming the same loss to offset income in two taxing jurisdictions). If there is no international tax regime, such rules make no sense. Similarly, rules such as those promulgated by the Treasury in 1998, which prevent taxpayers from using tax arbitrage to reduce *foreign* taxes, are very controversial.

In the following, I will briefly survey some examples that in my opinion strengthen the view that an international tax regime does exist and that it rises to the level of customary international law. As usual, the

---

[1] Repealed in the 2004 tax act.

hard question is whether countries not only follow a rule, but do so out of a sense of legal obligation *(opinio juris)*.

a. Jurisdiction to Tax.

Can a country simply decide to tax non-residents that have no connection to it on foreign source income? The answer is clearly no, both from a practical perspective and, I would argue, from a customary international law perspective. The fact that this rule is followed from a sense of legal obligation is illustrated by the behavior of the U.S. in adopting the FPHC and CFC rules described above. The deemed dividend rule was adopted precisely because the U.S. felt bound by a customary international law rule not to tax non-residents directly on foreign source income, even though they are controlled by residents. The U.S. no longer feels bound by this rule, but that is because enough other countries have adopted CFC legislation that expands the definition of nationality that customary international law has changed. The spread of CFC legislation is a good example of how rapidly customary international law can in fact change.

b. Non-discrimination.

The non-discrimination norm (i.e., that non-residents from a treaty country should not be treated worse than residents) is embodied in all tax treaties. But is it part of customary international law? The behavior of the U.S. in the earnings stripping episode suggests that the U.S. felt at the time that the non-discrimination norm was binding even outside the treaty context. Otherwise, even if it did not wish to override treaties, it could have applied a different rule to non-treaty country residents (as it did in the branch profits tax context three years earlier). Thus, I would argue that the non-discrimination norm may in fact be part of customary international law even in the absence of a treaty.

c. The Arm's Length Standard.

The standard applied in all tax treaties to the transfer pricing problem of determining the proper allocation of profits between related entities is the "arm's length standard", which means that transactions between related parties may be adjusted by the tax authorities to the terms that would have been negotiated had the parties been unrelated to each other. This standard has been the governing rule since the 1930s.

In the 1980s, the U.S. realized that in many circumstances it is very difficult to find comparable transactions between unrelated parties on which to base the arm's length determination. It therefore began the process of revising the regulations that govern transfer pricing. This culminated in 1995 with the adoption of two new methods, the comparable profit method and profit split method, that rely much less on finding comparables (and in the case of profit split sometimes require no comparables at all).

What is remarkable about the process by which these regulations were adopted is the U.S. insistence throughout that what it was doing was consistent with the arm's length standard. It even initially called profit split the "basic arm's length return method." But as I have pointed out elsewhere, once you abandon the search for comparables, it is meaningless to call a method "arm's length", because without comparables nobody can know what unrelated parties would have done.

Nevertheless, despite initial objections, the OECD ultimately came to accept the gist of the new methods in its revised transfer pricing guidelines, which were issued a short time after the new U.S. regulations and represent the widely followed consensus view of transfer pricing. The new methods are thus accepted under the rubric of "arm's length".

As Brian Leppard has suggested, the U.S. insistence that it was following the arm's length standard indicates that it felt that the standard is part of customary international law. Such a finding has important implications because the U.S. states explicitly follow a non-arm's length method, formulary apportionment, which has been twice upheld by the U.S. Supreme Court. If the arm's length method is customary international law, these cases may have been wrongly decided, as customary international law is part of federal law and arguably preempts contrary state law.

d.   Foreign Tax Credits vs. Deductions.

Many economists argue that countries should only give a deduction for foreign taxes rather than a credit. However, countries generally grant either an exemption for foreign source income or a credit for foreign taxes paid. Remarkably, in most cases (following the lead of the US) this is done even in the absence of a treaty. It is likely that at this point countries consider themselves in practice bound by the credit or exemption norm, and a country would feel highly reluctant to switch to a deduction method instead. Thus, arguably preventing double taxation through a credit or exemption has become part of customary international law.

e.   Conclusion.

If customary international tax law exists, this has important implications for the U.S. and other countries. As Justice Gray wrote over a century ago in the *Paquete Habana* case, "[I]nternational law is part of our law, and must be ascertained and administered by the courts of justice of appropriate jurisdiction as often as questions of right depending upon it are duly presented for their determination. For this purpose, where there is no treaty and no controlling executive or legislative act or judicial decision, resort must be had to the customs and usages of civilized nations." To the extent legislation exists, it can in the U.S. override customary international law as well as treaties. But in the absence of treaties or legislation, resort can be had to customary international law; and I would argue that it can also be used to ascertain the underlying purposes of treaties.

To the extent that customary international tax law exists, this suggests that it is a mistake to deny the existence of an international tax system or regime. Admittedly, even if an international tax regime exists, it does not follow what we should do about it-this has to be investigated in each particular case. But we should not pretend that there are no binding, widely accepted international tax norms that we should flout only when significant national interests are at stake.

5. Conclusion.

Clearly, international tax law is part of international law, even if it differs in some of its details from generally applicable international law. I believe both international lawyers and international tax lawyers can benefit from viewing international tax law in this way. For international lawyers, the tax field is an interesting arena to test some of their ideas. It offers them a different view of nationality and territoriality jurisdiction, which can perhaps be profitably carried over into other fields (I believe it would help, for example, to take control generally into account in determining the nationality of corporations). It also offers interesting examples of how customary international law can change rapidly, as in the CFC case. Finally, it suggests that even a basic rule like *pacta sunt servanda* may sometimes have its exceptions if one wishes to preserve the rationale of the underlying treaty.

I believe, however, that it is international tax lawyers who can benefit the most from viewing their field as part of international law. For example, knowing the VCLT can prevent mistakes such as those committed in *Xerox*. And understanding that international tax law can be seen in significant part as customary international law can help clarify some of the constraints facing a country like the U.S. as it struggles to adapt its international tax laws to the business realities of the 21st century.

11.5 REVIEW QUESTIONS—CHAPTER 11

This is a unique chapter because treaties cover all the topics discussed in prior chapters and some. Therefore, the following questions will refer back to questions in prior chapters and put them in the context of a treaty.

1. Assume in Chapter 1, review question 3, that A is not an Argentinean citizen but rather a citizen and resident of a country that concluded a treaty with the U.S. following the U.S. Model. How may your answer change?

2. Assume in Chapter 2, review question 1, that A is not a Brazilian citizen but rather a citizen and resident of a country that concluded a treaty with the U.S. following the U.S. Model. How may your answer change?

3. Assume in Chapter 4, review question 3, that C is not a Nicaraguan citizen but rather a citizen and resident of a country that concluded a

treaty with the U.S. following the U.S. Model. How may your answer change?

4.   Assume in Chapter 5, review question 1, that FC is not organized under the laws of Argentina but rather under the laws of a country that concluded a treaty with the U.S. following the U.S. Model. How may your answer change?

5.   Assume in Chapter 8, review question 1, that countries T, B and Y concluded a treaty with the U.S. following the U.S. Model. How may your answer change?

CHAPTER 12

THE FUTURE OF THE INTERNATIONAL TAX REGIME

In the previous eleven chapters, we studied the current international tax regime and how it is reflected in the U.S. domestic tax rules. You may want to re-read the introduction at this point for a summary overview.

In this chapter, we will first review how the U.S. international tax rules fit in with the international tax regime (a topic first raised in the introduction), and then discuss two major problem areas facing the international tax regime: tax competition and tax arbitrage.

12.1 THE U.S. AND THE INTERNATIONAL TAX REGIME

Yariv Brauner, An International Tax Regime in Crystallization

56 Tax L. Rev. 259 (2003).

I. Introduction

The grand illusion of a single, worldwide tax system that would eliminate all international inefficiencies and assist all the nations of the world in maximizing their relative advantages is commonly accepted as utopian. Academic and professional literature in the field of international taxation has grown exponentially in the last decade, but no significant work has been done to prove or disprove the validity of this hypothesis. Although some scholars and tax executives in certain international organizations have discussed global tax harmonization, no single organization has seriously attempted to promote it. Some countries have suggested a multi-country tax, mainly in the context of the European Union (EU) but this has garnered no support. Other, somewhat related, multilateral tax initiatives have drawn more attention and success. One such initiative is the promotion of proposals for multilateral tax treaties. Such treaties expand the application of the highly successful network of bilateral tax treaties that currently governs the taxation of income generated in cross-border transactions. This multilateral treaty effort has arisen in a period governed by a trend of "modelization" of the international tax rules, which started with the model (bilateral) tax conventions of the United Nations and the Organization for Economic Co-operation and Development. Subsequently, an idea developed to apply the modelization model to tax codification. The collapse of the Soviet Union and the increasing influence of international organizations on developing economies presented an opportunity to explore this approach. Experts from developed countries formulated a basic infrastructure for tax systems in emerging economies. Neither of these approaches was actually "global" in its reach. Tax treaties are mainly bilateral and therefore limited in scope, and only a few, though powerful, countries have signed the popular OECD Model Treaty. Nevertheless, it still represents the closest existin`g analogy to a global (though partial) set of tax norms, and it widely influences the laws and treaties of OECD members as well as nonmember states. I suggest that the next step should build on this partial success and accommodate the realities and challenges that countries face at the turn of the millennium.

In this Article, I explore the benefits of a truly global approach to meeting these current challenges. I examine the possibility of worldwide adoption of a single set of international tax rules. I seek to avoid an "all-or-nothing" perspective for the analysis of a possible world tax regime. That is, I seek a middle ground between harmonization of all aspects of all the tax systems in the world or no harmonization of any of the rules. This approach governs the current debate between proponents of global tax harmonization and proponents of unilateral solutions leading to global tax competition. I reject unilateral tax competition and propose a partial and gradual rule-harmonization solution to current international tax challenges. I analyze each component of the current regime in isolation, exploring the extent to which each rule already is globally harmonized and whether it could be part of a unification proposal in its current state, or theoretically any time in the future. A gradual, partial rule-harmonization effort would aim at eventual harmonization of all international tax rules except for the nominal tax rates, which the various countries would remain free to determine. I accept that it may not be possible to do so in one stroke, and therefore I support an effort to harmonize any one of these rules, as politically possible, and gradually reach full rule harmonization. I argue that the structure of the international tax rules allows for such flexibility and gradualness. I refer to my approach as "rule harmonization" in contrast to "rate harmonization," since the harmonization of the tax rates is much more complicated, and its net benefits uncertain. My intention is not to offer a specific prescription, but to present a workable framework for thinking about a world tax regime and possibly negotiating it.

I build the proposed framework on two contemporary realities, which allows me to evaluate the proposal's chance of success if implemented. First, most rules comprising international taxation are very close to being de facto harmonized. Second, the OECD's experience leading the recent global think tank on taxation of electronic commerce, after the practical concession of all the nation states that they could not deal with it alone, proved the necessity of a forum for global tax coordination. This experience also singled out the OECD as the most appropriate and practical institution around which a tax harmonization effort could be built, due to its expertise and experience in coordinating international tax cooperation. More specifically, I envision that the OECD would take the lead in designing a multilateral treaty, which would not be restricted to its members. Such a treaty should include a full set of international tax rules, as embedded currently in tax treaties, following the example of the OECD Model Treaty and commentaries.

I predict that the first set of rules to be harmonized will be the source rules, but the effort may begin with any one or any combination of rules. Key elements of the success of such a treaty would be: (1) the participation of a significant part of the major economic and trade forces in the world; (2) acceptance of non-negotiable rules as domestic legislation, such as the interpretation and arbitration clauses, which also would apply to trade with nontreaty partners; (3) a flexible but binding interpretation system similar to the OECD model commentaries; and (4) an easily accessible conflict resolution system, which would be open to the individual residents of the treaty partners.

The main benefit of my approach is efficiency; harmonization reduces differences between tax systems and reduces arbitrage potential that may distort business decisions. Additionally, harmonization reduces wasteful compliance and enforcement costs. Harmonization opponents, concentrating on effective tax rate competition, have complained mainly about the potential harm of competition. My approach would leave tax rates intact. Like any partial and gradual solution, my proposal arguably suffers from damaging second best effects, that is, that the harmonization of one set of rules may increase inefficiencies somewhere else in the system. I argue that this should not be the case with my approach.

Other merits of my proposal are that it is politically workable, flexible, and based on current practice. It therefore should not be rejected as too extreme or unprecedented. Furthermore, the time is also right to consider a global approach to international tax coordination since increasingly large portions of international business involve, to one extent or another, cross-border transactions and multinational enterprises, a concept not internalized by the laws of most, if not all, countries. Finally, the electronic commerce revolution has taken the world by storm and threatens to continue to grow. A significant information and services industry, through or with assistance of the Internet, has recently grown into a multi-billion dollar industry that did not exist before, and there are no unilateral solutions to the hardship electronic commerce inflicts on existing tax systems. . . .

II.　International Tax Rules

Every "foreign" tax course starts with the cliche that there is actually nothing foreign about a course that teaches the basic international tax rules of the relevant country. This cliche emphasizes the constant tension between the "domestic" tax rules of a country and the international rules that affect cross-border transactions involving multinational enterprises. Basically, there are three sets of international tax rules: (1) the domestic rules dealing with taxation of nonresidents, (2) the domestic rules dealing with taxation of residents generating income abroad, and (3) some complementary rules (that are not purely domestic and are mainly found in tax treaties) that may, or may not, change the result under one of the former sets of rules. In general, tax treaties aim to relieve double taxation of income generated in a transaction involving the parties to the treaty—at their election. The typical international income tax system currently consists of several layers of rules that apply to transactions and taxpayers independent of each other, but in a certain, rigid order. These sets of rules, in that order, are: (1) definition of "income" subject to tax, (2) measurement of the tax base and transfer pricing rules, (3) classification of types of income, (4) source (and allocation) rules, (5) taxing provisions, including rates and timing, (6) relief of domestic taxation under domestic rules, (7) relief of domestic taxation claiming tax treaty benefits, and (8) means of collection—mainly withholding tax rules.

These sets of rules may be visualized as a pyramid of rules or as a long corridor of analysis, where the result of the application of any set of rules allows the taxpayer to continue its analytical journey to the next set of rules, but only through a specific path. In analyzing an international tax question one cannot skip any of the above sets of rules.

In spite of the rigidity of the structure, it is a highly confusing system because of the interplay between the different rules. Some rules apply both to purely domestic and to international tax analyses. For instance, the tax base definitions, the measurement rules, and characterization rules must exist in any income tax system for purely domestic transactions. The taxing and collection provisions and tax rates also may belong to this group, even though they may be modified in certain international circumstances. The source rules apply only to cross-border transactions. The result is that the international tax system of any country "shares" some of its components with the purely domestic tax system. The relief provisions, embedded mainly in tax treaties, possibly apply at different levels of the rules pyramid. They may take off (from the domestic system) an item of income at the classification stage, the sourcing stage, or the tax stage.

Despite the complexity of the international tax system, both the structure itself and, to a lesser extent, the content of each of the sets of rules, are extremely similar throughout the world. This achievement is mainly due to the success of the bilateral treaty network and the OECD Model Treaty. In this project, my intuition is that rules that have significant implications for domestic tax policy would be more difficult to harmonize globally than the "pure" international tax rules. The latter, such as the source rules or the double taxation relief rules, tend to find better representation in tax treaties, which, in general, closely follow the OECD Model Treaty and therefore should be easier to harmonize. In this Section, I discuss the various stages of international tax analysis in their order of application to show the current level of similarity between the various systems of the world. For each set of rules, I analyze the potential for global harmonization at present and draw conclusions about this effect on my rule-harmonization approach.

A.   Income

Most income tax systems do not define income as clearly as one would expect. Moreover, even though there is a general acceptance of the Schanz-Haig-Simons economic definition of income, that is, consumption plus change in net wealth as an important starting point, or even as the "correct" way to define income, there is no agreement that it is the appropriate basis for defining income for tax purposes. All income tax systems today deviate from the basic formula. The debate over this issue has at least two levels: a normative one and a practical one. Some oppose the very notion of "income" as the proper basis for taxation. Others argue that although tax should be levied on "income," the pure SHS definition of income is not practical; for measurement, enforcement, and simplification reasons, the definition must be amended in order to produce a workable and politically acceptable income tax system. Practically, all income tax systems at least adjust the SHS definition to include a realization requirement n31 and annual assessment. As expressed by a leading comparative tax scholar: "The degree of commonality in income tax is striking." This is true even with respect to this most basic and fragile set of rules—basic, since it defines the boundaries of the system, and fragile, since they are exposed to the strongest political influences and therefore to the most stubborn sovereignty claims by countries except for tax rates. Since this is the source of exclusions, exemptions, and deductions (the politician's tools of trade), it is really striking that these rules are fairly harmonized, with only minor, potentially problematic differences. The possible hurdles are found in the details of the various items comprising income. The tax laws of most countries do not provide a comprehensive definition of income. In general, they require that most receipts be included in income, though some statutory exceptions exist. I propose to follow the standard SHS definition (subject to realization) as the baseline definition of income, with the following possible exceptions.

The first possibly problematic category to harmonize is income from gifts and windfalls. These nontrivial receipts should be included in income under the classic formula, but since they are probably insignificant as a matter of fiscal policy and extremely hard to track and enforce, many countries exclude them for administrative reasons. I suggest that a harmonized system should exclude them from the income tax base for practical reasons. A separate gift tax might or might not be levied.

A second category of items that are not always included in income is employee benefits, excluded in some countries as a matter of social policy. These may or may not be significant in dollar value, but, like any other deviations from the baseline definition, they should be included in the harmonized income tax base. I understand that political pressure might require special treatment in some countries. The difference from the current state is that such deviations from a baseline would then be more explicit and transparent, and therefore open to stricter scrutiny. Capital gains, the third possibly problematic category, is no different, and should be included in the harmonized income tax base even if a country chooses not to tax them for the same reasons. Other items do not seem to be problematic, and even the above problematic categories do not seem to create major disputes or significant administrative costs at the bilateral level.

This set of rules is probably the most elusive in any study of tax harmonization. On one hand, it is practically harmonized, and any tax professional can easily tell with a fairly high level of assurance if a certain item should be included in income in a country different than her own. On the other hand, the specific categories that I labeled above as problematic reflect the strong political aspects involved. Since these are the tax base rules, the base of the pyramid and its infrastructure, they are the likeliest target for populist politicians. They are the least transparent and provide the most potential for tax avoidance—once you are out of the system, you are out and none of the other rules may apply. I am not sure therefore that it would be politically possible to include the tax base in the debut of any harmonization effort, even though it does not seem to be technically problematic (even in the current bilateral treaty regime). As Klaus Vogel concludes: "There is at international level a basic common understanding of what 'income' . . . means."

An interesting recent development may signal a greater likelihood of the possibility of global harmonization of the tax base. The EU commission has suggested allowing companies in member states to use a consolidated tax base. The basis for the suggestion is the conclusion reached by various studies that effective tax rate differentiation between member states is not attributable to differences in the tax base, but rather to differences in national statutory rates. The commission concludes that it is possible to harmonize the tax base of different countries. This is important since the differences in the tax bases among EU countries represent the bulk of differences that may be found worldwide, and involve some of the most influential countries that account for a significant portion of international trade. If it is believed that tax base harmonization is possible in the European Union, it is more likely that it can be achieved globally.

In conclusion, the income tax base currently is fairly harmonized. It is possible to completely harmonize it without significant disputes, since there are only political rather than technical or ideological reasons for most exclusions. The use of the tax system to implement social policies is under debate, but the issue should be diverted to the tax rates level where it is most transparent and less distortive, being at the tip of the pyramid of rules and affecting the tax outcome of no other sets of rules.

It also should result in significant administrative gains and reduced arbitrage opportunities.

B.   Measuring the Tax Base and the Transfer Pricing Rules

1.   Tax Accounting

Once the substantive boundaries of the income concept are set, items need to be measured for tax purposes. Tax systems differ both in the substantive accounting rules and the philosophy behind them. In general, civil law countries use tax accounting rules that closely follow their financial accounting rules. These rules are conservative in principle and do not aim at economic accuracy. Rather, their intent is to protect creditors, namely the banks, and the integrity and stability of the financial system. Others, like the United States, employ separate and sometimes significantly different tax accounting rules. These rules include adjustments to the U.S. financial reporting standards, which are not entirely similar to parallel standards in the rest of the world. In addition, the U.S. tax system has an elaborate separate set of time value of money rules, some elective twists like the installment sale method, and the overriding rule that the accounting method chosen by the taxpayer should "clearly reflect income." The goal of these special rules is to try to reflect the true economic value of the reported figures. These rules are therefore not necessarily conservative.

Naturally, this dissimilarity results in additional compliance and transactional costs for multinationals. Nominally, it may result in either double taxation or undertaxation of income from the perspective of the countries involved. Nonetheless, this has never been on the agenda in bilateral treaty negotiations, which represent a basic compromise under which the definitions and measurement rules of each country are used to determine taxation in each of the parties to the convention. The treaty "assigns" to each country a "piece" of the pie and each country applies its measurement rules to that piece. Although successful, this system is only a compromise, since it is artificial to view each piece of the pie separately, or each so-called item of income separately. Taxpayers' choices may be distorted as a result of the divergence of the measurement rules, increasing the obvious inefficiencies generated by the inflated compliance and administrative costs. On the other hand, since the treaty negotiation process generally excludes these rules, they do not add unnecessary burdens inherent to the bilateral negotiation processes.

It is unrealistic to expect that countries would be willing to include the tax measurement rules at the top of the agenda of international tax harmonization. These are, like the tax base rules, primarily domestic rules with deep historical, and almost ideological roots, arising from the foundations of some countries' economic structure. Changes in the accounting rules have many significant implications in areas of the law apart from taxation and the transition period might be painful and have adverse affects in fields like corporate and securities law. Moreover, such changes are very hard and at least equally painful to reverse. At the first glance one would think that if harmonization were possible, it would follow the civil law countries' regime, since they follow the already available financial reports and their systems enjoy important advantages, such as simplicity, transparency, effectiveness, and mainly efficiency. This approach saves significant compliance and transaction costs, double expertise, and work. It also seems easier to envision one globally applicable financial and tax accounting standards along the same lines. Nevertheless, there has not been such a trend. It seems more likely that some of the European countries will adopt measurement rules that will be increasingly similar in concept to those of the United States. The accounting systems in these countries face contemporary criticism that they do not accurately reflect the economics of businesses and transactions; if adopted, such changes may make harmonization a much simpler task. The economic structure of these countries is changing. The banking system plays a lesser role and private equity investments play a larger role, similar to the traditional U.S. structure. This is understandable as the United States plays a more significant role in the integration of global markets, in general, and the western markets in particular.

In conclusion, it is unlikely that the tax accounting rules would be one of the first sets of international tax rules to be harmonized in a world tax regime, but they might be included at a later stage in the process. The fact that they were not harmonized should not affect the harmonization of the rest of the rules, but taxpayers might still face different dollar values for an item of income in two different countries, resulting possibly in either double taxation or nontaxation.

2.   Transfer Pricing

A somewhat different picture is to be found in a specific set of measurement rules, the transfer pricing rules. Although arising mainly from enforcement needs, they basically provide a standard for measuring income in cases of payments between related parties. As multinationals' activities increase, there will be an increasing amount of business and payments between related parties, escalating the importance of the transfer pricing rules. Currently there are more than 30 countries that have adopted transfer pricing rules, following the United States. The decisive majority of these countries have adopted the arm's length standard as the core of these rules, as has the OECD. The adoption of the arm's length standard, and the documentation requirements by most of the major economic powers in the world, have allowed for its penetration into the international tax systems of many other countries, which either adopted the standard into their law directly or indirectly. Such indirect means may have included interpretation by assimilation in cases of Lacunae, or using the arm's length standard as a result of the application of the "associated enterprises" articles in the treaties. These articles basically were adopted from the language of article 9 to the OECD Model Treaty.

The arm's length standard, in particular, has been harshly criticized, and some predicted that it eventually would become extinct. Nevertheless, the OECD has reaffirmed the arm's length principle as the international standard. The OECD's Transfer Pricing Guidelines discuss why, in its view, the benefits of the arm's length standard outweigh its drawbacks.

In any case, the arms' length standard is at the center of current consensus, with little resistance at the governmental level. Nonetheless, there are a few serious hurdles to overcome before one can really harmonize the transfer pricing rules globally. First, the arm's length standard offers several allowable determination methods, using approximations and comparables that are by definition inaccurate. The level of accuracy or appropriateness of each method for each situation is hard to determine. Various countries have issued different guidelines with respect to "best method" determinations. Harmonization of the basic standard without resolving the question of the "best method" is possible, but eventually will allow arbitrage. Adopting the OECD guidelines, refined to accommodate developments and changes in the business environment, seems like a likely compromise.

Second, documentation requirements are central to current transfer pricing practice. Distinct documentation requirements in different countries increase the already heavy administrative burden in the transfer pricing area. Transfer pricing service providers are promoting to their clients an integrated global documentation approach that will eliminate some of these (unnecessary) inefficiencies, with limited success at present. There is no reason that this should be left to the professional services firms, or the individual countries in a world tax regime. Mandating a single form of documentation that would serve worldwide inspection would reduce both the costs of compliance and administration of these rules. Finally, the harmonization of the transfer pricing rules would mandate co-ordination with the general dispute resolution and common interpretation mechanism of the world tax regime. Partly as a result of the differences described above, courts have become involved in transfer pricing disputes. Unilateral interpretation in transfer pricing will result in either double taxation or undertaxation since that difference amounts to a certain amount of income, which is either taxed in both countries involved, or not taxed at all. This result is contrary to existing acceptable international tax norms. I conclude that the transfer pricing rules could be part of the initial stage of a world tax regime initiative, but this process may not be effortless.

C.   Classification of Types of "Income"

The need for classification-of-income rules arises from the pathologies of the income tax system. In the domestic context, they may be required in order to enable differential tax treatment for certain items of income, such as capital gains and/or dividends. In the international context, many tax classifications may result in large varieties of tax, or even in extreme situations, no tax, double tax, or worse. In most cases, the need for such classification rules is the result of other tax rules adopted by political pressure and/or inefficient measures, obviously, in countervention to the traditional coherent definition of income. As globalization speeds up, and contemporary phenomena challenge current tax concepts, the importance of classification rules increases. The two most obvious examples are the increasing use of more complex financial instruments, which emphasizes the inherent difficulty in distinguishing between debt and equity, and the advent of e-commerce, mainly that which involves the transfer of intangibles and digitized products, which places added pressure on the distinction among services, sales, and licensing transactions. For most purposes the United States, like other countries, does not have a single, clear set of classification rules. At first glance, most items are easy to characterize and are supported by definitions in other legal fields or possibly implied from other tax rules. Nevertheless, as the e-commerce experience shows, creative use of classification rules may result in undertaxation. E-commerce income of an entity located in a low-(or no-) tax jurisdiction may easily escape taxation on income generated from a high-tax country, if characterized as sale proceeds or payment for services rather than royalties. The original vague characterization rules were developed mainly in the courts, and in a mainly "tangible" world; they were (and still are) vague, fact dependent, and obviously courts may apply them differently, a fortiori by courts in different countries. Creative tax attorneys, in such environment, could develop what I call "hybrid intangible transactions," characterized in one way in the country of source and in another in the country of residence, effectively leading to less than full taxation in any of the countries involved. Multi-country transactions multiply these risks.

Two major efforts have arisen as a result, and they illustrate the usefulness of global harmonization efforts. The United States promulgated proposed regulations for the classification of income from cross-border transactions involving software late in 1996. The regulations, commonly called the "software regulations," provide tests to distinguish among sales, services, licensing, and leasing income when software is involved in a cross-border transaction. The software regulations influenced more than just U.S. taxpayers. Other countries have used their tests to one extent or the other, especially when the relevant transactions involved the United States. The OECD followed this regulatory effort and recently published its set of rules for the characterization of income from e-commerce activity as part of its overall effort to deal with the taxation of income from e-commerce. The report does not really differ in result from the software regulations, but it is larger in scope and there is one main issue that is clearly not part of the consensus among OECD members, namely, the treatment of technical services. Such controversies nevertheless are few. The less controversial rules are almost identical in any case, and the more controversial still present relatively simple arbitrage opportunities to sophisticated tax planners. These harmful opportunities may be handled best through international cooperation rather than unilateral anti-avoidance measures. Harmonization of the rules is possible, as the e-commerce experience has shown. As with other bottom-of-the-pyramid rules, there may be political pressure by arbitrage beneficiaries and their agents who enjoy these rules, particularly since they involve definitions, words, and languages that may be interpreted and translated in many different ways. Efficiency would be served well therefore by the elimination of this wasteful, unequal, and distortive enjoyment, in particular where there seem to be no real, ideological, or significant technical reasons that would prevent such harmonization attempt. But harmonization of these rules alone will not suffice, since they involve definitional language. They must be supported, therefore, by an interpretative body that will apply the rules and maintain their integrity.

D.   Source Rules

Source rules perform the function of dividing items of "income" between countries. Therefore, unification of source rules would be an extremely significant step towards a world tax regime worthy of its name. The main hurdle stems from the inherent tension in source rules between the commonly called "source countries"—usually net capital importers—promoting more taxation at source, and "residence countries"—usually capital exporters—promoting as little taxation at source as possible. The use of labels, such as "domestic income" and "foreign income," is counterproductive since there are many cases where income just cannot be considered to entirely "belong" to one country or the other, and since the focus of these rules is on division, settlement, and compromise rather than adversity. These labels may be convenient and useful to bureaucrats and politicians involved in the tax policymaking and debate process, but, on the other hand, they may transform the policy analysis and debate into a political, or even patriotic debate. Instead of division of income in a compromise manner, countries are forced into a defensive manner of "protecting" their income.

The source rules are a set of arbitrary rules that were carefully crafted to support a specific compromise. They do not follow sound economic principles, particularly not the cornerstone of income tax thinking—the SHS definition of income. Fortunately, these compromises (over the rules, not the magnitude of taxation) are fairly similar worldwide, making a harmonization effort relatively easy because of the increasing importance of tax treaties, especially the OECD Model Treaty, on the domestic international tax rules of the world. Many nations have in effect incorporated the OECD Model Treaty source rules into their own systems. Some even have expanded their net of taxation to include treaty-sourced income that would not have been sourced to them under domestic rules.

Nevertheless, there are two areas where debate still exists. The more complicated is the treatment of income generated from the provision of personal services (hereinafter "service income"); the other is the taxation of capital gains. The former usually is taxed like business income, especially since the elimination of Article 14 of the OECD Model Treaty, which treated personal services separately from business income. The controversy is over the source of "technical services," which are taxed in the same manner as royalties in some countries. This is, and should be, a question of characterization and therefore should have no bearing on the harmonization of the source rules for services. It is relatively clear in which country these services are performed, and that should be the source of the income. Cases like remote (cross-border) technical support should be addressed separately in the interpretation guidelines.

In some countries capital gains still are taxed at source. I could not find any proof that this policy is beneficial to any of these countries, or that any country has ever raised a logical argument in support of it. These exceptions should be eliminated, preventing some arbitrage opportunities and needless administrative and complexity costs.

Other than these two areas, powerful, globally harmonized source rules are already in place. The basic notion behind them is that "active" income should be taxed solely in the residence country and "passive" income may be taxed first in the source country, leaving residual taxation to the residence country. Currently, there is some basic understanding that "business income" should be taxed in the business' residence country, and another country may tax a business to the extent that it has a "taxable presence" in that country. The definitions of residency and taxable presence are not globally unified, although in the bilateral treaty context they seem very close. The best example is the worldwide acceptance of the permanent establishment concept. This powerful consensus serves as a significant basis for any harmonization effort. The differences in application of these rules in some circumstances should not pose a significant threat to this effort.

A powerful consensus also exists with respect to the source rules for dividends. They are sourced at the country of the dividends' payor, which allows the source country to get the "first bite" of taxation. The major disputes in this area relate to situations involving more than two countries or to features of specific bilateral treaties. The rules for sourcing interest income are a bit more complicated than the dividend income sourcing rules. The basic rule sources the interest income to the country of the payor, again allowing the source country the first bite. Most countries consider the residence of the payor as the country of source. There are many more cases of branches paying interest because banks and other financial institutions traditionally do business outside their country of formation in a branch form, rather than in an incorporated form, usually for nontax reasons. This may raise a problem in the bilateral context since the branch country is not part of the treaty, but there should be no problem for a multilateral treaty like a world tax regime. If interest is sourced to the country of the payor, which can be identified, then it should not be difficult to determine the source of interest income (no matter what form the payor chooses to use).

The source rules for royalty income are slightly more complex only because they deal largely with elusive intellectual property. Other than that, at the source rules' level, the de facto harmonization is as robust as in any other area. Royalties are paid for a license: the right to exploit or use rights owned by others. The widely accepted rule is that royalties may be taxed first by the country in which the rights are used or exploited. As with dividends and interest, this is just the source country's right to take the first bite of taxation of this item. The source rule for royalties faces a problem similar to that of the interest source rules— many countries mutually refrain from imposing withholding taxes on royalties under their current bilateral tax treaties. The belief that royalty income should be taxed only by the residence country of the owner of the rights also reflects the difficulty of distinguishing between royalty income and business income generated from licensing. The new economy, and the intensive use of intangibles and licenses in the new business environment, emphasizes this problem. It is fairly complex, unlike other cases, to determine where rights are exploited, since geographical borders mean very little these days. The elimination of withholding tax on royalty payments in effect changes the rule to a residence-based source rule, similar to the sale of personal property. Global acceptance of this rule also would relieve the stress on the characterization rules (between a sale and a license of intellectual property) and in substance would not modify the current consensus. Nevertheless, it is possible to use the current consensus.

In conclusion, the source rules are close to being de facto harmonized already. Certain differences n86 could be solved in a world tax regime, but most of them would not be relevant since they arise from the bilateral nature of the current regime.

E.   Taxing Provisions

Tax rates are the most fiercely defended component of each country's tax system. Tax rates are probably also the most subject to change, as well as the most political feature. All taxpayers know at least the top tax rate to which they are possibly subject and every politician is sensitive to that. Thus, at least externally, tax breaks tend to be discussed in closed rooms—especially when they are "special" enough. Not surprisingly, therefore, one should expect that tax rates would be the component of the tax system most associated with sovereignty, and least likely to be completely harmonized. Moreover, the phenomenon of the growing proximity of tax rates, at least among the major economic forces in the world, is deterministic. The two big fears have not come true. Although tax rate schedules have grown more similar in the last 20 years, there has not been a "snowball effect," resulting in tax rates too low for countries to collect enough revenues, nor has there been complete harmonization of rates that jeopardize the basic ability of governments to alter their rate schedules. It is a common belief that the top corporate tax rates have dropped, tax bases have broadened, and tax burdens in general have risen. This is generally true. The basic income tax reforms in the 1980's and 1990's were to lower the corporate tax rates to the 30%-plus level, to lower the top personal income tax rate to as close as possible (politically and fiscally) to that level, and to broaden the tax base. Broadening the tax base had the most politically explosive potential because that meant giving up the giveaways, which are the strongest weapon in the hands of any politician. Therefore, these income tax reforms were complemented by an increased burden of consumption taxes—mainly of the VAT type—and of social security contributions. Tax systems following the above-mentioned pattern became less progressive. The tax burden of the lower income part of society has grown more than that of the rich. In addition, as businesses grow to be increasingly global, they become more sensitive to differences in tax burdens between countries in general, and tax rate disparities in particular. This allows the global economy the efficiency benefits of competition that is direct and transparent, in contrast to the use of loopholes and unintended, relatively small, nonideological differences in the nontransparent parts of the tax rules' pyramid. The harmonization of the tax rates is not only politically impractical, but under my approach is unnecessary for the stability of a world tax regime. Such a regime that would include all sets of tax rules except for the rate schedule may not be worse than one with a single rate schedule, since the pie countries divide is one of income and not tax revenues. Countries may put a heavier or lighter burden on their share of the pie, if well defined (and agreed upon, globally), without affecting the share of other countries. This would neutralize some emotional and rhetorical opposition to harmonization.

F.   Unilateral Relief Provisions

Most countries provide some relief from domestic taxation to taxpayers who have earned income abroad, to the extent of the foreign tax paid on such income. This relief is normally unilateral, that is, it is not dependent on an applicable tax treaty, but usually is synchronized with the countries' treaty obligations. The two most prominent methods of relief are the foreign tax credit (FTC) and the exemption of foreign source income. These provisions are purely international in that they are required only for cross-border transactions. In compatibility with the primary international tax norm of capital export neutrality (CEN), countries always have supported such activities by their constituents. A country does not want tax to interfere with its taxpayers' decision whether to invest or do business abroad or domestically, allowing them to choose better investments or businesses abroad if they generate higher yields. Hopefully, based on the close to zero mobility of humans, such yield will be repatriated and expand the domestic economy and tax base.

In some cases, most notably the U.S. worldwide tax system, there is no need for such yields to be repatriated in order for the residence governments to tax them. Nevertheless, this income may be subject to income tax in the country where it is generated (for simplicity the "source" country). So, if the residence country concedes taxation of this income for the sake of CEN, it may not always achieve its neutrality goals. If the tax at the source is higher than at home, there still would be an incentive to stay domestic, even with higher pretax yields abroad. If the tax at the source is lower, then there is a tax incentive to go international. Allegedly, the primary method to achieve CEN, or relief of double taxation, is the FTC. Why "allegedly?" Because, almost unanimously, countries with a FTC grant it only up to the level of domestic taxation. They allow full relief for tax paid at source if that tax is at a lower level than the domestic tax. They collect only the residual tax, but will not refund money to taxpayers who invest or do business abroad subject to higher levels of tax.

The United States was first to implement the foreign tax credit as a domestic, unilateral method to relieve its taxpayers of double taxation. I use its system to illustrate the policy dilemmas surrounding this regime. A FTC is limited to the taxpayer's "foreign source income." [n94] Even then, policymakers have a fear of "averaging," that is, taxpayers investing in high-taxed activities receiving full credit, since they have other low-taxed foreign income against which to "wash" the credit. Averaging allows taxpayers to pay as few U.S. residual taxes as possible. That may not be so bad, since it follows CEN, but proponents of limitations may argue that taxpayers may choose to invest and do business in one location just for FTC purposes, which defies the purpose of CEN. The problem with this argument is that this phenomenon still exists. Averaging is possible, and depends on a nonrelevant factor like ownership percentages. It is possible to average income from high-tax countries with income from low-tax countries, and to average low-taxed types of income with high-taxed types. In theory, it is possible to eliminate averaging completely, if the FTC mechanism is performed item by item, but that has proven to be administratively impossible, as well as extremely inefficient and burdensome on taxpayers. Currently, the United States chooses to fight item averaging and not to worry about country averaging. Together with the reduction of the corporate tax rates, this policy is believed to place U.S. taxpayers in an excess credit position, which forces them to attempt to create additional low-tax foreign source income in the appropriate basket, mainly active business income. The other method of unilateral relief is the exemption method, which exempts from domestic taxation certain income, most typically active business or employment income. Other categories of income usually are subject to the credit relief mechanism.

In a world where tax rates do not vary significantly, the differences between these two relief mechanisms are not very significant.

Nevertheless, in certain cases they matter, and they create arbitrage incentives that apply pressure on the source rules. If the source rules (and classification rules) were harmonized, this pressure would be weaker even if the two different methods of unilateral relief continued to exist, which I think they will for some time. This is because the two methods are thought to represent different basic policies (CEN/CIN), even though practically no country implements a pure version of either of them. A strong indication of the difficulty of harmonizing these rules is the fact that even the OECD Model Treaty left this issue for countries to decide, providing two optional prototypes. A world tax regime can follow this solution, at least temporarily, subject to some adjustments aimed primarily at the reduction of complexity, especially of the FTC rules. I do not attempt here to provide a prescription for simplification of these rules, but stress a few points. FTC limitation methods should be unified. Countries may insist on reserving rights to enact domestic anti-avoidance rules if necessary, and that should be acceptable, but only within the regime. Then, with respect to passive income, which usually is subject only to credit relief, even full harmonization seems possible. This should not generate effective pressure on classification arbitrage, since realistically the classification rules should be harmonized prior to the relief provisions. Another long shot is the possibility of developing tax sharing mechanisms to replace the unilateral relief mechanisms, which were impossible in a bilateral treaty world, but seem to be less utopian now. In any case, since the world tax regime would be a treaty with direct effect on domestic law, this is discussed in the next Section.

G.   Treaty-Based Relief of Domestic Taxation

The unilateral relief of double taxation usually is embedded into any applicable tax treaty. Both the FTC and the exemption methods are acceptable in the various model tax treaties, and each applies depending on the specific treaty partners. Very similar provisions apply either unilaterally or through a bilateral tax treaty. This is strong evidence and an example of the "evolutionary" harmonization process, whereby unilateral domestic tax rules were integrated into treaties, which, in turn, through their "modelization," influenced other domestic tax systems and the like. The treaty-based relief is just an additional "safety net" that in certain cases may expand the application of the unilateral relief rules. In a world with a unified tax regime the duality of treaty and domestic rules would be eliminated, so this no longer would be a concern. Only a single set of relief provisions would remain.

H.   Means of Collection

Once again, little variety is found in the concepts. International businesses expect to be taxed on a net basis (including an obligation to file a local tax return) in any country within which they perform their business activity. Individuals performing significant personal services outside their residence countries face the same basic requirements, except that the return-filing requirement may be relaxed in some countries because of the conventional obligation of employers to withhold taxes on salaries paid to their employees. Foreigners investing in a country should expect to be taxed, if at all, by means of a withholding tax. The domestic payor of that income to the foreigner usually is obliged to withhold from the payment a flat tax on a gross basis, which is normally the final tax on such income. Some foreigners also may need to file local information tax returns. This part of the current regime therefore seems fairly simple to harmonize in any world tax regime including the one proposed in this Article, which is based on the current bilateral treaty network.

It is important not to confuse withholding taxes as a means of collection with the general rate schedule. Withholding taxes have become the international norm for taxing employees and foreign investors because of their administrative virtues. Since they are levied on a gross, rather than net, basis, one would expect them to be an extraordinary last measure to approximate the normal tax levied on a net basis when there is a serious doubt whether such tax can be collected. In reality they became very popular in spite of their inherent inaccuracy. Nevertheless, as international business and investments grew more important, countries understood that, without cooperation, they will increase the rates of their withholding taxes to defend their revenue, despite the understanding that their trade partners then will be pushed to do the same in their respective countries. This classic dilemma could have been relaxed only in a cooperative effort such as the tax treaty negotiations process. The leading policy choice, including that of the United States, has been to reduce the level of withholding tax rates mutually. The reasons for such policy could be to reduce barriers to international trade and investment or, more likely, to ensure that the withholding tax at source will not exceed the residence country tax. Clearly, this trend has grown stronger recently, especially in treaties between close allies. Understandably, this trend reduced differences and arbitrage opportunities, and it makes life easier for any harmonization effort since sometimes negotiations over withholding taxes are conducted parallel to the generally applicable rates, which are at the heart of the stubbornness of countries negotiating tax treaties. Congress at times has attempted to effectively increase source taxation with legislation that is portrayed as a bad kid doing wrong hoping that such wrong would not be discovered, ignoring the effect of countermeasures by U.S. trade partners. Julie Roin has promoted the increase of withholding tax rates through renegotiation of the U.S. tax treaties. Although it is beyond my scope to challenge this view, it is worth noting that once a world tax regime is implemented, it would be much harder to promote increases in withholding tax rates. Roin's approach has not been adopted, and withholding tax rates continue to decline, creating a favorable environment for a world tax regime effort. Due to the political sensitivity of anything seemingly related to rates, I do not believe that these rules could be included in the initial harmonization attempt.

I.   Conclusion

In spite of some differences, most of the components of the current international tax regime are highly harmonized, and where they are not, they are within a tight margin of possible rules with which any international tax professional is fairly familiar. In particular, this review suggests that the rules at the bottom of the pyramid—tax base, measurement, classification, and source rules—are usually easier and closer to harmonization, which is good news for a world tax regime designed to enhance transparency and efficiency. Rules that are more purely international, like the source rules and the transfer pricing rules, seem to be closest to harmonization already. The tax accounting rules are the least likely of these rules to be harmonized soon but, as noted above, are moving in that direction as well. The middle of the pyramid rules, including the taxing rules and the means of collection, appear to be fairly harmonized and likely candidates for a world tax regime, with the exception of the nominal tax rate schedules. The nominal rates generally would not be harmonized under my proposal. The relief provisions at the top of the pyramid are a more complex problem since they are at the core of the current bilateral regime. The bilateral treaty network would be eliminated upon completion of the world tax regime, but I estimate that the way they approach scope and relief would continue to rule the proposed world tax regime. This is because of the evident importance of bilateral treaties as the foundation of the current regime. There should be little debate over the fact that current tax treaties practice is at the heart of the world tax regime, and its underlying principles direct and affect the rest of the relevant sets of rules. In light of the (almost) consensus about the impressive extent of similarity and even unity within the multitude of tax treaties and their importance in the structure of the current regime, I propose to build the future world tax regime on their success. The important lesson from the experiment is that rule harmonization is just around the corner. It is possible however complex it may be.

. . .

NOTES AND QUESTIONS

1.   How do the U.S. rules we studied fit in with the international tax regime described by Brauner?

2.   What do you think about the advisability of further harmonization along the lines proposed by Brauner? What are some counter-arguments?

3.   Is the OECD the best institution to promote harmonization? Are there any feasible alternatives?

4.   Some have suggested that if the world abandoned the income tax and employed only a destination-based VAT, harmonization would be easier. What do you think?

12.2   THE TAX COMPETITION PROBLEM

Avi-Yonah, Globalization, Tax Competition, and the Fiscal Crisis of the Welfare State

113 Harv. L. Rev. 1573 (2000).

I.   Introduction

The current age of globalization can be distinguished from the previous one (from 1870 to 1914) by the much higher mobility of capital than labor (in the previous age, before immigration restrictions, labor was at least as mobile as capital). This increased mobility is the result of technological changes (the ability to move funds electronically) and the relaxation of exchange controls. The mobility of capital is linked to tax competition, in which sovereign countries lower their tax rates on income earned by foreigners within their borders in order to attract both portfolio and direct investment. Tax competition, in turn, threatens to undermine the individual and corporate income taxes, which traditionally have been the main source of revenue (in terms of percentage of total revenue collected) for modern welfare states. The response of developed countries has been first, to shift the tax burden from (mobile) capital to (less mobile) labor, and second, when further increased taxation of labor becomes politically and economically difficult, to cut the social safety net. Thus, globalization and tax competition lead to a fiscal crisis for countries that wish to continue to provide social insurance to their citizens at the same time that demographic factors and the increased income inequality, job insecurity, and income volatility that result from globalization render such social insurance more necessary. The result is increasing pressure to limit globalization (e.g., by re-introducing exchange controls) which risks reducing world welfare. This article argues that if both globalization and social insurance are to be maintained, it is necessary to cut the intermediate link by limiting tax competition in a way that is congruent with maintaining the ability of democratic states to determine the desirable size of their government.

From its beginnings late in the 19th century to the recent rise in payroll taxation, the welfare state has been financed primarily by progressive income taxation. The income tax differs from other forms of taxation (such as consumption or social security taxes) because, in theory, it includes income from capital in the tax base even if it is saved and not consumed. Because the rich save more than the poor, a tax that includes income from capital in its base is more progressive (taxes the rich more heavily) than a tax that excludes income from capital (e.g., a consumption tax or a payroll tax). However, the ability to tax saved income from capital (i.e., income not vulnerable to consumption taxes) is impaired if the capital can be shifted overseas to jurisdictions where it escapes taxation.

Two recent developments have dramatically augmented the ability of both individuals and corporations to earn income overseas free of income taxation: The effective end of withholding taxation by developed countries and the rise of production tax havens in developing countries. Since the United States abolished its withholding tax on interest paid to foreigners in 1984, no major capital importing country has been able to impose such a tax for fear of driving mobile capital elsewhere (or increasing the cost of capital for domestic borrowers, including the government itself). The result is that individuals can generally earn investment income free of host country taxation in any of the world's major economies. Moreover, even developed countries find it exceedingly difficult to effectively collect the tax on the foreign income of their individual residents in the absence of withholding taxes imposed by host countries, because the investments can be made through tax havens with strong bank secrecy laws. Developing countries, with much weaker tax administrations, find this task almost impossible. Thus, cross-border investment income can largely be earned free of either host or home country taxation.

When we switch our attention from passive to productive investment, a similar threat to the taxing capacity of both home and host jurisdictions emerges. In the last decade, competition for inbound investment has led an increasing number of countries (103 as of 1998) to offer tax holidays specifically geared to foreign corporate investors. Given the relative ease with which an integrated multinational can shift production facilities in response to tax rates, such "production tax havens" enable multinationals to derive most of their income abroad free of host country taxation. Moreover, most developed countries (including the U.S.) do not dare impose current taxation (or sometimes any taxation) on the foreign source business income of their resident multinationals for fear of reducing the competitiveness of those multinationals against multinationals of other countries. If they did, new multinationals could be set up as residents of jurisdictions that do not tax such foreign source income. Thus, business income can also be earned abroad largely free of either host or home country taxation.

If income from capital can escape the income tax net, the tax becomes in effect a tax on labor. Several empirical studies have in fact suggested that in some developed jurisdictions the effective tax rate on income from capital approaches zero, and nominal tax rates on capital have tended to go down sharply since the early 1980s (when exchange controls were relaxed). As a result, countries that used to rely on the revenues from the income tax are forced to increase relatively regressive taxes. The two fastest growing taxes in OECD member countries in recent years have been consumption taxes (from 12% of total revenues in 1965 to 18% in 1995) and payroll taxes (from 18% to 25%), both of which are more regressive than the income tax. Over the same period, the personal and corporate income taxes have not grown as a percentage of total revenues (the personal income tax accounted for 26% of total revenues in 1965 and 27% in 1995, while the figures for the corporate income tax are 9% and 8% respectively). The total tax revenue as a percentage of GDP in developed countries went up sharply during the same period (from an average of 28% in 1965 to almost 40% in 1994), and this increase is largely accounted for by the rise of consumption and payroll taxes. Moreover, there is evidence that as the degree of openness of an economy in OECD member countries increases, taxes on capital tend to go down while taxes on labor go up (the income tax is imposed on both capital and labor so that its stability may mask this trend).

At some point, developed jurisdictions find themselves politically unable to raise income taxes on labor, consumption taxes, or payroll taxes any further. High rates of income tax on labor discourage work, high payroll taxes discourage job creation and contribute to unemployment, and high consumption taxes (e.g., on luxury goods) drive consumption overseas. If developed countries are unable to tax income from capital, and alternative taxes are not feasible, the only recourse is to cut the social safety net. But that net is needed more than ever because of both demographic factors and the increased income inequality, income volatility, and job insecurity that globalization tends to cause. Thus, globalization leads to an increased need for revenues at while simultaneously limiting the ability of governments to collect them.

This dilemma threatens to undercut the social consensus that underlies modern industrialized societies and create a backlash against globalization, despite its overall benefits. The previous age of globalization collapsed in the face of just such a backlash in the 1920's. To prevent such a collapse and maintain the social compact underlying the modern welfare state, it is necessary (inter alia) to limit tax competition so that cross-border income from capital is taxed rates approximately the same as those that are imposed domestically on labor income. However, any limits on tax competition must (as a normative and practical matter) be balanced against the desire of democratic countries to control the size of their public sectors. . . .

II.   International Tax Competition and the Taxation of Capital

A.   Taxation of Savings: Portfolio Exemptions, Traditional Tax Havens, and the Global Tax

In 1984, the U.S. unilaterally abolished its 30% withholding tax on foreign residents earning "portfolio interest" income from sources within the U.S. "Portfolio interest" was defined to include interest on U.S. government bonds, bonds issued by U.S. corporations (unless the bondholder held a 10% or more of the shares of the corporation), and interest on U.S. bank accounts and certificates of deposit. This "portfolio interest exemption" was available to any non-resident alien (i.e., any person who is not a U.S. resident for tax purposes) without requiring any certification of identity or proof that the interest income was subject to tax in the investor's country of residence.

The enactment of the portfolio interest exemption was the result of three factors, all of them rather fortuitous. First, as a result of the Reagan tax cuts of 1981, which dramatically lowered the U.S. effective tax rate, and the accompanying defense build-up, the U.S. government faced a significant budgetary deficit which could only be financed by borrowing abroad, especially from Japan (which had a large savings surplus). Second, the Japan-U.S. tax treaty imposed a 10% withholding tax on interest, unlike most U.S. tax treaties with developed countries which have a zero withholding tax on interest. Third, the U.S. in 1984 decided to terminate its tax treaty with the Netherlands Antilles which had a zero withholding tax on interest and no limitation on benefits to Antilles residents. The Antilles treaty allowed U.S. corporations to channel overseas borrowing through an Antilles finance subsidiary and thus avoid having a withholding tax imposed on the interest payments.[1] When the treaty was terminated. . . . The enactment of the portfolio interest exemption solved both the U.S. government's and the U.S. multinationals' problems in one stroke. For the former, it encouraged additional foreign investment in the U.S. and for the latter, it provided a mechanism for borrowing abroad without having to bear the cost of any withholding tax.

Arguably, none of these reasons is valid today. The U.S. government is in budgetary surplus, and Japan is an unlikely source of funds (and if it were, given the current desire of Japan to attract foreign investors, the tax treaty could be renegotiated to reduce the withholding rate on interest). Moreover, under current conditions, both the U.S. government and U.S. corporations can probably afford to borrow abroad without bearing the cost of any withholding because of the size of the U.S. market and the widely held perception of U.S. bonds as relatively safe investments in turbulent economic times. However, the portfolio interest exemption is still with us.

The result of enacting the portfolio interest exemption has been a classic race to the bottom: One after the other, all the major economies have abolished their withholding tax on interest for fear of losing mobile capital flows to the U.S. The following table shows current withholding rates in EU member countries and the U.S. on interest paid on banks accounts, securities (government and corporate bonds), and on dividends paid to foreign residents in the absence of a treaty:

---

[1]   In 1984, such taxes were likely to be shifted to the borrower, increasing its costs.

Country	Bank accounts	Securities	Dividends
Belgium	0	10	15
Denmark	0	0	15
France	0	0	15
Germany	0	0	15
Greece	10	10	0
Ireland	0	0	0
Italy	10	10	15
Luxembourg	0	0	15
Netherlands	0	0	15
Portugal	15	15	15
Spain	0	0	15
United Kingdom	0	0	15
United States	0	0	30

As the table indicates, most developed countries levy no withholding tax on interest paid to non-residents on bank deposits, government and corporate bonds. Withholding taxes are levied on dividends despite the fact that dividends (unlike interest) are not deductible and therefore the underlying income has already been taxed once. However, the discrepancy between interest and dividends may in reality be less than the rates given above indicate for two reasons: First, a significant portion of the return on equity comes in the form of capital gains which are not subject to source-based taxation in any of the countries included in the table. Second, the withholding tax on dividends is generally easy to avoid for sophisticated investors. For example, one technique is to construct a "total return equity swap" in which the foreign investor receives payments equivalent to dividends from an investment banker in the source country who in turn hedges by holding the underlying stock and receiving the actual dividends. Most countries do not withhold on the dividend equivalent amounts, and the underlying dividends are free from withholding because paid to a domestic entity. This situation has led to calls for a "portfolio dividend exemption."

The standard economic advice to small, open economies is to avoid taxing capital income at source because the tax will be shifted forward to the borrowers and result in higher domestic interest rates. However, the countries in the table include large economies (the U.S., Germany, and the U.K.) in which the tax is not necessarily shifted forward. Rather, the principal reason for the lack of withholding taxes in most of the countries included in the table above is the fear that, if such taxes were imposed, capital would swiftly move to other locations that do not impose a withholding tax. Thus, the Ruding Committee, writing about the European Community, concluded in 1992 that "recent experience suggests that any attempt by the EC to impose withholding taxes on cross-border interest flows could result in a flight of financial capital to non-EC countries."

The experience of Germany is a case in point: In 1988, Germany introduced a (relatively low) 10% withholding tax on interest on bank deposits but had to abolish it within a few months because of the magnitude of capital flight to Luxembourg (over $100 billion DM). In 1991, the German Federal Constitutional Court held that withholding taxes on wages but not on interest violated the constitutional right to equality; and the government, therefore, was obligated to reintroduce the withholding tax on interest but made it inapplicable to non-residents. Non-residents may, however, be German residents investing through Luxembourg bank accounts and benefiting from the German tradition of bank secrecy vis-à-vis the government.

The current situation resembles a multiple player assurance ("stag hunt") game: All developed countries would benefit from re-introducing the withholding tax on interest because they would gain revenue without fear that the capital would be shifted to another developed country. However, no country is willing to be the first one to cooperate by imposing a withholding tax unilaterally; and thus, they all defect (i.e., refrain from imposing the tax) to the detriment of all.

In global terms, this outcome would make no difference if residence jurisdictions were able to tax their residents on foreign source interest (and dividend) income as required by a global personal income tax on all income "from whatever source derived." However, as Joel Slemrod has written, "although it is not *desirable* to tax capital on a source basis, it is not administratively *feasible* to tax capital on a residence basis." The problem is that residence country fiscal authorities generally have no means of knowing about the income that is earned by their residents abroad. Even in the case of sophisticated tax administrations like the IRS, tax compliance depends decisively on the presence of either withholding at source or information reporting. When neither is available, as in the case of foreign source income, compliance rates drop dramatically from over 90% to about 30%.

In the case of foreign source income, withholding taxes are not imposed for the reasons described above. As for information reporting, even though tax treaties contain an exchange of information procedure, it is vitally flawed in two respects: First, the lack of any uniform world-wide system of tax identification numbers means that most tax administrations are unable to match the information received from their treaty partners with domestic taxpayers. Second, there are no tax treaties with traditional tax havens, and any exchange of information can be effectively foiled by simply routing the income through a tax haven. For example, if a Mexican national invests in a U.S. bank through a Cayman Islands corporation, the exchange of information article in the U.S.-Mexico tax treaty would not avail the Mexican authorities. The IRS has no way of knowing (given bank secrecy) that the portfolio interest that is paid to the Caymans is beneficially owned by a Mexican resident covered by the treaty.

The resulting state of affairs is that much of the income from portfolio investments overseas escapes income taxation both in the source and in the residence countries. Latin American countries provide a prime example: It is estimated that following the enactment of the portfolio interest exemption about $300 billion fled from Latin American countries to bank accounts and other forms of portfolio investment in the U.S. Most of these funds were channeled though tax haven corporations and therefore were not subject to taxation in the country of residence. For all developing countries, estimates of the magnitude of capital flight in the 1980's average between $15 billion and $60 billion per year. Nor is the problem limited to developing countries: Much of the German portfolio interest exemption benefits German residents who maintain bank accounts in Luxembourg, and much of the U.S. portfolio interest exemption benefits Japanese investors who hold U.S. Treasuries and do not report the income in Japan. Even in the case of the U.S., it is questionable how much tax is actually collected on portfolio income earned by U.S. residents abroad other than through mutual funds. One estimate has put capital flight from the U.S. in 1980–82 as high as $250 billion.

Thus, in the absence of withholding taxes or effective information exchange, income from foreign portfolio investments frequently escapes being taxed by any jurisdiction. This is particularly significant because the flows of portfolio capital across international borders have been growing recently much faster than either world gross domestic product or foreign direct investment. It is currently estimated that international capital flows amount to $1 trillion *a day;* and although this figure is much larger than income from capital, it gives a sense of the magnitudes at stake.

This situation has led knowledgeable observers like Richard Bird, to write that "the weakness of international taxation calls into question the viability of the income tax itself. . . . If something is not done to rectify these problems soon, the future of the income tax is bleak." Other authors have written articles like "Can Capital Income Taxes Survive in Open Economies?" and "Is There a Future for Capital Income Taxation?" In section (c) below, we will try to assess the possible revenue losses from portfolio investment abroad, and whether they really amount to a threat to the income tax. In Part V, we will consider possible solutions.

B. Taxation of Multinationals: Headquarters and Production Tax Havens, and Permanent Establishments

Income earned by multinationals from cross-border transactions is likely, to a significant extent, to escape the income tax altogether. There are only three types of jurisdictions that may, under currently accepted rules, impose a corporate income tax on income from the sale of goods or provision of services across national borders. They are

1) The demand jurisdiction (where consumption of the goods or services takes place), which may impose a tax if the goods or services are provided through a "permanent establishment" (i.e., some physical presence in the demand jurisdiction) or through a subsidiary to the extent of the income attributable thereto:

2) The supply jurisdiction (where production of the goods or services takes place), which may impose a tax on the income attributable to such production:[2] and

3) The residence jurisdiction (where a corporation is incorporated or managed or controlled), which has a residual right to tax income that is not taxed at source.

Out of these three jurisdictions, the demand jurisdiction is the one most likely to want to tax multinationals on income derived in it, but under currently accepted rules, it does not have the right to tax such income in an increasing number of cases. The other two jurisdictions that do have such a right (the supply and corporate residence jurisdictions) are unlikely to want to tax the income of multinationals for fear of driving them away.

(i) Demand Jurisdictions and the Permanent Establishment Threshold.

Out of the three jurisdictions that have the right to impose an income tax on multinational enterprises, Demand jurisdictions are the ones most likely to have a significant

---

[2] The demand and supply jurisdictions have the right to tax based on source.

corporate tax rate because large consumer markets typically have corporate income taxes imposed on foreign as well as domestic corporations. However, under the current international tax regime (as embodied in the tax treaty network) in order for a seller to be taxed in a demand jurisdiction it is necessary for it to have a physical presence there (a "permanent establishment" or, in U.S. terms, a "U.S. trade or business").

Traditionally, multinationals had to establish such a physical presence (a branch or a subsidiary) in demand jurisdictions in order to gain significant market share or to avoid tariff barriers. However, the tariff barriers have all but disappeared, and the rise of electronic commerce makes it increasingly feasible to sell large quantities of goods or services into a demand jurisdiction without establishing a physical presence in it. Most authoritative discussions of taxation of electronic commerce conclude that the most common forms of such commerce (a web page or even a server located in a jurisdiction) do not amount to a permanent establishment and thus do not give the demand jurisdiction the right to tax the companies involved. Therefore, while multinationals currently pay some tax in demand jurisdictions in which they have subsidiaries engaged in distribution, this tax base is rapidly diminishing in the face of technological developments and cannot be relied on in the long run if the permanent establishment threshold remains unchanged.

(ii) Supply Jurisdictions and Production Tax Havens.

Supply jurisdictions have traditionally imposed significant corporate income tax rates, equal to those in demand jurisdictions (in fact, most production used to take place in the same jurisdictions as most consumption, i.e., in the developed world). However, a crucial development in the last decade or so is weakening their importance. That development is the rise of production tax havens: jurisdictions that grant tax holidays specifically to local production facilities of foreign corporations while continuing to have an income tax imposed on domestic corporations and individual residents. This last feature distinguishes such production tax havens from traditional offshore tax havens that have no corporate income tax (and sometimes no significant tax of any kind). This distinction is crucial because it means that a foreign investor in a production tax haven can enjoy the benefits of government services financed by non-tax haven levels of taxation imposed on relatively immobile production factors such as labor and land while itself paying little or no corporate income tax.

Tax competition has led to the proliferation of production tax havens. There are currently at least 103 countries that offer special tax concessions to foreign corporations that set up production facilities or administrative facilities within their borders. They include developed countries such as Belgium, Ireland, and Israel, and developing countries such as Malaysia and India. The extent of the tax holiday varies, but generally the statutory tax rate is reduced to 10% or less for foreign corporations investing in specified types of facilities or areas within the jurisdiction. A higher tax rate averaging 30%—40% (the norm for OECD members) is imposed on local corporations, and a personal income tax at even higher rates, as well as a VAT, is imposed on resident individuals.

Studies by economists have shown that such tax incentives are quite widespread and that they succeed in bringing investments to such countries. For example, Altshuler and Newlon have studied U.S. multinationals' tax returns for 1986 and found that, out of 1,827 foreign subsidiaries ("CFCs"), 659 were located in countries with a tax rate below 20%. These CFCs had assets of $51 billion and earnings of $5.2 billion in 1986 which represented over 40% of the total assets and earnings of all the CFCs. Almost three quarters of U.S. multinationals studied had CFCs in both high and low tax jurisdictions. Similarly, Hines and Rice have documented the extent of U.S. investment in foreign tax havens for 1982. They show that while the havens had only 1.2% of world population and 3.0% of world GDP, their share of the foreign operations of U.S. MNEs was 26% of assets, 21.4% of equity, and 30.6% of net income (but only 4.3% of employment and 4.2% of property, plant, and equipment).

Two specific examples may help to illustrate this phenomenon. Intel Corporation, a top ten multinational, has operations in more than thirty countries around the globe. The company states that "[a]n Intel chip developed at a design center in Oregon, might be manufactured at a wafer fabrication facility in Ireland, packaged and tested in Malaysia, and then sold to a customer in Australia. Another chip might be designed in Japan, fabricated in Israel, packaged and tested in Arizona, and sold in China." Specifically, outside the U.S., Intel has major manufacturing facilities in Puerto Rico, China, Malaysia, the Philippines, Ireland, and Israel. Thus, outside the U.S., all of Intel's manufacturing facilities are located in countries granting tax holidays.

This phenomenon is not confined to new-fangled high tech corporations like Intel. For example, new auto assembly plants built by General Motors cars built since 1990 are located in Gravatai, Brasil (Opel cars); Rosario, Argentina (Chevrolet Corsica); Silao, Mexico (Chevrolet Suburban, Silverado); Gliwice, Poland (Opel Astra); Rayong, Thailand (Opel Astra); Jakarta, Indonesia (Opel Blazer, Vectra, Astra); and Shanghai, China (Buicks). Except for Mexico, all of these locations are in production tax havens.

The rise of electronic commerce is likely to make it easier to locate production in tax havens. The Intel example, involving traditional "hard" goods (as opposed to digitizeable "soft" goods), is a case in point: Intel's ability to coordinate production across the globe and locate its production facilities in production tax havens like Malaysia is based on modern communication technology including corporate intranets. Where goods can be conveyed in digital form, such as software, it is even easier to locate the entire operation in tax havens: The software can be written anywhere (e.g., in India or Israel where Microsoft has major operations) and transmitted elsewhere over secure corporate intranets. Information services in general have no inherent source, and on-line pornography, which is still one of the most profitable of the information services, is run largely from Guyana for both regulatory and tax-related reasons.

Are these locations influenced by the tax regime in the host country? There have been several studies by economists that examined the importance of tax differentials in location decisions. Hines has recently summarized ten quantitative studies of U.S. direct investment abroad and ten quantitative studies of foreign direct investment in the U.S. He concludes that although taxes are not the only determinant of the location of investments, "[t]he answer that emerges in a variety of contexts and from a variety of approaches is that, in spite of all the other economic and political considerations that are clearly important, taxation exerts a significant effect on the magnitude and location of FDI." Hines estimates that the studies are generally consistent with a—0.5 elasticity of investment with respect to tax rates at the currently prevailing rates. These statistical findings are corroborated by Wilson who interviewed managers from nine firms regarding sixty-eight location decisions and concluded that "tax considerations largely dictate location decisions for business activities . . . such as administrative and distribution centers." As for production locations, taxes are an important consideration in the location decision although they rarely dominate the decision process.

The economic studies have also demonstrated the ability of multinationals to shift profit to low-tax jurisdictions through transfer pricing or otherwise. For example, Harris and his colleagues have concluded on the basis of a sample of 200 U.S. manufacturing firms for 1984–1988 that having a subsidiary in Ireland or in the four Asian "dragons" (Taiwan, Korea, Singapore, and Hong Kong), all jurisdictions offering a tax holiday for foreign investors, is associated with lower U.S. taxes as a fraction of U.S. assets or U.S. sales "in a way that is consistent with tax-motivated income shifting." Hines surveys several studies on the financial behavior of multinationals, including the use of debt and transfer pricing, and concludes that "[t]he evidence indicates that the financial behavior of multinational corporations is quite sensitive to tax considerations, though not completely determined by them. . . . In some instances it may be less valuable to test the standard hypothesis that taxes influence financial behavior than to test the alternative hypothesis that *only* taxes influence financial behavior."

Some recent studies based on actual data derived from U.S.-based multinationals tend to bolster the view that (a) tax competition among countries has driven effective tax rates down, and (b) U.S. investment abroad has become more sensitive to tax rates. Altschuler, Grubert, and

Newlon used data on manufacturing affiliates of U.S.-based multinationals taken from U.S. Treasury corporate tax returns for 1984 and 1992 to assess that view. . . . Average effective tax rates for CFCs in about sixty countries were calculated based on dividing total income taxes paid by their total earnings and profits (a measure defined by the Internal Revenue Code that approximates "book" income). The study found that average effective tax rates for manufacturing affiliates fell by more than 15% between 1984 and 1992. The statutory tax rates likewise fell by 14%, indicating that rate reductions were not compensated by base broadening measures. The authors also found that the elasticity of investment to tax rate differentials in open economies increased from 1984 to 1992, indicating that the location of real manufacturing capital by manufacturing firms may have become more sensitive to tax rates in this period. This result held when countries with populations of less than 1 million, including most traditional tax havens, were excluded from the calculations. The authors concluded that their results were "consistent with increasing international mobility of capital and globalization of production."

Another study by Harry Grubert focused directly on the questions whether there is evidence of tax competition and whether U.S. multinationals respond to it. It too is based on U.S. Treasury data for 1984 and 1992. He Grubert found that the mean average effective tax rate for multinationals fell by almost 10% from 1984 to 1992, but there was no notable convergence in tax rates. He interpreted this as suggesting that there was no tax competition, but that conclusion does not follow from the data: It is possible that countries with high tax rates in 1984 reduced them because of competition with countries with low tax rates, but that the low tax countries responded with further decreases, resulting in a lower average rate overall but no convergence. Significantly, Grubert found that tax reductions were greater in countries with a population of less than 15 million suggesting that small, open economies were more sensitive to capital movements (countries with less open economies cut their tax rates less). Using firm-level data, Grubert also found that the firms with low foreign tax rates in 1984 also had the lowest rates in 1992, suggesting that those firms were highly mobile or more aggressive in their tax planning.

Whether the tax competition phenomenon is negative or positive is beyond the scope of this discussion. However, it is important, however, to note here that from the point of view of the investing multinational, there is no added cost to investing in a low tax jurisdiction. This is in contrast with the standard Tieboutian analysis of tax competition in the state and local context in which individuals choose jurisdictions based on their preferred level of government services and bear the cost of reduced services if they choose the lower tax jurisdiction. Here, the level of services provided by the host country is fixed before the tax holiday and is based on the revenues that were collected without regard to the tax holiday. Typically, the holiday jurisdiction would try to provide the same level of services with the tax holiday in place, funding the additional infrastructure necessitated by the multinational's presence by increasing taxes on relatively immobile factors of production (i.e., land and labor). From the point of view of the multinational, having decided to make the investment somewhere, getting the tax holiday is a pure windfall since it can typically choose among several jurisdictions with similar levels of government services but different tax rates.

(iii) Corporate Residence Jurisdictions and Headquarters Tax Havens.

The international tax regime allocates primary jurisdiction to tax active business income to the source jurisdiction. In situations where the source country refrains from exercising its right to tax (which it commonly does for the reasons described above), residual taxation is possible by the corporate residence jurisdiction. However, it is unlikely that corporate residence jurisdictions will actually impose a current tax on the foreign source active business income earned by multinationals whose headquarters are located in those jurisdictions (or whose parent corporation is incorporated therein).

The reason is that most corporate residence jurisdictions either exempt foreign source active business income earned by their multinationals or permit them to "defer" tax on the income earned by their foreign subsidiaries until it is actually repatriated to the parent in the form of dividends or otherwise. For example, under current U.S. rules, deferral applies to active business income earned by subsidiaries of U.S. parent corporations abroad. Significantly, deferral does not depend on whether or not the income was taxed abroad.

Under deferral, a U.S. based multinational can avoid paying taxes indefinitely on its active foreign source income as long as it does not need to repatriate it. Under the well known Cary Brown formula, deferral is equivalent to exemption of the yield on the amount deferred. Thus, the income earned on foreign-source profits of U.S. multinationals becomes effectively exempt from U.S. tax. Put another way, if deferral lasts long enough, the present value of any tax imposed when the income is eventually repatriated approaches zero.

The obvious solution to this problem would be to repeal deferral, that is, to apply Subpart F to all income, as the Kennedy administration originally suggested in 1961, rather than just to "Subpart F" (i.e., generally passive) income. This solution has been repeatedly suggested by various administrations, incorporated in several recent legislative proposals, and endorsed by academic commentators, but commentators, 65 but it has never gotten off the ground. In fact, the recent trend has been in the opposite direction: Code section 956A, which limited the ability of multinationals to avoid repatriation by imposing current taxation on excess passive assets held abroad, was repealed in 1996. The extension of "check the box" to foreign entities means that U.S.

multinationals can generally choose whether to have deferral based on the specific tax characteristics of the foreign entity and not its foreign legal status as a corporation vel non.

Why has deferral been so successfully maintained against all criticism in the U.S., and why have other jurisdictions maintained an exemption for foreign source active business income? Consider what would likely happen were the U.S. to end deferral: parent corporations of new multinationals, especially in new industries like electronic commerce, would not be incorporated in the U.S. Instead, they would be incorporated in a country like Belgium which does not tax holding corporations (although it taxes other corporations quite heavily and even has a classical system like the U.S.).

Gordon and MacKie-Mason have shown that a firm's decision *whether* to incorporate is significantly affected by tax considerations. Similarly, the decision *where* to incorporate can also be influenced by tax considerations. This can be shown in several ways. First, one can consider the evidence presented by Wilson based on interviews with corporate management that "tax considerations largely dictate location decisions for . . . administrative and distribution centers." This is precisely the type of operation envisaged by Belgium: a corporate headquarters engaged in supervising worldwide manufacturing operations (located in production tax havens). Belgium is in effect marketing itself as a "corporate headquarters tax haven." Like production tax havens, such headquarters tax havens are proliferating because of tax competition.

Second, one can consider industries that are taxed exclusively on a residence basis because taxation at source is considered too difficult or too likely to lead to multiple taxation. Prominent examples are the shipping and commercial insurance industries which are not subject to source-based income taxation because there is no permanent establishment and production can be located in tax havens. One finds that in those cases the corporate residence is frequently also in a tax haven (Liberia and Panama are prominent examples for shipping, Bermuda for insurance) and therefore no income tax is levied (excise taxes are typically levied at source as a minimal but not adequate substitute).

Third, there is evidence that even the current loose U.S. anti-deferral rules may have induced attempts to change corporate residence to avoid them. The U.S. has recently changed its tax rules to impose a tax on publicly-traded U.S. corporations that wish to change the residence of their corporate parent to another jurisdiction. This was prompted by a well-publicized case of a cosmetics distributor that was able to reincorporate tax-free in the Cayman Islands to avoid application of Subpart F to its future subsidiaries.

Reincorporating in Panama or in the Caymans may be a step most U.S. multinationals would be unwilling to take. But establishing the corporate headquarters and formal corporate residence in Belgium, even when the entrepreneurs are U.S. residents, would seem to carry little business risk. Moreover, the shares of most multinationals are currently traded on several exchanges so that it would not appear to matter much which country the parent is incorporated in (since the shareholder protection laws of the trading jurisdiction will typically apply). While this may be unlikely for old, established U.S. corporations like General Motors or even Intel, the major players in a new industry have yet to be incorporated, and future incorporation decisions may well be influenced by tax considerations.

The Treasury Discussion Paper on taxation of electronic commerce suggests that because of such considerations, "a review of current residency definitions and taxation rules may be appropriate." But it is hard to see what definition of corporate residence can be adopted that will avoid these problems. Looking at the corporation's place of management and control seems difficult because the rise of corporate intranets means that there is no longer any need for corporate boards to meet in one physical location, and corporate management can be dispersed in many different countries (including headquarters tax havens) and communicate via secure e-mail or video conferencing. Looking at the residence of shareholders to establish corporate residence is likewise problematic because (as stated above) the shares of most multinationals now trade on several exchanges, and so there would be many corporate residences and no clear way to divide the tax base among them. As long as residence jurisdictions compete with each other for the location of corporate headquarters, effective residence-based taxation seems unlikely.

To sum up: Corporate income from cross-border transactions is increasingly unlikely to be taxed anywhere. In demand jurisdictions it will not be taxed because of the absence of a permanent establishment. In supply jurisdictions it will not be taxed because production will be situated in production tax havens. Finally, in corporate residence jurisdictions it will not be taxed on a current basis because of deferral, and it may never be taxed if corporate residence can be established in headquarters tax havens. Thus, unless current rules are changed, such income will increasingly escape tax altogether, leaving a heavier burden on labor and land and wider gaps in the already strained social safety net.

NOTES AND QUESTIONS

1. The above text suggests that there are two principal problems facing the international tax regime: Effectively enforcing residence-based taxation of passive income, and preventing tax competition from eroding source-based taxation of active income. What do you think is the future of international taxation if neither problem is resolved? What is the future of the income tax? Is this outcome problematic?

2. Neither of these problems is amenable to a unilateral or bilateral solution. The current international tax regime can be distinguished from the international trade regime by its emphasis on unilateral or bilateral solutions. Do you think this is a problem? If so, which is the best multilateral forum to resolve it? Plausible candidates that have been put forward are the OECD, the WTO, or an entirely new "world tax organization." What are the advantages and drawbacks of each?

12.3   THE TAX ARBITRAGE PROBLEM

Ring, One Nation Among Many: Policy Implications of Cross-Border Tax Arbitrage
44 B.C. L. Rev 79 (2002).

INTRODUCTION

The central challenge in international tax is navigating the relationship between an individual country's tax system and the rest of the world—a question of how nations should balance competing demands of revenue, domestic policy, retaliation, and global goals. The question grows more pressing as the pace of intersections among tax regimes escalates. The difficulty of this exercise manifests itself quite clearly in the emerging questions about cross-border tax arbitrage. Does cross-border tax arbitrage represent egregious abuse of the tax system? Is it the natural outcome of a multi-jurisdictional world? What is the proper view of cross-border tax arbitrage and how should its analysis be framed?

In its simplest terms, cross-border tax arbitrage refers to a situation in which a taxpayer or taxpayers rely on conflicts or differences between two countries' tax rules to structure a transaction or entity with the goal of obtaining tax benefits (for example, reduced or no taxation) overall. Had the structure or transactions taken place entirely domestically, the net tax benefit (which was created by the conflict between the two countries) would not exist. Thus, taxpayers in the arbitrage transaction or structure exploit the intersection of the two countries' tax systems to eliminate or reduce substantially their income tax. Particular areas of tax law can prove to be especially fertile "breeding ground[s] for arbitrage," either because one country's tax rule is rather unique or because it is difficult to apply predictably.

The starting point for analysis of cross-border tax arbitrage, as with most other international tax analyses, is recognition of the power of globalization. The international scope of business, along with related changes in communication, cash flow restrictions, and regulatory practices, has increased the ease and volume of cross-border activity. The reality of these changes helps shape international taxation as a topic, and has contributed to the burgeoning growth of arbitrage.

The opportunity for cross-border tax arbitrage arises where transactions are subject to two or more countries' tax regimes. This regulatory intersection between two countries presents the potential for conflicting rules. Despite many common features in our trading partners' tax systems, the multitude of factors that produce tax law, including social policy, administrative constraints, and political compromise render conflicting rules a likely possibility. Conflict in rules produces one of two results: taxation by both countries (double taxation) or taxation by neither (nontaxation). Domestic tax laws and bilateral treaties include mechanisms for limiting double taxation, which is generally viewed as a barrier to cross-border activity. Where the conflict in rules leads to nontaxation, taxpayers (and governments, perhaps because of reduced taxpayer advocacy on the issue) have traditionally paid less attention. The internationalization of the economy, however, combined with developments in technology, has fueled taxpayer recognition of these tax-law conflicts as an opportunity for profitable tax planning. Tax differences exploited by taxpayers to achieve nontaxation produce cross-border tax arbitrage.

What should be the federal government's response to such arbitrage? At the end of the 1990s, the U.S. Treasury Department ("Treasury") identified cross-border arbitrage issues as a high priority; the international community is now displaying a growing interest. When exploring these issues, it is critical to specify precisely what is included in and what is excluded from the concept of cross-border tax arbitrage. As noted above, arbitrage is generally considered the "exploitation [of] differences between the tax system[s] of two different jurisdictions to minimize the taxes paid to either or both." What is excluded from the concept here are those transactions that can be characterized as cross-border "shelters." Such transactions already face scrutiny and examination under the developing shelter rules. The arbitrage question differs because it confronts those transactions that are benefiting from inconsistent treatment across jurisdictions, but presumably have more substance than shelters. . . .

The core tax policy issues for cross-border tax arbitrage can be separated into two discrete sets of questions: (1) why and when is the arbitrage problematic; and (2) whether and how a country, in this case the United States, should respond. Answering these questions demands a comprehensive consideration of tax policy goals, competing values, and practical constraints. Two rather polar responses can be readily imagined. The first, favored by many taxpayers, argues that the United States has no legitimate interest in whether and how much tax is paid to a foreign country. If the U.S. tax rules are followed (and the transaction is not otherwise challenged as a shelter), then no further government action or response is appropriate. In fact, the United States should be quite satisfied that domestic taxpayers might be able to reduce their foreign tax burden. The second response, evident in the U.S. government's effort in the late 1990s to eliminate certain arbitrage opportunities, reflects a generalized but not fully articulated sense that it can be inappropriate to manipulate the differences between countries' tax rules to reduce or eliminate tax.

The very source of conflict between these positions is the reason that neither constitutes an adequate response. Both positions, at least in their extreme form, grant paramount priority to one of the tax system's goals without adequate acknowledgment of the validity of the others. The view that no action is warranted where U.S. rules have been followed gives dominant weight to national regulatory independence, and perhaps implicitly to administrability, while giving seemingly no weight to the economic distortions and equity harms generated. Conversely, a blanket desire to eradicate cross-border tax arbitrage elevates the elimination of distortions at the expense of other factors, including administrability and domestic policy. A comprehensive policy for cross-border tax arbitrage must integrate and balance all competing goals. As a result, however, any resolution reached here will inevitably have an air of compromise. It will neither seek full elimination nor full acceptance of cross-border tax arbitrage. Steps taken to control arbitrage will reduce domestic autonomy and increase harmonization, but these steps will not fully curb arbitrage. Despite these limitations, the analysis of the arbitrage question should be undertaken in a principled manner and proposals measured against established tax criteria.

Ultimately, this Article contends that the government can legitimately respond to some instances of arbitrage but that the continued existence of many more will be an ineluctable feature of a multi-jurisdictional business environment. The conclusion is not surprising; it acknowledges the strengths behind the polar positions articulated above. More specification, however, is needed to translate this broad determination into policy guidance. This Article proposes a balancing test that identifies and evaluates the competing goals in each arbitrage case to derive an appropriate response. In addition, this Article offers insights as to the factors that are most likely to be salient and the types of risks that are most likely to arise with particular antiarbitrage policies.

It is important to be quite clear about the value and the limits of this analytical framework. First, it provides a structure for discussion of arbitrage that targets the core issues. Second, it weaves the divergent strands of the arbitrage argument into a single debate by fostering recognition of the multiplicity of national and international goals. Third, it offers an approach for the policymaker attempting to answer, in a coherent and reasonably uniform manner, the question of whether to intervene and, if so, how. The balancing test, however, is not self-applying. There will continue to be very significant questions of policy to debate. That outcome is not a failing of the framework but rather a reflection of the nature of the endeavor, which demands the accommodation of a variety of competing policy goals in a wide range of circumstances. Furthermore, evaluating the examples under the balancing test is not a static exercise; it may change as tax rules, policy goals, or other features of the tax system change. The balancing test, however, should enable comprehensive consideration of arbitrage without reliance on ad hoc case assessments, along with the development of a sophisticated understanding of the arbitrage problem and the responses that can be crafted.

Through the detailed investigation of this major example of an international regulatory clash (cross-border tax arbitrage), the fundamental question of all global regulatory systems can be clarified and distilled: What vision of international regulatory relations should animate government policy? In making regulatory decisions in the absence of full information, countries must determine the nature of the relationship between and among nationally based regulatory regimes. A nationalist-driven perspective emphasizes competition; a more global perspective encourages cooperation. In reality, neither approach likely serves national or international interests because neither nationalism nor globalism constitutes a defensible, definable goal. The real question is whose interests are to be taken into account in making a policy decision and what outcomes will serve those interests. In tax matters, nations are the dominant actors and can be expected (at least loosely) to promote national interests. The paths most likely to advance these interests will vary by time and context, and may include a range of more or less cooperative behaviors. It is through the detailed investigation of cross-border tax arbitrage that we can gain more insight into this universal regulatory question. . . .

I. THE SCOPE OF CROSS-BORDER TAX ARBITRAGE

A. The Basic Definition

Before attempting to evaluate cross-border tax arbitrage, it is necessary to establish a working definition. This step is purely a positive decision of how to classify a transaction or structure. Whether and when it should be limited is the central question and is taken up in the remainder of this Article.

Various definitions of cross-border tax arbitrage have been offered by government officials, tax scholars, and practitioners. Generally, these definitions encompass situations in which countries' tax rules governing a particular transaction or structure differ sufficiently that the conflict results in tax benefits that would not exist had the transaction or entity occurred entirely domestically in either country. In cases of cross-border tax arbitrage, taxpayers avail themselves of conflicting rules and gaps between national tax systems to reduce their tax burden.

Two other problem areas in tax are likely to overlap with arbitrage, but they remain distinct: cross-border tax competition and tax shelters. Unlike tax competition, cross-border tax arbitrage can occur where two countries each operate robust tax systems and aim to tax economic activity comprehensively. The fact that two such tax regimes would still differ (as would be expected in a multi-jurisdictional world) means that the opportunity for conflicting rules, and thus arbitrage, exists. Thriving examples of cross-border tax arbitrage persist independent of any traditional tax competition. Moreover, current proposals for eliminating "harmful" tax competition would not impact most arbitrage opportunities. . . .

In contrast to arbitrage transactions, tax shelters typically prompt questions about shams and economic substance, reflecting the nature of corporate tax shelters to test the limits of ambiguities in domestic tax law. The primary concern for shelter regulations is how to identify and stop transactions that generally lack substance without chilling desirable conduct. The challenge lies not in the abstract goal, but in the more concrete task of ascertaining what constitutes a shelter and how that will be determined. Much attention has been devoted to developing shelter gatekeeper-oriented rules that emphasize reporting and documentation. Although it is certainly possible for a cross-border tax arbitrage to be a sham, that is not the core of the arbitrage question. Achieving a cross-border benefit is generally more attractive and secure than a shelter benefit because the former derives from the conflict of clearly applied rules in two different countries, not from a stretch of domestic law, which may be subject to domestic anti-abuse rules. To the extent there is overlap in a case, it makes sense to view the transaction under the rubric for shams because the degree of substance in the activity will be the threshold question. Thus, this Article begins with the premise that the transactions under scrutiny would pass the initial test for substance and not merit classification as shams or shelters. The relationship between corporate tax shelters and cross-border tax arbitrage, however, highlights some of the potential challenges in any effort to limit cross-border tax arbitrage. The U.S. instinct in dealing with corporate tax shelters has not been to advocate or implement a general anti-avoidance rule (with its potential chilling effect) as seen in Australia and Canada. Nonetheless, the recent domestic legislation targeting corporate tax shelters and enacting understatement penalties and registration requirements has ignited debate over the breadth of the rules and the ability to discern boundaries. As always, a tension exists between designing broad reforms that may reach too far and designing targeted rules that may encourage taxpayers' participation in a regulatory cat-and-mouse game as they seek the next transaction just beyond "the law."

B. The Origins of the Arbitrage Problem: Why Countries' Tax Rules Vary

An initial question that arises from the basic definition of cross-border tax arbitrage, which is significant later in assessing possible responses, is why do countries have different tax rules? Clearly no single reason prevails. In fact we have only to look at the motivations behind domestic tax law to imagine the range of reasons. Rules vary because of: (1) different policy choices—the political consensus about tradeoffs may vary among societies with different values, traditions, and expectations; (2) different judgments about the impact of given rules—to the extent that all rule making requires decisions to be made without full knowledge of the potential impact, it is quite plausible for different decision-making groups (countries) to arrive at alternative determinations; (3) politics— here used in the sense that different political systems permit or facilitate different access to rule-makers and allow different forms of power and influence; (4) randomness; (5) path dependence; and (6) resources—a country could determine that an otherwise attractive rule is unrealistic due to administrative, resource, and technical skill constraints. The scope of reasons listed here suggests that one could readily anticipate a notable degree of variation among countries' tax regimes, even when they share many fundamental principles and goals. To the extent that cross-border tax arbitrage depends on the existence of conflicting rules, a steady supply seems quite likely.

The enumeration of sources of tax-law variability is important for policy purposes. The reasons that countries' rules vary can play a critical role in thinking about potential responses to arbitrage and what those responses would entail. For example, where tax rules differ because of policy goals, any plan to coordinate rules would require the countries to balance their domestic policy choices against the benefits from coordination with other countries. If path dependence played a major role in establishing conflicting rules, then changing the relevant arbitrage-related rule could have more widespread impact. That is, when the arbitrage-related rule is changed, the country may need to review its other domestic rules that were part of the original regulatory path. National-level policies may need to be reevaluated once benefits from multilateral coordination (loosely defined for the present) are factored into the equation of creating policy. . . .

If administrability motivated a country to select a particular rule, then unless the country's move to a different, internationally coordinated rule offers discernable benefits to the country, the move might be ill advised. Where there are competing judgments about the impact of particular rules, a coordination or harmonization effort may require countries to be persuaded about the likely advantages of the alternative rules. Implicit in these tensions are more fundamental questions about the value of regulatory diversity and the benefits that arise from a system that tolerates experimentation.

C. Case Studies

To develop the framework for cross-border tax arbitrage, it is useful to specify a few case studies to provide context for the analysis and to serve as illustrations. This section outlines four sample arbitrages in some detail. There is no intention to suggest that these are exclusive categories of arbitrage, nor is the mission here to reach a conclusion about their treatment. The case studies help ground the more abstract discussions of arbitrage. For most of these examples, a detailed discussion is available in the literature. The purpose of this section is to convey enough information about the arbitrage's structure, operation, impact, and incentives to provide a useful hook for the later analysis of cross-border tax arbitrage. . . .

1. Original Issue Discount in the United States and Japan

The United States has grappled with the taxation of original issue discount ("OID") for several decades. The question centers on the timing of interest income to the holder of an OID bond. Prior to 1969, the United States waited until the maturity of the OID bond to tax the holder on the interest income, although the corporate issuer was taking current deductions for the OID. This "wait and see" rule provided nonparallel treatment and a significant deferral opportunity because the holder was perceived to have a virtually guaranteed receipt (unlike, for example, with a stock investment). Thus, in 1969, Congress required current annual inclusion in the holder's income of a pro rata amount of the gain to be received at maturity.

The ratable inclusion method, however, overstates income in the early years and understates it in the later years. In theory that result favors the borrower who could take larger interest deductions sooner and disadvantages the bond holder who reports a larger portion of income sooner. In practice though, the effect will not be a wash if the taxpayers holding OID bonds are those for whom the timing of income is not significant, such as tax exempts. In light of these concerns, Congress made significant changes to the OID rules in 1982 (and 1984), requiring interest to be calculated on a yield-to-maturity basis reflecting the debt instrument's internal rate of return. The overall pattern of tax reform in the area of OID demonstrates an attention to the time value of money and the importance of more accurately representing it in taxation (even if in all areas of the Code this principle is not pursued with equal vigor).

The opportunity for cross-border tax arbitrage with OID bonds occurred where U.S. issuers of OID bonds paired with buyers in a country that did not require current accrual of the holder's interest income. Japan, in particular, was a market into which U.S. issuers sought to sell their bonds. The basic tax picture was rather attractive. The U.S. issuer received current annual interest expense deductions, while the Japanese holder paid no tax on the foreign bond interest under Japanese law until the interest income was actually received (for example, at the end of the bond period). U.S. income tax also was not imposed on the holder, presumably because the bonds in question qualified for the portfolio interest exemption. (In any event there would be no U.S. withholding tax on the OID until the U.S. issuer made payments to the holder.) Thus, the parties benefited by pairing current U.S. deductions with deferred income recognition in Japan. Had the borrowing been entirely domestic, with either the U.S. issuer selling to U.S. purchasers or Japanese investors buying from Japanese issuers, this timing benefit might not have been available.

2.   Double-Dip Lease

Perhaps one of the most ubiquitous of cross-border tax arbitrage transactions is the "double-dip lease." At the core of this transaction is the ability to have two jurisdictions each treat their taxpayer (either the "lessor" or "lessee") as the "owner" of a leased asset. By virtue of owner status, the taxpayer is entitled to depreciation deductions (typically accelerated) and any investment tax credits. (The key to creating an arbitrage benefit is the availability of accelerated deductions and/or credits, not the fact that two taxpayers are recovering their respective investments.) For example, imagine that Plane Co., located in France, leases an asset (such as a plane) to Flight Co., located in the United States. Assume that France determines Plane Co. is the owner of the plane (perhaps because France uses a formalistic rule based on legal ownership of an asset). Also assume that the United States considers Flight Co. to be the owner of the plane (because the United States uses a rule based on the economic substance of the lease transaction to determine asset ownership). Thus, two different taxpayers "own" a single plane and both take accelerated depreciation deductions (plus any available credits). The result derives from the conflict between France's and the United States' rules for asset ownership.

If the leasing transaction had occurred entirely domestically (either in the United States or France), only one owner would be identified and only one taxpayer would be permitted the depreciation deductions. The taxpayer deemed to be the lessee would generally take business deductions for the cost of the lease/rental payments made annually. Those deductions, however, would typically be less advantageous than ones classified as "depreciation" because of the acceleration permitted for depreciation. In addition, investment tax credits may be available for owners but not lessees. Thus, even in the domestic case both taxpayers recover their investments (through depreciation deductions by the owners and through rental deductions by the lessee). It is the availability of the second set of accelerated depreciation deductions (and investment tax credits) in the cross-border scenario that creates cross-border tax arbitrage. In addition to the double-dip benefits, cross-border leasing can offer financing and withholding tax advantages as well. It is worth noting that conflicting ownership rules could lead to a case in which neither country recognized their taxpayer as the owner entitled to depreciation deductions. In that case, though, the "burden" borne by the taxpayers is not classic double taxation; it more properly constitutes a "loss" of special tax benefits designed with business incentives in mind. Specifically, if each country in the cross-border lease considers the other country's taxpayer as the owner, no taxpayer receives accelerated depreciation deductions. The key loss is the difference in timing. The other likely "loss" from non-owner status is access to investment tax credits—a tax technique to spur investment activity generally, or in targeted sectors. Thus, the "penalty" from tax-law conflict in the cross-border leasing context arguably is not "inappropriate," uneconomic taxation, although it is burdened more heavily than a domestic transaction because no party receives accelerated depreciation deductions or investment tax credits.

3. Dual-Resident Companies

In this arbitrage based on residence rules, corporate groups in two different countries can use a double-dip strategy with a dual-resident company (DRC) to deduct losses twice. Specifically, a corporation resident both in the United States and a foreign jurisdiction (most notably the United Kingdom) serves as a member of a consolidated group of related companies in each jurisdiction. (The dual-resident status is possible if the two countries apply different tests, for example, incorporation versus management and control, and the facts of the case allow a single corporation to satisfy the relevant test in each country.) If this DRC has losses, then there is an opportunity to use those losses against the income of the U.S. group and the income of the U.K. group. For example, the DRC might borrow to fund the acquisition of U.S. subsidiaries. The DRC would have little income but substantial loss due to interest deductions on the debt. The DRC losses would be shared with affiliated groups in both the United States and the United Kingdom. Thus, a single corporation's losses (those of the DRC) reduce two sets of income and ultimately two sets of taxes, creating the double-dip effect.

4. Hybrid Entities

Once we define cross-border tax arbitrage as a situation in which a transaction or structure receives different treatment under two jurisdictions' tax laws, the range of possible arbitrages seems almost infinite. An active (and highly contested) source of arbitrage exists with entity classification. When two countries classify an entity differently— for example, the United States views a business operation as a branch, but the foreign jurisdiction deems it a corporation—substantial arbitrage opportunities result. Although such conflict has always been possible, the adoption of the "check-the-box rules" effective January 1, 1997 provided these results with much greater certainty and much less complexity. Prior to these new rules, entity classification (in particular the distinction between a partnership and an association taxable as a corporation) turned on an analysis of six factors. This multi-factor test applied to both domestic and foreign business organizations.

Ultimately, Treasury determined that because classification was virtually elective for a subset of taxpayers, then perhaps it should be elective directly, with a lower cost and broader availability. The final check-the-box regulations specify certain domestic and foreign entities as "per se" corporations. No election is possible, and there is no flexibility regarding their taxation. For the remainder of business organizations not subject to the per se classification, however, the taxpayer is generally allowed to elect its tax status either as a corporation or a pass-through (partnership or branch, depending on the facts).

The extension of the election regime to foreign business organizations generated considerable debate. Although both domestic and foreign entities were analyzed under the old six factor test, some tax commentators expressed serious concern about extending any elective classification system to foreign entities due to the risk of inconsistent entity classification between countries and the potential arbitrage it could facilitate. The Internal Revenue Service (IRS or "Service") itself acknowledged this risk, but ultimately issued the final check-the-box regulations with treatment for foreign entities that mirrored the regime for domestic entities. In both cases, certain types of enumerated business operations automatically receive corporation status (for foreign entities, the regulations provide a country-by-country list). The remainder may choose their classification. With these new regulations came new opportunities for hybrid entities.

As an arbitrage category, "hybrid entities" is much larger and more varied in its content than the other examples offered in this Article. Nonetheless, it is helpful to have at least one or two versions in mind to support the later discussion of a framework for cross-border tax arbitrage. Two examples are described below.

a.   Subpart F And Entity Classification

One common use of hybrids is to avoid some of the limitations and restrictions of the Subpart F regime. For example, imagine a U.S. person has a wholly owned operating entity in Country X, a high-tax jurisdiction. This entity constitutes a controlled foreign corporation (CFC), thereby subjecting the U.S. person to Subpart F's antideferral rules. Despite the fact that the CFC is a separate legal entity and is not a U.S. corporation, some or all of its income might be taxable currently to its U.S. shareholder, even in the absence of a distribution from the CFC. If the CFC earned passive income, that income would likely be included on the U.S. shareholder's U.S. income tax return immediately, eliminating the deferral benefit from operating offshore. In contrast, most active income earned by the CFC would not be captured by the Subpart F rules and, therefore, would not be subject to U.S. tax until the CFC made a distribution to the U.S. shareholder. Under the facts of the proposed hypothetical here, however, the active income earned by the CFC still faces unattractive taxation because the CFC itself is located in a high-tax jurisdiction. Even though current U.S. tax is avoided, high Country X tax is not. This is where a hybrid structure could be useful.

The U.S. person directs the CFC to set up an entity (Entity Y) in Country Y (a low-tax jurisdiction). Entity Y is treated as a corporation by Country X but is disregarded under U.S. tax law. Entity Y makes a loan to the CFC, and the CFC deducts the interest payments because Country X views the payments as made to a separate corporation. These interest deductions reduce the CFC's operating income subject to Country X's high tax rate (assuming no Country X thin capitalization rules apply). The interest payments received by Entity Y bear little or no tax because

Country Y is a low-tax jurisdiction. The remaining question is the U.S. tax treatment. [Generally, interest income is passive and captured by Subpart F, but only if earned by a CFC. Here, taxpayer would argue that because Entity y was disregarded, the cash flow was purely internal and should also be disregarded]. Thus, Country X tax on the CFC's operating income is reduced, no significant Country Y tax is due, and no U.S. Subpart F income is created in the process. The success of this structure turns on the use of hybrids and the discrepancies in entity classification.

b.   Domestic Reverse Hybrids

Another type of hybrid, a "domestic reverse hybrid," produces a different benefit. Consider a foreign corporation with a U.S. operating subsidiary. When the U.S. subsidiary pays a dividend to the foreign parent, there is no deduction and the payment is likely subject to U.S. withholding tax under the applicable treaty. On the other side, the dividend will probably benefit from a foreign tax credit or exemption in the foreign parent's jurisdiction. If instead of owning the operating subsidiary directly, the foreign parent establishes a U.S. hybrid holding company to own the U.S. operating subsidiary, a tax benefit results. The key to obtaining this benefit is that the U.S. holding company is a hybrid—that is, the U.S. holding company is considered a corporation for U.S. tax purposes, but is a pass-through entity under the rules of the foreign parent's jurisdiction. In this alternative scenario, the U.S. operating subsidiary pays a dividend to the U.S. hybrid and the hybrid pays interest to the foreign parent. The following tax treatment results: Under U.S. tax law, the first payment is a dividend and is excluded from the hybrid's income and is not deductible by the payor. The interest payment from the U.S. hybrid to the foreign parent is deductible and can receive the lower withholding rate negotiated in the treaty (if there is one) with the parent's jurisdiction. The foreign jurisdiction, however, again views the payment received by the foreign parent as a dividend from the underlying U.S. corporation (not as interest from the hybrid entity). The "dividend" again benefits from the foreign jurisdiction's applicable foreign tax credit or exemption rules. Thus, for U.S. tax purposes, the hybrid transaction effectively replaces a direct dividend distribution from an operating U.S. subsidiary to its foreign parent (which is not deductible by the U.S. subsidiary and faces U.S. withholding tax) with an interest payment to the foreign parent (which is deductible on the U.S. side by the hybrid entity and has reduced U.S. withholding under the treaty). The arbitrage benefit derives from the fact that in both scenarios the foreign jurisdiction views the payment to the foreign parent as a dividend, yet in the hybrid scenario the United States "relinquishes" its taxing power because it views the payment as interest and assumes that the other jurisdiction does as well (and will correspondingly tax it). The conflicting classification of the U.S. hybrid entity lies at the center of this profitable mismatch. . . .

NOTES AND QUESTIONS

1. How does the description of the relationship among country tax rules in this article compare with the description in the Brauner article? What is the reason for this difference?

2. Do you think tax arbitrage is a problem? Why or why not?

3. If tax arbitrage is a problem, can anything be done about it? Under what circumstances? The OECD has included arbitrage as part of its focus in the BEPS Action plan. See, e.g., OECD, *Neutralising the Effects of Hybrid Mismatch Arrangements, Action 2—2015 Final Report,* available at http://www.oecd.org/tax/neutralising-the-effects-of-hybrid-mismatch-arrangements-action-2-2015-final-report-9789264241138-en.htm.

12.4   THE INTERNATIONAL TAX REGIME AFTER BEPS AND THE TCJA

From 2013 to 2015, the US participated in the OECD/G20 effort to limit BEPS. However, until recently, the general view was that following the conclusion of the BEPS negotiations and the change of Administration the US is stepping back from the BEPS process. While the EU was charging ahead with implementing BEPS through the Anti-Tax Avoidance Directive (ATAD), the US stated that it was already in compliance with all BEPS minimum standards and therefore other than Country by Country (CBC) reporting it had no further BEPS obligations. The US refused to join the Multilateral Instrument (MLI) to implement BEPS into tax treaties, and did not join the common reporting standards (CRS) to further automatic exchange of information, leading the EU to call it a tax haven. The US did adopt BEPS provisions in its model tax treaty, but those have not been implemented in any actual US treaty. Thus, most observers believe that the US has abandoned the BEPS effort.

But this view is wrong. TCJA clearly relies on BEPS principles and in particular on the single tax principle. This represents a triumph for the G20/OECD and is incongruent with the generally held view that the US will never adopt BEPS. This can be seen in both the outbound and inbound provisions of the TCJA.

For outbound transactions, GILTI means that Amazon, Apple, Facebook, Google, Netflix, and their ilk will have to pay tax at 10.5% on future GILTI because they have CFCs that produce "tested income" (and no loss) in excess of 10% over their basis in offshore tangible assets, which is zero or close to it (since they derive almost all of their income from intangibles). This imposes residence taxation in cases where there is no or low taxation at source. For inbound transactions, the BEAT means that a minimum tax of 10% will apply to many payments to foreign related parties. This imposes source taxation where there may not be taxation at residence.

TCJA also contains two anti-hybrid provisions that directly implement the single tax principle, similarly to the ATAD. The first,

Section 245A(e), disallows the participation exemption for hybrid dividends that are treated as deductible payments at source. The second, Sectionection 267A, limits the deductibility of payments on hybrid instruments or to hybrid entities. These provisions clearly implement OECD BEPS Action 2 in accordance with the single tax principle.

Overall, The TCJA contains multiple provisions that incorporate the principles of the OECD/G20 Base Erosion and Profit Shifting (BEPS) into domestic US tax law. Together with the changes in the 2016 Model US tax treaty, these provisions mean that the US is following the EU and China in implementing BEPS and in particular its underlying principle, the single tax principle. However, while TCJA in general is consistent with the spirit of BEPS, as noted above it retains and to some extent exacerbates the shifting potential of prior law. In particular, the GILTI provision encourages shifting of real activities offshore to benefit from the hurdle rate exemption, and the participation exemption allows any resulting profits to be repatriated tax-free. It remains to be seen whether GILTI and BEAT together act as a more effective curb on the artificial shifting of profits than pre-TCJA law. The following text discusses how the TCJA fits in with the post-BEPS international tax regime.

Avi-Yonah and Mazzoni, BEPS, ATAP and the New Tax Dialogue: A Transatlantic Competition?

46 Intertax 885 (2018).

The Tax Cuts and Jobs Act (TCJA) signed into law by President Trump on 22 December 2017 contains multiple provisions that incorporate the principles of the OECD/G20 Base Erosion and Profit Shifting (BEPS) into domestic US tax law. Together with the changes in the 2016 US Model Tax Treaty, these provisions mean that the United States is following the European Union in implementing BEPS and particularly its underlying principle, the single tax principle (all income should be subject to tax once at the rate derived from the benefits principle, i.e. active income at a minimum source tax rate and passive at the residence state rate). This represents a triumph for the G20/OECD and is incongruent with the generally held view that the United States will never adopt BEPS.

1.1. Introduction: The US and BEPS

Since its launch in 2013, the United States has actively participated in all aspects of the BEPS Project. However, until recently, the general view was that following the conclusion of the BEPS negotiations and the change of Administration, the United States was stepping back from the BEPS process. While the European Union was charging ahead with implementing BEPS through the Anti-Tax Avoidance Directive (ATAD), the United States stated that it was already in compliance with all BEPS minimum standards and therefore other than country-by-country reporting (CbCR) it had no further BEPS obligations. The United States decided not to sign the Multilateral Convention to Implement Tax Treaty Related Measures to Prevent Base Erosion and Profit Shifting (MLI), which would have obliged it to implement BEPS into tax treaties and did not join the Common Reporting Standard (CRS) to further automatic exchange of information, leading the European Union to call it a tax haven. The United States has adopted BEPS provisions in its model tax treaty but they have not been implemented in any actual US treaty. Thus, most observers believe that the United States has abandoned the BEPS effort.

This view is not wholly correct. The current tax reform legislation clearly relies on BEPS principles and particularly on the single tax principle. This represents a triumph for the G20/OECD and challenges the generally held view that the United States will never adopt BEPS.

This chapter proceeds in four parts. Sections 1.2., 1.3. and 1.4. analyse the three BEPS provisions included in TCJA: a one-time 'transition tax' on untaxed accumulated earnings and profits (E&P) of certain non-US corporations (new § 965) and two anti-base erosion and income shifting provisions, namely a foreign minimum tax on 10% US shareholders of controlled foreign corporations (CFCs) to the extent the CFCs are treated as having 'global intangible low-taxed income' (GILTI) (new § 951A) and a base erosion and anti-abuse tax (BEAT) that will be imposed in relation to deductible payments made by certain corporations to their non-US affiliates (new § 59A). Section 1.5. discusses one of the key BEPS Action items that caused the most concern in the United States, i.e. Action 6 on the prevention of treaty abuse through inclusion of a principal purpose test (PPT). In section 1.6., the authors argue that Congress could have done more, especially with regard to the anti-hybrid rules for certain related-party amounts of the new § 267A since it does not have any significant impact on foreign-to-foreign hybrid planning. To this extent, it should be noted that in order to limit the application of Subpart F exceptions to transactions that use reverse hybrids to create stateless income, the Obama Administration proposed a rule that would provide that §§ 954(c) and 954(c)(6) do not apply to payments made to a foreign reverse hybrid held directly by a US owner when those amounts are treated as deductible payments received from foreign related persons. Section 1.7. provides some conclusions.

1.2. Past Accumulations

Section 965 of TCJA provides for a one-time deemed repatriation tax on previously untaxed accumulated foreign earnings. TCJA splits E&P between cash and illiquid assets with cash amounts taxed at a 15.5% effective rate and illiquid assets taxed at an 8% effective rate. The taxpayer may elect to pay this tax over an eight-year period. However, if a US shareholder becomes an 'expatriated entity' within the meaning of § 7874(a)(2) at any point within the ten-year period following enactment of TCJA, the benefits of the reduced rates would be recaptured. In that event, the US shareholder would be subject to an additional tax equal to

35% of the amount of the deduction allowed in respect of the transition tax. No foreign tax credits are permitted to offset this additional tax.

The accumulation of offshore profits by US multinationals in low-tax jurisdictions has been the focus of significant concern and a primary driver of the BEPS effort. The EU ATAD and State aid as well as the UK diverted profits tax (DPT) and current discussion on the digital economy all reflect these concerns. Indeed, these earnings, accumulated since the 2004–5 tax amnesty and currently exceeding USD 2.6 trillion, are located in just seven low-tax jurisdictions and they are highly concentrated: just four companies (Apple, Microsoft, Pfizer and GE) hold approximately one quarter (24%) of the offshore profits. Ten companies have 38% of the profits and fifty companies hold three quarters of the earnings.

In the authors' opinion, there are four arguments for why such low rates are inappropriate for past earnings. Firstly, as a policy matter, there is no justification for not taxing these profits in full, because they do not raise competitiveness issues (since they have been earned) or behavioural response issues (since the behaviour has already happened) and because they mostly represent earnings on intellectual property developed in the United States with hefty taxpayer support.

Secondly, there are a few outstanding issues with dual rates, including: (i) what may be considered a 'cash or cash equivalent' for the purposes of this tax and (ii) whether there would be a look-back rule for 'cash or cash equivalent' assets recently invested to take advantage of the lower rate, or a more general anti-abuse rule targeting transactions carried out to achieve the lower rate. The reason is simple: taxpayers are incentivized to manipulate their foreign cash positions by converting cash to more illiquid investments and by legitimately distributing some of their cash through dividend payments or other means. The new law includes both a look-back rule and a subjective intent-based anti-abuse test, the PPT. Indeed, § 965(c)(3)(A) provides a formula for calculating how much E&P should be attributed to cash assets and therefore subject to the higher 15.5% rate. The benchmark is the 'aggregate foreign cash position' calculated as the greater of either 'the pro rata share of the cash position of all specified foreign corporations as of the last day of the last taxable year beginning before January 1, 2018, or the average of the cash position determined on the last day of each of the two taxable years ending immediately before November 2, 2017.' In addition, § 965(c)(3)(F) states that, 'If the Secretary determines that a principal purpose of any transaction was to reduce the aggregate foreign cash position taken into account under this subsection, such transaction shall be disregarded for purposes of this subsection [emphasis added].' The Conference Report accompanying TCJA, states that, 'The provision also authorizes the Secretary to disregard transactions that are determined to have the principal purpose of reducing the aggregate foreign cash position [emphasis added],' thus, viewing those two formulations as having the same meaning. But if 'a principal purpose' shall be defined as being one of its 'first-in importance' purposes, the authors believe that the effectiveness of § 965(c)(3)(F) would be substantially undermined. In this regard, the extensive report prepared by the Tax Section of the New York State Bar Association (NYSBA) on the 1994 proposed partnership anti-abuse regulation stated,

If a transaction were subject to attack only if 'the' principal purpose were tax avoidance, the result would be a substantially increased willingness on the part of taxpayers to engage in aggressive transactions. In our experience, a taxpayer usually is able to assert some nontax purpose for a transaction, even if that purpose is on its face borderline. Any such claim would have to satisfy a much lower threshold of 'believability' if the test were whether 'the' principal purpose of the transaction is tax avoidance . . . The history of § 269, the corporate anti-abuse rule that applies only when 'the' principal purpose of a transaction is tax avoidance, demonstrates the weakness of such a test. The Service has been unable to successfully apply $ 269 with any regularity, as indicated by the dearth of judicial decisions under that section as well as our experience that agents in the field rarely attempt to apply the section. We believe those results may be attributable to § 269's requirement that 'the' principal purpose of a transaction be tax avoidance, which often allows the taxpayer to prevail by asserting a relatively weak business purpose [emphasis added].

Thirdly, studies have highlighted that repatriated earnings in 2004 were used to send cash back to shareholders, either in the form of dividends or stock buybacks, instead of being invested in new US jobs and infrastructure as President Trump sold TCJA on the promise that, 'the plan is going to bring trillions of dollars back into the United States, money that's offshore . . . But you look at the great companies—Apple and so many others. They have billions of dollars overseas that they want to bring back. Now they're going to be able to bring it back, and we'll [sic] spending that money, and they'll be spending that money right here. And it will be jobs and lots of other good things [emphasis added].' Thus, it is highly likely that repatriated funds will be used for already planned projects, such as pay down [sic] existing borrowings, set off a new wave of M&A, rather than being invested in expansion. For example, Cisco expects to spend much of the newly repatriated cash on share buybacks and dividends over the next two years. On the other hand, Apple announced in January that it would invest USD 30 billion in capital spending in the United States; over five years that would create more than 20,000 jobs. However, analysts questioned whether Apple's commitments were new and impacted in any way by the tax reform since the company would have been able to make this investment with existing cash flow—without needing to tap into cash holdings.

Last but not least, this money is not trapped offshore. Under the previous § 956(c)(2)(A) and (F), a foreign subsidiary's untaxed earnings might have been invested without triggering the deemed dividend rules regarding stock of a domestic corporation, a debt obligation of a US person or a US bank deposit, as long as the issuer was not a US shareholder or did not have a 25% or other proscribed relationship with the foreign subsidiary. The US Senate Permanent Subcommittee on Investigations on the 2004 tax holiday has showed that at the end of FY2010, of the USD 538 billion in undistributed accumulated foreign earnings of 20 US multinational corporations, nearly half (46%) of the funds that the corporations had identified as offshore and for which US taxes had been deferred were actually deposited in the names of CFCs in accounts at US financial institutions. Recent data compiled by Bloomberg shows that the top 10 US multinationals have boosted their investments in government bonds to USD 113 billion from USD 67 billion and have received at least USD 1.4 billion in interest payments over the past five years.

1.3. Future Accumulations

In TCJA, the shift from a worldwide system of taxation to a quasi-territorial one is accompanied by some sort of a foreign minimum tax, the so-called global intangible low-taxed income (GILTI) provision, the stick. The intent is to discourage erosion of the US base by moving or holding intangible assets outside the United States. Under the new § 951A(a), a US shareholder of any CFC must include in its gross income for a taxable year its GILTI in a manner generally similar to inclusion of Subpart F income. GILTI means, with respect to any US shareholder for the shareholder's taxable year, the excess (if any) of the shareholder's net CFC tested income over the shareholder's net deemed tangible income return. Net deemed tangible income return is, with respect to any US shareholder for a taxable year, the excess (if any) of 10% of the aggregate of its pro rata share of the qualified business asset investment (QBAI) of each CFC with respect to which it is a US shareholder over the amount of interest expense taken into account in determining its net CFC tested income for the taxable year to the extent that the interest expense exceeds the interest income properly allocable to the interest expense that is taken into account in determining its net CFC tested income. Net CFC tested income means, with respect to any US shareholder, the excess of the aggregate of the shareholder's pro rata share of the tested income of each CFC with respect to which it is a US shareholder over the aggregate of its pro rata share of the tested loss of each CFC with respect to which it is a US shareholder. The tested income of a CFC means the excess (if any) of the gross income of the corporation—determined without regard to certain exceptions to tested income—over deductions (including taxes) properly allocable to such gross income. QBAI means, with respect to any CFC for a taxable year, the average of the aggregate of its adjusted bases, determined as of the close of each quarter of the taxable year, in specified tangible property used in its trade or business and of a type with respect to which a deduction is generally allowable under § 167. To put it simply, the formula for GILTI can be expressed as:

GILTI = Net CFC Tested Income − [(10% × QBAI) − Interest Expense]

As a result, the formula generally exempts from inclusion a deemed return on tangible assets and assumes the residual income to be intangible income that is subject to current US tax.

The tax rate for future GILTI is determined by taking the 21% corporate tax rate and allowing a deduction of 50%, to give a net rate of 10.5%. This rate can be partially offset by foreign tax credits but in a separate basket (but with cross-averaging within the basket). The provision is effective for taxable years of foreign corporations beginning after 31 December 2017.

What this means in plain English is that Amazon, Apple, Facebook, Google, Netflix and their ilk will have to pay tax at 10.5% on future GILTI because they have CFCs that produce 'tested income' (and no loss) in excess of 10% over their basis in offshore tangible assets, which will be zero or close to it (since they derive almost all of their income from intangibles). Other MNEs (e.g. GE or Intel) will pay less because they have more tangible assets offshore. This creates an obvious incentive to move jobs (not just profits) offshore. In this regard, a Baker McKenzie Client Alert observed that, 'the GILTI rules create a surprising and unexpected incentive for U.S. multinationals to increase the amount of tangible assets held by their CFCs, which in most circumstances will presumably be situated outside the United States. Assuming a more or less steady amount of overall income potentially subject to Section 951A (and deductible under Section 250), increasing QBAI held by CFCs may be one of the most effective ways to manage or reduce GILTI.'

To address these issues, TCJA proposes two solutions. Firstly, § 951A(d)(4) includes a very broad anti-abuse provision which reads as follows: '[f]or purposes of determining QBAI, the Secretary is authorized to issue anti-avoidance regulations or other guidance as the Secretary determines appropriate, including regulations or other guidance that provide for the treatment of property if the property is transferred or held temporarily, or if avoidance was a factor in the transfer or holding of the property [emphasis added].' Secondly, § 250(a)(1)(A) provides a 37.5% foreign-derived intangible income deduction (FDII), the carrot, with the result that the portion of a US corporation's intangible income derived from serving foreign markets is effectively taxed at 13.125%. The intent is to encourage US multinationals to remain in the country and keep their assets, earnings, jobs and functions there.

Section 250(b)(1) defines the FDII of any domestic corporation as the amount which bears the same ratio to the corporation's 'deemed intangible income' as its 'foreign-derived deduction eligible' income bears to its 'deduction eligible income'. In other words, a domestic corporation's FDII is its deemed intangible income multiplied by the percentage of its deduction eligible income that is foreign derived.

Deemed intangible income is the excess of a domestic corporation's deduction eligible income over its deemed tangible income return.

The 'foreign-derived deduction eligible income' is defined as income derived in connection with (1) property that is sold by the taxpayer to any foreign person for a foreign use or (2) services provided to any foreign person, or with respect to foreign property. Foreign use means any use, consumption or disposition which is not within the United States. For purposes of the provision, the terms 'sold,' 'sells,' and 'sale' include any lease, exchange or other disposition. Special rules for determining foreign use apply to transactions that involve property or services provided to domestic intermediaries or related parties. Section 250(b)(5)(B) and (b)(5)(C) operate—to make sure that property is ultimately sold to a foreign person for use or consumption abroad or services are provided to a person, or with respect to property, located outside the United States. If property is sold to a related foreign party, the sale is not treated as for a foreign use unless the property is sold by the related foreign party to another person who is unrelated and is not a US person and the taxpayer establishes to the satisfaction of the Secretary that such property is for a foreign use. Transactions implicating this rule might arise where, for example, a US corporate taxpayer who owns intellectual property (IP) rights domestically in film or television programming licenses those rights to a wholly owned foreign subsidiary, which, in turn, sub-licenses the content in its local market to third parties. A similar restriction also exists with services provided to a related party located outside the United States. Income derived from such a transaction does not qualify as foreign-derived deduction eligible income unless the taxpayer establishes to the satisfaction of the Secretary that the service is not substantially similar to services provided by the related party to persons located within the United States.

There are three obvious problems with the FDII deduction.

According to a group of thirteen tax law professors, taxpayers may be able to take advantage of the reduced rate on export income through 'resale' transactions where goods are sold to independent foreign distributors who subsequently resell back into the United States. In their opinion, Treasury should address such 'roundtripping' transactions in regulations with rules similar to those under Treas. Reg. 1.954–3(a)(3)(ii), which determine the place of use, consumption or disposition of property for foreign base company sales income purposes. In particular, Treasury should require US manufacturers to conduct a real investigation of how much the independent foreign party will sell back into the United States. Another major issue that Treasury should focus on is the level of further processing required to qualify as foreign use. Assuming that roundtripping transactions are permitted to the extent that the property sold is somewhat further processed abroad, what would be the minimum amount of further processing necessary to allow reimportation into the United States? In the authors' opinion, Treasury should apply standards similar to the 'substantial transformation' and/or 'substantial contribution' tests provided by Treas. Reg. 1.954–3(a)(4)(ii) and 1.954–3(a)(4)(iv). If substantial transformation and/or contribution may sound like high standards, the authors believe that property should be, at least, significantly or materially modified before being reimported into the United States. Additional guidance will be needed for computer software transactions where software is licensed to be merely imprinted in physical CDs and then sold back into the United States. In the authors' opinion, income derived from such a transaction should not qualify as foreign-derived deduction eligible income since the software is merely imprinted in physical form and not significantly modified.

Secondly, the authors believe that the FDII regime is clearly inconsistent with the modified nexus approach adopted by the OECD in the BEPS because it does not require any activity to be carried out in the United States other than exporting. Taxpayers can get the lower rate by importing goods and immediately exporting them. As stated by Schler, 'the provision does not require that anything be manufactured in the U.S. The formula is based only on profits from exports. A U.S. corporation could buy goods from a related or unrelated foreign supplier, resell them around the world, and have FDII for its profits on foreign sales. Not a single employee need be in the United States.'

Thirdly, the FDII regime has a blatant and obvious WTO problem: it is a subsidy contingent upon export performance, which is explicitly prohibited by Art. 3.1(a) of the Subsidies and Countervailing Measures Agreement (SCM). This was precisely the type of export subsidy struck down in the 'Domestic International Sales Corporation,' 'Foreign Sales Corporation' and 'Extraterritorial Income' cases, resulting in massive potential sanctions and forcing the United States to repeal the subsidy and enact a domestic manufacturing provision (§ 199) that did not violate the SCM because it was not contingent upon export performance. The FDII has a very low chance of surviving a WTO dispute not only because it clearly satisfies the definition of a 'prohibited subsidy' under the SCM agreement, but also because it is inconsistent with the main arguments advanced by the United States during the US-FSC litigation. The authors would expect that this provision will be struck down by the WTO and the United States will be left with only the GILTI provision. As stated above, the GILTI provision is inadequate but this can be fixed by a future Democratic administration by the setting of the GILTI rate as the same as the domestic rate (21%).

1.4. Base Erosion

The Conference Agreement followed the Senate's BEAT with some changes, an alternative to the House excise tax proposal. Under the new § 59A(a), an 'applicable taxpayer' is required to pay a tax equal to the 'base erosion minimum tax amount' for the taxable year. The BEAT generally applies to corporations (other than RICs, REITs or S corporations) that over a three-year period have average annual gross receipts of at least USD 500 million and a 'base erosion percentage' for the taxable year of at least 3%. The 'base erosion minimum tax amount' is the excess of 10% of the taxpayer's 'modified taxable income' over the taxpayer's 'regular tax liability' (defined in § 26(b)) reduced (but not below zero) by the excess (if any) of credits allowed against such regular tax liability over the sum of: (1) § 38 credit properly allocable to the § 41(a) research credit; plus (2) the portion of the applicable § 38 credits not in excess of 80% of the lesser of the amount of such credits or the base erosion minimum tax amount. To determine its modified taxable income, a corporation computes its taxable income for the year without regard to any 'base erosion tax benefit' with respect to any 'base erosion payment' or the 'base erosion percentage' of any allowable net operating loss deduction allowed under section 172 for the taxable year. A 'base erosion payment' is defined as any amount paid or accrued to a foreign related person that is a related party of the taxpayer and with respect to which a deduction is allowable, including interest and royalties; amounts paid in connection with an acquisition of property subject to the allowance of depreciation (or amortization in lieu of depreciation); premiums or other consideration paid or accrued for any reinsurance payments and, for inverted corporations only, also the cost of goods sold (COGS). On the other hand, payments for services if such services qualify for the services cost method under Treas. Reg. § 1.482–9 and only if they are made for services that have no markup component, as well as any qualified derivative payment, are not treated as base erosion payments.

A couple of preliminary observations are in order. Firstly, the real purpose of BEAT seems to be somehow ambiguous and confounding. If BEAT intends to prevent the erosion of and protect the US tax base, why does it make a distinction between payments to foreign related parties and payments to unrelated ones and include only the former in calculating the new tax? Stevens and Barnes argue that the definition of base erosion payment apparently reflects the US government's lack of confidence in policing transfer pricing. In this regard, it should be noted that § 59A(i) provides that the Secretary of the Treasury is to prescribe such regulations or other guidance necessary or appropriate, including regulations providing for such adjustments to the application of this section necessary to prevent avoidance of the provision, including through: (1) the use of unrelated persons, conduit transactions or other intermediaries or (2) transactions or arrangements designed in whole or in part: (A) to characterize payments otherwise subject to this provision as payments not subject to this provision or (B) to substitute payments not subject to this provision for payments otherwise subject to this provision. In the authors' opinion, principles similar to those under the anti-conduit regulations may be applied to identify whether a foreign related party is the actual beneficial owner of a base erosion payment.

Secondly, it offers tax planning opportunities with unintended consequences. Rather than manufacturing the goods itself and paying the foreign affiliate a royalty for the use of software, trademark or other intellectual property, a US corporation may prefer to purchase the finished products from a foreign affiliate. The fact that a royalty payment is excluded from a US company's COGS but included in the expanded tax base creates incentives to move jobs offshore.

Finally, can the BEAT be seen as violating the non-discrimination provision of Article 24? Article 24 has two relevant provisions: Article 24(4) and (5). Under Article 24(4),

Except where the provisions of paragraph 1 of Article 9 (Associated Enterprises), paragraph 8 of Article 11 (Interest), or paragraph 7 of Article 12 (Royalties) apply, interest, royalties, and other disbursements paid by an enterprise of a Contracting State to a resident of the other Contracting State shall, for the purpose of determining the taxable profits of such enterprise, be deductible under the same conditions as if they had been paid to a resident of the first-mentioned Contracting State. Similarly, any debts of an enterprise of a Contracting State to a resident of the other Contracting State shall, for the purpose of determining the taxable capital of the first-mentioned resident, be deductible under the same conditions as if they had been contracted to a resident of the first-mentioned Contracting State [emphasis added].

Does the BEAT violate this provision? The first author has already argued elsewhere it does not because the BEAT is not equivalent to the denial of a deduction. Interest, royalties and the other items covered by the BEAT remain fully deductible. Instead, the tax benefit conferred by deducting them is subject to the 10% BEAT. The non-equivalence of the BEAT and denying the deduction can be seen from the fact that denying a deduction would increase the tax on the deductible item by 21%, not by 10%.

In addition, the BEAT can be seen as conceptually similar to a broadly applied thin capitalization rule. In fact, the BEAT replaces the old earnings stripping rule (former IRC § 163(j)). And thin capitalization rules, even though they do frequently involve denying the interest deduction for interest paid to foreign but not domestic related parties, are widely used and generally regarded by the OECD as non-discriminatory.

The other relevant provision of Article 24 is paragraph 5, which states that a country may not apply less favourable treatment to any entity owned or controlled by non-residents in comparison with domestically held entities.

Arguably, this paragraph is violated by the BEAT because a foreign-owned US party will be subject to the BEAT but a US-owned one will not. But there are two counter-arguments. First, the BEAT applies regardless of the ultimate ownership of the US corporation and thus also to payments from a US party to a foreign party that is owned by the US party (e.g. a CFC), which shows that one of the intentions was to protect the US corporate tax base, not to discriminate against foreign-owned US parties.

Secondly, the first author argued that the foreign related party and the US related party are not comparable for applying a non-discrimination analysis. The reason is that the United States knows that a US related party is in fact subject to tax on the relevant deductible items, such as interest, royalties, and in some cases, cost of goods sold. But the United States does not know that the foreign related party is similarly subjected to tax by its country of residence because in many cases these countries will not tax, particularly when it comes to foreign-source interest or royalties. It should be expected that the enactment of the BEAT would lead multinationals to establish related parties that receive deductible payments from US parties precisely in those jurisdictions that exempt such payments because otherwise they would risk double taxation since a credit would normally not be immediately available.

The guiding spirit behind the international provisions of the TCJA is the single tax principle and under that principle it is perfectly appropriate for the United States to deny a deduction for items that it has no reason to believe will be taxed on a residence basis. No violation of Article 24(5) should arise under those circumstances. Therefore, rather than engaging in retaliatory actions, EU treaty partners should adopt similar measures and apply them to US multinationals.

1.5. BEPS Action 6: Should the US Reconsider the Rejection of the PPT?

One of the key BEPS Actions that generated the most controversy in the United States and eventually led the United States not to join the MLI was Action 6, primarily due to the inclusion of a general anti-abuse rule based on the principal purposes of transactions or arrangements (the PPT rule). Under that rule, if one of the principal purposes of transactions or arrangements is to obtain treaty benefits, these benefits will be denied unless it is established to grant them would be in accordance with the object and purpose of the provisions of the treaty. In order to understand why the United States opposed this subjective intention-based test and preferred a more objective detailed LOB provision, which has been part of its treaty policy since 1981, it is necessary to go back to the beginning of the 21st century when the US Senate refused to approve the ratification of negotiated treaties with Italy and Slovenia that originally contained a 'main purpose' clause.

The Italian negotiators wanted to include a very broad anti-abuse provision which would have denied treaty benefits in situations not covered by the LOB clause. At that time (second half of the 1990s), Italy did not have effective domestic anti-abuse rules, which could have been used to deny treaty benefits in the case of abusive transactions, and was therefore increasingly relying on explicit anti-abuse provisions in its treaties. Indeed, Italian domestic anti-abuse provisions were so weak that, in three cases of the early 2000s, the tax authorities tried unsuccessfully to fight dividend washing transactions through the principle of fraude à la loi set forth by Article 1344 of the Civil Code. In particular, Italian negotiators wanted to incorporate a provision similar to Article 30 of the 1995 treaty with Israel, which reads as follows: 'The competent authorities of the Contracting States, upon their mutual agreement, may deny the benefits of this Convention to any person, or with respect to any transaction, if in their opinion the receipt of those benefits, under the circumstances, would constitute an abuse of the Convention according to its purposes.

However, in a hearing before the US Senate Committee on Foreign Relations, Phil West, International Tax Counsel for the US Department of the Treasury, declared that this broad, subjective anti-abuse rule in the Israel-Italy treaty was rejected for several reasons:

First, it provided a less certain standard against which a taxpayer could meaningfully evaluate its transaction. Second, since the narrower rule ['main purpose' test] before you appears in a significant number of treaties around the world, and promises to appear in more, it is more consistent with international norms and will likely be the subject of more interpretive law than the other standards . . .

We gravitated toward the 'main purpose' standard of our proposed rule because it corresponds to the U.S. 'a principal purpose' standard which is applied in a number of our statutory provisions and regulations.

A compromise was thus reached on the inclusion of the 'main purpose' clause in Articles 10 (Dividends), 11(9) (Interest), 12(8) (Royalties) and 22(3) (Other Income). Article 10(10) of the 1999 treaty with Italy provided that:

The provisions of this Article shall not apply if it was the main purpose or one of the main purposes of any person concerned with the creation or assignment of the shares or other rights in respect of which the dividend is paid to take advantage of this Article by means of that creation or assignment.

Lindy Paull, Chief of Staff of the Joint Committee on Taxation, told the US Senate Committee on Foreign Relations that:

While the main purpose tests are intended to prevent inappropriate benefits under the treaty, such tests inject considerable uncertainty into the treaty provisions because such tests are subjective and vague. This uncertainty can create difficulties for legitimate business transactions, and can hinder a taxpayer's ability to rely on the treaty.

The US Senate Committee on Foreign Relations, in turn, stated that the inclusion of such tests represented a fundamental shift in US treaty policy, which was based on clear, bright-line objective tests (such as ownership and base erosion tests, and public company tests, as well as active business tests). In this regard, the Committee complained that it had not been afforded an opportunity to weigh the relevant policy considerations. Accordingly, the Committee placed a reservation on the main purpose test, citing subjectivity, vagueness and uncertainty as sources of the serious concerns about the provision. The reservation had the effect of striking the objectionable provision from the instrument of ratification.

In the authors' opinion, Phil West's memorandum to Senator Hagel (R-NE) appears to be contradictory while seeking to give meaning to the term 'a principal purpose.' On the one hand, West cited Judge Posner's ruling in Santa Fe Pacific Corporation v. Central States, Southeast and Southwest Areas Pension Fund, a labour law case governed by the Employee Retirement Income Security Act rules. On the other hand, he listed § 877(a)(2) among the IRC provisions using 'a/one of the principal purposes' anti-abuse language. Firstly, Santa Fe was not a tax case and did not interpret any provisions of the IRC. Secondly, its conclusions totally oppose those of several judicial decisions involving §§ 367 and 877. Santa Fe might have caused enough confusion to lead the Senate to reject the inclusion of the 'main purpose' test in the tax treaties with Italy and Slovenia.

Under the Multiemployer Pension Plan Amendments Act of 1980, an employer that withdrew from a multi-employer pension plan could have been required to pay the plan a sum equal to the vested but unfunded benefits of the employer's employees. The purpose was to avoid situations where the other employers would have had to pay for those benefits. A parent and its subsidiaries were considered to be a single employer with the consequence that if a subsidiary withdrew from the plan, its withdrawal liability could have been assessed against the parent. But in the event that the parent had sold its subsidiary, the parent would have not been liable for withdrawal liability unless 'a principal purpose' of the transaction was to 'evade or avoid' parental liability. In determining whether a principal purpose of Santa Fe was to evade or avoid its parental liability, the Court held:

The imposition of withdrawal liability in a sale of business situation requires only that a principal purpose of the sale be to escape withdrawal liability. It needn't be the only purpose; it need only have been one of the factors that weighed heavily in the seller's thinking. We can find no decisions discussing situations in which there is more than one principal (major, weighty, salient, important) purpose, but we would be doing violence to the language and the purpose of the statute if we read 'a principal' as 'the principal.' The clear import of 'a principal' is to let the employer off the hook even if one of his purposes was to beat withdrawal liability, provided however that it was a minor, subordinate purpose, as distinct from a major purpose. To let the employer off even if avoiding such liability was a major purpose would ill serve the statute's goal of preventing one employer from unloading his pension obligations onto the other employers in a multiemployer plan.

However, such interpretation of the term 'a principal purpose' contrasts starkly with settled case law involving IRC provisions, such as

§§ 367 and 877. As mentioned above, Phil West adopted Judge Posner's interpretation of the term 'a principal purpose' while, at the same time, he made reference to § 877 as one of the many Code provisions which contains such language. A 1984 Tax Court case, regarding whether the petitioner had tax avoidance as one of her principal purposes in expatriating, clearly illustrates West's inconsistency.

Until 20 August 1996, when it was amended by the Health Insurance Portability and Accountability Act (P.L. 104–191, § 511(g)), § 877 generally provided that a non-resident alien individual who lost his US citizenship should be subject to tax on his US-source income, for the 10-year period following such loss, at the graduated tax rates applicable to US citizens rather than more favourable rates applicable to non-resident aliens, unless the loss did not have as one of its principal purposes the avoidance of US taxes. Section 877(e) specifically assigned the burden of proving the lack of a tax avoidance motive to the expatriate if the respondent established that it was reasonable to believe that the individual's loss of US citizenship would result in a substantial reduction in taxes. In Furstenberg v. Commissioner, the taxpayer was able to carry her burden under § 877(e). Furstenberg was the daughter of Robert Lee Blaffer, one of the founders of Humble Oil & Refining Co., the predecessor of Exxon Corporation. Because of the financial success of her father, the petitioner travelled extensively with her family, visiting Europe, in particular, France, where she spent several summers. By the time of her expatriation (23 December 1975), she was divorced from her second husband, Richard M. Sheridan, an international executive of Mobil Oil Corporation. The genesis for the expatriation was her third marriage to Prince Tassillo von Furstenberg (17 October 1975), a member of the Austrian aristocracy, whose ancestors were princes of the Holy Roman Empire in 1664. At the time of their decision to marry in early 1975, Furstenberg explained to the petitioner how important she was to him, given his Austrian heritage and ties, the fact that she should have adopted Austrian citizenship. Prior to expatriating, she met with her accountant and informed him that she intended to marry Furstenberg, adopt Austrian citizenship and live with her husband in Paris. He told her that adopting Austrian nationality would 'complicate' her taxes and warned that French taxes could be very high. The Petitioner had no further discussions with her accountant in 1975. Her income in 1975 and 1976 came from two trust distributions she received and from the sale of securities. The distribution from Trust No. 1, a complex inter vivos trust established by her parents, occurred on the day of her expatriation. In addition, in 1976 and 1977, after her expatriation she sold various securities realizing net capital gains in the amounts of USD 2.601.680.06 and USD 7.219.440.35 respectively. After careful consideration of all the evidence, the court was convinced that tax avoidance was not one of her principal purposes in expatriating. Interestingly, the Tax Court held the following:

Although we have never specifically interpreted the phrase 'one of its principal purposes' in the context of section 877, we find instructive the following definition set forth in Dittler Bros, Inc. v. Commissioner, 72 T.C. 896, 915 (1979), affd. without published opinion 642 F.2d 1211 (5th Cir. 1981), in which the Court was called upon to determine, under section 367, whether or not a certain translation was 'in pursuance of a plan having as one of its principal purposes the avoidance of Federal income tax. . . .'

The Court then quoted the definition of the term 'principal purpose' as articulated in Dittler Bros., according to which:

[T]he term [principal purpose] should be construed in accordance with its ordinary meaning. Such a rule of statutory construction has been endorsed by the Supreme Court. Malat v. Riddell, 383 U.S. 569, 571 (1966). Webster's New Collegiate Dictionary defines 'principal' as 'first in rank, authority, importance, or degree.' Thus, the proper inquiry hereunder is whether the exchange of manufacturing know-how was in pursuance of a plan having as one of its 'first-in-importance' purposes the avoidance of Federal income taxes.

To better understand the logic of Furstenberg's conclusions it is necessary to closely examine Dittler Brothers, Inc. v. Commissioner of Internal Revenue, which interpreted the term 'principal purpose' within the context of § 367.

Prior to the Deficit Reduction Act of 1984, § 367(a)(1) provided that certain outbound transfers of appreciated property would be non-taxable only if the exchange did not have the avoidance of Federal income taxes as one of its principal purposes. This determination was made by the IRS in accordance with guidelines set out in Rev. Proc. 68–23, 1968–1 C.B. 821. Section 1042(d) of the Tax Reform Act of 1976 afforded taxpayers a remedy through a declaratory judgment procedure in the Tax Court in cases where the IRS issued an adverse ruling or failed to make a determination as to whether a transfer had tax avoidance as a principal purpose. However, the scope of a Tax Court declaratory judgment was limited as to whether the IRS acted reasonably.

In Dittler Bros., the taxpayer had special know-how and trade secrets regarding the manufacturing of 'rub-off' lottery tickets. In order to expand its sales into foreign markets, Dittler entered into a 50–50 joint venture with a UK holding company, known as Norton & Wright Group Ltd. (NWG), which had developed a substantial market for the sale of lottery tickets. Dittler had previously granted two non-exclusive licences of its secret process to foreign companies, but since only nominal royalties were produced, both licences were cancelled. Dittler and NWG created two Netherlands Antilles corporations. NWG's representatives requested the joint venture to be located there primarily due to potential tax benefits: a low rate of Netherlands Antilles tax plus Netherlands tax exemption for dividends received. The first corporation, known as Stansfield Security N.V. (SSNV), was owned 50% by Dittler and 50% by Norton & Wright (Holland) B.V. (NWBV), a NWG's wholly owned Netherlands subsidiary. The second corporation, known as Opax Lotteries International N.V. (OLINV), was wholly owned by SSNV. Dittler and NWBV each contributed USD 25.000 to SSNV as partial consideration for their respective 50% stock interest. In addition, Dittler transferred its secret process for the printing of rub-off tickets to SSNV while NWBV transferred, along with its cash contribution, specific marketing and customer information. Subsequently, SSNV transferred 80% of its cash, the manufacturing know-how and the marketing information to OLINV for 100% of its stock. This contribution qualified SSNV as an investment holding company under Netherlands Antilles law. Under the terms of a shareholder agreement, 75% of the net profits after taxes of OLINV would be declared and paid out as a dividend distribution to SSNV. SSNV would in turn declare and pay, pro rata, dividend distributions to its shareholders from the dividends received from OLINV. Accordingly, the fight with the IRS concerned whether the retention of 25% of OLINV's after-tax earnings was pursuant to a plan having as one of its principal purposes the avoidance of Federal income taxes.

The Tax Court determined that Dittler was denied a favourable ruling on two grounds. Firstly, the IRS concluded that neither SSNV nor OLINV would devote the property received (manufacturing know-how) to the active conduct of a trade or business, within the meaning of § 3.02(1) of Rev. Proc. 68–23, 1968–1 C.B. 821. Secondly, the transaction created a potential for tax avoidance in that income from the exploitation of the manufacturing know-how would be diverted to a passive recipient in a benign foreign tax country.

Perhaps the most significant part of the judgment is when the Court stated that:

> Neither Congress in its hearings nor respondent in his rulings
> has ever defined what is meant by a 'principal purpose.'

Although we have never interpreted the term principal purpose within the context of section 367, we have interpreted the meaning of principal purpose in a somewhat analogous provision under section 269. That section, unlike section 367, focuses on whether the principal purpose for which an acquisition was made is the evasion or avoidance of Federal income tax. For section 269 to apply, principal purpose has been interpreted to mean a tax-evasion or avoidance purpose which outranks or exceeds in importance, any other purpose. VGS Corp. v. Commissioner, 68 T.C. 563, 595 (1977): Capri, Inc. v. Commissioner, 65 T.C. 162, 178 (1975).

In contrast to section 269, section 367 speaks in terms of a plan having as one of its principal purposes the avoidance of Federal income taxes. When these two statutory provisions are laid side by side, it becomes apparent that the subjective tax-avoidance motive in section 269 acquisitions must be greater than the tax-avoidance motive in section 367 transfers. Consequently, section 269 is instructive in the instant case by defining the nature and scope of the tax-avoidance purpose.

However, because of the statutory variance between section 269 and section 367, with respect to the intendment of the respective statutes, we believe that the term 'principal purpose' should be construed in accordance with its ordinary meaning. Such a rule of statutory construction has been endorsed by the Supreme Court. Malat v. Riddell, 383 U.S. 569, 571 (1966). Webster's New Collegiate Dictionary defines 'principal' as 'first in rank, authority, importance, or degree.' Thus, the proper inquiry hereunder is whether the exchange of manufacturing know-how was in pursuance of a plan having as one of its 'first-in-importance' purposes the avoidance of Federal income taxes [emphasis added].

In conclusion, the issue centres on the correct meaning on the term "principal purpose." In other words, is 'a principal purpose' standard met only when the avoidance of tax exceeds in importance any other purpose as stated in Dittler? Or is the standard also operative when the tax-avoidance motive was only one of the factors that weighed heavily in the taxpayer's thinking as argued in Santa Fe? Obviously, on the one hand, taxpayers would prefer the former interpretation, which is more lenient, because this allows them to preserve treaty benefits by asserting a relatively weak business purpose, while, on the other hand, tax authorities would prefer the latter, stricter, interpretation because it permits them to deny treaty benefits if tax avoidance was just more than a trivial or de minimis purpose.

Analysis of the legislative history and regulations of § 129 of the 1939 IRC, predecessor to § 269, as well as the extensive case law before and after Dittler, clearly suggests that any standard using a principal purpose is met only when the purpose of evading tax exceeds in importance any other purpose.

Therefore, if the United States' ultimate goal were to incorporate these new anti-abuse rules in its Model Treaty and, at the same time, provide certainty to its business community that other countries' tax authorities will not inappropriately invoke the main purpose provisions to challenge legitimate business transactions, why cite the ambiguous Santa Fe ruling? In the authors' opinion, the United States should have requested the inclusion of an additional provision in the Protocol to the tax treaty with Italy, clarifying the scope of the 'main purpose' provision, which reads as follows: 'As was discussed and understood among the negotiators, the following Articles 10(10); 11(9); 12(8) and 22(3) should be operative only if the tax evasion or avoidance purpose outranks or exceeds in importance, any other purpose.'

The rejection of 'main purpose' tests in the tax treaties with Italy and Slovenia based on the incorrect interpretation of the term given in

Santa Fe could be considered a posteriori to have been a strategic mistake. Oddly, in 1999, the United States did not take advantage of the opportunity to play a leadership role in shaping the future direction of this important principle. The fact that the PPT rule is currently included in more than 1,100 matched agreements demonstrates how important it was to the United States in 1999 to adopt such a standard in the tax treaties with Italy and Slovenia. However, as mentioned, the inclusion of this standard should have been explicitly based on the Dittler ruling, the only approach able to ensure a consistent and reasonable application of the standard. In 1999, the United States lost the chance to unilaterally impose its own interpretation of the PPT rule. Today, with the United States refusing to sign up to the MLI, the concerns of Ms Paull and of Sen. Hagel as to whether other countries' tax authorities would appropriately administer this provision are more important than ever.

1.6. Anti-Hybrid Provisions

Similarly to the ATAD, TCJA contains two anti-hybrid provisions that directly implement the single tax principle. The first, § 14101 of the Senate amendment, the new § 245A(e), disallows the participation exemption for hybrid dividends that are treated as deductible payments at source. The second, § 14223 of the Senate amendment, the new § 267A, limits the deductibility of payments on hybrid instruments or to hybrid entities. These provisions clearly implement OECD BEPS Action 2 in accordance with the single tax principle.

In particular, on the one hand, § 245A(e)(1) provides that the dividend received deduction is not available for any dividend received by a US shareholder from a CFC if the dividend is a 'hybrid dividend'. Hybrid dividend is defined as, 'an amount received from a controlled foreign corporation for which a deduction would be allowed under this provision and for which the specified 10-percent owned foreign corporation received a deduction (or other tax benefit) from taxes imposed by a foreign country'. In addition, if a CFC receives a hybrid dividend from another CFC, the hybrid dividend is treated as Subpart F income. Finally, § 245A(e)(3) provides, by reference to § 245A(d)(1) and (2), that no foreign tax credit or deduction is allowed for any taxes paid or accrued with respect to a hybrid dividend.

On the other hand, § 267A(a) denies a deduction for any 'disqualified related party amount' paid or accrued pursuant to a 'hybrid transaction' or by, or to, a 'hybrid entity'. A disqualified related party amount is any interest or royalty paid or accrued to a related party to the extent that: (i) there is no corresponding inclusion to the related party under the tax law of the country of which such related party is a resident for tax purposes or is subject to tax, or (ii) such related party is allowed a deduction with respect to such amount under the tax law of such country. A hybrid transaction is defined as 'any transaction, series of transactions, agreement, or instrument one or more payments with respect to which are treated as interest or royalties for Federal income tax purposes and which are not so treated for purposes of the tax law of the foreign country of which the recipient of such payment is resident for tax purposes or is subject to tax'. Finally, a hybrid entity is any entity which is either: (i) treated as fiscally transparent for Federal income tax purposes but not so treated for purposes of the tax law of the foreign country of which the entity is resident for tax purposes or is subject to tax, or (ii) treated as fiscally transparent for purposes of the tax law of the foreign country of which the entity is resident for tax purposes or is subject to tax but not so treated for Federal income tax purposes.

It may seem strange that the United States took this action while making the CFC-to-CFC look-through rule § 954(c)(6) permanent and thereby facilitating foreign-to-foreign profit shifting from high- to low-tax jurisdictions abroad. The fundamental question is whether all of this is consistent with the spirit of BEPS. Eventually, the United States will tax at residence if there is no tax at source (§ 245A(e)) and will tax at source if there is no tax at residence (§ 267(a)). But what about the case where both source and residence are foreign? The United States will not impose tax and will leave this situation to the foreign jurisdictions to resolve by adopting their own anti-BEPS rules, like the new ATAD II. Again, a strategic mistake made by the United States?

Early commentators highlighted how TCJA prevents the use of hybrid instruments or entities that could reduce the US tax base but does not have any material impact on 'foreign-to-foreign hybrid planning, the type of United States multinational planning that many countries blame on the United States check-the-box rule.' In the same vein, a Baker McKenzie Client Alert stated:

The new provision is a very limited version of the much broader anti-hybrid provisions recommended by the OECD under BEPS Action 2. In particular, the rules only apply to interest and payments, and only to outbound payments. There is no equivalent provision that subjects hybrid income paid by a foreign related party to tax in the US where that income would otherwise escape US tax. Moreover, the definitions of 'hybrid entity' and 'hybrid transaction' are relatively narrow, so that the new Code Section would not seem to apply, for example, to permanent establishment hybrid mismatches [emphasis added].

Thus, neither § 245A(e) nor § 267A(a) will significantly impact foreign reverse hybrid entities, i.e. entities that are treated as opaque by a foreign investor and transparent under the jurisdiction where they are established, such as a Dutch CV-BV or a Luxembourg SCS-Sarl structure. This might have adverse consequences for both US multinationals and tax authorities, considering that ATAD II also includes specific rules aimed at reverse hybrid mismatches, namely Article 9a.

Over the past few years, US multinationals have widely used either a Dutch CV-BV (Starbucks) or a Luxembourg SCS-Sarl structure (Amazon) in order to defer US taxation on their non-US earnings. A US multinational establishes a limited partnership under Dutch (CV) or Luxembourg (SCS) law, which is a fiscally transparent entity under local law but elects to be treated as a corporation for US tax purposes. The CV/SCS licenses international IP rights from the US parent company and further develops such IP under a research and development (R&D) contract (CRA) or cost-sharing (CSA) arrangement with the US parent. It then grants an IP licence to a Dutch (BV) or Luxembourg (Sarl) principal. The BV/Sarl may either (i) sell products throughout Europe and retain local in-country service companies for support services or (ii) grant sub-licences to European operating companies. The tax consequences are the following: (i) service or operating companies across Europe remit local country tax on routine income; (ii) the BV remits 25% tax on net sales or licensing income reduced by royalty payments to the CV; (iii) there is no Dutch withholding on royalties under domestic law; (iv) the CV is treated as a pass-through for Dutch purposes and thus is not subject to Dutch tax; and (v) the US parent achieves deferral of US tax on its non-US profits as a result of the CV/SCS's hybrid treatment. On the one hand, the United States treats the CV/SCS as a corporation and, as a consequence, income that it earns will not generally be subject to current US tax. Moreover, even if the CV/SCS is treated as a CFC, interest and royalty income earned from the BV/Sarl, which otherwise would qualify as Subpart F income, may nonetheless not be subject to current US taxation as a result of either § 954(c)(3) or § 954(c)(6). On the other hand, payments to the CV/SCS are also generally not subject to tax in the foreign jurisdiction in which it is established or organized (either Netherlands or Luxembourg) because the foreign jurisdiction views the CV/SCS as a fiscally transparent entity and therefore treats its income as derived by its owners, including its US owners.

It should be noted that as from 1 January 2020, the benefit of tax deferral for US MNEs derived from setting up those structures in Netherlands or Luxembourg will likely disappear due to the general hybrid mismatch rules of ATADII, whose territorial scope has been extended to third countries. In particular, Article 9(2)(a) of ATADII states that, 'To the extent that a hybrid mismatch results in a deduction without inclusion, the deduction shall be denied in the Member State that is the payer jurisdiction. . ..'

This means that where the CV/SCS owns IP and licenses such IP back-to-back through the BV/Sarl in exchange for a royalty payment or enters into loan agreements with the BV/Sarl and/or its subsidiaries to lend surplus cash back to group companies, the payments of interest and royalties by the BV/Sarl to the CV/SCS should no longer be deductible. In those cases, indeed, the interest or royalty deduction will be denied in the payer's jurisdiction, i.e. the Netherlands and Luxembourg.

In addition, as mentioned above, ATADII also provides specific rules aimed at reverse hybrid mismatches. Article 9a(1) states that,

Where one or more associated non-resident entities holding in aggregate a direct or indirect interest in 50 percent or more of the voting rights, capital interests or rights to a share of profit in a hybrid entity that is incorporated or established in a Member State are located in a jurisdiction or jurisdictions that regard the hybrid entity as a taxable person, the hybrid entity shall be regarded as a resident of that Member State and taxed on its income to the extent that that income is not otherwise taxed under the laws of the Member State or any other jurisdiction.

This specific rule, which takes precedence over the general reverse hybrid mismatch rule of Article 9(2)(a), will become effective as from 1 January 2022. The Netherlands unsuccessfully tried to postpone the effective date to 1 January 2024 'to give third countries, like the United States, sufficient time to amend their legislation to neutralize the effects of a hybrid mismatch in the country of the payment recipient.' Indeed, according to the OECD BEPS Action 2 Report (Recommendation 5), mismatch arrangements can also be addressed through changes to domestic law. The residence state of the foreign investor, in this case, the United States, could improve its CFC regime in order to ensure that income earned by the CV/SCS will be currently subject to US tax. As will be described below, this could be done by closing the two biggest loopholes of the Subpart F regime, namely the same-country exception of § 954(c)(3) and the look-through exception of § 954(c)(6). However, such proposal should consider whether US MNEs will end up being less competitive than foreign multinationals since they will not be able to redeploy their foreign earnings overseas without an additional US tax burden.

Regardless of the actions that have been undertaken by the United States, as a result of Article 9a(1), since the parent company is located in a jurisdiction, the United States, that treats the CV/SCS as a corporation, the CV/SCS would be treated as a Dutch or Luxembourg resident entity and taxed on the interest or royalty income received from the BV/Sarl, respectively.

In this regard, the first question that should be asked is whether rules addressing hybrid mismatches are actually necessary. In the authors' opinion, the answer to this is theoretically no, but practically yes. Theoretically no because a textual interpretation of Article 24(4) of the Netherlands-United States Income Tax Treaty (1992) suggests that the Netherlands does not have to allow for an exemption from or a reduction of Dutch tax. Article 24(4) of the treaty reads as follows:

In the case of an item of income, profit or gain derived through a person that is fiscally transparent under the laws of either State, such item shall be considered to be derived by a resident of a State to the extent that the item is treated for the purposes of the taxation law of such State as the income, profit or gain of a resident.

As mentioned above, the CV is viewed as a pass-through entity for Dutch purposes, but as a company for US tax purposes, when it receives interest or dividends from its operating subsidiary, BV. As a result of this hybrid treatment, income earned by the CV generally would not currently be subject to tax in either the United States or the Netherlands. Consequently, Article 24(4) provides that the withholding rate should not be reduced.

This view was initially also confirmed by J.G. Wine, State Secretary for Finance in a letter of 3 May 2005 to the President of the Senate of the States General, where he argued that the Netherlands was no longer obliged to reduce the withholding rate on dividends and interest paid by the BV to the CV. He justified this result based on the purpose of the hybrid entity provision, according to which differences in the qualification of an entity should not lead to situations of double taxation or double non-taxation. However, in the same letter he also mentioned he was investigating the possibility of granting certain tax benefits to US MNEs that made use of such structure. If real and substantial activities had been performed in or via the Netherlands, Article 24(4) would not have been applied. Therefore, on 6 July 2005, the State Secretary for Finance published Decree IFZ2005/546M, according to which treaty benefits will be granted to an entity that is classified as transparent for Netherlands tax purposes and as non-transparent for US tax purposes, provided that the Netherlands subsidiary carries out real activities. In this regard, a company may request an advance tax ruling confirming that real activities are carried out. The Decree considered the following points as being relevant for the purposes of determining whether real activities are carried out: (i) whether the dividend distributing company is (for tax purposes only) established in the Netherlands; (ii) whether directors and/or employees are active in the Netherlands; (iii) whether these directors have sufficient professional knowledge; (iv) where important decisions are taken; (v) where the company's primary bank account is kept; (vi) where the bookkeeping takes place; (vii) the amount of equity and debts; (viii) which activities are carried out in or through the Netherlands; (ix) whether the employees active in the Netherlands are sufficiently qualified; (x) where real risks are run and (xi) whether the remuneration for the activities carried out and the risks run is at arm's length. Granting treaty benefits to entities that do not qualify based on the literal interpretation of Article 24(4) is the reason why the present authors believe that hybrid mismatch rules are necessary in practice. In the absence of any tax holiday granted to foreign direct investors, Article 24(4) is perfectly adequate since it provides that dividend withholding tax should not be reduced. Indeed, similar provisions to Article 24(4) have been included in the treaties with Canada, Denmark, France, Iceland, Ireland, Italy, South Africa, Thailand and Venezuela. In particular, examples in the Technical Explanation address the issue of reverse hybrid entities. The language contained in the Technical Explanation to Article IV(7)(a) of the Canada-United States Income and Capital Tax Treaty (1980) is very clear:

> For example, assume USCo, a company resident in the United States, is a part owner of CanLP, an entity that is considered fiscally transparent for Canadian tax purposes, but is not considered fiscally transparent for U.S. tax purposes. CanLP receives a dividend from a Canadian company in which it owns stock. Under Canadian tax law USCo is viewed as deriving a Canadian-source dividend through CanLP. For U.S. tax purposes, CanLP, and not USCo, is viewed as deriving the dividend. Because the treatment of the dividend under U.S. tax law in this case is not the same as the treatment under U.S. law if USCo derived the dividend directly, subparagraph 7(a) provides that USCo will not be considered as having derived the dividend. . . .

Canada is therefore not obliged to grant treaty benefits, e.g. reduction or elimination of dividend withholding tax imposed under domestic law. Here, the taxable event is the distributive share of dividend paid to CanLP. Because the distributive share of dividend income is not taxed in the United States, there is no reduction in Canadian withholding tax on the share belonging to USCo.

The second question that should be asked is what would be the interaction between US tax reform and ATADII? In particular, what would be the effect of the new GILTI regime on the CV/BV reverse hybrid structure? Would the hybrid mismatches be shut down? Some practitioners have pointed out that since there will be a 10.5% immediate tax, it could be argued that the United States has resolved the issue of stateless income made possible by the CV/BV structure. In their opinion, due to GILTI, the United States no longer allows profits from IP, such as royalty fees, to be transferred out of a Netherlands-based entity without being taxed anywhere. Only time will tell if that is true, but, in that event, EU Member States should refrain from taxing those profits through either the denial of deduction or by including the payments in the taxable income of the reverse hybrid.

In conclusion, it should be noted that all these problems, especially avoiding taxation by other countries of what the United States believes is its income, would have been resolved if TCJA had adopted a similar provision to that proposed by the Obama Administration, according to which § 954(c)(3) and § 954(c)(6) would not have been applied to payments made to a foreign reverse hybrid held by one or more US persons when such amounts were treated as deductible payments received from foreign related persons. Indeed, as a consequence of that proposal, the IP income of a CV would currently be subject to US tax. However, the proposal would have modified some of the core provisions of the Subpart F regime denying the possibility for US MNEs to engage in foreign-to-foreign profit shifting. When the US Congress, on behalf of US multinationals, forced Treasury to withdraw Notice 98–11, 1998–1 C.B. it used two arguments to justify foreign-to-foreign profit shifting.

Firstly, it was said that reduction of foreign taxes through hybrid entities is a good thing for the US Treasury because if US MNEs pay less tax to foreign administrations, that means they will pay more tax to the United States when earnings are eventually repatriated. Secondly, foreign-to-foreign profit shifting is also good economically because US MNEs will have at their disposal more resources that could be used to expand their domestic business operations, thereby increasing the well-being of US workers and customers. It is therefore clear why TCJA did not include the Obama Administration's proposal. In the authors' opinion, the United States finds itself confronted by a difficult choice: (i) either tax MNEs' offshore income now by eliminating deferral or (ii) do nothing and risk that other countries, such as EU Member States through ATAD II, might tax what the United States believes is its tax base. Basically, it is like a zero-sum game; if US tax authorities gain, US multinationals lose and vice-versa.

1.7. Conclusion: The Future of BEPS

The authors believe that with TCJA, the future of BEPS as the underlying standard of the international tax regime (ITR) is assured. As long as the United States stood aside, it was not clear that the European Union would be able to implement BEPS on its own, and China is only now just beginning to adopt BEPS measures. But TCJA represents the incorporation of BEPS into US domestic tax law. Moreover, TCJA should not be considered as a 'tax war': it is a long-overdue response to the BEPS by US and other multinationals and a correct application of the single tax principle to prevent double non-taxation. It turns out that the immense effort of the OECD in 2013–15 was not in vain and a new and better ITR is on the horizon.

INDEX

References are to Pages